THE PACIFIC, ASIA AND THE

ORIENT

...STAGE OF HISTORY, PAST

PRESENT, AND FOR THE

TIME TO COME

OLSON'S ORIENT GUIDE

OLSON'S

ORIENT

GUIDE

BY HARVEY S. OLSON

Illustrated by CY FERRING

J. B. LIPPINCOTT COMPANY
PHILADELPHIA AND NEW YORK

TO MY DEAR MOTHER,

THE GREATEST TRAVELER OF THEM ALL

Contents

PART I

PART II

8   *Contents*

Illustrations

9

PART I

CHAPTER 1

Planning and Preparing for Your Trip

ANCIENT CHINESE in flowing robes and contemporary Madison Avenue ad men in gray flannel suits share at least one common cliché: "One picture is worth a thousand words." I must hasten to assure you, however, that even if I were able, miraculously, to bring you ten thousand times ten thousand vivid pictures of the Orient or if I were gifted with the most vividly brilliant descriptive powers, it would still be impossible for me to convey an absolutely accurate introspective image of the utterly amazing, sometimes mysterious, always fascinating lands of the Far East.

Until the jet age exploded over the *Pacific* in 1960, pathetically few Americans had visited the Orient. Even now, when interest in travel to the far side of the world is growing faster than crab grass in August, there is a mass misconception as to what awaits the visitor in the Far East. I shall do my best to set this right.

I have always been a meticulous plu-perfectionist and firmly believe that a guidebook, like a railroad timetable, must be absolutely accurate. Facts must prevail, with opinions, however well founded, being secondary. The one thousand and six pages of my European guidebook, *Aboard and Abroad,* are jam-

13

packed with pertinent information on every facet of life and travel in the Old World. It has been read, enjoyed, and found to be completely factual, thorough, and unbiased by hundreds of thousands of foreign travelers. This Orient guidebook is built from the same set of plans and on the same solid foundations as *Aboard and Abroad*.

To illustrate the complexities of the problems of doing justice to this objective opus, I can quote Joe Grace, a friend of mine living in **Tokyo,** who says, "The only thing that amazes me out here is to find something Oriental that is completely normal."

A trip to the Orient represents a large investment. It is an investment which should pay generous dividends for years and years to come. The value, the size, and the frequency with which those recurring dividends are declared will be in strict proportion to the thoroughness of the planning which goes into your proposed trip.

A businessman forming a new company or merging with another company would seldom, if ever, proceed without seeking and following the advice of a skilled lawyer. A family building a new home invariably retains a trained architect and chooses a reputable contractor. One making investments in stocks or bonds seeks the advice of an established broker and, if ill, sees a doctor.

A new bride planning her first dinner party leans heavily on Fanny Farmer or a similar authority. She does not throw a variety of ingredients into a pot and then pray for a delectable dish, but knows, instead, that the repast can be balanced, delicious, and nourishing following the proper directions.

There is no knowledge of matrimony as sagacious as that of a bachelor, and there is no counsel on the rearing of children as fervently bestowed as that of a spinster relative. The most intense, and seemingly inescapable, tips on a trip to the Orient will frequently emanate from a neophyte who has usually spent, at most, a mere three weeks there!

All too frequently, for reasons that will ever remain nebulous and incomprehensible, those planning a trip to the Orient will, and do, entrust their travel plans and their fondest dreams to the amateur advice of friends, relatives, and neighbors who have, perchance, made one trip abroad. Don't smile snidely. It happens thousands of times every season.

America is full of self-appointed "Mother's-little-helper" types of travel advisors. No matter what carefully conceived travel plans you make or what efficient, smooth-flowing itinerary you work out, you will be amazed and disappointed by the deluge of your relatives, friends, neighbors, and associates who will descend telling you what a particularly poor choice you have made. Irrespective of where in the world you plan to go, these "one-trip wonders" will come up with other captivating cities, gems of scenic beauty, and sites of historical interest that "you simply can't afford to miss." I suggest that you ostensibly listen to their well-meant advice, pretend to pay attention to the pearls of their wisdom cast before you, smile, and, as soon as you can politely do so, change the subject, quit their company, and ignore the conversation. No matter how many times these well meaning "touts" may have been to the Orient, their experience and know-how cannot begin to match the skill of the professional travel agent who has planned your trip for you. You must, from the very beginning, reconcile yourself to the fact that you can't possibly include everything on any one trip anywhere. If your itinerary has been well planned, it will encompass all that should be included within your budgeted time and money. No matter how much you do or see, you will inevitably find yourself, some place in the Orient, near a point of outstanding beauty or interest that has not been included in your well-planned trip. Steel yourself to this fact. The world is bursting with fascinating places begging to be visited. Unless you devote the rest of your life to traveling, you cannot see all that this intriguing planet has to offer. Be content, please, to include the best of what the Orient has to present on your itinerary, bearing in mind that it is not only of utmost importance to select the most rewarding places to visit but to do so in an order of

ascending climaxes rather than in a series of descending anticlimaxes.

The happiest travelers, both in prospect and retrospectively,
are those who place themselves in the hands of a capable travel
agent, make their desires known to this counselor, and let him
carry on from there, thus assuring the success of their trip.

After you have selected a well-qualified travel agent, work
closely with him (and America also has scores of outstanding
female travel agents) from the moment the germ of the idea of
the trip has been planted until the golden harvest of glorious
dreams is reaped. The travel agent's continued success, his very
livelihood, is dependent upon the satisfaction received and value
derived by his clients from the trips which he has planned. He
must produce the goods. A conscientious travel agent has made
a life's work of pleasing travelers. Whether this is your first or
your fiftieth trip to the Orient, you will want to take advantage
of the services of a good travel agent.

Your travel agent will sell you steamship, air, or rail tickets;
cruises; and preplanned prepaid tours at precisely the same
price as if you had purchased them directly from the operators.

Should you elect to forgo the pleasures and advantages of
packaged arrangements, your agent will, if he is intelligent
enough to be entrusted with your precious plans, charge you
for his time and out-of-pocket expenses in setting up your trip.
Whatever he charges you for his professional services, it will
be far less than the hourly rate used in computing the fees for
doctors, dentists, and lawyers.

WHAT PLAN TO FOLLOW

There are three roads for the prospective traveler initiating
his first steps in planning and preparing for a trip to the Orient
to consider. They are the following: (1) potluck, (2) an F.I.T.,
and (3) a personally escorted all-expense tour.

POTLUCK. Otherwise intelligent people who say, "We don't
want to make any advance travel plans; we want to go where

we please, when we please, and stay in each place to our heart's content; we don't want to leave any place until we have grown tired of it" are, to express it in General Anthony C. McAuliffe's vernacular, "nuts." It is indubitably true that the happiest diners, the happiest travelers, and the happiest investors are those who "quit when they are ahead." The glutton who eats twice as much as his tummy can comfortably hold, the traveler who remains in a locale until he is satiated, and the investor who insists on pressing for that last eighth of a point of profit when the zenith has passed are all being less than intelligent.

There are three important factors present in potluck travel that must be considered. (1) Unless you are most unusual, you will adore almost every place in the Orient and you will not willingly leave any place. (2) Few people have both unlimited time and money at their command, most of us being definitely restricted by one or the other, more frequently by both. (3)

There is scarcely any place in the Orient today where the hotel or transportation situation is adequate to the peak season demands. In **Bangkok, Taipei, Manila, Saigon,** and **Singapore,** for example, the hotel situation is desperate, the rooms available being but a handful when the requirements are for scores of hundreds. In **Hong Kong, Tokyo,** and **Kyoto,** the pressure on the hotels has been eased a bit by the recent opening of new hotels. Airline reservations are sure to be at a premium during the spring and fall peak seasons, and part of the wintertime. Without advance reservations, you are bound to encounter difficulties. If you insist on using that most miserable inefficient implement, the "do-it-yourself travel kit," don't ever say that your "Uncle Harvey" didn't warn you against it.

Should you elect to travel "potluck," there are certain minimum requirements which I implore you to fulfill: (1) see a good travel agent, (2) make the key air or steamship reservations, and (3) make at least the first hotel reservation in advance to insure that your whole trip will not go sour from its very inception.

THE F.I.T., which magic letters stand for "Foreign Independent Travel," is an ideal arrangement for one or more individuals who believe that they prefer not to travel with a tour group but who wish the ease and luxury of having all arrangements made in advance. Your travel agent is equipped to work out an F.I.T. for you, which he will, no doubt, place through one of the large reliable travel wholesalers. The F.I.T. will include reservations and tickets for all transportation by whatever mode and in whichever class you prefer; prepaid hotel reservations; preplanned sightseeing by private car or motorcoach, depending on your budget and desires; and the services of smart, English-speaking interpreters at the airports, railroad stations or docks wherever you go. Your F.I.T. fixed price, payable in advance, can cover every necessary traveling expense including all meals or, if you prefer, it can call for breakfasts only, or breakfast and one other meal each day. I, personally, prefer the latter plan, called demi-pension.

The F.I.T. gives you the advantage of knowing, when you leave home, that you have confirmed reservations every place, that you will be able to complete your itinerary within the allotted time, and you know exactly how much your trip is going to cost.

An F.I.T. is a bit more expensive than a conducted tour, but for those not desiring group travel the slight additional cost should not be a deterrent.

I know from experience that there are certain people who are happier when traveling alone, not being emotionally equipped for travel with a group. One's travel agent can be helpful in advising whether an F.I.T. or a conducted tour would be best for you.

THE PERSONALLY ESCORTED ALL-EXPENSE TOUR. From my long, intense, and concentrated experience, I have mined the nugget of knowledge that for the vast majority of travelers the most pleasant, economical, and efficient way to see foreign lands pleasantly with the maximum return for the dollar expended is to join a well-planned tour operated by an experienced, reliable company. Americans visiting the Orient who are the happiest and get the most out of their trips are those who travel in small, congenial groups with an experienced tour conductor to look after all the many details. A tour conductor is kind, gracious, thoughtful, and considerate, a person of culture and refinement.

There are almost as many varieties of tours as there are automobiles. There are "dirt cheap" economy tours, and there are luxury tours that are finer than any conceivable potluck or F.I.T. arrangement. Economy class tours around the Orient sell for as little as $1,700.00 or $1,800.00 for a six- to seven-week program, while all first class luxury tours sell for as much as $3,500.00 to $3,900.00. It is possible for excellent values to prevail in both brackets.

One of the outstanding advantages of a tour is that the conductor can, and does, assume all of the cares and worries of the entire group. The only documentation the tour member needs to carry to traverse the entire Orient area is: a passport, air or steamship ticket, and a tour membership certificate.

On a tour, one need not stand in line for hours to reconfirm transportation or hotel reservations or seek out sightseeing terminals. The tour conductors handle all the transportation details, and sightseeing arrangements for the tour parties begin right at the hotel, not at some remote motor-coach station.

All too frequently there are Americans who think there is some stigma attached to tour or group travel. There isn't. If you could but see the top-drawer social registerites, as well as other nice, but well-to-do, people who take fine luxury tours to the Orient, you would never worry about the alleged stigma of a tour. Orient travelers on economy tours are less socially conscious and quite properly never give a thought as to whether or not taking a tour is THE thing to do. Too much aloneness can be much more devastating than too much togetherness. It is a matter of record that couples blissfully married for years and years can, when traveling alone (together), soon be at each other's throats. This never happens on a tour.

On a conducted tour, all reservations and arrangements have been made months—sometimes more than a year—in advance. Hotel and transportation people are honored to have the privilege of handling tour groups. They realize the value of a tour company's repeat business, and to do other than to please tour operators must prove costly. An individual can, at best, visit a foreign hotel a few times during his life's span. A tour operator sends business to the Orient month after month, year after year. The one- or two-time guest, however important in his community, wields no weight of influence 12,000 miles from home. The F.I.T. wholesaler and important tour operator has the first choice of select accommodations.

Your travel agent can guide you in selecting a tour. If you are interested in price and price alone, you must be very careful. Some operators, particularly at the "rock bottom" level, are much better and more reliable than others. Read carefully what the tour rate includes. Some of the less expensive tours can, and do, use better grade hotels but reserve only the poorest rooms.

In the Orient there are a number of hotels which have had sections rebuilt or added new wings. Others have a wing, or wings, originally built for the landed gentry, while other sections were designed for the servants. The rate spread in some hotels is AS MUCH AS 400% between the least attractive rooms in the old, old section and the best rooms in the new part of the new wing.

It is obvious that the economy tour rates must include drastically less than the luxury tours since they sell for considerably less than the base operating costs of luxury tours.

Some very cheap tours may offer only special economy "strip" table d'hôte menus and frequently include breakfasts only in their rate rather than all meals. There are many other ways to cut corners.

On luxury tours, the best rooms in the best hotels are included, à la carte meals are provided wherever desired, frequent night life entertainment is included, as are many other costly but worthwhile features.

I know many sophisticated world travelers who have been abroad a score or more of times who wouldn't think of traveling outside of our own country in any other way than on a good tour.

Recently in **Tokyo** I happened to spy two good, old friends of mine standing forlornly outside the *Imperial Hotel*. I had no previous idea that they were in the Orient. When I dashed over to speak to them, they fell upon me like a long lost debtor. They were lonesome and unhappy. When I questioned them as to their plans for the evening, they said they had none and were wondering where to eat, how to get there, and what to do afterwards. I shepherded them to an outstanding restaurant where one of my tour groups was taking dinner. We all dined together and later went to an exciting night club. My friends were delighted with their evening of good food, fun, and companionship. It was their first pleasant excitement since

leaving home five weeks before. They enjoyed the experience
so much, and having learned from the group how well everything was going, they wanted to join my tour. Unfortunately,
they couldn't. It was filled to capacity.

In advance, it would have been impossible to have sold this
couple a conducted tour, even a luxury tour. But when, traveling alone, they arrived in the Orient, they felt lonesome and
"out of things." With no fixed program, they were desolate.
When they saw a good tour in operation, they were captivated.

All too frequently, I have seen couples, two or three ladies,
or solitary individuals in hotel lobbies, standing in front of
their hotels, or wandering aimlessly around a foreign city
wondering what to do, how to do it, how to get there, where
to eat, and where to have fun. I have taken scores of them
under my protective wing. Invariably, such unfortunates have
been enchanted to have me make plans for them, although, in
advance, they couldn't have been less interested.

In the luxury tour field, I can particularly recommend the
Olson Travel Organization of Chicago, Hemphill World
Cruises of Los Angeles, Donald L. Ferguson Ltd. of Katonah,
New York, and Harvey R. Mason Travel Service of Kenil-
worth, Illinois. In my estimation, these are by far the best of
the luxury operators. In the economy category, it appears to
me as though Sita spread-eagles the field.

Of the wholesalers, I can cast my vote wholeheartedly for
Lissone-Lindeman U.S.A. Inc. of New York City, Chicago,
Los Angeles, San Francisco, and Miami.

HOW TO TRAVEL

I have always been a great believer in one traveling the way
one is accustomed to living at home. Admiral Struble, U.S.N.,
loves to tell the story of the time that he had his wife and two
daughters aboard the battleship which was his first "big time"
command. As we all know, few, if any, nabobs or potentates
live better than do captains and admirals in the United States

Navy. When the Admiral's (then Captain) wife and two daughters reached home after their rich dinner in the Captain's quarters, the one daughter said to her mother, "Mamma, why is it that when we are at sea with Daddy we live so well when we live so poorly at home?"

I suggest that if you live well at home, travel in the same manner. It just doesn't make sense for one to have a houseful of comforts and luxuries and then go halfway around the world to "rough it." As Epictetus, the Greek Stoic philosopher, said hundreds of years ago, "Too many live as if they were going to be here a thousand years." Since we do not have a thousand years to live, my philosophy is: "Why not live and enjoy the best of life for the short period we are privileged to be here."

In the air section of *"Crossing the Pacific,"* I have discussed the matter of class of air travel at some length. There is almost $600.00 difference between the economy and first class air ticket round trip from the West Coast to **Bangkok** or **Singapore.** I can give you a written guarantee that, if you can afford it, the added comforts of first class are well worth the difference in cost. This is not an opinion. It is a fact. Time and again I have bumped into people in **Tokyo** who have arrived in economy class from the States who have immediately rushed to the airline office to try to change their return passage to first class which, alas, all too frequently is not possible. The transpacific jet flights, though extremely swift, are still long. Ten to fourteen hours aloft in limited quarters can be something of a trial.

A PASSPORT, the most important document in the traveler's possession, is documentary evidence, issued by the United States Government, identifying the bearer as a citizen and granting him permission to leave the country.

A VISA is a passport endorsement made by an official of the country to be visited showing that the holder of the passport has received approval to enter the country in question. While visas in **Europe** are almost a thing of the past for all non-Iron

Curtain countries, they are still required for visitors to some countries in the Orient.

To visit the Orient, it is necessary that each traveler, regardless of nationality, have in his possession a valid passport of his country and visas for each country requiring such documentation.

United States citizens may apply for a passport through the clerk of any United States District Court or State Court authorized by law to naturalize aliens. There is one court in the county seat of every county of the United States which is authorized to accept passport applications. United States citizens may obtain passports at the following Federal Passport Agencies:

Chicago (4)—Room 252, U.S. Courthouse, 219 South Clark Street Telephone HA 7-4700, Ext. 278.

New York City (20)—630 Fifth Avenue

Boston (11)—148 Tremont Street

Honolulu—217 Federal Building

Los Angeles (17)—500 South Figueroa Street

Miami (32)—320 S.E. First Street

San Francisco (2)—Airlines Terminal Bldg., 375 O'Farrell Street

New Orleans (12)—124 Camp Street, International Trade Mart

Seattle (1)—1410 Fifth Avenue

Washington (25), D.C.—Passport Office, Department of State, 22nd and E Street, N.W.

Passport offices are closed on Saturdays.

United States passports may be obtained by persons who are citizens of the United States by birth, by naturalization, and a woman by marriage if wedded before 1923.

In applying for a passport, you must have in your possession one of the following: your birth certificate, your baptismal certificate, or a notarized affidavit of birth which affidavit must be filled out by a relative (preferably) or other person having knowledge of your birth. If available, the birth certificate must be used. If a birth affidavit is used, it must be accompanied by a letter from the Bureau of Vital Statistics of the community in which you were born certifying that record of your birth is not available. A husband and wife may share one passport. Minor children may appear on a passport with a parent or parents. When a husband and wife, and/or children, apply for a joint passport, each must be in possession of the necessary documentary proof of birth. Women claiming citizenship through marriage must submit marriage certificate and proof of husband's citizenship. A person who claims United States citizenship through naturalization must submit the certificate of naturalization with his passport application. One who has been adopted will have to produce his, or her, adoption papers in addition to proof of birth.

When one applies for a passport, he, or she, must establish proof of identity which may be by possession of a driver's license, a Federal, State, or municipal government card or pass, or a business card. If none of these is available, then a witness must be present who must be over twenty-one and must have known the applicant for at least two years. Your photograph, physical description, or signature must appear on the document you submit for identification.

Before applying for a passport, it is necessary to have passport pictures in your possession which must be unretouched front-view photographs on lightweight, unglazed paper with light background. The passport pictures should be no larger than 3x3 inches, and not smaller than 2½x2½ inches, and may be either in color or in black and white. Black-and-white pictures which have been tinted or otherwise colored are not acceptable. While only two photographs are required to accompany your passport application, to be on the safe side have a dozen pictures made. Sometimes pictures must be submitted with visa applications, and it is well to carry a few passport pictures with you. Sometimes visa regulations in the Oriental countries change after you have left the **United States.**

Group photographs are preferred when minor children appear on a passport with their parent, or parents. When a husband and wife share the same passport, they should be photographed together. Two passport photographs should be signed by the applicant. It is an obvious economy for a wife and family to share a passport. Not only is the $10 per additional passport saved by having one passport, but the cost and documentation of securing visas is proportionately reduced. Offsetting this economy is the possible future complication of amending the passport if one of the family should wish to travel abroad alone.

In Chicago, the College Studio, 20 East Jackson Boulevard, specializes in passport photos. They do excellent work, and their price is modest. Almost all large cities have reliable studios specializing in passport photos. Even in small communities, passport photos do not present a problem. Any qualified photographer can produce unretouched pictures of the proper size.

Miss Frances G. Knight, an extremely capable executive, is in charge of the Passport Office, Department of State, Washington, D.C. She diligently studied passport procedures when she assumed her present job. It was she who streamlined departmental operations and procedures to their present state of efficiency.

Passports previously were valid for only four years, but those issued since September 14, 1959, are valid, initially, for three full years and may be renewed for an additional two years, with the total validity not to exceed five years from the original date of issue.

Before Miss Knight's regime, it took from two weeks to a

month or more to get a passport after ordering it. Two, or at the most three, days is now par for the passport course.

When applying directly to the Federal Passport Agency in Chicago, New York, Washington, D.C., Boston, Seattle, New Orleans, Miami, Los Angeles, San Francisco, or Honolulu, the passport fee is $10.00, which is payable by postal money order or in currency.

The total fee for passport and application if not applied for directly to a Federal Passport Agency is either $10.00 or $11.00. If ordered through a court $9.00 must accompany the passport application to Washington and is to be in the form of a postal money order payable to the Secretary of State, Washington, D.C., and $1.00 in cash is paid to the clerk of the court or agent before whom the application is executed. State courts may at their discretion collect $2.00 rather than $1.00 to process a passport application.

One must always appear in person to apply for a new passport, but in renewing a passport, one may send it by registered mail, together with a letter requesting the renewal, to the *Passport Division, Department of State,* **Washington, D.C.** with a $5.00 money order. You must sign the letter requesting the renewal.

After one renewal, or a period of five years from the original date of the passport's issue, an entirely new passport must be obtained following the same procedure and paying the same fee as for the original passport.

Once one has a passport, it should be zealously guarded at all times. In securing a second or subsequent passport, the old passport is the only documentation or identification required. The expired passport must be shown when applying for a new one. After it has served its purpose, the old passport will be mutilated and returned to you.

It is well to apply for a passport well in advance of a trip to the Orient, thus allowing ample time to secure the required visas.

It is strictly against government laws to deface your passport in any way. The blank pages are for visa stamps, when needed, not for bridge scores.

Immediately upon receipt of your passport, sign it where indicated and fill in the required information promptly. Since your passport is so precious, guard it every minute of the day and night. Keep it with you at all times when traveling. Never, never pack it in a suitcase. You can well imagine what can happen to people who are careless with their passports. Hours of delay, frustration, and embarrassment are encountered if you need your passport and it is not available to the authorities. If you are unlucky enough to lose your passport, it presents a real calamity. You cannot leave the country where your passport is lost until it has been replaced. While our Embassies in all foreign countries are extremely sympathetic and helpful, securing a replacement passport is a time-consuming, burdensome chore which may be expensive. But you must, if your passport is lost, get a new and provisional one before you can continue your travels.

MEDICAL AND VISA REQUIREMENTS. The following requirements for visa applications and medical documentation may sound formidable, but neither procedure is as complicated as it would appear on the surface. Your travel agent can be ever so helpful with visas. Since all regulations and requirements change rapidly in this volatile world of today, it would be well to check with your travel agent to see if there have been any changes in the following.

MEDICAL. Each passenger arriving in the United States from the Orient, or elsewhere abroad, is required to submit to the U. S. Public Health authorities a properly executed "International Certificate of Vaccination" showing that you have been vaccinated against smallpox within 3 years of the date of your return to the States. The certificate must be so worded as to indicate that the vaccination was successful, or showed immunity.

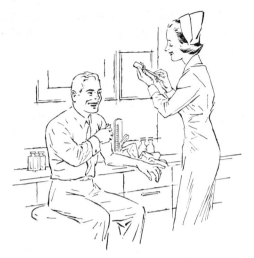

When applying for your passport, ask for an *International Certificate of Vaccination,* a U. S. Public Health Service form distributed by the Passport Department. Your doctor can enter on this form the details of all inoculations except yellow fever; the latter must be administered by the Public Health doctor, who must also enter it on the Certificate. Yellow fever shots must be obtained not less than 10 days or more than 6 years prior to entry into the country for which the shot is required.

For a visit to all of the Oriental countries covered in this book, one must have only a cholera inoculation in addition to the smallpox vaccination. Your health certificate must show that you have been inoculated against cholera less than 6 months before starting your trip. (The cholera shot is not always required.) Your doctor may advise typhoid, paratyphoid, and/or yellow fever inoculations. The latter is not usually required, but most countries stipulate that if a traveler passes through an area where yellow fever is epidemic he must have an inoculation before entering a country free of this disease.

After your doctor has signed your International Certificate of

Vaccination for any shots he has given you, the Certificate should be stamped by your local board of health, which can be done in person or by mail.

MEDICAL REQUIREMENTS

CAMBODIA: requires valid smallpox vaccination certificate.

HONG KONG and MACAO: require a valid smallpox vaccination certificate. If the traveler arrives from an area where there is a yellow fever or cholera epidemic, these two inoculations are required.

JAPAN: No inoculations are required unless the traveler is arriving from an area where there is yellow fever or cholera epidemic. In this case, these two inoculations are required.

MALAYSIA and SINGAPORE: require valid smallpox and cholera certificates, the latter of which is good for 6 months from the date of inoculation.

THE PHILIPPINES: require a valid smallpox vaccination.

TAIWAN: requires only a valid smallpox vaccination.

THAILAND: requires a valid smallpox vaccination certificate as well as (sometimes) a cholera certificate. If one enters Thailand from an area where there is a yellow fever epidemic, this certificate is also required.

VIET NAM: requires a smallpox vaccination certificate and, if entering from **Cambodia,** a cholera inoculation.

MEDIC ALERT FOUNDATION INTERNATIONAL, Turlock, Calif. performs a worthwhile function for travelers with medical problems or allergies. It provides a stainless steel identification emblem which lists blood type and any medical problem such as diabetes, allergy to penicillin, taking anticoagulants, wearing contact lenses, neck breather, etc. If you are concerned about a medical problem that could cause complication in an emergency, communicate with Medic Alert Foundation. The cost is $5.00 for a stainless steel disk or $7.50 for a sterling silver disk. This is the only charge.

VISAS

Your travel agent will gladly assist you in processing forms and securing required visas.

JAPAN: entry involves various visa procedures. No visa is required if your stay is to be less than 72 hours, but I suggest you'd better get a visa even if you only plan to be in Japan 48 hours. People often change their minds and wish to remain longer, and one can easily and unavoidably be detained because of air schedule emergencies. I believe it is wise for each traveler to apply for at least a Transit Visa which is good for 15 days. If you wish to remain longer than 15 days, you may secure a Tourist Visa, good for 60 days with multiple entries. A full visa is good for 4 years, with unlimited exits and entrances. There is no charge for Transit or Tourist Visa, no photographs are necessary, but one must execute three visa application forms.

If your trip to Japan is strictly for business, you must secure a Commercial Visa, good for 180 days. It is best to ask your travel agent for current regulations governing this Commercial Visa.

THE PHILIPPINES: require no visa for a stay of less than 72 hours, provided the visitor's onward travel is confirmed. A Transit Visa is good for a stay up to 2 weeks and is valid for 6 months from date of issue. Visa applications are required in triplicate accompanied by 3 passport-size photographs. The cost of Transit Visa is $5.00. For a Philippine stay up to 59 days, a Tourist Visa is required. Ask your travel agent for the requirements in effect at the time when you might need such a visa.

SINGAPORE and MALAYSIA: require no visa for U.S. citizens who remain less than 90 days. It is necessary for visitors who spend two weeks to register with the police. Those staying more than a month have to apply for a Registration Identity card.

CAMBODIA: requires no visa for a stay of 48 hours. A

Tourist or Visitor's Visa covers a stay up to 7 days, which is valid for 3 months from the date of departure from the U.S.A. and may be renewed gratis for another 3 month period. The cost of a Cambodian visa is $3.50. **Cambodia** requires one visa for each passport even though the passport might be a collective one, and one fee is all that is necessary, but each individual on a passport must complete application forms in triplicate. A passport picture must be attached to each of the forms (3 photos each person). If a stay longer than 3 months is anticipated, ask your travel agent for the latest regulations covering this contingency.

THAILAND: requires no visa for a stay of 15 days or less. No photographs are required. For a longer stay, your travel agent can supply you with the current regulations.

TAIWAN: requires no visa for a stay of less than 72 hours, but does require one for a longer stay. The visa application form must be filled out in duplicate accompanied by two passport photographs. There is no visa fee for U.S. citizens.

VIET NAM: requires no visa for U.S. citizens wishing to stay less than a week.

HONG KONG: does not require a visa for U.S. visitors traveling by air and staying less than 48 hours in **Hong Kong.** A **Hong Kong** Transit Visa is necessary for a stay of from 2 to 7 days, the fee for which is $2.00. If one's stay in **Hong Kong** is from 7 days to 3 months, a Tourist Visa is required for which the fee is $2.00 and is good for multiple entries into **Hong Kong.**

MACAO: requires a visa, the fee for which is $3.67 for single passports or $5.67 for family passports. This visa is good for a stay of 20 days. No photographs or application forms are necessary to obtain this visa. For a longer Macaoan stay, consult your travel agent as to rules and regulations.

See Chapter 8, Pages 467–70 for a list of Foreign Consulates and Embassies in the U.S.

CLIMATE

Much of the territory covered in this guidebook lies in the tropics where, understandably, it is frequently hot. The climate, however, should not be a deterrent to your planning a trip to the Orient nor need it be a discomfort factor when traveling. Be prepared, dress comfortably, stay out of the sun at midday, and particularly at noon, don't overindulge in food or alcohol, and you will get along just fine.

Hong Kong is never really terribly hot, **Japan** only in the summer months, the other places no more uncomfortable than **Chicago, Washington, D.C.,** or **St. Louis** in the summertime.

All good hotels and many restaurants are air conditioned. There are many fine swimming pools and invitingly cool beaches.

The following tables will be helpful to you in planning your itinerary and wardrobe:

CLIMATE IN BANGKOK (THAILAND)

Month	High Temperature, Maximum	Night Temperature, Minimum	Average Temperature	Average Humidity	Monthly Rainfall
Jan.	91°F.	68°F.	79.5°F.	72%	Nil
Feb.	93	71	82	70	Nil
March	94	74	84	74	1.02 in.
April	97	77	87	72	.05
May	93.5	77	85	77	4.5
June	92	77	85	77	3.16
July	91	77	84	80	5.08
Aug.	89	77	83	81	9.76
Sept.	89	75	82	84	18.00
Oct.	88	75	82	86	17.7
Nov.	89	72	80.5	83	3.76
Dec.	87	68	77.5	75	.50

CLIMATE IN HAWAII

Month	High Temperature, Maximum	Night Temperature, Minimum	Average Temperature	Average Humidity	Monthly Rainfall
Jan.	77°F.	67°F.	72°F.	80%	4.31 in.
Feb.	77	67	72	78	2.49
March	77	68	72.5	77	2.30
April	78	69	73.5	75	2.05
May	80	71	75.5	75	1.01
June	81	72	76.5	74	0.63
July	82	74	78	74	0.86
Aug.	83	74	78.5	75	1.09
Sept.	83	74	78.5	75	1.34
Oct.	82	73	77.5	76	2.28
Nov.	80	71	75.5	78	2.08
Dec.	78	69	73.5	78	3.48

CLIMATE IN HONG KONG

Month	High Temperature, Maximum	Night Temperature, Minimum	Average Temperature	Average Humidity	Monthly Rainfall
Jan.	75.3°F.	63°F.	69°F.	68%	0.15 in.
Feb.	78.7	63.5	71	80	1.82
March	81.5	71	76	86	2.02
April	84.7	72.3	78	82	6.78
May	91	80.4	85.5	81	8.42
June	84.5	78.5	81.5	80	4.76
July	93.6	79	86.5	83	19.37
Aug.	92.1	74.3	83	84	14.29
Sept.	92.1	76.9	84	79	10.42
Oct.	87.2	72.5	80	72	4.33
Nov.	82.7	67.6	74.5	69	1.67
Dec.	78.2	67.5	72.5	70	1.03

CLIMATE IN THE PHILIPPINES

Month	High Temperature, Maximum	Night Temperature, Minimum	Average Temperature	Average Humidity	Monthly Rainfall
Jan.	83.5°F.	75.2°F.	79°F.	78%	0.90 in.
Feb.	85.1	76.3	80.5	74	0.42
March	88.2	78.6	83	70	0.68
April	90.7	81.1	85.5	69	1.28
May	89.8	81.7	85.5	75	5.03
June	88.2	80.8	84.5	80	10.04
July	84.9	79.5	82.5	85	16.38
Aug.	84.9	79.5	82.5	85	17.07
Sept.	84.6	79.0	81.5	86	13.76
Oct.	84.9	78.3	81.5	85	7.66
Nov.	84.2	76.5	80	83	5.54
Dec.	83.5	75.6	79.5	82	2.71

CLIMATE IN SAIGON (VIET NAM)

Month	High Temperature, Maximum	Night Temperature, Minimum	Average Temperature	Average Humidity	Monthly Rainfall
Jan.	93°F.	59°F.	76°F.	75%	.56 in.
Feb.	98	64	81	72	.20
March	98	64	81	72	.44
April	98	69	83	75	2.12
May	97	70	83	82	8.24
June	95	70	82.5	85	12.60
July	94	69	81.5	85	11.64
Aug.	94	68	81	85	10.64
Sept.	93	70	81.5	87	13.36
Oct.	92	68	80	86	10.44
Nov.	91	64	77.5	83	4.80
Dec.	92	66	79	79	2.24

CLIMATE IN SINGAPORE

Month	High Temperature, Maximum	Night Temperature, Minimum	Average Temperature	Average Humidity	Monthly Rainfall
Jan.	87.8°F.	73.3°F.	81°F.	85.1%	9.93 in.
Feb.	87.4	73.5	81	83.3	6.89
March	87.9	74.4	81.5	84.2	7.89
April	87.1	75.4	81	84.6	7.72
May	87.6	76.1	81.5	84.4	6.84
June	87.5	76.5	81.5	82.5	6.73
July	87.1	76.4	81.5	82	6.59
Aug.	86.9	76	81.5	82.5	7.53
Sept.	86.7	75.5	81	83.1	7.05
Oct.	86.7	75.1	81	84.1	8.18
Nov.	86.2	74.7	81	86	9.89
Dec.	85.9	73.8	79.5	86	10.46

CLIMATE IN TAIWAN (FORMOSA)

Month	High Temperature, Maximum	Night Temperature, Minimum	Average Temperature	Average Humidity	Monthly Rainfall
Jan.	66.4°F.	54.1°F.	60.2°F.	84%	3.51 in.
Feb.	65.5	53.6	59.5	84	5.50
March	70.2	57.2	63.7	84	7.22
April	77.0	63.1	70.1	82	6.65
May	83.5	69.1	76.3	82	8.93
June	88.9	73.4	81.1	81	11.98
July	91.9	75.7	83.8	78	8.97
Aug.	91.1	75.6	83.3	78	11.80
Sept.	87.9	73.0	80.5	79	8.87
Oct.	81.3	67.8	74.6	80	4.45
Nov.	75.2	62.4	68.8	81	2.37
Dec.	69.3	57.0	63.1	83	2.88

CLIMATE IN TOKYO

Month	High Temperature, Maximum	Night Temperature, Minimum	Average Temperature	Average Humidity	Monthly Rainfall
Jan.	48°F.	30°F.	39°F.	61%	2.30 in.
Feb.	48	32	40	58	5.00
Mar.	54	35	44.5	59	3.50
April	64	48	56	62	7.00
May	70	54	62	69	8.50
June	76	63	69.5	78	5.50
July	83	69	76	79	3.75
Aug.	88	73	80.5	79	6.50
Sept.	89	66	77	76	7.00
Oct.	71	56	63.5	72	8.60
Nov.	61	44	52.5	64	4.75
Dec.	52	34	43	61	7.60

THE QUESTION OF CLOTHES . . . AND SOME AN-SWERS. There is always the problem of what clothes to pack when one is planning a trip to faraway lands. The tendency for all of us travelers, male and female alike, is to burden our-selves with too many clothes and too much baggage. One can always supplement wardrobes along the way if this becomes necessary, particularly in the Orient.

Much of the Orient is in the tropics; hence, lightweight, very cool clothes must constitute the base for any travel wardrobe. Woolens, essential for **Japan** during the late fall, winter, and early spring, can also be worn in **Taiwan** and occasionally in **Hong Kong** in the winter.

Hawaii has a very equable climate—cottons and synthetics can be worn the year around except in the mountain areas where it can be crisply cool in the winter.

The weather in the **Philippines** is warm the year around, with April and May being the warmest months. Light cottons and synthetics are always the order of the day.

The average year-around temperature in **Singapore** is circa 80 degrees accompanied by intense humidity. The evenings, at times, can be pleasantly cool.

The Orient is not a "dressy" part of the world by any means. One seldom sees hats or gloves worn, and during the hottest weather many women dispense with stockings and go bare-legged. Men usually wear jackets and ties for cocktails and dinner. It is practical for a woman to have a sweater or stole to throw over her shoulders in the air conditioned places.

For evening wear in the **Philippines,** men choose, for the most part, the elegant, long-sleeved, high-necked, beautifully embroidered native shirts, officially called *barongs* but better known as "Manila shirts," worn properly without coat or tie.

While evening dress in **Hawaii** is strictly informal, men do wear shirts and ties with jackets in the nicer restaurants, night clubs, and hotel dining rooms.

Except in **Hong Kong** and **Japan,** men usually wear only shirts and slacks during the day, even for traveling, choosing either a long-sleeved or sport shirt. Just be sure it's plain white, except for **Hawaii** where gaudy, multihued Aloha shirts are worn.

For women, cocktail dresses are the most popular for evening. Except on very special occasions, one seldom sees formal clothes worn in the Orient.

WARDROBE SUGGESTIONS FOR MEN

2 suits. One dark that can be worn in the evenings; the other can be either light or dark, but both must be cool and lightweight except for **Japan** where, in winter, heavier suits are comfortable.

1 topcoat for winter in **Japan**, **Taiwan** or **Hong Kong**. Otherwise not necessary.

3 pairs of slacks.

1 lightweight sport coat.

1 raincoat, lightweight or water-repellent gabardine depending on the time of year.

1 sweater without sleeves (cashmere is an excellent choice).

1 hat, if you wear them, for late fall or winter in **Japan, Taiwan, or Hong Kong.**

2 or 3 pairs of shoes. Be sure to take one pair of comfortable walking shoes.

3 shirts of dacron or other synthetic fabrics.

3 sport shirts (2 white).

3 sets of underwear, nylon or dacron.

3 neckties.

6 handkerchiefs.

1 belt.

2 pairs of nylon pajamas.

6 pairs of socks.

1 dressing gown in tie silk, cotton, or nylon.

1 pair swimming trunks.

1 set toilet articles.

1 razor and ample supply of blades (adaptor transformer kit if you use electric razor. Most countries in the Orient have 2-prong electrical outlets with variable current and voltage).

PRACTICAL AND USEFUL ADDITIONS

1 brush-top cleaning fluid.

2 bars of your favorite soap.

2 deodorant. *Ban* is effective and easy to carry.

1 first-aid kit (include a thermometer).

1 small Traveler's Sewing Kit (with a few extra buttons).

2 washcloths.

1 small traveler's alarm clock with luminous dial.

1 pair of dark glasses.
1 extra pair of glasses if you wear them.
1 ballpoint pen with refills.
1 extra supply of any regularly used medicines.
1 cigarette lighter, fluid and flints, if you use a lighter. Matches are plentiful.
2 plastic bags for wet swim suits, shirts and soap.
1 Scotch tape and dispenser (a most useful item).
2 folding plastic hangers (for use in drying your synthetic shirts).
1 plastic bottle of liquid Ivory soap—lasts a long time—handy. Can be used for laundering and shampooing.

COTTON is the coolest fabric for the tropics, but nylon, dacron, and related synthetic fabrics are certainly the most practical, as they can be so easily laundered and dry rapidly. Never hang synthetic shirts on wooden hangers as they will become discolored from the paint. The folding plastic hangers are a great boon.

SHAVING SOAP. Concentrated whipped cream-like shaving lather, put up under a variety of trade names, and push button dispensed, is wonderful. Shaving is made easier by this luxuriant lather which is impervious to hard water. One can is good for 50 shaves or more.

NECKTIES. Sport shirts are worn so frequently in the tropics during the day a man does not need many neckties. Take 2 or 3 ties to wear evenings in the nice restaurants and hotel dining rooms. If you need additional ties, attractive ones can be purchased inexpensively all along the way.

HATS are not worn much by westerners in the Orient except in **Japan,** and occasionally in **Taiwan** and **Hong Kong** during the winter.

TOPCOATS are not at all necessary if you are traveling in the summertime. A topcoat is a necessity in **Japan** and sometimes in **Hong Kong** and **Taiwan** in the winter.

BEACH WEAR. If you swim, by all means take along your trunks. There are many beautiful, inviting beaches, as well as convenient swimming pools in the hotels.

LADIES' CLOTHING

Warm weather clothes are worn all year in the tropical countries. Cottons are the coolest, but the synthetics are the most practical because of their easy care. Silk is also cool and practical. Sweaters, or a scarf, to throw over your shoulders in the cool of the evening or while in air conditioned areas are most convenient. A fur coat can be comfortable in Japan in winter, where a woolen suit and topcoat will also be most comfortable. This latter is also true of **Taiwan** and **Hong Kong** in the winter.

WARDROBE SUGGESTIONS FOR WOMEN

1 knitted dress.
2 blouses. Woolen, nylon, or cotton.
1 raincoat. Plastic for rainy season.
1 pair of rubbers for rainy season.
2 dresses. Cocktail.
1 dress with jacket. Silk.
2 dresses, sleeveless, with jackets. Cotton.
2 dresses. Nylon.
1 or 2 suits. Silk, cotton, or woolen, depending on the season. Silk and cotton always worn in the tropics. Woolen worn in **Japan** and **Hong Kong** in winter. Take 1 wool and 1 cotton for winter travel.
1 topcoat. Woolen. Depending on season. Never needed in tropics or **Japan** in summer. A must for **Japan** in fall, winter, or spring.
2 sweaters. One a little dressy for evening wear. One for **day** wear.
1 stole. Woolen.
1 hat. Small, which can be easily packed.
1 head scarf or decorated veil.
1 robe. Nylon, tie silk, or cotton.
12 pairs of nylon hose.
2 girdles or garter belts.
3 bras. 1 strapless.
3 pair panties.
3 slips. Nylon.

3 nighties. Nylon.

4 pairs of shoes. 1 pair of plain pumps for evening, 2 pair street shoes (one could be light in color for the tropics), 1 comfortable walking shoes. Plastic bag containers for shoes.

2 pairs of gloves.

2 handbags. 1 large enough for traveling. 1 for afternoon and evening.

2 pairs of peds.

1 pair of traveling slippers in case.

1 bathing suit.

1 shower cap.

VERY PRACTICAL ADDITIONS

3 lipsticks.

1 box face powder.

2 deodorant.

2 toothbrushes.

2 boxes "Argenta" hand lotion pillows.

2 "Venus" sanitary napkins (large travel packages).

1 sanitary belt.

1 bottle brush-top cleaner.

1 liquid soap like Ivory in plastic bottle. Easy to carry, lasts a long time—can be used for laundry and shampoos.

1 plastic bag for carrying soap flakes if you prefer them to liquid soap. As soap flakes are used, the packing space becomes available for other items.

1 sewing kit.

1 first-aid kit.

1 small traveling alarm clock with luminous dial.

1 pair of dark glasses.

1 extra pair of glasses, if you wear them, and tissues for cleaning.

2 washcloths.

3 bars of your favorite toilet soap.

1 manicure kit containing your favorite nail polish.

1 hairbrush.

2 combs.

1 or 2 small plastic containers to carry extra bobby pins, hairpins, and safety pins.

1 ballpoint pen with refills.

1 cigarette lighter, fluid and extra flints, if you use a lighter. Matches are plentiful in the Orient.

3 extra plastic bags for carrying wet swimming suits, or other damp articles.

1 Scotch tape and dispenser. Handy for sealing envelopes, mending, etc.

Wash-n-Dri cleansing tissues.

WARDROBE NOTES

SUITS. A woolen suit for cold weather, cotton and silk suits practical for the tropics. Try to take one basic color and fit accessories to this color.

RAINCOAT AND TOE RUBBERS can be used during rainy seasons.

COAT. A warm coat is necessary for cold weather in **Japan** and winter in **Taiwan** and **Hong Kong.**

KNITS. A knitted dress is always practical, as it never wrinkles. Purchase either lightweight or heavier material, depending on the season in which you will be traveling.

DRESSES. Nothing is more practical for hot weather than a real silk dress, perhaps with jacket. Sleeveless cottons with jackets are wonderful. Nylons are lighter, more porous, and cooler than they used to be and can't be beat for practicability. They can be laundered in a jiffy. One or two cocktail dresses will suffice for evening wear.

A HEAD SCARF OR DECORATED VEIL is practical for sightseeing as protection against the wind.

GLOVES are not generally worn in the Orient, though they are occasionally used in **Singapore,** or in **Japan** and **Hong Kong** during the cool weather. Cotton or lightweight kid are best.

PURSES. Two purses will be ample . . . one large with zipper compartment for passports, tickets, traveler's checks, and money, and one that can be used for evening—beaded or fabric is nice.

BATHING SUITS. If you like to swim, or "sun all over," you will surely want to take along a bathing suit. There are many beautiful beaches in the Orient, and many of the hotels have fine swimming pools. Bring your favorite suit (or suits). There are no prudish restrictions as to the anatomical area to be covered.

ROBES. Tie silk robes are easily packed, practical, and cool. Nylon is easily cared for and practical. Like silk, it stands up under rigorous traveling.

SPECIAL FOOTWEAR. When entering Japanese homes or Japanese inns, the shoes must be left at the entrance. Throughout Japan you will be provided with slip-on foot covering that is quite adequate. However, if you are squeamish about wearing slippers that have been worn by others, bring your own portable variety. In most department stores you may buy the type of "all size" cloth foot covering similar to that which many airlines dispense on long overnight journeys. These expandable "slippers" fit snugly and are easily carried in a man's pocket or a woman's purse. As I have mentioned elsewhere, I fervently urge that you do not fail to enter a few of the Buddhist temples. In **Kyoto** and **Bangkok,** particularly, there are temples so beautiful as to be indescribable. You should enter them. In **Kyoto,** slippers will be furnished. In **Bangkok,** no. Therefore, if you have your all-purpose portable slippers with you, you probably will be happy. On the other hand, in **Bangkok** things are so clean and the climate so temperate that you wouldn't mind going in your stocking feet, or bare feet if the ladies are not wearing hose. If you are traveling by air, it might be well to stick a pair of the airline slippers in your overnight bag. (These are usually handed out free to the passengers.)

LINGERIE. Thanks to the easily laundered synthetics, women can conveniently travel very lightly. Three sets of lingerie are really sufficient.

HOSE. Be sure to take enough hose to last the trip. It is sometimes difficult to get the right size hose for American women in the Orient, so one should take a sufficient quantity.

CONVENIENT ADDITIONS. There are many small, zippered, practical sewing, toilet article, and jewelry kits on the market. Bring one or two along.

PLASTIC CONTAINERS. It is a good idea to carry as many cosmetic items as possible in plastic bottles or containers. Take several such bottles or containers along. They are so convenient for storing small items.

TISSUE PAPER. Bring along a large roll of tissue paper to insert in your clothing when packing.

DRUG STORES. There are numerous exceptionally well-stocked drug stores and pharmacies throughout the Orient where one can buy almost all the American name-brand drugs, toiletries, cosmetics, and hygienic needs. Well-equipped drug stores are to be found in all Japanese cities, as well as in **Bangkok, Singapore, Saigon, Hong Kong, Manila,** and, of course, **Hawaii.** Travelers need have no fear of running out of their favorite toilet articles, cosmetics, or drugs.

DRY CLEANING AND LAUNDRY are done quickly and efficiently in almost all of the hotels in the Orient. The service in **Hawaii** is exactly as on the Mainland—quick and efficient. In **Japan** one can get one-day laundry service, but dry cleaning may take a couple of days. Good cleaning and laundry services are obtainable in the **Philippines.** In **Singapore** the laundry service is good, but dry cleaning is not on a par with **ours and** is likely to be expensive. There is excellent laundry service in **Thailand,** but dry cleaning does not compare with ours.

Hong Kong offers excellent laundry and dry-cleaning facilities. Pressing service is amazingly good, much better and faster than anything known in the States. One-hour pressing service is routine.

BEAUTY PARLORS are excellent throughout the Orient. You need have no worries. Your everlasting ethereal beauty will have as many artificial aids in the Orient as you have at home. The finest beauty parlors are in the best hotels. Should you be staying at a lesser hotel, not equipped with a beauty parlor, consult the hotel pages of this book and make an appointment by telephone with the beauty shop at one of the recommended hotels. Everything is available in these excellent salons: set, shampoo, permanent, manicure, depilation . . . EVERYTHING. Many of the beauty operators have been trained in America.

THE BARBER SHOPS are also very good indeed. As with the gals, the Oriental barber shops offer all the comforts and luxuries we are accustomed to at home. The barbers are adept at hair cutting, shaving, shampooing, and facial massage. The manicurist will be chic and skilled at her work. There are shoe-shine boys too. The best barber shops as well as the superb beauty salons are found in the top-grade hotels. In **Tokyo** I particularly like the barber shop in the basement arcade of the *Nikkatsu Hotel* and office building.

LUGGAGE. Another important decision to be made involves luggage . . . quality, size and how much to take. For a six- or seven-week, or even longer, trip, two suitcases and an over-night case should do the trick nicely. An ideal size case is 29x19x9 inches. Fiber cases with trays, which may or may not be used, are exceptionally sturdy and cheap, although they are a bit heavy if you are flying. Unfortunately, good luggage takes an awful beating. I have seen fine new leather cases badly frayed, with strips of leather torn off and locks damaged, after only one or two airport and airplane handlings.

Some travelers prefer the Val Pak, which is particularly practical for ladies. These cases comfortably carry 10 to 12 dresses and a coat on hangers. The Val Pak can be hung on a hook in the closet or room and does not ever have to be completely un-packed. Each article can be taken off the hanger, as needed, and the clothing is never wrinkled.

The ladies' invaluable cosmetic case comes in leather or synthetic coverings, and will hold all make-up requirements as well as other personal accessories which one might have need of in a hurry en route, such as nightie, robe, or slippers. Very often these same things are needed when one reaches the hotel and before the large bags have arrived. The airlines bags which hold all toilet articles, clean shirt, pajamas, cosmetics, nightie, and even some reading material are neat and utilitarian for both men and women.

Choose luggage that will go right along with you in the trains, planes, and cars. Luggage shipped ahead, or separately, may get lost, stranded, or misplaced for days, weeks, or forever.

If one does a lot of shopping, a good idea is to buy a lightweight suitcase at the last stop, put all one's purchases in it, and ship it home, air express, at a reasonable price.

TIPS ON PACKING. I have found that if one uses the flat, box-like suitcase, shoes in plastic bags can be put on the bottom. Small articles can be placed in the shoes, and other articles of clothing may be placed around them. When either men or women are packing dresses, suits, and coats, lay the garments out flat on a bed and place tissue paper generously on the clothing after which the ladies' dresses can be tightly rolled and the men's suits folded over the tissue paper, keeping the articles of clothing fresh and wrinkle free during their travels. Another idea is to keep the garments in their plastic bags just as they are returned from the cleaner, fold the garments and put them in the suitcase. This also helps to keep clothing from wrinkling.

Garments do not wrinkle at all should you choose to buy a Val Pak—but be sure to buy the best. The Val Paks of inferior quality are less than satisfactory.

CARRYING FUNDS. No matter what kind of arrangements you have made for your trip, you will need a certain amount of money with you. The best way to carry funds is in the form of traveler's checks, the best known of which are American Express Company and Thomas Cook & Son. These inexpensive checks, easily cashed anywhere in the world, may be purchased in denominations of $10, $20, $50, $100, and $500 from your travel agent or local bank. In Chapter 8 under *Helpful Hints,* I have commented further on this important subject.

CURRENCY REGULATIONS imposed by the various foreign governments are covered in Chapter 8 under *Helpful Hints* (Foreign Exchange).

A BIBLIOGRAPHY OF TRAVEL

AROUND THE WORLD
Around the World with Elmer or How to Haggle in 17 Countries. Wheeler, E.; Fleet Publishing Corporation.

CAMBODIA
Angkor. MacDonald, M.; Praeger.
Cambodia: Land of Contrasts. Tooze, Ruth; Viking.

CEYLON
Ceylon. Tresidder, A. J.; Van Nostrand Co., Inc.

EUROPE
Aboard and Abroad. Olson, Harvey S.; J. B. Lippincott Company.

FORMOSA (TAIWAN)
Still the River Grows Green. Caldwell, J. C. and Rignery, H.

GENERAL
After You, Marco Polo. Shor, Jean Bowie; McGraw-Hill.
All the Best in Japan with Manila, Hong Kong, and Macao. Clark, Sydney; Dodd, Mead and Company.
Far East Travel Guide. Caldwell, J. C.; John Day Company.
Fodor's Guide to Japan and East Asia. Fodor, E. and Fisher, R. C., eds.; David McKay Company.

McKay's Guide to the Far East and Middle East. Gellhorn, Eleanor Cowles; David McKay Company.

Orient Holiday. American President Lines.

New Horizons World Guide. Pan American World Airways.

South Asia Travel Guide. Caldwell, J. C.; John Day Company.

Travel Guide to the Orient and Around the World. American President Lines.

HAWAII

All About Hawaii. Thrum; Honolulu Star-Bulletin.

Fodor's Modern Guide to Hawaii. Fodor, E.; David McKay Company.

Hawaii. Michener, James; Random House.

The Hawaii Book. J. G. Ferguson Publishing Company.

HONG KONG

Hong Kong and Macao. Ingrams, H.; London: M.M.S.O.

INDIA & PAKISTAN

A Passage Through Pakistan. Linck, O. F.; Wayne State University Press.

Drums Behind the Hill. Bower, E. G.; William Morrow & Company.

Indian Handbook for India, Pakistan & Ceylon. Murray, John.

Pakistan & Afghanistan. Linck, O. F.; Wayne State University Press.

Your Holidays in India. Shahani, R. T.

JAPAN

A Guide to Kyoto, Nara, Osaka, Kobe. Japan Travel Bureau.

A Guide to Tokyo and Environs. Japan Travel Bureau.

Hiroshima. Hersey, John; Bantam Books.

Japan, the Official Guide. Japan Travel Bureau.

Japan, the Pocket Guide. Japan Travel Bureau.

Japan Travel Dictionary of Tourist Resorts. Okada, R.; Japan Travel Bureau.

Japanese Arts—What & Where. Kikuchi, Sadao; Japan Travel Bureau.

Japanese Etiquette. Nakajima, Bun; Japan Travel Bureau.

Japanese Inn. Statler, Oliver; Random House.
Kimono. Ken-ichi Kawakatsu; Japan Travel Bureau.
Meeting with Japan. Maraini, Fosco M.; Viking Press.
Tell Me About Japan. Japan Travel Bureau.

MALAYSIA

The Hostile Sun. Stacy, T.; Duckworth (London).

NEPAL

The Mountain is Young. Suyin, Han; Putnam.

PHILIPPINES

Bare Feet in the Palace. Keith, A. N.; Little, Brown & Company.
The Philippine Islands, a Guide. Abrahamsen, H. M.; Pacific Books.

THAILAND

Anna and the King of Siam. Landon, Margaret; Garden City.
Thailand. Busch, N. F.; Van Nostrand.

VIET NAM

Saigon Journey. Stafford, Ann; Taplinger Publishing Company.
Viet Nam. Van Tung, Tran; Praeger.

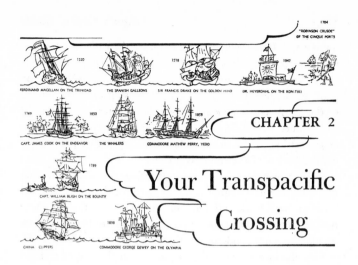

CHAPTER 2

Your Transpacific Crossing

OF LIFE's most ecstatic experiences, none is more completely captivating than sailing across the azure blue waters of a vast mysterious ocean. In the storehouse of one's memories, no room is more treasured than the cherished one reserved for mental souvenirs of travel to faraway places. To tread the soil of foreign lands is to set in motion superchargers of emotional stimuli. Each new country visited in the mysterious Orient, every Far Eastern city, will unfold strange and awesome panoramic vistas. New travel adventures on the far side of the world will bring into brilliant focus the pages of the erstwhile dimly obscure past. An investment in foreign travel is an immediate source of rewarding pleasure and one that will pay recurring and increasing dividends with each passing year.

Foreign travel offers one art, architecture, culture, and history generously blended with fun, romance, and adventure, but of all the excruciatingly exciting experiences of traveling abroad, none is more spine tingling than blithely sailing across broad expanses of brooding bodies of water.

I remember warmly and with crystal clarity that July day in 1929 when first I scrambled up the gangplank of a mighty *Atlantic* liner. Irrepressible emotion surged through every fiber of

51

my massive frame when I sensed, rather than felt, for the first time the throb of powerful engines turning over far below decks. I can never obliterate the scene from my mind, as on my maiden voyage I stood rapturously at the ship's rail and gulped in the lavish portrait of a glowing west. After the purple sea had claimed the setting sun, I will ever remember the romance of the setting as the moon etched a silvery path on the shimmering waters of the limitless ocean.

My first over-the-ocean flight, a laborious one in a lumbering DC-4, found me chugging tediously for more than sixteen hours between **New York** and **London** punctuated by the inevitable fueling stops at gray **Gander** and shamrock studded **Shannon.** As plodding and ponderous as that flight was in the "Model T" of long distance aircraft, it gave me a great thrill, greater I am sure than any received by contemporary astronauts in their magnificent conquest of outer space.

As one plans and prepares for an exciting Orient adventure, the first and most important choice one must make is "How shall I travel? Shall I fly all the way, shall I go by ship all the way, or should I blend the two modes of transportation?"

The choice is not an easy one. The jets are amazingly rapid, efficient, and comfortable. The ocean liners of the transpacific fleets offer endless joys. Each precious moment aboard a ship is charged with the ultimate in pleasure. While I shall do my best to render all possible assistance in making a proper decision, I must confess that I am not an entirely impartial observer. Long before I went on active Naval Reserve duty in World War II, I had become thoroughly addicted to the salty ships that sail the sea. I am a dedicated seagoing adventurer.

As thoroughgoing a deep sea devotee as I am, however, I have flown across various oceans scores of times and adored each experience. I full well appreciate that the distance involved in crossing the seemingly endless *Pacific* by ship can well impose insurmountable barriers. If time is of the essence in your busy schedule and a choice must be made between "taking a boat ride" or seeing the Orient thoroughly, there is no problem.

Fly. If time is only a minor problem, by all means fly one way and taste of the luxury of ship travel the other. If time is no factor, by all means take advantage of the wonderful transportation afforded by the transpacific ships both ways. How to cross the *Atlantic* poses a much more difficult problem. One reaches **Europe** by ship in five days or less. The jets devour the transatlantic miles in a matter of fleeting hours, but the time differential between flying and sailing is basically not great . . . at the most a few days each way. The *Pacific* presents an entirely different pot of porridge. The eager jets span the *Pacific* from **San Francisco** to **Tokyo** in twelve hours or less, while in the fastest ships the journey requires some two weeks of delightful ocean travel.

During decades of concentrated travel, I have culled countless gems of ocean experience. My travels have been both as a conscientious professional in pursuit of his duties and as an avid amateur enchanted by every rapturous minute of a glamorous career. I am delighted to share with you the gleanings gathered in my fantasy of "Olson in Travel Wonderland."

My friend and adviser, the canny old Scot, has said that there are two salient features of advice: (1) it's usually no good, and (2) it is seldom followed. Be that as it may, in this chapter I will pass on to you pertinent pointers on transpacific travel both by the ships of the surface fleet and the services of the jet aircraft. Take some and leave some, and whatever your choice, bon voyage, happy traveling; may your trip be replete with blue skies, smooth seas, soothing sunshine, and glorious travel adventure aboard, aloft, and abroad.

YOUR CROSSING BY SHIP

I know of no more supercharged exciting experience than sailing day. For months, even years, one will have schemed and planned, thought and dreamed, of a grand *Pacific* adventure. Then suddenly, almost unexpectedly, the voyager finds himself in **Los Angeles** or **San Francisco** preparing to board a sleek ocean liner.

Even before reaching the pulsating dock churning with gay activity, one will have been wound tight with pleasure packed excitement such as when the band plays the "Stars and Stripes Forever" on the Fourth of July or in that excruciating moment when one's loved one says, "I do."

The pier area assumes an aura of gay expectancy for this extra special occasion . . . sailing day . . . a gay springboard to the ecstasy of Orient travel.

The taxis, yellow, red, black, blue, and purple, add to the paint pot luster of the occasion as they converge to disgorge their handsome cargos of fellow travelers and their guests.

Porters dart in and out handling countless pieces of baggage ornamented like Christmas trees with decorative, rainbow-like baggage tags and labels. Flowers adorn the ladies' shoulders . . . gift boxes, books, and magazines are tucked under their arms. What a heady experience. Ooh, la, la!

Soon tickets and passports will have been presented, and you will be aboard your dream vessel. It is not at all unlikely that hundreds of guests will have come aboard to add to the electricity of the moment. Gay farewell parties will be in progress.

In a matter of minutes, or so it seems, the deep throated blast of the ship's horn signals the impending casting off of the lines. Page boys and stewards bang on gongs and echo the time honored haunting shout, "All ashore that's going ashore."

Soon a slight stirring below decks indicates that powerful engines have started to turn. Lines are cast off, and the great vessel slips out into the bay or harbor. The moment of departure is the climax of all. Serpentine confetti streams from ship to pier, and there are shouts of "Bon voyage, bon voyage . . . have a wonderful time." Perhaps a nostalgic slightly hidden tear or two mingles with the tinkling laughter as, at last, the grand adventure has been transformed from a nebulous dream to pleasure packed reality.

All too many of us have become hopelessly enmeshed in our confining daily routine. We get up at a fixed hour, take breakfast, lunch, or dinner by the clock; we beat a path from our homes to our offices, clubs, or stores; we talk with the same people, and do the same things day in, day out, week in, week out. Life at sea is a continuous floating house party. This exciting shipboard activity enables us to jump clear of the chains that have bound us to our work-a-day traditional activities. Now one may live a completely new vibrant life of luxury and ease.

The health-giving effect of the tangy salt sea air imparts to the digestive tract a voracious appetite that is legendary. The yum-yum quality of transpacific seagoing cuisine is more than adequate to your newly found super-stimulated insatiable desire to eat. And don't worry about the calories; there is plenty of opportunity for all types of refreshing exercise to whip the "battle of the bulge" before it begins. You may enjoy swimming, ping pong, brisk walks on the sun-splashed deck, shuffleboard, and deck tennis, as well as "vigorous" deck chair snoozing.

One of the untold delights of life at sea is the opportunity to linger lazily abed late in the morning. The epitome of the lap of luxury is to be able to press a button to order a voluptuous breakfast: fresh strawberries and cream, raisin pancakes with maple syrup and a side order of pork sausages, blueberry muffins, or creamed chicken on toast with toasted English muffins. After breakfast you can cuddle up and doze until your fancy urges a visit to the ship's pool for a crisp plunge or a séance in the sun.

Most *Pacific* liners offer an outdoor midday buffet to swimmers and loungers. The choice is from among a taste-tempting myriad of hot and cold dishes.

There is so much shipboard entertainment from which to choose, there are never enough hours in the fun-filled days at sea.

Even after a hearty breakfast, one is offered bouillon or a sherbet at eleven in the morning, a large lunch either on deck or informally in the main dining room, high tea, and after a fine dinner there inevitably will be a generous midnight buffet just to be sure that the inner man or woman is not forgotten. One enjoys a rapturous life fit for a king or queen en route by ship across the vast *Pacific*.

For your guidance in choosing a ship for your transpacific crossing, I have included the following brief resumés of the background and services of the transpacific fleets:

AMERICAN PRESIDENT LINES

AMERICAN PRESIDENT LINES is the leading steamship line, and my favorite, providing *Pacific* and around the world services. The traditions of this renowned company were founded in 1867, when, shortly after **Japan** was opened to foreign ships, the *Pacific Mail Steamship Company* vessel *"Colorado"* sailed from **San Francisco** to **Yokohama** and **Hong Kong**. The *Colorado,* and her sister ships by whom she was soon joined, were wooden side-wheeler paddle ships. In 1874, iron-hulled, propeller-driven ships entered the *American Mail Pacific* service, and in 1904 the *"City of Peking"* and *"City of Tokyo"* made their debut. These two vessels subsequently became the first of the famous *"Presidents,"* being rechristened the *"President Johnson"* and *"President Fillmore."* The continuity of the early history of the present *American President Lines* was kept intact and the scope of the early services enlarged by the addition of five "535" type *Presidents,* which were owned by the United States Shipping Board and operated by the *Pacific Mail Line* as managing agents. The "535" category was so named because the hull length of the *Presidents Cleveland, Lincoln, Pierce, Taft,* and *Wilson* was 535 feet each.

In 1925 another significant step was taken toward the inspiring goal which ultimately placed all of the transpacific, around the Orient, and around the world *Presidents* under the house flag of the *American President Lines.* The United States Shipping Board advertised the "535's" for sale with the stipulation that the sale and purchase of these vessels carried the rights, as well as the obligation, to continue a fortnightly service between **San Francisco** and the Orient.

The *Dollar Steamship Lines,* founded by Robert Dollar and continued under the leadership of the intrepid Captain Stanley Dollar, were the successful bidders for the ships. The *Pacific* services continued without interruption under the *Dollar Line* flag.

The Dollar interests were no newcomers to the field. Their house flag had flown on freighters from California to the Orient since the turn of the century, and in 1924 the *Dollar Line* inaugurated the first combined freighter-passenger service around the world in seven "502" type vessels also acquired from the United States Shipping Board. This celebrated service is today a part of the famed worldwide operation of the *American President Lines.*

The first of the transpacific luxury liners, the original *Presidents Hoover* and *Coolidge,* were placed in service in 1930 and 1931 respectively. Both of these vessels were wartime casualties, but their names were carried on by postwar additions to the APL fleet. The second *President Hoover* was retired by the company in the spring of 1964. In 1940 and 1941, seven ships of the *President Polk* type were constructed for the round the world market.

In 1938, as a result of a sweeping reorganization, the name of the line was changed officially from the *Dollar Steamship Lines, Inc.* to *American President Lines, Ltd.* The union was so closely fused as to enable the then new APL to acquire the offices and personnel of the *Robert Dollar Co.*, managing agents of the *Dollar Steamship Lines.*

The *American President Line*'s contribution to the war effort was herculean. As was the case with other American operators, APL was placed under the wartime control of the War Shipping Administration during which crisis the *Line* efficiently operated more than one hundred vessels, carrying the American flag proudly to farflung world ports.

The end of the conflict saw the return of the ships to their former owners, but as a result of the ravages of war the APL received only the *Presidents Polk* and *Monroe* of its former around the world fleet, the ancient *President Johnson*, ex *Manchuria*, three C-3 type World War II freighters, and the *Presidents Grant, Pierce*, and *Taft.*

To enable APL to play a vital role in the moving of the large backlog of traffic, APL operated several now extinct government-owned austerity-type passenger vessels of great capacity. The list of these one-time troop carriers included the *General Gordon, General Meigs*, and *Marine Lynx;* the last of which, the *General Gordon*, was retired in 1950.

The celebrated twin luxury liners, *President Cleveland* and *President Wilson*, made their seagoing debuts in 1947 and 1948.

In 1947, the dynamic, perspicacious Mr. George Killion was appointed to run the APL, then owned by the government and operated under the aegis of the Department of Commerce, and from that date the present and future success of APL was assured. Mr. Ralph K. Davies, a business genius and currently chairman of the board, and Mr. Killion were the nucleus of the group known as A.P.L. Associates which purchased the present company from the United States Government.

Messrs. Davies and Killion have proved to be an executive team of great stature. Their combined ability to foresee the future and to build soundly and dramatically to meet the demands of the contemporary market while planning far ahead has seen the APL grow from a handful of outmoded ships to the present great fleet of twenty-eight magnificent vessels proudly sailing the transpacific, *Atlantic Straits,* and round the world routes. Many other ships are in the planning, drawing board, and construction phases. These gentlemen have excelled in surrounding themselves with skilled experts in the passenger, freight, and operation departments, while they themselves have provided an extraordinarily sound business management based on the bedrock of solid business acumen. They have given APL imaginative leadership in sales, operation and public relations.

It is a matter of great personal pride that I have known and long shared a warm friendship with John Marshall Diggs, APL's sagacious vice president in charge of passenger traffic. I have admired John's meteoric progress as he moved steadily upward from an office boy in a steamship company office in **New York** to become APL's top passenger executive. He is a fellow *Purdue* Boilermaker, a native of Winchester, Indiana, and has indeed added luster to the Horatio Alger legend of the local boy who made good in the big city. I know of no one in the steamship business whose knowledge of the needs of the passengers is more profound or more appreciative than is John Diggs'.

Each day something new, something different, is done in APL to add to the already fine services enjoyed by their fortunate passengers.

The APL passenger vessels now engaged in the transpacific service are the two class beauties, the *S.S. President Cleveland* and *S.S. President Wilson,* and the newest addition to luxury cruising on the *Pacific,* the magnificent all first class liner, *S.S.*

President Roosevelt, named after either "Teddy" or FDR, depending on your political leaning.

All APL liners sail from **San Francisco** with seasonal sailings of the *Wilson, Cleveland,* and *Roosevelt* calling at **Los Angeles** en route to **Honolulu.**

The *Wilson, Cleveland,* and *Roosevelt* speed from **San Francisco** directly to **Honolulu** in five days, or in six days when proceeding via **Los Angeles.** After a day's stopover in **Hawaii, Yokohama** is eight days further along. After a day in **Japan's** great seaport, **Hong Kong** is reached four days later. The interval in this glamorous port is from nine A.M. to a ten P.M. departure. From **Hong Kong,** the picturesque run to **Manila** is accomplished in thirty-seven hours, a daylong stopover being allotted to the **Philippines.**

I am thoroughly delighted that the itinerary of the APL *Pacific* vessels includes a return, second call at **Hong Kong** before the ships proceed via **Yokohama** for second calls at **Honolulu** and **San Francisco.** The **San Francisco** back to **San Francisco** complete around the Orient cruise in the *Wilson* and *Cleveland* is thirty-nine fun-filled days, or forty-four days including **Los Angeles** and port calls at **Keelung, Nagasaki,** and **Kobe** during the extended spring and fall voyages. Instituted in 1964, these popular, extended, voyages give the Orient traveler the added bonus of interesting ports which are not regularly featured on cruises to the Far East. A daylong visit in **Keelung** allows one a delightful glimpse of the emerald beauty of **Taiwan** (*Formosa*) and its capital city, **Taipei.** After their second call at **Hong Kong,** the *Presidents Cleveland, Wilson,* and *Roosevelt* sail to historic **Nagasaki** and, on the following day, they wind their way through narrow channels and picturesque islets in the *Inland Sea* of **Japan.** Views of these manicured islands, with their carefully tended farms and gardens, are close at hand from the decks of your luxury APL liner. These special, extended, voyages truly offer one an added reward to the thrills of sailing the sparkling Pacific in a majestic ocean liner.

The splendid APL around the world passenger services may be used efficiently in connection with your journey to the Orient exclusive of the rest of the world. Space permitting, passage in the *Presidents Monroe* and *Polk* may be reserved from **New York** or **San Francisco** to the Orient. These *Presidents* sail from **New York** to the West Coast via **Port Everglades,** Florida, the *Panama Canal Zone* and **Acapulco, Mexico** in sixteen days. Their around the world route is from **San Francisco to Yokohama** via **Honolulu,** thence on to **Kobe** and **Hong Kong** before embarking for the journey to **Saigon, Singapore, India,** and **Europe** before returning to **New York.**

Description of the APL Passenger Ships

The S.S. PRESIDENT ROOSEVELT, which made her maiden voyage in 1962, is the most modern and luxurious all air conditioned, one-class, yachtlike beauty of APL's transpacific fleet. 622 feet in length, 76 foot beam, 18,300 gross tons, with a speed of twenty knots, the passenger capacity of the *Roosevelt* is 456. The *Roosevelt's Marine Veranda* is, by day, a shaded luxurious lounge overlooking the pool and, by night, an ultra smart supper club for your dining and dancing pleasure. Replete with stabilizers and blocks of sunswept deck space, I can think of no more delightful way to approach your Oriental holiday than in the *S.S. President Roosevelt*. I recommend the *S.S. President Roosevelt* highly.

The PRESIDENT CLEVELAND and PRESIDENT WILSON. These twin sisters par excellence are 610 feet in length with a 76 foot beam and of 18,962 gross tons. Each has a passenger capacity of 684 of whom 304 may be accommodated in first class and 380 in economy class.

The *Cleveland* and *Wilson* are replete with chic modern shops where all manner of goodies may be purchased, library, nursery, hospital, children's playroom, kennels for pets, and a photographic shop with developing service. The renowned *California Dining Room* has attained international repute for the excellence of its service and cuisine. Room service is never ending . . . you have but to press a button. The invigorating swimming pool, much larger than most ship bathing facilities, is a favorite gathering place. There are sun and game decks, soothing main lounge, exciting marine veranda, glass enclosed promenade decks, a "live" ship's orchestra for dancing and concerts, motion pictures daily, and facilities for every conceivable type of deck sport. The daily newspaper contains stock reports, world news items, and sports results.

The *Cleveland* and *Wilson* have a wide variety of accommodations ranging from the most luxurious of suites and deluxe lanais to modest first class staterooms without private bath for the economy minded.

Nothing is left to chance in these *Pacific Presidents*. Your every physical want has been anticipated. The barber and beauty shops are comparable to the best ashore. The children's game room and nursery are "heir conditioned" for just what junior would like to order.

The S.S. PRESIDENT POLK and the S.S. PRESIDENT MONROE are globe circling sister ships which accommodate 96 first class passengers each. All *Polk* and *Monroe* rooms are outside, and each has either a tub or shower bath. The rooms are "wired for sound," with radios for receiving broadcasts, many of them weird and exotic, from stations throughout the world as well as internal carefully chosen tape recorded broadcasts. A commodious outdoor swimming pool, large deck areas, a handsome bar, and intimate dining rooms are among the around the world amenities at your disposal for your deep sea enjoyment. While these ships are basically built for the world service, both the *Polk* and the *Monroe* may be used, space permitting, for your cherished trip to the Orient. (These much loved globe-circlers may be retired by the end of 1965.)

DINING ABOARD. APL officials and their purring with delight passengers are equally enthusiastic about the cuisine of these liners. The management takes understandable pride in the varied international flavor of its cuisine. One may be succulently tempted with Indian curries and taste-titillating French dishes, while the pastas of **Italy** and the specialties of **Hawaii, the Philippines, China,** and **Japan** are all offered with equal ease. On an American ship, you have every right to expect that the chefs would be proud of their skill in producing clam chowder, barbecues, and juicy savory steaks. They are. The luncheon buffets served on deck are particularly lavish.

Two dining room sittings prevail on most sailings, with the first breakfast sitting being served at 7:30 A.M., lunch at twelve noon, and dinner at six P.M., while the second sittings provide breakfast at 8:30 A.M., lunch at one P.M., and dinner at 7:15 P.M. Passengers traveling "en famille" frequently prefer the first sitting with the children (children under twelve are required to eat at the first sitting).

Informality is the order of the voyage. Slacks and sports shirts, skirts and sweaters, sports dresses or what-have-you, are quite in order for breakfast and lunch, while at dinner gentlemen are asked to wear coats or jackets and sports dresses or light summer dresses are in order for the gals. For the Captain's and other gala dinners, evening dress is optional. Since you will not be required to have dinner clothes elsewhere, it would probably not be wise to burden your bulging suitcase with a dinner jacket for just one or two special events aboard. Outfits for the costume balls may be happily improvised aboard ship.

AMUSEMENTS ABOARD. Nothing delights me and most voyagers more than the relaxing daily choice of daytime snoozes, uninterrupted reading or writing, and active or semi-active participation in athletic endeavors at sea. APL is particularly lavish in providing facilities for complete entertainment of their guests. Athletically, there are facilities for shuffle board, deck tennis, volley ball, swimming, and ping pong. For the less active, more sedentary passengers, there are bridge, pinochle, rummy, canasta, horse races, bingo, and the daily auctioning of the ship's pool. The library is well stocked with books, pe-

riodicals, and magazines. The cinema is always a well received diversion. The bar service is ubiquitous.

Deluxe Cargo Liners

The APL boasts of eight deluxe *Mariner Class* and two deluxe *Sea Racer Class* cargo liners, each of which carries twelve passengers in unbelievably luxurious stateroom accommodations. For your travel comfort, the deluxe *Mariners* offer single rooms, twin-bedded double rooms, and combination bedroom-sitting room suites of outstanding comfort. Each room has the most spacious shipboard fully tiled bathrooms I have ever seen, complete with overhead and mirror side lights, modern tub and shower, hot and cold fresh water (gobs of it), and circulating ice water.

Designed by the renowned architects Anshen and Allen, with interior motifs by Eleanor La Maire, Michael Taylor, and H. Clifford Burroughs in association with James R. Patterson, the fully air conditioned *Mariners* are the very latest word in seagoing luxury. Unique in the seagoing world is the glassed-in, air conditioned *Sky Room* and library from which passengers, cradled in the lap of luxury, may enjoy the limitless vistas to the salty horizon. The *Sky Room,* as well as all other decks, is reached by a modern elevator.

The APL management calls your attention to the fact that because these vessels are working freighters, there are certain deck space and personal service limitations. I have found, notwithstanding, one's every wish is readily interpreted in terms of cheerful service, and ample sunny and open deck space will enable one to enjoy outdoor activities and deck chair lounging, in chairs provided without charge. A launderette, electric dryer, and self service iron and ironing board offset the lack of laundry and valet service.

The dining room, conveniently located on the main passenger deck, is surrounded by picture windows on three sides. The staterooms, all of which are outside, are fitted with large picture windows rather than view-limiting port holes. The wardrobe space is commodious.

It is difficult, if not impossible, to convey the ultra smartness and luxury liner deluxeness of the passenger accommodations in these *Mariner Class,* all air conditioned cargo liners. After many more than one hundred ocean crossings, I was privileged to sail the *Pacific* in a deluxe *Mariner,* the *President Hayes.* I have never enjoyed a finer voyage in any class of ship on any ocean. The rooms are large and luxurious offering every conceivable convenience, the atmosphere is intimate and congenial, and the food is excellent. I am ecstatically happy about them. I know that you will be, too.

These super cargo liners, 563 feet in length with a beam of 76 feet, are of 9,216 tons and skim across the *Pacific* at an amazing speed of 20 knots, fast even for passenger liners. Because the accommodations are so excellent, the rates so favorable, and the romance of this type of travel so great, reservations in these freighter beauties are difficult to secure. Should one plan an APL cargo liner voyage, one should see his travel agent post haste . . . or sooner!

The transpacific deluxe *Mariners* proceed from **San Francisco** to **Yokohama** in ten days (eleven calendar days) and continue to **Nagoya** and **Kobe, Japan,** proceed to **Pusan, Korea, Okinawa** in the *Ryukyus,* and **Keelung, Taiwan** *(Formosa),* before returning to **Kobe, Nagoya, Shimizu,** and **Yokohama.** They then speed back to **San Francisco** where they arrive some seven weeks after having departed from their home base.

The world cruising deluxe *Mariners* sail from **New York** to the West Coast approximately every two weeks via the *Panama Canal.* They arrive in **Los Angeles** on the eleventh day, leave on the twelfth, and arrive in **San Francisco** on the fourteenth day where they lay over two to four days before proceeding directly to **Yokohama.** Another deluxe *Mariner* call is made in **Japan** at **Kobe** before proceeding to **Korea, Taiwan, Hong Kong, Singapore,** and around the world.

The APL deluxe *Mariners* include the transpacific *Presidents Garfield* and *Taylor* and the around the world *Presidents Adams, Arthur, Buchanan, Coolidge, Hayes,* and *Jackson.*

SEA RACERS. The *Presidents Tyler* and *Lincoln* are the two newest of the super deluxe cargo liners known as the *"Sea Racer"* Class. They are air conditioned and were put into service in 1961. From the gay mosaic tile bathrooms to the elegant *Continental Restaurants* with their spectacular fourteen-foot murals, the *Sea Racers* are worthy of the attention of the most discriminating ocean traveler. All of the fine features of the deluxe *Mariners* have been incorporated in the *Sea Racers,* plus a host of new developments for the comfort of the passengers.

The basic format of the new super-duper cargo liners *President Lincoln* and *President Tyler* is much the same as the super *Mariners* with the notable exception that these marine beauties do not have an elevator because the main lounge, card room, and dining room are all on the main passenger deck. Deck space is located both on the port and starboard sides of the main passenger deck. A boat deck lounge in the *Tyler* and *Lincoln,* enclosed on three sides, offers an ideal vantage point for viewing the sea, the stars, the lovely moon, or the glamorous harbors into which the *Sea Racers* sail.

These two around the Orient vessels have fascinating forty-four day itineraries to **Yokohama, Nagoya, Kobe, Pusan, Korea, Okinawa** *(Ryukyus)*, **Keelung** *(Formosa)*, **Kobe, Nagoya, Shimizu, Yokohama,** and a glorious rapid return directly to **San Francisco.**

C-3 CARGO LINERS. In addition to the deluxe *Mariner* and *Sea Racer* classes of cargo liners, excellent passenger accommodations for twelve are provided in each of the nine so-called "C-3" type cargo ships, slightly smaller vessels which follow the same route, on a slower schedule, as the *Sea Racers*. The C-3 *Presidents* are the *Harrison, Johnson, Van Buren, Grant, Jefferson, Madison, McKinley, Taft,* and *Pierce*.

The cargo liners have rather stringent rules relative to children. Youngsters six years and under twelve years will be carried as passengers only when accompanied by a parent or guardian, while children under six years will be accepted as passengers only if accompanied by two or more adults over twenty-one years of age. Baby foods and other infant needs are not generally carried aboard the cargo liners. Should you have an infant you intend to take with you on a cargo liner, be sure to have your agent notify the APL as to the specific requirements for your adored one.

Fares (First Class)

The sample fares I will quote herewith are based on double occupancy. Rates for three passengers occupying a room are correspondingly less, while the tariff for single occupancy is correspondingly more expensive. Rates, of course, are subject to change without notice.

One-way first-class fare in the *Presidents Wilson* and *Cleveland* from **San Francisco** or **Los Angeles** to **Yokohama** in a room without bath is $490 each for two. The **Hong Kong** fare in the same room is $608. An outside A Deck room with private shower and toilet runs at $753 to **Yokohama,** $934 to **Hong**

Kong. An upper deck deluxe room may be had for $1,101 to **Yokohama,** $1,254 to **Hong Kong,** while two persons in a super-duper bedroom-sitting room deluxe suite accommodation may figure their fare at $1,923 each for two to **Yokohama,** $2,386 each to **Hong Kong.** The complete round the *Pacific* cruise, thirty-nine to forty-four days, runs from a minimum of $1,156 each for an inside room with bed and upper without facilities to $4,534 each for a deluxe suite. $1,900 to $2,200 will buy truly luxurious accommodations for the complete cruise, California back to California.

Reduced fares, frequently as much as 25%, are offered from time to time, particularly at Thanksgiving and Christmas times. These bargains offer an enticing inducement to spend the holidays at sea or in the Orient.

Orient interport fares from **Yokohama** to **Hong Kong, Manila, Hong Kong, Kobe,** and back to **Yokohama** are subject to a 25% reduction from the quoted one way fares provided the passage originates in the Orient and the elapsed time from beginning to the end of the voyage is ninety days or less. A 10% round trip reduction applies under other conditions.

The *President Roosevelt* fares from **San Francisco** to **Yokohama** range upward from $526 basis two to a room and from $652 to **Hong Kong.** The complete all first class cruise fares in the *S.S. President Roosevelt* are from $1,240, California back to California.

In the globe circling *Presidents Polk* and *Monroe,* one way fares from **San Francisco** to **Yokohama** run from $825 to $1,115 each for two based on double occupancy, with the **Hong Kong** rates ranging from $1,000 to $1,350. (It is anticipated that these two *Presidents* will be retired by the end of 1965.)

In the deluxe super *Mariner* cargo liners, the fares from **San Francisco** or **Los Angeles** to **Yokohama** run at $470 each for two persons accommodated in luxurious double rooms, while single staterooms carry a rate of $505. The suite costs $565 each for two. The **Hong Kong** rate of $530 is based on double occupancy, while $570 covers the single occupancy passage. The complete around the *Pacific* cruise in the *Mariner* cargo liners runs at $855 basis two, $925 for single occupancy, and $980 each, basis double occupancy, for suite accommodations California back to California.

From **San Francisco** or **Los Angeles** to **Yokohama** in the *President Tyler* type deluxe *Mariner,* the double room rate is $420 each for two, $455 for a single, or $485 each for a suite. From the West Coast to **Hong Kong** via **Japan** is $475 basis double, $515 for a single, and $545 each for a suite. For the complete transpacific Orient cruise, the fare is $975 in a double, $925 in a single, or $980 each in a suite.

In the C-3 type cargo liners, the **San Francisco-Yokohama** rate, basis two, is $375, and $425 each to **Hong Kong**.

Economy Class (Presidents Cleveland and Wilson Only)

For students, young people, and families traveling the *Pacific* "just to get there" and who are searching for a real buy, the economy class is just made to order. The rates are extremely low . . . as little as $325 to **Yokohama** in a dormitory or $420 in a room for two. **Hong Kong** fares are from $357 to $461. Full cruise fares are from $673 to $869. The so-called E-2 and E-1 family style cabins accommodate four to eight persons in upper and lower curtained berths. The economy class sleeping quarters, dining room, veranda lounge, main dining room, and bar are all air conditioned (as is every nook and cranny of these glistening beauties). The splash and sparkle of a luxuriously refreshing swimming pool offers economy class passengers an invitation to while away pleasant sunning hours on their Pacific voyage. The economy class food is prepared basically in western style, but by virtue of the number of Orientals who use this type of accommodation, a number of Far Eastern dishes are available for one's choice. The economy class dormitories are limited to men. Family groups traveling together (and, under certain conditions when space is available, a man and his wife) may have a four berth stateroom to themselves.

P & O ORIENT LINES

"It is time to run away to sea" . . . so say the highly skilled publicists of the *P & O Orient Lines*. Indeed, this fits my own

philosophy. It has ever been my firm conviction that one should "travel now . . . it's later than you think," and to run away to sea in the superb ships of the *P & O Orient Lines* will fulfill the romantic dreams of the most avid wanderer of the globe.

The offerings of the *P & O Orient Lines* are the most extensive of the passenger operations in the world today. The present format of this vast seagoing enterprise came about early in 1960 by virtue of the merger of two British companies, the *Peninsular and Oriental Steam Navigation Co.* and the *Orient Steam Navigation Co., Ltd.*

The colorful history of both of the parent organizations dates back to the mid-1800's when shipping service was begun from **London** to **Europe's** *Iberian Peninsula* and was soon extended to **Egypt** (then, believe it or not, known as the Orient). As the Empire grew, so did the fleets, until by the end of the 19th century **India, China,** and **Australia** were established routes of the *P & O Lines*.

The end of the Second World War marked the turning point in the old traditional service. Political changes and unheralded immigration to **Australia** brought new demands on a fleet decimated by the global conflict. Both companies embarked on vigorous building programs of large liners to handle the burgeoning trade. These new postwar ships became the backbone of their respective fleets.

In 1954, the *Orient Line* directors, sensing an increased interest in *Pacific* travel, extended operations from **Australia** and **New Zealand** to **North America.** Service was soon increased to include routes through the *Panama Canal* to **Europe.** Shortly thereafter, the *P & O Line* introduced its postwar fleet and, with the *Orient Steam Navigation Co.,* established a joint service under the tentative name of *Orient and Pacific Lines.*

Coincidental with the opening of new North American head-quarters in **San Francisco** in 1960, the two companies officially joined hands in an extensive worldwide service to be known thereafter as the *P & O Orient Lines.*

The word "posh" currently in vogue to describe something that is elegant or elite owes its inception to the original *P & O* and *Orient Lines.* During the halcyon days of the British Empire before the sun began to set on imperialism, air conditioning was an unknown quantity at sea. Rich Indians and titled Britons, as well as elegant and sophisticated non-titled but equally well-heeled travelers who were proceeding from **Britain** to **India,** not only wished to be as comfortable as possible but were quite prepared to pay for an added feeling of well-being. From **England** through the *Mediterranean, Suez Canal,* and *Indian Ocean* to **Bombay,** the port side was the shady side during the hot season. Conversely, on the return trip, the starboard side was the shady side.

Because of the heavy demand for the port side out and the starboard side home, the steamship lines varied their rates considerably with the shady side being the expensive section in both directions. When the maharajahs, lords, ladies, and other elegant travelers sent their servants to the travel agent's offices, they merely gave their servitors a note to hand to the agent indicating the date on which they intended to travel outward and homeward. In heavy letters at the bottom of the note, they always inscribed, "Port Out, Starboard Home." Soon instead of writing out the full inscription, it became standard procedure to write the initials only: "POSH." In order that there be no misunderstanding as to the location of the staterooms, the tickets were also stamped "P.O.S.H." Now, more than a century later, we use this term to indicate something that is extra special. Apocryphal? I think not. True? I believe so.

Headed by the most highly publicized ships since the advent of the greatest of them all, the *R.M.S. Queen Mary* and the

R.M.S. Queen Elizabeth, the *P & O Orient Lines'* spanking new 45,000-ton *Canberra* and the 42,000-ton *Oriana* have captured the imagination of travel agents and travelers alike. *Canberra* and *Oriana,* products of the finest British shipbuilding skill, head a fleet of twelve vessels which also includes the 30,000-ton *Iberia,* the 24,000-ton *Chusan,* the 28,000-ton *Himalaya,* the 28,000-ton *Oronsay,* the 28,000-ton *Orcades,* the 29,000-ton *Orsova,* the 30,000-ton *Arcadia,* the 14,000-ton *Chitral,* the 14,000-ton *Cathay,* and the 20,000-ton *Orontes.*

The itineraries followed by many of these "run away to sea" ships are so globe encompassing as to fall largely outside of the scope of this around the Orient guidebook. One of the services into which a number of these ships are assigned includes a route that originates on the North American continent at **Vancouver.** From this point the vessels sail to **San Francisco, Los Angeles,** and **Honolulu** to **Yokohama, Kobe, Hong Kong,** and **Manila.** These vessels then proceed from the Orient to **Singapore, India,** the *Suez Canal, Mediterranean Sea,* and to **England.** Other of the sister ships return over the same course in reverse. An excellent around the Orient itinerary can be established using the *P & O Orient Lines* ships. The advertising campaigns and promotional activities of this aggressive company, superbly designed and skillfully carried out, have opened the doors to romance at sea for thousands of travelers.

The *P & O Orient Lines* vessels are skillfully routed and re-routed to place their ships into each of the world ports at the proper time to accommodate peak season travelers. The *P & O Orient Lines* ships follow greatly dissimilar itineraries. To illustrate: I was talking with a crew member of the *Oriana* not long ago and he said, "Serving in this ship is just like being a passenger who has truly 'run away to sea' as a vagabond." He continued, "We left **London** in April, made calls in the *West Indies* and came through the *Panama Canal* to the West Coast and on to **Hawaii,** the *Fiji Islands,* **New Zealand,** and **Australia,** and returned by way of **Vancouver.** Now we're starting on that itinerary again, and when we get back in July, we will run through the *Panama Canal* to **London** after which we sail through the *Mediterranean* and *Suez* to **India, Australia,** and **New Zealand,** back to **London** over the same route in reverse. Then we come out to **Los Angeles** and **San Francisco** again to make the **Australian-New Zealand** trip."

The progressive business people of the *P & O Orient Lines* do not limit themselves to traditional routes, but send their ships where the demand is known to be great.

Apart from the West Coast, **Honolulu, Japan, Hong Kong,** and **Manila** services, the *P & O Orient Lines* operate from **London** through the *Mediterranean* and *Suez Canal* to **Bombay, Colombo,** and **Penang** to **Australia** and **New Zealand.** Others of these ships sail from the West Coast of the **United States** to **Honolulu,** the *Fiji Islands,* **New Zealand,** and **Australia,** with connections to **England** via **Singapore, India,** and the *Suez Canal.* There are also connections which may be made from **Australia** to **Manila** and **Hong Kong** where further connections may be made for return voyages to the States, thus making a complete circle possible.

The following is typical of the *P & O Orient Lines* schedule from **Vancouver** through to **Manila:** first day, depart from **Vancouver** with second morning arrival in **San Francisco;** after a two-day layover in **San Francisco,** the ship continues on the overnight run to **Los Angeles; Honolulu** is reached on the fifth day after departure from **Los Angeles,** which is the ninth day after the ship's departure from **Vancouver;** the voyage from **Honolulu** to **Yokohama** consumes eight days, while **Kobe** is just overnight further along; **Hong Kong** greets the ship three days later, and the arrival at **Manila** is scheduled twenty-five days after the departure from **San Francisco.**

Because of the rotating nature of the *P & O Orient Lines* schedules, it is not generally known long in advance which of the ships will be on the Orient run. It is possible, of course, that *Canberra* and *Oriana* will be in this Orient service by the time you read these pages. Their original itineraries were from the West Coast to **Honolulu,** the *Fiji Islands,* **New Zealand,** and

Australia and back, with *Panama Canal* to **England** and **England-Australia** runs interspersed.

CANBERRA, pronounced British fashion "Can-brra" with the accent on the first syllable, is the largest passenger ship ever to have sailed the *Pacific* on scheduled runs. *Cunard*'s great *Queens* were carrying troops in the *Pacific* from time to time during the war, but no ship has ever before been scheduled which rivals this behemoth in size . . . 820 feet in length, 102 feet in beam, with an overall height from keel to the navigational bridge of 130 feet. She carries 2,235 passengers in two classes, 550 of which are accommodated in first class. Her surface speed is 25 knots. In July of 1961, *Canberra* reached the Pacific Coast of the United States on her maiden voyage and was vociferously acclaimed by the travel fraternity, civic leaders, and hordes of avid curiosity seekers.

ORIANA which made her appearance six months prior to the advent of *Canberra* is but slightly smaller with a gross tonnage of 40,000, a length of 804 feet, and a beam of 97 feet. She is 121 feet 6 inches from keel to navigational bridge. Maintaining a surface speed of 27.5 knots, *Oriana* holds all the speed records from **Gibraltar** east and across the *Pacific* to the West Coast of **North America.**

Both *Canberra* and *Oriana* are air conditioned with the humidity thermostatically controlled throughout. Their specially designed bulbous bows insure a minimum of pitching, while stabilizers control the now nonexistent roll.

All first class *Canberra* and *Oriana* staterooms have a private tub or shower bath. One bit of equipment which tickles the funny bone of this unreconstructed bachelor is the iron and ironing board with which the staterooms are provided. Needless to say, I did not use mine.

The tourist class staterooms are for two or four persons. More than half of the tourist rooms are equipped with private shower and toilet facilities.

Running ice water is provided in all staterooms. These floating beauties cost in excess of $40,000,000 each to build.

The theater, two decks high, is equipped with a wide screen on which stereophonic movies are shown. There are four swimming pools in each ship, two being allotted to tourist class, one to first class, and, as an innovation, one exclusively to the crew. The launderettes are equipped with the latest type of washing and drying equipment. The newspaper carries squibs of news of world affairs as well as international sports results. The nursery and teenage rumpus room (replete with soda fountain, juke box, and indestructible floors and walls) have proved to be extraordinarily popular.

The *Oriana*'s luxury penthouse perched loftily on the main games deck commands a magnificent panoramic marine vista. The *Grill Room* is a dimly lit sophisticated dining room which, on payment of a small fee, may be used interchangeably with the first class restaurant.

The *Oriana* is now in Orient service. I hope that one day *Canberra* will follow a similar itinerary.

Fares

As on other ships, the *P & O Orient Lines* fares vary depending on type of accommodation, size of the room, its facilities, location, and general desirability.

The minimum first class fare, calling for a double room with bed and upper berth, provided with hot and cold running water but without other conveniences, is $437 from the West Coast to Yokohama.

All *P & O Orient Lines* West Coast fares to Honolulu, Australia, and the Orient for any type of stateroom are the same regardless of whether one boards the ship at Vancouver, San Francisco, or Los Angeles. Obviously I need not point out that the fullest value prevails if one sails from Vancouver, which bargain one of Scottish descent couldn't resist. If proceeding to Honolulu or beyond, Vancouver embarkees are given several additional days of "board, room, and tuition" at no additional cost, plus, of course, the transportation on the coastal run from Vancouver to San Francisco and Los Angeles. The minimum fare to **Hong Kong** is $515 and to **Manila** $549, while a bed-room-sitting room suite is $1,490 to **Yokohama**, $1,756 to **Hong Kong,** and $1,872 to **Manila.**

A superior outside double room with twin beds and bath and a comfortable outside single, also with bath, carry approximately the same rate per person—$935 to **Yokohama**, $1,102 to **Hong Kong,** and $1,174 to **Manila.**

Tourist class accommodations in the *P & O Orient Lines* are excellent. The emphasis is on simplicity and comfort in all of the tourist class two-, three-, and four-passenger staterooms, as well as throughout the gay tourist class restaurants, lounges, and bars.

Tourist class fares, as in first class, are based on the type of accommodation, with West Coast to **Yokohama** rates ranging from $336 to $480, from $396 to $566 to **Hong Kong,** and from $422 to $603 to **Manila.**

The rates quoted above are one-way tariffs; round-trip fares may be computed simply by multiplying the above rates by two and deducting 10%. As of now, however, one may not readily make the return trip in the same vessel. The ships that make the West Coast–Orient run continue on to **Europe,** the return voyage being made in other of the *P & O Orient Lines* ships. With this dynamic company, however, these arrangements are subject to change.

CHILDREN'S AND INFANTS' FARES. Experts who compute steamship fares and compile marine regulations would, in my opinion, be diabolically adept at building haunted houses or manufacturing mystery jigsaw puzzles from which three key pieces have been withheld. To illustrate, the following is the verbatim *P & O Orient Lines* regulation governing children's and infants' fares: "The fare charged is based on the child's age at the time of initial embarkation, except for infants, in which case the fare is based on the child's age at embarkation for the initial or any subsequent leg of a journey." Tsk, tsk.

"Full fare is required of children over twelve, half fare when three years and under twelve years, quarter fare when under three years and over one year. The first child under one year is free, and each additional child under one year is charged one-quarter fare.

"Children under the age of sixteen must be accompanied by a parent or guardian."

Oh, boy! You figure it out, or leave Junior at home.

ROYAL INTEROCEAN LINES

The *Royal Interocean Lines* operates several magnificent passenger ships. The *Ruys, Tegelberg,* and *Boissevain* are of 14,300 tons carrying from 104 to 131 first class passengers at a speed of 17 knots. The deluxe staterooms offer their own private enclosed deck space, lounge, bathroom, and luggage room, while other staterooms, practically without exception, have private facilities. These three vessels and the 17,200-ton *Tjitjalengka* which carries 64 first class passengers all have extensive sports decks, sparkling tiled swimming pools, smoking rooms, bars, and gay dining rooms.

The other R.I.L. passenger vessels are the *Straats Banks* of 9,000 tons carrying 46 first class passengers at 17 knots, the *Tjisadane* of 16,700 tons carrying 36 first class passengers at 14 knots, and the *Tjinegara* of 16,000 tons carrying 40 first class passengers at 17 knots.

Yet other R.I.L. passenger liners are the *Straat Bali,* the *Straat Mozambique,* the *Straat Magelhaen,* the *Straat Van Diemen,* and the *Straat Rio.* The *Straat Mozambique* and the *Straat Magelhaen* carry six passengers each and the others twelve at a speed of 17 to 18 knots.

It is unfortunate that these perfectly delightful ships do not sail to the Orient from the **United States,** but they may well be used to good advantage for transportation between ports in the Orient.

The *Tjiluwah* and *Tjiwang* of 8,630 tons carry 104 first and 118 tourist class passengers. All of the air conditioned first class rooms are outside and are equipped with private toilet and shower facilities. These liners sail from **Melbourne,**

Sydney, and **Brisbane** to **Yokkaichi, Nagoya, Yokohama, Kobe,** and **Hong Kong** and return. The first class fare from **Yokohama** to **Hong Kong,** for example, is $162 per person sharing a double room with shower or $178 for a single room with shower. The **Hong Kong–Sydney** rate is $647 for a single room with shower or $588 each on the basis of sharing a double room with shower.

The principal R.I.L. passenger service is on the South American–African–Far Eastern run. The numerous vessels of this service depart on approximately a fortnightly basis from **Buenos Aires, Santos,** and **Rio de Janeiro** to **Capetown** and **Port Elizabeth** or **East London, Durban,** and **Mauritus** before going on to **Malaysia, Singapore, Manila, Hong Kong, Kobe,** and **Yokohama.** These excellent vessels offer unlimited possibilities for Orient interport services.

The *Royal Interocean Lines* is Dutch, and its service is the spotless, immaculate, perfect performance that you come to expect and always receive from the Netherlanders. The ships' staffs are a happy blend of Dutch and Chinese. The Dutch, having had generations of experience in the Far East, are masters of the combined cuisine of the Orient and **Europe.** The first class ships listed above each carry a doctor, have all of the amenities of the great ocean liners, plus intimate facilities for your comfort, convenience, and safety, and provide complete steward and stewardess service. Each has a swimming pool, moving picture presentations, and boasts of a shop for the sale of a wide variety of souvenir bargains and daily necessities. Other attractions include a hair dresser, nursery, and sports deck.

The *Royal Interocean Lines* has reciprocal interchange and interline arrangements with most of the other steamship and airline companies and may be included in round trip or around the world reductions just as would apply if one used a single service throughout. In addition to the passenger vessels mentioned, R.I.L.'s fleet includes a number of passenger-freighters, many of them air conditioned, carrying up to twelve passengers. These liners make frequent calls throughout the Orient and might well fit into your program. Your favorite travel agent will be able to give you the information on their sailings.

LLOYD TRIESTINO LINE

This famous Italian line's monthly service between **Genoa** and **Hong Kong** includes calls at **Naples, Karachi, Bombay,** and **Singapore.** The fully air conditioned motor vessels *Asia* and *Victoria* offer deluxe first class service, with fares from **Genoa** to **Hong Kong** beginning at $526. The voyage to **Genoa** from **Hong Kong** takes 26 days. Two ultramodern smart new vessels, the *G. Marconi* and *G. Galilei,* provide a luxury service from **Italy** to **Australia** (3 weeks from **Naples** to **Melbourne**). These two class beauties are highly recommended. First class rates range from an offseason minimum of $568 (**Italy to Brisbane**) to an inseason maximum of $1,380.

MESSAGERIES MARITIMES

This distinguished French company operates an *Indian Ocean* service, a **New Caledonia–Australia** service, and a **Far Eastern** service that may well be of interest to the readers of this book.

The *S.S. Viet Nam, Cambodge,* and *Laos* are in the Far Eastern service. These vessels are triplets—that is, identical sisters built from the same plan. 532 feet in length with a breadth of 72 feet, they maintain a service speed of 21 knots. Each carries 441 passengers, of whom 117 are in first class, 110 in tourist class, and 214 in economy class. The M.M. home port is **Marseilles,** and its ships sail by way of **Port Said, Aden,** and **Bombay** to **Colombo, Singapore, Saigon, Hong Kong, Kobe,** and **Yokohama,** with the itinerary being repeated in the reverse direction with the exception of **Kobe.** Passengers may travel between any of the ports mentioned.

Minimum first class fares from **Singapore** to **Hong Kong** and/or **Manila** are approximately $146, with the luxury deluxe staterooms carrying a rate of $240 each person. The first class fares from **Singapore** to **Kobe** or **Yokohama** begin at $196 each.

MATSON LINE

A tome of any type treating with any section of the *Pacific* would be remiss in its objectivity without mention of the world-renowned ships of the *Matson Line*. The scope of this guide-book is the area "around the Orient" which the *Matson Line* does not serve, limiting its schedule to the glamorous run to **Hawaii** and the *South Pacific*. There is no question but what one's voyage to or from the Orient should be broken one way or the other at **Hawaii,** the glamorous "gateway to the Orient." It is an exciting adventure to sail from **Los Angeles** or **San Francisco** to **Hawaii** before continuing on to the Orient by ship or plane. In reverse, a delightfully soothing post-itinerary inter-lude may be spent in **Hawaii** as a "dessert" to your Orient travels. The return voyage to California in one of *Matson*'s liners will provide a grand finale to your Orient adventure.

The S.S. LURLINE, regal monarch of the *Pacific,* provides frequent all first class service from **San Francisco** and **Los Angeles** to **Honolulu** and back. One may live in the lap of luxury aboard this chic vessel. The *Lurline* sails alternately from **San Francisco** and **Los Angeles** at four P.M. and arrives at ten A.M. the fifth morning in *Honolulu Harbor* after a gracious voyage punctuated with rich overtones of ultra-smart living. The lanai suites in the *Lurline* provide this ultra-smart living at a one way rate of $1,470 each for two.

One-way first class rates to **Honolulu** begin at $230, which price includes a place in an inside triple room without facilities. An outside double room without bath may be purchased for $300 to **Hawaii** or $540 round trip, while a so-called double outside "standard" room with twin beds, private shower and toilet sells from $395 to $475 each to **Hawaii,** or from $711 to $855 round trip.

The outdoor tile swimming pool is surrounded by acres of lush deck space. The noontime snacks on deck are in the form of a kingsize buffet picnic. An evening snack buffet begs you to sample its luscious offerings. The completely air conditioned

Lurline, 632 feet in length with a beam of 79 feet and a gross registered tonnage of 18,655, carries 761 first class passengers at a speed in excess of 22 knots.

The S.S. MARIPOSA and S.S. MONTEREY, providing frequent service to **Hawaii** and the *South Pacific,* and designed especially for this area, are 563 feet in length, have a beam of 76 feet, a speed of 20 knots, and are of 18,497 registered tons. Air conditioned throughout, these two sleek all first class *Pacific* beauties accommodate 365 passengers each. *Mariposa* and *Monterey* accommodations are spacious; there are acres of deck space, an outdoor tiled swimming pool with adjacent pool terrace, oodles of public rooms, and commodious stateroom accommodations. Except on special occasions, the *Mariposa* and *Monterey* skip **Honolulu** en route to **Papeete** and **Auckland,** but on the return from **Pago Pago** both ships call at **Honolulu** before proceeding homeward to **San Francisco. Honolulu** to **San Francisco** first class *Mariposa* and *Monterey* rates commence at $295 each for a place in a four-berth room and go as high as $715 each to share a lanai suite.

HAWAIIAN MONARCH LINE, LTD.

HAWAIIAN MONARCH LINE, LTD., which joined the ranks of steamship corporations in 1964, concentrates exclusively on the operation of cruises between the four major islands of **Hawaii.** The former APL liner *S.S. President Hoover,* rechristened the *S.S. Queen Liliuokalani,* is the *Hawaiian Monarch Line's* prized possession. The former 202-passenger liner has been converted into an 80-cabin, 160-passenger luxury resort cruise ship with three-quarters of a million dollars spent on refurbishing. All staterooms are outside with private bath. The *Queen Liliuokalani* sails from **Honolulu** on Fridays at 6:00 P.M. on her seven-day cruise itinerary and returns to **Honolulu** at 7:00 A.M. the following Friday. The ticket price ($50 to $100 per day) includes everything from gourmet meals to escorted land tours. All of the joys of a sea-going voyage are offered amidst the setting of the lovely **Hawaiian Islands.**

CARGO LINES

STATES LINE, STATES STEAMSHIP COMPANY. The *States Line* operates a series of modern cargo vessels from the West Coast to **Japan, Okinawa,** the **Philippines,** and **Hong Kong** on a fortnightly basis with a monthly program of sailings to **Manila, Saigon,** and **Bangkok,** which vessels return by way of **Hong Kong.** Service to the Orient, often via **Honolulu,** is provided in the C-3 type cargo vessels *S.S. Texas, S.S. New York,* and *S.S. Ohio,* and in the *Mariners S.S. M.M. Dant, S.S. C.E. Dant, S.S. California, S.S. Oregon, S.S. Washington,* and *S.S. Hawaii.* Direct **Manila** service is provided in the C-3 type cargo vessels *S.S. Michigan* and *S.S. Idaho.* The C-3 class liners are of approximately 491 feet, with a standard beam of 69 feet 6 inches; the gross registered tonnage is from 7,771 to 7,948 tons. Accommodations are based on two or three to a stateroom.

The *Mariner Class* ships are 563 feet 7¾ inches long with a beam of 76 feet and a gross registered tonnage of about 12,711 tons. The ships of the *Mariner Class* each carry six fully air conditioned double staterooms with private shower and toilet. The *Mariners* proceed from **San Francisco** to **Honolulu** in five days, another ten days to **Yokohama,** and continue to **Manila** and **Hong Kong.** The *S.S. Michigan* and the *S.S. Idaho* take twenty days to **Manila.** They make calls at other Philippine ports and arrive in **Saigon** in about thirty days and in **Bangkok** in thirty-five days. On return, the vessels call first in the Pacific Northwest, where passengers must debark. The *S.S. Michigan* offers a master suite for a surcharge of $50 per person.

States Line Fares. The fare from California to **Yokohama** is $375 each for two or three sharing a double or triple room; from California to **Yokohama** via **Honolulu,** $400; from California to **Okinawa** via **Japan,** $400; from California to **Okinawa** via **Honolulu** and **Japan,** $425; from California direct to **Manila,** $400; to **Manila** via **Japan,** $425; and to **Manila** via **Honolulu** and **Japan,** $450.

The California–**Hong Kong** rate via **Japan** is $425; via **Honolulu** and **Japan,** $450; and to **Hong Kong** via **Honolulu,**

Japan, and **Manila,** $475. From California to **Saigon (South Viet Nam),** the fare is $450, $490 via **Manila,** or $560 via **Manila** and **Bangkok.** The California–**Bangkok** direct rate is $475, or $525 via **Manila** and $550 via **Manila** and **Saigon.**

The *S.S. California, Oregon, Washington, Hawaii, C.E. Dant* and *M.M. Dant* are all 1961-1962 vintage vessels.

PACIFIC FAR EAST LINE, INC. ("Route of the Bears") provides frequent freighter-passenger service from the West Coast to the Orient in C-2 and standard cargo liners as well as in fabulous new deluxe *Mariners,* each of which ships carries a maximum of twelve passengers. Voyages from the West Coast to the **Philippines** and **Hong Kong** returning by way of **Japan** are provided at fifteen day intervals, while seven to ten day intervals separate the sailings to **Japan, Okinawa, Formosa, Korea,** and, occasionally, **Saigon** and **Bangkok. San Diego, Los Angeles, San Francisco,** and **Portland** are all used as ports of departure and return for the *"Bears."*

The 22,560-ton deluxe *Mariners Golden Bear, Japan Bear, Hong Kong Bear,* and *Korean Bear* sail to **Yokohama, Hong Kong, Manila, Cebu, Iloilo, Kobe,** and **Nagoya.** The outward run to **Yohohama** is speedily accomplished in ten days.

Two standard cargo liners, the *American Bear* and *China Bear,* and three super cargo liners, the *Oregon Bear, Washington Bear,* and *California Bear,* provide service to **Japan, Korea, Okinawa, Formosa, Hong Kong, Thailand,** and **Viet Nam.**

The *India Bear,* the *Alaska Bear,* the *Hawaii, Canada,* and *Guam Bears* provide the so-called **"Guam** service." These ships reach **Guam** in eighteen days from **Los Angeles** and **San Francisco.** There are occasional **Guam** departures from **Portland,** with calls being made at **Honolulu** and *Wake Island.* The final outward destinations of the **Guam** *Bears* are **Yokohama** and **Kobe.** Additional calls will be made if there is sufficient inducement for the cargo hatches.

Passenger accommodations in the new *Mariner* cargo liners are luxurious, including individual air conditioning, wall to wall carpeting, and staterooms with picture windows. The staterooms and public rooms are gaily and smartly decorated.

C-2 and standard cargo liner fares are quoted on the basis of double occupancy. Typical per person rates are $375 from the West Coast directly to **Yokohama,** $400 to **Yokohama** via **Guam,** $390 to **Kobe** via **Yokohama,** $400 to **Kobe** via **Guam,** $460 to **Kobe** via **Yokohama, Hong Kong,** the **Philippines,** and **Hong Kong.** Fares from the West Coast to **Korea** begin at $400 on the direct route or $550 if the voyage is via **Bangkok** and **Japan.** The **Hong Kong** rate varies, depending on itinerary, from $505 to $735, **Okinawa** $400, **Formosa** (*Taiwan*) $425, **Guam** $350, and **Manila** via **Japan** and **Hong Kong** $520 to $760.

Per person rates in the deluxe cargo liners, basis double occupancy, are $420 from the West Coast to **Yokohama** directly; $690 if via **Hong Kong,** the **Philippines, Hong Kong** (second call), and **Kobe;** $440 to **Kobe** via **Yokohama;** and $670 to **Kobe** via **Yokohama, Hong Kong,** the **Philippines,** and **Hong Kong** (second call). The West Coast to **Hong Kong** rate via **Yokohama** and the **Philippines** is $625. Single room rates are slightly higher than for sharing a double room. The fare for the magnificent suites is some thirty-five per cent higher than the double room rates.

The *Pacific Far East Line,* Route of the Bears, unlike many other freight lines, does publish a sailing schedule.

OSAKA SHOSEN KAISHA (O.S.K.) LINE (c/o Williams, Dimond & Co., 530 West Sixth Street, Los Angeles, California) provides monthly passenger freighter service from **San Francisco** to **Yokohama.** The sailing time to **Yokohama** is two weeks. Occasional sailings from the Orient continue on to **New York** via the *Panama Canal,* while others terminate at **Los Angeles.** All rooms have private shower and toilet facilities. The fares are $375 and $400 per person from the West Coast to **Yokohama.** Passenger vessels of the O.S.K. South American service are divided into two and three classes and call at **Los Angeles** and **San Francisco** en route from **Rio** and **Buenos Aires** via the *Panama Canal* to **Yokohama**—either directly or with an occasional call at **Honolulu.** The voyage from the West Coast to **Yokohama** is of two weeks' duration. The new *Sakura Maru* (**South America**–Orient service) is fully air conditioned and carries 152 passengers in cabin class and 800 in third class. The *M.S. Brazil Maru* and *M.S. Argentine Maru* carry twelve passengers in cabin class, 68 in tourist class, and 902 in third class. The *America Maru* and *Africa Maru* carry twelve cabin class passengers and 542 in third class, while the *Santos Maru* carries twelve passengers in cabin class, 50 in special third class, and 558 in third class. Cabin class passenger fares from the West Coast to **Yokohama** are from $375 to $400 depending on the ship and type of accommodations. Tourist class and special third class fares are from $300 to $350 per person in double staterooms.

AMERICAN MAIL LINE, 1010 Washington Building, Seattle, Washington, provides sailings in C-3 and *Super Mariners* approximately every ten days from **Seattle** to **Japan** ($375–$470), **Hong Kong** ($450–$560), and the **Philippines** ($425–$540), with monthly C-3 sailings to **Hong Kong** ($425), **Singapore** ($475), **Cochin** ($610), **Bombay** ($610), **Madras** ($660), **Calcutta** ($660), and **Chittagong** ($660). Cruises range from $875 for the shorter, more frequent service to $1,098 for the longer.

BARBER LINE, 17 Battery Place, New York 4, New York. Thrice-monthly sailings of Norwegian cargo liners are provided from **New York** via the *Panama Canal* to **San Francisco, Manila, Hong Kong, Bangkok,** and **Singapore,** with connections for around the world. Monthly sailings are also included in the Barber schedule from **New York** and **Los Angeles** to **Hong Kong, Manila,** and **Japan.** One way fares from the Pacific Coast are: to **Manila,** $400; **Hong Kong,** $450; **Bangkok,** $500; and **Singapore,** $560. The round trip Pacific Coast–Orient fare is from $850.

FERN-VILLE FAR EAST LINES, 17 Battery Place, New York 4, New York. These Norwegian cargo liners sail semimonthly from the States to **Singapore, Port Swettenham, Penang, Belawan, Ceylon,** and **Port Said.** U. S. East Coast one-way rates are: **Singapore/Belawan,** $550; **Ceylon,** $425; and **Port Said,** $325.

HANSEATIC-VAASA LINE (Williams, Dimond & Co., 225 Battery Street, San Francisco, agents). The *M.S. Karpfanger, Kersten Miles,* and *Simon Van Utrecht* are of German registry, while the *S.S. Holthav* flies the Norwegian flag. All originate their voyages in **Hamburg** en route to **Hawaii** via **Los Angeles, San Francisco,** and **Vancouver.** Round trip fares from **Los Angeles, San Francisco,** or **Vancouver** to **Hawaii** are from $405. Full cruise rate (approximately 3 months) from $1,072.

IINO LINES (Bakke Steamship Corp., 311 California Street, San Francisco, agents). These Japanese freighters sail monthly from **New York** via the *Panama Canal* to **Los Angeles** and thence directly to **Yokohama.** The *Muneshima Maru,* the *Takeshima Maru,* the *Tsuneshima Maru,* and the *Yasushima Maru* carry a rate of $350 each to Japan.

ISTHMIAN LINES, INC., 90 Broad Street, New York 4, N.Y. There are two dozen *Isthmian* cargo liners flying the American flag and sailing from **New York** via the *Panama Canal* and **San Francisco** to **Manila, Surabaya, Djakarta, Saigon, Bangkok,** and **Singapore** before continuing around the world.

JAVA PACIFIC & HOEGH LINES (represented by Dutch World Service, 457 Post Street, San Francisco, California). These cargo liners sail from **San Francisco, Seattle,** or **Vancouver, British Columbia** to **Hong Kong,** the **Philippines, Malaysia,** and on to **Pakistan, India,** and beyond.

KLAVENESS LINE (Overseas Shipping Co., 310 Sansome Street, San Francisco, agents). The *Bougainville, Sunnyville, Bonneville,* and *Bronxville* are of Norwegian registry and proceed on the 22nd of each month from **San Francisco** and on the 24th of each month from **Los Angeles** en route to the **Philippines, Hong Kong, Singapore,** and ultimately to **Penang,** with a return to **Los Angeles** being made via **Singapore, Djakarta,** the **Philippines,** and **Hong Kong.** The full cruise is of eleven weeks' duration with fares from $1,175.

KNUTSEN LINE (c/o Bakke Steamship Corp., 311 California Street, San Francisco). These cargo vessels, seven in all, commence their voyages of adventure in **San Francisco** for

Manila, Hong Kong, and Singapore as well as to the west coast of Australia. Sailings are monthly with one-way rates of $425 to Manila, $400 to Hong Kong, $525 to Singapore, and $375 to Japan.

MATSON NAVIGATION COMPANY, 215 Market Street, San Francisco, California. The *S.S. Hawaiian Farmer*, the *S.S. Hawaiian Packer*, the *S.S. Hawaiian Retailer*, the *S.S. Hawaiian Refiner*, the *S.S. Hawaiian Pilot*, the *S.S. Hawaiian Rancher*, and the *S.S. Hawaiian Wholesaler* provide a frequent regular schedule from San Francisco and/or Los Angeles to various Hawaiian ports. The fare is $180 each way.

PACIFIC ORIENT EXPRESS LINE, 432 California Street, San Francisco, California (General Steamship Corporation, Ltd., agents). The *M.S. Varda*, the *M.S. Ventura*, and the *M.S. Vigan* depart from Los Angeles on the eighth of each month for the Philippines, Hong Kong, Okinawa, Kobe, Osaka, Nagoya, Shimizu, and Yokohama, with the return being to Vancouver, British Columbia. The entire cruise is of sixty days' duration. Full cruise fares begin at $1,050. You may secure one-way quotations to the port of your choice on request to the agent.

WATERMAN STEAMSHIP CORPORATION, 310 Sansome Street, San Francisco, California. This famous American line operates the *Iberville, Jean Lafitte, Madaket, Maiden Creek, Wacosta, Kyska, Wild Ranger,* and the *Choctaw*. Sailings from the West Coast for Japan and Korea are approximately every ten days. One-way fares to Japan are $375 and to Korea $400.

WE'RE OFF TO SEA

Now that you have made your all important decision to go by ship and have chosen the dream ship for your Orient interlude, there are a few simple but fundamental facts of life at sea that we should discuss together. I am full well aware that many of my Orient-bound guidebook readers are old hands at international travel. Many of you have made numerous ocean crossings to Europe, the Mediterranean, and other sections of the world and are fully familiar with shipboard procedures. Even for the most sophisticated travelers, however, a periodic review of some of the interesting facets of life at sea will not be amiss. I know that the first-time traveler will find the following pages invaluable.

LABELING YOUR LUGGAGE. Your travel agent will have given you baggage tags and labels for each of your pieces of baggage. Be sure to fill out both the tags and labels completely and accurately and affix one of each to each of your pieces of luggage including lady's train case, gentleman's briefcase, typewriter, and/or all your other miscellaneous dribs and drabs of luggage. There should be one baggage tag and one pasted-on label on each piece of luggage that will accompany you to your ship. Docks, piers, and dock areas frequently are teeming with numerous ships that are preparing to depart for the far corners of the globe. Be sure that your baggage is so clearly marked that it will reach your ship and accompany you where *you* are going. Don't give a careless stevedore an excuse to place your luggage on the wrong ship.

EMBARKATION HOURS. Be very careful that you study closely, and commit to memory, the day, date, and precise hours of the embarkation of your ship. This might sound like over simplification and too basically fundamental a piece of advice. It isn't. You would be amazed to know how many people miss ships every week of the year because they have the wrong day or date in their own mind. It is not unusual for a ship to sail first thing in the morning, or even at one minute after midnight, but with the embarkation the night before. If, for example, a ship is scheduled to sail at the crack of dawn on June 19th, that date will have been listed on the sailing schedule and your ticket issued for June 19th, but you must be aboard your ship the night of June 18th, or else you won't sail.

Be sure to check with the steamship line's port office for possible last minute changes in the sailing hour. Such late changes of sailing plans are not unheard of.

AT THE PIER. Docks are always bustling with stimulating beehive-like activity. While this is fun, it can, in the last analysis, be confusing. As you approach the pier in your taxi or car, make doubly certain that your baggage tags and labels are solidly affixed, that your name and the stateroom number appear on each piece of baggage, that you have your passport, steamship ticket, and inoculation certification all readily available. You will be asked to produce this documentation on embarkation. If, perchance, you have inadvertently packed any of these precious papers, by all means stop the cab at once and break out the suitcase harboring the cached documents and assemble everything that will be required when you reach the gangplank. On your arrival at the pier, courteous and efficient porters will be immediately on hand to take charge of your baggage (be sure to make a mental or written note of his number or name). In some instances, the baggage chore will be taken over by the ship's stewards, but most probably your baggage will be handled by a stevedore. The stevedores are well paid by the steamship company, but if you offer yours an additional gratuity in advance, he will personally shepherd your luggage right to the area from which it will be whisked immediately to your stateroom. Such instantaneous service is comforting. Even the most sophisticated travelers champ at the bit until their luggage is on hand in their staterooms.

Try to arrange your affairs so that you may board your ship early. Beat the crowd. Most travelers appear during the last of the two or three embarkation hours. It has been my experience that it is well worthwhile to go aboard as soon after the formalities have begun as is possible. If you arrive at the ship before the peak of the embarkation period, you will avoid the inevitable heavy surge of traffic which will cause a jam-up a bit later, porters and stewards will be immediately available, the line for the presentation of tickets and documents will be much shorter, or even non-existent, and once aboard the demands on the attention of the room stewards and stewardesses will be much less.

NOW THAT YOU'RE ABOARD. If you have followed my sagacious advice and come aboard early, I would suggest that you have your steward or stewardess help you unpack at once. If garments to be pressed are sent to the valet shop early, you will be able to appear neatly pressed the first evening for dinner. It is great fun, a study in human nature, to watch the passengers as they arrive and to inspect objectively this electrically charged panorama of sailing day.

DINING ROOM AND OTHER SHIPBOARD RESERVATIONS. Almost all of the transpacific ships serve their passengers in two meal time sittings. Perhaps you have already asked your travel agent to make your dining room reservation for you; if not, it would be well for you to proceed to the designated area to take care of this important chore with the chief steward at once. Even though you may have indicated your choice of sitting and size of table through your travel agent, and the home office of the steamship company, it will be necessary for you to reconfirm the reservation on arrival at the ship. There is much to be said in favor of both the first and the second sitting, sometimes called the early and late service.

I prefer the late sitting for a number of reasons. Dining in the second sitting is a much more leisurely and, I think, more pleasant experience. You may arrive late for your meal, and remain later, without causing anyone any inconvenience. Those in the first sitting must be out of the dining room in time for it to be cleared and set up for the second sitting. Rush, rush . . . just what we're trying to avoid. I have found that when leading the maritime life of luxury and ease that late meals are particularly attractive. The luncheon hour is normally not so important as many of the ships serve a buffet that may be taken on deck. Passengers traveling with youngsters will no doubt wish to dine at the first sitting; as a matter of fact, almost all of the vessels require that children under twelve years of age eat in the early sitting. If the demand for reservations in the second sitting becomes too heavy, some lines require passengers occupying less expensive accommodations to take their meals at the first sitting. Whatever sitting you desire, however, it will be well to make your reservation promptly.

Tables in the dining room vary in size from intimate arrangements for two persons up to tables for six or eight or even more passengers. One of the real joys of foreign travel is to meet new acquaintances and make new friends, many of whom will warmly endure for the rest of your life. Even if you are on your honeymoon or otherwise feel as though you would like to be segregated from the world at large, I think you would be happier at a table for four or six than you would with just one friend or your ever loving spouse. This is merely my opinion; do as you please. The steamship line aims to please and will be delighted to make whatever type of reservation will make your voyage the dream trip of your lifetime. Just tell them what you want and prepare to enjoy yourself.

Ship's officers are intelligent and interesting fellow travelers. Being vibrantly human, they also eat, and usually do so in the main dining room. Officers' tables are much sought after. Procedures for assigning seats at the officers' tables not only vary from line to line but from crossing to crossing. There is no hard and fast fixed procedure. It is considered to be a feather in one's cap to be assigned to the Captain's table. Sometimes, however, the Captain's table is the least interesting of all. By virtue of his demanding duties, the Captain does not come down to a number of meals. If the weather is bad, he may not show up for days on end. Persons chosen to share the Captain's table are usually long-time travelers or economic V.I.P.s. Some of them may be extraordinarily interesting; others may well be bloated stuffed shirts. In any event, I know of no steamship company which will accept a request to be seated at the Captain's table. Such participation must be strictly by invitation. There are other officers such as the Purser, the Assistant Purser, the Doctor, and the Chief Steward whose tables are usually gay and lively. Your experiences may be just as rewarding, or even more so, if you are not at a table with one of the ship's personnel. I would suggest, however, that when you make your reservations you suggest to your travel agent that he request a seat for you at one of the ship's officers' tables. A great deal of the potential fun and interest of such an experience depends on the personality of the officer. If the one you have chosen turns out to be a dour introverted individual, you might better be elsewhere. If he is a hilarious story teller, only believe a portion of what he says but you will enjoy the voyage.

Visit the deck steward as early as possible to select your deck chair and its location. You might have a particularly attractive mental image of just where you wish your deck chair. Tell the deck steward; he is there to please you. Perhaps you wish it in the bright sunlight, perhaps in a shaded area. Some people like to sun in the fresh breeze, others enjoy brooding in a secluded nook away from both sun and breeze. Your desires will be met if you but make them known.

ELECTRICAL APPLIANCES. Voltage and amperage vary in different ships. In vessels of foreign registry, even the electrical plug will probably be different. Before you try out your favorite traveling iron or electric razor, by all means ring for your steward or stewardess and ask if there are any special ground rules relative to such appliances. Usually there are. If special precautions are to be taken, your steward or stewardess will ask the chief electrician for whatever is necessary in the reduction coil-transformer-adapter plug department. Just don't experiment on your own. It is acutely embarrassing to short circuit one entire side of a ship as well as a bit scarey to have sparks flying in your face.

SHARING A STATEROOM. A man and his wife traveling together will, of course, be assigned to a double stateroom in whatever class they travel across the Pacific. A man or a woman traveling alone or two men or two women traveling together might well be called upon to share the intimate life of living together at sea with one or more total strangers. This sounds abnormal. It isn't. Hotels and inns seldom, if ever, ask strangers to share living quarters, but it has been a custom of the sea to do so ever since vessels have sailed the oceans of the world. In the interests of the economy of space, living quarters must normally be sold to capacity. Single rooms are usually available, but they are frequently a good deal more expensive than the fare charged for sharing a double, triple, or four berth stateroom. First class rooms are for one, two, or three persons, while in economy or tourist class the accommodations are for two, three, four, or more passengers. Some Pacific liners offer dormitory-like rooms for men only and women only which accommodate a good many travelers together. Such an arrangement has obvious disadvantages but is much less expensive than the smaller rooms.

In my long, concentrated, experience during which I have crossed the various oceans of the world many more than a hundred times and have personally supervised the travel destinies of scores of thousands of persons, I have known of only a few remote instances where any degree of incompatibility was evinced as a result of strangers sharing ship's accommodations. If you are called on to share a room, just be kind, courteous, and, above all, a good sport. It is entirely possible that the person, or persons, with whom you might be called upon to share a room might be scrutinizing you with a more jaundiced eye than you are casting in their direction. I have found that little niceties go a long way when sharing accommodations. I repeat: be a good sport.

SHIPBOARD VISITORS. Part of the fun of sailing day is generated by the effervescent conversation and tinkling laughter of the departing passengers and their guests. From time to time there may be special circumstances which will limit the number of shipboard guests you may invite to see you off. Be sure to ask your travel agent to check with the steamship line to see if for any reason the number of guests has been limited for your sailing, which will save you the embarrassment of inviting guests who will not be permitted aboard. Usually visitors may, and do, come aboard freely. On some ships, it is customary for visitors to make a small contribution of fifty cents or so to seamen's charity.

Visitors will be asked to leave the ship approximately thirty minutes before sailing time.

FAREWELL PARTY (Aboard Ship). Among the gayest most festive parties that are held anywhere are those which take place in passengers' staterooms before the hour of departure. If you are expecting a group of friends to see you off and you wish to have a party, there are a few advance plans you should make. Ships in port may have their bars open if state laws permit. Bars are open on most ships sailing from California. Otherwise, maritime rules and customs regulations require that ship's liquor stores be locked for the period of the vessel's stay in port. Ask your travel agent to advise the steamship line of your desire to have a party and the number of guests. If you don't know how many friends will be on hand, guess. One or more stewards will be assigned to your stateroom for your pre-sailing cocktail party who will provide you with ice, glasses, sparkling water, and other mixing ingredients. With sufficient notice and under certain conditions, your party steward can provide either hot or cold hors d'oeuvres. You can be sure of having peanuts and other crunchy little tidbits with-

out any special problem. Should you wish to be so ostentatiously lavish, you may arrange to have a caterer come aboard
to handle the arrangements for your farewell party, and provide
all the goodies, liquid and solid. Nowadays the embarkation
hours are almost too short to permit such an elaborate setup,
though I can well remember the days when, in New York,
many ships sailed at midnight with the embarkation beginning
at seven P.M. You can imagine how gay such parties were. Now
they are happily effervescent and spontaneous but usually not
so lavish or long.

REFRESHMENTS AT SEA. During the course of your
voyage, you will be delectably inundated with magnificent service and a seemingly never ending chain of epicurean delights.
The passenger liners maintain twenty-four hour a day room
service. You may phone or buzz, per the custom of your ship,
for your steward or stewardess at whatever the hour of the day
or night and be promptly and cheerfully served with whatever
food or beverage meets your fancy. If, at three o'clock in the
morning, you should have a sudden urge for a chicken sandwich
and hot chocolate, you may have it, though there are off hours
limitations. I don't presume that the night steward would be
able to whip up pheasant under glass or a steaming bowl of
Hungarian beef goulash, but he can and will produce sandwiches, fresh fruit, toast, sweet rolls, coffee, tea, or milk. You
may take breakfast in the intimate confines of your stateroom or
in the cheerful dining room. At eleven o'clock in the morning,
it is a tradition of the sea that bouillon and crackers be served.
In the *Pacific,* it is not unusual that you may have a choice
of a cooling sherbet or ice instead of bouillon. In the late
afternoon, tea with scones, cakes, finger sandwiches, and other
appetizers are served. There will be a tantalizing buffet served
from 10:30 or eleven P.M. until past midnight including luscious
hot and cold concoctions. For all of this service and all of these
calories, there is no extra charge. It is all included in the price
of your ticket. Apart from coffee, tea, milk, and various fruit

juices, all beverages including Coca-Cola, ginger ale, other soft drinks, beer, wine, and hard spirits are extra.

SHIPBOARD LANGUAGE. You will wish to speak the language of the sea knowingly. Read these pages carefully, and ere you have been on the vast expanse of the broad *Pacific* twenty-four hours, you will have attained conversational eminence in nautical terminology. One always refers to the right and left sides of the ship as the "starboard" and "port." At sea one never goes upstairs or downstairs but "above" or "topside" or one goes "below." To go to the rear of the ship is to go "aft." When you walk toward the front of the ship, you are going "forward." The front extremity of the vessel is either the "bow" or the "prow" or the "stem" which words may be used interchangeably, though one hears "bow" more frequently used. The aft extremity of the ship is the "stern" or "fantail" which latter expression is not normally used in connection with passenger liners. It is a navy term. The anchor is frequently called the "hook." The anchor or "hook" is "raised" or "dropped." The official command for its raising is "anchor aweigh" or "anchors aweigh" if more than one is being used. A sleeping room is a "stateroom" or "cabin."

The ropes with which a ship is tied to a pier or a dock are known as "lines" or "hawsers." A pier juts into the water whereas a dock does not. The ceiling of a ship's stateroom or public room is an "overhead," the floor is always a "deck," the wall is a "bulkhead." The openings in the ship for light and air are "port holes" and should be so called, though now some of the *Pacific* ships are actually equipped with picture windows which may be called windows. The sheltered side of the ship is the "lee side" and the windy side is the "weather side." A ship that is moving forward is to be "under way" and a ship that is not moving and not tied up is said to be "dead in the water." A stairway is a "ladder" and a hallway a "companionway." The approximate center of any deck is called "amidships." The names of decks like fancy foods can be very confusing. For example, the fabled crepe suzette was named after a nephew of King Edward VII when he was Prince of Wales. You can have potatoes known as *pommes de terre Frère Jacques,* which means they were named after Brother Jack, and innumerable fancy French dishes are known only by the name of the chef who originated them or some favorite hot-shot client who especially liked the concoction. On some ships, A Deck can be almost the top deck while on other ships it is buried down with the porpoises. One bit of consistent inconsistency is that the Main Deck is supposed to be the uppermost deck that runs continuously from stem to stern, though even this rule is violated. The Boat Deck must be the one on which the majority of the life boats are stored. The Sun Deck is normally one of the uppermost in such a location that the sun will strike all of its area all day. Almost any ship worthy of its name will have a glass enclosed Promenade Deck.

STEWARDS AND STEWARDESSES. These ubiquitous, helpful members of the ship's crew will be on hand at all times to help make your voyage just perfect in every way. The room steward normally does the heavy work in the room and is of particular help to the male traveler, while the stewardess, working as a team with the steward, concentrates on the ladies' needs. Your steward and stewardess will be on duty from early morning until late at night with a night steward at your beck and call for nocturnal needs. The room steward and stewardess will be helpful in arranging for your pressing and laundry, and in certain ships where electric washers and dryers are available, your stewardess will supply soap and an electric iron on request. The dining room steward, your waiter, will serve you cheerfully. He will explain unknown dishes to you and make suggestions of exotic dishes that will be palatable to one of western tastes. He will be delighted to take your order for any special dishes you might wish for an ensuing meal which might or might not be on the menu of the day. The deck steward will be available to see that your deck chair is where you want it when you want it there, and will provide you with a lap robe if desired. (There is a nominal charge for the deck chair and robe).

Should yours be a stateroom without private bath, you will have a bath steward.

All of these well trained, thoroughly disciplined servitors are on board to make you comfortable and happy. Don't fail to take advantage of their desire to please.

TIPPING. I am frequently asked what to do about the "tipping problem." So far as I am concerned, there is no such problem. A problem in this connection is something that exists only in certain limited minds. Tipping is here; it's here to stay. It has been with us for eons and eons. I have read of the gratuities given to servants in Luxor 2,500 years before the birth of Christ, and should this grand old earth survive the various atomic assaults that are being planned for us, there is no question but what recorded history in A.D. 5000 will mention tipping. So it is here . . . why make a problem of it?

I have found that tipping is largely the mirror of the character of the person giving the gratuity. Interestingly enough, the French word for "tip" is *pourboire* which means "to drink." Even now Americans in a facetious mood when giving a tip will say, "Buy yourself a drink" or "Buy yourself a cigar." The French introduced the expression into their language centuries ago . . . "Have a drink on me," so to say.

I shall make suggestions, recommendations, and comments on tipping, which subject is not the least squeamish so far as I am concerned. I have found that a penny pinching penurious Scrooge-like individual is going to give precisely and exactly the minimum tip with the worst grace possible irrespective of what I say, and a kind, gentle person is going to give more than I suggest. One will be happier, though poorer; the other, richer and more wretched. I am sure that I shall influence nobody, but I shall tell you what is customary and what makes sense.

Not only should a tip reflect the personality of the giver but should be a reflection of the promptness and the cheerfulness of the service and the aura of pleasant relationship between the servant and the passenger that has been established. I don't for a minute believe in tipping for tipping's sake. A tip is a reward for good and cheerful service and should be so regarded.

The longer your ocean voyage, the less should be your per diem tipping budget. Such a "rule of thumb" is quite true of most anything that is done in traveling. If, for example, a man flies from New York to Chicago for one day, he can quite easily spend $150 in the day. If he goes to New York for two weeks, his per diem expenditure will be down to $30 or $40. Be guided accordingly. The longer you are on the same ship, the less your per day tipping budget will be strained.

In first class, the dining room steward, room steward and/or room stewardess should be given a minimum of $10 each for a short voyage; if the voyage is fifteen days or more, however, I would be inclined to suggest that the per diem gratuity be figured at $1.25 to $1.50 a day, and if the voyage is extended to a month or more the gratuity may be graciously reduced to $1.00 to $1.25 per day. The important thing in giving a tip is that it should be given warmly. I am sure that a steward or stewardness or other servant would rather receive a dollar given from the heart than $20 thrown at them begrudgingly. To be completely practical about the transpacific crossing, if you should ride from San Francisco to Yokohama, for example, and if you have been aboard for sixteen days, I would suggest you would want to give your first-class room steward (stewardess for the ladies) and your dining room steward about $25 each if the service has been up to your expectations, which I am sure it will be. I would say that $20 would be a minimum for good service. You would then want to tip the bath steward a dollar a day if you have not had a room with private bath. The shoe shine boy ("Boots" in a foreign vessel) should have about $3.00 a week. Provided you have used his service, the wine steward in the dining room should have about 12½ to 15% of the wine bill. The bar steward, if you have run up a tab, should have about twelve and one-half to fifteen per cent of your bill. In tourist and/or economy class, the suggested schedule of tips in the foregoing can be reduced fifty per cent with a clear conscience.

Line Officers—those in direct command of the ship, such as the Captain, Staff Captain, and Mate and those under them— not only do not expect gratuities but would be highly embarrassed if offered a tip. The Engineer and Purser and their staffs should not be tipped. Gratuities are given in the Steward's department *only*. The Chief Steward himself is an excellent person to remember with a gratuity, particularly if you have requested or received unusual or special attention. If you have requested special dishes to be prepared and/or have given parties in which the Steward's department has actively participated, you could well remember the Chief Steward with a $5 to $10 gratuity. It would not be remiss to give a gratuity to the chef if he has been active in preparing special dishes for you and your party.

On short voyages of a week or less, tips are traditionally given on the last day out. I prepare envelopes on the outside of which I write, "To Charles, my efficient, cheerful steward, from Harvey S. Olson." You may do this for each of the persons whom you wish to remember. Hand over the envelopes with a smile, a handclasp, and a spoken word of appreciation. On longer voyages, it is not remiss to pass out the gratuities once a week.

At the risk of being completely redundant, may I say again, and again, whatever you give, give from your heart because you wish to reimburse somebody for having done a good job well.

BOOTS. On British ships, the man who shines your shoes is called "Boots." This is a term peculiar to the tight little isle and its marine adherents. On American vessels, the room steward performs this little service. By whatever name, you may leave your boots (shoes) outside the door of your stateroom every night. They will be picked up while you are sleeping, shined to a bright turn (or, in the case of sports shoes, the white will be made much whiter), and returned to their place outside your door in the morning. These well trained men are equally adept with brown, black, or two toned shoes.

SHIP'S POOL. On almost every transpacific ship, part of every afternoon or evening will be devoted to the auctioning of the ship's pool. Even though you might not wish to participate in the gamble, you will find this form of transpacific lottery to be exciting. A ship's pool auctioneer will have been chosen by the smoke room steward and upon this individual will depend the success of the auction and the resultant fun to be had therefrom. The Captain will have, in advance of the auction, sent down a range of nautical miles within which he expects his ship to run within the next twenty-four hours. This might be from, let us say, 480 to 500 nautical miles. Each of these numbers is auctioned off and on completion the low field, all numbers under 480, and then the high field, all numbers over 500, are auctioned collectively. If you have purchased the number that coincides with the exact day's run, 497 for example, you will be awarded eighty per cent of the total pool. Ten per cent of the pool will go to the person who bought 496 and ten per cent to the person who bought 498. On certain ships, an additional ten per cent will be deducted for seamen's charities, which would mean that the total pool would be divided with the winner receiving seventy per cent, and ten per cent each going to each of the side numbers and a worthy seamen's charity. In addition to the ship's auction pool, there are so-called "hat pools," or simple pools based on the last digit of the number of the ship's run. For example, the gamut of zero to nine will each be sold for one dollar, five dollars, or in some instances ten dollars. If, for example, you had number seven and 497 was the day's run, you would collect $100 on a $10 hat pool, $50 on a $5 pool, or $10 on a $1.00 pool.

HORSE RACING is frequently conducted on ships the world over. The rules of the game vary slightly from ship to ship, but basically dice are thrown and mechanical horses go up and down the course on a billiard-table-green cloth that has been marked into lanes for the six horses. Parimutuel tickets are sold, and the amount of money bet is divided by the number of tickets sold on the winning horse, with the ultimate undivided reimbursement being directly proportional to the number of tickets on the winning horse. Horse racing is now also being conducted on some ships featuring films of actual past contests, the movies of which are run for the edification and profit (or loss) of the passengers. Horse racing is good fun.

WHAT TO DO AT SEA

Where will the endless hours at sea go? What will I do? How can I pass the days at sea pleasantly? Will I be bored? All good questions, but needless. By the second day out, so many things will have been planned for your enjoyment and you will have become so intrigued with the life on the water that you will soon be of the opinion that you need forty-eight hours to complete your daily program of activity, let alone your anticipated sleeping program. Among the many activities that will be yours are:

BINGO or KENO. Whatever name is given to this game (and on some British ships it is called "Housey-Housey"), it is an old standby to while away pleasantly an hour or so after a hearty dinner at sea. Stakes are modest, usually twenty-five or fifty cents a game, and you may buy one or more cards as your pocketbook and urge to participate might dictate. Just as at your favorite club or church, the rules vary from game to game. Sometimes one line is filled, other times two lines, and sometimes the entire card . . . it's lots of fun.

TOURNAMENTS. Not only may the various games and facilities be enjoyed in small informal groups but almost invariably there will be organized tournaments with suitable prizes for winners of tournaments in deck tennis, shuffleboard, deck quoits, swimming, and bridge. Don't hesitate to participate. You will find that you are much better than you had thought you were. In such competitions, you will meet new friends and have a great time. You can't lose. It costs nothing to enter the competitions.

DECK SPORTS. Deck tennis, the most active of the outdoor activities, is played on a court quite similar to badminton. Instead of being played with a shuttlecock and racket, however, it is played with enlarged ropelike quoits. Deck tennis, played both in singles and with partners, is scored according to the tennis system, while the play is similar to volley ball or badminton.

DECK QUOITS AND SHUFFLEBOARD. Adequate facilities are always on hand for these two old standbys. Neither is too arduous for even the most sedentary. Try them. They'll get you out in the sun and the breeze and will stimulate your appetite, make your eyes sparkle, and give your skin a fresh new tone.

SWIMMING. The pools on the transpacific liners are of the deck variety, usually large enough to permit vigorous swimming, and are open during the daylight hours. Most lines limit the number of hours for children so that the youngsters and the adults are not simultaneously endangering each other's lives.

MOVIES. Late run color pictures are shown regularly on the transpacific liners. Frequently releases are made to ships at sea even before metropolitan theaters are permitted to show them. The variety is good. There is no charge for this entertainment.

DANCING is a nightly feature on almost all of the passenger liners.

COCKTAIL PARTIES (AT SEA). Very soon after you sail, you will be exposed to the pleasant procedure of the seagoing, floating variety, cocktail party. In many ships, the officers will entertain the passengers en masse or in smaller groups. You will be invited to cocktail parties either in the staterooms of new found friends or in one of the public bars. Ship's personnel are most anxious to help make these affairs festive. They provide hors d'oeuvres and all the trimmings. It is customary to reciprocate when you have been a guest, so after you have been to a few such gatherings, you may wish to invite a congenial group to enjoy a convivial gathering.

CARD GAMES. To the best of my knowledge, there are no longer international sharpies riding the ships of either the *Atlantic* or the *Pacific Ocean* to fleece passengers of large sums of money in fixed card games. It is still a safe rule, however, not to gamble with strangers for more than a pittance. This is a sane and sagacious seagoing rule just as it is on railroad trains or in other public gatherings at home. You may participate in the bridge tournaments at no cost or you will find others who enjoy bridge at a fifth or a tenth. Whatever is your "cup of tea" in cards, you will find others to share your pleasure.

GALA PARTIES. Because the *Pacific* voyages are long and the urge to give you the best possible trip is great, the shipboard entertainment routine is highly organized. You will find that there will be special Captain's parties, fancy dress parties, and nightly dancing parties to add additional verve to the already crowded social program. Don't bother to bring anything from home for the costume party. The stewards and stewardesses will help you assemble something attractive and hilarious, although if your competitive instinct is keen and your heart is set on winning a prize for the most original costume, it would not be amiss to bring some basic materials from home. Be sure whatever you bring is expendable so that you won't have to lug it all over the Orient.

SHIPBOARD CLOTHING. Life at sea in the *Pacific* area is comfortably informal. Daytime shipboard attire is as widely and colorfully varied as there are creative types of minds. Don't forget to bring your swimming costume; it may well be *the* indispensable part of your basic wardrobe, whether or not swimming is your forte. Men will find their daytime garb consisting largely of swimming trunks or sport shirt with slacks or shorts and sandals or loose, cool shoes. The gals will wear wash dresses or shorts and halter. There is no formality of any kind at either breakfast or lunch, although a tee shirt or swimming suit is frowned upon in the dining room. There is no dinner dressing problem to worry about. Females generally will be quite happy evenings in a light summer dress or sports dress, while the men will wear a business suit or sport jacket and slacks, shirt and tie. That's all there is to it. Even for the special dress parties and Captain's dinners, formal dress is completely optional. If you make the complete cruise around the Orient, interrupted only by shore excursions, a white tuxedo jacket might be a worthwhile addition to your wardrobe. If you are leaving the ship for a trip of exploration through the Orient, however, you will have no further need for formal clothes and you'll probably find them a cumbersome nuisance.

WATCHES AND CLOCKS. Crossing the *Pacific* you are going to have lots of fun trying to answer the age old question "What time is it?" . . . even "What day is it?" In traversing the *Atlantic Ocean* or the *Mediterranean Sea,* you may be a bit mystified from time to time with the advancing or retarding of clocks, but in the *Pacific* you will frequently be in the midst of a three-ring circus. Not only will the clock be retarded regularly as you proceed westward from San Francisco or Los Angeles, but all of a sudden, though with adequate advance fanfare, you will cross the International Date Line, and to all intents and purposes will have a day lopped completely from the calendar. Under *Helpful Hints,* I have indicated the simultaneous times of day at various points in the Orient and the United States. Watch the ship's newspaper and posted announcements for the periodic retarding of the clock and the all important day when you will cross the International Date Line and jump from Tuesday to Thursday. What happened to Wednesday? Who knows?!

KING NEPTUNE CEREMONY. Should your ship cross the equator, it will be the occasion for great hilarity and ostentatious ceremony. King Neptune will come aboard, and uninitiated polliwogs will be given proper indoctrination into the realm of the monarch of the deep. A suitably etched scroll will be given to those who have passed through the ceremony to prove to posterity that they have crossed the equator. It's good fun. Be a good sport.

SHIP'S NEWSPAPER. Practically all passenger liners publish a newspaper to disseminate the latest reports of world events as they transpire. British ships will put more emphasis on cricket than baseball, the American ships vice versa. The stock market trends, when clocks are to be advanced or retarded, the schedule of the day's athletic activities, the cinema schedule, and local trivia will all be noted in the ship's paper.

SHIP'S OFFICERS

The Captain of a ship at sea is the most omnipotent man in the world. He is lord and master of all he surveys. He is an absolute dictator. Napoleon, Caesar, and Genghis Khan in their halcyon days of power never were bigger figures in the wide world than a captain on his ship. The Captain's word at sea is final law. His decisions are absolute. The responsibility for the safety of the ship and his passengers is the Captain's responsibility. In foul weather, it is not unusual for a master to be on the bridge for forty-eight hours, seventy-two hours, or even longer at a stretch. Of all the dedicated men of the world, none are more so than ships' Captains. They have lived their entire life for their moment of glory when they are given their own ship. They guard their trust zealously. A Captain may perform marriages, hold a court of inquiry, or he may even place passengers or crew members in the brig.

THE PURSER. The busiest place on a ship is the Purser's office, a combined general inquiry bureau and the ship's business office. Strong boxes for valuables are in the Purser's office, and here, if desired, one may make arrangements to change a stateroom, purchase shore excursions, or report a lost or a found article. The Purser and his staff are courteous, efficient, and well informed. From this office, you will, in due course, receive the customs declaration forms, necessary landing instructions for going ashore, and the necessary documents for your debarkation. From early morning until late at night, there are a stream of passengers parading to the Purser's office.

The CHIEF STEWARD is charged with the ship's housekeeping. He arranges the dining room sittings and, with the head chef, plans the menus. It is he who will make arrangements for special parties or assist you in planning the hors d'oeuvres for your own private soiree. He supervises the activities of the stateroom stewards and stewardesses as well as the waiters in the dining room . . . a very important officer.

The CHIEF ENGINEER is responsible to the Captain for the maintenance of the engines in a highly efficient state of operation. It may or may not be true, but it is rumored that the best engineering officers in the world are Scotsmen. True or not, a good many engineers are Scots. I have never known a Chief Engineer who did not love his precious machines with passionate ardor.

DOCTOR. All passenger vessels carry a licensed doctor. These men are unusually skilled in a wide variety of specialties. They are called on to treat emergencies including such diverse ailments as broken bones, sunburn, acute hangovers, tummy aches, and childbirth. Ships' doctors are an unusually cheerful lot for whom I have an abiding respect.

FREIGHTER TRAVEL

The general comments on the preceding pages apropos of life at sea on the *Pacific* have been written about passenger liners. Much of it applies to activities aboard the passenger-carrying cargo liners. There are, however, some notable differences which should be mentioned. Because freighters are working ships, certain passenger refinements may not be available, though I have found the service astoundingly good. Meals are served in one sitting with breakfast at 7:30, luncheon at 11:30 A.M., and dinner commencing at 5:30 P.M. at sea or 5:00 P.M. while in port. These odd dining hours appear a bit awkward, but it is surprising how quickly one becomes accustomed to such a different eating schedule.

Champagne and other spirits may usually be purchased by the bottle from the purser. A steward will provide glasses, ice and siphons without charge. Other "mixers" may be purchased

Room steward service is available from 8:00 A.M. to 7:00 or 8:00 P.M. The galley is left open around the clock for passengers to raid the refrigerator. You can fix your own late hour snacks. It's fun. Coffee is always piping hot. Dress is even more informal aboard the cargo liners than it is on the *Pacific* passenger liners. Cargo liner passengers may, and usually do, dine informally—women in cotton dresses, men in shorts or slacks and sports shirts—for all meals, dinner included. Deck chairs and blankets are provided without charge. Shuffleboard and deck quoits are included on the sports agenda. Laundry, dry cleaning, and pressing services are not available, but light washing may be done in the stateroom, and the management thoughtfully provides an electric iron and ironing board. Laundromats and electric dryers are on hand for your use in some of the more deluxe cargo liners. The most important differential between passenger liners and cargo liners is the matter of sailing dates and hours. While the APL cargo liners are on fixed itineraries and fairly fixed schedules, some of the other cargo liners will add or delete anticipated ports of call depending on the cargo carried. No cargo liner of any company can maintain an absolutely fixed schedule. The amount of cargo to be handled in Singapore might take two days to handle, conceivably three or four days. In the next port of call where the vessel had originally been scheduled to remain for three days, the cargo might only require a day to handle. If you are planning a cargo liner voyage, be sure that you check with the management a few days prior to your scheduled sailing date to ascertain whether or not there has been a change. Once en route, keep in close touch with the ship's officers when approaching each new port as to their anticipated length of time there.

Cargo liners which accommodate twelve or less passengers do not carry a doctor. They do, however, carry complete medical supplies, and at least one, and usually two, officers are qualified in first aid. Stewards but not stewardesses provide the day to day service.

PREPARING TO LAND

Before arrival at each new port, the Purser's office will advise you of any special formalities or technicalities that will be involved in going ashore. In "Planning and Preparing for Your Trip" I have outlined the various bits of documentation required, such as visas, money formalities, and health require- ments. The purser will reaffirm these details. The papers that the purser hands you to fill out should be taken care of at once. The lazy man's philosophy of "put off until tomorrow what you don't have to do today and maybe tomorrow you won't have to do it" doesn't apply here. If the purser has given you the papers, they must be executed. You can help him, and ultimately save yourself annoyance, by working on these papers promptly. They are not voluminous and usually quite simple. Money declarations in currency controlled areas are important. Neither the purser nor the foreign currency control officer cares a tinker's damn how much money you are carrying. They are interested only in having you enumerate the amounts accurately. If called on to list how much you have in dollars, how much in foreign currency, and how much in traveler's checks, state the amounts honestly and accurately. Whatever papers you are told you will need to land should be kept in your passport. These normally will include your landing card, money declaration, and frequently a customs declaration form. On returning to the **United States,** the purser will definitely present you with the United States Customs form, the details of which I have covered elsewhere, but since there have been certain radical changes recently in the handling of customs declarations, I would like to reiterate here that your duty free allowance on purchases made abroad is now only $100. Bear in mind that you need to declare only a fair wholesale price on these items— not what you paid for them. In filling out the customs form, you need not list the packages valued at ten dollars or less which you have mailed from foreign ports. You must, however, list separately each item purchased abroad which you have with you other than items which cost (fair wholesale price) less than five dollars each, which up to a value of fifty dollars may be lumped together. If you are within the one hundred dollar duty free allowance and you have items following, you must list such items to follow on the declaration if you wish to avoid paying duty. It is hoped that by mid-1963 the duty free allowance will be raised to the more realistic five hundred dollar figure. Time will tell. In the meantime, one hundred dollars is the limit.

PART WAY SHIP . . . PART WAY AIR

I am a devotee of planning an itinerary in such a way that the outward leg of a trip may be made by ship and the homeward portion by air if this can conceivably be arranged. I am full well aware that there are roadblocks to such idyllic planning and that in the *Pacific,* particularly, it isn't always possible. Nevertheless, there is a great deal to be said in favor of starting a long trip fully refreshed, and there is absolutely no question but that crossing the *Pacific* by ship will instill you with more avid zest than if you took a ton of vitamin pills. You will leave your ship thoroughly refreshed and in fine fettle to absorb the wonders of the Far Eastern lands.

Another significant, and compelling, reason for sailing out and soaring home is purely psychological. Outward passages are supercharged with gay anticipation of the grand travel adventures which lie ahead. You and your fellow voyagers will eagerly devour each exciting moment as you approach the Orient. Everyone is freshly exuberant and ready for each new frolic. An atmosphere of utter excitement permeates the ship. Most of the "days" are twenty-five hours long while speeding westward across the *Pacific,* but even then they are scarcely long enough to do all of the exciting things that are to be done aboard your ship.

Sailing from **San Francisco** or **Los Angeles** is a much more pulsating experience than sailing from any Oriental port (though **Hong Kong** is an exciting port either to approach or to leave). Nowhere else will there be the hundreds of shipboard visitors to create such a pleasant hubbub and hullabulloo. To sail from the **United States** is an experience that everyone must enjoy at least once in a lifetime. I, for one, never grow jaded or bored with this experience . . . and I have sailed away scores of times. I love every second of this thrill-filled day. Don't miss this opportunity if you can possibly help it . . . please . . . pretty please with sugar on it.

Should your time permit you to sail only one way across the *Pacific,* I might point out that it is much more fun to sail westward on the outbound voyage. This is due to a purely psychological but nevertheless important factor which should weigh heavily as an ingredient in the recipe of your decision. Actually, to fly overseas from **Chicago, New York, Seattle, Los Angeles,** or **San Francisco** is not in itself an unusual or spine tingling experience. As your plane is being called for **Honolulu, Tokyo,** or **Manila,** other planes will be in the process of being announced for Denver, Seattle, Portland, Des Moines, Cleveland, Pittsburgh, Toledo, and Boston. One does not have to spend thousands of dollars or travel halfway around the world to enjoy this type of travel experience. You yourself will be effervescently bubbling over with the zestful excitement of the moment, but as you hustle down the long corridors of the airport, you will be rubbing shoulders with those who are not the least bit excited about your "trip of a lifetime."

Conversely, the situation does a 180-degree turn should you reverse the procedure. If you sail home from **Hong Kong** having flown to the Orient, your fellow passengers will be in a state of well earned relapse. They are more anxious to rest, relax and dwell in solitude over the joys they have experienced in the weeks immediately preceding this homeward voyage. They will spend more time in their staterooms, and the spontaneity of the response to party invitations will be notably less than on the outward voyage. Fun it will be. All ocean voyages are

fun. But it will of necessity be much less of a breathtaking experience than if you had sailed outward.

On the other hand, should you fly home from **Hong Kong,**
there will be excitement galore. The airport will be brimming
over with Chinese, Japanese, British, Filipinos, Australians.
Indians, Malayans, and others. As you await the departure of
your plane, others will be called for **Bangkok, Saigon, Singapore, Bombay, Taiwan, Tokyo, Honolulu, Seattle,** and the
airports of the world. It will be an exotic and a much to be
desired experience.

I am firm in my conviction that an Orient itinerary should
start in **Japan** and finish in **Hong Kong.** You can't do better
than to start your trip by sailing from **San Francisco** to **Yokohama** in one of the *American President Lines* ships. In two
glorious weeks, you will enjoy a grand seagoing adventure.
You will arrive in **Yokohama** filled to the bursting point with
the *joie de vivre* and avid anticipation you've dreamt about.
You may, on the other hand, ideally sail from **San Francisco**
to **Honolulu** in a ship of the *American President Lines,* the
Matson Line, or from **Vancouver** in *P & O Orient Lines,* and
fly from **Hawaii** to **Tokyo.** If you follow this procedure, you
may visit **Japan,** then fly on to **Manila, Singapore, Bangkok,
Saigon, Hong Kong,** and back to **Honolulu,** to sail back to the
West Coast. Another variation of this latter scheme which I
think is a good one is to sail from **Los Angeles** to **Honolulu,** fly to **Tokyo,** complete your trip through the Orient, and
then sail home from **Hong Kong.** In this way, you will have
had the experience of sailing from the States, transcended
several of the longer journeys by air, and accomplished another
purpose, namely, using the return voyage for a combination
transportation and rest cure from your strenuous Orient journeys.

Another highly recommended itinerary gambit is to sail
into *Hong Kong Harbor* from anywhere. The approach to
Hong Kong Harbor either by day or by night is utterly fantastic.
For miles and miles before reaching the harbor, one will have

seen the heights of **Victoria** emerge mystically from the sea, and almost as soon as this peak enters the field of vision, the color packed local journey will have begun as the ship picks a path gingerly through jillions of small sampans, Chinese junks, plodding freighters, darting *walla wallas,* and majestic liners. One gets the impression that there are more small Chinese boats darting about *Hong Kong Harbor* and its approach than there are ants scrambling about the biggest sand dune in the world. What color, what mysticism. Should the approach be by night, it will be even more breathtakingly enchanting. The lights twinkling in the hills overlooking the harbor, the gently bobbing stern lights of the junks and sampans, and the aura of Oriental charm that envelops the soft lush evening paint an unforgettable mental picture.

One may approach *Hong Kong Harbor* from **Yokohama** or **Manila** in the *American President Lines* ships or from **Singapore, Saigon, Bangkok, Korea,** or **Australia** in the vessels of a number of lines, most of which I have discussed in this chapter.

By virtue of careful advance planning, you will find that a number of interesting interport voyages may be made, such as from **Kobe** or **Yokohama** to **Manila** or **Singapore,** from **Singapore** to **Saigon, Saigon** to **Bangkok** or **Hong Kong,** or **Hong Kong** to **Honolulu** to fly home from there.

Plan as much of your trip by ship as time will permit. You will be glad you did.

FARE REDUCTIONS. Many of the *Pacific* ship lines and airlines interchange round-trip reduced rate fares, a most useful arrangement in making possible the planning of a superb Orient itinerary. The round trip reduction amounts to ten per cent, a not inconsiderable sum when one takes into consideration the fact that the one-way first class air fare from the West Coast to **Singapore** is $880. The double one way fare is $1,760, with the ten per cent reduction permitting a saving of $170 each person. By virtue of the air-sea interchange, one may sail from **San Francisco** to **Honolulu,** fly from **Honolulu** to **Tokyo,** sail

from **Yokohama** to **Hong Kong, Manila,** or **Singapore,** fly
from **Singapore** to **Bangkok,** continue by air to **Siem Reap** and
Saigon, returning to **Hong Kong,** and then sail from **Hong
Kong** to **San Francisco** or **Los Angeles** (not a bad itinerary,
incidentally). In the compilation of the rate for such a combination of air and sea, ten per cent will be deducted from
each local fare quoted. I have long been scathingly scornful of
the lack of applied intelligent perspicacity in compiling steamship and airline rate structures. Many of the fares are completely
and idiotically unrealistic. In due deference to whatever guiding
genius conceived the air-sea, and interline, interchange, I
humbly apologize for all of the unkind remarks and evil
thoughts that I have long held against ocean and air rate men.

TWENTY-FIVE PER CENT REDUCTIONS are available
between Oriental ports. A ninety-day excursion in the APL,
first class, for example, is available from **Yokohama** back to
Japan (**Yokohama–Kobe** or **Yokohama**) via **Hong Kong,
Manila,** and **Hong Kong.** Ten per cent reductions are available
in all classes between Orient ports good all the year round. To
be eligible for the twenty-five per cent reduction, the business
must originate in the Orient.

SPECIAL CHRISTMAS CRUISES are usually offered at
reduced rates. Inquire of your travel agent. He will know.

YOUR CROSSING BY AIR

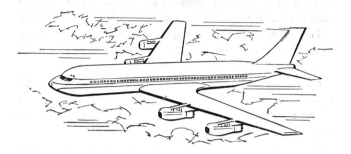

The years 1854 and 1961 are most significant ones in the annals of Orient travel. As noted elsewhere, Commodore Perry arrived in *Yokohama Harbor* in 1854 bearing with him official documents proposing treaties between the **United States** and **Japan** which when accepted—as they were—engendered a new brisk international business intercourse and opened the door, if only a crack at first, to pleasure travel between these two great, widely separated countries. The latter date is particularly portentous, for it was then that the jet age hit the *Pacific* area with a mighty swoosh that revolutionized all previously known travel concepts and imparted emotional stimuli that captivated the fancy of potential travelers the world over, particularly throughout our own **United States.**

A few short years ago, travel to the Orient was a babe in swaddling clothes. Today it is a colossus, a giant daily growing larger, more prosperous, and more enthusiastic. Until recently, the number of Americans visiting the Orient could be counted in the thousands; they are now counted in the multiple tens of thousands, and in my crystal ball I can foresee the day, in the not too distant future, when the numbers of our fellow Americans who make the exotic trek to the Orient will be numbered in the multiple hundreds of thousands.

Less than a decade ago the fleetest of the transatlantic prop aircraft consumed fifteen or more hours flying from **New York** to **Paris.** Today the jets wing their way from **San Francisco** to **Tokyo** in 10 or 11 hours, even though it is about twice as far from **San Francisco** to **Tokyo** as it is from **New York** to **Paris.**

The jet age has contributed much more than distance-shrinking incredible speed, however; it has created an entirely new atmosphere of international travel thought. The utter nonchalance with which the jets link the far corners of the world in a matter of but moments is one of the greatest phenomena of the twentieth century. The time has already passed when the sheen of the novelty of jet air travel could easily have worn off—were it not here to stay. On the contrary, world travelers have embraced this mode of transportation with a fiery, fervent, enthusiasm unmatched by any other event since the **Yukon** gold rush.

If you yourself have not experienced the sheer joy of the magic carpet experience of being whisked through the limitless skies at 10 miles a minute with the effortless ease of reclining on a downy silk bed, there is in life an ecstasy that is yours to embrace. Whatever you do, don't fail to take advantage of this utterly indescribably exhilarating travel pleasure.

Phnom Penh is a name that not one American in a hundred recognizes on sight, and I doubt if one in a thousand is able to spell it. Not only is this strange sounding city the capital of **Cambodia** but it owns a modern, gleaming white, busy as a beaver airport. In **Bangkok,** capital of **Thailand,** the huge new airport is a joy to behold. The *Singapore Airport* is new and modern, and a terminal has recently opened in **Manila.** The traffic in and out of **Saigon, South Viet Nam's** *Tan-Son-Nhut Airport* is unbelievably heavy. At **Tokyo's** *Haneda International Airport,* I have seen as many as 16 arriving and departing jets on the strip at one time. **Hong Kong's** beautiful new strip and airport building never calm down. A hopeless romanticist like me tingles from the top of my pate to the soles of my feet when I hear the multi-lingual announcements signaling the departures of planes to **Honolulu, Guam, Wake, Karachi, Djakarta, Sydney,**

Darwin, Singapore, Bangkok, Phnom Penh, Rangoon, Bombay, Delhi, Cairo, Athens, Rome, Paris, Anchorage, Hamburg, Copenhagen, and London. Just to spend an hour or two in such an Oriental airport atmosphere is to enjoy vicariously the eternal pleasure of travel through foreign lands.

The air activity to and through the Orient is the most rapidly expanding in the world today. Everywhere air progress is being made: better and faster planes appear daily, new and more modern efficient airports are being opened, and greater sales efforts are exerted to keep the planes full.

Because of this tremendously expanding air effort, it takes a brave man indeed to attempt to outline in a guidebook the future services, rates, and activities of the airlines. New cities are being served, new and faster schedules are being made, and new rates are being charged. Were I blessed with the century long clairvoyance of Jules Verne or if I had a crystal ball which permitted me to read the pages of the future, I would still not be able to keep abreast of the shifting panorama of the international air services. I shall exhibit my unflagging courage, however, and on the following pages outline the contemporary services of the airlines flying to and through the Orient. I beseech one and all, however, that before attempting to finalize Orient travel plans that you discuss your entire contemplated trip with your skilled travel agent. He can and will give you the latest word on the rates, schedules, and equipment to be used.

AIRPORT NAMES AND DISTANCES FROM THE HEART OF TOWN

Honolulu—*International*, nine miles
Hong Kong—*Kai Tak*, four and one-half miles
Kuala Lumpur—*Airport Kuala Lumpur*, four miles
Los Angeles—*International*, eleven miles
Manila—*International Airport*, five miles
Osaka—*Itami*, nine miles

Penang—*Bayan Lepas,* eleven miles
Saigon—*Tan-Son-Nhut,* four and one-half miles
San Francisco—*International Airport,* nineteen miles
Singapore—*Civil,* seven miles
Tokyo—*International (Haneda),* eleven miles
Taipei (Taiwan)—*Taipei International,* four miles
Bangkok—*Don Muang,* eighteen miles

ALOHA AIRLINES is a domestic service operating entirely

within the *Hawaiian Islands.* This remarkably progressive airline flies F-27 and Viscount Rolls-Royce jet-powered prop planes between *Kauai* and **Honolulu** to *Molokai, Maui,* and to **Hilo.** *Aloha Airlines* schedules frequent flights, with daily departures directly from **Honolulu** to **Hilo, Honolulu** to *Maui* and *Kona,* **Honolulu** to *Maui* and **Hilo,** and **Honolulu** to *Molokai* and *Maui. Aloha Airlines* features a family plan in effect every day of the week. One parent buys a full fare ticket, and the other parent and all children under 22 may travel on half fare tickets on *Aloha* flights departing **Honolulu** airport after 11:00 A.M. (local standard time) and all flights departing from neighboring island airports any time prior to 2:00 P.M. (local standard time). *Aloha's* jet powered F-27's are pressurized and have refrigerated air conditioning. Refreshments are served on all flights. *Aloha* service is excellent.

AIR FRANCE, the world's largest airline, long one of my

very favorites, flies the very latest model Boeing 707 intercontinental jets to and through the Orient. My cumulative *Air France* travels over a period of three decades total many times around the world. I have always found *Air France* to be reliable and dependable, its crews gracious and courteous, and the food out of this world. I regret only that this great airline does not fly directly from the North American continent to the Orient. Their services in the Orient are so extensive, however, that you may on many occasions find it convenient and attractive to fly with *Air France*. *Air France* offers over the Pole service from **Tokyo** to **Paris** via **Anchorage,** Alaska, and **Hamburg, Germany,** on which flights one may leave the Japanese capital late in the evening and arrive in **Paris** the same (I mean the same) morning. Such is the magic of the International Date Line and the speed of the intercontinental jets. In the other direction, one leaves **Paris** in the early afternoon and arrives in **Tokyo** late the following afternoon.

Air France connections and service within the Orient are extremely helpful in planning smooth itineraries. On the non-Polar **Paris–Tokyo** route, *Air France* in co-operation with U.T.A. flies from **Europe** to **Teheran** via **Istanbul** or **Athens,** then on to **New Delhi** or **Karachi, Calcutta, Bangkok, Saigon,** and **Manila,** and from **Bangkok** to **Tokyo** via **Phnom Penh** and **Hong Kong,** and **Bangkok** to **Tokyo** via **Hong Kong.** Another service offers flights from **Saigon** to **Hong Kong** and **Tokyo.** *Air France,* with its affiliated U.T.A., flies to **Djakarta** and **Australia** with connections to the *Fiji Islands.* U.T.A., as noted later, flies from our West Coast to **Tahiti,** the *Fiji Islands,* **Australia, Viet Nam,** and on to **Europe.**

What a thrilling climax it would be to your Orient trip to fly over the Pole from **Tokyo** to **Paris** for a few days in the gay French capital before proceeding by direct service to **New York, Chicago** or connecting flights within the States.

AIR-INDIA, as of October 15, 1964, was 32 years old, and various members of my staff and a number of friends and clients have used *Air-India* to complete satisfaction. The pilots are efficient, the crews are courteous, the food and passenger attentions are the best. *Air-India* offers a variety of routes from **New York** to **Europe,** the *Mediterranean* countries, **Bombay,** and beyond. From **India,** one schedule in-

cludes **Calcutta, Bangkok, Hong Kong,** and **Tokyo,** while another service is from **Bombay** to **Singapore** and **Djakarta.**
Connections are available from **Djakarta, Singapore,** and **Bangkok** to **Hong Kong** and **Tokyo.** You will be happy with *Air-
India,* whose planes are powerful, well-kept Boeing 707 intercontinental jets. *Air-India* offers a daily service from John F.
Kennedy Airport, **New York** to **Europe** and **India,** with connections to the Far East.

ALITALIA. The Italian airlines fly DC-8 jets to and through

the Orient from **Rome** to **Australia,** with
principal service from **Rome** via **Teheran,
Karachi,** and **Bombay** to **Bangkok, Hong
Kong, Singapore, Tokyo,** and **Sydney, Australia.** *Alitalia's* Orient expansion program
has burgeoned to the point that this fine airline now serves 84 cities in 49 countries and
spanning six continents.

AIR VIET NAM is a relatively small but
aggressive airline. Air services are provided
from **Saigon** to **Phnom Penh, Siem Reap,** and
Bangkok. I have an abiding confidence in
these much needed *Air Viet Nam* services.

BRITISH OVERSEAS AIRWAYS CORPORATION

(BOAC). The sun never sets on the services
of BOAC. This vast, far-flung company provides a profusion of efficient services over a
wide variety of routes to and in the Orient.
The transpacific–U.S.A. services of BOAC
are performed in late-model long-range 707
jet aircraft.

The numerous BOAC routes coupled with affiliated *Cathay
Pacific* and *Qantas* enable the Far East, and world traveler, to
complete the most complex travel plans under one efficient system.

BOAC flies from **London** and **New York** to **San Francisco,
Honolulu, Tokyo,** and **Hong Kong,** with other transpacific

flights operating to and from **Darwin** and **Sydney, Australia.**

BOAC international flights within the Orient join **Tokyo** with **Hong Kong, Calcutta,** and **Karachi** and **Tokyo** with **Hong Kong** and **Rangoon, New Delhi, Istanbul,** and **Europe.** BOAC affiliates follow an interesting route from **Tokyo** and **Osaka** to **Taipei** and **Hong Kong.** There is a service from **Hong Kong** to **Seoul, Korea,** and flights operate directly from **Hong Kong** to **Singapore** and from **Hong Kong** to **Bangkok.** From **Singapore** one may fly to **Kuala Lumpur** and **Kota Bharu** in **Malaysia** en route to **Bangkok** with other flights from **Singapore** to **Penang, Calcutta,** and **Singapore** directly to **Bangkok.** Other BOAC flights interlace the Far East and continue to **India,** the Near East, **Africa,** and **Europe.** BOAC services are impeccable.

CANADIAN PACIFIC AIRLINES, flying the most advanced of the DC-8's with a passenger capacity of 141, offers sleek jets equipped with new Rolls-Royce Conway Mark 15 engines with a non-stop range of 5,700 miles, with full load.

Because of **Vancouver's** favorable position at the apex of the Great Circle, the **Tokyo** flight has been shrunk to a mere ten hours of flying time. Imagine, if you can: from the North American continent to the heart of **Japan** in a third of a day.

Canadian Pacific routings are from **Vancouver** to **Tokyo** and **Hong Kong** as well as from **Vancouver** to **Honolulu, Nandi, Auckland,** and **Sydney.**

The *Canadian Pacific Airlines* is a branch of that great far-flung organization operating a vast steamship, hotel and railroad empire, and airlines throughout the world. My first memorable trip to **Europe** was made with the *Canadian Pacific* in 1929. I remember them with warmth for their many kindnesses throughout the years.

CATHAY PACIFIC AIRWAYS (CPA). This airway, virtually spanning the Far East, was founded in 1946 and is proud of its claim to operate more services into and out of **Hong**

Kong than any other carrier in the world. On other routes, it also provides frequent flights and fast service. *Cathay Pacific* now serves **Hong Kong, Bangkok, Singapore, Manila, Tokyo, Taipei, Rangoon, Calcutta, Saigon, Kuala Lumpur, Phnom Penh, Brunei,** and **Kyoto-Osaka.** Services to **Djakarta** and **Vientiane** have been temporarily suspended. See your own travel agent to ascertain if these cities have been reinstated on the *Cathay* schedules.

Among the *Cathay Pacific Airways* routes are **Hong Kong–Manila, Hong Kong–Bangkok–Singapore, Hong Kong–Seoul, Hong Kong–Taipei–Osaka–Tokyo, Hong Kong–Bangkok–Rangoon–Calcutta, Hong Kong–Bangkok–Kuala Lumpur, Hong Kong–Saigon–Kuala Lumpur, Hong Kong–Saigon, Hong Kong–Vientiane, Hong Kong–Phnom Penh,** and **Hong Kong–Manila–Brunei.** *Cathay Pacific* flight crews and ground employees are cordial and courteous in all of their dealings.

CIVIL AIR TRANSPORT (CAT). The Mandarin jets of

CAT are the talk of the international aviation world. These Convair 880M's enable CAT to span the Orient quick as a flash. The personalized in-flight passenger service of CAT is traditional. Interiors of CAT planes are of a rich colorful Chinese décor, while the charming, trim stewardesses dress in eye-captivating costumes. The Mandarin jets have an authentically styled moon-gate as their cabin entrance. CAT routes include **Seoul–Tokyo–Osaka–Okinawa–Taipei, Bangkok–Hong Kong–Taipei, Hong Kong–Taipei, Manila–Taipei** and **Taipei–Manila–Hong Kong–Bangkok.** The charm of the Orient with all of the efficiency of the modern age are combined in the CAT services. You will like them. I do.

GARUDA INDONESIAN AIRWAYS operates a compact, frequent, efficient service from **Djakarta** to **Singapore, Malaysia,**

Bangkok, **Manila, Tokyo,** and
points in **Indonesia.** *Garuda* has
now added swift Convair 990A's
to the new **Djakarta–Tokyo**
service which operates via **Hong
Kong** and **Bangkok.**

HAWAIIAN AIRLINES (HAL) provides fast, frequent,
comfortable, inter-island services in luxurious 4-engine DC-6B's, 4-engine Rolls-
Royce jet prop Royal Viscounts, and is-
land-proven Super Convairs, air conditioned throughout. The Super Convairs

and DC-6B's each have a roomy club lounge. HAL serves
Kauai, **Honolulu,** *Molokai, Lanai, Maui's* **Kahului** and **Hana,**
Upolu Point, **Kamuela**, *Kona,* and **Hilo.**

HAL's family plan provides that a full fare ticket for one
parent entitles the other parent and all children under 22 to
travel on half fare tickets on all flights departing *Honolulu Airport* between 11:00 A.M. and 11:59 P.M. and on all flights
departing neighboring island airports between 12:01 A.M. and
2:00 P.M. The family plan applies to 4 P.M. from **Hilo.**

HAWAIIAN AIR TOUR SERVICE. HATS is a most unusual and commendable organization. In addition to being operators of air charters and
air taxi service to all airports in the islands,
the best known service of this splendid organization is an all encompassing air tour
which leaves *Honolulu Airport* daily at
dawn and returns at dusk after a 900 mile
circuit over the eight principal islands which comprise the Hawaiian group: *Lanai, Kahoolawe, Hawaii, Maui, Molokai,
Oahu, Kauai,* and *Niihau.*

The unusual flight route follows *Waikiki Beach* in a slow
climb through the pink-tinted cloud mists that are so characteristic of morning in the Islands. One has most spectacular and
photogenic views of sheer cliffs, waterfalls, great plantations,

orchid gardens, volcanic pits, yawning canyons, sparkling bays and inlets. The HATS "All Islands Tour" is, according to renowned travel expert R. W. ("Burt") Hemphill, the most exciting and thrilling trip in the entire *Pacific*. The bargain rate for this unusual tour is $75.00 plus $2.63 tax.

JAPAN AIR LINES (JAL). I drool ecstatically every time I even think of the taste titillating food, personal attention, beautiful planes, and all round excellence of JAL flights. I have been flying the far-flung airways of the world for more than three decades and have made fast friends and become enamored of air services in various sections of the world. But *Japan Air Lines* is different . . . that's all there is to it. Ecstatically different. One is in the gracious Orient the moment one enters the sleek, sturdy, incredibly luxurious, and speedy JAL DC-8 or 880 Convair jet. With JAL, one is an honored guest to be pampered and pleased, to be lavishly served by dainty stewardesses in native kimonos. Passengers are given, among other things, scented fans, special sleep socks, piping hot towels, and are provided with handsome happi coats.

One cannot fail to be favorably impressed by the exquisitely served cocktail appetizers and succulent meals prepared both in the Oriental and western styles. First class JAL service is known as *Kiku (Chrysanthemum),* the most elegant to be found aloft, while the thrifty economy class is known as *Sakura (Cherry Blossom).* Service in both classes is so highly personalized as to make one a pampered darling from the moment one becomes interested in JAL services until long after the return from the Orient.

DC-8C jets provide service from **Los Angeles, San Francisco,** and **Seattle** to **Honolulu** and **Tokyo. Los Angeles** and **San Francisco.** Seventeen flights weekly leave from these cities and three originate in **Honolulu** for **Tokyo.** Sleek, faster-than-a-bullet Convair 880 aircraft are used from **Tokyo to Fukuoka,** to **Okinawa** and to **Sapporo** in northern **Japan.** The Convair

880's also serve from **Tokyo** to **Hong Kong, Bangkok, Singapore, Djakarta, Osaka,** and **Seoul.** JAL now offers through DC-8 service from the West Coast to **Hong Kong** via **Honolulu** and **Tokyo.**

Two of my very favorite airlines, JAL and *Air France,* have pooled their facilities to operate from **Europe** to **Japan** and vice versa via the North Pole, and from **Europe** to **Japan** and return via **Asia.** The **Tokyo** to **Paris** service is operated via **Anchorage, Copenhagen,** and **London** in the JAL DC-8 aircraft, while, in the pool service, *Air France* provides Boeing 707 intercontinental jets from **Tokyo** via **Anchorage** and **Hamburg** to **Paris.** The same itineraries are maintained in reverse. The joint AF-JAL services via **Asia** follow slightly different itineraries from day to day with basic routings being **Tokyo–Hong Kong–Phnom Penh–Bangkok–New Delhi–Teheran** and **Tel Aviv** to **Paris** while another routing is from **Tokyo** to **Hong Kong,** then **Saigon–Bangkok–New Delhi–Teheran** and **Rome** to **Paris;** yet another route includes **Tokyo–Hong Kong–Bangkok–New Delhi–Teheran–Istanbul** and **Rome** to **Paris** and from **Tokyo** to **Manila–Saigon–Bangkok–Karachi–Teheran** and **Rome** to **Paris.**

As noted under Japanese transportation, I have previously mentioned and will reiterate only briefly that JAL domestic services enable you to fly **Tokyo–Sapporo, Tokyo–Osaka** and **Fukuoka** to **Okinawa.** These domestic services are rapidly being taken over by jet aircraft and soon will all be operated entirely in jets.

I like JAL.

K.L.M. (ROYAL DUTCH AIRLINES), Route of the Flying Dutchman. KLM was the world's first airline, and theirs is the "senior service" in flights across water to foreign lands. KLM, whose service is traditionally solid and good, operates a Polar route from **Amsterdam** via **Anchorage** to **Manila** and **Tokyo**, and a European flight via **Asia** to **Tokyo** via **Cairo, Karachi, Bombay, New Delhi, Colombo, Calcutta, Rangoon, Bangkok, Saigon, Kuala Lumpur, Singapore,** and **Manila** to **Tokyo.** The flights are excellent and frequent enough to be helpful in working out transportation problems in your Orient itinerary. My first memorable **Tokyo–Manila** flight was with KLM. They literally killed me with kindness.

LUFTHANSA, the great old German airline, flying Boeing 720 jets, proceeds from **Europe,** the Near East and **India** to **Bangkok, Hong Kong** and **Tokyo,** plus a magnificent polar service from **Hamburg** via **Anchorage** to **Tokyo.** Their service is superb.

MALAYSIAN AIRWAYS, LTD. operate jet flights from **Singapore** to **Bangkok, Hong Kong** and **Djakarta.** These cities are linked with frequent services to **Penang, Kuala Lumpur, Jesselton,** and other Malaysian cities.

NORTHWEST ORIENT AIRLINES. This rapidly burgeoning airline flies Intercontinental 320-B fan jets twice daily from **New York, Chicago** and **Seattle** to **Tokyo** with connections to **Seoul, Okinawa, Taipei,** and **Manila,** in large, fast, well

serviced aircraft. The appointments are
cheerful and the food is excellent. Basic
Northwest Orient Airlines schedules are:
New York–Chicago–Anchorage–Tokyo and
New York–Chicago–Seattle–Tokyo with
through service to **Seoul** or to **Okinawa–**

Taipei–Manila. Breathtaking, incredibly fast direct flights op-
erate from **Chicago** and **New York** via **Anchorage** to **Tokyo.**
Within the Orient, *Northwest* operates **Tokyo–Taipei, Tokyo–
Okinawa–Taipei, Tokyo–Okinawa–Manila, Tokyo–Seoul.**

PAN AMERICAN WORLD AIRWAYS (PAN AM), the
world's most experienced airline, operated
the first transpacific air service years before
any other airline even dreamed of entering
this field. The then lumbering, cumbersome
flights were made in flying boats, equipped
with commodious berths. Stops were made
at **Honolulu, Guam, Wake,** and **Midway** en

route. All this has now changed radically. The present route of
the jet clippers of this worldwide organization is one of the
most complex and efficient that one could conceivably contem-
plate. Juan Trippe's great airline began modestly enough
from **Miami** to **Havana.** That was scarcely more than three
decades ago. Now *Pan American* has grown to what could
very easily be the largest transportation service the world has
ever known. The ubiquitous, intrepid World War II traveler,
Kilroy, has nothing on *Pan American.* If Kilroy can get there,
Pan American can and does. The flying clippers not only circle
the globe but seek out its remote byways and serve them well.

Pan American approaches the Orient from **Los Angeles, San
Francisco, Portland,** and **Seattle,** with a minimum of two flights
daily, each way. On the Orient flights from the West Coast,
Pan American flies both via **Honolulu** and a Great Circle
course directly to **Tokyo,** with no scheduled stop, though a fuel
stop is sometimes necessary at **Anchorage.**

From the West Coast *Pan American* flies to **Hawaii, Tahiti,**

Nandi, Auckland, Sydney, Tokyo, Hong Kong, the **Philippines**
directly, **Bangkok, Viet Nam, Djakarta,** and, in conjunction
with *Air Viet Nam,* to **Siem Reap.**

Pan Am's round the world services continue from **Bangkok**
to **India,** the Near East, **Europe** and back to the States. One may
also approach the Orient via **Europe** with *Pan American,* as
each of the services operates in reverse. *Pan Am* flies all latest
type Douglas and Boeing jets. Their service reflects their vast
experience and their ability to plan and serve with consummate
skill.

PHILIPPINE AIRLINES (PAL). The PAL schedules include flights to virtually all the larger islands
of the Philippine group, two weekly first and
tourist class flights **Hong Kong–Manila–San
Francisco** and return, and a daily tourist
service to **Hong Kong.**

There are numerous classes of PAL domestic service: the
Rolls-Royce service (Viscount and Friendship planes), Eco-
nomico service in DC-3's, night Mercury and the Maya service.
To prove there is something new under the sun, PAL has a
rate structure that includes a 20% discount for every woman
passenger in a group of five, and a 10% discount for every
woman passenger traveling alone on its Rolls-Royce service.
The age of chivalry does, indeed, thrive in the **Philippines.**
There are special fares for students, families traveling together,
and for a husband and wife traveling together. I have found
that PAL offers something special for almost everybody. The
routes and schedules of PAL are so extensive as to make it less
than rewarding to try to list them. Let it suffice to say that if
it's a city on the map in the **Philippines,** PAL serves it. The
PAL schedules are not only all-embracing in their coverage but
their standards of service are uniformly high.

QANTAS EMPIRE AIRWAYS LTD. This pleasantly aggressive, reliable, globe-circling Australian airline services **Indonesia,** the **Federation of Malaysia, Singapore, Thai-**

land, **Manila, Hong Kong,** and **Japan** in the Orient, as well as providing their Empire services from **Australia** and **New Zealand** to India, the Near East, and **England.** West Coast schedules include flights from **San Francisco** and **Vancouver** to **Honolulu, Australia,** and **New Zealand.** Other *Qantas* routes include flights from **Australia** to **Manila, Hong Kong,** and **Tokyo** and return, as well as from **Australia** to **Djakarta, Singapore, Kuala Lumpur** and/or **Bangkok** to **India,** the Near East, and **England.** *Qantas* service is impeccable, thorough, and courteous. Equipment for the vast *Qantas* fleet includes latest type long-range jets.

ROYAL AIR CAMBODGE, the airline of **Cambodia,** provides a very necessary and efficient service between **Bangkok, Siem Reap, Phnom Penh,** and **Saigon,** with a weekly service from **Phnom Penh** to **Hong Kong** and return. Local services  are provided in prop aircraft, while the **Phnom Penh–Hong Kong** flights are in 707 Boeing jets, first and tourist class. (Royal Air Cambodge flights between **Cambodia, Thailand,** and **South Viet Nam** have been temporarily discontinued. Check with your travel agent for resumption of these services.)

SWISS AIR TRANSPORT. The Swiss Navy has long been the butt of travelers' jokes. The Swiss Air Force and the *Swiss Air Transport* are not. *Swiss*  *Air* flies from its home bases of **Zurich** and **Geneva** via **Rome, Athens, Cairo,** and the Near East to **Bombay, Calcutta, Bangkok,** and **Hong Kong.**

THAI AIRWAYS INTERNATIONAL, LTD., Route of the Royal Orchid Service, links ten key cities of the Orient in late model Douglas prop and Caravelle jet planes. Services include **Bangkok** to **Saigon, Bangkok** to **Kuala Lumpur,** and **Sin-**

gapore to **Djakarta, Hong Kong** to **Bangkok, Bangkok** and

Rangoon to **Calcutta, Tokyo** to **Taipei** and **Hong Kong, Bangkok** to **Kuala Lumpur,** and **Singapore** to **Djakarta.** Thai aircraft are decorated in Oriental style, its hostesses are multilingual, beautifully garbed, and attractive. I have found the *Thai Airways* people more than friendly, accommodating, and efficient.

TWA (TRANS WORLD AIRLINES). Our own American

airline, TWA, basically does not serve much of the area we are talking about, but it does have an excellent service from **Rome** and **Athens** through the Near East (to **Cairo, Tel Aviv,** and **Dhahran**) and on to **Bombay.** TWA flights are traditionally good, and should you be coming from **Europe** or the Near East to **Bombay,** or returning, TWA will serve you well.

U.T.A. (UNION DES TRANSPORTS AÉRIENS) is

represented in North America by *Air France* as general agent. Flight schedules, tariffs, and information may be secured through all *Air France* offices who also will be delighted to make reservations on U.T.A. flights. Flying latest model DC-8 jets, U.T.A. flies non-stop **Los Angeles** to *Tahiti, Los Angeles–Honolulu–Tahiti–Fiji–New Caledonia–Australia–Indonesia–Viet Nam–Thailand–Cambodia–Pakistan* and on to **France** via the Near East. One may connect in various places with *Air France* for a complete French flag around the world service. U.T.A., in common with other French carriers, is "high" on service and food.

INTERNATIONAL JET FARES

FIRST CLASS

U.S. and CANADA west coast to:

City	One Way	Round Trip
Bangkok	$880.00	$1,584.00
Hong Kong	$820.00	$1,476.00
Manila–Taipei	$780.00	$1,404.00
Saigon	$870.00	$1,566.00
Singapore	$880.00	$1,584.00
Tokyo	$700.00	$1,260.00

CHICAGO to:

	One Way	Round Trip
Bangkok	$996.60	$1,817.10
Hong Kong	$936.60	$1,709.10
Manila–Taipei	$896.60	$1,637.10
Saigon	$986.60	$1,799.10
Singapore	$996.60	$1,817.10
Tokyo	$816.60	$1,493.10

NEW ORLEANS to:

	One Way	Round Trip
Bangkok	$1,004.40	$1,832.80
Hong Kong	$944.40	$1,724.70
Manila–Taipei	$904.40	$1,652.80
Saigon	$994.40	$1,814.80
Singapore	$1,004.40	$1,832.80
Tokyo	$824.40	$1,508.80

NEW YORK CITY to:

	One Way	Round Trip
Bangkok	$1,040.20	$1,904.40
Hong Kong	$980.20	$1,796.40
Manila–Taipei	$940.20	$1,724.40
Saigon	$1,030.20	$1,886.40
Singapore	$1,040.20	$1,904.40
Tokyo	$860.20	$1,580.40

INTERNATIONAL JET FARES (Cont.)

ECONOMY CLASS JET FARES

U.S. and CANADA west coast to:

City	One Way	Round Trip
Bangkok	$550.00	$990.00
Hong Kong	$500.00	$900.00
Manila–Taipei	$490.00	$882.00
Saigon	$545.00	$981.00
Singapore	$550.00	$990.00
Tokyo	$435.00	$783.00

CHICAGO to:

Bangkok	$635.00	$1,160.00
Hong Kong	$585.00	$1,070.00
Manila–Taipei	$575.00	$1,052.00
Saigon	$630.00	$1,151.00
Singapore	$635.00	$1,160.00
Tokyo	$520.00	$953.00

NEW ORLEANS to:

Bangkok	$651.60	$1,193.20
Hong Kong	$601.60	$1,103.20
Manila–Taipei	$591.60	$1,085.20
Saigon	$646.60	$1,184.20
Singapore	$651.60	$1,193.20
Tokyo	$536.60	$986.20

NEW YORK CITY to:

Bangkok	$669.00	$1,228.00
Hong Kong	$619.00	$1,138.00
Manila–Taipei	$609.00	$1,120.00
Saigon	$664.00	$1,219.00
Singapore	$669.00	$1,228.00
Tokyo	$554.00	$1,021.00

JAPAN AND ORIENT FARES

FIRST CLASS

From HONG KONG to:

City	One Way	Round Trip
Bangkok	$122.50	$232.80
Fukuoka (Japan)	$204.20	$367.50
Manila	$80.00	$152.00
Osaka	$216.60	$411.60
Saigon	$120.20	$228.40
Taipei	$89.60	$161.30

From TOKYO to:

City	One Way	Round Trip
Bangkok	$313.60	$595.90
Fukuoka (Japan)	$31.80	$63.60
Hong Kong	$216.60	$411.60
Manila	$232.40	$441.60
Osaka	$15.90	$31.80
Saigon	$308.00	$585.20
Sapporo (Japan)	$29.70	$59.40
Singapore	$352.80	$670.40
Taipei	$152.20	$274.00

ECONOMY CLASS FARES

From HONG KONG to:

City	One Way	Round Trip
Bangkok	$86.80	$165.00
Fukuoka (Japan)	$150.10	$270.20
Manila	$64.00	$121.60
Osaka	$155.40	$295.30
Saigon	$91.60	$174.10
Taipei	$70.00	$126.00

JAPAN AND ORIENT FARES (Cont.)

ECONOMY CLASS (cont.)

From TOKYO to:

City	One Way	Round Trip
Bangkok	$226.80	$431.00
Fukuoka (Japan)	$31.80	$63.60
Hong Kong	$155.40	$295.30
Manila	$175.90	$334.30
Osaka	$15.90	$31.80
Saigon	$210.00	$399.00
Sapporo (Japan)	$29.70	$59.40
Singapore	$249.20	$473.50
Taipei	$109.20	$196.60

As of going to press, the above rates have been completely verified as being accurate. Air schedules, rates, and even classes of travel change faster than a woman's mind. Long before the ink is dry on these pages, one or more, if not all, of the rates listed above could well have changed—even radically. Don't plan a trip to the Orient on the basis of these rates. They should be used only as a guide as to the relative costs, though conceivably they may be completely accurate when you read this. (Are you confused? Why not?)

AIR DISTANCES

The following brief table will illustrate the horrendous distances which modern jets shrink "to size."

From SAN FRANCISCO to:

Bangkok, Thailand	9,166	miles
Hong Kong	8,116	"
Honolulu, Hawaii	2,400	"
Manila, Philippine Islands	7,800	"
Saigon, Vietnam	8,807	"
Singapore	9,490	"
Tokyo	6,260	"

INTERNATIONAL AIRLINES SERVING THE PRINCIPAL CITIES IN HAWAII AND THE ORIENT

BANGKOK:

Air France
Air-India International
Air Viet Nam
Alitalia
BOAC-British Overseas Airways Corporation
Cathay Pacific Airways, Ltd. (CPA)
Civil Air Transport (CAT)
Garuda Indonesian Airways
Japan Air Lines Company, Ltd. (JAL)
K.L.M. Royal Dutch Airlines
Air Laos
Lufthansa German Airlines
Malaysian Airways, Ltd.
Pan American World Airways System
Qantas Empire Airways, Ltd.
Royal Air Cambodge
SAS-Scandinavian Airlines System, Inc.
Swiss Air Transport Company, Limited
Thai Airways International, Ltd.
TWA-Trans World Airlines, Inc.
U.T.A. (Union des Transports Aériens)
Union of Burma Airways

HAWAII:

BOAC-British Overseas Airways Corporation
Canadian Pacific Airlines, Ltd.
Japan Air Lines Company, Ltd. (JAL)
Northwest Orient Airlines, Inc. (NWA)
Pan American World Airways System
Qantas Empire Airways, Ltd.
United Air Lines, Inc.

HONG KONG:

Air France
Air-India International
Air Viet Nam

BOAC-British Overseas Airways Corporation
Canadian Pacific Airlines, Ltd.
Cathay Pacific Airways, Ltd. (CPA)
Japan Air Lines Company, Ltd. (JAL)
Korean National Airlines, Inc.
Lufthansa German Airlines
Malaysian Airways, Ltd.
Northwest Orient Airlines, Inc. (NWA)
Pan American World Airways System
Philippine Air Lines
Qantas Empire Airways, Ltd.
Royal Air Cambodge
Swiss Air Transport Company, Ltd.
Thai Airways International, Ltd.
Union of Burma Airways

KUALA LUMPUR (Malaya)

BOAC-British Overseas Airways Corporation
Cathay Pacific Airways, Ltd. (CPA)
Garuda Indonesian Airways
K.L.M. Royal Dutch Airlines
Malaysian Airways, Ltd.
Qantas Empire Airways, Ltd.
Thai Airways International, Ltd.
SAS-Scandinavian Airlines System, Inc.

MANILA (The Philippines)

Air France
Cathay Pacific Airways, Ltd. (CPA)
Civil Air Transport (CAT)
Garuda Indonesian Airways
K.L.M. Royal Dutch Airlines
Northwest Orient Airlines, Inc. (NWA)
Pan American World Airways System
Philippine Air Lines
Qantas Empire Airways, Ltd.
SAS-Scandinavian Airlines System, Inc.
Swiss Air Transport Company, Ltd.

SAIGON (Vietnam)

Air France
Air Laos
Air Viet Nam
Cathay Pacific Airways, Ltd. (CPA)
K.L.M. Royal Dutch Airlines
Pan American World Airways System
Royal Air Cambodge
Thai Airways International, Ltd.
U.T.A. (Union des Transports Aériens)

SIEM REAP (Cambodia)

Air Laos
Air Viet Nam
Royal Air Cambodge
Thai Airways International, Ltd. (temporarily discontinued)

SINGAPORE

Air-India International
BOAC-British Overseas Airways Corporation
Cathay Pacific Airways, Ltd. (CPA)
Garuda Indonesian Airways
Japan Air Lines Company, Ltd. (JAL)
K.L.M. Royal Dutch Airlines
Malaysian Airways, Ltd.
Pan American World Airways System
Qantas Empire Airways
Thai Airways International, Ltd.
Union of Burma Airways

TAIPEI (Taiwan . . . Formosa)

Cathay Pacific Airways, Ltd. (CPA)
Civil Air Transport (CAT)
Japan Air Lines Company, Ltd. (JAL)
Northwest Orient Airlines, Inc. (NWA)
Thai Airways International, Ltd.

WHAT CLASS TO CHOOSE

Even though it might be rigged, the most difficult $64,000.00 question that I could conceivably attempt to answer is: "What class of aircraft travel shall I choose?"

This is an enigma if ever there was one.

I am a thorough going believer that people should travel as they live, and I am as intolerant of squandering money needlessly as I am of false economy. But such philosophy doesn't help too much in solving the problem of how to travel in the air. This debate has raged furiously ever since planes started to offer more than one class of travel. The subject of "class of air travel" is one on which almost everyone not only has a fixed opinion, but it is one on which most people get as emotional as they did in the '30's about Franklin D. Roosevelt. With FDR there was no such thing as being lukewarm. You loved him or you hated him; you didn't ignore him. So with air travel: rich people, middle class people, lower income people— all know all there is to know on the subject of what class to travel in the air.

It is obvious, therefore, that I am in the process of wasting our time by adding my opinions, but I shall, nevertheless. *You* might just be the *one* person in a million who has not already molded a convictior. on the subject.

The gargantuan distances involved in reaching the Orient necessarily involve expensive steamship and air fares. Air fares maintain a fixed ratio between first class and economy class, which means that the dollar differential between the classes increases acutely with the additional miles traveled.

The difference between the first class and economy fare from the West Coast to **Tokyo** and back is $477.00 per person, while it costs $594.00 more in first class round trip from the West Coast to **Singapore** or **Bangkok**. Obviously if you are going to **Singapore** and **Bangkok,** you can very properly rationalize that $594.00 per person—$1,184.00 per couple—is a sum of money that is not plucked off plum trees in August. It is a very considerable package of *e pluribus unum.* Is it worth it?

My hearty, immediate, vociferous, and opinionated answer is, "Yes, if you can afford it." Or I might go so far as to say, "Yes, if you have it."

Perhaps the most overworked cliché apropos of air travel is the "I am not going to spend all that extra money for free cocktails and more food."

If there were nothing involved in the choice between economy and first class than calories and beverages, there would be nothing to it, but there is a good deal more.

The configuration of all jets is subject to the whims of the airlines who purchase them. During slack seasons, or if the operators wish their passengers to be ultra comfortable, the planes are set up for 126 passengers of whom 30 would be in first class and 96 in economy class. When the managements get a bit more avaricious, they will arrange to seat up to 160 passengers with 40 in first class and 120 in economy class. While the number of first class passengers is roughly 25 per cent of the passenger complement, the first class area normally occupies fully 40 per cent of the aircraft. The difference in creature comforts between the two classes is imposing and should receive your best attention when making your decision.

Laterally there are six passengers abreast in economy class, three on either side of the aisle, while in first class the passengers are seated four abreast—two on either side of the aisle. Longitudinally, the space ratio is much the same as laterally. The first class passengers have a full 33⅓ to 50 per cent more leg room, and in first class there is always at least one lounge frequently supplemented by a comfortable, cheerful bar. On the long flights one may be called on to be seated for a dozen or more hours on end. Not only are the first class passengers infinitely more comfortable, but the aura of well being creates an entirely different and more attractive psychological environment.

Who travels first class? Lots of people, but never the ones

you would expect. I have a friend and client who, already rich, had a windfall of two and three-quarter million dollars recently. In preparing for her trip to the Orient, she said, "Harvey, I wouldn't spend that extra $595.00 to go first class if it were the last thing that I ever did." She didn't, either!

Considering the amount of money involved, it is amazing to me, on the other hand, that first class is proportionately as well, or better, filled than economy on almost all flights. Very frequently, the first class is sold out long before economy class is.

While I would not for the world suggest that you let the food or cocktails influence you, they are important factors. In economy class you may buy cocktails and you get enough to eat. In first class the meals are exotic creations that in themselves are delightful epicurean experiences. I chuckle every time I think of a recent JAL afternoon flight from San Francisco to Honolulu. The first time I took this flight I was fortunate in having had only a sandwich for lunch. JAL had carefully explained in advance that since the flight left at 2:00 P.M. and arrived at 4:30 P.M., no meal would be served en route, just "light snacks."

As soon as we reached cruising altitude fifteen or twenty minutes after taking off from San Francisco International Airport, two stewards and two stewardesses assigned to the first class section to serve the 30 passengers there circulated with happi coats, slippers, hot towels and gifts. They started taking cocktail orders and within a few minutes started to serve a procession of the most delectable hot and cold dishes I have ever seen or gorged myself on. By running their little legs off at top speed for three and one-half hours, they just barely got the "light snacks" served before descending on Hawaii. Dinners on all transpacific flights in first class are multi-course affairs that are just out of this world. That's all there is to it.

If the additional cost does not place an unusually heavy burden on your budget, I can assure you that you will be well pleased if you go first class. On the other hand, if budget is a problem, you will find that you will arrive at your destination exactly the same time as the first class passengers and that you will have received an unusually fine travel value in economy class.

PLANE CONFIGURATION

In the now obsolete propeller planes, the rear of the aircraft was considered the most comfortable, and safest, place to ride. First class sections were always aft. Not so in the jets.

With the exception of the *Caravelle,* which is not yet in service in the Far East, jet engines are forward in much the same position as in the propeller planes. The entire economy class is back of the engines. It is the gospel truth that jet flight is infinitely smoother than in a propeller plane. In these amazing man-made aluminum birds, noise and vibration have been reduced incredibly.

But don't for a moment believe that there is neither noise nor vibration in jets. One notices both. The first class seats, the last of which normally is abreast the engines, are so situated that they are almost entirely free from both noise and vibration. The farther aft one sits, the more swishing noise and more vibration one feels on the take off and while gaining altitude. Sitting in the rear is a little bit like being in a wind tunnel during an experiment. This slight bother is rapidly alleviated after the first tremendous ascension thrusts have taken their effect and the aircraft is soaring freely. In economy class it makes little difference whether one sits at the forward or the aft end of the section; there is slightly more noise near the engines and slightly more motion aft. In first class the comforts are much the same wherever one may be seated, though I have always preferred the very front seats where it is so quiet and motionless as to make one feel as though he is in his own den or library.

SEAT RESERVATIONS. There is no universal airlines practice relative to advance seat reservations. Ask your travel agent the procedure followed by the line of your choice. Precise first class seats may be reserved at the time of making your reservation with many of the airlines, others will list your preference. Tourist or economy class reservations usually may not be made in advance. There are exceptions to both of the foregoing procedures. The best thing to do is to have your travel agent check the procedures of the airline of your choice, and if reservations may be made in advance, do so. If not, don't fret; as previously mentioned, there isn't enough difference between the various locations within a class to cause any considerable concern. If one is traveling with a spouse or family, the important thing is that seats should be together; otherwise, there is little reason to request specific seats.

BERTHS. There is no reason why jets could not be fitted with berths; some are. There are at least two impelling reasons why they are not sold, however. The first, and probably most important, is that air travelers demonstrated long ago that they just did not want to share either an upper or a lower berth. Virtually without exception, berths in prop planes were sold on the basis of one berth to one person. An upper and a lower berth occupy the same space as four first class or six economy class seats. Jets cost between four and one half and five million dollars to build. It is an economic necessity that the airlines receive maximum income on every flight. Since few air travelers will pay a double fare or close to it in order to have the added comfort of sleeping horizontally, the airlines cannot afford to provide berths. The second factor involved in the absence of jet berths is that with the jets' cruising speed being between 550 and 655 miles per hour, there just aren't enough long journeys to warrant the added expense to the passengers or added bother to the airlines.

Both *Northwest* and *Japan Air Lines* have a few berths built into their jets for emergency hospital use. The sick person must have a doctor's certificate to be assigned a berth, and must pay a $100.00 supplement over the first class fare.

AIRCRAFT STATISTICS

Jet aircraft are phenomenal. Latest model DC-8's, for example, have a wing span of 142 feet 7 inches, a length of 150 feet

6 inches (more than half the distance of a football field), a height of 42 feet 4 inches, and have a gross weight of 315,000 pounds, without passengers, luggage, mail, or freight. Late model jets have a range of 6,500 miles non-stop, and it is anticipated that shortly this will be increased to more than 7,000 miles that planes may fly without refueling. The horse power exceeds 60,000. Colossal!

BAGGAGE ALLOWANCE. The first class baggage allowance is 66 pounds and 44 in economy class. It will be well to note that if you are flying overseas, you will be given a 66 pound first class or 44 pound tourist class allowance from your home town to the airport of your embarkation for your overseas trip rather than the domestic allowance of 40 pounds. On long flights, it is expedient that you should pack carefully and carry light weight luggage. Excess baggage rates, irrespective of the class you travel, are computed on the basis of 1 per cent of the one way first class fare per kilogram of baggage. A kilo is 2.2 pounds. The one way fare from the West Coast to **Tokyo,** for example, is $700.00. One per cent of this sum is $7.00 which divided by 2.2 produces the West Coast to **Tokyo** (one way) excess baggage rate of $3.18 per pound.

You wouldn't be normal if you weren't piqued by the payment of the excess baggage charges. Of all travel experiences, none is more universally annoying than having to pay extra for baggage. The system is here to stay, however, and it is best to learn how to live with it. The simplest way is to keep within the allotted weight.

The miscellaneous trivia you carry aboard the plane with you normally does not count against your 44 or 66 pounds baggage allowance. Women's purses are exempt, as are reasonable quantities of books, magazines, a small camera and pair of binoculars, umbrella, a foot rug, and coats. The overnight flight bags provided by some airlines are usually not exempt from the allowed weight. Brief cases, attaché cases, a second or third camera, ladies' train cases, radios, and other cumbersome or bulky articles must be weighed. A general rule of thumb relative to cabin baggage is that you may carry aboard only that which will fit under your seat. There is a wide latitude in the thinking of airline personnel on the matter of what should be done about excess luggage, however. Even within the same airline, one seldom finds two consecutive "weigh-ins" that are the same. I have, for example, seen two people checking in for the same flight, one of whom had several odd pieces of cabin baggage weighing at least 18 or 20 pounds plus 71 pounds of baggage that was weighed. His check-in man did not ask him to weigh the brief cases or the extra camera and said that since he was so close to being within the limits, he would make no charge. The man at the next counter had 69 pounds of baggage and no cabin baggage, and his clerk went to all the time and trouble to write up an excess baggage slip for 3 additional pounds. The foregoing occurred on a flight between **Hong Kong** and **Tokyo.** I myself have paid for as few as 2 or 3 additional pounds and have had, on other occasions, 28 or 30 pounds excused. One must go on the assumption, however, that the rules will be followed and that anything over 66 pounds in first class and 44 pounds in economy class will be subject to excess baggage payment.

RECONFIRMATION. The matter of reconfirming continuing flights is one which is vitally important. The procedure is simple. When you arrive at an airport, don't leave that airport without reconfirming your departing flight. Since it must be done ultimately—and usually 48 to 72 hours in advance, the easiest time to do it is on your arrival. This way you won't forget it. At the airport the procedure is always simple because the airline on which you are flying out must have a desk there. Most foreign lines are much more persnickety about reconfirmation than are some of our domestic lines. If, as is frequently the case these days, the airline has a waiting list, they will confirm to those on the waiting list the moment the reconfirmation period has expired, whether it be 24, 48 or 72 hours before the flight departure.

CHECK-IN PROCEDURE. Because of the numerous details to be processed on international flights, carriers like to have passengers check in at the field a minimum of an hour before scheduled flight departure or an hour and a half to two hours before the scheduled flight departure if one is checking in at their downtown office. Be on time. The airlines are very strict about enforcing their check-in times. If you are late, your place can, and probably will, be sold. One may proceed by taxi or car from downtown directly to the airport which is slightly simpler than taking a taxi to the downtown office, checking in there, and then proceeding by airport limousine to the field. If one is alone, it will be more expensive to go to the field by cab. This is particularly true in **San Francisco** where the taxi fare from downtown to the *International Airport* costs more than $6.00. If there are two or more in a party, taxis will normally cost little more than the limousine. When checking in either at the airport or the local office, be sure to have immediately available your passport, International Health Certificate, and airline ticket. These papers must all be scrutinized by the official in charge.

In foreign lands, check-in procedures are very similar to our own. When reconfirming one's flight, inquire as to whether or not there will be a limousine departing for the airport either from one's hotel or the downtown office of the airline and what time one is expected to be where. In every instance when departing for another country, one will be required to show one's passport, air ticket, and International Health Certificate. Have them immediately available always. I must caution you about the *Tokyo Airport:* in miles the distance is not great. Only eleven. If catching a plane at any of the rush hours, morning, noon or evening, one must allow at least an hour and a quarter to get from downtown **Tokyo** to *Haneda Airport* by car. The new helicopter service is much faster. Thus, if one is to leave **Tokyo** at 10:00 A.M. and is expected at the airport an hour before departure, be sure to leave, by car, not later than 8:00 A.M.; 7:45 would be better. If one is checking in at a downtown airline office to go out by airport limousine, be sure to inquire specifically what time to report. **Tokyo** traffic is hard enough on the nervous system without the added hazard of the possibility of missing a plane. The *Bangkok Airport* is 18 miles from the center of town. It's quite an expensive taxi ride. Other airports are more conveniently located.

IN-FLIGHT PROCEDURES. On arrival in the cabin of your plane, stow your flight bag, brief case, train case or any other solid object under your seat. Don't place solid objects in the overhead rack. Curiously enough, foreign airlines are not fastidious about keeping the overhead racks clear of heavy objects and will frequently permit "solids" to be stored therein. If, perchance, the once in a million happenstance occurred that you should hit a cold front or air pocket and the plane be jostled about, heavy objects can become dislodged from the overhead rack and give someone, maybe you, a resounding whack on the head. It is much more comforting to have the heavy or solid pieces under foot. The cabin personnel will hang up your top coat, jacket, or other garments you wish to keep wrinkle free or you may deposit them in the overhead rack. As soon as the initial chores are cared for, take your seat and fasten the seat belt firmly. Observe the no smoking injunction until flight altitude has been attained and the "No Smoking" sign has been extinguished. Remain seated and "hooked in" until such a time as the "Fasten Your Seat Belt" sign has been turned off.

Soon after flight altitude has been reached, which in the jets will be somewhere between 28,000 and 40,000 feet, the cabin personnel will demonstrate the use of the life jackets and oxygen masks. There is only one chance in about 50 million that you will ever be called on to use either one. But pay close attention. There is nothing else to do for the moment, anyhow.

After the oxygen masks–life jacket demonstration, one is free to get up, walk around, find the bar or lounge, or otherwise make one's self comfortable. Proceeding first to **Honolulu,** there will be no advance preparation for landing formalities. If the first stop is **Tokyo, Manila,** or any other foreign country, the cabin attendant will hand out various forms which should be dealt with promptly and thoroughly. There will be a landing card, customs, and money declaration form. Fill out the latter accurately and completely. Follow carefully any special instructions given by the airline's personnel. I, for one, would almost rather give up my left arm than my passport. If **Tokyo** is your destination, however, one's various forms and passport will be picked up to be turned over to the Immigration Authorities in the Japanese capital on arrival there. When one reaches the Immigration Desk, the passport will be returned. Before arrival at other terminals, there will be similar documents which, after they have been filled out, should be put in one's passport to be dealt with by the Immigration and Customs Authorities on arrival. On long flights, such as from the West Coast to **Honolulu, Tokyo** or **Manila,** one will have plenty of time on his hands. One may read, write, drink, eat, snooze, talk, or play cards. Be comfortable. Enjoy this ecstatic experience. Time always seems to pass rapidly in the air and, ere you realize it, the journey is almost over; the "No Smoking" and "Fasten Your Seat Belt" signs will appear. Obey them promptly. Soon one will be on the ground, and a new world of travel experience will unfold before you.

AIRCRAFT PERSONNEL. The big jets seating from 120 to 160 or more passengers will be served by as many as six or eight eager young men and young women. The girls are called either stewardess or hostess, the men, steward or, on some airlines, purser. Their collective job is to make their passengers happy, to see that one's every want is not only cared for but anticipated. If you should be traveling with an infant and need special assistance, you have but to tell them what you need and they will be only too happy to comply. Whatever one's desires might be, these nice people will do their best to satisfy them. On the Flight Deck, there will be the captain, the co-pilot, flight engineer, and navigator.

Flight personnel neither expect nor would they be anything but embarrassed if offered a gratuity. Don't offer one.

CHAPTER 3

Suggested Itineraries

Paeans of praise must be heaped upon those introspectively perspicacious travelers who sagaciously devote as much or more of their pre-trip time to choosing a good tour or setting up an intelligent itinerary as they do to the equally important but secondary subjects of where to stay, what to do while in the various Oriental settings, what to buy—and where.

To heap a golden harvest into the warehouse of one's travel memories, the seeds of intelligent planning must be carefully planted and lovingly nurtured.

It is essential that a successful itinerary should be the product of a happy blend between a practical mind skilled in setting up efficient transportation arrangements and the warm emotions of a heart that beats in tune with the potential series of delightful travel climaxes possible to achieve in the Far East.

All too many trips to the Orient fail to earn the generous dividends begging to be declared due to downright careless planning, lack of knowledge, or sheer ornery stubbornness.

It is a proposition of primerlike simplicity to comprehend that the value of any trip abroad is enhanced in direct proportion to the care with which the itinerary is planned, the type of hotel accommodations chosen, restaurants selected, the comprehensiveness of the sightseeing program, and the planning of intelligent shopping expeditions. Where to go, in what sequence to see the points of dazzling interest, how to get there, and how long to stay in each place combine to become the most important factors contributing to the success of the dream trip of your lifetime.

I am firmly convinced that for one's first, and frequently subsequent, trip to the Orient, there is no substitute for a well planned personally escorted, all expense tour. Good tours give outstanding values. The skilled operators who have set up Orient tour programs have been guided by their long experience in the field and their knowledge of just what itineraries and plans will produce the greatest rewards for the traveler's dollars invested.

Should you elect, however, to proceed independently, I must iterate and reiterate my oft pronounced recommendation that you place yourself in the hands of a skilled travel agent and be guided by his recommendations. You will most certainly, unless your case is utterly unusual, wish to have a completely pre-planned, prepaid F.I.T., if you don't take a group tour.

HOW MUCH TIME is required for the best possible coverage of the Orient? Without wishing to invite accusation of being unduly flippant, I can answer best by saying, "How high is up?" Fortunately, however, my solution is much simpler than that reply might indicate. There are certain facts about foreign travel known to experts that are incontrovertible. I have learned long since, for example, that the ability to absorb the zestful joys and pleasures of travel, and the historical and geographical foreign gems, is limited by a point of satiation that is resoundingly reached somewhere between six and ten weeks after departure from home. As with other "rules of thumb," the foregoing does not apply to all travelers the world over but it does to most of them. I know. Having personally handled the arrangements for more than 60,000 starry eyed world travelers and having talked or corresponded personally with most of them, I am in a position to talk factually about matters that otherwise might be mere conjecture. To focus more brilliantly the time element, I can assure you that those individuals who return from trips of from six to eight weeks do so as fresh as a daisy, have been at full functional capacity throughout the trip, and stayed long enough to get the full "per diem" value from their expenditure.

THE PRO RATA TRANSPORTATION EXPENSES are an important factor in determining the length of a trip. The Orient's high spots, its highways and byways, scenic splendors, historical vignettes, and geographical wonders can be absorbed ideally in 45 or 46 days from the West Coast back to the West Coast traveling by air between areas. When traveling by ship, of course, the ideal period of time can be lengthened because neither one's physical plant nor mental capacity is being taxed while sailing the sparkling *Pacific* waters. If we agree, as I hope we do, that from six to eight weeks is the ideal extremity what, then, should be the shortest period of time to devote to such a trip? The farther one travels, the more important the pro rata transportation expenses become. From the West Coast to **Bangkok** or **Singapore** (the "turn around" points on a trip around the Orient) the round trip first class air fare is in excess of $1,600.00, while the economy class air fare costs approximately $1,000.00 for the same journey. This Orient fare represents an almost 100 per cent increase over the cost of flying from **New York** to **Europe** and return. In my European guidebook, *Aboard and Abroad,* I dwell rather lengthily on the importance of making a European trip long enough to make the per diem cost commensurate with the values to be received. Whatever I have said on this subject apropos of a trip to **Europe** must be multiplied by two insofar as the Orient is concerned.

I shall illustrate the foregoing in the following two examples: (1) In this jet age one can fly from **Chicago** to **New York** in a matter of an hour and twenty minutes. It is entirely practical to make a one day business trip from **Chicago** to **Manhattan** leaving the Windy City at seven or eight o'clock in the morning, arriving in **New York** in mid-morning, working all day, returning from **Manhattan** after dinner to be home in **Chicago** or its suburbs well before midnight. Such a one day trip costs a businessman something over a hundred dollars depending on the extent of his luncheon and dinner entertainment. The same man can go to **New York** on Monday morning and return Friday night, spending the entire week in **New York** and, including his round trip transportation, spend less than two hundred dollars. In the first instance he has a per diem of a hundred to one hundred twenty-five dollars while in the latter case he spends forty dollars a day or less.

If one devoted three weeks to a tour around the Orient, the amortization of the air fare in economy class is approximately $50.00 a day or $80.00 a day in first class, which is costly for transportation alone.

If, on the other hand, the trip is lengthened to six weeks or more, the economy class air fare breaks down to less than $25.00 a day for the entire trip and less than $40.00 per day for those traveling first class which represents a much better value in either class. (N.B. These figures refer only to transportation and DO NOT include hotels, meals, sightseeing, local transportation, or shopping!)

There is an increasing number of people who today are taking shorter trips abroad than ever before. Sometimes the too brief foreign sojourns are warranted by the real necessity to return to one's business or family. I have found, however, from the most concentrated experience that businessmen are all too loath to commit themselves to be gone from their affairs as long as they, in their own hearts, really realize they can be gone—if they really wish. There is a trace of the "indispensable man" in all of us. A businessman must take himself in hand and say, "I am going to take time to do this trip right. I plan my business, my investments, and my home life intelligently; why shouldn't I do so when it comes to an important trip to the Orient?" I have seen men in **Bangkok, Singapore, Hong Kong,** and **Tokyo** shake their heads and say sorrowfully, "Why didn't we plan to stay longer? Everything is going fine at home and in the office while we have either hurried through these wondrous places much too rapidly or passed up places we now know are truly fabulous."

Face up to the realities that you can be gone both from your home and your office longer than you initially thought you should be away. Few, if any, businesses fold up because of the temporary (or permanent) absence of one key man.

The timing of an Orient holiday must be considered carefully and assiduously in advance. Without exception you are going to find almost every place that you visit in the Orient so intriguing and captivating that you will want to stay there longer. If not, your trip is bound to be a failure. One simply cannot plan a good trip on a hit or miss basis. Do bear in mind that it is difficult, if not impossible, to amend your travel plans en route. There just aren't enough hotel rooms and available air reservations to be had in the Orient to permit willy-nilly last minute changes of bookings. The planning must be done accurately and intelligently in advance.

At *Purdue University* I majored in civil engineering where I learned that differential and integral calculus, chemistry, physics, and geometry are exact sciences. Mathematical equations, chemical formulas, and physical properties, once established, never vary. The travel business, on the other hand, is an inexact science at best. Honest, well conceived opinions on itineraries, hotels, restaurants, and modes of travel vary even among travel experts.

I have been extraordinarily successful, however, in pleasing people on trips abroad basing present recommendations on my own travel experiences plus those of the tens of thousands of others who have gone before. A "do it yourself" travel amateur in possession of all too meager knowledge is almost sure to "louse up" a trip to the Orient. It is, at times, almost awesome for me to realize how accurately I have been able to forecast just what people should do abroad, how they should do it, how long they should take doing it, and where they should eat, sleep, and shop. Invariably they come back and tell me that they would not have varied one day, or portion thereof, on the entire itinerary I suggested.

In urging you to follow my suggested basic "Around the Orient" itinerary, I am making the recommendations of what I would do were I making my own first Orient trip again, what I would have any beloved member of my family do, and what I would plan for a valued client.

Whether or not you follow my advice is entirely up to you. If you do, I know you will have a wonderful trip.

An experienced hostess, proud of her accomplishments, invariably begins a perfect meal with an inviting, attractive appetizer and tops it off with a frothy, palate-pleasing dessert. In between there should be a tasty main dish and succulent side dishes. It would never do to start a meal with a baked alaska nor would it be particularly appetizing to finish a meal with a soup or shrimp course.

A trip must also be planned to include an appetizer, main course, and dessert—and be a series of ascending climaxes, not one of descending anticlimaxes.

There are three outstanding high points in the Orient: **Japan, Thailand,** and **Hong Kong.** To put two, or all three, of these at the beginning is to take the frosting off the cake virtually before one really begins one's Orient travels. To place the three of them together at the end is also too strong a series of ethereal-like climaxes tied too closely together.

Just as **London, Paris,** and **Rome** are **Europe's** highlights, and should be separated on an itinerary, so **Japan, Hong Kong,** and **Bangkok** should be used to greatest advantage in planning an itinerary.

THE PERFECT ORIENT ITINERARY

Here's how I would do it:

GETTING there and getting back (2 days).

JAPAN (19 days): **Tokyo** and environs, **Osaka, Kobe, Takarazuka,** *Inland Sea,* **Beppu, Hiroshima,** *Miyajima,* **Kyoto,**

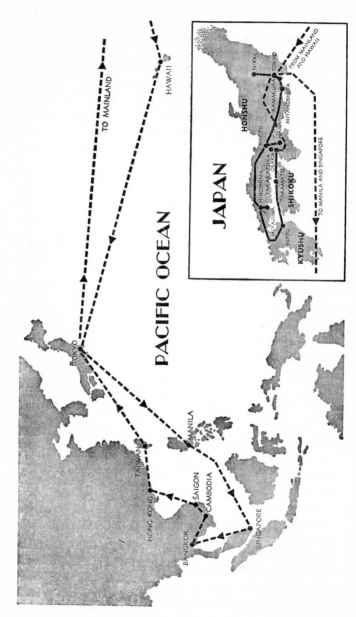

Nara, *Hakone National Park (Mt. Fuji)* **Kamakura, Yokohama, Tokyo** (again), and **Nikko.**

TAIWAN *(Formosa)* (1 day): **Taipei.**

THE PHILIPPINES (3 days): **Manila, Tagaytay,** and **Baguio.** (*Corregidor* and *Bataan* optional).

SINGAPORE AND MALAYSIA (3 days): **Singapore,** city and island, rubber plantation, with **Johore Bahru, Malaysia** to be visited from **Singapore.**

THAILAND (4 days): **Bangkok.**

CAMBODIA (1 day): **Siem Reap** (**Angkor Thom** and *Angkor Wat*). (Political conditions permitting.)

VIET NAM (2 days): **Saigon.** (Political conditions permitting.)

HONG KONG (8 days): *Kowloon, Victoria Island,* and the *New Territories.*

MACAO (Portuguese colony) (1 day): from **Hong Kong.**

HAWAII (3 days). *Waikiki* and around *Oahu.*

JAPAN

JAPAN is an ideal introduction to the Orient. Arrive in **Japan** either by ship or plane but plan to start your trip in **Tokyo** to best place your finger on the pulse beat of the Oriental atmosphere and unusual way of life.

To make the most effective use of the nineteen worthwhile days that I have recommended you spend in **Japan,** devote the first three days to **Tokyo.** If you have come by plane you will have arrived in the evening and, even though the flight was smooth and easy, you will want to rest the first morning. In the afternoon I would recommend that your sightseeing tour includes the *Imperial Palace Grounds,* the *Kanda* section, the *Korakuen* or *Rikugien Garden,* the *Kodokan Judo Hall, Tokyo University,* and *Ueno Park,* where I recommend you take tea at the *Seiyoken Restaurant,* the *Asakusa Shopping Center,* a view of *Ryogoku Bridge,* the *Nihombashi* and *Ginza* shopping districts, and the *Kabuki Theater.* By all means waste no time in choosing either tempura or sukiyaki for your first luncheon in **Japan** and the other one for dinner. These meals will be excitingly different and will not only introduce you to the two best known native specialties but will also indoctrinate you in the adept use of chopsticks.

You will want two full days of sightseeing in the capital on this first visit. There is much to see and observe. As soon as you feel brave enough, try an exploratory stroll—it will take a little while to get accustomed to the seething traffic proceeding on the left side of the street. Making one's way through the streets, lanes, and narrow alleys is, of itself, an exciting travel adventure. Walk about, drink deeply of the scene, stop in one of the coffee houses and listen to the music, try a lunch at a tiny *Sushi* restaurant or *Yakatori* bar. You can do it and you'll dream about it for years. Enjoy scintillating **Tokyo** by night and you'll experience grand adventure. **Tokyo's** allotted time will slip by all too fast.

Osaka, Takarazuka, and **Kobe** should be given two days of your time. The flight from **Tokyo** to **Osaka** is rapid and pleasant. I am suggesting that you fly south and return by train thus ultimately losing nothing of the gorgeous scenic effects. Both **Kobe** and **Osaka** are interesting, but the hotels in **Osaka,** I believe, are superior. I recommend the *Osaka Grand Hotel.* One will particularly wish to see the impressive *Osaka Castle,* the *Tsutenkaku (Sky) Tower* for a panoramic view of **Osaka,** and the *Dotombori* and *Sennichimae* pleasure quarters of **Osaka** which are jam packed with countless theaters, cinemas, restaurants, and cabarets, the *Shinsaibashi-suji* shopping center of the city, and the *Nakanoshima Park* picturesquely situated between the *Dojima* and the *Tosabori Rivers*. While in **Osaka,** a half day excursion to the lovely resort town of **Takarazuka,** home of the famous *Takarazuka Girls Opera* troupe, is one of the most fascinating experiences in the entire itinerary. Here is a practical helpful hint: **Takarazuka** is not far from the *Osaka airport* and it's much more practical to proceed there directly from the landing field than it is to make the long trip to town and come back again. Send your luggage to the hotel and proceed by car to the amusement center.

The amazing *Takarazuka Girls Opera,* which performs both revues and operettas fantastically, was highly publicized in James Michener's book *"Sayonara."* There is a *Takarazuka Company* which performs in **Tokyo** should, by any chance, you miss the experience of enjoying a performance at the home theater. **Kobe,** 20 miles west of **Osaka,** is a great port city on the fascinating *Inland Sea.*

THE INLAND SEA BY STEAMER is one of the most colorful experiences **Japan** has to offer. The local ships are superb, offering every possible comfort and amenity for the voyagers, who are also treated to a seemingly never ending series of majestic panoramic vistas of islands dotting the sea. The voyage may be accomplished pleasantly either from **Osaka** or **Kobe** (the same ship makes both ports). One boards the vessel, before 8 A.M. in **Osaka** or before 9 A.M. in **Kobe,** for breakfast, luncheon, and dinner aboard, with the arrival in **Beppu** being towards 9 in the evening. The daylight trip from **Beppu** leaves about 8:30 A.M. and arrives in **Kobe** about 9 P.M. **Takamatsu** is the principal port of *Shikoku,* an island situated between the *Inland Sea* and the *Pacific Ocean.* Unless your time is ample, **Takamatsu** is not sufficiently compelling interest for a special stopover. If through some "break" in the *Inland Sea* steamer's schedule you should be able to work out a four or five hour stopover here, you will find the view from the heights prepossessing. A word of caution: Some of the vessels calling at **Takamatsu** are of prewar vintage and are not nearly of the high standards required by American visitors.

The daylight trip from **Osaka-Kobe** usually includes a stop at **Matsuyama,** also on the island of *Shikoku,* which is well worthwhile, with the approach in the late afternoon being particularly compelling.

The best of the *Kansai Line* ships are the *Murasakai Maru, Kohaku Maru,* and the *Kurenai Maru.*

BEPPU is one vast hot spring emanating steam and literally flooded with mineral baths. If, as I have suggested, you arrive in **Beppu** one evening, that night and the next day and night will be adequate to see this enchanting resort city and its attractive environs. The outstanding points of interest that you must see are the *"Jigoku"* Hot Spring Hell, the *Onsen* Hot Spring Swimming Pool, the *Sunayu Sand Bath Hotel* where the sand is steaming hot, being warmed by the hot spring, the unusual *Monkey Mountain* with its well trained pets, an amusement center on the hill commanding a magnificent view, and the *Oita Prefectural Produce Museum* with its beckoning exhibits of local products. The *Shotengai* shopping street is emblazoned with colorful signs and attractive shops. **Beppu's** behemoth *Daibutsu,* Big Buddha, is one of Japan's largest. The hot springs, wells, and boiling mud pools include the vermilion colored *Chinoike* (Pond of Blood) which is a sizzling hot spring 540 feet deep.

The hotels and inns of the area are not exceeded elsewhere numerically or qualitatively. I particularly recommend the *Suginoi,* high on a hill overlooking the harbor and the spa area. In the *Suginoi* one may live either in Japanese or western style (in the same apartment) and may dine with chopsticks on Japanese fare or with knives and forks on Continental or American cuisine.

Be sure to feed the monkeys in their park on the side of a mountain. You may purchase tangerines or peanuts, their favorite diet, at little kiosks along the way. Be careful. They are "clever as monkeys." If you hold a full bag of peanuts in your hand, you can be certain that the little rascals will steal the entire sack. If you take one peanut in your hand and place the balance in a sack in your coat pocket, they will make a pass at your hand but will steal the bag from your pocket faster than a New York subway "dip."

HIROSHIMA AND MIYAJIMA. If one leaves **Beppu** by limited express train after breakfast, he will arrive in **Hiroshima** shortly after an excellent lunch aboard the train. The balance of the afternoon can be spent sightseeing in the ill-fated city and its environs.

The *Peace Park* is a focal point for all visitors where one finds the skeleton of the *Industrial Exposition Hall,* currently a monument, which was in the direct "hypo center" area of the atomic bomb explosion. *Peace Tower* includes the *A-Bomb Museum* which contains a great collection of the souvenirs, reminders, and photographs of the A-bomb damage. Under the arch of the *Memorial Cenotaph* is a solemn stone box containing the names of thousands of the bomb victims. A huge radiation research center is located on *Hijiyama Hill* where Japanese and Americans work together to determine the ultimate effects of atomic radiation and from which point a magnificent view of the city, harbor, and *Miyajima* in the distance may be had. Under American auspices, a new multimillion dollar research hospital was opened in **Hiroshima** in 1961, an impressive sight.

It is a moral duty for all of us to see the horror resulting from the explosion of the atomic bomb that is said to have been only a fraction of the nuclear power of present-day bombs.

The ancient **Hiroshima** *Feudal Castle* was demolished in the atomic blast; the original moat remains, however, while the grounds have been converted into a sports area. A replica of the castle has been constructed.

The next morning affords one the opportunity to experience one of Japan's finest sightseeing adventures—a visit to the island of *Miyajima,* an illustrious scenic center in its own right but particularly appealing because of its unusually attractive *Shinto Shrine* which is built on supports in the sea. At high tide the water rises to the level of the shrine's base creating the illusion that the shrine is afloat and lending its name, *"Floating Shrine."* One reaches *Miyajima* by a fierce dragon-like ferry from the port of **Myajimaguchi.** A huge *torii* in the sea silhouettes the shrine within which is the famous *Senjo-kaku* or *Hall of a Thousand Mats.* Nearby we see the colorful, painted *Five-storied Pagoda,* and one can visit the *Daiganji Temple* built in A.D. 802. *Myajima Island* is in a fairyland-like setting. Its village streets are narrow; its shops are beckoning. On the **Hiroshima** side there is a most fantastic Japanese hotel *(ryokan)*, the *Issaen Inn.* If time or desire rules against staying overnight in this Japanese inn, you might try luncheon or dinner there. It will be unusually good.

The trip from **Hiroshima** to **Kyoto** is made by the limited express train, *"Kamome,"* which scoots along at great speed. Arrival in the ancient capital is some time after having taken an excellent dinner on the train. Four nights must be devoted to **Kyoto,** Japan's most fascinating city.

While in **Kyoto,** not less than two full days should be devoted to sightseeing in the ex-capital, not including a day's excursion to nearby **Nara.** While in **Kyoto** be sure to visit the *Gion* (geisha) district, and if time permits do see a public geisha performance. The *Kiyomizu Temple,* better known as the *Eleven-faced Kannon* (Goddess of Mercy), is one of the best known in Japan. You must see the *Old Imperial Palace.* If your taste turns to adventure, you may "shoot" the *Hozu Rapids* for the nearby nine mile stretch between **Kameoka** and **Arashiyama.** *Lake Biwa,* frequently called the "Lake Lucerne of Japan," may be reached from **Kyoto** in a matter of twenty minutes or less. Northeast of **Kyoto** one may visit *Mt. Hiei* reached through the *Taya Pass* or by cable car.

NARA may be visited from **Osaka, Kobe,** or preferably **Kyoto,** from which old capital the drive is twenty-six miles over a reasonably good road. The trip to **Nara** can be made in a half day, but there is so much to see I suggest that you make **Nara** a leisurely full day trip. You can consume a fine luncheon in an excellent setting at the *Nara Hotel* and later visit the *Deer Park,* temples, and pagodas.

The best known of **Nara's** attractions is the mid-8th century *Todaiji Temple* which houses the great *Daibutsu Buddha.*

The ideal place in one's itinerary to visit the great *Hakone National Park,* the *Hakone Mountains, Mt. Fuji,* and *Lake Hakone (Reed Lake)* is between **Kyoto** and **Tokyo** when completing the splendid circle tour described in the foregoing.

Proceed by limited express train from **Kyoto** to **Numazu** where one can be met by a private car or motor coach to drive along the shores of *Lake Ashi-no-ko* (yet another name for *Reed Lake* or *Lake Hakone*) where the inverted reflection of *Mt. Fuji* is, on a good day, reflected mirror-like in the crystal clear waters. This spa area has numerous excellent places at which to stop. Try either the storied *Fujiya Hotel* at **Miyanoshita,** the nearby, new, excellent *Kowaki-en,* or the magnificent *Hakone Kanko Hotel* overlooking the lake. One should visit the *Five Lakes,* the *Big Hell* (a gorge in the mountains where boiling waters and sulphurous fumes are amazingly ejected from crevices in the rocks and bare earth), and drive past *Long Tail Pass* for another base-to-summit view of *Mt. Fuji.* A motor launch trip on *Lake Hakone* and a funicular cable car ride in the park are both suggested for your consideration.

From the *Hakone National Park,* I suggest returning to **Tokyo** for three more nights via

KAMAKURA and YOKOHAMA. The route first meanders through the *National Park* to *Sagami Bay* where, for a short distance, it follows the shore line and then turns inland to **Kamakura,** where one visits the impressive *Daibutsu,* the great image of Lord Buddha, and other historic shrines. The drive back to **Tokyo** continues through the port of **Yokohama** and passes the *Tokyo Tower,* tallest steel structure in the world.

One of the remaining days in **Tokyo** should be devoted to an excursion to **Nikko.** I have found that, while **Nikko** affords one of the most interesting excursions in all of the Far East, a one day excursion there is quite adequate. One need not spend overnight in this shrine and scenically endowed area. The *Tobu Electric Railway* from its own station is most comfortable; the trains are air conditioned in the summertime and well heated in the winter. In **Nikko** the points of greatest interest include the *Sacred Bridge,* the *Toshogu Shrine,* and the myriad nearby shrines, temples, and religious relics. Americans are always interested in the *Sacred Stable* with its "Hear no evil, See no evil, Speak no evil" monkeys carving, the *Sacred Library,* the *Yomeimon Gate,* the *Insect Eaten Bell,* the *Belfry* and *Drum Tower.* Be sure to take luncheon at the charming *Nikko Kanaya Hotel.*

High above **Nikko,** in the *Nikko National Park,* is *Lake Chuzenji* situated amid magnificent mountain scenery replete with rushing waters and sylvan waterfalls. Here one finds the *Kegon Waterfall* and the *Futaarasan Shrine.* The trout hatchery just north of *Lake Chuzenji* is most unusual, and the *Yudaki Hot Waterfall* is particularly photogenic. The almost perpendicular drive up to *Lake Chuzenji* is over a road indented with 36 sharp hairpin curves, a drive that is a pleasure to see throughout the year but particularly so in the spring and fall.

For your last day of sightseeing in **Tokyo,** one must be sure to include as many of the points of interest I have covered in Chapter 12 as possible. Don't miss the *Marunouchi Quarter,* the *Meiji Shrine, Meiji Shrine Outer Garden, National Diet Building, Nicolai Cathedral,* and *Tokyo Station.* Without my reminding you, I know that you will be sure to see a *Kabuki* or a *Noh drama,* preferably the former, as the latter drags a bit. During your free time, you should visit at least one of the large department stores and shopping arcades, or need I mention it?

From **Tokyo,** I suggest that you proceed to

TAIWAN

TAIWAN *(Formosa).* Flights to **Taipei,** Taiwan's capital, may be boarded either in **Osaka** or **Tokyo.** Twenty-four (or at the most forty-eight) hours is adequate for **Taipei** and surrounding area. Here is the one chance in the world today to see the real **China,** as yet untainted by Communism. Do try to stop at the *Grand Hotel.* It's fabulous. For dinner I think you'll enjoy a Mongolian barbecue, prepared and served like nowhere else.

From **Taipei** our suggested itinerary carries us to

THE PHILIPPINES

THE PHILIPPINES where you will be pleasantly surprised. Almost everyone is. So many friends have said, "What is there to see in the Philippines?" Actually, there is a great deal. The verdantly beautiful country has a charm and fascination quite its own. Its people are unusually interesting. Three nights will be adequate for **Manila** . . . two could suffice if you are pressed for time.

The balance of the first day and evening can be kept free for shopping and independent exploration, with dinner, perhaps, at the *Jai Alai* and later visits to one or more of the many amusing night clubs. The next morning should embrace a sightseeing excursion of **Manila** including, particularly, the walled city of *Intramuros,* the *University of Santo Tomas,* oldest institution of learning in the country, *Dewey Boulevard,* the *New Luneta Park,* **Quezon City,** and the *Rizal Avenue* and *Escolta* shopping centers, busiest in the **Philippines.** You must be sure to see the magnificent residence of the Republic's President and the well-groomed *Forbes Park* residential area, known as "Millionaires' Row."

That afternoon, drive to the scenic *Tagaytay Ridge* where luncheon can be taken at the *Taal Vista Lodge* overlooking *Lake Taal* and *Taal Volcano.* En route one sees the famous *Bamboo Pipe Organ* in *Las Piñas Church* and countless open air fruit and flower markets, stilted houses, and water buffaloes plodding in the fields.

For the second day, one may visit *Corregidor* and *Bataan,* or fly to mountainous **Baguio,** and/or visit the incredible *Banaue* rice terraces. They are all richly rewarding experiences.

SINGAPORE

SINGAPORE, *the Crossroads of the World.* You will, no doubt, arrive in the late afternoon. Try to spend 3 nights in summery Singapore, but two nights could suffice. The better part of one day can be spent interestingly in nearby **Johore**

Bahru, Malaysia, where one can visit a rubber plantation, the *Zoo,* the *Botanical Gardens, Istana Besar,* the chief palace of His Highness the Sultan, *Bukit Serene,* the residence of His Highness the Sultan, the picturesque *Mosque,* and the waterfront along *Jalan Ibrahim* and *Jalan Scuda.* On returning to Singapore, after visiting **Johore Bahru,** I recommend a stroll along the *Esplanade, Nicoll Highway, Collyer Quay,* and *Raffles Place,* which will prove intriguing beyond expression. For your first evening out, after dinner, visit one of the *"Worlds"* (amusement parks). On your way home, stop at the *Albert Street* or *Bedok Corner* Chinese eating stalls or a *Beach Road* Malayan food stall.

For your full day's sightseeing, in the city and on the rest of the *Island of Singapore,* be sure to include the *Botanical Gardens* with their tremendous collection of gorgeous orchids, *Van Kleef Aquarium, McRitchie Reservoir,* the *Haw Par Villa, Tiger Balm Gardens, Siang Lim Sian Si Temple, Sri Mariamman Temple,* the *Holy Sultan Mosque, Mount Faber, Chinatown,* the Malay stilt villages, the cool greenery of the *Royal Island Club,* the *Singapore Turf Club,* and the shopping centers at *High Street, North Bridge Road, Orchard Road,* and *Stamford House.*

From **Singapore** it is a relatively short flight to

THAILAND

BANGKOK **(Thailand)** is the world's most colorful, and one of its most interesting, cities. Here one needs but time. Four, preferably five, nights should be an irreducible minimum for **Bangkok,** where you will want most definitely to have a minimum of two full days of organized sightseeing to explore every nook and cranny of the city and environs, plus a half day on the *klongs,* and as much more time for independent exploration as possible. Every minute in **Bangkok** will be an enchanting one. The palaces, temples, and public buildings of **Thailand** are the most richly ornate and exotically colorful on which I have ever feasted my well-traveled eyes. You will be utterly amazed at the modern aspect of **Bangkok.** There are smart boulevards, chic residential areas, attractive public buildings, and lovely hotels. No one, including myself, has ever adequately described the seething setting of the *klongs,* and visitors invariably are pleasantly surprised at the fascinating area in which they find themselves. There is so much to absorb in **Bangkok.** You will, of course, wish to attend a performance of Thai classical dancing and see the native handicrafts exhibited in the government buildings. The dolls are the finest in the world but expensive. Thai shopping, particularly for bronze ware and wind (temple) bells, is intriguing. You absolutely must attend an incredible Thai boxing match in which the boxers may, and do, use their feet as well as their hands. Be sure to dine one evening high over the river in the *Normandie Grill,* in the glittering elegance of the *Rama's Tropicana,* or at *Nick's Hungarian Restaurant No. 1.*

CAMBODIA

CAMBODIA. **Siem Reap,** a cleared area in the jungle, has a population of approximately 6,000 souls who lead a primitive life. One may visit **Siem Reap** comfortably from **Bangkok** in a day. There is a sufficiently good air schedule to permit one to leave **Bangkok** after breakfast, spend the day in **Siem Reap,** and fly back again for a late dinner. I prefer to do it another way, however, as follows: when your **Bangkok** stay is completed, pack up and leave on the morning plane for **Siem Reap,** where you will arrive about 10:30 A.M., which will give you adequate time to visit **Angkor Thom** before 'uncheon. Go directly to the hotel from the airport. After checking in, proceed to **Angkor Thom** where many of the temples and buildings have been fully reclaimed from the jungle. Return to your hotel for luncheon and a short siesta, after which you can depart, at 3:00 or 3:15 P.M., for *Angkor Wat,* one of the most amazing structures in the entire world. At *Angkor Wat,* you may ride an elephant as part of your sightseeing fun. Several hours in *Angkor Wat* are needed to explore the temple, which is in a remarkable state of preservation. Air schedules to **Cambodia** currently are curtailed. Check with your travel agent to see if political conditions permit travel here.

SOUTH VIET NAM

SOUTH VIET NAM. **Saigon** is the Paris of the Orient where you should spend two memorable nights. The *Caravelle Hotel* is as fine a fully air conditioned hotel as I have ever seen. In **Viet Nam** the females' costumes are the cutest imaginable, their white silk (long) pants contrasting with vivid hued blouses and flowing silk streamers of blue, red, crimson, violet, pink, and orange. **Saigon's** boulevards are wide and spacious, the residential section handsome, and the smart restaurants serve magnificent food. The *Central Market* is fascinating, and the adjacent Chinese section of *Cholon* is colorful and worth visiting. **Bien-Hoa** and **Thu-Dau-Mot,** village art centers for pottery and lacquer, may be visited by car in a day. Check with your travel agent to see if political conditions permit travel to **South Viet Nam.**

HONG KONG

HONG KONG. The grand finale, the climax to end all climaxes, **Hong Kong** will be the scintillating gem of all your Far Eastern travel adventures. No matter how long you spend in **Hong Kong,** it is too short a time to be in this British Crown Colony, a melting pot of the Far East and a shopping center beyond all belief. Hong Kong's setting is jewel-like by day and a veritable fairyland of twinkling lights in the romantic nocturnal atmosphere. I recommend eight days for **Hong Kong.** You may choose to stay on the **Kowloon** side. Or, with the completion of the fine new hotels recently opened in **Victoria,** you may prefer to stay on the **Hong Kong** side—*Victoria Island.* Either way, you will be ferrying back and forth since there is much of interest on both sides. If you do stay in **Kowloon,** you will be near the *Star Ferry,* which frequent boat service will transport you to the island in a matter of minutes from the mainland, the ferries shuttling back and forth like busy water bugs every few minutes. Your organized sightseeing will take a minimum of three days, including one day for **Kowloon** and the *New Territories*, one day for **Victoria** including *Aberdeen, The Peak, Tiger Balm Gardens, Repulse Bay,* etc., and one day for an excellent trip offered by launch through the harbor, typhoon shelters, *Aberdeen,* and around the island. It will take several days to get fully familiar with *Nathan Road, Austin Road, Granville Road, Gascoigne Road, Chatham Road,* and *Canton Road* in **Kowloon,** as well as *Connaught Road Central, Chater Road, Des Voeux Road Central, Lockhart Road,* and *Hennessey Road,* and the vast labyrinth of the Chinese section of **Victoria.** One of your very first evenings, you must be absolutely certain to have cocktails and dinner at **Kowloon's** *Carlton Hotel,* and, while on the **Victoria** side, do enjoy the priceless view from *Victoria Heights.*

MACAO

MACAO (Portugal). This wicked city, which lies forty miles west of **Hong Kong,** about three hours by boat, can probably amuse you for a day and evening. A peninsula on the Chinese mainland, not far from Canton, Portuguese Macao is also a melting pot and has attained some reputation as being a very wicked city, which is probably exaggerated, though it is the only gaming city in the Orient and somewhat sinister in aspect.

HAWAII

HAWAII can be the steppingstone to the Orient, just as it can be a glorious finale. It serves both as an appetizer and as a dessert. I have purposely put it last, however. You will have been traveling strenuously, and your stay in **Hong Kong** will have been an active one from morning until late evening day after day. You will welcome the opportunity to relax completely in this paradisiacal setting where the climate, the tropical atmosphere, and all the services have been geared to provide the most perfect traveler's haven in the world. I have allotted three days for this stay, but now, since you have stopped traveling, my comments apropos of how many days one can enjoy and absorb in foreign lands without super-satiation no longer apply. Once you have had your tour around the island and conceivably an inter-island excursion, you will just want to absorb the health giving rays of the sun, loll about, and be just as lazy as ever you can. Three days will be a proper climax. Take longer if you wish.

For your first trip to the Orient, the foregoing is the finest possible itinerary. It has all the elements of perfection. Each allotment of time has been carefully weighed and found just right . . . a perfect six and one-half week itinerary.

This itinerary lends itself beautifully to a combination of land and sea travel. If your time permits, I heartily recommend that you sail from **San Francisco** to **Yokohama** or from **Hong Kong** back to **Honolulu** and/or **San Francisco.** The *American President Lines* frequently has space available between **Kobe, Hong Kong,** and **Manila.** One of the most spectacular sights in the world is the approach to **Hong Kong** through its harbor. To include this voyage is to add another star-studded page to the diary of your world travels. With the *Presidents Wilson, Cleveland,* and *Roosevelt* in service, the APL provides frequent service to and from these exotic Orient ports. You will have little difficulty fitting in a sailing one way or the other—or, even better, for the round trip.

ALTERNATIVE ITINERARY No. 1

It is really quite difficult to improve on perfection. Very. I have found, however, that someone is always trying to "gild the proverbial lily." Why not me?

Before I make my first alternative itinerary suggestion, I must hasten to point out that there are so many completely captivating places in the world one could spend 365 days a year for

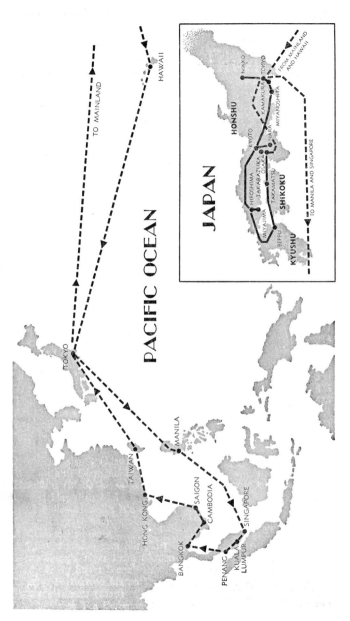

PACIFIC OCEAN

TO MAINLAND

HAWAII

TOKYO

MANILA

TAIWAN

HONG KONG

SAIGON

CAMBODIA

SINGAPORE

BANGKOK

PENANG

KUALA LUMPUR

JAPAN

HONSHU

NIKKO

TOKYO

KYOTO

TAKARAZUKA

HIROSHIMA

OSAKA

NARA

AMAKUSA

MIYANOSHITA

MIYAJIMA

TAKAMATSU

SHIKOKU

BEPPU

KYUSHU

FROM MAINLAND AND HAWAII

TO MANILA AND SINGAPORE

one hundred years and visit a new, intriguing, fascinating, and attractive place *every day.*

There is no time while you are traveling on Itinerary No. 1 that you are more than minutes from places of outstanding scenic splendor, warm local color, rich human interest, historical significance, or cultural importance. I know much about many of them, all about some of them. But I must reemphasize the value of skilled guidance. Don't get "mouse trapped" into following every ethereal will-o'-the-wisp. There are the limiting factors of time and money and the inability of the mind to absorb more than "just so much." If you are not careful, one, two, or all three of these foregoing will become active in mitigating against YOUR having a successful trip.

One must guard zealously against the well meant, but usually worthless, advice of "one-trip wizards" who "know it all" and tell you "oh, you just can't miss **Nagoya,** your trip will not be complete without it" or "you must go to **Bali, Java,** and **Djakarta**—you'll be so close to them when you are in **Singapore**" or "you simply can't pass up **Nagasaki.**"

To all this, I say "horse feathers."

One can only do so much. Do it well, and do it intelligently. If, however, you have four extra days at your disposal and wish to make a perfect trip pluperfect, you can follow the following alternative routing:

THE FEDERATION OF MALAYSIA. From **Singapore,** penetrate the Federation of Malaysia either by day train for a superbly colorful ride, or a short plane ride, to the lusty, brilliant, beautiful, old but brashly new capital, **Kuala Lumpur.** Three days in Malaya will be abundantly filled with strange and attractive experiences. Spend two of them in **Kuala Lumpur** and one in **Penang.** While in K.L., as the city is affectionately known, be sure to visit the busy *Mountbatten Road* shopping thoroughfare, the unique *Railway Station, Istana Negara,* the Sultan's *Mosque,* the *Cathedral of St. John,* the *Sunday Market,* the outdoor stall-like restaurants, the *Bukit Bintang "World" Amusement Park,* the *Selangor Turf Club,* and the *Selangor Club Padang*. The nearby *Batu Caves* are worth an hour or two of your time.

PENANG is a daylight train ride or a short flight from **Kuala Lumpur.** In the island state, one is literally lost in local color. Places to be sure to include are the *Kek Lok Si Monastery and Temple* at **Ayer Itam** near **George Town,** the *Captain Kling Moslem Mosque,* the Ceylon-type *Burmese Temple,* the *Snake Temple* at **Sungei Kwang,** 9 miles from **George Town,** the *Nattukottai Chettiar Temple,* the *Sri Mariamman Temple,* the *Siva Temple* in **Dato Kramat,** the *Subramanian Temple,* **Penang's** hustling harbor, *Penang Hill,* the *Botanical Gardens,* the *"Great Worlds" Amusement Parks,* and the *Chinatown* shopping center.

From the island state of **Penang** to BANGKOK (**Thailand**) is a long, interesting train ride or a relatively short fascinating flight.

ALTERNATIVE ITINERARY No. 2—Three Weeks

Here is the "Short Term Olson Special" for those who really must limit themselves to three weeks.

TOKYO	4 days (including **Nikko**)
KYOTO	3 days (including **Nara**)
OSAKA	1 day
SINGAPORE	2 days (via **Hong Kong,** and including **Johore Bahru, Malaysia**)
BANGKOK	4 days (including side trip to **Siem Reap** for *Angkor Wat*)
HONG KONG	5 days (including **Macao**)
TRANSPACIFIC	2 days

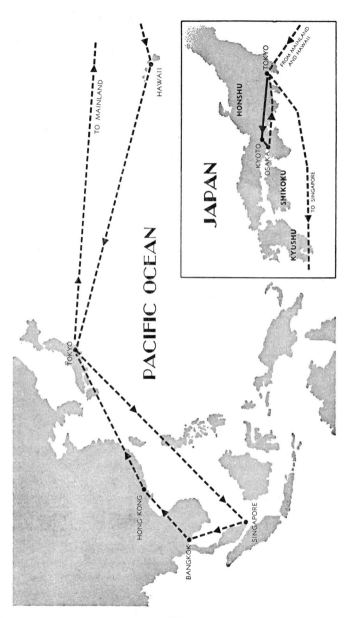

ALTERNATIVE ITINERARY No. 3

This splendid four-week itinerary is most inclusive and gives one a wide coverage of the Oriental points of outstanding interest.

TOKYO	5 days	(including **Nikko**)
HAKONE NATIONAL PARK	2 days	(*Mt. Fuji*)
KYOTO	4 days	(including **Nara**)
OSAKA	1 day	(including **Takarazuka**)
SINGAPORE	2 days	(including **Johore Bahru, Malaysia**)
BANGKOK	5 days	(including *Angkor Wat*)
SAIGON	2 days	
HONG KONG	5 days	(including **Macao**)
TRANSPACIFIC	2 days	

AROUND THE WORLD

For those continuing on around the world, the itinerary should be planned, insofar as the Orient is concerned, as follows:

HAWAII	(3 days)
JAPAN	(14 to 19 days)
TAIWAN	(1 day)
THE PHILIPPINES	(2 or 3 days)
HONG KONG	(6 days—including **Macao**)
SAIGON	(2 days)
SINGAPORE *	(2 days)
BANGKOK *	(5 days—including *Angkor Wat*)

BANGKOK or SINGAPORE to India, **Pakistan,** the Near East and **Europe.**

* **Singapore** and **Bangkok** may be visited in the reverse of the above order. The routing depends on the day of the week, and the available flights.

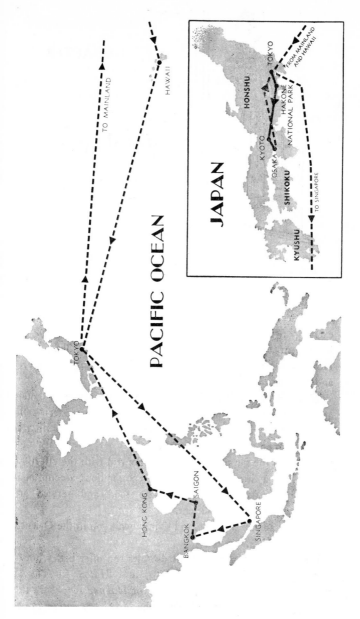

PACIFIC OCEAN

TO MAINLAND

HAWAII

TOKYO

HONG KONG

SAIGON

BANGKOK

SINGAPORE

JAPAN

HONSHU

TOKYO

FROM MAINLAND AND HAWAII

KYOTO

HAKONE NATIONAL PARK

OSAKA

SHIKOKU

TO SINGAPORE

KYUSHU

CHAPTER 4

Hotels in the Orient

HOTELS IN the Far East are fascinating. Frequently there are too few rooms to meet the ever expanding demands generated by increasing numbers of foreign and domestic visitors. But each month sees new hotel construction begun or plans made for exciting new hostelries. Old bottlenecks brought about by insufficient accommodations have been broken in **Tokyo** and **Hong Kong**; new ones are building up in **Bangkok, Singapore,** and **Manila.**

With the exception of the *ryokan* (Japanese style hotels and inns), hotels in the Orient follow the same western style pattern with which we are familiar from our travels in the States, **Europe,** or **South America.**

Hotels on the far side of the world are run with the effortless precision of a fine Swiss watch, the commodious accommodations are spotlessly clean, and the food and service are dramatically good and efficient.

Glorious adventures in grand living await you in the Orient's handsome hotels.

Neither **Europe** nor the **United States** can offer better hotels than the *Imperial, Palace, Okura,* and *Hilton* in **Tokyo;** the *Fujiya* and *Kowaki-en,* **Hakone,** or *Hakone Kanko* in the *Mt. Fuji* area not far from **Tokyo;** the *Miyako* or *International* in **Kyoto;** the *Peninsula* or the *Ambassador* in **Hong Kong;** the *Rama* in **Bangkok;** or the *Caravelle* in **Saigon.**

The extremes of the Oriental hotel situation are represented by **Tokyo** on the one hand and by **Bangkok** and **Singapore** on the other. In the latter crossroads of the world, there are no large hotels; the few there, headed by the venerable, justly renowned *Raffles, Goodwood Park,* and the new *Singapura Intercontinental,* are entirely inadequate to the increasing demand for accommodations. In **Bangkok** the plight is even more desperate. In **Thailand's** capital the number of hotels I would deem worthy of recommending may be counted on the fingers of one hand, with at least one digit to spare. I am sure I need not point out again, or more forcefully, that if your plans do, as they should, include **Bangkok** or **Singapore,** DON'T FAIL to have a confirmed hotel reservation in both places before you leave home. I might also point out parenthetically that this tidbit of sagacious advice is equally and universally sound for reservations the world over.

In **Tokyo** there are literally scores of good hotels, and, although the requirements continue to expand more rapidly than a helium balloon under a summer's sun at midday, one can generally expect to find a clean room in a good hotel. In the Japanese capital the four truly deluxe establishments (*Imperial, Okura, Hilton,* and *Palace*) continue under severe reservation pressure. I heartily approve of seeking out the best hotels, restaurants, and services, but I hasten to assure you that should you stop in the *Hotel New Japan, Nikkatsu, Kokusai Kanko, Tokyu Ginza, Azabu Prince,* or *Marunouchi,* you will be "snug as a bug in a rug" and enchanted with your **Tokyo** home. The hotels I have under "Good" in the **Tokyo** listing may be used with confidence, and there are many others, quite satisfactory, that I have not catalogued.

Beppu, a tiny resort bathed by the *Inland Sea* on **Japan's** island of *Kyushu,* has more good charming inn-type hotels than Chicago's Near North Side had B-girls before the erudite Californian, Orlando Wilson, rode out of the West as a crusading

Lochinvar to become the Windy City's purging, purifying police commissioner.

Nagoya, Nagasaki, Osaka, Karuizawa, and **Yokohama** all boast excellent hotels.

The best in the **Philippines** hotel world does not compare favorably with elite hotels elsewhere. The number and quality of the hotel rooms in **Manila** will, I am sure, soon be increased materially.

New hotels in **Hong Kong** are thrusting skyward almost as fast as fresh vegetables in **Singapore,** where twelve crops a year are not unusual. Only a very few years ago the deluxe traveler to the British Crown Colony was limited in hotel choice to the celebrated *Peninsula,* in **Kowloon;** or the remotely situated, stately *Repulse Bay* on **Victoria's** far shore.

Even though the *Peninsula* continues to reign as matriarchal queen of the Colony's hotels, one need no longer be considered an outcast if staying at another hotel. The *Marco Polo Peninsula Court,* under the same management as the *Peninsula,* is simply superb. In **Kowloon** the *Ambassador, Miramar, Park, President, Merlin,* and *Carlton* are all excellent establishments.

The two relatively new establishments in the center of **Victoria,** the *Mandarin* and magnificent *Hilton Hotels,* opened in 1963, have few, if any, peers. With the addition of these 1,500 deluxe rooms in **Hong Kong** (1,000 in the *Hilton* and 500 in the *Mandarin*), the onetime near-desperate hotel situation is, temporarily at least, eased.

Without exception the food and service in the hotels listed in this chapter are just out of this world. In the hotel bedrooms or dining rooms, one may choose from palate pleasing menus including local dishes and the best European and American cuisine. In Japanese hotels one may dine sitting on *tatami* mats or on chairs, using chopsticks or knife, fork, and spoon.

Breakfast may be ordered the previous evening for delivery to your room at a specified moment in the morning. You can be rib-rocked certain that the waiter, waitress, or room boy will be tapping at your door at the precise moment requested and that the table will be smartly covered with starched linen, and shiningly set with clean plates, sparkling silver, and adorned with a flower. The food will be perfectly prepared, piping hot or crispy cool, as desired.

Room boys, floor clerks, and hovering maids insure an instantaneous response to your ring for service. One hour for pressing is routine, as is one day laundry service.

The rooms are, for the most part, air conditioned, large, and tastefully decorated, with latest style bathrooms including tub and shower bath, direct and indirect lighting, electrical outlets, circulating ice water, heated towel racks, and frequently twin "his" and "hers" washstands. The toilet paper is soft and strong. Bidets are found—sometimes. Soap is usually provided.

Radio and/or television sets are standard hotel room accoutrements in the Orient, and writing desks, unlike most of ours, are well stocked with various kinds of envelopes, paper, and post cards. Telephones, found in the bedrooms, are, in addition to normal communication functions, used to summon servants, although some hotels provide an efficient push-button system for this purpose.

The concierge, or hotel porter, so helpful in **Europe** is not generally known in this section of the world. This does not pose a problem, however. Information, mail, and reception desks are manned by English speaking personnel, anxious to please. These eager employees will assist you by: writing directions for your taxi driver; stamping letters or post cards; sending cablegrams; answering questions on local lore or customs; wrapping packages; suggesting shops, cinemas, or restaurants; arranging for barber, beauty, or massage appointments; and being towers of strength in your time of need.

Tips and taxes are usually added to your hotel bill. If you are making your own reservations and paying your own bills, be sure to inquire, when confirming the rate, how much the gratuities and local imposts will increase your account. 10% is the normal gratuity fee, while the government tax is usually the same. A $25.00 a day room thus becomes $30.00 daily.

Hotel rates are quoted on the basis of room only, or including one or more meals which latter arrangements are known in the trade as bed and breakfast, demi-pension, (breakfast and one other meal), or full pension (room plus all meals). Larger city hotels tend to sell their rooms either with breakfasts or without requiring the inclusion of any meals. Hotels in smaller cities and resort areas usually require at least demi-pension. Where available, demi-pension affords a good, and flexible, arrangement. One has the economy of the included meals and the freedom to take either lunch or dinner at a restaurant of one's choice. Should you select a plan including one or more meals, be sure to ascertain if the rate includes breakfast served in the room, what the meals include, and whether or not the second meal must be taken in a special dining room. Full pension is sometimes required.

Meal hours in Japanese hotel dining rooms are much the same or a little earlier than ours are in the States, while in the other countries the meal hours are similar to ours or a bit later.

Many hotels in the Far East have new wings or sections offering vastly superior accommodations than the original building. The prices charged for a room in a new, new wing can easily be as much as double, triple, or even four times what your Aunt Agatha paid 5 years ago in the old wing of the same hotel. The rates in the new sections are frequently double or more the current rates in the older unit. Don't let this disturb you. If you can afford it, choose the "new wing"—it will be worth it.

The following observations reflect my opinions. I hope they will prove both useful and interesting to you.

HAWAII

The ROYAL HAWAIIAN. The *Royal Hawaiian Hotel* has long been a symbol of the quintessence of hotel perfection. Its justly deserved fame is so worldwide that the *Royal Hawaiian* is frequently linked with such posh international establishments as the *Negresco Hotel* in **Nice,** the *Villa d'Este* at *Lake Como,* the *Royal Danieli* in **Venice, Rome's** *Excelsior, Raffles* in **Singapore,** and the *Imperial* in **Tokyo.** The *Royal Hawaiian* exudes an aura of nobility. Although it is the oldest of Hawaii's deluxe hotels, it has kept pace with the modern world, and its services and facilities are as efficient and endearing as its setting—on *Waikiki* with a pluperfect view of *Diamond Head*—is unexcelled. Its reputation for luxury is thoroughly established. Superbly and picturesquely set in its own vast garden, the *Royal Hawaiian* is apart from but an integral element of its exciting surroundings. The lobby, lounges, bars, and shops all have an air of quiet elegance. A portion of the gleaming white sand beach which spreads luxuriously before the hotel is kept private for *Royal Hawaiian* guests. The *Surf Room* terrace, where cooling drinks and snacks may be enjoyed, is popular and convenient for bathers.

HILTON HAWAIIAN VILLAGE. Created in the fertile brain of Henry J. Kaiser, the *Hawaiian Village* is under the general managership of my old friend, Ed Hastings, a *Hilton* vice president.

The principal units of this complex, completely air conditioned operation on *Waikiki Beach* are the new seventeen story *Diamond Head Tower,* which is luxury personified; the fourteen story *Ocean Tower,* on the beach; the thirteen story *Village Tower,* surrounded by a cluster of gracious gardens; and the *Waikiki Beach* lanais and thatched roof cottages. In connection with the *Ocean Tower,* beach apartments are available for families of up to five persons.

There is a wide variety of dining rooms, shops, swimming pools (six in number), bars, and recreational areas. For your entertainment, the *Hawaiian Village* complimentary services include hula lessons (daily), floral demonstrations (Tuesday), film showings (Tuesday and Thursday), the Polynesian flag ceremony (daily), and the Chinese Dragon night (Thursday). The *Hawaiian Village* luau preceded by the impressive *imu* ceremony is popular with hotel guests and other visitors.

KAHALA HILTON. A Hilton jewel lavishly set amidst a tropical palm-shaded lagoon, splashing fountains, and fiery bougainvillea, the *Kahala Hilton* is one of the world's truly great hotels. It has 300 lovely rooms. Trellised balconies overlook the sparkling Pacific. Fifteen minutes from *Waikiki* in the exclusive *Kahala* section bounded on three sides by the Waialae Country Club, the *Kahala* provides a cabana-fringed fresh-water swimming pool with sun bathing to be enjoyed on its $850,000 man-made white sand beach. One may dine casually on the *Hala Terrace* facing the beach (beach clothes permitted during the day) or enjoy an elegant gourmet adventure in the stately, fountain-graced *Maile Lanai Room,* to the strains of a small society orchestra. Fresh maile is flown in daily from *Hilo* with maile leis awaiting you at each table. For cocktails and dancing, try the sophisticated *Maile Lounge.*

The SHERATON-MAUI. This ultra-lovely hotel offers 212 luxurious ocean view rooms, elegant dining and dancing in its uniquely designed *Top of the Rock,* and a superb 18-hole championship golf course.

The ROYAL LAHAINA BEACH HOTEL. The complex spreads over 1,000 beautiful acres and includes 32 deluxe golf cottages. Nine holes of its idyllic 18-hole golf course play along the ocean. There is a beach club. Both the *Sheraton-Maui* and the *Royal Lahaina Beach Hotel* are in the lush setting of **Kaanapali,** on the Island of *Maui.*

The MAUNA KEA BEACH HOTEL. Opened in March, 1965, at **Kailaua-Kona** on the Island of *Hawaii,* Laurance Rockefeller's deluxe 14-million dollar, 500-acre beach resort is located 1½ miles from the deep sea port of **Kawaihae** and some 150 air miles from **Honolulu.** This fabulous layout is a dream come true for the sports minded. The delightful 18-hole golf course is set against the magnificent backdrop of the mountains and is washed by the sea. There are riding and hunting facilities, a wonderful beach, and a spacious ranch house 12 miles away at **Waimea,** 2,500 feet above sea level. The site is close to the vast Parker cattle ranch.

HONG KONG

PENINSULA HOTEL. Among the world's most revered hotel names is **Hong Kong's** *Peninsula,* a queen among the world's regal luxury hotels. Even now her rooms are luxurious and comfortable, her lobby a buzzing beehive of activity at tea time and the cocktail hour, and her restaurants the most celebrated in **Hong Kong.** The mezzanine shops are among the finest in the world. Overlooking the harbor, a few steps from the **Kowloon** side of the *Star Ferry,* the superb situation of the *Peninsula* provides its clients scintillating views as well as every modern convenience. Though facing severe competition for the first time in her history, the *Peninsula* has been thoroughly renovated and will long rank as one of the world's great hotels.

THE MANDARIN. The 27-story deluxe *Mandarin Hotel,* in the *Star Ferry* area, towers nearly 300 feet above the harbor and offers incomparable vistas of the heart of **Hong Kong,** the busy harbor, and **Kowloon.**

The *Mandarin* restaurants serve an enormous variety of Continental and American cuisine, plus exotic Chinese specialties. In the prestigious *Saddle and Sirloin,* the connoisseur may choose escargots provençale and chilled vichyssoise, prime New York cut sirloin steak, and bring the meal to an exotic climax with peches flambées. The *Button,* a roof garden restaurant by day and an intimate supper club by night, is as much a culinary delight as it is a fairyland-like setting. On the restaurant floor are the *Harbor Room* and *Harbor Bar.*

The *Captains' Bar,* the *Clipper Lounge,* the *Look-Out,* and the *Chinnery* provide quiet spots for a refreshing drink or pleasant visit.

Sports facilities range from swimming in a rooftop pool to tennis on the grass courts of the *Cricket Club.*

The many smart services offered include a barber shop, beauty salon, sauna baths, complete shopping arcade, florist's kiosk, cable office, a tourist information office, and baby-sitting facilities.

The HONG KONG HILTON, opened in 1963, is one of the

Orient's plushest, most superbly situated hotels with eye-popping views of majestic *Victoria Peak* and **Hong Kong's** incomparable harbor. Twenty-six stories high, this 1,000-room hotel boasts an 80-foot outdoor swimming pool, a 25th-floor supper club graced with first-rate entertainers, five restaurants, and a lush tropical Oriental garden on the roof of the 4th-floor setback. The *Hong Kong Hilton,* completely Oriental in décor, offers impeccable international service. It has some 50 fine shops on the ground and first floors.

JAPAN

TOKYO

IMPERIAL HOTEL. Nothing so thoroughly delights me, and my fellow professional travelers, as to enter the gracious portals of an exquisitely run hotel, of which, relatively speaking, there are all too few in the world.

A great hotel very frequently is the image of its head man, whether he be called president, manager, general manager, or by some other title.

The *Imperial*'s president is Mr. T. Inumaru, one of the great hoteliers of the world. He is energetic, personable, gracious, and perspicacious. Inumaru reminds me for all the world of my good friend, Commendatore Riccardo Zucchi, general manager of the *Royal Danieli* in **Venice, Italy,** the hotel that is a palace. They both have that easy charm which enables them to meet kings, queens, statesmen, and V.I.P.s just as easily and cordially as they make nickel-and-dime big shots from Hometown U.S.A. feel important.

Inumaru is Mr. Imperial himself; in the garden stands a bust of him inscribed with great affection by the employees of the hotel. In his long distinguished career, Inumaru has been an apprentice cook in **Shanghai, London,** and in **New York,** a page boy in *Claridge's* in **London,** and has traveled widely in America. He understands the American mind and our tastes. His hotel's service reflects this knowledge.

The main building of the *Imperial* is the product of the architectural genius of Frank Lloyd Wright. Coincidentally and providentially, the *Imperial Hotel* had been designed by Wright to withstand the most severe earthquake. Within months after the hotel was opened, the most horrendous earthquake to rend asunder any city or country in the world hit **Japan.** The carnage was unbelievable and the state of destruction almost complete. Mr. T. Inumaru's lustrous character was polished bright and shiny as a result of his heroic actions and humanitarian deeds following this catastrophic disaster. Immediately that it was ascertained that the hotel had withstood the terrifying tremors of the earth's surface, Mr. Inumaru announced to all his guests that they could remain in the hotel so long as would be necessary until proper transportation arrangements could be made. He told them that they would not be required to pay for their lodging and board during that interim which subsequently lasted a week's time. Simultaneously, the doors of the *Imperial* were thrown open to refugees from all walks of life who were permitted to sleep in every nook and cranny of the hotel and were fed so long as food remained in the larders and storage rooms. When all other food was exhausted by the tremendous demands that were made by thousands of empty stomachs, Mr. Inumaru miraculously produced enough rice to supply a never ending flow of rice soup which gave sustenance and courage to all concerned. When **Tokyo's** rehabilitation period began, Mr. Inumaru directed the food distribution for the metropolitan **Tokyo** area, in the execution of which job he again covered himself with glory.

Four decades ago this young man was a knight in bright and shining armor whose deeds won him and his hotel the respect and the admiration of travelers the world over as well as the love of his fellow countrymen.

The first annex was opened in September of 1954, and the new "second wing" first received guests in 1958. The new building is an outstanding luxury hotel. The rooms and bathrooms are superbly appointed with every conceivable modern convenience. 1923, however, is not long ago as hotel ages are calculated. It was in that year that *Grosvenor House* was built in **London,** and it is still considered one of the most modern of the hotels of Europe. While the main building (the original one) does not have all of the super-duper appointments of the new building, it does exude a great charm; its rooms are comfortable and pleasant.

The "information, please" service at the *Imperial* is unique. Two young ladies share a desk in the lobby. They are multilingual and have at their command one of the most amazing masses of local lore imaginable. They know "just everything." They are called upon to suggest what to wear to a local night club, what presents to give to a local host or hostess, where to buy magazines of Kodachrome film (not easy in **Tokyo**), and to arrange hair appointments. They will write the names and addresses of the places you wish to visit in Japanese so that the taxi driver will take you unerringly and swiftly to your destination and back.

ROOM TELEPHONE SERVICE. This ingenious system, thought to have been created in Mr. Inumaru's fertile mind and now copied some years later by other "progressive" hotels, is worthy of description. Each room phone is equipped with what appears to be a standard dial but is quite different. The dials have five slots: A, B, C, D, and E. Dial A and you are immediately in touch with the operator. Dial B and you are talking with the housekeeper-maid service. Dial C and you have room service. Dial D and you will be talking with the laundry-valet service, and should you wish to talk to the front desk, you have but to dial E.

In the lower right-hand corner of the phone, there is a light bulb next to which are the words "Special Message." When this light glows red, it indicates you are to dial A and ask for the mail desk. The message, or record of some event which transpired in your absence, has been reported to the mail desk and your phone alerted accordingly.

The telephone operator is on duty constantly, while room service and maid service are available from seven A.M. to midnight. Laundry and valet service are available from eight A.M. to seven-thirty P.M. One day laundry, pressing, and dry cleaning are quite normal.

The bedstands are equipped with radio and an internal broadcasting circuit which the management uses to broadcast transcribed overseas news in the rooms at eleven A.M., three P.M., and five P.M. A small but to me important bit of equipment is the bedstand switch which not only controls the excellent reading lamps but the overhead light as well. Have you ever noticed how few, if any, American hotels are so equipped?

The *Imperial Hotel,* in addition to being one of the world's great hotels, presents an epicurean series of delights in seven restaurants where one can dine delightfully at all hours. For your convenience the restaurants and bars are listed here. (See Chapter Five for full descriptions of the restaurants.)

RESTAURANTS

Phoenix Room (north side of lobby of new building). Early breakfasts served six to seven A.M., regular breakfasts until ten A.M. Luncheon twelve noon to two P.M., dinner six to nine P.M.

Cafe Terrace (south side of lobby, new building). Continuous service from ten A.M. to midnight. Dancing nightly seven P.M. to midnight except Sundays.

Imperial Viking (basement, new building). Smorgasbord. Luncheon noon to two P.M. Dinner six to nine-thirty P.M.

Main Dining Room (front lobby, main building). Breakfast from seven to nine-thirty A.M., luncheon only, noon to two P.M.

Grill Room (north wing, basement, main building). À la carte service from eleven-thirty A.M. to ten P.M. Cocktails and other beverages served in the adjoining lounge. Chic, smart.

Prunier (above *Grill*). Seafood specialties. Luncheon twelve noon to two P.M., dinner five to nine P.M.

Sukiyaki and Tempura Rooms (south side of Banquet entrance). Luncheon twelve noon to two P.M. Dinner five-thirty to nine P.M. Sukiyaki and tempura are served to please you either in western or Japanese style rooms.

BARS

Phoenix Lounge (lobby, new building). Cocktails from eleven-thirty A.M. to twelve-thirty A.M.

Skoal Bar (basement, new building). Four-thirty to ten P.M.

Garden Bar (south court, off front lobby, main building). Nine-thirty A.M. to eleven P.M. Charming. Coffee, tea, and light snacks are served.

HOTEL OKURA. An Intercontinental hotel, the *Okura* stands on the heights of **Akasaka**. Few, if any, hotels have had such a lavish outpouring of money and tender loving care in the development of their architectural splendors as the *Okura*. Topped by the twelfth-story *Sky Lounge* where, in soft light, soothing music is presented for your listening pleasure by the *Okura's Champagne Orchestra,* one can dine splendiferously while enjoying the panoramic vista of downtown **Tokyo** and *Tokyo Bay* immediately below. The *Okura* presents for your approval 520 western style guest rooms, all graciously appointed with the last word in efficiency and decorative charm. There are thirty Japanese style suites as well. In addition to the *Sky Lounge,* there are the *Japanese* and *Chinese Restaurants,* the *Emerald Room, Grill,* and *Main Dining Room.* The *Shopping Arcade* has been artistically designed and includes representatives of the finest merchandising organizations in **Japan.**

TOKYO HILTON. Deluxe, smart, and serene, the *Tokyo Hilton Hotel* adjoins the famous *Sanno Shrine* in the **Akasaka** district. The architecture and décor ideally blend the contrasts of modern with classic Japan. Entering the lobby one enjoys, through a clear glass wall, a breathtaking scene of an exquisite Japanese landscaped pond and garden which span the entire length of the main lobby floor. The *Origami Coffee House* and *Genji Japanese Restaurant* overlook this lovely setting. The Hilton boasts 500 exquisite air conditioned western style single and double rooms of a quiet, modern décor; Japanese style rooms; and typical lavish Hilton suites. For relaxing, a dip may be enjoyed in the large outdoor swimming pool (separate pool for children) topped off with a massage in the hotel's invigorating steam baths. The International Shopping Arcade and specialty shops offer intriguing merchandise of great variety.

RESTAURANTS AND BARS. For rotisserie and grill specialties and famous Kobe beefsteaks, try the *Keyaki Grill.* The *Origami Coffee House* (off main lobby facing the Japanese garden) offers attractive food at reasonable prices around the clock. The *Genji Japanese Restaurant* (main floor facing the Japanese garden) features tempura, sukiyaki, and traditional Japanese barbecue. The sophisticated *Star Hill Supper Club* (top floor) provides Continental cuisine, with soft music for candlelight dining and dancing. The *Tea Lounge* (off main lobby) daily offers traditional tea ceremonies and tea concerts. The *Lipo Bar* affords an Oriental atmosphere, piano music nightly.

TOKYO AIRWAIT HOTEL (*International Airport*). The 70-room *Tokyo Airwait Hotel* is located on the third floor of the renovated terminal building. Rates start at $2.78 for three hours plus 50¢ for each additional hour for a single room. Double rooms cost $5.56 for three hours, and 70¢ for each additional hour. Overnight rates are $7.78 single, $12.50 double.

PALACE HOTEL. The view from the *Palace,* which rises majestically opposite the *Imperial Palace Plaza,* not only encompasses the *Imperial Palace* but on clear days affords a magnificent view of *Mount Fuji.* Its four hundred and fifty western style rooms are refreshingly air conditioned, completely soundproof, and equipped with circulating ice water, radio, and television sets. All have tub and shower baths. The *Grill Room* offers luxury dining at its best. The view from the *Sky Lounge* is spectacular. The *Club Gold* is an intimate night club for dining, dancing, and entertainment. The *Coffee Shop* is excellent. There are more than twenty shops in the *Palace Hotel Shopping Arcade.* The *Palace* was opened in 1961.

KYOTO

MIYAKO HOTEL. **Kyoto's** abnormally wonderful *Miyako Hotel* is years ahead of anything that we know in our own contemporary hotel world. The service and amenities of this hotel snuggled cosily against a steep, wooded hill are worthy of special description.

Bed reading lamps are almost universally inadequate. Not so in **Kyoto.** In this ultramodern, yet warm and gracious establishment, the reading lights, one for each bed, are mounted beside and slightly above the beds on flexible arms adjustable to each reader's tastes.

One button on the bedstand controls the room's remote lights, another the bedstand lights. The push button I like best and which always gives me a chuckle is the "right away" button for urgent service. There is another to be used for routine service. There is an innovation in the *Miyako* bedstands that I have thought about for years but never dreamed anyone would ultimately introduce to hotel living. It is a faint foot light under the bedstand. This dull glowing bulb could not conceivably disturb one's slumber, but it is a friend in need on awakening in a strange room in the middle of the night. Beneath its friendly subdued beams, a rapid orientation will bring order from this sometimes chaotic "just awake" situation. The soft light clearly silhouettes the proper buttons to push, if needed.

The bedstand also houses the air conditioning control, telephone, full-range radio, and four separate sets of canned music selections including choices of native Japanese music, international classical music, American classical music, and American popular music.

The excellent dining room and cosy bar lounge are on the third floor, while on the eighth floor the grill enjoys a wide view of the city.

Because of its mountainside setting, one can leave the lift on the eighth floor for a plunge in the swimming pool, delightfully situated in a glen-like setting. One floor below are the Turkish baths.

The *Miyako* Japanese inn is not far from the swimming pool in a completely separate, thoroughly enchanting building. As in other Japanese inns, one replaces shoes with slippers on entering this inn.

Should you wish to indulge in the experience of sleeping one night in Japanese style, the *Miyako Inn* might be an excellent place to try. If for any reason you find the experience not to your liking, which is possible, you have but to dress and transfer to a western style luxury bedroom in the main building.

In the *Miyako* Japanese inn, you may also, after having made sure to make an advance reservation, enjoy a sukiyaki meal. Here the reservations will be accepted for two or more persons, though sukiyaki is better served for four or more. You will dine sitting on the floor.

In the chapter on shopping, I have discussed the delights of a shopping spree in **Kyoto,** but I cannot leave the description of the *Miyako* without a word about its shopping arcade. This purchaser's paradise is reached either from the street entrance of the new section or down a short flight of stairs from the lobby. There are thirty-two varieties of high class merchandise dispensed in the arcade with virtually all of the best **Kyoto** shops being represented.

Under antique and modern art goods, for example, there are many of the great names of Japan to be found in the arcade including *Yamanaka and Company,* which name is well known in America. *Yamanaka,* before the war, had shops in **Chicago, New York,** and on the Pacific Coast. The arcade includes a tailor, a florist, and shops selling wood block prints, warrior's helmets and armor, textiles, porcelain and Satsuma, pearls and lacquerware, kimonos and happi coats, handbags and purses, dolls (real pretty ones), damascene and silver, cloisonné, cameras and binoculars, and—believe it or not—brassieres, girdles, and lingerie.

Three of the principal department stores have show windows in the arcade.

INTERNATIONAL HOTEL. The **Kyoto** *International Hotel* is sparklingly new. Opened in August of 1961, it is ideally situated in front of the *Nijo Castle.* The view from each of the three hundred and fifty completely air conditioned rooms is excellent. To the west one has a panoramic view of the *Nijo Castle* and to the north looms the picturesque peak of *Mount Hiei.* This ten story beauty boasts of all rooms with tub and shower bath. Circulating ice water in each bathroom is another modern touch. The cocktail lounge and *International Room* face the graceful Japanese garden in which is to be found a Genghis Khan barbecue. The American soda fountain and magnificent night club are in the basement. Complete shopping facilities are available.

MIYANOSHITA

FUJIYA HOTEL is a charming hostelry of the Old School. As Lonesome George Gobel would say, "They don't hardly build them that way no more." Spacious and exuding character, the *Fujiya,* oldest resort hotel in Japan, offers something very special to its guests. It is one of the finest and best appointed hotels in Japan, with 141 wonderful western style rooms and a quaint Japanese style annex. The *Flower Palace* has 48 twin-bed rooms, each beautifully decorated with the flower for which it is named. The *Forest Lodge* wing, opened in 1960, is a most modern four-story concrete building which contains 45 smart rooms, all with bath. Water from the natural hot springs is piped into all guest rooms. This magnificent resort hotel is a self-contained entity, with the following tourist amenities: a shopping arcade (gift shop, arts and crafts, and fashion displays), restaurants with outstanding cuisine, fascinating Japanese cottages set amid an exotic garden punctuated with ponds and waterfalls, a library containing four thousand books, a ballroom, travel bureau, hotel newspaper, magnificent outdoor and indoor hot spring swimming pools, and tennis courts. The *Fujiya's Sengokuhara* championship length eighteen hole golf course is five miles away. Its comfortable club house has 28 western style and Japanese rooms available for sleeping guests and is under the *Fujiya* management.

The *Fujiya's* environs are outstandingly lovely, even for the *Hakone* district, replete with exhilarating walks, verdant glens, lush forests, and majestic mountains.

Should you be planning an all day trip from the *Fujiya,* you may take a box lunch prepared by the *Fujiya's* skilled chefs with you.

Massages for both men and women are available at any time until eleven P.M. Normal laundry service is two days, but one day service is available at supplemental charges. Rapid pressing service is also available.

The mineral baths in the hotel are: the *Roman Aquarium Bath*—also called the *Gold Fish Bath*—popular with children; the *Mermaid Bath,* a large bath sporting a sea background decorated with a statue of a mermaid; the *Bath of Eternal Youth and Perpetual Spring;* the *Dream Pool,* which is a small swimming pool in a hot spring setting; the *Indoor Pool* with tepid water; and the *Outdoor Pool,* one hundred feet in length, open only in the summertime. Reservations are necessary at all but the swimming pools.

The *Kikka-So* Japanese style inn annex is an ex-royal house formerly used as a summer place by Prince Takamatsu. It is across the *National Road* from the *Fujiya Hotel* and has been used as an inn since World War II. Sukiyaki and tempura meals are served in the Japanese gardens. A miniature one room ceremonial tea house called the *Reiju-an* ("Longevity Cottage") is located on the grounds. Ceremonial tea is available to guests who so desire. There is also a cosy bar. Leave your shoes outside.

I give the *Fujiya Hotel* high marks on all scores, but add an accolade for a practice which I wish hotels in the so-called western world would follow; namely, no dogs are allowed either on the grounds or in the hotel's buildings.

HAKONE NATIONAL PARK AREA

HOTEL KOWAKI-EN. For those who prefer the ultra-modern while still retaining many of the amenities in a smart, chic atmosphere, I can heartily recommend the *Hotel Kowaki-en,* an important cog in the Western International Hotels, Incorporated, chain. From the *Kowaki-en,* you can enjoy a breathtaking view of the *Hakone* mountain range. There is a tennis court and an 18-hole golf course for your athletic outlets, and a night club for your dancing, cocktails, and television pleasure. An outdoor heated swimming pool will add to the pleasure of your stay. Western and Japanese style rooms and dining facilities are available.

HAKONE KANKO HOTEL. This elegant hotel, superbly situated overlooking *Lake Hakone* (alternatively known as *Lake Ashi* or *Reed Lake*), commands a spectacular and unique view of the incomparable *Mount Fuji* and the *Hakone Mountains.* The *Hakone Kanko* is an unusual and most gratifying blend of an ultramodern luxury hotel and charming Old World, gracious Japanese hostelry of another era.

The impeccably appointed guest rooms are huge, with soft, thick carpeting in perfect harmony with the tasteful decorative scheme. All *Hakone Kanko* guest rooms have radio, television, tub and shower baths, easy chairs, davenports, and efficient writing desks. The balconies are provided with decorative tables and chairs. Of the 116 perfectly beautiful rooms, 8 are Japanese style, the balance being of western design. Both the main dining room and the lobby are graciously appointed and punctuated with floor to ceiling windows. The hot spring bath is one of Japan's most beautiful.

In the wintertime guests may skate on the nearby attractive outdoor rink, while in the other seasons four golf courses in the immediate vicinity are available for visitors. Clubs may be rented. Local fishing would make even Isaak Walton drool.

The longest ropeway in the world descends from a point adjacent to the hotel down to the *Big Hell* hot spring. The views from the cable cars encompass a wide area of breathtaking panoramic vistas.

The *Hakone Kanko*'s cuisine, both Japanese and western style, is delicious and beautifully served. The bar is well stocked and its prices are moderate.

I know of no finer resort hotel than the fireproof, earthquakeproof, and full soundproof *Hakone Kanko*.

ATAMI

The ATAMI NEW FUJIYA is a lavishly luxurious seaside resort as well as a modern Japanese inn. This lush, plush establishment has some 300 air conditioned rooms, of which 140 are western style and 70 combine the best features of a Japanese and western hotel. Deluxe features include an all-weather indoor-outdoor swimming pool overlooking the ocean, bowling alleys, a private movie theater, a health club with hot spring baths, and western style and Japanese cuisine.

The KAN-ICHI HOTEL. The entire top floor, which serves principally as a dining area, is circular and revolves continuously, affording a panorama of the town and its beaches.

IZUSAN SPA

The SAGAMIYA INN is extraordinarily interesting. In addition to its private baths, the large, luxurious *"Sennimburo"* —hot water swimming pool—will attract your attention and, I hope, your patronage. *Sennimburo* means "one thousand people's bath." Maybe they can't all get in at the same time, but a thousand people do bathe there. Honest Injun.

BEPPU

Because of its superb setting over *Beppu Bay,* its mineral springs, and gay atmosphere, **Beppu** is a favorite resort of both Japanese and overseas visitors. There are an amazing seven hundred-plus Japanese style inns and western style hotels in **Beppu.** This is incredible considering the fact that the population of the city is scarcely over a hundred thousand souls. In the descriptions which follow, I have particularly singled out the *Suginoi Inn* because of its excellence, setting, and charm. In the **Beppu** listing, however, you will find other establishments which are highly recommended. This is a great hotel and inn area.

The SUGINOI INN will make your eyes pop. It can't help but do so. It is possessed of great charm, superb service, and unique layout. Until recently, the *Suginoi Inn* was strictly Japanese style, but, in 1961, a new luxurious western style wing was added which retains every ounce of the charm of the old rustic inn but adds a lustrous magnificence of its own. The Japanese inn wing continues to function. These words, incidentally, were inscribed in the *Suginoi Inn.* My bedroom is equipped with a balcony fully twenty feet in length from which the view over *Beppu Bay* encompasses a delightful panoramic vista. The sliding floor-to-ceiling glass panels are tastefully adorned with Japanese draw drapes. Half of the commodious room is richly covered with wall-to-wall carpeting. The radio located on the writing desk gives a wide assortment of musical entertainment. The twin beds are soft and comfy. The bath is furnished with both tub and shower. The entire hotel is air conditioned. To the rear of the bedroom, raised approximately fifteen inches above the floor of the western style bedroom, is a Japanese style room separated from the basic room by artistic rice paper sliding doors. This old Japanese style room is typical; the floor is covered with mats, cushions surround a dwarfed table, and should you decide to sleep Japanese style, it will be on the floor.

You will be killed with kindness and overwhelmed with service in the *Suginoi*. There are a minimum of three kimono'd Japanese girls in constant attendance to tend to your every wish. They will be on hand to serve you sukiyaki or tempura should you wish to enjoy a typical Japanese meal in your room. The service of the sukiyaki dinner is a good part of the fun. The girls add zest to the occasion with their graceful motions accenting the charming preparation and serving of the food. They also keep the *sake* and other beverages flowing.

In both the new western wing and the old Japanese wing, your shoes must be checked at the door. A pair of slippers will be assigned to you. In the old wing, there is no dining room and meals must be taken in the bedroom. As a nod to the overseas guests, however, the new wing boasts of an excellent grill room. Here the cuisine selection is from among steaks, chops, cutlets, roasts, and other western dishes but with a variety of Japanese dishes including tempura and sukiyaki.

The second floor contains a tastefully decorated cocktail lounge with juke box, television and radio. It adjoins a refreshment bar. There are two steaming thermal baths on the second floor fed from the local springs. Communal mixed bathing is not indulged in here, although the ladies' and gentlemen's sections are separated by only an opaque glass partition. These piping hot baths are stimulating. If you are a *Suginoi* guest, you will have in your room two Japanese style kimonos one of which fits over the other. They are worn in public. You may don this combination to proceed to the second floor public bath where the bath attendant will provide a basket of bamboo in which to check your robe and slippers. Before you step into the bath, please, pretty please, soap and bathe yourself in the approved Japanese manner. It is a cardinal sin of Oriental etiquette to bathe in the bath. A wooden bowl has been provided specifically to aid in your pre-bath cleansing processs. Dip it into the communal bath, scoop up some hot water, and then proceed to the edge of the marble drain to give yourself a complete lather bath, followed by a rinse with additional hot water garnered in your wooden bowl. Only after you are hygienically clean may you enter the steaming bath. You will probably "sweat it out" with forty-five or fifty fellow bathers.

The lobby of the *Suginoi* is warmly and richly decorated and possessed of a wonderful panoramic vista. The foyer is a combination of Japanese and western design and ornamentation. The carpeting is thick and the decorative wall covering is of ancient Japanese art. The varied bright hues of the furniture add to the picturesqueness of the setting.

The roof garden is attractive.

KAMENOI and SEIFU. These charming establishments are considered to be of *Suginoi* calibre, but are rather smaller. The *Seifu* is sparkling new. Both are a combination of Japanese style inn and western style hotel, with both type of cuisine.

The SHOWAEN and the SHIN BEPPU are high-class Japanese inns. Locally they are considered to be on a par with the above and both are worthy of a visit if you wish to see the best of the Japanese inns.

The SHIRAGIKUSO is just below the category of the above and, while fundamentally a Japanese inn, has a new wing, western style, almost as attractive as the *Suginoi.*

The AKAGANEGOTEN (HOTEL COPPER) and the KINSUIEN (PRIVATE MUSEUM) are simply delightful, but are strictly inns with Japanese cuisine and sleeping mats. The *Kinsuien* is above an interesting museum. Here on the first floor one may see the antiques and curios of Old Japan and on the second floor find a Japanese inn.

HIROSHIMA

The HOTEL ISSAEN is a superb Japanese inn located on the *Inland Sea* overlooking *Miyajima*. The grounds and gardens are reminiscent of an Old World now long extinct. This completely Japanese style hostelry is small, intimate, and thoroughly charming. You leave your shoes at the entrance and wear slippers in the corridors, which are removed when entering the sleeping rooms. Japanese meals prevail. The sukiyaki and tempura are particularly appealing. There are two western style sleeping rooms with real beds. The balance are typically mat covered rooms. Should you be in the **Hiroshima** area and seek true Japanese atmosphere, I can heartily recommend the *Issaen Inn* to you (locally it is called the *Hotel Issaen*).

If you choose not to stay in this charming old inn, you might wish to stop for lunch or dinner. It will be well worth your while. It has been the lodging place of at least one Japanese emperor who stopped here when visiting the famous *Itsukushima Shrine* at *Miyajima*. The ferry for *Miyajima* is a short distance from the *Hotel Issaen*.

RYOKAN (Japanese-style Hotels and Inns)

The typical Japanese style *ryokan* is as different from an American or European hotel as the Japanese people themselves are from their western visitors. Mature American adults of fixed living habits will quite probably find life in a *ryokan* rather too different to adjust to with any sort of ease, comfort, and pleasure. Adventuresome oldsters and all youngsters, however, will welcome these attractive inns on their itineraries not only as a delightful and unique travel experience but also as an essential adjunct to their travels for those wishing to understand the real background of every day living in **Japan.** Life in the *ryokan* presents a captivatingly different world punctuated with charm and good taste.

I have an excellent suggestion for those of you who think

you would enjoy life in a Japanese inn but aren't just too certain about the whole thing. In **Japan** today, there are many of the new hotels which include both western and Japanese style rooms, while other hotels, such as the *Miyako* in **Kyoto**, offer guests a separate section consisting of genuine old world Japanese inns. The *Suginoi*, a deluxe hotel-inn at **Beppu**, goes one step farther; one is offered there an entire *ryokan* wing set in a delightful Japanese garden plus a new, unusual, section in which the rooms are equipped with western style beds and bath and a Japanese style room ensemble. In this wing of the hotel, the western type rooms have the *tokonoma* alcove above the main room set up as an authentic *ryokan* room (a room within a room) replete with *tatami* mats, low slung table, and sitting mats. The bed gear for sleeping on the floor is hidden away during the day.

I would suggest that, after you have gotten used to the different ways of the Orient, you request a Japanese style room in a hotel which offers both types of accommodations. Then, if for any reason you find the Japanese room not to your comfort or liking, you can without creating too much furor switch to western style accommodations.

The *Japan Ryokan Association* is an august, official, and reliable body catering to the comfort and general well-being of foreign guests. Everything has been done to offer the best service, facilities, furnishings, and equipment to enable visitors from other lands to have a correct idea of Japanese domestic life. Of the more than 700 *ryokan*, approximately half are under government registration. The *Japan Ryokan Association*'s **Tokyo** address is Kokusai Kanko Building, Marunouchi.

The principal features of the *ryokan* are:

THE GENKAN (ENTRANCE HALL) of the *ryokan* is where guests are personally received on arrival the first time by the manager and one or more charming, pretty women who seem to be available in legion in **Japan**. One of the female managerial assistants, bowing gracefully, will pass the guest along to a maid, usually very attractive, who will carry the baggage and conduct the guest through the hall, the floor of which is of highly polished wood or stone, to the bedroom.

At the *genkan* entrance to the *ryokan* one removes one's shoes *(de rigueur)* and will be given a pair of slippers, the shoes being carefully guarded, usually shined, and returned when the guest wishes to go out.

THE GUEST ROOMS, which are partitioned with decorative sliding panels, are beautifully proportioned and are identical with the living quarters in many authentic Japanese homes. The floor is matted with *tatami,* made from rice straw surfaced with fine woven reed covering, most comfortable for the stockinged feet, which is convenient since the heeless type slippers provided on your arrival must not be worn in the bedroom but left outside the door.

The *tokonoma,* an alcove whose floor is 9 to 12 inches above the main room, is considered to be the holiest section of the house. One of the *tokonoma*'s walls is traditionally adorned with a scroll in the form either of a painting, or a five- or six-line verse in tiny Japanese writing. *Tokonoma* scrolls vary with the seasons. In the springtime the painting may be of a crystal clear waterfall tumbling over rugged rocks, while at the New Year a flight of cranes may be displayed indicating a wish for long life to the visitor. A charming arrangement of flowers is found on the *tokonoma*'s floor, while in the center of the main section of the room a low table called an *ozen* is surrounded by four cushions, or *zabuton*. Many westerners find it extraordinarily difficult to assume the Japanese posture of sitting on their knees, or even cross-legged, but in due course some become accustomed to this gymnastic habit. Not me! In some of the best, and newest, inns, western style chairs can sometimes be supplied on request, but don't count on it. You can usually obtain a back and arm rest to assist you in sitting on the floor if you need it.

The *ryokan*'s bedroom, where one sleeps on the floor, is usually equipped with a washstand normally found in an alcove on the side of the room. If hot water is not available in the faucet, the ever fawning maid will fetch it in by the kettleful **when** required. Items from one's baggage are laid either on **the** floor or in baskets provided for that purpose, while men's **suits** and ladies' frocks are placed on room racks or closet hang-**ers.** Unless the inn is thoroughly westernized and provided **with** central heating, the room will have a small electric heater **or a** charcoal brazier.

THE BEDDING is kept out of sight in a closet during the daytime, but the maid will make up the sleeping pad when-ever it is required. The entire "bed" consists of two thick quilts made of layers of silk or cotton laid one over the other on the *tatami,* which arrangements western visitors may consider too spartan . . . much! I do. If so, extra quilts can be added to in-crease one's comfort. The bed coverings are gaily colored, pad-ded quilts, while one sleeps on a white cotton sheet spread over lower quilts. At some *ryokan,* with a nod to the westerner's well-being, a thin spring or foam rubber mattress is placed under the floor quilts. Other *ryokan* have one, two, or a handful of western style bedrooms, but this is unusual, particularly in the country places.

THE SERVICE is always excellent. Directly after the guest has entered the room, the chambermaid *(jochusan)* will follow with a cup of aromatic, piping hot green tea. Male visitors should not become embarrassed when the girl, either by word or accurate motions of the hand, requests him to divest himself of his shirt and pants! This is the normal procedure after arrival. She will quickly produce a light kimono *(yukata),* drape him in it, and tie the sash. If the *ryokan* visit is other than in the summer, the *jochusan* will add a second, heavier, kimono over the lighter one.

Because the guest room is a gracious sitting room, cozy dining room, and intimate bedroom, it is necessary for the maid to be more or less constantly at the guest's service. As a matter of fact, the *ryokan* guests will find themselves attended to even when such service apparently is not requested or, ostensibly, needed. Such attention should be gratefully understood and appreciated, however.

MEALS. *Ryokan* food is always basically Japanese, but European cuisine can be prepared in many of the inns, if requested and the desired dishes are not too elaborate. If ordered the day before, ham, eggs, toast, and coffee can frequently be had for breakfast. The most popular dishes served in the *ryokan* for the visiting foreigner, however, are sukiyaki and tempura.

A typical *ryokan* breakfast consists of: smoked fish, rice wrapped in thin layers of seaweed, mushroom soup with pickled cucumbers, cabbage, turnips, and the ubiquitous green tea.

A typical dinner (other than sukiyaki or tempura) includes fish, raw, smoked, or steamed, clear soup with preserved turnips, radishes, and rice. Those who are allergic to fish can order western food (grilled chicken or steak is usually available), for fish, always deliciously prepared, is the base of all *ryokan* Japanese dishes except sukiyaki. *Sake,* other wine, beer, and whisky can be served in the guest rooms at any time.

It is rare for a real *ryokan* to have a public dining room because the Japanese, practically without exception, dine in the privacy of their own rooms when resting at an inn. Existing *ryokan* dining rooms are patronized almost exclusively by overseas guests. Room meals are cooked and dispensed by a minimum of two bowing and scraping well trained "on the knees" girls. The meal's ingredients are prepared in the kitchen, but the hot dishes are cooked on a brazier in the room.

BATH AND TOILET. *Ryokan* members of the J.R.A. have private bathrooms available with some of their rooms. As I have noted elsewhere, western notions of prudishness relative to nudity have caught on with the Japanese in the big cities, but nudism is still regarded in many Japanese households and *ryokan* as a healthy and natural state of affairs unconnected with any false modesty. Mixed group bathing is normal at some *ryokan,* particularly in remote rural areas, in which westerners wishing "to do in Rome as the Roman does" can participate if they can overcome their prejudices. Inns in the hot spring resort areas, particularly, have large *hot* water pools where numerous persons of all ages indulge in enjoyable and healthful mixed bathing. The charm and unconscious grace of most young Japanese women should be sufficient to put westerners at their ease.

If the guest has his own private bathroom, it must be remembered that the tub (not a western style bath) is for soaking and warming one's body, not cleaning it, the normal bathing functions being performed before one gets into the tub. To get straight into the bath by Japanese standards would not be "polite." Special wooden vessels are provided for cleaning purposes, as well as a small wooden stool or plank to sit or stand on while "scrubbing up." If one dislikes these more primitive methods, hot showers are sometimes available, though not often, as the Japanese are not fond of showers. The more modern first-class *ryokan* have guest rooms with western style private bath and toilet, but in most of the others these facilities are close at hand "down the hall." The Japanese-style toilets, equipped with an elliptical slit in the tile floor, are always separate from the bathrooms.

Some *ryokan* provide a public lounge, billiard room, ping pong tables, bar, ballroom, coffee shop, and souvenir arcade.

THE CHARGES differ according to the class and location of the inn, the size and superiority of the room, quality of furnishings, and whether the accommodation includes private bath and toilet. *Ryokan* rates include room and two meals (breakfast and dinner), although room charges only are available, if desired, at about 70% of the demi-pension rate.

Meal charges run from a dollar to a dollar and a half for breakfast, a dollar and a half to three dollars for lunch, and three to five or six dollars for dinner. Japanese meals are offered on a table d'hôte basis, while western style plates, if available, are served á la carte.

Tipping in the *ryokan* follows the same procedure as in the hotels, with the managements prefering that no cash tips be distributed to their help. In many instances a tip will be refused, but a 10 per cent gratuity service fee will be added to one's bill which money is said to be divided equitably among the employees. Tipping has made inroads in the *ryokan* also, and if your maid has been polite and her attentions good, a little something can be left or given to her in an envelope, never openly.

SINGAPORE

RAFFLES HOTEL. **Singapore** is the *Raffles Hotel,* and the *Raffles* is **Singapore.** This esteemed establishment is unquestionably one of the world's most famous hotels. For years and years, travelers and stay-at-homes alike have known of this magnificent hostelry. Its legends have long conjured vivid mental images of international society, mystery, and intrigue. Big, old, and rambling, *Raffles* reeks with atmosphere. Establishments with long embellished reputations frequently tend to disappoint. Not so in **Singapore.** I think you will be enchanted with the *Raffles.* Almost all of the rooms are enormous. The

baths, some of which are divided into dressing room and bathroom, are commodious. The sleeping rooms in one wing are
air conditioned, and many of them are made more attractive
by the addition of lanai type porches. One has but to push
a bell to bring an eager houseboy gliding rapidly in to take
one's order. In a matter of seconds, one's needs or wishes will
have been fully satisfied. The room boy is at your beck and
call for cleaning, pressing, shoe shining, stationery, cool drinks,
food, or what-have-you. Pressing is performed practically in-
stantaneously, while one-day laundry service is routine. The
beverage and food room service is rapid. The food is delicious
and the beverages served most attractively. The air conditioned
Elizabethan Room, Grill and Bar, about which I have written
at greater length under "Restaurants," are the best in town.

The courtyard is colorful and attractive, decoratively adorned
with palm and blooming trees. Its grass is like a golf green
gaily festooned with tables protected from the sun's rays by
bright umbrellas. At night this carefully manicured plot is
romantically mysterious. The lights are soft, and the conversation and laughter of the guests taking cocktails or after dinner

coffee and liqueurs in the courtyard add to the romance of the setting. The foyer, lounge bar, main dining room, and other public rooms are kept pleasantly cool by large, constantly rotating fans. Some of the non-air conditioned rooms leave something to be desired.

Other **Singapore** hotels are:

CATHAY. **Singapore's** popular air conditioned, modern hotel is centrally and beautifully located. The views rom the higher rooms overlooking the harbor on one side and the gardens of the Governor's mansion on the other are attractive. It is unfortunate that a cinema occupies the area where the entrance and lobby should be. The foyer, desk, dining room, and bar are all on the third floor. The unbelievably tiny entrance affording access to the lilliputian lift to the lobby is situated in the rear of the hotel. Apart from its unattractive approach, the hotel is well run, neat, and clean. The efficiently designed rooms are inviting and comfortable.

PRINCE'S HOTEL GARNI. My fellow "Boilermaker" and fraternity brother, John Carmichael, and his wife **Ruth** have lived in **Singapore** for many years. They are ecstatic over the *Prince's Hotel Garni;* it is their favorite local hotel. Built as an apartment building at the close of World War II when the demand for housing was acute, it was later converted into a hotel. It is the only reputable hotel that I know of in which there is no lobby. The service is outstanding, however, and it is "spit and polish" spick-and-span clean. The rooms are rather small, but this is compensated for by converting them each **day** into comfortable sitting rooms.

GOODWOOD PARK HOTEL. Inanimate though they are, some hotels exude charm. The *Goodwood Park* does. Though not as centrally located as either *Raffles* or the *Cathay,* the completely air conditioned *Goodwood Park* has a great deal to commend itself to you. The new wing is modern and pleasant, the restaurant is extraordinarily good, and the cool refreshing tiled swimming pool is chic and inviting. The local elite favor the *Goodwood Park*. There is dancing nightly in the *Arundel Room*.

HOTEL SINGAPURA INTERCONTINENTAL. Located in Orchard Road, one of **Singapore's** finest locations, this brand-new hostelry is completely air conditioned, including its American coffee shop, European style supper club, and cocktail lounge. The *Singapura's* 195 attractive rooms are a useful addition to the **Singapore** hotel community. The *Four Lions* restaurant is an attractive supper club overlooking the swimming pool. Featuring Continental and Eastern cuisine, the *Four Lions* offers music, dancing, and entertainment. The *Raya Cocktail Lounge* and *Pebble* (piano) *Bar* are popular **Singapore** meeting places.

TAIWAN (FORMOSA)

GRAND HOTEL, **Taipei.** Commanding a magnificent view of the city high above the gently meandering *Tamsui River*, **Taipei's** grand *Grand Hotel* is one of the most beautiful, charming, and efficient hostelries in the Far East. Originally the site of a huge Japanese Shinto Shrine, it was remodeled after war-time damage into the super-deluxe hotel it is today. Its ornate Chinese décor, with furnishings in black, Chinese red, and gold, its intricate ceiling artwork, and carved wood panelings exude an authentic Old China flavor. The *Grand Hotel* provides sizzling central steam heat in the chill winter and refreshing air conditioning in the warm summertime.

The *Grand Hotel*, rich in colorful hues reminding one of a Chinese palace, is uniquely divided into four sections: (1) the *Grand Hotel* itself, less exclusive but no less luxuriously comfortable; (2) the *Golden Dragon Annex;* (3) the *Jade Phoenix*, further up the mountainside; and (4) the new *Chi-Lin Pavilion*, which for sheer opulence and magnificence has no peer in the Far East. The pavilion, which has added 64 rooms and six suites to the *Grand Hotel,* operates both as a hotel and a government guest house. The main building offers an elegant *Club Room,* a night club open every evening featuring Filipino music, and tasty western style cuisine. The *Grand* has a beauty parlor downstairs, a gift shop upstairs, and movies are shown nightly.

A cocktail lounge and a dining room serving Chinese delicacies are located in the *Golden Dragon Annex,* while the *Jade Phoenix* section has a coffee shop.

The lovely Chinese gardens embrace two popular, beautifully kept red clay tennis courts, a swimming pool, and special bungalows for guests who seek the last word in service and comfort.

The *Grand Hotel* is almost always booked solidly months, or more, in advance.

MAYFLOWER HOTEL, **Peitou.** If you would like to spend a carefree day or two "taking the waters" (mineral springs) at the scenically colorful, though naughty, hot spring resort of **Peitou,** be sure to make a reservation in the splendid *Mayflower Hotel,* perched on a hill where it was built in 1949 and run by the charming and wealthy Madame Yu Shen. This hotel's décor is unspoiled, and its service not only untarnished but impeccable. The *Mayflower's* attractive restaurant features Peiping, Cantonese, and local Taiwan dishes which are served round the clock. Madame knows the foreign taste well. This is rightly called **Taiwan's** most luxurious hot spring hotel, a Chinese establishment with Japanese atmosphere and solid western style comforts and convenience.

THAILAND

BANGKOK

The number of foreign visitors to **Thailand** is increasing by leaps and bounds. The requests for hotel accommodations are incredibly numerous. Many of the visitors are from America. Many others are from Europe or from other continents. The hotel building program has not begun to keep pace with the wildfirelike spread of the demand. My friend, Kusa Panyarachun, is managing director of the *World Travel Service, Limited.* A few brief years ago, the staff of *World Travel Serv-*

ice consisted of Kusa, his wife, and one guide-interpreter-station man. As of 1962, the staff of this organization numbered two hundred and fifty. But the greatest trial and tribulation Kusa's company faces, as do the *Everett Travel Service* and other local tour operators, is the utter dearth of good hotel rooms. The scheduled opening, in 1965, of the *Bangkok Intercontinental* and the *Bangkok Hilton* will alleviate somewhat this critical situation. Firm advance reservations in this fascinating city are highly important as the demand still exceeds the supply.

The understatement of the age is for me to say, "Don't come to Bangkok without a confirmed reservation." Now I know as some of you read this, there will be cocked eyebrows, and you will say, "But Uncle Wise Guy got off the plane and went straight to the best hotel in town and had no trouble getting in." Perhaps that's true. It's also true that somebody wins first prize in the Irish Sweepstakes every year. But the chances are remote. Jimmy, the sagacious *World Travel Service* guide, made an interesting observation when I was talking with him about the hotel situation in his home city. He said, "You know, Mr. Olson, people are funny. I can remember when American visitors used to come to **Bangkok** and insist on a fan in their room. Now, even if they get a room with two fans, if it's not air conditioned they want to take the next plane out." The important thing is that all planes in and out of **Bangkok** at the time when you would be visiting this "never-never" land are booked solidly for months, even years, in advance. If you arrive in Thailand and don't find a proper hotel reservation, you will have no choice but to sweat it out . . . and I mean *sweat it out.*

HOTEL RAMA. This is the newest, finest hotel in **Bangkok.** It is a simply delightful hostelry that will afford you every conceivable comfort. The ten-story *Rama* was opened in January of 1961. The original Swiss management who supervised the plans and construction thought of just about everything to make the hotel modern and cheery. It is air conditioned from the moment you step into the lobby through all of the public rooms and bedrooms. The air conditioning is thermostatically controlled in each and every bedroom to suit your pleasure and comfort, with blower speeds of high, medium, and low. The individual room thermostats may be shut off completely and the windows opened if you prefer, though I don't think you will follow this procedure. All of the one hundred eighty bedrooms are tastefully decorated. Half of them overlook an open courtyard and the swimming pool. The others are fully outside and overlook the city. I personally prefer the court rooms, but there is really no advantage of one side over the other. The *Rama* beds are comfortable and invite deep sleep, the baths are equipped with both tub and shower plus an individual air exhaust, and all rooms are equipped with venetian blinds and draw drapes. The swimming pool, on a second floor terrace opposite the main dining room and cocktail foyer, is readily reached from the main elevators. You may undress in your room, get off the lift at the second floor, and plunge into the good-sized pool. There are ladies' and gentlemen's dressing rooms adjacent to the pool where you may change if you prefer. The pool is surrounded by tables festooned with gay umbrellas where you may enjoy your favorite beverage while sunning or swimming.

If you wish to be super elegant, the *Rama* can offer for your choice eighteen private suites designed in the Thai, Chinese, Japanese, and Indian styles. One day laundry service and twenty-four hour dry cleaning service are available. The *Rama* would be considered a strictly first class hotel in either America or Europe.

The other two first class hotels are the ERAWAN and the ORIENTAL. Which of the latter two is the better is strictly a matter of opinion.

ERAWAN HOTEL. The *Erawan* is a large, rambling five story edifice with one hundred and seventy-five air conditioned rooms, each with individually controlled temperature. The hotel was opened late in 1956 and is considered to be quite modern. The rooms are tastefully decorated, having bathrooms containing both tub and shower. The courtyard is colorful and bedecked with tables, umbrellas, and deck chairs overlooking a tastefully designed swimming pool. Entrance to the courtyard is from the open lobby which is partially air conditioned and also is so designed that it captures the natural breezes. The dining room, bar, and night club are all fully air conditioned and quite comfortable.

ORIENTAL HOTEL. The *Oriental* is **Bangkok's** only hotel overlooking the river. From the front and side rooms, one enjoys a constantly changing panoramic vista of teeming activity on the busy stream. The old section was established in 1895 making it the oldest hotel in **Bangkok**. The new *Tower Wing* is quite modern with rooms being air conditioned and provided with either private tub bath or shower. The lobby and restaurant are of the open air variety, not air conditioned, but there is an excellent air conditioned *Bamboo Bar*. The chic *Normandie Grill* atop the new section is among **Bangkok's** finest.

VIET NAM

SAIGON

CARAVELLE. The Caravelle jet aircraft, introduced by *Air France,* is the most magnificent object that has ever floated through the sky. It is graceful, sleek, and chic. The hotel in **Saigon** of the same name must also be described with superlatives. It taxes one's credulity to believe that a hotel of this deluxe character could possibly be found half a world away from Hometown U.S.A. I am as completely enchanted with the *Caravelle* as I am captivated with **Saigon**—Paris with Oriental overtones. The hotel was opened in 1960. It is completely airconditioned from the foyer, overlooking a pleasant square, to the ninth floor terrace restaurant and bar. The rooms are gaily, tastefully decorated. The bathrooms include all modern conveniences—plus the mysterious bidet. The service is superduper. Two room boys are assigned to each room, and you have but to push a button for anything your heart desires. The lads literally break world speed records rushing to your assistance. The restaurant, covered in another chapter, is the best in town. High atop the *Caravelle* is a completely open observation terrace. It is a favorite setting for evening cocktails and is reached by circular stairway from the terrace adjacent to the dining room. The eighth floor *Jerome et Juliette* cocktail lounge (fully air conditioned, of course) is smart and attractive.

The *Caravelle* would be a deluxe hotel by any standard in any country. You will love it, and every minute you spend in it.

MAJESTIC HOTEL. The *Majestic* is an older establishment that is possessed of great charm and atmosphere. Air conditioned rooms are cooled with individual units. The terrace dining room commands an excellent view, and while not air conditioned is pleasantly wafted with fans and gentle breezes enhanced by the height over the river. The sidewalk terrace cafe is busy as a beehive at the cocktail hour populated with fascinating personalities from all over the world. The roof terrace boasts of an excellent bar, the longest I can ever remember having seen. There is a completely open observation roof opposite the bar with a vast panoramic view of the city and a sweep of the river.

RECOMMENDED HOTEL LIST

CAMBODIA

Deluxe	Superior	Good
	Siem Reap	
	Grand Hotel d'Angkor	L'Auberge Des Ruines
		De La Paix (Annex of the Grand)
		Temple Motel

CAMBODIA *(Continued)*

Deluxe	Superior	Good
	Phnom Penh	
	Monorom	Raja
	Le Royal	(Annex of Le Royal)
		Sukhalay
		Mondial
		International
		De La Poste

STATE OF HAWAII

ISLAND OF OAHU

Honolulu

Royal Hawaiian	The Waikikian	The Reef Tower
Kahala Hilton	The Breakers	The Reef
Hawaiian Village	Surfrider	Moana
Princess Kaiulani	Hawaiiana	Waikiki Biltmore
Halekulani	Alexander Young *	The Edgewater
Ilikai †	New Coral Strand †	Hawaiian King
		Colony Surf
		The Palms †

Kaneohe

Pali Palms

ISLAND OF HAWAII

Hilo

The Hilo Naniloa

Hilo Hukilau

* The best of the downtown hotels.
† Combination hotel and apartments (lovely).

STATE OF HAWAII *(Continued)*

ISLAND OF HAWAII (Continued)

Deluxe	*Superior*	*Good*

Kailua-Kona

Kona Inn	Waiaka Lodge	Kona Hukilau
King Kamehameha		Kona Palms
Mauna Kea Beach		Kona Sunset

Hawaii National Park

Volcano House

ISLAND OF KAUAI

Coco Palms	Tropical Inn	Polynesian Inn
Resort Hotel	Kauai Inn	
The Kauai Surf	Hyatt House *(Poipu Beach)*	
Hanalei Plantation		
Waiohai *(Poipu Beach)*		
Sheraton-Kauai † *(Poipu Beach)*		

ISLAND OF MAUI

Hana

Hana-Maui

Kahului

Maui-Palms
Maui-Hukilau

Kaanapali Beach

Sheraton Maui
Royal Lahaina

Wailuku

Iao Needle *   Wailuku

* In *Iao Valley.*
† Expected to open in early 1966.

STATE OF HAWAII *(Continued)*

ISLAND OF MAUI (Continued)

Deluxe	*Superior*	*Good*

Hawaii National Park
(Haleakala)

Silversword Inn

ISLAND OF MOLOKAI

Seaside Inn

ISLAND OF LANAI

Lanai Inn

HONG KONG

Kowloon

Deluxe	Superior	Good
Peninsula	Miramar	Grand
Marco Polo-	Ambassador	Astor
Peninsula	Park	August Moon
Court	Carlton †	Imperial
	President	Shatin Heights *
	Merlin	Vanda §
		Palm Court
		Fortuna
		Palace
		Empress

* A considerable distance from town, too far for those staying only briefly.
† Four miles from town but with regular transportation to and fro.
§ Near airport.

HONG KONG *(Continued)*

Deluxe	*Superior*	*Good*
	Victoria and Environs	

Deluxe	*Superior*	*Good*
Hilton		Victoria
Mandarin		Sunning House
Repulse Bay		

JAPAN

Tokyo

Deluxe	*Superior*	*Good*
Imperial	Nikkatsu	Nikko
New Japan	Kokusai Kanko	Dai-ichi
Palace	Tokyu Ginza	Shinagawa Prince
Okura	Marunouchi	Grand
Otani	Kegon *	Fairmont
Akasaka Hirano	Shiba Park	Tsukijien
Seiko-En *	Tokyo Prince	(Tsukiji) *
Fukudaya		Azabu Prince
(Yotsuya) *		Diamond
Kyoine		Airwait †
(Yotsuya) *		
Tokyo Hilton		

Akakura

Deluxe	*Superior*	*Good*
		Akakura Kanko

Aso

Deluxe	*Superior*	*Good*
		Aso Kanko

* *Ryokan* (Japanese-style inn).
† In the airport.

JAPAN *(Continued)*

Deluxe	Superior	Good

Atami

New Fujiya		Atami
		Kan-ichi †

Beppu

Suginoi	Shiragikuso *	Akaganegoten *
Seifu	Shin Beppu *	(Hotel Copper)
Kamenoi		Kinsuien *
Hakuun Sanso		

Fuji Lakes Area

	Fuji View (*Lake Kawaguchi*)	Fuji New Grand (*Lake Yamanaka*)
	Mount Fuji	Motel Ashinoko

Fukuoka–Hakata (Kitakyushu)

	Hakata Imperial	Hakata Nikkatsu
	New Hakata	

Gifu

	Grand Hotel Gifu	Nagaragawa

Hakone Park Area

Fujiya **(Miyanoshita)**	Fujiya Hotel	Hakone Highland
Kowaki-en	Sengoku Annex	Keiunso *
(Hakonemachi)	Hakone	
Hakone Kanko	**(Hakonemachi)**	
(Sengokuhara)		
Naraya *		

Hiroshima

	Hiroshima Grand	Matsumasa *
	New Hiroshima	
	Issaen *	

* *Ryokan* (Japanese-style inn).
† Revolving top floor.

JAPAN *(Continued)*

Deluxe	Superior	Good
	Izusan Spa	
	Sagamiya *	
	Karuizawa	
Mampei	Seizan	Green
	Tsuruya *	Park
	Kawana (Ito)	
	Kawana †	Ito-Kowakien *
		Sankoen *
		Hatoya *
	Kobe	
	International	Oriental
	(Kobe Kokusai)	
	New Port	
	Kumamoto	
	Kumamoto Hotel	Tsukasa Honten *
	Castle	
	Kyoto	
Miyako	Kyoto Station	Sumiya *
International	Goshonoso *	Tawaraya *
Kyoto	Biwako	Tozankaku *
Mt. Hiei	Hiiragiya *	
	Lake Toya	
		Manseikaku *

* *Ryokan* (Japanese-style inn).
† Golf course.

JAPAN *(Continued)*

Deluxe	Superior	Good
	Miyajima (Island)	
		Iwaso Inn *
	Nagasaki	
Grand	New Nagasaki	Yataro *
	Nagoya	
Nagoya Miyako	New Nagoya	Fujikyu
	Nagoya Kanko	
	International	
	Nara	
	Nara	
	Nikko Park Area	
Nikko Kanaya	Nikko Kanko	Lakeside **(Chuzenji)**
(Nikko)	**(Chuzenji)**	
	Noboribetsu	
	Grand	
	Oshima (Island)	
	Oshima Kanko	Oshima Kowaki-en
	Osaka	
Osaka Grand	New Osaka	
Osaka Miyako	International	
	Sapporo	
	Grand	Yamagataya *
	San-ai	

* *Ryokan* (Japanese-style inn).

JAPAN *(Continued)*

Deluxe	*Superior*	*Good*
	Sendai (and Matsushima)	
	Matsushima Park	Sendai
	Sendai Central	
	Grand	
	Takamatsu	
	Kawaroku *	
	Tokiwa Honkan *	
	Takarazuka	
		Takarazuka
	Toba	
	Toba International	
	Unzen	
Unzen Kanko		Yumei
		Kyushu
	Yokohama	
	New Grand	Bund
	Silk	Tokyu

MACAO

	Macao	
	Estoril	Riviera
	Bela Vista †	Pousada de Macao
	Tai Yip Villa	(Macao Inn)
	(Pousada Taiyip)	

* *Ryokan* (Japanese-style inn).
† Scheduled to close at any moment.

FEDERATION OF MALAYSIA *

Deluxe	Superior	Good

Cameron Highlands

		Cameron Highlands
		Smoke House Inn
		Eastern Hotel

Ipoh

	Station	Bali
		Hollywood
		Winner

Kuala Lumpur

Federal	Station	
Merlin	Majestic	

Malacca

		Valiant
		Sea View

Penang

Eastern and Oriental	Metropole	
Town House		

THE PHILIPPINES

Manila

Manila	Bay View	Luneta
Filipinas	Mabuhay	Shellborne Arms
Hilton †		Swiss Inn

* Singapore listed separately, see p. 225.
† Scheduled to open in 1965.

THE PHILIPPINES *(Continued)*

HOTELS OUTSIDE MANILA

Deluxe	*Superior*	*Good*
	Baguio	
	Pines	Plaza
	Banaue	
		Beyers Inn
	Bontoc	
		Bontoc
		Pines Kitchenette
		Inn
	Butuan	
		New Narra
	Cagayan de Oro	
		Ambassador
	Cebu	
	Bay View	Capitol
	Magellan	
	Davao	
	Davao Insular	Apo View
	Hundred Islands	
		National Park
		Park View

THE PHILIPPINES *(Continued)*

HOTELS OUTSIDE MANILA (Continued)

Deluxe	Superior	Good
	Iligan	
		Bascon
	Iloilo	
		Admiral
		Ledesma
	Laoag	
		Texicano
	Legaspi	
		Mayon
		Eden
		Casino
	Naga	
		Rainbow
	Tacloban	
		Grand
	Tagaytay	
	Taal Vista Lodge	
	Tarlac	
		Je-na's
	Vigan	
		Vigan
	Zamboanga	
		Bayot

SINGAPORE (MALAYSIA)

Deluxe	*Superior*	*Good*
Raffles	Adelphi	de L'Europe
Singapura Interconti- nental	Prince's Hotel Garni	("The Cockpit")
	Cathay	Ocean Park
Goodwood Park		Seventh Story
Ming Court *		Majestic
Hilton *		

TAIWAN (FORMOSA)

Changhua
Pakuashan

Kaohsiung
Grand
Garden

Peitow
Mayflower   Hsin Hsiu Ko
Wen Hua Chuang

Sun-Moon Lake
Evergreen

Taichung
Railway

Tainan
Hwa Chow Grand
Long Beach

* Expected to open in late 1965.

TAIWAN (FORMOSA *(Continued)*

Deluxe	*Superior*	*Good*
	Taipei	
Grand	Friends of China	Park
New Taipei	Club Park	Green Garden
Ambassador	Orient	Lucky
President	China	Palace
Mandrin *	Nanking	
	Prince	
	Taiwan	

THAILAND

	Bangkok	
Rama	Erawan	Princess
Bangkok	Oriental	Plaza
Intercontinental *	Royal	Grand
	Manida	Trocadero
		Thai Hotel

VIET NAM

	Saigon	
Caravelle	Majestic	

	Dalat	
	Dalat Palace	Dalat
		Cam Do

* Scheduled for 1965 opening.

CHAPTER 5

On Dining Out in the Orient

For most of us, eating has long since ceased to be the mere fulfillment of the physical need for nourishment. From my own experiences and those shared with scores of thousands of gracious fellow foreign travelers, I have learned that dining abroad can be a delightful social and epicurean experience. This is particularly true if the foreign visitor has been properly advised as to the how, when, where, and why of dining out in the Orient.

The contrasts in Oriental cuisine are endless and as stimulating to the imagination as they are appetite-arousing. In your travels in the Far East, a never ending series of ecstatic dining pleasures await you. The variety of types of food that will be available to you are seemingly without end. The quality will be perfect and the service impeccable. One of the sheer delights of foreign travel lies in the contrasts that such experiences afford. The different types of food and the service that await your pleasure in the Orient are unique.

Each of the countries features its own succulent native dishes. The local specialties themselves are varied and interesting. In addition, however, with few exceptions most hotels and many restaurants feature a superb western style cuisine which includes sizzling steaks, elegant chops, succulent ribs

and roasts, roast chicken, crisp salads, and just about anything and everything that would please you in your favorite
restaurant at home.

But the taste-animating story of Oriental eating is much more
all-encompassing. In addition to the local fare and the western
style kitchen, each of the countries boasts of extraordinarily fine
European restaurants and establishments featuring Continental
specialties. French, German, Italian, Spanish, Hungarian, and
Scandinavian restaurants abound in the Orient. Scandinavian
smorgasbord tables at the *Raffles Hotel* in **Singapore,** at the
Osaka Grand in **Osaka,** and at the *Imperial* in **Tokyo** are
among the finest that I have ever encountered.

I can assure you that whether you dine at a great gay
sophisticated restaurant in such metropolitan centers as **Tokyo,
Kyoto, Hong Kong,** or **Singapore,** or whether you choose to
dine in a wayside Japanese inn, you will be served graciously,
pleasantly, and to the limit of your heart's content.

To illustrate the complete degree to which western-style
dining habits have been absorbed in the Far East, a breakfast
would, I believe, be most typical. The room service menu of the
Imperial in **Tokyo** includes, according to season, seventeen different fresh fruits and juices including orange, tomato, or tan-
gerine juice, strawberries (the biggest, most luscious, sweetest,
and most eye-appealing that you have ever seen or tasted),
melon or pineapple, followed by a wide variety of hot and cold
cereals, eggs cooked in every conceivable fashion garnished
with ham, bacon, or country sausage. There is kippered herring,
fried salmon or halibut, a breakfast minute or rump steak,
creamed chicken on toast, calves' liver, corned beef hash, and
breakfast potatoes. Should you lean more to the carbohydrates,
you may have a choice from waffles, French toast, and hot cakes
served with honey or hot maple sirup, and raisin bread, Danish
pastry, corn muffins, cinnamon rolls, or toast. On the *Imperial's*
room service à la carte menu, you may have for lunch or
dinner such a choice as oysters, any style, Chateaubriand,
curried shrimp, spaghetti, fillet of sole. *sole meunière.* or grilled

lobster. There are sirloin steaks, veal chops, combination salads, hamburger, chicken and club sandwiches, hot and cold roast beef plates, and old fashioned strawberry shortcake.

I have particularly emphasized the easy availability of our western type of food because there are such appalling misconceptions as to what type of food awaits the visitor to the Orient. There are many otherwise well informed and sophisticated travelers whose footsteps have not yet turned to the East who believe that fried rice, bamboo sprouts, and butterfly brains are the only staple items available on the far side of the International Date Line. It just isn't so, of course.

It is, however, quite true that in the Japanese home a day seldom goes by in which the family does not partake of rice at least once, usually twice, and in which fish is not served. This is because of their love for rice and fish. An Italian counts the day completely lost unless he consumes a mountain of his beloved spaghetti. So with the Oriental; rice, like our bread, is his staff of life. It is consumed in lieu of bread.

Other much loved and widely consumed items of the Japanese diet are bean sprouts and pastes and sauces made from soy beans. The Japanese themselves and most foreign visitors are fond of sukiyaki made of thin beef strips simmered in a tasty soy sauce garnished with various fresh vegetables, served with a raw egg, and accompanied by rice. They enjoy tempura, too, a dish composed of seafood and vegetables. All elements are dipped in a special characteristic batter, then deep fried in vegetable oil to a light succulent golden brown. A fine grated radish and spicy soy sauce is used as a delicious appetizing condiment for the tempura.

Despite their proclivity for imitation, the Japanese have originated their own cooking schemes for steaks, chops, and fowl which far exceed our own sizzling treatment of these tasty subjects. There are steak restaurants, such as *Misono,* in which the tables are built around the chef's grill, which is actually a part of your table. Unlike our custom of just putting the huge hunk of meat on the grill and letting it simmer, the

Japanese style is for the chef to surround the magnificent cut of *Kobe beef* with bean sprouts, celery, potatoes, and other vegetables, and from time to time place a metal bowl over the steak to trap the heat. When the steak has been well basted, the chef, using a special shredding knife, shreds the steak into small pieces, each of which is prepared to the exact point of perfection to tantalize your taste buds. When the steak is prepared like this, it may be handled successfully even with chopsticks. The aroma is tantalizing and the flavor exquisite.

By nature I am a gourmet and relish every conceivable type of food from the simplest hot dog and humblest hamburger to glamorous *duck à l'orange, Fettuccine Alfredo, crepes Grand Vefour, sole Belle Meunière,* Hungarian beef goulash, veal stroganoff, smorgasbord *à la Viking, Kobe and Matsuzaka beef,* tempura, sukiyaki, and the appetite-arousing Chinese specialties, particularly the Cantonese variety. The foregoing is to name but a few; I could (and might) write a book on my various international epicurean adventures. If food is served piping hot or fresh from the refrigerator, prepared in the eastern or western hemisphere, presented on plates, in bowls, or on sandwiches, eaten with knives, forks, fingers, or chopsticks . . . I like it.

I am as zestful a diner as I have ever known, and I would venture to say that I have eaten in as many different places in the world as anyone alive today. Being very human, I must have my pet places which I revisit and savor, but I conscientiously assay and evaluate the wonders of scores of new restaurants each year. Obviously, no one person can have sampled personally every restaurant in every city in the Orient, as well as in Europe. Not even one of Olson's ample avoirdupois. It is certainly soul-satisfying and stimulating to make the effort, however. Fortunately, I have a host of trusted epicurean friends and advisors whose collective tastes and culinary judgment I have learned to respect. I have sampled or visited every restaurant and night club listed on the following pages myself, or have had a first hand detailed report from reliable traveler-gourmets.

The special write-ups preceding the general listings are high on the list of my own personal "very favorites."

HAWAII

The ROYAL HAWAIIAN HOTEL MONARCH ROOM is set in the sandy lap of *Waikiki Beach*. As I inscribe these words, I look down from Room 476 to a sparkling setting, international in its sophistication, and hear the melodic tunes of Moxie-Whitney and his orchestra. Every night except Sunday and Monday, the famous *Kamaaina* dinner is served, which is a six-course repast featuring green turtle soup, breast of *Kahunakaku chicken, Liliuokalani salad,* pineapple delight, and other native specialties. All this plus a superb floor show and dancing. You must "dress up" for the *Kamaaina* dinners. For the men, however, this means a business suit or dinner jacket and for the ladies, their nicest party dresses.

The generous daily buffet lunches in the *Royal Hawaiian* SURF ROOM are always popular.

HAWAIIAN VILLAGE. Of the numerous restaurants in the *Hawaiian Village,* the *Tapa Room* reigns supreme. This restaurant-night club features charcoal broiled steaks and Polynesian specialties, as well as outstanding entertainment every night. The atmosphere is intimate and charged with gaiety.

The *Ale Ale Kai Room,* just off *Waikiki Beach,* is completely informal and offers excellent service and fine food and drink. The *Hawaiian Village*'s *Golden Dragon* and *Dragon Bar* feature traditional Oriental cuisine.

HALEKULANI HOTEL. For a more sophisticated experience, may I suggest that you watch the sunset from the terrace of the *Halekulani Hotel,* under a setting of huge trees, to the tune of a sunset serenade. Hawaiian, Continental, or other beverages are available. You may take dinner in the restaurant or on the terrace with a choice of numerous American or native dishes. Luncheon at the *Halekulani* consists of an excellent buffet.

CANLIS' CHARCOAL BROILER, 2100 Kalakaua Avenue *(Waikiki)* is, in my estimation, the finest restaurant in Hawaii both as to cuisine and décor. Really elegant and expensive, this outstanding establishment compares favorably with the best restaurants in Europe or on the Mainland. Taxi drivers and other self-appointed experts have a tendency to point out that *Canlis'* serves only steaks. Nothing could be farther from the truth. Their New York cut sirloin steak is indeed their *pièce de résistance* specialty, but included on the menu are such other outstanding delicacies as Burma jungle fowl, genuine fresh caviar, Alaska king crab in shell, fresh Louisiana prawn shrimp, avocado cocktail, French lamb chops, steak tartar, ground fillet of beefsteak, mushrooms, calves' liver steak, fried seafood, and whole broiled lobster tail, to name but a few. The "original" *Canlis'* Idaho baked potato served with gobs of butter, parmesan cheese, green onions, and minced bacon is extraordinarily good. Everything is à la carte, but ten dollars will buy a complete dinner, everything included. You can get by for much less.

The WAIOLI TEA ROOM, Honolulu, just northwest of the intersection of University Avenue and East Manoa Road, is set amidst a garland of exotic Oriental flowers and trees. "The Land of the Singing Waters" *(Waioli)* is named after the mission home of the Salvation Army located on the northern tip of *Kauai*. A complimentary fruit juice cocktail is offered to all visitors. The *Waioli* menu is fixed, but it is varied and superb. First, you visit the salad bar which presents a wide variety of mouth-watering salads. This is followed by the main course, usually fried chicken. Afterwards, you may visit the taste-provoking dessert bar. The spotless and immaculate kitchen is open to visitors. The beautiful setting is in the *Manoa Valley*. Don't fail to visit the grass hut, originally owned by Princess Kaiulani and according to legend occupied by none other than Robert Louis Stevenson on his visits to

Hawaii. Jams, jellies, and other Hawaiian products may be purchased in the gift shop. Profits from the *Tea Room* are used by the Salvation Army for its work in **Honolulu.**

Many "do good" projects are noteworthy only by the worthwhileness of their end results . . . but not this place. It stands on its own merit. The *Waioli Tea Room* is highly recommended for luncheon or tea, for the charm of its setting, the lovely spirit of the surroundings, and the excellence of its food. At noon a daily blessing is offered in song by gracious and beautiful Hawaiian girls. The *Tea Room* is closed Sundays, Mondays, and holidays.

The INTERNATIONAL MARKET PLACE is on Kalakaua Avenue midway between, and across the street from, the *Royal Hawaiian* and *Moana Hotels.* Under "Hawaii," I have mentioned the *International Market Place,* but it is so well known for its international accent on food that it must be included here. Don the Beachcomber has his skilled hand in several of the restaurants. The best known of his interests are:

(1) COLONEL'S PLANTATION BEEFSTEAK AND COFFEE HOUSE. Here you may indicate the thickness to which you desire your steak to be cut. You pay for what you select. The sour dough French bread is served warm. The baked potato à la Idaho and crisp fresh green salad set off the steak just right. The rosé wine is outstanding.

(2) TREE FOR TWO. This is a bit of a "gag," but a famous one. A small thatched cottage is located in a banyan tree and equipped with a delightfully intimate table for two. Honeymooners should adore this. The cuisine is good, the price is high. Thirty-five dollars covers the meal, wine included.

(3) BORA BORA COCKTAIL LOUNGE. Well known and worthy of an interesting and intimate visit.

Also in the *International Market Place:*

DUKE KAHANAMOKU'S, formerly "Don the Beachcomber's," features delectable American cuisine and exotic Oriental dishes. Set in a typical tropical motif of soft lights and romantic atmosphere, it offers good music and dancing, interesting floor shows. Sunday nights are devoted to the luau. The "Duke" is well remembered as an all-time Olympic swimming champion, vintage of Johnny Weissmuller and Norman Ross, and more recently famous as the local police chief.

THE LUAU

The luau is as typically native to Hawaii as is smorgasbord to the Scandinavians; wurst, pork shank, and sauerkraut to the Germans; *knocchi, fettucine,* spaghetti, and other *pastas* to the Italians; *paella* to the Spanish; and *escargots* to the French. The luau, leaf of the taro, is more ceremonial than any of the others aforementioned. The largest of the basic ingredients of the luau is a whole pig *(puaa kalua)* cooked in an underground oven *(imu)* with great ceremony. However, the basic luau is more varied than a combination of imaginative hamburger, hash, and chili con carne. Other components usually included are *lomi lomi* salmon, hand massaged local fish mixed with fresh tomatoes and onions, the *moa, chicken luau,* mixed with

Hawaiian spinach and/or taro tops, and coconut cream served in fresh coconuts. Poi, the basic staple sustenance of Hawaii, is taro root which has been pounded into a paste. It is usually eaten with the fingers. There will be the barbecued Hawaiian steak prepared in soy sauce and spices and charcoal broiled to a delicate consistency. There are baked yams *(uwala kalua)* which have been steamed and wrapped in *ti* leaves. The *limu,* dried seaweed, are eaten as a relish. The Hawaiian rock salt, *paakai,* is a seasoning. To all of this you add the *halakahika,* the luau-style pineapple, the baked bananas *(plantains),* banana muffins, and coconut cake. These are all generously laced with Polynesian rum punch.

THE LUAU, where served:

The principal ceremonial luaus are served at:

(1) *The Royal Hawaiian Hotel.* 6:30 P.M. on Sundays by the sea in front of the *Royal Hawaiian.*

(2) *Queen's Surf, Waikiki Beach.* Sundays, Tuesdays, and Thursdays at 6:30 P.M. (Tuesdays July and August only and Thursdays February through October only.)

(3) *Duke Kahanamoku's, International Market,* Kalakaua. Sundays at 6:30 P.M.

(4) *The Hawaiian Village.* Wednesdays and Sundays at 6:30 P.M. except during the Christmas holiday period when the schedule is irregular (depending upon when Christmas and New Year's fall).

Reservations are urgently suggested for the luau.

Each of the aforementioned includes not only the extraordinarily exotic menu but also entertainment throughout the feast featuring Polynesian music and dancing, the hula, and unusual music.

HONG KONG

The number and variety of palate-tempting, taste-exciting restaurants in **Hong Kong** is gratifyingly large. By virtue of its being a British Crown Colony, the European influence in **Hong Kong** is a definite factor in the local cuisine. On the other hand, the population of **Hong Kong** being predominantly Chinese is, no doubt, its most important food factor, while its proximity to **Japan** and **Macao** permit other exciting culinary influences to be exerted. In addition to the exhilarating joy of **Hong Kong** shopping and sightseeing, restaurant sampling will add another sparkling facet to your visit to this tiny never-never land.

It is advisable for parties of from 4 to 10 persons to gather to enjoy Chinese cooking. When ordering hors d'oeuvres and the main course, for example, a great deal of the fun is derived from sampling a wide variety of dishes. Each person may order one or two different specialties and then all divvy up portions of their choice.

Because **Hong Kong** offers the world's greatest variety and selection of Chinese cuisine, it might be worthwhile to outline briefly the selections within the general category of Chinese cooking.

CHINESE CUISINE includes:

CANTONESE which is the blandest, most subtle, and least greasy of the varieties of Chinese cooking. Most of the Chinese restaurants in America are Cantonese, but a real Chinese menu will not include chop suey or chow mein while chicken and vegetables predominate in Cantonese cooking. Cantonese kitchens feature: egg roll, egg foo young, sweet and sour pork, barbecued chicken, fish fried with ham, winter melon cup, shark's fins, minced pigeon, barbecued pork, lobster, braised young pigeon, fried rice, egg and corn soup, baked chicken, garoupa, beef with oyster sauce, and bean curd and minced pork. Walnuts, mangoes, and mushrooms are generously used in Cantonese preparations. Cantonese cooking also embraces *Fukien* food.

PEKING *(Peiping* or *Northern)* cooking is particularly noted for the crisp *Peking duck,* in which preparation the duck is roasted in its entirety to a point where the skin is crisp and succulent and is then served separately before the body meat.

The Cantonese ducks are very large and must be cooked whole, another reason why parties of four or more should assemble to try Chinese food. *Peking* specialties include: roasted shrimps and tomato, steamed prawns, sweet and sour pork, creamed cabbage, fried shrimp balls, chicken in paper, sea slugs with shrimp, fried kidney, diced chicken in heavy sauce, and the aforementioned painstakingly prepared duck.

The SZECHUAN kitchen features highly spiced beef, pork, chicken, and vegetables—similar to Indian, Mexican, and/or Thai dishes. Among the tart specialties served in the *Szechuan* restaurants are: duck smoked with camphor and tea leaves, diced chicken with walnuts, braised chicken legs, *Szechuanese* bean curd, diced pork with fish flavor, stewed fish with garlic, carp with hot bean sauce, steamed pork with rice flour, shredded chicken with hot sauce, and spiced ox tendon.

SHANGHAI culinary preparation, known also as *East China* food, is light and delicate, accentuating sweet, gently spiced dishes with meat, chicken, duck, and seafood as a base. *Shanghai* cuisine is best known for its boiled chicken, fried prawns, steamed carp, fried eel, sweet and sour fish, braised turtle, fried frogs' legs, shark's fin soup, steamed abalone, and bird's nest soup.

Originally many of my friends, and I, turned up our respective noses at the thought of shark's fins. Don't! They're good, particularly when served either with sauces, shredded chicken, or other ingredients. They make an ideal appetizer.

Among the Chinese soups that are highly regarded are duck soup, bacon and cucumber soup, dried mushrooms and chicken soup, chicken wing with mushroom soup, bird's nest soup, and a divine concoction of Peking mushrooms and crisp rice.

Duck is served in half a dozen or more different ways including shredded, braised, barbecued, roast *Peking,* and *Szechuan* style.

Chicken gets the most varied treatment, being served fried, whole, roasted *Cantonese* style, fried in rolls, diced with hot peppers, diced and fried with walnuts, boiled, and *Shanghai* style—the so-called *"Beggar's Chicken"*—to name but a few.

Pork is served braised, barbecued, sweet and sour, and plain fried with a variety of condiments.

Beef is served with oyster sauce or slowly scorched.

Seafood is available in a voluminous number of choices including prawns, garoupa, abalone, fried fish rolls, braised shark's fins, and steamed crab.

Bamboo shoots are served in a variety of ways, as are cabbage and rice. Rice can and does appear any place in the meal including fried as a dessert or as an accompaniment to one or another of the courses. It is also a standard side dish to replace bread.

Noodles are popular in all Chinese cooking.

Some of the Chinese delicacies, which might not even strike you as being such, can be very expensive. After you have worked out a menu with your waiter, ask him to give you a complete price for the meal. This might save you a rude shock later.

The HOTEL MIRAMAR RESTAURANT and NIGHT CLUB have excellent menus prepared for groups of four, eight, and twelve persons, and include:

Chinese Menu for Four Persons, with generous helpings for each, includes shark's fins with shredded chicken in soup, fresh shrimp and walnuts, pan-fried barbecued chicken, sliced garoupa in sweet and sour sauce, and fried rice Yang-chow style. The cost is H.K. $70 . . . less than $12 U.S., or $3 U.S. each.

Chinese Menu for Eight Persons includes fried stuffed crab pincers, fresh shrimp and walnuts, shark's fins in superior soup, barbecued chicken, black mushrooms with vegetables, roasted pigeons in lemon juice, delicious rice wrapped in lotus leaf, and sweetened mango and milk in gruel. The cost is H.K. $150 . . . approximately $25 U.S., or $3 U.S. per person.

Chinese Menu for Twelve Persons includes lobster salad, delicious fried chicken liver roll, minced pigeon with lettuce, stuffed chicken with shark's fins, barbecued duck, boiled chicken with ham garnish, double boiled winter melon, red garoupa in sweet and sour sauce, rice wrapped in lotus leaf, and mango ice cream cake—costing H.K. $250 . . . approximately $41 U.S., or a little over $3 U.S. per person.

More and more one gets the idea of why Chinese meals should be enjoyed ensemble with one's friends and/or acquaintances.

The FLOATING RESTAURANTS

Three of the most fascinating and unusual restaurants which are talked of throughout the Far East are floating in the waters of **Hong Kong's** bays. At *Aberdeen* we find the colorful and glamorous SEA PALACE and TAI PAK. Recently *Tai Pak* has opened another floating restaurant, of the same type and category as the original, in *Castle Peak Bay*. There is little to choose between these unusual restaurants. They are fascinating, wonderful, and not expensive. In each place, there are large pools of water in which the carefree fish swim happily about waiting to be selected to provide you with a succulent meal. You indicate your choice, and your meal is netted for you to be turned over to a skilled chef. I am emotionally torn as to whether to suggest that you try one of the floating restaurants for lunch or dinner. If your time permits, do both. At noon, the entire area is a beehive of activity with the picturesque junks of the fishing fleet passing hither and yon; the little sampans in which you will be rowed out from the shore are manned by colorfully costumed women who frequently have their babies or older children with them who placidly amuse themselves while mama rows the diners to either the *Sea Palace* or the *Tai Pak*. They will wait patiently for you to finish dining. The fee for this water taxi service is borne by the restaurant. The floating restaurants are extraordinarily popular with the wealthy Chinese, and while they are indeed tourist attractions, they are so excellent as to attract the best of the local trade. By night these restaurants are gaily lighted, and the local boat lights mysteriously twinkle in the murky distance.

The HONG KONG LADY is the brainchild of Don the Beachcomber (Don Beach). Unlike the *Tai Pak* and the *Sea Palace* which are stationary floating restaurants, the fluorescent painted *Hong Kong Lady,* patterned after a Mississippi River showboat, will, when in operation, take her dining passengers on a colorful voyage through *Victoria Harbor.* Innumerable delays have been encountered in placing the *Hong Kong Lady* in service. When, if ever, she will be ready is a question mark.

SADDLE AND SIRLOIN, first floor, *Mandarin Hotel,* is deservedly popular as one of **Hong Kong's** outstanding restaurants, as it has been for many years past. This culinary paradise is continuing in a new and even more luxurious setting in the *Mandarin Hotel.* Offering grilled specialties, the *Saddle and Sirloin* presents the most "choosy" diner with taste-tempting Chateaubriand and prime sirloin steaks, beef fondue, shish kabob, crisp salads, and other Continental and American dishes topped off by exotic desserts. *Peche flambée* (flaming peach) is one of the glamorous sweet dishes on the *Saddle and Sirloin's* groaning menu. One may personally select grill favorites and then watch the savory repast sizzle on the open grill. Reservations are absolutely essential. Open for lunch from noon until 3 P.M. and for dinner until midnight.

GADDI'S, ground floor, *Peninsula Hotel,* is quite generally considered to be the finest restaurant in **Hong Kong.** It is smart, chic, and attractive. When you enter this plush environment, you could very easily, if you did not know that you were halfway around the world, believe that you were in one of **France's** smartest establishments. The cuisine is cosmopolitan, the service is impeccable, and the prices are high. Dancing is to the music of a fine Filipino orchestra. Lavish luncheons; no breakfasts.

The MARCO POLO, across the street in the *Peninsula Court,* ground floor, is the famous "twin" of *Gaddi's.* There is little to choose between *Gaddi's* and *Marco Polo,* and everything said about *Gaddi's* can go double for *Marco Polo.* Music and attractions.

AMBASSADOR HOTEL RESTAURANT. The view by day from the *Ambassador* restaurant across the waters of the harbor to the heights of **Victoria** is scintillating. It encompasses a sweeping panoramic vista of all **Kowloon** and toward the *New Territories*. This photographer's paradise is also a gourmet's delight. The food and service are excellent, and the environment delightful. The *Ambassador Coffee Shop* is both modern and inviting. I recommend the restaurant and coffee shop without hesitancy.

The DYNASTY ROOM, *Ambassador Hotel*. This highly authentic Oriental bar and restaurant features Cantonese style Chinese food in a setting high atop this deluxe establishment. The site, view, and description of the locale are comparable in every way to the *Ambassador* restaurant described in the foregoing paragraph. I highly recommend the *Dynasty Room*.

The PRINCESS GARDEN RESTAURANT, *Princess Theater,* is, to my utter shame, a Chinese restaurant which for completely inexplicable reasons I have missed. Many of my friends, and particularly that international gourmet, Vernon Brooks, tell me that it is simply "out of this world." By the time these words are read, I will have been back to **Hong Kong** again and will have sampled it myself. In the meantime, I might point out that Vernon recommends particularly the special deluxe hors d'oeuvres, the barbecued Peking duck, the sweet sour fish, the quick fried shredded duck and bean sprouts, the duck soup, and the toffee apples. The variety of the Peking cuisine is endless. The *Princess Garden* is also a night club of some repute. The floor show takes place at midnight. The local Chinese wine, *shiao shing,* will remind you of *sake,* which the Chinese claim is a derivative of their own.

The HIGHBALL, 74-78 Nathan Road, Manson House, features Cantonese cuisine. This is a night club which shares its shows with *Blue Heaven*. There are usually three or four acts, and floor shows are featured from 10:15 P.M. to about 2:00 A.M. I recommend, however, that you try the *Highball* for luncheon. It is unique. Waitresses roam the room with delicious hot Chinese specialties, sort of a roving smorgasbord. To the best of my knowledge, this type of service is unique to the *Highball* and certainly well worth your trying.

The CARLTON HOTEL TERRACE, Taipo Road on the heights overlooking **Kowloon** and across the bay to **Victoria,** affords a most romantic vista. Try to be there at twilight for cocktails and stay for dinner. The setting is an absolute fairy-land. The cuisine is western, the music, dancing, and floor show are excellent, but I think the view is the real treat. Quite unusual.

The WINTER GARDEN, 221 Nathan Road, features Shanghai-Peking food. The fried shrimp and cabbage and ham soup are particularly flavorsome, as is the assorted meat with crisp rice.

SHATIN HOTEL, *Shatin Heights.* About fifteen minutes by car beyond the *Carlton Hotel,* the *Shatin* enjoys a superb view over a tremendous valley and inland sea beyond. I would recommend it as a pleasant drive from **Kowloon** for lunch or tea, though the lunches can get a bit crowded with numerous visitors arriving at the same time. There is an excellent bar and the tea service is fine.

In **Hong Kong** you will not wish to drink water from the tap. In your hotel the room boy will provide carafes of bottled water, while in the restaurants you will choose usually mineral or boiled water.

BALLROOMS in **Hong Kong** were first established in 1930. *Wong Choy* was the forerunner of the several hundreds that have been opened since. There are more than eighty of these "poor man's paradises" in business today, employing an average of about one hundred hostesses each. These dance halls are open from four P.M. to three A.M., with the four to 8:30 period known as a tea dance and from 8:30 onward as a night dance. Fees are handled by a fairly complex system: a coupon must be purchased for each twenty minutes that a hostess spends with the customer. The cost varies from sixty cents H.K. to more than five dollars H.K. each. Sometimes a hostess may "fudge" a bit during the busy hours and refuse to spend the full twenty minutes with her patron. Tea and melon seeds are the more popular refreshments consumed in the ballrooms.

If the hostess approves, customers are permitted to take partners from the floor to visit other night clubs or restaurants. The number of coupons required is larger if the girl leaves the premises. There are, of course, all kinds of girls in **Hong Kong,** but the ballroom hostesses most definitely are just that. Don't get any ideas. Popular hostesses have been known to make as much as $3,000 H.K. a month. When one considers that a skilled artisan has difficulty making more than $800 H.K. a month, it is understandable why these well educated girls have little interest in extra curricular activities . . . at least for money.

The *Metro* and the *Blue Sky* are the most popular ballrooms for foreign visitors, while the locals seem to like the *Tonnochy* and the *Oriental* best.

JAPAN

Japanese bars and night clubs are among the most enthusiastically attended of any in the world. It has been estimated by reliable authorities that fully ninety-seven per cent of the Japanese businessmen of all strata do not go directly home from their places of business but instead repair to their favorite Turkish bath, bar, bistro, restaurant and/or night club.

The zeal with which the Japanese exhibit their desire to be entertained is virtually a mania. Of the world's capitals, none sparkles with more brilliancy after dark than does **Tokyo,** and of the world's great cities none are more effervescently exuberant in the pursuit of pleasure than the cities, towns, villages, and hamlets of **Japan.** Even in such a remote port city as **Takamatsu,** the night clubs are gay, garish, and uninhibited. It would be impossible to make even an off-the-cuff guess as to how many females are employed nightly entertaining the Japanese and their ever increasing fun-hungry guests. The floor shows in the various night clubs vary greatly from nude and naughty to gay, elegant presentations such as one would find at the *Copacabana, Latin Quarter, Hanabasha, Aoi Shiro,* or the *Queen Bee*. While in **Japan,** you need never lack for any type of entertainment. There is an establishment for every mood, taste, and virtually every pocketbook. While not cheap, the Japanese night clubs are a bit less expensive than those of **New York** or **Paris** . . . just a bit.

Despite this wide popularity of dining out and seeking nightly entertainment, the restaurant and night club hours open for business vary considerably and are worthy of comment. Outside of **Tokyo,** many excellent restaurants close by ten P.M., with the last order taken not later than nine P.M. In the capital, on the other hand, while some outstanding restaurants close early, others, particularly tiny bars and restaurants featuring foreign cuisine, are open to the wee small hours and some of the snack bars never close.

Night clubs throughout **Japan** follow a pattern quite unique to this island empire. Practically without exception, all Japanese night clubs are neatly secured by midnight or at the latest twelve-thirty A.M. Others close as early as eleven-thirty P.M. Floor shows are presented abnormally early by our standards, some as early as six P.M., others at eight-thirty P.M. or nine, with second shows from ten to eleven-thirty P.M. Before planning your night out, be sure to consult the following pages for details of openings, closings and floor show hours, or, if in doubt, ask at the desk of your hotel. It is disappointing to seek out a highly recommended bright light emporium at midnight to find that you have come just in time to see the hostesses depart. The number and types of rendezvous are endless. There are tiny bistros with a handful of tables and twin pianos up to the largest, brassiest establishments in the world. Have fun, and, if you wish, play games!

JAPANESE SPECIALTIES

SUKIYAKI is a local favorite, steeped in tradition, originating back in feudal days when samurai warriors feasted on their hunting kills in the wilderness. I heartily recommend that you become familiar with this unusual dish with all its ancient atmosphere and palate-pleasing ingredients as soon after your arrival in Japan as is possible. I am sure you will wish to have sukiyaki in a variety of surroundings. In the big Japanese cities, you will have a choice of whether you wish to have it served at a western style table or in a traditional Japanese style sukiyaki room which is really much more fun. In the traditional Japanese style, the floor is covered with *tatami* matting and the décor is refined and restful, though a bit severe. In the Japanese manner, one enters the dining room in stocking feet and sits before a low table surrounded by cushions and, sometimes, arm rests. Because of the complexity of the sukiyaki preparation and service, parties of from four to eight persons are ideal for this type of meal. As many as a dozen, however, can conveniently be served together. In the center of the table is a cheerful brazier, sometimes heated by charcoal and at others, with a bow to the modern age, by electricity or gas. At each place a pair of ubiquitous chopsticks will be found as well as a small wine receptacle for hot sake, a plate, and a small bowl containing soy sauce. A charming young woman dressed in kimono and obi, her ancient Japanese costume, will act as cook or cook-waitress. It is not unusual for a party of four or six to have two or three "waitresses" who serve ceremoniously from the table's center to the accompaniment of profuse breath-drawing and bowing. All sukiyaki service is from a kneeling position, and the dexterity with which these girls can move about on their knees is incredible.

The attractive sloe-eyed "cook" first places a piece of suet in a heavy pan which is sizzlingly heated over the fire. Adjacent to the brazier, she has an attractive bowl which has been painstakingly and attractively prepared with a view toward

entrancing eye appeal as well as to the ultimate tongue gratifi-
cation. The bowl contains small pieces of lotus root, scallions,
bamboo shoots, bean curds, mushrooms, and other greens. In
another inviting bowl are the thin bits of ambrosial beef. The
vegetables and beef are placed in the sizzling pan together and
cooked in a sweetened soy sauce. By cooking small portions
of the thin beef, it seems to be only a matter of seconds before
the first, of many, helpings is ready to distribute to the guests.
Each person is served a small portion by the kneeling dexterous
attendant. The bottom of the sukiyaki bowl will have been
covered previously with a beat-up raw egg in soy sauce and
chopped radishes. Initially at least, most Americans prefer the
sauce and radishes but *without* the egg, even though the hot
food half-cooks it rapidly. I'm an intrepid explorer and whipped
up the raw egg at the time of my sukiyaki initiation and liked
it. You have your choice. While beef is the usual basic ingredient of sukiyaki, chicken, pork, veal, or even oysters and
wild fowl may be used alternatively. No sooner has the first
helping been distributed than the cooking pan is refilled and
this delightful process continues until all the guests are
satiated . . . and more.

The *sake* cups are filled up, too, as frequently as the law of
supply and demand dictates.

After the sukiyaki has been dispensed with, hot green tea is
served together with a tiny bowl of Japanese pickles. For
dessert, there is a variety of choices. In season, large fresh
strawberries with cream are my favorites; at other times,
candied ginger, small cakes, and fresh fruit are served.

The hot towel ceremonial plays an important part in the
sukiyaki service. These handy cloths are distributed before,
during, and after the meal.

TEMPURA. As mentioned previously, fish and rice are to
the Japanese what spaghetti and ravioli are to the Italians:
indispensable. One of the most delectable of the fish preparations is tempura. This palate-pleasing concoction is served in
completely native Japanese settings as well as in western style

and also in a combined, modified western-Japanese fashion. Tempura consists of practically every variety of small fish or shell fish and vegetables which have been dipped in batter and fried in deep fat. Many tempura bars are circular, with a chef rising from a trap door in the center of the "kitchen." The service is continuous until you are bloated.

KOBE AND MATSUZAKA BEEF. The Japanese are inordinately proud of these two succulent, tender beef specialties of the country which are reputed to be the finest meats in all the world. Certainly one would have to travel far and wide to find anything more superlative. There are several unusual qualities to these two types of beef, the first of which is that with labor being so penuriously inexpensive, carefully trained men can, and do, work amazingly tedious hours at massaging the beef cows twice a day in such a way as to inhibit hard muscles from forming. In this manner, plus the fact that they are also kept in pens to keep them from getting muscular, the meat is kept tender even while on the hoof. The second feature is that the cows are slaughtered prior to having wasted any of their strength on reproductive activities. Last, but not least, the cows are fed great quantities of beer daily except Saturdays and Sundays. Most unusual. But the results are taste titillating.

MAMMOTH JAPANESE STRAWBERRIES, a cross in size between a huge radish and a medium-size carrot, are grown in Shizuoka Prefecture near the region's capital city of **Shizuoka,** located about an hour's drive from the *Fujiya Hotel* in *Hakone* where the winter climate is milder than **Tokyo's.** These juicy, mouth-watering berries are produced through a peculiar process known as *stone wall cultivation.* The slanted walls, built with special crannies, or nooks, where the stones meet, always have a southerly exposure. Winter days in Japan are usually sunny, and the heat of the sun is absorbed by the stones, permitting the plants imbedded in each cranny to be cosy and warm by night as well as by day since the walls, which retain the heat absorbed during the day, radiate heat by night. When the strawberries take root and blossom, a polyethylene, or vinyl, transparent sack is placed over the bloom so that each plant is provided with its own portable hothouse. These huge, wonderful, sweet strawberries are in season from late December through mid-April. The Shizuoka area is also renowned for its famous "mandarin oranges," or tangerines. This delicious fruit, exported in cans, is served fresh locally from November through February.

WILD PINE MUSHROOMS (MATSUTAKE) appear in the fall and are generously used as seasoning, particularly with wild game, soup, and tempura. The Japanese, connoisseurs all, are enormously fond of *Matsutake*—so am I.

YAKITORI RESTAURANTS. *Yakitori* restaurants are as completely Japanese as are fish, rice, and the symbol of the rising sun. They are tiny joints which specialize in skewered chicken—and its by-products. These petite family-run restaurants accommodate from six to twenty paying guests who are usually served on a wooden counter while seated on stools. The skewered barbecue bits include the livers, ground chicken meat, the wings, legs, thighs, and skin of the chicken. Skewered duck, green peppers, and mushrooms in season are also usually available at *Yakitori* restaurants. The *Yakitori* sauces, soy thinned with special *sake*, are mouth-wateringly appetizing. My favorite *Yakitori* restaurants include: TORI GIN, half a block up the alley behind *Ketel's* German restaurant, marked by a big red paper lantern hung outside. The place has four branches, all huddled close by. You'll get all you can eat for less than $2.75, with beer and sake alongside. Try the FUNACHU, any one of many branches, two of the best being opposite *Asakusa's Kokusai Theater* and on Avenue B opposite Mita police station. I think you'll enjoy TATSUOKA in the alley parallel to the Ginza behind *Matsuzakaya Department Store* (phone 571-3581 or 5214), which features chicken supreme, from Nagoya. Besides the *yakitori*, try the *"Matsu"* course for $2.75, the *"Take"* meal for $2.20, or the *"Ume"* repast for only $1.65, plus 10 per cent tax and service charge. *Nagoya chicken* is to the bird what *Kobe beef* is to the cow.

BATAYAKI is a first cousin to sukiyaki, the only notable exception being that *batayaki* is prepared in a sauce less pungent than that used for sukiyaki. The *batayaki* variety is also of a soybean base but mixed liberally with butter: hence the name *"bata,"* the Japanese pronunciation of our "butter." The Japanese prefer grated radishes as a base for eating *batayaki*. For *batayaki* at its best, I suggest: TARUTARAN on the *Sumida River* near *Asakusabashi* or MATSUZAKAYA on the Ginza.

OKARIBAYAKI is less well known but typically Japanese. It is comprised of finely sliced wild game and adorned with chrysanthemum leaves, sprouts, and vegetables, all prepared in a special *okaribayaki* grill. For my money, FUJINO is the best of the *okaribayaki* restaurants, but other lovers of this samurai swordsmen's delight swear by OHTORI, in a tiny alley near the Ginza Sembikiya (everyone knows this place).

This latter place serves a bubbling hot, utterly delectable hunter's dish, the *kamonabe:* duck chunks and vegetables served together with hot noodles in a marvelous and piquant sauce.

SUSHI RESTAURANTS. Along with sukiyaki and tempura, the more daring may wish to try Japan's premium dish, *sushi* or *sashimi*—that is, raw fish that can be described as fish fillets rolled in rice, in a kind of rice sandwich. Many *sushi* shops are laid out much in the tempura shop style. Patrons sit at one side of a gleaming wood counter and watch countermen dexterously rolling riceballs, mixed with raw fish, shell fish, and vegetables and flavored with horse radish. Before you, under glass, are the wares: perch, mackerel, seabream, flounder, shrimp, yellowtail, tuna, octopus, cuttlefish, mullet, crab, salmon, ad infinitum. At your signal, the man scoops up a glob of vinegared rice from his wooden tub and moulds the fish of your choice into the mass, touching it off with a dab of soy sauce applied with a paint brush.

Sushi is eaten with the fingers usually, the *sashimi* raw fish strips with chopsticks. A side dish of ginger plus strong dark tea helps.

Raw fish, ugh? Not at all. The Dutch like raw herring dripping brine; Americans go for raw oysters . . . Japanese like the rest of the fish family raw. It's that simple to understand.

Places? Try the OZASA behind the *Imperial* on 4th Street or the SUSHI-SEN a few yards away up a tiny alley. There are literally thousands of these shops, often several per block. Other good ones include the one in the *Nikkatsu Hotel* basement or anywhere in the *Tsukiji* fish market area.

KABAYAKI RESTAURANTS. Don't squirm and wriggle like an eel; just plunge your chopsticks into the pretty lacquered box where the scented eels, baked and simmering, lie on their bed of pearly rice. This is an unusual treat, a really tasty Japanese delicacy, and good for the health so swear the natives besides being mm-m-mm good.

Eels are served broiled or roasted over charcoal, on spits, dipped in sweet *sake*-sugar-soy sauce. Golden brown, they melt in the mouth. With rice or by themselves on the bamboo skewers, this is simply marvelous food. OHWADA is tops among the *kabayaki* restaurants. It's located on the second lane east of 5th Street between Z and Annex Avenues (phone 571-0793). Open daily nine A.M. to 6:30 P.M.; closed Sundays. A very famous eel place is CHIKUYO with two branches, one on Z, the other on Y at *Kyobashi* next door almost to the *Modern Art Museum*. Or you may wish to dine in style at the YAMA-NO-CHAYA *(Mountain Tea House)* on *Diet Hill* behind the *Sanno Hotel* (phone 581-0656/0585). Wonderful!

TORI NO MIZUTAKI RESTAURANTS. Here's a dish from Old **Nagasaki,** a simmering chicken broth filled with succulent vegetables, herbs, sake, spices, egg yolks, all dished up from a large pot. A meal in itself accompanied by rice, tea, and pickles. It's a party dish, like sukiyaki or tempura, enjoyed best with good friends and good talk. The best restaurant I've found is the fabulous JISAKU on the *Sumida River* near *St.*

Luke's Hospital. An elegant Japanese style restaurant that can summon up *Geisha* entertainment from the chic *Tsukiji* quarter nearby if you wish.

SAKE, pronounced "sah-kay" with the emphasis on the first syllable, is a rice wine which is a Japanese institution. Its service is a ritual. The wine is heated before it is served, and when drunk by the Japanese always dispensed from a special ceramic *sake* bottle, frequently of dove gray or blue on white design. This narrow-necked dispenser has the capacity of about a pint. The *sake* "glass" is of the same ceramic design but is minute in size and has a capacity of a good sized thimble. A limited number of more modern, less traditional Japanese will serve *sake* chilled in the summertime, but whether ordered by a son of Nippon or a foreigner, the *sake* is heated unless special instructions are given to the contrary. Unless you are in a Japanese style inn, you may order the *sake,* should you so desire, in its original clear glass bottle and drink it from a tumbler of your own choosing. This is not considered to be in the best Japanese Emily Post tradition, however. For years, I have heard horrendous tales of the potency of this national brew. Either I have an extraordinarily high resistance to alcohol or these stories are grossly exaggerated. I don't know which. I believe the latter to be true. The taste is pleasingly sweet. If the *heurige*—new wine—of Austria were heated, it would have about the same sweet-waterish taste of *sake*. On the other hand, the *heurige* does pack much more of a wallop. A sukiyaki meal and *sake* are as inseparable as Damon and Pythias.

BEER. The *Asahi* beer is a great favorite with the Japanese. It is advertised and served universally. I am far from an authority on this subject, but purely in the interests of research I have consumed a bottle of *Asahi*. To my uneducated tongue, it would seem that there is no great difference between an American beer and *Asahi*. The bottles are rather larger than our normal beer bottles and the price a bit less.

WESTERN ALCOHOLIC BEVERAGES. The bars in all western style hotels and restaurants, as well as many Japanese inns, are well stocked with pretty much the same alcoholic beverages that would be found in your favorite domestic bistro. Scotch whisky predominates, followed by bourbon and gin. Various liqueurs are available as is Scandinavian akvavit. The "shot" is a bit smaller than in your favorite stateside bar and the price is a bit higher, but neither noticeably exaggerated. There is no need to go thirsty.

SOY SAUCE. The Random House *American College Dictionary* defines soy sauce as "a salty, fermented sauce much used on fish and other dishes in the Orient, prepared from soy beans." I cannot emphasize too strongly how important a part this sauce plays in the Japanese cuisine. It is not only used in connection with fish but as a sauce for sukiyaki. It is also used generously in preparing chicken and steak and is utilized as a garnish as well as an ingredient.

As a matter of fact, I can think of no place where this tasty bit is not likely to appear. I, for one, like soy sauce. However, it might or might not appeal to your palate. I suggest that you try it. If you find that it does not enhance the flavor of your meal, be sure to tell the waiter whenever ordering: "No soy sauce." If you don't you will almost certainly find it in (or on) some part of your lunch or dinner.

CHOPSTICKS. Sooner or later, you will be called upon to dine with chopsticks in the Orient. My principal advice in regard to these gracious dining implements is "relax and enjoy them."

Curiously enough, even the most inept westerners ultimately find little or no difficulty with these typical Oriental implements. The very first time I tried them I was soon deftly picking up such difficult objectives as isolated peas and beans singly and in groups.

The trick is to get started with the proper grip and to keep your fingers completely relaxed. Place the one chopstick between your thumb and index finger. Anchor it firmly in the bottom of the crevice. The chopstick should be resting in its socket in your hand about two-thirds up the length of the implement. Rest the chopstick on the finger next to the little finger. Hold the other chopstick as you would a fountain pen lightly and easily between the index and second finger. With the least bit of practice, you will soon be stoking the Oriental vittles with ease, grace, and gratifying results. Bear in mind that many of the Oriental ceramic dishes in which your food will be served are small and relatively deep. They may be held in the left hand in front of and close to your chest to make the chopstick journey shorter and less hazardous.

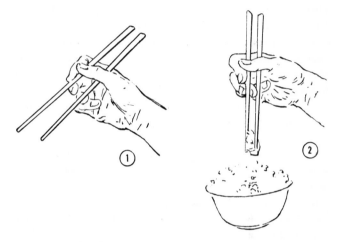

In **Japan** the chopsticks employed in public restaurants are usually made of wood. In the homes throughout the Orient as well as in restaurants outside of **Japan,** these eating devices are frequently made of bone, plastic, or of ivory. These are a bit more difficult to cope with, they're slipperier, but can also be mastered with a modicum of patience.

If you wish to look like an old pro, be sure that each time you have your implements set for action that you place them on the napkin or table surface to be sure that the ends are precisely even. It is impossible to eat efficiently if the chopsticks are not evenly matched.

When not in use, the chopsticks should be put to rest on the table leaning on a small ivory or porcelain "chopstick pillow" designed for this task.

HOSTESSES, as such, are no novelty to most semi-sophisticated seekers of entertainment, but the Japanese variety are quite unique both as to their number and decorative qualities. There are myriads of unusually attractive gals who swarm gracefully through all Japanese night clubs and most bars. These hostesses are not to be confused with *Geisha* girls. Not at all. They are a separate, select clique all their very own. Some are daintily attired in native silk kimono-type garb, others in Chinese dresses slit almost to the thigh, and yet others in the smartest of western formal or informal dress. These girls have been selected because of their beauty and often because of their ability to converse intelligently in English, though in some instances their linguistic and mental attainments are not their outstanding attribute.

These entertaining young ladies are well informed as to the local lore. They can be helpful in recommending shops, sight-seeing information and itineraries, and pleasant off-hour pastimes.

In some of the night clubs, the hostesses will come to your table only if invited. In the more intimate type of bars and other night clubs, they will join you at your table without special invitation.

If, when a hostess joins you at your table, she immediately presents you with a hot towel, please don't be insulted. This is a polite gesture. Use it. You will find it refreshing. If your stay is a lengthy one, you are quite apt to have more piping hot towels presented.

Not only are these lovely creatures gifted conversationalists but they dance lightly and gracefully. They will answer questions or chatter amiably as the situation requires.

Three, four, or five hundred hostesses in a night club are commonplace. In at least one, the *Metro* in **Osaka**, one thousand and one hostesses are employed.

I need not mention that night clubs are commercial institutions. Irrespective of how much pleasure they afford, everything has a price tag. The hostesses are paid by the hour. Usually three dollars per girl per hour in the better establishments, less in others. This amount will be added to your bill. It does not necessarily include the gratuity.

I am a Jack Benny type "thirty-nine year old" bachelor and could in good conscience pursue the matter of the hostesses to a more exciting finale. But I haven't. Several of my close friends and associates are authorities on such subjects as "dames." From them, I have had more comprehensive reports than from my own personal experiences. I am told that because of the very high rate of pay for their company in the night clubs and bars these girls are extremely independent in their personal relationships. They earn as much money as many executives, often receiving generous tips which are relatively "tax-free" income. They can pick and choose their friends and their pleasures. It seems inevitable, however, that birds, bees, and butterflies will always be with us. So will extracurricular activities. There are rules . . . and there are exceptions. Like other services and commodities, the price varies greatly.

TOKYO COFFEE BARS. Throughout **Tokyo** there are thousands of small, intimate, and quite delightful "coffee bars" steeped in local color and atmosphere. The unusual thing about these little charmers is that each of them features a different type of music more or less à la Muzak. The GINZA TACT, near the *Imperial,* features "music and coffee." This is strictly classical music. You may come, have refreshments, and despite the featured "music and coffee" you may be served alcoholic beverages as well while you request your favorite classical music. Such language is universal. Other of the coffee bars feature "cha-cha-cha," "rock and roll," operatic, or Japanese music, but each one confines its entertainment to its own particular specialty. Prices are low. You may spend an hour or more over a simple cup of coffee and be enthralled by your favorite type of music.

The TENNESSEE (Avenue Z, off the Ginza) is the head-quarters for the bebop Japanese teenagers. It features American jazz and hillbilly music. The kids sip coffee to cowboy rhythms belted out by Japanese artists who have memorized the words from records, but I'll bet a fortune cookie they have no inkling of their meaning. There's a similar spot—the MIMATSU—also on Avenue Z.

RESTAURANTS AND NIGHT CLUBS

TOKYO

FRANK'S STEAK HOUSE, Honsho-cho, 9 Banchi, Yotsuya, Shinjuku. (Phone 351-7071 or 351-7729). It would be difficult, if not impossible, to find a more taste-titillating or elegant restaurant. For many years, *Frank's* has been a favorite of the elite and celebrated in **Tokyo**. Now it is even more so. Recently an enthusiastic group of epicureans took over the management, superbly redecorated the entire domain, and brought the cuisine to a point of virtual perfection. The charcoal steaks, especially known as the house specialty, are unsurpassed. The cocktail lounge is intimate, well stocked, and a spot where you are certain to see well-known international personalities. There are small, enchanting private dining rooms should you wish to have a special party. *Frank's* tasty New York cut, T-bone, chopped prime beef, *filet mignon,* sirloin steak, and tenderloin steak are served sizzling from the broiler. From the flaming swords one may choose *filet mignon en brochette,* chicken kabob, and assorted seafood kabob.

The appetizers, seafood, and salad selections are enough to make this international diner dizzy with wonderful memories and breathtaking anticipation. Don't miss *Frank's.*

CHO-YA, off D between 10th and 15th (phone 481-5577). A pearl in a sea of pearls. Here, behind an unpretentious fence, hides a dream teahouse where some of the country's best suki-yaki is prepared at your table and served with the simple elegance and grace that charms the western fancy. When the *jochu-san* (Japanese kimono'd waitress) ties your husband's shoe laces upon your departure, he'll be spoiled for life. Best for parties of four to twelve, a phone reservation is a must, and an interpreter in the party is desirable. A five minute taxi ride from the *New Japan* or *Imperial Hotel*. (The foregoing description of *Cho-ya* has come from the heart, and the pen, of that intrepid and sophisticated traveler, Ralph Michaels.)

The CRESCENT, Avenue A between 15th and 21st (phone 431-1222/3125). Here in the heart of the capital of the Land of the Rising Sun is a French restaurant par excellence . . . one of the best in the entire Far East. Set in an old English-type cottage, the atmosphere is intimate and charming. Though the staff is Japanese, the chef and his assistants have been trained in **France.** The *escargots, Fois gras naturel, soufflé fromage,* French onion soup, and roast *filet* of beef are as Gallic as you would find in the finest Parisian or Provençal restaurant—or even at my favorite *Jacques'* in **Chicago.** *Magnifique!* The hors d'oeuvres, main dishes, and desserts are a bit of Paris transplanted. For **Japan,** the *Crescent* is reasonably expensive, but by the standards of fine restaurants either on the Continent of Europe or in the United States, it is quite reasonable. Including a drink or two and a full dinner, six or seven dollars a person will cover the tab. Italian, German, and American dishes are also featured on the menu. The view of *Toyko's Tower* from the second floor is superb and recalls the *Eiffel Tower*—and **Paris.** Don't miss it. You can dine no more elegantly in the Orient than at the *Crescent.* Do try it. Reservations for dinner are essential; for luncheon, they are advisable.

THE LITTLE CLUB, 10th between D and F (phone 481-6023). This chic, ultrasmart, sophisticated, and intimate restaurant is located upstairs of the *Copacabana Night Club.* The menu would do credit to the *Grand Vefour* in **Paris, Manhattan's** *Twenty-One,* **Chicago's** *Pump Room,* or **San Francisco's** *Ernie's.* It's *the* place for soft lights, unsurpassed atmosphere, and superb cuisine. My friends and neighbors, Ralph and Ruthie Michaels, are well traveled connoisseurs of impeccable taste. I bow to their enthusiasm. In their well-educated collective opinion, no finer evening may be enjoyed than to dine graciously and well in *The Little Club* and then spend the balance of the evening dancing and being pleasantly entertained in the *Copa*. Not expensive as such super-duper places go. Seven to ten dollars a person will cover a full course dinner, including your favorite beverages. Charming English-speaking hostesses are available from the *Copa* downstairs to wine, dine, and converse with you. Just ask the head waiter. She might be particularly helpful in advising the ladies in your party on shopping, local customs, and sightseeing.

COPACABANA, 10th between D and F (phone 481-5806/8). This svelte night club, like its sister restaurant, *The Little Club,* is elegant. The *Copa* is frequented by smart Japanese and well-informed foreigners. I like its intimate atmosphere . . . not big and brassy but large enough to permit a good-sized dance floor. The band is excellent and the floor show adequate. There are many smart international travelers who will tell you, and I would not disagree, that the *Copa* is the best night club in **Tokyo**. The hostesses are particularly high class and well informed.

CLUB HANABASHA, 10th between D and F (phone 581-1221/8). The *Hanabasha* is situated almost next to the *New Japan Hotel* and cater-cornered across the street from *The Little Club-Copacabana*. Many discriminating night club goers rate the *Hanabasha* equally as chic and attractive as *The Little Club*. It is certainly one of the very best. While the atmosphere of *The Little Club* is intimate and cosy, however, the *Hanabasha* is big and brassy. The pace at *Hanabasha* is rapid. There are two bands which play continuously. They operate on a revolving series of stages, and as the one band leaves, the other one picks up the melody. Not long ago I was there when, for the grand finale, the two bands, some forty pieces, played in unison "When The Saints Come Marching In" . . . stirring!

(N.B. Word was received just as this edition went to press that *Hanabasha* has been closed.)

THE MIKADO Night Club, according to my discerning friend, Joe Grace, is really *something*. Lush, plush, and lavish are the best descriptive words for this incredible "Lido of the Orient." The well paced floor show consists of a combination of sprightly European and exotic near nude Japanese acts. *The Mikado's* veritable horde of Japanese show girls are beautifully complemented by a brace of European lovelies.

The gargantuan shows are presented at seven and nine, with the second show being the happier choice since all guests at the first show must vacate the premises in time for the nine o'clock show patrons to be seated. Uniquely *The Mikado* employs no hostesses. But, then, there is no dancing at all. One sits, eats, and enjoys considerable expanses of undraped female forms.

Mikado's main menu is "fixed" and, while there is an à la carte choice, it is minuscule, and one endears oneself with the waiter not at all by choosing from it. It must be borne in mind that this is a huge emporium seating 1,500 goggle-eyed, hungry guests. Everything on the table d'hôte menu is standard except the main course which includes a choice of steak, chicken, lobster, or open-faced sandwich dinner with corn *potage,* vegetables, salad, ice cream, and coffee or tea. The cost of the foregoing dinner, including tips and taxes, is about $8.40. For an extra $3.25 per table one can obtain a superior location, well worth the small additional charge. Foreign and domestic wine and liquor may be purchased in addition.

Located not far from the *Imperial Hotel, The Mikado* is in a side alley so narrow and difficult of access as to present guests arriving in and intending to depart in taxis a very considerable problem of ingress and egress. When one leaves *The Mikado,* so do 1,499 others, and cabs immediately become scarcer than hair on Yul Brynner's head.

Should you choose *The Mikado,* it would be well to have your own private car which can be hired inexpensively for all, or part, of the evening, and which can be awaiting your departure at a prearranged site.

CHINZANSO, Avenue M near 15th (phone 941-0116).

About fifteen minutes from the center of town by taxi. Great fame has descended on *Chinzanso* by virtue of its unique setting. The garden consists of seventeen acres of landscaped loveliness replete with a pagoda, rose arbor, stone garden lanterns,

temple and shrine, and dim mossbound ponds. In the spring, summer, or fall, this beautiful outdoor restaurant is a must, preferably for lunch, weather permitting. The specialty of the house is Genghis Khan barbecued beef and chicken which consists of grilled meats and fowl, and vegetables served for four or more persons who are seated at the table around a brazier. During inclement weather, the braziers are brought inside. Don't fret about your frock or suit coat. Generous full-size napkins are provided. In this rather considerable layout, there is a special tempura bar and Japanese-style dining room. The outdoor grill accommodates more than four hundred diners simultaneously. In June there are brilliant "firefly festivals" every night.

INAGIKU, Off 18th between W and X (phone 671-0828). *Inagiku* is extraordinarily interesting as it combines the atmosphere of an old Japanese restaurant with a semi-modern effect.

There are cocktail lounges in which one sits and sips on the floor, sans shoes, while in the restaurant itself a concession has been made to the modern age. Here the circular tempura bar has been provided with comfortable western style stools on which one may dine while seated upright . . . and dine, I might add, on tempura the likes of which may some day serve as a substitute for the food of the gods. The chefs enter their domain, incidentally, by means of a trap door in the subterranean depths of the restaurant. Chopsticks? But of course. *Inagiku* is a great favorite among the younger successful Japanese businessmen. I like it, too.

MISONO, Near 10th Street and Hardy Avenue (phone 591-7823). This is one of my very, very favorite places. Famous for grilled steaks, chops, and chicken, I would heartily recommend that you give top priority to trying the steaks. There are only four tables in the restaurant. Each seats approximately nine people and has its own hot plate grill on which steak and vegetables are grilled. The steaks are cut into small squares which may be readily handled with chopsticks. When the meal has been succulently completed on the grill, the chef pushes the entire assortment to you, or your party, where it is kept warm on the edge of the grill. You take the portions you desire onto your plate by chopsticks and when ready to replenish it is still piping hot. Obviously, reservations are essential. Even with reservations, if your party is less than nine, you will have somebody else at your table. But this is fun. Closed the first and the sixteenth of each month. You'll find other branches of MISONO off Avenue A between 15th and 30th Streets and near the *Hotel New Japan*.

The IMPERIAL HOTEL. I have written up each of the *Imperial Hotel* restaurants and bars separately on the following pages. I would like to comment specifically and additionally on these extraordinary interesting establishments as a group. Were you to remain in **Tokyo** for a month and never dine outside the *Imperial Hotel,* you could dine more graciously, with a greater variety and in more delightful surroundings, than in any other one place that I have ever been. The *Grill* is perfectly charming, the *Cafe Terrace* outstanding, the seafood in *Prunier* is mouth-watering, and the *Sukiyaki Room* is my very favorite of all. The *Viking* makes you feel as though you were in **Copenhagen** or **Stockholm,** and the *Tempura Room* is both convenient and endowed with delectable cuisine. Please read the individual write-ups of these *Imperial* restaurants, and try as many of them as your time and your eating capacity permit.

FRANCE-YA, near *Gotanda Station* off B Avenue and 45th Street (phone 491-6371), is an ecstatic *coin de Paris,* tiny and distinguished, presided over by owner-chef Imai, a prewar NYK luxury liner *chef de cuisine* and a connoisseur of sauces and wines. Imai's steaks will tantalize your taste buds. Other specialties of the house include French onion soup (yum-yum), buttered seabream, superb Chateaubriand, shrimp and lobster cocktails, mushrooms in wine, and mouth-watering strawberry shortcake. The bar and cellar are excellent. Although this tiny, rather shabby-looking home converted into a dining establishment accommodates only a few clients and is not air conditioned, its delectable food is well worth the discomfort.

RAKUMAN, on *Roppongi Hill* near the corner of D Avenue and 15th Street (phone 401-9476), is a Japanese style cottage restaurant which serves succulent food in a *shibui* manner. The décor of this three-roomed establishment is genuinely Japanese, rich in traditional style. The palate-tempting meats and fowl are cooked before one's wondering eyes on a gas-heated, blackened and polished stone and are accompanied by perfectly prepared and beautifully served vegetables. The hostess at the *Rakuman* is a gracious gentlewoman who personally supervises everything from greeting her guests to seeing that they are comfortable and more than pleased with her cuisine. Reservations are absolutely essential here. While prices are relatively low, one may dine in a strictly native atmosphere.

FUJINO, behind *Shimbashi Station* two blocks from the *Dai-ichi Hotel* (phone 591-6717), is a hunting-style bistro charmingly situated in a genuine Japanese style house which has been modernized without sacrificing its essential atmosphere. The grill, a perforated gleaming helmet-like arrangement kept at a constant sizzly heat, is presided over by a rural kimono'd farm girl who deftly serves one's dinner farm style with chopsticks. *Fujino* meals include the "three heroes of the feast"—chicken, beef, and pork—as they are called by the Chinese sages. There is absolutely nothing "fancy" here, but the meals are authentically typical of Old Japan for those who enjoy native cuisine in its normal setting.

FURUSATO, atop *Shibuya Hill* near the corner of F Avenue and 40th Street (phone 461-6515), affords one the opportunity to enjoy really rustic dining in an old farmhouse, brought piece by piece from Gifu Prefecture and reassembled on the outskirts of this quiet residential section. The original interior has been preserved including its fire-blackened great beam, while the walls are hung with farmers' rice-thatch raincoats and hats alongside crude centuries-old tools. *Furusato's* substantial country food is served Japanese style. At the sound of a gong and drum, a rustic folk dance begins, affording a glimpse into rural Japan. Open daily. Reservations essential.

SHIROBASHA ICE CREAM PARLOR, near the *Imperial Hotel,* was a colossal emporium five stories high, a veritable frozen paradise, with a large orchestra borne from floor to floor by a special elevator. This unusual establishment no longer exists. The building has been torn down and replaced by a gleaming office building. Because of its fame, and since so many visitors to **Tokyo** seek out the *Shirobasha Ice Cream Parlor,* I deemed it worthwhile to call its demise to your attention.

MONBAN, across from the *Grand Palace Cabaret* in the Nishi Ginza three blocks from *Shimbashi Station* (phone 571-9017), is an innovation in Japan. Meals, resembling a Japanese smorgasbord, consist entirely of hors d'oeuvres served tempura style piping hot. Service is at counters and small tables. Eighteen different concoctions are molded by skilled fingers and placed before guests in any quantity one's appetite can conjure. Specialties include gingko nuts wrapped in seaweed, chopped up celery leaves and cuttlefish, white river fish dipped in citron, deep fried pork, seabream seasoned with anchovy, chestnuts rolled in bacon, lobster mashed with quail egg, flounder served with lemon mayonnaise. Alongside one's plate is a wooden pail full of crisp salad vegetables. The popular comedienne, Kiyoko Tange, and a group of her fellow stage performers have sponsored *Monban.* Open daily from noon to eleven P.M. Try it for lunch, not dinner.

LIU YUAN. On A Avenue, one block from the *Crescent Restaurant, Liu Yuan,* the largest, most elaborate and best Chinese restaurant in **Japan,** has as its official address No. 9, 5-Gochi Shibakoen, Minato-ku, **Tokyo,** telephone (501) 8009-7915. From the rice barrel in the kitchen to the tip of the gold pagoda's top, *Liu Yuan* is the most Chinese thing in all of **Japan.** The food is absolutely superb—even better than elsewhere, since in **Japan** the quality of the vegetables and almost all of the meat is much better. Cantonese and Shanghai style cookery, the two cuisines best liked by American visitors, predominate in *Liu Yuan. Liu Yuan's* system of service, menu, presentation and pricing is unique. The restaurant's first floor is open to the general public for "drop in" business where a party of four can reasonably expect to spend no more than $4.00 each for a good selection of Chinese à la carte dishes. *Liu Yuan's* rates, despite its elegance and superb cuisine, compare favorably with other **Tokyo** Chinese restaurants.

The restaurant's second floor is devoted to rooms for private parties, some of which rooms overlook *Tokyo Tower* which, particularly at night, makes an impressive view. One may reserve a room for a maximum of ten persons. The minimum price in the second floor rooms including a meal of shark's fin soup, a fish course, meat course, shellfish dish, vegetable mixture, dessert and tea is approximately $28.00. This price applies whether the party is for four persons or for ten diners ($7.00 each for four, or $2.80 each for ten persons). On the third and fourth floors, the charges are double and triple that on the second floor, being $56.00 on the third floor and $84.00 on the top floor. The higher one ascends, the more one pays and the more extensive the menu becomes.

Oddly enough, Chinese restaurants are unusually popular in Japan. It is thought that there are almost as many Chinese restaurants in **Tokyo** as there are in **Hong Kong.**

PAPAGAYO currently is one of the most noted and popular of the **Tokyo** clubs. Less starkly sensuous than the establishments in *Asakusa,* its performers are nevertheless almost completely nude. The shows, which take place continuously between nine P.M. and midnight, are quite sure to make you gasp. Just in case your erotic tastes are not completely satiated between nine and midnight, you may come for the early show, every night except Sunday, which runs between six and seven P.M. The food is of the Mexican variety and excellent. Hostesses? You bet!

The QUEEN BEE. In the very heart of the entertainment wonderland of the Ginza, the *Queen Bee* is, if not the best, certainly one of the best known night clubs in **Tokyo.** It is fascinating and exciting. The hostesses are garbed in both formal and informal western style dresses, in their native Japanese costumes, and in Chinese dresses with slits practically to their hips. Many of them are amazingly beautiful, and all of them are solicitously attentive. The floor shows go on at nine and ten-thirty P.M., and the closing hour is at half past midnight. It opens at five P.M. The cuisine in addition to splendid Japanese dishes includes fine French and Chinese specialties. A unique feature of the *Queen Bee* is the gay, ornate rotating bar for men only, which seats about fifty lusty males. It is situated to the rear of the terrace tiers and is surrounded by scores of avid hostesses who beg with their eyes to be chosen as a partner by one of the "bar riders."

ASAKUSA has been mentioned briefly under the **Tokyo** write-up, but should be included here because it is also an amazing entertainment area, a combination of Coney Island, Miami Beach, Riverview Park, and the Montmartre.

Here one finds a jungle of bars, restaurants, snack shops, coffee houses, souvenir shops, movie houses, and brashly daring strip shows that draw thousands of sparkling-eyed enthusiasts. Some of the strip joints are limited to "men only"; others are overly erotic . . . sensuality at its pagan peak. There's nothing left to one's imagination. Better try *Asakusa* with a guide or Japanese friend. It's on the rough "native side" with few foreign visitors.

Here one also sees the frantic *pachinko* parlors, where pin-ball games are played by avid males with the rat-a-tat-tat rapidity of World War II machine guns. Gambling is usually involved, but for soap, canned goods, cigarettes, and the like . . . no cash.

The SHOW BOAT—near Ginza. A five-story building entirely devoted to fever-pitch entertainment. This hot spot, gleamingly futuristic in décor, is a Japanese version of a replica of a Mississippi river boat. The dimly lit center is a large five storied well in which the dance band is transported up and down from floor to floor creating a cacophony of noise. The postage-stamp-size dance floor is absurdly small for so large a place. Over four hundred hostesses dressed in nautical attire are always in attendance, while girls dressed as streetcar conductors pick up the tabs from customers' tables.

HIROSHIMA

CASA BLANCA and GRAND PALACE. These are both large, cavernous cafes featuring reasonably priced drinks, moderate entertainment, and three or four hundred hostesses each. The entertainment is so-so and the music enthusiastic.

Here is an opportunity to taste of true middle class Japanese entertainment. Few foreigners go night clubbing in Hiroshima, hence you can become a part of the Japanese scene . . . mostly "men only" drinking, dancing, and being entertained by the hostesses. It's different.

NOTE: As **Hiroshima** goes—cabaret-wise, bar-wise, night club-wise—so goes the Japanese nation. In any major city, and in almost every small one, too, the night world revolves at a dizzying pace, from 5:30 P.M. until eleven P.M. or midnight legally, or until dawn if you want to find it.

Cities like **Sendai, Fukuoka, Sapporo, Nagasaki, Kumamoto, Gifu, Toyama, Nagano**—to mention a few in case you happen to wander in—all have two to five (or more) big flashy night spots.

Even remote *Shikoku Island*'s quartet of cities—**Matsuyama, Kochi, Tokushima,** and **Takamatsu**—also have the full complement.

Japanese like night life. To deny that is to say there is no sand on the *Sahara,* no drop of salt water in the *Mediterranean,* and no snow atop *Mount Everest.*

KYOTO

DEN-EN. Change, particularly in the Orient, is not only inevitable but accomplished rapidly. *Den-En* was one of my top favorites—as a night club. Glamorous, chic and sophisticated, it had everything. But, alas, *Den-En* has lately changed hands and it is now a teen-agers' "jump and jive" joint. What a pity. Better skip *Den-En* unless you're a teen-ager.

HAMAMURA RESTAURANT. Heartily endorsed by my friend, the knowledgeable traveler Chris O'Malley, who says, "The best sukiyaki I've ever eaten; the atmosphere is charming, much like that of *Cho-Ya* (Tokyo), and the entertainment was delightful. The total bill came to only ¥1500 each person. An outstanding value."

OSOME, BEL-AMI, and GION are three truly delightful **Kyoto** night clubs. I have only just looked into each of them and cannot vouch for the bands or the floor shows, but my good friend, Mr. S. K. Kawana, manager of the *Miyako Hotel,* tells me that they are on a par with the very best.

OSAKA

ALASKA, across from the *Osaka Grand*. This restaurant is as excellent as its name is improbable. Its setting is vaguely reminiscent of the *Tour d'Argent* in Paris. Situated high atop the *Asahi* office building overlooking the canal-river, the evening view is romantically punctuated with flickering lights. The bar is cosy and intimate. The menu selection is the widest I have encountered anywhere. The appetizers include caviar, *pâté de foie gras,* shrimp, fruit cocktail, sardines, stuffed celery, and crab meat, to name a few. The soups are varied and excellent. The seafoods are international. Eggs and omelets are offered in profusion, as are all kinds of spaghetti, frankfurters and sauerkraut, chicken livers, smoked pork chops, weiner schnitzel, and assorted cold cuts. But from the grill come the most mouth-watering delicacies including Kobe sirloin steak from beer-fed, hand-massaged beef. Other specialties include mixed grill, minute steak, tournedos, and ham steak. There is a wide variety of special rice dishes for your choice. The salads and vegetables are excellent. Everything is à la carte, but you may select an excellent meal for between six and seven dollars, not including caviar, but including appetizer, salad, main course, vegetable, and dessert, plus coffee and cocktails. There is another *Alaska* restaurant in Osaka's *Hanshin Department Store.*

HOTEL OSAKA GRAND. The dining rooms of the *Osaka Grand* are delightful. The *Pine Grill* in the basement is as attractive a room as an epicure could wish to choose. The *Maple Room,* second floor, features Japanese food exclusively including tempura, sukiyaki, *kabayaki,* and the "house specialties," the *teishoku* (full "menu of the day") dinners.

The *Smorgasbord Restaurant* on the fourteenth floor commands an excellent view and is a genuine import from the Norseland including all the usual hot and cold delicacies plus ice cold akvavit.

The *Empire Room*—main dining room—on the third floor

serves breakfast from seven to nine-thirty A.M., luncheon from noon to two P.M., and dinner from six to nine P.M. You may order table d'hôte or à la carte. Steak lunches and dinners are featured.

The *Pine Bar* is a convivial gathering place before lunch or dinner as well as between ten P.M. and midnight when special snacks are served. The variety of such snacks varies from *sole meunière* and *filet mignon* through spaghetti *alla bolognese,* to cold meats and fowl.

The *Osaka Grand* is well recommended to you both as a hotel and as a place to dine.

The METROPOLITAN INTERNATIONAL CABARET THEATRE (better known as THE METRO). When you walk into the *Metropolitan,* your eyes will pop saucer size. It is unique in the world. To try to impress you with its size, I can say that this startlingly cavernous institution employs one thousand and one kimono'd and western dressed hostesses. Each time I tried to count the number of tables, I ran out of abacus digits. It is safe to say, however, that between the main floor and the loges-mezzanines there must be in the vicinity of five hundred tables with a capacity of well over two thousand guests.

The management makes quite a "to-do" about the floor show. By our standards, the show is only so-so. However, the costumes are brilliant, the hostesses are amazing, the décor is delightful—as night clubs go—and it's the least expensive thing I have ever found in Japan. The floor shows on week nights and Saturdays are at eight-thirty and ten P.M. and from nine-thirty P.M. on Sundays. The soft drinks run less than fifty cents, beer and *sake* at about a dollar. Whisky, brandy, and similar beverages sell for a dollar and a quarter. Good champagne is about three dollars and fifty cents a bottle.

CLUB KYO. This cosy little bistro is not a night club in the sense that we know such places. Rather it is an intimate bar with soft lights and live piano music. The owner is both gorgeous and clever. Her gals are enthusiastic in their efforts to see that their male and female guests are well cared for. Expensive.

THE ARROW. The atmospheric *Arrow* is a small night club (as contrasted with the cavernous *"Metro"*) which boasts of a lovely garden which one may enjoy either from the bar or from a table in the night club proper. The spectacular shows and concerts are presented both inside the club and in its lovely garden, weather permitting. The *Arrow* is a bit on the expensive side plus a dollar-and-a-half cover charge. It opens at six P.M. daily, with show time being at nine and ten-thirty P.M. Harry Belafonte and Nat "King" Cole have appeared here.

NOTE: Several other mammoth night clubs in the spectacular style of Cecil B. De Mille beckon. They, too, are great, dim, barnlike, female-filled palaces featuring all too corny floor shows. **Osaka** is adequately described, and not just by **Tokyo** city slickers either, as a "city with a village mind." These spots prove it.

If you crave more after hours entertainment, however, try these: CABARET UNIVERSE, CABARET BIJINZA, CLUB LE RAT MORT (watch out here: some call it a "bit of a clip"), CLUB AZAMI, and—if you can get in since it's basically a private preserve for girl-loving **Osaka** millionaires—try the elegant BOTAN, located down in the Kita-Shinchi *North Station* area.

THE PHILIPPINES

TAGAYTAY

TAAL VISTA LODGE, at **Tagaytay,** is scenically situated high over *Lake Taal* and encompasses an eagle's eye view of the awe-inspiring volcanic crater and the smouldering valley below, one of the most spectacular settings in the Far East. You may enjoy a cool refreshing drink on the terrace and choose from either a native Filipino menu or enjoy a good American style meal, as your fancy may dictate. The food is more than satisfactory, which, coupled with the view, makes the hour and a half drive each way more than worthwhile. The motor trip from **Manila** to **Tagaytay** is frequently mentioned as being of an hour's duration, but don't go that fast. If you do, you won't enjoy the colorful settings to their best advantage. The unique native homes on stilts form an interesting roadside backdrop, while gay gardens bedecked with a wide variety of tropical flowers lend verdant richness to the area. Fresh fruit and vegetable venders are to be seen along the road, as are plodding water buffaloes pulling ancient plows. Because of its altitude, the temperature is always cooler at **Tagaytay** than in **Manila.** Apart from its restaurant, the lodge accommodates a limited number of sleeping guests.

SINGAPORE

Everything about **Singapore** is exciting. Just to be at this crossroads of the world is to be supercharged with exhilarating stimulation. Local restaurateurs take great pride in the fact that you may, in **Singapore,** order and expect to be served delectably such a wide variety of dishes as Australian oysters, French *escargots,* Borneo bird's nests, steak from Scotland, Indian curries, Indonesian *rijsttaffel,* Scandinavian smorgasbord, Malayan dishes, as well as Continental and British cuisines at their best.

There is a most unique restaurant setup in **Singapore** consisting of a profusion of colorful street dining stalls which are certainly worthy of your inspection if not your dining patronage. These stalls display great quantities of attractive food and are located principally on *Albert Street* (Chinese cuisine), *Peoples Park* (Chinese cuisine), *Beach Road* (Malayan cuisine), *Bedok Corner* on the sea front (Chinese cuisine), and *Koek Road* (Chinese cuisine). There are many others. The stalls have acquired a certain right of eminent domain through squatter's procedures. Don't be fooled, however, that these are just little pushcarts. They're not. You will see as wide a palate-pulsating assortment of intriguing food as ever you would want to see. In the "good old days," men in top hats and tails, brilliantly gowned women, and natives rubbed shoulders at these stalls. Now, well dressed Europeans and Americans are side by side with the natives. Be sure to at least look at the outdoor stalls, if not to dine.

There are three highly colorful and fascinating amusement parks in **Singapore** known as the _Happy World, Great World,_ and _New World_. My friend, Dick Banks, who has lived in **Singapore** for some considerable period of time, gives the _Happy World_ his best marks, though all three are quite interesting. These are basically amusement parks where Chinese operas are performed, cinema theaters are found in quantity, innumerable restaurants abound, amusement concessions of all kinds are operated, and bizarre types of shopping booths will invite your patronage. Entertainment is the order of the day at each of the three _"Worlds."_ Here, too, you will see a great cross section of the world's population laughing and having a good time. Be sure to see the _"Joget Modern"_ which is a special Malay dance where the partners attempt to be as close as possible without touching each other. There are dance halls with partners available if desired.

The **Singapore** drinking water is quite pure. You may consume it directly from the tap. Your room boy will also have brought you vacuum carafes of ice water—also quite pure.

LIQUOR. But of course one will want to try a **Singapore** _Gin Sling_. Everyone does. I detest gin, but all of my life I had dreamed of walking nonchalantly to the _Raffles_ bar and ordering the world-renowned local specialty. I did, and what fun it was.

This state has been a British bastion for more than a century, and their habits prevail. If one orders a whisky, it will of course be Scotch whisky. In the bigger and better bars, one can find bourbon, though sometimes it takes a bit of searching. Unless requested, ice will normally not be served with drinks, but there is plenty available; one has but to make one's wishes known. A Scotch and soda is known in smart **Singapore** circles as a *stengah*, which means literally half Scotch and half soda.

The ELIZABETHAN ROOM in the *Raffles Hotel* is one of the most cosmopolitan restaurants in the world. Neither the bar in the foyer nor the restaurant itself is large. They are both distinguished meeting places for sophisticated travelers, however. *Raffles* serves smorgasbord luncheons à la the Vikings on Monday and Thursday in the *Elizabethan Room*. Other days the luncheon and dinner cuisine is varied, with western dishes being excellently prepared.

PRINCE'S, on Orchard Road, is considered by many to be **Singapore's** best—at least one of its most famous. It is definitely on the elegant side and, as in the *Elizabethan Room* at *Raffles,* many of the guests dress quite formally. Coat and tie are *definitely* required. The wine list and the Continental menu are renowned for their superiority. Reservations are essential. Dancing nightly.

PULAU SELEGU ISLAND FLOATING RESTAURANT and NIGHT CLUB. *Pulau Selegu* is a tiny five-acre island which is reached in about five minutes by boat from *Jardin Steps*. Planned, owned and operated by the enterprising Christina Loke (she was the well-known Mrs. Loke Wan Tho), this multimillion-dollar fun spot is expected to be completed in 1965. The exact opening date had not been announced as this edition went to press. In addition to the glamorous floating restaurant and an exclusive night club, island attractions will include a series of chic chalets, a sea-water swimming pool, badminton courts, and bowling alleys. The night club is to be limited to members only, but visitors may become temporary members by producing their passports.

TAIWAN (FORMOSA)

TAIWAN CUISINE. The Taiwan cuisine provides an endless variety of succulently prepared, authentic Chinese specialties, including: *Cantonese, Hunan, Peking (Peiping), Szechuan,* and *Shanghai*. For descriptions of these cuisines please see page 236 (**Hong Kong** Dining).

The MONGOLIAN BARBECUE, a colorful Chinese concoction from the Northlands, offers a generous feast, prepared with great flourish, and known, alternatively, as a Genghis Khan barbecue. The Mongolian barbecue brazier is more vigorous than the regular charcoal grill, shooting its searing flames skyward in a brilliant display. The groaning hors d'oeuvres tables are generously decorated with platters of spicy, marinated raw beef, venison, wild boar, mutton, and heaping mounds of green uncooked vegetables. The diner makes his choice of the uncooked victuals, selects his all-important sauces and seasoning, and passes to the end of the table where he hands his choices to a clever chef presiding over the charcoal-filled broilers. The seething flames, the sizzling meats, and the spitting oils present an unusual sensory experience. When cooked, the Mongolian feast is something extraspecial for your chopsticks. As when coping with Swedish smorgasbord, you are expected to go back to the Mongolian grill again and again. Try rice wine with the Mongolian barbecue. It is taste stimulating and, while it seems weak, has a high degree of potency.

The CANTONESE BREAKFAST is delicious, consisting of hot or cold Cantonese pork sausage, steamed dumplings filled with mincemeat, ground pork or beef, steamed gingerbread, watermelon, and sometimes a clear chicken soup or broth, and always tea . . . tea . . . tea.

Do-it-yourself gourmets will automatically approve and swear by the SHANSI RESTAURANT on Chung Cheng Road, where the feast is *Huo Kuo,* a chafing dish, which literally means "Hot Pot." The meal begins with a variety of "appetizers" including cold pickles, fish, and fried shredded chicken with slivers of cold boiled ham, chicken, and beef with sliced cucumbers, which are meant to whet the appetite.

Each guest for the "Fiery Pot" is next given his own bowl for mixing the dipping sauce to his own taste. In it will go a choice of raw egg, bean paste, vinegar, ginger juice, sesame seed, soy sauce, shrimp oil, hot sauce, and/or onions. Any and all of the foregoing are combined to create a tangy dressing for the meats, a portion of which is cooked with the meal and part of which is used, uncooked, as a condiment. The "Fiery Pot," placed in the middle of the table over the glowing charcoal coals, exudes an aromatic, appetite stimulating aroma from the cooking beef, pork, lamb, and sometimes game, such as venison, when in season.

The GIRLIE RESTAURANT is a unique specialty of **Taiwan.** For entertainment the Chinese rely, oddly enough, on these "girlie restaurants" or perhaps the somewhat more elegant "wine restaurants," also Taiwanese specialties.

In the absence of floor shows, the attraction of the "wine" and "girlie" restaurants is the becoming bevy of sensuous girls who act as tea and wine pourers, conversationalists, dance companions, confidantes, and, upon occasion, after hours girl friends.

Colorfully lit on the outside and well decorated, there is no outward manifestation of the joys that lie waiting within the gaudy portals . . . and for reasonable prices, too.

The following article has been reproduced in its entirety, without editing, as it appeared in the July 4, 1961 edition of the *China Post Tourism Magazine.* It explains so much more interestingly than I can this specialty of **Taiwan.**

Tourists of Taiwan who are interested in taking a look at Taiwan's entertainment and night life can hardly afford to miss a visit to the island's famous 'girlie restaurants.'

The signboards of these 'girlie restaurants' suggest no mystery and excitement at all because one place is called a cafe and another is called a restaurant. There is nothing on the signboards to advertise what is really in store inside those colorfully lighted and decorated establishments. Local residents and old Taiwan hands, however, all know what excitement and fun can be obtained there.

To many local people, girlie restaurants are the ideal places for them to fulfill their social obligations with plenty of enjoyment to satisfy both the host and the guests.

A girlie restaurant in Taiwan is tantamount in nature to a Geisha house in Japan. In addition to serving delicious Chinese dishes and drinks, the girlie restaurant features charming hostesses who like the Japanese Geisha girls will keep company of their patrons, sing for them and dance for them. Many hostesses of the girlie restaurants are accomplished singers of either popular songs or Peiping opera. And most of them are excellent dancers, from the old fashioned slow fox trot to the most modern off-beat cha cha. The patrons need not pay anything extra for the singing and dancing because these are part of the service.

Many foreigners regard girlie restaurants as places of mystery. Actually, the local people consider a girlie restaurant as a high class restaurant-rendezvous for social activities like any luxurious night club in New York or Tokyo. Therefore, even the fair sex may patronize a girlie restaurant and satisfy their curiosity.

Patrons of the girlie restaurant may have any number of hostesses to wait on them. However, there will be one or two, depending on the number of patrons, hostesses who will serve more or less like waitresses. The hostesses make their living on tips from the patrons. The prevalent amount of the tip for a hostess is NT $80 (U.S. $2). The restaurants stay open until midnight, and you may go there any time between six P.M. and that time, have a few bottles of beer or other drinks, order a dish of your favorite Chinese food, and enjoy tender services of the hostesses until the closing hour. For all of this enjoyment, you will probably have to pay from NT $300 to NT $400 (U.S. $7.50 to $10).

Quite a number of hostesses of girlie restaurants in Taiwan have had a secondary education and speak fairly good English. Usually dressed in the Chinese gown, these girls are good companions to kill your leisure hours in a gay and enjoyable way. Do not miss the girlie restaurant if you want to learn something about night life in Taiwan.

Tung Yuan Kuo Cafe & Restaurant, 87 Yenping North Road, Taipei, the largest and most extravagant girlie restaurant on the island, is staffed with more than 150 pretty hostesses.

WINE RESTAURANTS. In the official government publication, "Welcome to Free China," wine restaurants are described as follows:

'Wine restaurant' is a misnomer and an understatement. Misnomer because a 'wine restaurant' only serves good Chinese dishes and the celebrated Taiwan beer, no wines or liquors. Understatement because the food and the beer are only the secondary provisions offered.

To be frank, a 'wine restaurant' is where one is able to sit in well decorated rooms, enjoy the food and drinks, and at the same time converse with sunshine with charming companions.

'Wine restaurants' are to be found in all major cities of Taiwan with those in Taipei, Kaohsiung and Taichung considered the best. In the small towns, the tea rooms take over.

A 'wine restaurant' is usually a three or four storied building with colorful decorations and flickering neon signs. On every floor, there is an open space in the center where those who wish may dance. Around the space, there are many partitioned nooks. The bigger rooms have round tables for feasts and banquets, with space reserved for rest and conversation. In smaller rooms, only square tables with half a dozen chairs are provided.

When a customer arrives at the restaurant, he is ushered into a room. Then there will come a waiter and waitress. The waiter is to take orders and the waitress on duty to serve the food and drinks. But the customer is always encouraged to call upon the services of other waitresses. They will sit down by his side, engage in conversation, exchange greetings, and comment on the weather. A friendship is either begun or renewed.

When you have seated yourself in a room, tell the waiter or waitress on duty the names recommended by your friend. The owners of the names come pronto. But you must be prepared for their constant departures because a popular waitress may have to circulate among eight or more rooms. She may be able to sit with you for fifteen minutes, only to leave and come back one hour later, with apologies of course.

When the customer is leaving, he has to pay two bills, one for the food and beer consumed (in general, a four man party needs about NT $1,000 (U.S. $25) if only one or two dishes are ordered) plus a tip for the waiter, and the other to the waitresses themselves.

Ask the management for waitresses who are able to speak English or Japanese. Each restaurant has a number of waitresses well versed in these two languages.

The CENTRAL THEATER-RESTAURANT, 120 Chung-shan N. Road, Section II, Taipei (phone 53165), is in a modern three story building housing a large downstairs dining and dancing area and a mezzanine dining balcony overlooking a large stage. Cantonese cuisine is featured. Breakfast from 8:00 A.M., luncheon from 11:00 A.M., dinner from 6:00 P.M., with snacks from 9:30 P.M. to midnight. The floor shows, 9:00 and 11:30 P.M., run the gamut from Chinese opera, local folk songs and dances to acrobatics and modern western music.

THAILAND

The food in **Thailand,** and most particularly in **Bangkok,** is remarkably good. I would suggest now, however, and under-score later as forcefully as possible, that you do not attempt to become a devotee of native Thai cuisine. Don't be a guinea pig in your "home away from home" halfway around the world. Take your Uncle Harvey's word for it: Thai cooking is just "too hot to handle." Unless you have a cast iron tummy, a throat lined with flexible asbestos, and a mouth of marble, you will find that the Thai food will literally "burn you up." There is such a choice of other food available in **Thailand** that it will not deprive you of your dining pleasure if you do not indulge in the local fare. The number of different places to dine is relatively limited, but those that I do recommend are outstanding. You most certainly will not suffer lack of quality, quantity or variety.

Lest your hometown friends should inquire as to the basic ingredients of a Thai meal, I will pass them along to you. The foundation of all Thai meals, in common with all of the Oriental countries, is rice. Thai rice is served fried, boiled, in soup, as a stuffing, and frequently as a hot side dish with green onion shavings, sliced cucumbers, soy sauce, and grated chili peppers. In savoring a full dinner, a Thai family normally will start with soup and will then have fish, vegetables, and a good selection of meat curries, consumed with rice. A favorite Thai soup prepared on a charcoal brazier is *Gang Tom Yam* which includes leaves of the makroot, lemon grass, watercress, prawns, chicken, fish, and *pri-kee-noo* peppers.

Haw Mok, a flaming hot Thai specialty, is made by pounding dry chili peppers, shrimp paste, lemon grass, onions, garlic and salt, and blending them with steamed coconut milk and soy sauce decorated with egg and slices of raw fish. It is served in a large banana leaf.

The hot Thai curry *Gang Pet* includes beef, pork, shellfish, coconut milk, chili peppers, ginger, caraway seeds, the paste of lemon grass, garlic, mashed shrimps, lots of pepper, and wild rice. The Thais are particularly fond of their desserts, particularly concoctions of sweets made from milk, sugar, coconut, and rice. Favorite Thai dishes to top off a meal are: *Salim,* made of thin strips of egg noodles in sugary coconut milk, and *Songakaya,* a coconut milk pudding, served both hot and cold, made from both the whites and yolks of eggs, palm sugar, sticky rice, mangoes, and other fresh fruit.

Tropical fruit is available in abundance. In the preparation of the spicy Thai meals, there is a profound emphasis on various types of spices, particularly a deadly red or green pepper called *pri-kee-noo.* To use this lethal little condiment is like osculating a spark plug with the engine running.

When dining, the Thais use a spoon and fork, a knife being unnecessary since the food consists of vegetables, rice, and precut curried meats which present no need for anything to fall under the knife at the table. The meat invariably has been either skewered or sliced by the chef; in any event, it arrives all ready to be consumed.

In **Thailand** one may have any type of fish that one wishes. Local chefs will prepare seafood in American, European, or

Thai style. The area abounds in shrimp, crab, and prawns from the gulf, while the inland bodies of water are productive of eels, terrapin, and frogs.

There are excellent Thai, Chinese, Japanese, and European restaurants in **Thailand,** as well as establishments featuring genuine American dishes.

It has been mentioned elsewhere, and should be reiterated, that whenever you are planning to sample a Chinese or Thai dinner, it is always better to have four to six or more in your party. The variety is so great and the portions so large that if you do not have a number of persons with whom to share the offerings, you are apt to be disappointed and/or glutted.

Beer drinkers will be pleased to know that the Thai variety of their favorite brew is both good and cheap and that there is also a choice of imported beer from America, **Hong Kong, Holland, Japan, Denmark,** and **Germany.**

One should not drink the water out of the taps. Excellent bottled water is available at all good restaurants and in your hotel. Be sure to use it.

BANGKOK

NICK'S NUMBER ONE. This is the most famous restaurant in **Bangkok** and, outside of the hotels, certainly by far the best. Please don't be oversold in advance, however. If you are, you're sure to be disappointed when you first see the layout . . . but not when you leave. Just don't expect much physically, and you'll come away enchanted with your luncheon or evening. The restaurant and kitchen are housed in an ancient building reached in ten or fifteen minutes by car from the center of town. Nick's establishment reeks with antiquity. During the rainy season, June until September, meals are taken indoors. The remainder of the year the taste-thrilling dishes are served in a series of garden bowers, of varying sizes, which furnished with tables seating from four to a dozen or more diners. The setting is unique and superb. You will find the outdoor dining comfortably cool in the evening. No bugs, and the breeze is pleasant. Nick is a fabulous Budapest-born character. He was educated in **Vienna, Paris,** and **Lausanne, Switzerland,** and has traveled the world over many times. He speaks French, Hungarian, German, English, and Thai, to name a few. His cuisine is varied, but I particularly liked his *Kobe steak* garnished with Roquefort cheese. He features Hungarian dishes as well as an international cuisine. Ask him or his beautiful Thai wife what they recommend. They're very reliable. I can recommend *Nick's Number One* highly.

The MAIN DINING ROOM, *Rama Hotel,* is an attractive room with pluperfect service. The waiters are handsomely garbed young men, most of whom speak high school English or better. The two cheerful, cute Thai hostesses and the head waiters all speak excellent English.

The daily table d'hôte menus are imaginatively gotten up and more than adequate. The excellent à la carte fare features American and European specialties. I would hasten to mention that should you wish to have something that is not on the menu, don't hesitate to mention it to the hostess or head waiter. I have found that they can come up with most anything your heart, or more particularly your tummy, might desire. One of the features of every meal is a large attractively arranged fruit platter with choice of such elegant local produce as fresh pineapple which is cut before your eyes, fresh papaya, watermelon, and bananas. I have found that a luncheon of cold *gazpacho* and a variety of fresh fruit is excellent.

HOTEL RAMA COFFEE SHOP. The *Rama Coffee Shop* is unique and one of the most unbelievable eateries I have ever encountered. If you could photograph it devoid of the cute, colorfully costumed Thai waitresses, you would never believe that it was halfway around the world from your home town. The menu is eye-opening in its variety. You may have as an appetizer a seafood cocktail, chilled papaya, consommé, cream of tomato soup, or Spanish *gazpacho* . . . and believe it or not, the *gazpacho* is every bit as tasty as if it were served in its native Catalonia. The morning specialties include every conceivable type of egg concoction as well as pancakes, waffles, sausages, sweet rolls, fruit, ham, or bacon.

The cold buffet and sandwich selection includes Swiss cheese salad with spring onions, sliced beef vinaigrette, frankfurters with potato salad or tomatoes and cucumber salad, cold cuts with mixed salad, ham, roast beef, salami, chicken or cheese sandwich as well as three decker club sandwich, hamburger sandwich, cheeseburger sandwich, and all types of cheese. You may have ham steak with pineapple, broiled sirloin steak, or prawns.

For dessert, there are caramel cake, caramel fruit salad, caramel pineapple pie, Danish and French pastries, layer and English cake. In the ice cream department, there is no end to the selection including banana, chocolate, coconut, and pineapple flavors plus sherbets and sundaes, milk shakes, and Coca-Cola, Pepsi-Cola, Seven Up, and all sorts of fruit juices. Unlike most coffee shops, the menu also includes all types of cocktails, brandies, spirits, and beers.

The most expensive item on the menu is a dollar and ten cents. Pancakes are fifty cents, ham and eggs sixty cents. Utopia . . . um-m-m!

The TROPICANA NIGHT CLUB, *Rama Hotel,* is superbly situated overlooking the colorful second floor court area. It is tastefully designed, the décor is rich, and in my opinion it's the best in **Bangkok.**

The RAMA *Cocktail Bar,* located off the lobby, is colorfully decorated, intimate, and cheerful.

Thai classical and folk dances are featured at the *Rama Hotel* every Tuesday, Thursday, and Saturday beginning at nine P.M.

The MAIN DINING ROOM, *Erawan Hotel,* is an air conditioned, cheerful room with excellent cuisine.

LE CHALET, *Erawan Hotel.* The atmosphere of the air conditioned *Chalet* is Swiss. Here you may enjoy fondue as in **Switzerland,** which my old friend and sidekick, Harvey Mason, says he thinks is better even than at *Alpnochdorf* near **Lucerne,** but I think that such a statement is heresy, notwithstanding that it is the expert opinion of one who knows the Orient and Europe intimately. The cuisine of the *Chalet* is made up of a variety of Continental specialties.

The AMBASSADOR CLUB, *Erawan Hotel*. The air conditioned *Ambassador Club*, adjacent to the *Chalet*, is pleasant for after dinner drinks and dancing from eight until midnight. The floor shows are at nine and eleven P.M. On Tuesdays and Fridays, Thai classical dancing is featured.

The NORMANDIE GRILL, *Oriental Hotel*, enjoys a wide sweeping view across the river to the *klongs* and from the rear the terrace overlooks the city of **Bangkok.** The charcoal grill is used to prepare specialties from **France,** but there are many American dishes as well.

RECOMMENDED RESTAURANTS AND NIGHT CLUBS

STATE OF HAWAII

Honolulu

CANLIS' CHARCOAL BROILER—2100 Kalakaua Avenue. Known locally as *"The Broiler,"* this small, charming, and elegant local and tourist favorite specializes in steaks, chops, and seafoods. See special write-up, page 232.

COLONEL'S PLANTATION BEEFSTEAK AND COFFEE HOUSE—International Market Place. You pick your steak and are charged by weight. The *pièce de résistance* comes after your entree when you may choose from the multi coffee confections (there's nothing like *Frosted Coffee Hawaii* on a warm afternoon).

COLONIAL HOUSE (formerly Woody's) and the COCK'S ROOST—International Market Place. Both good. The latter specializes in sandwiches at lunch and prime ribs of beef in the evening.

LE COQ D'OR—1900 Kalakaua Avenue. Small, intimate, chic, and possessed of an outstanding wine cellar. Luncheon served Monday through Friday in the dining room, sandwiches in *Le Bistro*. Soft piano music in *Le Bistro* nightly. Because it is fashionable and small, reservations are essential.

STATE OF HAWAII (cont.)—Honolulu

DUKE KAHANAMOKU'S (formerly *Don the Beach-comber's*)—2318 Kalakaua Avenue. Here both Oriental and American cuisines are cooked to perfection. Sunday night is devoted to a luau, and there's dancing every night. The floor shows later in the evening feature native entertainment.

ELLIOTT'S CHUCKWAGON—1015 Kapiolani Boulevard. Call 581-161, and Elliott will send a limousine to your hotel to whisk you to his restaurant (and bring you back of course). "All you can eat" of the prime rib roast of beef (and it's so good this will be quite a lot) costs only $2.95.

THE EMBERS—311 Lewers (located just off Kalakaua). Charcoal broiled steaks, excellent *Embers* salads, and lobsters are the specialties. Cocktails daily from five P.M., dinner from six to eleven P.M., entertainment Friday and Saturday nights. Piano music in the bar nightly.

FISHERMAN'S WHARF—Ala Moana Boulevard overlooking *Kewalo Basin*. Typical of outstanding wharf restaurants famous for a wide selection of fruits of the sea including lobster thermidor, *chioppino,* poached opakapaka, and mahimahi. *Fisherman's Wharf* has two "decks"—the upper deck which is the captain's bridge featuring the *Mermaid Bar,* and the main deck which offers the *Seafood Grotto* and the *Snug Bar.*

GOLDEN DRAGON—*Hawaiian Village Hotel.* All of the Chinese and Japanese dishes served in this, one of the many fine restaurants of the *Hawaiian Village,* are both authentically prepared and temptingly served.

HALEKULANI HOTEL COFFEE SHOP. This is probably *the* most popular spot for breakfast or mid-day refresher snacks. You may dine here in your swimming togs if you desire.

HOST INTERNATIONAL DINING ROOM—*International Airport.* Overlooking the gorgeous *Aloha Gardens* at the new airport terminal, the *Host Room* features multilingual waitresses, a most palatable international cuisine, and sumptuous views. The *Host Coffee House,* serving snacks and sandwiches, is in the same area.

STATE OF HAWAII (cont.)—Honolulu

THE HOFBRAU—2448 Kalakaua opposite *Kuhio Beach*. German cuisine is featured including à la carte and table d'hôte. Light lunches are available. Organ music at the cocktail hour. Trio music from 9:30 until closing.

ISHII GARDEN—1720 Huna Lane. One of the loveliest of the Japanese tea houses of the Islands. Beware, however: reservations require that you have a minimum of four in your party.

JOJAN—Waialae-Kahala area. The food (broiler specialties featured) is quite good, and the inside floodlit waterfall is sure to intrigue you. One of **Honolulu's** newest dining establishments that seems to be catching on rapidly.

KOPPER KETTLE—Royal Block, Kalakaua Avenue, around the corner from the *Royal Hawaiian*. A snack bar-coffee shop brimming with activity from seven A.M. to midnight. Short orders, lunch, dinner, salads, sandwiches. Free parking in the rear. Not expensive.

KYO-YA—2057 Kalakaua Avenue. Another Japanese tea house with delicious full sukiyaki dinners a specialty.

LE SALON ROUGE—1441 Kapiolani Boulevard. Here is a bit of epicurean France transplanted to our island paradise. The menu ranges from *escargotis* to *flambées* with numerous delights interspersed between.

LAU YEE CHAI—2020 Kuhio Avenue. One of the most beautiful of the Chinese restaurants of the Islands. You'd better fast for at least twenty-four hours before dining here since I literally had to be rolled out after one of their seven course dinners. There's an outdoor dance floor.

M'S COFFEE TAVERN—112 Merchant Street (downtown) and M'S RANCH HOUSE—5156 Kalanianaole Highway (about twenty minutes' drive from *Waikiki*). The *Tavern* is a favorite for luncheons in town with wide praise accorded the meals, especially the choice desserts. The *Ranch House* features a good grill selection and is noted for its excellent service.

MAILE LANAI ROOM—*Kahala Hilton Hotel*. For elegant dining in regal splendor, the *Maile Lanai Room* is unsurpassed.

STATE OF HAWAII (cont.)—Honolulu

It ranks as one of **Honolulu's** top Continental restaurants. A small orchestra provides rhythmic accompaniment to the room's gently dancing fountains. Outdoor terrace for moonlight dancing. Open for luncheon and dinner. Cocktails in the smart *Maile Lounge*.

THE MERRY MONARCH—298 Beach Walk at Kalakaua. The menu is international in flavor, but I call your special attention to the Hawaiian-Haole dishes. Cocktails from 3:30 P.M., dinner from 5:30 P.M. Expensive and justifiably so.

MICHELE—*Colony Surf Hotel*. This distinguished restaurant offers French cuisine par excellence. *Michele* is located in a most attractive room overlooking the sea. The sophisticated décor is brilliantly matched by unsurpassed service and foreign food at its best. A piano bar adjoins the restaurant.

MOCHIZUKI—647 Kunawai Lane. A Japanese tea house in a garden setting, again where a minimum party of four is required.

QUEEN'S SURF—2709 Kalakaua Avenue. American cuisine is featured on the regular menu, but the luaus which are a Sunday attraction are among the best on the island. Luaus on Tuesdays and Thursdays, too, at various times of the year. This is an island favorite. The BAREFOOT BAR of the *Queen's Surf* is perhaps the most amusing of the after dinner spots. Shows are at ten P.M. and one A.M. The Bar opens at nine P.M.

THE RED VEST—2310 Kuhio Avenue. This is one of my "special sleepers," particularly recommended by those discriminating gourmets, John and Virginia Diggs. Small, chic, and elegant—clams and artichokes, broiled steaks and chops, as well as salads, are all featured specialties *de la maison.* Soft piano music in the bar. Luncheon from 11:30 A.M., dinner from five P.M.

LA RONDE enjoys a most unique and unusual setting atop the sparkling new *Ala Moana Building*. Opened in 1961, it is not only new but also chic and smart. *La Ronde* consists of the entire top floor of the building which makes a complete

STATE OF HAWAII (cont.)—Honolulu

circular revolution each hour. Your view from *La Ronde* encompasses a wide sweep of *Waikiki,* the shimmering waters of the vast *Pacific,* the airport, *Diamond Head,* the downtown area of **Honolulu,** and the countryside beyond. The cosmopolitan cuisine emphasizes French cooking. *La Ronde* is a show place to be remembered.

ROYAL HAWAIIAN HOTEL. For luncheon buffets, the *Surf Room* is just about the best in Hawaii. Fabulous dinners are to be had in the *Monarch Room*—both Hawaiian and Continental cuisines. See special write-up, page 231.

LA SCALA—255 Beach Walk (*Waikiki*). Here one may enjoy Italian cuisine. Open for luncheon and dinner.

SURF RIDER HOTEL, CAPTAIN COOK ROOM. New and scintillating. Luncheon is served from noon to two P.M., dinners from six to ten P.M., with night owl specials until midnight. Cocktails in the *Captain's Galley.*

THE SWISS-HAUS—*Royal Tropicana Hotel,* 340 Royal Hawaiian Avenue near the *Waikiki Post Office.* In this coffee shop one finds cheese fondue and other Swiss specialties. Breakfast, lunch, and dinner are served.

TAHITIAN LANAI—*Waikikian Hotel* (beside the pool), Ala Moana Boulevard. A fine outdoor restaurant in an idyllic setting. Tahitian chicken, lobster, and broiled steaks for dinner are specialties. Cocktails in the *Papeete Bar.*

TOP OF THE ILIKAI—*Ilikai Hotel.* The top floor dining room and cocktail lounge is reached by a spectacular nonstop 27-story ride in the exterior glass elevator. From these impressive, heady heights, one can enjoy a lovely view of the sea and surrounding mountains. Broiler specialties.

TOPS—Ala Moana Boulevard at Ena Road. Another coffee shop, always open. Clean and attractive with display cooking. The *Clown Room* features cocktails. Carved sandwiches eleven A.M. to two P.M. Monday through Saturday.

TRADER VIC'S—926 Ward Street at King (across from the *Ward Plantation*). This original Polynesian restaurant is

STATE OF HAWAII (cont.)—Honolulu

truly unexcelled for fine Cantonese cooking—roast beef, charcoal steaks, and planked mahimahi, plus, of course, fabulous explosive rum drinks. Luncheon Monday through Friday 11:30 A.M. to 2:30 P.M., dinners nightly five to eleven P.M.

TREE FOR TWO—International Market Place. High in a banyan tree, this tiny thatched tree house is a honeymooners' paradise. Squab and champagne are served in utter privacy—quite expensively.

THE TROPICS—1607 Kona Street. Exceptionally well-prepared meats, a wide variety of Island specialties, and colorful salads. Not expensive.

WAIOLI TEA ROOM—3016 Oahu Avenue *(Manoa Valley)*. Delectable lunches and tea snacks. See special write-up, page 232.

THE WILLOWS—901 Hausten Street. A delightful setting for a particularly tempting luncheon. Both Hawaiian and American cuisine prepared to perfection. Although best known for curries, almost any order you may place will exceed your fondest expectations. The garden surroundings are lovely—and don't leave before you've had one of the pastries.

WISTERIA—1206 South King and Piikoi Streets. Japanese tea house. A bit more modest than those listed previously but with a fine Japanese fare.

WO FAT—115 North Hotel Street. This downtown Chinese restaurant is a favorite of the local Chinese. Definitely not small or intimate, for color and cuisine it is highly recommended.

HONG KONG

Kowloon

AMBASSADOR HOTEL ROOF RESTAURANT. The flawless cuisine, of the Continental variety, is served here against an almost overwhelming backdrop of Hong Kong and its harbor. See special write-up, page 240.

BOMBAY ORIENTAL—19 Prat Avenue. All kinds of Indian and Oriental plates, including *"Tandoori"* chicken.

HONG KONG (cont.)—Kowloon

CARLTON HOTEL—Taipo Road. Beautiful view. See special write-up, page 242.

CHAMPAGNE RESTAURANT—Kimberley Road. One of Hong Kong's finest dining spots for Shanghai dishes.

DYNASTY ROOM, *Ambassador Hotel*. Authentic and varied Cantonese cuisine. See special write-up, page 241.

GADDI'S—*Peninsula Hotel*. See special write-up, page 240.

GOLDEN CROWN—66-70 Nathan Road. Exquisitely beautiful authentic Chinese décor. Chinese cuisine exclusively.

GOLDEN PHOENIX—Nathan Road. This is one of the fine restaurants located above the *Dairy Farm Supermarket*. Here the dishes are European and very good, too.

HIGHBALL RESTAURANT—Manson House, Nathan Road. Cantonese dishes. See special write-up, page 241.

KOWLOON RESTAURANT—221D Nathan Road. Just about the best spot in Hong Kong for the specialties of the Province of Szechuan. I might mention here that they're rather hot and highly spiced but really good.

MARCO POLO—Peninsula Court. One of Hong Kong's most delightful restaurants and night clubs. See special write-up, page 240.

HOTEL MIRAMAR RESTAURANT and NIGHT CLUB is highly recommended. The food is delectable, with specialties

HONG KONG (cont.)—Kowloon

of the Peking and Cantonese styles. There is dancing and an evening floor show. Try it. You'll like it.

"PLAY PEN"—*Peninsula Hotel* (on the mezzanine). This is an ideal place to get one of those satisfyingly large, so typically British, breakfasts.

PRINCESS GARDEN—Princess Theater Building, Nathan Road. The Peking specialties served here have earned fame throughout the world. See special write-up, page 241.

PARIS RESTAURANT—Shaw Building, Nathan Road. Another fine restaurant offering Chinese plates.

RIKKI'S—Cameron and Carnarvon Roads. Besides the Russian offerings which are the specialty of the house, the barbecued steaks and chicken will melt in your mouth. Good cakes and pastries.

SIAMESE STARLIGHT ROOF—*Hotel President.* Lavish Thai décor, panoramic view of harbor. Fine cuisine.

TKACHENKO'S—3 Hankow Road. A less pretentious bit of Russia but good.

WINTER GARDEN—221 Nathan Road. There's no going to **Shanghai** these days, but all of the specialties of that exciting city are prepared here with care and most tasteful results. Also *Peking* dishes if you desire. See special write-up, page 242.

Victoria and Environs

BUTTON ROOM—*Mandarin Hotel.* Charming roof garden restaurant by day and romantic rooftop supper club by night. Local and western gourmet delights.

CAFE DE CHINE—China Building (top floor), Queen's Road. Fine view. Excellent Chinese dishes.

CAFE DE PARIS—8/8A Queen's Road Central (almost adjacent to the renowned "P.G."). Charming, intimate French restaurant . . . of the smaller variety. I personally found the cuisine to be quite good.

CHAMPAGNE ROOM—*Sunning House Hotel.* An intimate

HONG KONG (cont.)—Victoria and Environs

and enchanting spot for an evening of dancing. The orchestra is small but good. The excellent European menu is varied.

EAGLES NEST—*Hilton Hotel.* Luxurious top floor supper club. Sparkling view of Hong Kong and its harbor. Choice cuisine, dancing, and top entertainment.

GLOUCESTER LOUNGE—Gloucester Building, Pedder Street. You'll have a wide selection of excellent European dishes to choose from at this exceptionally pleasant restaurant. Ideal for morning coffee or afternoon tea.

JIMMY'S KITCHEN—Theater Lane, China Building (ground floor). Russian, American, and European epicurean choices. This restaurant is one of the most famous in Hong Kong. I would say from my own observations that Jimmy's fine reputation is highly deserved not only because of the flavorsome cuisine but also because of the gracious personal attention which he manages to render to each of his patrons.

THE LIDO—Repulse Bay. An interesting night club, fairly far out from town. Both European and Chinese dishes are available.

MAJESTIC RESTAURANT—Empire Apartments, King's Road. An excellent night club which features a good floor show and tasty Chinese food.

MAXIM'S—Telephone House, Des Voeux Road. A quiet, plush dining and dancing rendezvous with French overtones.

OPIUM DEN—*Hong Kong Hilton.* Smart cocktail lounge with sleek *cheongsamed* waitresses. Swinging entertainment nightly.

PARISIAN GRILL (known far and wide as the "P.G.")— 10 Queen's Road Central. This elegant and popular restaurant is deservedly Hong Kong's most famous. The director, Emile, is most justly proud of the French dishes prepared in his kitchen, but any of the many other European and Russian specialties to be had here are worthy of your attention. Reservations are absolutely essential. A visit to Hong Kong would not be complete without at least one meal here.

HONG KONG (cont.)—Victoria and Environs

RAINBOW RESTAURANT—Winner House (ground floor), 310 King's Road. One of the nicest of the hotel dining spots. The European cuisine is very fine. Music.

HONG KONG HOTEL-REPULSE BAY—Repulse Bay. If you get the chance, take an excursion out this way on Sunday and stop here for the Sunday noon smorgasbord served on the porch overlooking the bay.

SADDLE & SIRLOIN—*Mandarin Hotel*. Magnificent restaurant, one of Hong Kong's best. See special write-up, page 240.

SKY RESTAURANT—8A Queen's Road, Great China House (top floor). All of the Cantonese dishes are available for your dining pleasure.

SPANISH ROOM (PARAMOUNT)—Des Voeux Road Central. This restaurant features . . . guess what? . . . unusual Spanish food and music offered by a trio. Both are very good.

TAI TUNG—234 Des Voeux Road. Probably the most popular of the Cantonese restaurants of Hong Kong. You might try *dim sum* (those tiny buns filled with meat, seafood, and vegetables) here. It's a succulent specialty.

WINNER RESTAURANT—Winner House (top floor). A good Cantonese dining spot much frequented by the local Chinese and patronized by discriminating tourists as well.

The Floating Restaurants in Aberdeen

I'm sure you'll enjoy trying a meal on one of the floating restaurants located in *Aberdeen Harbor*. As you would expect, they specialize in seafood prepared in all sorts of exotic ways. See my special write-up on the SEA PALACE and TAI PAK on page 239.

ISTIMEWA RESTAURANT—147 Wong Nei Chong Road, Happy Valley. Decorated completely in Indonesian style with sylphlike Chinese waitresses in native costume. The only Indonesian restaurant in Hong Kong, *Istimewa*'s culinary ingredients, including spices, are imported from Indonesia. Specialties include *gado-gado, rendang, gulai-gulai,* and *achar.*

JAPAN

Tokyo

RESTAURANTS

AKAHANE—off Avenue D between 10th and 11th Streets (phone 481-4023). Wild game in a Japanese setting, with cosy *tatami* rooms fronting on a Japanese lawn. The accent is on fowl—the wilder, the tastier—including grouse, woodcock, quail, pheasant, and that grand Japanese specialty, the *yama dori* (mountain chicken). A picturesque place; expensive but well worth it.

ANTONIO'S—on Avenue D between F and 15th Street (phone 408-1971). An Italian mariner turned landlubber serves up his homeland's best in a fine Neapolitan atmosphere. Spaghetti, lasagne, fettucine, chicken cacciatore . . . Antonio has them all. Open from eleven A.M. until the wee small hours.

BANGKOK—basement of Miharabashi Building at 10th and Z (phone 541-6274). Siamese (Thai) cuisine is featured, but a word of warning: the food of ancient Siam, modern Thailand, is really "hot." Be very, very careful. The food here is highly spiced, and besides the Thai specialties, you'll find a good assortment of Chinese and South Sea dishes. Open 11:00 A.M. to 10:30 P.M.

CAFE TERRACE, *Imperial Hotel*—off Lobby, New Building. The décor is most unusual . . . colorful lanterns, Japanese red decorative fences separating the terraces, and a pool. The à la carte service is magnificent and the food at its zestful best. For dinner the pool is covered over for dancing. The *Imperial* orchestra is justly renowned. Open 10:00 A.M. to midnight.

CHACO—A between 10th and 12th (phone 591-2024). *Chaco* charcoal broiled steaks are prepared to the accompaniment of aromatic sizzle and visual delight right before your eyes. This popular new restaurant opens at 11:00 A.M. and closes at 11:00 P.M. or midnight, depending on the night.

CHIANTI—on 15th between B and D (phone 481-7546).

JAPAN (cont.)—Tokyo

As Italian as its name, this tiny Italian restaurant serves practically all of the specialties of its native land. The chef has a fantastic international background—a Chinese serving authentic Italian food in Japan! The cosy accommodations are extraordinarily limited. Be sure to make reservations. Open twelve noon to three A.M.

CHINA HOUSE—almost diagonally across from *Sun-ya,* Avenue A. One of the very finest Chinese restaurants in all of Japan.

CHINZANSO—Avenue M near 15th (phone 931-0116/9). Mouth-watering Mongolian barbecued dishes. The garden setting is particularly inviting in the spring and fall. See special write-up, beginning on page 259.

CHO-YA—off Avenue D between 10th and 15th (phone 481-5577). The sukiyaki and tempura are paragons of Oriental perfection. *Cho-ya* is a sparkling setting for a festive group party. I am devoted to this exquisite restaurant. Open five to eleven P.M. See special write-up, page 256.

THE CRESCENT—Avenue A between 15th and 21st (phone 431-1222 and 3125). Marvelous French delights. Splendid view of *Tokyo Tower* from second floor tables. See special write-up, page 257.

DOH-HANA—near Ueno Station, N between Ginza and 4th (phone 831-5509). *Doh-Hana* is graced with exquisite gardens and will offer you food at its zestful best in lovely Japanese style rooms. I recommend this to you as one of the very best sukiyaki and tempura restaurants. Traditional tea ceremonies performed. Open eleven A.M. to ten P.M.

FRANCE-YA—near *Gotanda Station,* off Avenue B and 45th Street (phone 441-1976). Tiny and ultra-plain but superb dining in an atmosphere essentially French. See special write-up, page 262.

FRANK'S STEAK HOUSE—Honsho-cho, 9 Banchi, Yotsuya, Shinjuku (Phone 351-7071 or 351-7729). One of my very favorites. See special write-up, page 256.

JAPAN (cont.)—Tokyo

FUJINO—behind *Shimbashi Station,* two blocks from the *Dai-ichi Hotel* (phone 591-6717). The finest traditional Japanese cuisine in lovely Old World surroundings. See special write-up, page 262.

FURUSATO—near the corner of Avenue F and 40th Street atop *Shibuya Hill* (phone 461-6515). Rustic gaiety in the heart of **Tokyo;** Japanese cuisine at the height of perfection. See special write-up, page 263.

GEORGE'S—near Avenue A and 15th Street. A romantic little island of enchantment, a short half block from the second *Misono,* also off Avenue A, characterized by soft lights and sweet romantic music. Steaks are a specialty, but be sure to try the mouth-watering Mexican hors d'oeuvres.

GRILL ROOM, GINZA TOKYU HOTEL—near the *Kabuki Theater,* Ginza (phone 541-2411). The *Grill Room* has several exquisite specialties. Perhaps the finest is their taste-animating roast beef. Also oysters on the half shell, oyster stew, and Blue River trout. Open daily from noon until eleven P.M.

GRILL ROOM, IMPERIAL HOTEL—basement of North Wing, New Building. A cosy, chic grill room with displays of food which invite your selection. À la carte service only. Open 11:30 A.M. to ten P.M. The adjoining bar is elegant.

GUEST HOUSE—on 17th Street off D, close to the *Chinese Embassy* (phone 4081-5763). This would have to be good, catering to the palates of the diplomatic Chinese from *Formosa,* and it is. There's an attractive main dining room with a picture window overlooking the handsome garden and a cluster of pleasant party rooms as well. The food, both bland and spicy, satisfies 'most any taste; the bar offers one of the finest selections in **Tokyo.** Open until midnight.

HAMASEIHO—near *Omori Station* on the road to *Tokyo Airport* (phone 771-5185). A tempura restaurant in a classic Japanese garden, this is the perfect spot for that farewell dinner before take-off. Host Sasazuka knows exactly how to serve

you hot food topped off with a brandy toast while still enabling
you to be whisked away in your airport-bound limousine in
time to meet your plane schedule. This is a very favorite haunt
of cinema celebrities, both foreign and local, with special party
rooms and discreet, English speaking service.

HANACHO—V near U, across from the *Meijiza Theater*
(phone 671-6271). The delectable cuisine of *Hanacho* is enhanced by the picturesque setting which reproduces the aura
of Old Japan. The recipes and rituals of antiquity are preserved. An especially good place to try that tempura meal you've
heard so much about. Open from noon until 9:30 P.M.

HANA-NO-KI—5th between Annex and Utility (phone
571-0073). *Hana-No-Ki* provides an outstanding French menu.
Luncheons are crowded. Reservations suggested. Most convenient to the *Imperial Hotel*.

HONG KONG—Avenue A between 10th and 12th (phone
591-3715, 5066). *Peking* cuisine is the specialty. Service is excellent. Open eleven A.M. to ten P.M.

HOTOTOGISU—near *Nakano Station,* easy to find (phone
381-0191). For Buddhists, vegetarians, and lovers of a unique
but ample table. Only vegetables, but, oh, in what taste and
profusion they are served! This garden restaurant's skilled
chefs do wonders with baking, roasting, stewing, frying, boiling, and, above all, flavoring. To see is to believe . . . and worth
the adventure.

IMPERIAL HOTEL, MAIN DINING ROOM—Front
Lobby, Main Building. A colorful, charming Old World restaurant. Breakfast is served from 7:00 to 9:30 A.M., luncheon
from noon to two P.M. Dinner is not served.

INAGIKU—17th between W and X. Outstanding tempura.
See special write-up, page 260.

INDONESIA RAYA—Ryokan Avenue near 10th (phone
501-8505). Indonesian atmosphere and cuisine. Open eleven
A.M. to eleven P.M.

IRENE'S HUNGARIA—off 5th between St. Luke's and

JAPAN (cont.)—Tokyo

Canal (phone 561-6327/1010). Deservedly famous, *Irene's,* in a dimly lit, mysterious basement, not only offers you the chicken paprika and Hungarian goulash as you would expect but also Gypsy steak and a complete Continental cuisine. Open 11:30 A.M. to 10:30 P.M.

ITALIAN GARDENS IN GINZA—Ginza near Z Avenue intersection (phone 571-7553). Suzi will recommend the best of the *Italian Gardens.* Try the spaghetti; it will melt in your mouth. Prices are lower between 10:30 A.M. and 2 P.M. Open 10:30 A.M. to 2 A.M.

KETEL'S—near Z Avenue between Ginza and 5th (phone 571-5056/1210). A truly typical German menu is featured at *Ketel's.* Because of its popularity, reservations are suggested.

KUNG CHIAO TING (PEACOCK)—*Hotel Ginza Tokyu Restaurant* (phone 541-2411). Very popular. A Chinese buffet service, an Oriental smorgasbord, is featured. The steam table menu changes daily, particularly attractive because you can see the finished product before making up your mind. Open from noon to 2:30 P.M. and from 5:30 to 9:30 P.M.

THE LITTLE CLUB—10th between D and F (phone 481-6023). A pure delight. See special write-up, page 257.

LIU YUAN—No. 9-5 Shiba Park, Minato-Ku (phone 581-6221). Superb Chinese cuisine. See special write-up, pages 264–265.

A. LOHMEYER—on 5th Street near Z Avenue (phone 571-1142). *Lohmeyer* features German style cooking with an extensive Teutonic menu. Other European specialties are available. Open 11 A.M. to 10:30 P.M.

MATSUBAYA—Asakusa (phone 841-1937, 871-6724). The classical tempura and sukiyaki are superlatively presented to the accompaniment of old-style *Geisha* dances. Open 6 P.M. until midnight. Closed the fourth Sunday of the month.

MISONO—three restaurants: one near Avenue A and 15th Street, another near the *Hotel New Japan,* and the other near

JAPAN (cont.)—Tokyo

10th and Hardy Streets (phone 591-7823). Steak is the order of the day . . . and night. See special write-up, page 261.

MONBAN—across from the *Grand Palace Cabaret* in the Nishi Ginza three blocks from *Shimbashi Station* (phone 571-9017). The meals here are composed entirely of hors d'oeuvres: all sizes, shapes, and varieties—and mountains of them. See special write-up, page 263.

NAIR'S—10th Street almost at Z Avenue (phone 541-8246). Want some mouth-watering curry, as hot or as cold as you wish? This is the place. Fresh chapaties and vegetarian dinners. You can buy your own curry powders and chutney here, too, from affable Mr. Nair. Open daily from noon to ten P.M.

NICOLA'S—on 15th Street between B and D Avenues, across from *Club 88* (phone 481-4702, 7983). Fifty varieties of pizza and the best in town. Nick holds the recipes and they're his creations. If you tire of the authentic Italian dishes, he'll point you toward his steak bar with justifiable pride. This is an outstanding spot for an inexpensive, quiet lunch, dinner, or late hours gaiety.

PAPAGAYO—Avenue B and 10th Street (phone 501-9604). This typical south-of-the-border Mexican hot spot should be most notably remembered as a night club because the excellent, though hot, Mexican dishes are interspersed with a lively naughty nude show.

PEACOCK—Maruzen Building Basement, Ginza between W and X (phone 271-2358/9). A top-flight restaurant which features fine steaks and chicken. French food is also a specialty of the house. Open eleven A.M. to ten P.M.

PEKING MANSION—in the New Building of the *Shiba Park Hotel* (phone 431-4131). The cuisine is fourteen carat genuine *Peking* prepared by **Tokyo** imported **Hong Kong** trained chefs. Not expensive. Reservations essential. Open eleven A.M. to ten P.M.

PHOENIX ROOM, *Imperial Hotel*—off Lobby, New Building. An excellent restaurant serving Continental breakfasts from

JAPAN (cont.)—Tokyo

six A.M. until seven A.M., full breakfasts from seven A.M. to ten A.M., luncheon from noon to two P.M., and dinner from six P.M. to nine P.M.

PRUNIER ROOM, *Imperial Hotel*—above the *Grill Room*. The French style seafood dishes are famous. Crowded for both lunch and dinner. Be sure to make a reservation.

PRUNIER ROOM, TOKYO KAIKAN—Avenue A between Y and Z (phone 271-2181). The service is marvelous and the seafood delectable. For the most discriminating gourmets. Open twelve noon to 9:30 P.M.

QUEEN BEE—Ginza between St. Luke's and Canal (phone 561-8331). The fame of the *Queen Bee* as a night club is widespread, but the management is justly proud of its Chinese and French cuisines (with more emphasis on the Chinese, please) served throughout the evening. See special write-up, page 265.

RAKUMAN—on *Roppongi Hill* near corners of D Avenue and 15th Street (phone 401-9476). Only three rooms in a Japanese style cottage, but, please, don't miss this dining paradise. See special write-up, page 262.

RAN-GETSU—Ginza, practically across the street from the *Matsuya Department Store* (phone 561-2313). In this colorful restaurant you will be served by kimono-clad girls in either a traditional Japanese style room or at comfortable tables with western style chairs. The sukiyaki of the house is made of *Matsuzaka* or *Kobe beef* (remember?—the beer-fed, hand-massaged type).

RENGAYA—D between 12th and 15th (phone 481-4856). This French restaurant is typified by its country style décor and presents perhaps the widest selection of French cuisine of all. The *Sole Bonne Femme* reminds me of Paris. The fricassee of chicken is excellent, and the braised tongue and crepes à l'Orange are particularly appealing. French cheeses prevail. The excellent wine of the house is made locally. Open 11:30 A.M. to two A.M.

RHEINLAND—on D Avenue between F and 15th Street

JAPAN (cont.)—Tokyo

at Kasumi-cho. Your host, Herr Dokteur Jakob Fischer, bon vivant, Japan expert, author and ex-Berliner, supervises this tidy establishment. Lots of *Gemütlichkeit,* fine German cuisine, and merriment the year round, with draft beer served in the garden in the summer. The Doctor converses in seven languages and is a mean hand at after-dinner chess. Open late.

RO-RAN—near Minamisakuma-cho bus stop on Mita Street (phone 501-9209). Another well recommended Chinese restaurant. All the best specialties. Closed Sundays.

SANWA—5th between Z and 10th (phone 571-3329). A venerable establishment featuring a French menu. The bar is mammoth. Open eleven A.M. to two A.M.

SEIKO-EN (CHONG-YAN-WAN)—near the famed *Tokyo Onsen* (Turkish Bath) in the Ginza Roku-Chome section (phone 561-5883). Korean food at its very best. Try *pulgogi,* the Korean barbecue of beef strips, cooked in ginger-soy-*sake* sauce. I think you'll also enjoy the iced oxtail and the many other superlative native soups.

SIN HO RAI—Kakyo Building Basement, Avenue Z between 15th and 18th (phone 541-7485). *Sin Ho Rai,* in the heart of **Tokyo,** specializes in **Taiwan** *(Fukien)* dishes, considered to be the most Chinese of all. Closed the first and third Sundays of each month.

STAR HILL CLUB—*Tokyo Hilton Hotel.* Sophisticated supper club. See special write-up, page 189.

SUEHIRO—Annex Avenue between Ginza and 10th behind *Matsuzakaya Department Store* (phone 571-9271). A chain of *Suehiro* restaurants, to be found throughout Japan, feature steak and sukiyaki. Very well known. Good food at reasonable prices. Not air conditioned.

SUKIYAKI ROOM, IMPERIAL HOTEL—Main Building. This is my very favorite of all. You have a choice: you may be seated on a chair with the sukiyaki ceremony performed on the table before you, or you may choose to try the taste-stirring sukiyaki in the Japanese style room upstairs where you will sit

JAPAN (cont.)—Tokyo

on the floor and be served by kimono clad girls. The setting and service are both the very best. Open for lunch from noon to 2 P.M. and for dinner from 5:30 to nine P.M.

SUN-YA—Avenue A between 10th and 12th (phone 431-4369). *Sun-ya* is particularly popular with Tokyo's foreign community. It is elegantly modern. *Shanghai* specialties are featured. There are those among the elite of the travel world who consider *Sun-ya* to be the best Chinese restaurant in the world. Could be!

SZECHUAN—Avenue A between 10th and 15th Streets (phone 591-7573). Tops in hot spicy western Chinese cooking. Try the shark fin soup, the soy-soaked jelly fish, the carp smothered in peppery vegetables, the hot chicken slices laced with ginger and spices, the shrimp in the shell garnished with chili, and scores of other bitey Chinese dishes. The bar is good, but try the Chinese yellow wine, *laoh-chiou,* served hot with a bit of rock crystal sugar. Open daily until eleven P.M.

TAKANAWA PRINCE HOTEL—facing the *Shinagawa Station* (phone 441-4121). The extensive garden is lovely, the cuisine that of Old Japan, with a modern European-type menu also being available.

TAKANE—in the *Tsukiji Geisha* area (phone 541-6585). The waitresses in this, one of the best known of the traditional Japanese tempura restaurants, are selected for their beauty. Their costumes are incomparably lovely kimonos. It is considered locally to be elite.

TEMPURA ROOM, *Imperial Hotel*—Main Building. As I have mentioned so frequently, everything in the *Imperial Hotel* is simply delightful. So is the *Tempura Room.* The luncheons are from noon to two P.M. and dinners from 5:30 to nine P.M.

TIMPACHI TEMPURA—near the *Imperial Hotel.* A Ralph Michaels favorite. 'Nuff said.

TEN-ICHI—5th at Z (phone 571-1949). Yabuki-san, the owner-chef, is known throughout the Far East for the perfection of his tempura. His tender loving care is given to each

JAPAN (cont.)—Tokyo

meal served. I know you'll like everything about this traditional establishment. Open from noon until 9:30 P.M.

IMPERIAL VIKING—New Building Basement, *Imperial Hotel.* Both the *Skal Bar* and the *Imperial Viking* of the *Imperial Hotel* are worthy of the praise of my Scandinavian ancestors. When you walk into the smorgasbord setup of the *Imperial Viking,* you have but to flash your mind's eye half way across the world to Scandinavia . . . you're there. The food is absolutely authentic.

ZAKURO—Kikai Boeki Basement, in front of *American Embassy* (phone 481-2478). Beef at its best in sukiyaki and many Japanese *teishoku* (table specialties) such as *sashimi* (raw fish), *domburi* (bowlfuls of rice mixed with eggs, chicken, vegetables, seafood, and eels), *ton-katsu* (Japanese style pork cutlets), *suimono* (clear soups), *miso-shiru* (bean-paste soups), and *momo yaki* (charcoal broiled chicken thighs). The atmosphere is traditional Old Japan, tailored to lovers of mellow, old things, while the décor leans toward folkcraft.

NOTE: Because of the wide assortment of Chinese specialties, parties of four or more are suggested to take best advantage of the cuisine at the Chinese restaurants we have listed. See **Hong Kong** for a complete description of Chinese fare.

SNACKS

GINZA SNACK—*Hotel Ginza Tokyu Restaurant* (Annex at Canal). The *Ginza Snack* never closes. You may have a light snack or an à la carte order.

HIBIYA ALASKA—second floor of Hibiya Mitsui Building, across the street from *Yurakuza* and *Hibiya Theaters.* Open all day every day serving inexpensive snacks.

MEIDIYA—Ginza between St. Luke's and Canal. Here you have an American style restaurant serving American specialties. Inexpensive. Open eleven A.M. to eight P.M., it is excellent for a "break" while out shopping. Very popular.

JAPAN (cont.)—Tokyo

NIKKATSU COFFEE SHOP—Basement, Nikkatsu Building. Located in the *Arcade* shopping area near the barber shop. The service is rapid, the choice wide. Convenient and inexpensive.

NIGHT CLUBS

CLUB AOI SHIRO—on F beside the *Jingu-mae Subway Station* near Yoyogi Street (phone 401-6134/6). This dining and dancing establishment, featuring so-so French and Chinese cooking, was started off on the right foot by the music of Smiley O'Hara a couple of years ago and has been on the beam ever since. Many foreign entertainers—Filipinos, Europeans, and Americans—come here regularly. The shows are really quite good, the hostesses are unusually refined, and the décor pleasant.

CLUB BAMBOO—Ginza. From two P.M. to midnight, this exotic club features fast moving floor shows and intriguing atmosphere for those "out for adventure." (Temporarily closed as of going to press. Check locally to see if reopened.)

COPACABANA—10th between D and F (phone 481-6023). This is my favorite; see special write-up, page 258. (The "Copa" is in the same building with the smart *Little Club* restaurant.)

CROWN—Ginzanishi, 5th between Annex and Utility. A mammoth night club with lots of exquisite hostesses. Chic and expensive. Excellent floor shows are presented nightly at 9:30 and 10:30 P.M.

CLUB HANABASHA—10th between D and F, near the *Okura* and *New Japan Hotels* and the American Embassy (phone 581-1221/8). One of the best; see special write-up page 258. N.B. It is with sadness that I report the closing of the *Club Hanabasha*. Word was received of its demise just as this revised edition went to press.

LI-PO BAR—*Tokyo Hilton Hotel* (phone 581-4511). The décor is dedicated to the great Chinese poet who died in 762 A.D. There is a piano but no dancing. It is open from noon until 3 A.M.

JAPAN (cont.)—Tokyo

MANUELA'S—10th near Avenue A (phone 591-0635). Perhaps the best, certainly the first, of the "wee small hours" spots. Run by a dynamic little lady from **Shanghai** who's a pretty mixture of several nationalities, the steaks sizzle, the tempura bar is wonderful, the combo's hot, and the big band highly danceable. Hostesses are available. Open until 4 A.M.

CLUB MARUNOUCHI—Nomura Building, W and 4th Street (phone 231-0622/3). This establishment features Chinese cuisine, a handful of hostesses, and some of **Tokyo's** best dance music provided by K. Ebihara, his trombone, and his Blue Coats. There is no cover charge for diners arriving before 9 P.M.

THE MIKADO. Gay, gaudy, and popular. See special write-up, page 259.

THE MIMATSU—Ginza and 10th. A large, exciting, highly regarded cabaret which each evening presents exhilarating floor shows. No longer a night club as such, *Mimatsu* is in a category of its own, best defined as a glorified coffee shop featuring jazz music and entertainment spectacles.

MONTE CARLO—Ginza, Utility at 5th (phone 571-5671). A select, expensive, and popular night club with floor shows at 9:30 and 10:30 P.M. Saturday and Wednesday nights are particularly exciting. On these evenings, so-called "bathtub reviews" are held, and the sophisticated place is glistening with sleek, completely nude female forms. This schedule does vary, however, so check. Open 6:30 to 11:30 P.M.

NEW LATIN QUARTER—Basement of *Hotel New Japan* (phone 581-1326). A big, brassy, brilliant night club with oodles of hostesses. The floor shows, which are excellent, are at nine and eleven P.M. While the *New Latin Quarter* unquestionably presents the finest foreign entertainment in **Tokyo**, it is also tops insofar as prices are concerned.

NIKKATSU FAMILY CLUB—Fourth Floor, *Marunouchi Nikkatsu Theater*. Here one may enjoy an unusually lavish and lively floor show. Basically, *Nikkatsu Family Club* is a membership arrangement. Members and their guests form the

JAPAN (cont.)—Tokyo

basis of the clientele. Hotel guests staying in either the *Nik-katsu* or the *Imperial Hotel* are welcome and may make reservations for this huge, attractive, always gay nightery through the information desk of either hotel. The orchestra is excellent. There is also dancing to the strains of a Hammond organ.

PAPAGAYO—Avenue B and 10th Street (phone 501-9604). A naughty nude show combined with "hot" Mexican cuisine.

QUEEN BEE—Ginza between St. Luke's and Canal (phone 561-8331). One of the most famous in the Orient; see special write-up page 265.

THE SHOW BOAT—near Ginza. Colossal; see special write-up page 266.

STARLIGHT LOUNGE—*Hotel Okura* (phone 481-8011). Cocktails on the tenth floor with postcard views of **Tokyo.** Enchanting by day, all-encompassing by night. A combo plays from six P.M. to eleven P.M. No dancing.

RESTAURANTS AND NIGHT CLUBS OUTSIDE TOKYO

Beppu

Apart from the hotels, which are in themselves magnificent, the principal restaurants in **Beppu** are the NUMBER ONE and NUMBER TWO TOYOKEN, both owned by the same man. The SWAN completes the trio of leading **Beppu** restaurants. These are intimate establishments of twenty to thirty tables serving à la carte meals with a wide variety of international dishes from which to choose.

The NARUMI is a Japanese style restaurant in which one removes one's shoes and dines on sukiyaki or tempura.

The TSURUMI and the GIN are cabarets which feature taxi dancing type hostesses. Both serve food but are principally known for their music, drinking, dancing, and entertainment. The striptease will be introduced twice each evening to excite the emotions. *Tsurumi* is the larger and brassier of the two.

JAPAN (cont.)

Hakone National Park

HOTEL KOWAKI-EN'S fabulous *Tatami Room* is as heartwarming and soul satisfying an experience as one can derive from gracious dining at its best. The *Tatami Room,* adjacent to the main dining room, is mat covered and furnished with low brilliant-hued tables. There are cushions on the floor and convenient back rests from which vantage points one may enjoy the finest of sukiyaki and other Japanese dishes. The *Night Salon* for dancing and cocktails is gay, yet cosy.

Miyanoshita

HOTEL FUJIYA. Memorable dining may be enjoyed at its best in the *Hakone National Park* at the *Hotel Fujiya.* Breakfast, lunch, and dinner are served in the main dining room, with breakfast from seven to ten A.M., lunch from noon to two P.M., and dinner from six-thirty to nine P.M. The *Grill Room,* where à la carte service is rendered most appetizingly, is immediately below the main dining room. It is open from ten A.M. to ten P.M. The *Kikka-so,* an ex-imperial residence situated across the famed Tokaido National Highway, is operated as an annex to the *Fujiya.* This completely Japanese institution, one which I can highly recommend, serves traditional sukiyaki banquets.

Kobe

RESTAURANTS

BALALAIKA. Cuisine as Russian as the Kremlin, and tasty.

CHIKUYOTEI—Kitanagasa-dori, Ikutaku. A Japanese restaurant famed for its eels. Open daily 11:00 A.M. to 9:00 P.M. Closed the second Monday of each month.

DONNALOIOA. A transplanted corner of Italy in the Meikai Building doors away from the *Oriental Hotel.* Run by

JAPAN (cont.)—Kobe

Joe (of course). Featured are ravioli, spaghetti, fettucine, and lasagne.

KING'S ARMS TAVERN. This is England, lads and lassies, replete with roast beef, Yorkshire pudding, steak and kidney pies, and fish 'n' chips, all authentic and succulent. This is an English pub, a club for the British colony, and there's a dart board, a roaring fireplace, and the Queen's picture smiling down on the gathered patrons. There's another tavern, same management, in **Tokyo,** right below the *American Embassy.*

KOBE STEAK—Kitanocho, Ikutaku. The steaks and chops are wonderful. Open daily 11:00 A.M. to 10:00 P.M.

GRILL MISONO (phone 3-2890). The granddaddy of that handsome pair of **Tokyo** steak houses, located on the *Bund.*

MITSUWA—Motomachi-dori, Ikutaku. A Japanese restaurant featuring sukiyaki. Open 11:00 A.M. to ten P.M.

RISTORANTE ITALIA—Ikuta-shinmichi, Ikutaku. Spaghetti, ravioli, lasagne, and other Italian specialties are temptingly offered.

NIGHT CLUBS

AOI SHIRO (phone 2-2950, 3371/2). A mammoth multi-hostessed establishment in Ikutaku.

CASINO—Sannomiya-cho, Ikutaku. The swing band tunes up at six P.M. The floor show begins at ten-thirty. Midnight is the closing hour.

CLUB CHERRY—near *Sannomiya Station* (phone 3-2345). "Plenty of Wine and Fine Women." The same old thing, but if you're on the town, this one's as good as any.

CLUB NIGHT AND DAY—Shimo Yamate-dori, Ikutaku. Good band, lots of hostesses, intimate atmosphere. Open daily 6:30 P.M. to midnight.

KITANO CLUB—Kitano-machi, Ikutaku. The orchestra is good, the entertainers attractive. Floor show nightly. The *Choral Kitano Restaurant* is upstairs and enjoys a sweeping view of bustling *Kobe Harbor.*

JAPAN (cont.)—Kobe

MOONLIGHT (phone 3-0157, 0886). A roaring cabaret, all stops out. In Ikutaku, like so many of the **Kobe** clubs, it's all here: blaring bands, moaning chanteuses, bevies of bosomy beauties, slim drinks, and high prices.

Kyoto

RESTAURANTS

AURORA RESTAURANT—*Kyoto Hotel*. A rooftop restaurant as deserving of high marks for its savory cuisine as it is for its well-remembered panoramic views.

KYOTO ALASKA—Atop the seven-storied Asahi Building at Sanjo-Kawaramachi (phone 23-7200). French style cuisine and **Kyoto** below you with its staggering misty views. One of the famed *Alaska* chain. Need I say more?

HAMAMURA—Somewhat like *Cho-ya* in **Tokyo** . . . and what higher accolades could be sought? Charming atmosphere, cosy local entertainment. The best sukiyaki Chris O'Malley has ever tasted is served here. Highly recommended.

HAMASAKU—In the *Gion Geisha* district's heart. Each mouth-watering Japanese delicacy is presided over by jovial Mr. H. himself. The best in fish, including in season that bubbling delight, blowfish, either in raw strips or in a fiery vegetable-fraught stew. A place for gourmets, and not limited to the Japanese vintage either.

HYOTEI—Behind the *Miyako Hotel* in the templed *Nanzenji* section (phone 7-1282/3). Operated by the 14th generation of Kaichi Takahashi who founded this tea room in a moss garden three hundred years ago in Old Kyoto. Famous, tasty Kyoto style dishes. This is one of Japan's great restaurants, so call and reserve in advance. It's small but elegant.

JUNIDANYA—In a fascinating, hard-to-describe old part of town (phone 6-0213). Famous for beef dinners and the best in that delicious, characteristically Japanese chicken stew, the *tori no mizutaki*.

JAPAN (cont.)—Kyoto

KARAFUNE—Gion Hanami-koji. Here in the heart of the *Gion* district is one of the great and unusual restaurants of Japan. The specialties are sukiyaki, tempura, and terrapin. Each of the numerous dining rooms is decorated with the finest examples of rare, ancient Japanese art. *Karafune* not only has a circular tempura bar and traditional sukiyaki service but is replete with artificial rainmakers and decorated with flags of countries from all over the world. The "Stars and Stripes" will inevitably pop up in the room in which you dine. There is an excellent bar. A specialty of the house is, believe it or not, ice cream tempura. Open every day from noon to eleven P.M.

KYOBOSHI (phone 6-0352). **Kyoto's** greatest tempura house with a branch in **Tokyo's** Nishi Ginza. Soft, succulent lobster, crab, shrimp, and sea bream will melt in your mouth. In the convenient *Nawate* shopping area, *Kyoboshi* is deservedly popular.

KY YAMATO. This is an extraordinarily charming, old, typically Japanese inn-restaurant. The rooms are all Japanese style. The temple lanterns across from the restaurant add romance to the setting. Sukiyaki is the outstanding specialty. Dinner is served by reservation only. Be sure to have your hotel representative call in advance of your arrival.

MISHIMA-TEI—Sanjo Teramachi. The daintily flavored sukiyaki at *Mishima-tei* is outstanding. Also known for a selection of Japanese specialties.

KYOTO PRUNIER—Shijo-Kiyomachi. Grill service only, but the best. Steaks, chops, roasts, broils . . . and seafood.

RASHOMON—On Kawaramachi near Shijo (phone 2-5253, 3307). Guests are cheerfully served charcoal broiled beef, pork, and chicken at the counter. In my opinion *Rashomon* is **Kyoto's** finest grill.

SUEHIRO—Kawaramachi-dori, Shijo Agaru. Here's that name again. Sizzling steaks and chops are the order of the day or night. (Japanese specialties, too) There is a branch on the second floor of the *Gion Kaikan Building*. Both open from eleven A.M. to ten P.M.

JAPAN (cont.)—Kyoto

YOTARO—In the premium shopping area of Old Gate and New Gate Streets near Nawate-cho (phone 6-1605). Tempura to make your mouth water.

And for hotel food, besides the *Miyako* and the grill at the *Kyoto Hotel*, journey up the mountain to the *Mount Hiei Hotel*, with views of **Kyoto** and *Lake Biwa*, Japan's "Lucerne." Try the fabulous leek-olive oil-sour cream salad dressing, the lake trout in *yuzu* sauce and vinegar, the delectable *ayu* river fish in season, and the *Tsuruga Bay* crabs.

NIGHT CLUBS

BEL-AMI—Ohashi Higashi Sanjo. Most impressive. Enthusiastic floor show. Food, drink, and service tops. 7:00 P.M. to midnight.

GION—facing *Maruyama Park*. Huge floor show, gorgeous hostesses. 6:30 P.M. to midnight.

OSOME—Kiyamache Oike-agaru. Typical night club. Hostesses. 7:00 P.M. to midnight.

Nagoya

RESTAURANTS

ALASKA—Second Floor, Toyoda Building (catty corner across from the *Nagoya Station*). This attractive restaurant offers western style menu with a wide variety of popular dishes including steaks, chops, salads, and both Italian and French cuisines. Open 11:00 A.M. to 9:00 P.M.

FLAMINGO—Tate Mitsukura, Naka-ku. The flourishing *Flamingo* offers Chinese cuisine at its best. Open 11:00 A.M. to 2:00 A.M.

MARUKO (phone 9-4015/6). A mightily good spot for sukiyaki is this attractive Japanese style eatery in the *Shin-sakae-machi* district.

TORIKYU—Nayacho Nakamura-ku. This restaurant is strictly Japanese in décor and cuisine. The emphasis is on chicken sukiyaki. Open 11:00 A.M. to nine P.M.

JAPAN (cont.)—Nagoya

YAEGAKI—*The* place for tempura, and don't hesitate to ask for the *Ise Bay* prawn and crab, the house specialties.

YACHIYO and YOSHIMI. These are **Nagoya's** best steak spots, in an area where the overshadowing wing is that of the *Nagoya chicken.*

NIGHT CLUBS

FERNANDO'S—in the Sogo Building on main Sakura-dori (phone 9-3463). I haven't been here personally, but the reports are that it's another of the better, more spectacular night clubs. There are lots of girls and a fine floor show. Small and intimate.

The THREE ACE—Imaike Building. This spot has a good band and entertaining floor show. It is open from 6:30 P.M. until midnight every night of the week except on the second Sunday of each month.

ZOMBI (phone 4-6512). A smart night club. Good music, good shows.

Osaka

ALASKA—across from the *Osaka Grand.* For fine international cuisine, a well stocked bar, and unparalleled views atop the Asahi Building, this is the place to dine. See special write-up page 268.

ASAHI—Sonezaki-shinchi, Kitaku. Strictly Japanese, the specialty is sukiyaki. Open eleven-thirty A.M. to ten P.M.

CHIKUYOTEI (phone 44-1884/5). In the mood for grilled, skewered, egg-folded eels? Here's your spot. Or try the nearby KITATEN GRILL (phone 34-1869).

DAITORO—a few blocks from the *Osaka Grand* and *New Osaka Hotels* (phone 34-2031). **Osaka** is famed for its Chinese cuisine and this is one of the best. *Peiping* style and tasty. Duck strips, roasted, are folded with herbs into a wheaten patty and down they slip, deliciously.

IPPOH—Dojima, Kitaku. Strictly Japanese, but here the

JAPAN (cont.)—Osaka

specialty is tempura. Open every day noon to nine P.M. Closed Sundays and (Japanese) holidays.

OSAKA GRAND. Simply wonderful dining. See special write-up page 268.

SUEHIRO—Homachi-ten. That name again. Known for its steaks and chops. Open daily 11:00 A.M. to 8:30 P.M. Closed Sundays and (Japanese) holidays.

TOKAI CLUB (phone 64-0285). Cantonese cuisine is the specialty here. The sweet-sour pork, shrimp and green peas, beef and green peppers can't be beat.

YEN KYO (phone 26-8100). Another quality Chinese restaurant, just the thing after shopping in Osaka's big *Daimaru Department Store*. Taste the spring rolls, the chicken in papers, and the vegetable bean curd dishes. Do look over the various fine soups listed on the menu.

YOTARO (phone 34-7404). The **Osaka** branch of the famous **Kyoto** tempura house.

Yokohama

RESTAURANTS

CHINATOWN. Just stroll down this "Miracle Mile" of *"Chuka Dori,"* the City's Chinese center, and follow the lead of eyes and nose. It's impossible to say this or that is the best place to eat because restaurant elbows restaurant the length of the street, both sides, and all are good. What do you fancy? Food from Shanghai, Szechuan, Peiping, Canton, Yunan: it's all here. Try TUNG FAT (a new **Tokyo** branch just opened, incidentally, on Avenue A near 10th Street), BOTAN-EN, KASEI-RO, KASHU-RO, or MANCHIN-RO . . . but don't slight any of the others.

HAMATEN—close to the *Grand Hotel* (phone 8-1389). *Sushi* and tempura are the specialties.

HOF BRAU—next to the *Seamen's Club* near *South Pier* (phone 8-5081). This salty spot serves chilled beer and good hot food at all hours to mariners, to tourists, and to you.

JAPAN (cont.)—Yokohama

KAORI—2-chome, Isezakicho (phone 8-2881/3). This is a versatile place where both sukiyaki and tempura are available for your dining pleasure, as are French and Chinese cuisines. You may dine in western or Japanese style.

ORIGINAL JOE'S (phone 8-4564/5). This man Joe gets around with his spaghetti mix, and here he shows up in **Yokohama.** A different Joe but the same wonderful Italian food found so easily in Japan. Try it. It's right next to *Chinatown* and open till late.

SUEHIRO—Bashamichi Street, near *Toho Theater* (phone 8-6054). The same name as we find in **Tokyo,** and a branch thereof. The steak room is on the second floor and the sukiyaki on the third floor.

NIGHT CLUBS

Two night spots particularly favored are the CAFE SUEZ, where assignations with pretty ladies are made via telephones attached to every table in the manner of smart European night clubs, and the NIGHT AND DAY (phone 2-0776/8), famous for its beautiful hostesses. "Our hostesses," reads the club's advertisement, "are the most desirable and beautiful young ladies in **Yokohama.**" Maybe.

BLUE SKY (phone 8-4757/9). Located right behind the *Grand Hotel,* I hear nothing but the best about this spot. It features fine floor shows, discreet hostesses, and rippling Latin American rhythms.

DEL MONTE. A bit of a joint, but on the safe side. Afro-Cuban music and raw floor shows. Open until the wee small hours of the morning.

MACAO

FAT SIU LAU *("Laughing Buddha")*—Rua Felicidade. Abundant European and Chinese dishes are skillfully prepared here. The famous specialty is roast pigeon which is a rich and succulent taste treat.

MACAO (cont.)

POUSADA DE MACAO. The specialty of the chef is an aromatic concoction known as *Chicken Africana*. This is tender barbecued chicken served with a mysterious sauce of limitless ingredients and accompanied by crusty hot rolls called *"casquieros"*—all of which makes for a delicious meal. This charming inn also offers a selection of Portuguese dishes (some of them laced generously with **Portugal's** famed wines) which are deserving of accolades.

While the restaurants listed above are to be considered the best in the area, you might enjoy any of the following: BELO, located on the main drag (Avenida Almeida Ribeiro); LONG KEI, a Cantonese establishment of some note; RUBY, which offers a varied European menu; and HELENA, atmospherically located on the waterfront.

FEDERATION OF MALAYSIA

All of the comments I have made apropos of variety of cuisine, native specialties, types of restaurants, and service in **Singapore** apply equally accurately to **Malaysia**. Native Malayan food, while generously treated with condiments and spices, is not "burny-burny" hot as is the Thai food. The restaurants of the Federation of Malaysia specialize in Indian, Chinese, Malayan, and western foods, all of which are good, with the Malayan and Indian curries being particularly delectable.

Western style night clubs do not exist in Malaysia.

Typical native dishes are:

CHICKEN IN THE COCONUT, a thick, spiced, soup uniquely served in the same coconut in which the chopped chicken has been brewed for seemingly endless hours.

FISH and CHICKEN cooked with sweet or sour sauce similar to, but different from, the normal Chinese variety.

MAHMEE or MEEHOON, a Chinese style Malay spaghetti.

FEDERATION OF MALAYSIA (cont.)

NASI BERIANI, an Indian dish of chicken or mutton with a base of turmeric rice.

SAMBALS is the collective name for the half dozen or more side dishes served with a Malayan meal.

SATAY, comprised of a variety of meats and chicken grilled over charcoal on bamboo sticks, served with chili-peanut sauce, eaten directly off the skewer either at a *Satay* stall or restaurant.

STUFFED LOBSTER. Super-duper.

Fruits:

LANGSAT, sour-sweet and juicy.

MANGOSTEEN, which is delectable, watermelon, papayas, and bananas.

RAMBUTAN, which is sweet.

Plus a wide variety of the fruits we know.

Kuala Lumpur

COLISEUM RESTAURANT—Batu Road. Known for its excellent Continental cuisine.

LE COQ D'OR—Ampang Road, near *Selangor Race Course*. One of **Malaysia's** most distinguished restaurants featuring French cuisine but also specializing in local dishes, particularly the "Chicken in the Coconut."

FEDERAL HOTEL—Bukit Bintang Road. Renowned for its Chinese cuisine in a superb atmosphere.

FEDERAL MALAY RESTAURANT—Princes Road. The best restaurant featuring Malay cuisine exclusively. It is clean and good.

GRIFFIN INN—Ampang Road, between *Le Coq d'Or* and the *Selangor Turf Club*. A charming establishment, well recommended for its selections of both Continental and Chinese cuisines.

HARLEQUIN—in the *Hotel Merlin,* Treacher Road. An excellent Chinese cuisine unmatched outside of **Hong Kong.**

FEDERATION OF MALAYSIA (cont.)—Kuala Lumpur

The MAJESTIC HOTEL—Victory Avenue. An excellent choice of western dishes.

STALLS and COFFEE SHOPS—Campbell Road.

TAJMAHAL RESTAURANT—Batu Road. All of the Muslim specialties.

Penang

DAWOOD RESTAURANT—611 Queen Street. Features both Indian and genuine Malay food.

EASTERN & ORIENTAL HOTEL offers an excellent western cuisine.

GARDEN HOTEL & RESTAURANT—571 Tanjong Bungah. An adept exponent of the art of Chinese cuisine.

HOLLYWOOD CAFE—Tanjong Bungah. A mouth-watering selection of Chinese cooking.

MEERA RESTAURANT—166 Campbell Street. Well known locally for its excellent Malay food with a choice of Indian food.

SUN HOE PENG—25 Lake Street. Recommended Chinese restaurant featuring Cantonese cooking.

THE PHILIPPINES

The Philippine cuisine embraces a wide variety of native dishes in addition to which we may enjoy European, American, Chinese, Japanese, and Javanese meals in abundance. I think you will be particularly interested in the following local Filipino specialties:

ADOBO, an agglomeration of chicken and pork, might be worth trying.

ALEMANGO, a "fruit of the sea," is a delicate stewed crab.

BAKERY SPECIALTIES are mouth-watering and unusual. They include: PAN DE SAL, which comes in tiny, delicately crusted, salted loaves; CUCHINTA and PUTO, two types of tasty, sweet, steamed rice bread; and ENSAIMADAS, a Fili-

THE PHILIPPINES (cont.)

pino version of sweet roll, garnished with Spanish sausage *(chorizo)* and/or grated cheese.

BALUT has to be seen, or eaten, to be believed. It is hot *boiled duck's egg* served complete (ugh) with embryo. Usually sold in the markets and on the streets. *"Balut sa puti"* means the embryo will be immature and (almost) palatable. I personally believe this is a dish strictly for the natives.

Tree-ripened, sun-drenched FRUIT is available in profusion, including pineapples, cantaloupes, coconuts, bananas, star apples, mangoes, calimancis, papayas and watermelons.

LECHON is as native to The Philippines as hamburger is to us. It is universally served on all festive occasions. This drawn baby pig is stuffed with tamarind leaves or papaya, roasted over red-hot coals, and served with a choice of tangy sauces (spicy liver sauce is preferred by the natives).

LUMPIA is delectable. Its ingredients consist of pork, vegetables, shredded coconut pith, and shrimp enveloped in wafer-thin pancakes. Served with its own tasty sauce.

MERIENDA is Filipino for afternoon tea, which can assume the proportions of a buffet dinner.

PANCIT (GUISADO) is composed of noodles garnished with pork, chicken, or seafood.

PANCIT (MALABON) is similar but with spices added—good and served most everywhere.

PANUT MOLO, a native soup of obscure origin, is wonderful.

SALTED DUCK'S EGGS served piping hot are unusually good. For eye appeal they are painted red, and for taste they are grated and mixed with onions, lettuce, tomatoes, and chipped smoked dried fish.

SINIGANG is an elaborate production of stew-like pork or fish.

SUGPO, a dish of steamed shrimps, is one you'll fancy if you are a devotee of seafood.

TUBA is to the Filipinos what akvavit is to the Scandina-

THE PHILIPPINES (cont.)

vians, vodka to the Russians, and moonshine whisky to our own hillbillies. Wow! A drink of sledgehammer ferocity.

Oysters are not at their best in the Philippines. I suggest that you not eat them.

It's all right to drink water from the taps in good restaurants and hotels.

The milk generally is not up to our standards. Better pass it up unless you are sure it has been pasteurized. The *Golden State Dairies* (of California) are doing a good job in improving this situation.

Manila

RESTAURANTS

ALBA—1123 Florida Street. Spanish cuisine is the specialty, meticulously prepared and graciously served.

ARISTOCRAT—2168 Dewey Boulevard (overlooking *Manila Bay*). Though an international variety of food ranging from snacks to multi-course dinners is available, the Filipino specialties are the reason for coming here. The *Orient Room* is air conditioned. Always open.

ATAMI—Padre Faura. The oldest Japanese restaurant in the Philippines, featuring only Oriental food and drink.

BULAKEÑA—Dewey Boulevard. A commendable establishment for sampling the exotic cuisine of the Philippines. Truly native in quality.

BUNGALOW—1000 California Avenue. Features *lumpia*, *lechon*, and other Filipino dishes. The cakes of the house are outstanding.

CAFE INDONESIA—Dewey Boulevard. Indonesian and Malayan food.

COUNTRY BAKE SHOP—Isaac Peral, Ermita. The bakery goods are palate pleasing and the coffee, aromatic perfection.

CUCINA ITALIANA—585 Padre Faura. All of the *pasta* delights of Italy lovingly prepared in native fashion for your gastronomic pleasure.

THE PHILIPPINES (cont.)—Manila

DI'MARK'S—Menlo Road, Pasay City (a Manila suburb). The flavor here is international but Italian dishes predominate, especially pizza. The charcoal broiled steaks are also recommended. Good bar. The Italian combo comes to life after eight P.M. or so.

FISH FUN-MALABON (20 minutes from the *Manila Hotel*). Excellent. Specializes in fish. Clean, modern.

JADE VINE—1153 M. H. del Pilar. American food in a genuine Philippine atmosphere. Also Chinese and Continental dishes and a buffet on Wednesdays and Saturdays. Air conditioned.

LA PARILLA—Dewey Boulevard. Continental foods, wine and service. Excellent restaurant. One of the best in Manila. Expensive.

MADRID—24-25 Highway 54, Mandaluyong. Restaurant and cocktail lounge. Well recommended.

MAX'S PLACE—Dewey Boulevard. Local dishes including mouth-watering fried chicken prevail.

NEW EUROPE—227 Isaac Peral. The Continental cuisine and charcoal broiled steaks are famous. Many believe this to be the best restaurant in Manila. Expensive.

CASA MARCO'S—Dewey Boulevard. Popular with jai alai players because of its Spanish and Basque food and atmosphere. Patrons join in singing to the guitar. Open all night. Interesting.

SWISS INN—Miramar Apartment Building, Dewey Boulevard. Popular as a luncheon rendezvous and highly regarded for excellent food at all times.

TOWN'S TAVERN—Isaac Peral. Pleasant atmosphere for luncheon. A wide choice of tasty European dishes await your selection here.

Quezon City

D. & E. COFFEE SHOP. Spick and span. Both Filipino and international dishes.

THE PHILIPPINES (cont.)—Quezon City

MAX'S PLACE. Same specialties as in **Manila.**

TRES HERMANAS. The dishes of the Philippine gourmet.

HOTEL DINING IN MANILA

HOTEL FILIPINAS—GOLDEN LOTUS, Dewey Boulevard. World renowned for "local color." Try the Chinese cuisine. American and European dishes are also available. Air conditioned.

MANILA HOTEL. The *Bamboo Room* features Philippine food and the *Moongate Room* specializes in Chinese food. The *Champagne Room,* sometimes doubling as a night club, is a cosmopolitan restaurant with music.

MABUHAY HOTEL—PEKING HOUSE. Chinese food is served exclusively.

BAY VIEW HOTEL—BAY VIEW HOUSE. Here we find excellent European dishes.

NIGHT CLUBS

There are scores upon scores of night clubs in Manila, many of them excellent. Much of the night life centers around the small "boite-type" night clubs where the entertainment fluctuates from quiet, if not dull, to noisy and rollicking. There are a number of little clubs along Dewey Boulevard near the city limits in which you might find a bit of "pub crawling" fun if you are so inclined. Since the night life situation varies considerably, it would be well to inquire at your hotel or from your travel representative as to whether or not there are any spots which are currently popular. One need not search far for Manila night diversion, however. The clubs are air conditioned and boast of the finest dance bands in the Orient. Unescorted gals do have a problem, though. They may not visit the night spots without at least one male escort in the group. Most night clubs thoughtfully provide hostesses, many of them beautiful, for the solitary males seeking company. Here are a few of the best night spots:

THE PHILIPPINES (cont.)—Manila

Dinner Dancing

ALBA'S SUPPER CLUB—Dewey Boulevard. Good food, elegant, modern décor. Gambling. Formerly the *"Key Supper Club," Alba's* now includes a fully equipped theater for staging internationally famous revues and variety shows.

CHAMPAGNE ROOM—*Manila Hotel.* Cosmopolitan restaurant and night club.

JAI ALAI SKYROOM—Taft Avenue. Here you may drink, dine, dance, and watch the jai alai (from the balcony) in elite air conditioned comfort.

Night Clubs

ANGELES—Near *Clark Air Base* (some hour and a half to two hours' drive from the heart of Manila). Of some interest to those seeking the bizarre. A grubby collection of cinemas, honky tonks, restaurants, daring side shows, and naughty adventure. Not recommended for the prim or the prissy.

BAYSIDE—1712 Dewey Boulevard. Small but interesting.

GUERNICA'S—M.H. del Pilar. Gay fun spot. Recommended.

JIMMY'S NIGHT CLUB—2016 Dewey Boulevard. How Jimmy does get around the Orient!

JUNGLE BAR—*Manila Hotel.* Music and refreshments in an unbelievable setting. Almost without light. Décor of jungle growth and waterfall.

NINA'S PAPAGAYO—1038 Avenida Mabini. Comes well recommended.

RIVIERA—Dewey Boulevard. Terrific band. Entertainment includes the excitement of the *"tapis vert"* (gambling).

SAFARI SUPPER CLUB—Corner Dakota and Harrison Boulevards. Outstanding food. Dancing nightly.

SHANGRI-LA—*Shelbourne Hotel.* Basement night club, popular with young Manila. Music and dancing both good.

THE PHILIPPINES (cont.)—Manila

GOLF CLUBS

The MANILA GOLF CLUB and the WACK-WACK GOLF AND COUNTRY CLUB are both short drives from the city. The *Wack-Wack* has two eighteen hole golf courses and a swimming pool.

Guest memberships may be made available through local members. If you are a devotee of the royal and ancient game, have your club secretary or manager write ahead to request guest privileges.

SINGAPORE

THE CAPITOL—Capitol Theater Building, Second Floor, North Bridge and Stamford Roads. A tempting selection of Chinese and Continental dishes is offered but best known for its tantalizing specialties of the Province of Szechuan. Dancing and a good floor show in the evening.

THE CATHAY—Cathay Hotel Building. Highly recommended for truly superior Chinese cuisine. The interior is quite appealing. Dancing nightly.

Christina Loke's PULAU SELEGU ISLAND FLOATING RESTAURANT and NIGHT CLUB. A short boat ride from Singapore. See special write-up, page 273.

"THE COCKPIT" (or the *Hotel de l'Europe,* as you please). A very good outdoor charcoal grill and barbecue is pretty special, and there's dancing and a floor show (indoors), too. If you happen to be in Singapore on Saturday or Sunday, I call your attention to the week-end luncheon feature; namely, Javanese *rijsttafel.* What a taste treat it is.

ELIZABETHAN ROOM—*Raffles Hotel.* The chef definitely has a superb way with Chicken à la Kiev, and an equally fine touch with the entire, varied selection of Continental dishes. One of Singapore's epicurean jewels. The *Elizabethan Room* is a smart, internationally renowned restaurant in a distinguished setting. See special write-up, page 273.

SINGAPORE (cont.)

ESPLANADE—Opposite *Pedang,* by the water's edge. A very good place for your introductory tasting of Malayan cuisine. They're a specialty here and prepared beautifully.

FOUR LIONS RESTAURANT—*Singapura Intercontinental Hotel.* Attractive supper club. See special write-up, page 208.

GRILL ROOM—*Adelphi Hotel.* French and Swiss cuisines are pleasantly served. Nightly dancing and floor show.

ISLAMIC RESTAURANT—795-7 North Bridge Road. Hot and exotic Indian curries are spicily served.

OCEAN PARK HOTEL—East Coast Road. The delicious barbecues are prepared outdoors by the sea. You'll find enticing Continental and Malayan dishes to choose from, as well as *nasi goreng,* the local specialty. Open-air dancing.

PAVILION—Orchard Road. Singapore may no longer be a British Colony, but Britannia rules this "little bit of England." Reminiscent of the chop houses of Britain, the food is well prepared, the setting plain and simple, and the service is flawless.

THE PEKING RESTAURANT—321-3 North Bridge Road (28 Clemenceau Avenue). Peking specialties. Dancing.

PRINCE'S—Orchard Road. One of Singapore's best and most famous. See special write-up, page 273.

ROSE D'OR—first floor, *Lido Cinema,* Orchard Road. Combination restaurant and night club. Continental and native cuisines. Short floor show. Dancing. Luncheon and dinner.

SATAY CLUB—Just off Beach Road (near the *New Alhambra Theater*). *Satay,* skewered meat rolled in sauce and grilled, is the specialty.

SZECHUAN DYNASTY ROOM—*Adelphi Hotel.* Szechuan dishes and a delightful atmosphere.

TANGLE INN—23-25 Tanglin Road. In the residential district of *Tanglin,* this pub-like inn is another last outpost of British life in Singapore.

WEST POINT GARDENS—Panjang Road on the sea. The outdoor dance floor and outstanding Chinese cuisine make this a glorious place to spend an evening. It opens at 9 P.M.

SINGAPORE (cont.)

The "WORLD" AMUSEMENT PARKS feature Cantonese restaurants, including: BEDOK, TAI THONG—*Happy World Amusement Park;* TAI TONG—*New World Amusement Park;* and WING CHOON YUEN—*Great World Amusement Park.* See special write-up, page 272.

Also, I think you might like the restaurants of those two fine department stores, ROBINSON'S and JOHN LITTLE'S, both located on Raffles Place, or the G. H. CAFE, Battery Place.

TAIWAN (FORMOSA)

Taipei

See **Hong Kong** section for descriptions of regional cuisines.

PEKING (Peiping) CUISINE

FENG TSE LOU RESTAURANT—125 Hanchung Street, phone 33904.

CHIH MEI LOU RESTAURANT—162 Chunghua Street, phone 34214.

SHANGHAI CUISINE

LAO CHENG HSING RESTAURANT—1733 Chungcheng Road, phone 24216 or 33385.

JANUARY RESTAURANT—1761 Chungcheng Road, phone 24898.

CANTONESE CUISINE

CENTRAL THEATER RESTAURANT—120 Chungshan N. Road, Section II. Two floor shows nightly. See special write-up, page 278.

KUO CHI RESTAURANT—*Park Hotel,* 159 Hsi Ning Road South, first floor, phone 30797.

MALAYA RESTAURANT—161 Hsi Ning Road South, 1st, 2nd, and 4th floors, phone 32144 or 32145.

TAIWAN (FORMOSA) (cont.)—Taipei

SZECHUAN AND HUNAN CUISINE

KUO KUANG RESTAURANT—6 Chengtu Road, Lane 27, phone 31075 or 31076.

GREEN HOUSE RESTAURANT—48 Hengyang Road, phone 25675 or 34794.

LEE YUEN RESTAURANT—23, Section I, Nanking Road, E., Taipei, phone 53291.

O'MEI RESTAURANT—109, Section I, Chungching S. Road, Phone 38251.

YU LOU TUNG RESTAURANT—49-5 Chengtu Road, phone 32187.

YU YUAN RESTAURANT—3rd and 5th floors of the Hsin Shing Theater Building, phone 31639.

WESTERN STYLE CUISINE

GRAND HOTEL—Yuan Shan, phone 48241. Great.

HONG KONG RESTAURANT—107 Chungshan North Road, Section II, phone 45032.

TERRY'S RESTAURANT—47 Chungshan North Road, Section II, phone 43531.

ROSE MARIE RESTAURANT—114 Po Ai Road, phone 24553 or 33044.

FRIENDS OF CHINA CLUB—New Park, phone 23817.

MONGOLIAN CUISINE

BAR-B-QUE INN—Pei An Road.

HUO KUO (Hot Pot)

SHANSI RESTAURANT—Chungcheng Road.

GENERAL

HOTEL TAIWAN—center of city. Mongolian barbecue in air conditioned rooms on ninth and tenth floors, Peiping and Shanghai style cuisine on seventh floor, genuine western food on eighth floor, and an excellent coffee shop on first floor.

THAILAND

Bangkok

RESTAURANTS

The best restaurants in BANGKOK listed according to their specialties are:

THAI CUISINE

THE PALMS RESTAURANT—Ploenchitr Road, adjoining *Erawan Hotel*.

SALINEE, opposite the Army T. V. Station—Don Muang Road.

CHINESE FOOD

THE GOLDEN DRAGON RESTAURANT—Sukhumvit Road, Bangkapi.

HOI THIEN LAO—Sua Pah Road.

PALMS RESTAURANT—Ploenchitr Road, adjoining *Erawan Hotel*.

JAPANESE SPECIALTIES

KAWACHIYA—New Road, adjoining *Oasis Club*. The very finest of Japanese food that may be had outside the home islands. Quite expensive.

MISCELLANEOUS

ARCADE TEA ROOM—*Erawan Hotel*. Open 9:00 A.M. to 10:00 P.M. The only genuine tea room in **Bangkok.**

THE CARLTON—Patpong area. This place is new and is quite popular.

LE CHALET—*Erawan Hotel*. Air conditioned restaurant and bar. Wonderful. See special write-up page 282.

DAIRY FARMS—335-337 Suriwongse Road. A soda fountain snack bar which offers "Chicken in the Basket," hamburgers, hot dogs, milk shakes, banana splits, and other ice cream delights.

THAILAND (cont.)—Bangkok

LITTLE HOME BAKERY—Three of them: at 99/105 Vorachak Road; on Suriwongse Road, near *Ciquita's Tavern;* and 139 Gaysorn Road, opposite the *Erawan Hotel.* Delicious pies, pastries, cakes, and bread to take out if you wish. Also a profusion of sandwiches. These light, airy, clean soda fountain-lunch rooms are convenient and efficient for luncheon and in-between-meal refreshments.

NICK'S NUMBER 1—Sathorn Road, No. 1. Magnificent. My favorite. See special write-up, page 280.

NORMANDIE GRILL—top floor, *Oriental Hotel.* Excellent. See special write-up, page 283.

LA (CIQUITA'S) TAVERN—329 Suriwongse Road, near the *Trocadero Hotel.* An intimate bar serving light snacks from 11:00 A.M. until the early hours of the morning.

RAMA HOTEL—Main Dining Room, Coffee Shop, Tea Room, and Tropicana. The best in Bangkok.

TRADER KEITH'S—*klongs* area waterside restaurant. Owned by the enterprising Cincinnati-born Ethan Emery, who came to Thailand to collect leopards. *Trader Keith's* has built a reputation in just a few years. Breakfast served 7:30 A.M. to 10 A.M., specialties are Bloody Marys, scrambled eggs, Danish bacon.

NIGHT CLUBS

ALEXANDRA NIGHT CLUB—corner of *Democracy Monument* and Rajdamnoen Avenue. A large choice of foods including Thai, Chinese and western cuisines. A Filipino band is accompanied by attractive vocalists. Dancing every night.

AMBASSADOR CLUB—*Erawan Hotel.* Wonderful. See special write-up, page 283.

BAMBOO BAR—*Oriental Hotel.* Fully air conditioned with dancing every night. A bit murky, but attractive.

CLUB KEYNOTE—81 Patpong Road. A night club-restaurant featuring barbecues, grills, steaks, and, if you please, dancing. Air conditioned. Open for lunch and dinner. Open until 2:00 A.M. Fridays and Saturdays.

THAILAND (cont.)—Bangkok

MOULIN ROUGE—Mansion 3, Rajdamnoen Avenue, corner of *Democracy Monument*. A new, modern, and air conditioned restaurant-night club—with music and dancing. Open from 11:00 A.M. to midnight except Fridays and Saturdays and the eves of holidays when it is open until 2:00 A.M.

TROPICANA NIGHT CLUB—*Hotel Rama*. Lush, plush, and attractive. See special write-up page 282.

You will see a number of advertisements for Thai night clubs. I wouldn't be too impressed if I were you. Outside of the good hotels and those listed above, the other alleged night clubs to the best of my knowledge are third- and fourth-rate joints crawling with hostesses whom we would, for the most part, call "B-girls."

VIET NAM

Saigon

Though the number of restaurants in Saigon is limited, the excellence of their fare is absolutely top drawer. The historical background of Saigon is French, and its fine restaurants reflect the best in French cordon bleu tradition.

Cholon is a part of **Saigon** but separated from it as an independent Chinese settlement. Almost like another city, there are a number of Chinese restaurants there, but I believe that you will be happier if you concentrate on the French food in the restaurants described below or on the special Vietnamese and Chinese food that may be had at the MAJESTIC HOTEL.

Of the restaurants in **Saigon** proper, the following are simply superb and completely out of this world:

The CARAVELLE. The finest restaurant in Saigon is the ninth floor terrace restaurant of the *Hotel Caravelle*. The view from this lofty eminence is excellent; the French cuisine is the taste-thrilling product of one of the finest Gallic chefs. The menu is succulently varied. The orchestra plays background

VIET NAM (cont.)—Saigon

music for both lunch and dinner. American and Continental specialties prevail on the menu.

L'AMIRAL ("THE ADMIRAL"). This is a tiny, elegant, sophisticated French restaurant, situated a short walk from the *Caravelle* or a short taxi ride from the *Majestic.* From the *Caravelle* you turn left as you leave the hotel for a few steps, then left for a block to the corner of the *Vietnamese Arts and Crafts Shop,* turn left and in the middle of the block on the opposite side is *L'Amiral,* a gastronomic bit of France transplanted. Every delicacy that you would find in the finest of the great restaurants of France you will find at *L'Amiral.* Because it is small, a reservation is rather necessary. By Vietnamese standards, this is a bit expensive but not by ours. If time permits and you wish to try a restaurant out of the hotel, you couldn't be more pleased.

CARUSO. Despite its Italian name, this restaurant is as French as the *Eiffel Tower* and the *Champs Élysées.* The bar and restaurant are small and intimate, the décor pleasant, the menu outstanding, and the prices reasonable. I've mentioned that this is a typical French restaurant; it is. In common with restaurants in France and French restaurants out of France, however, there are Italian specialties such as spaghetti alla bolognese that are served.

GUILLAUME TELL ("WILLIAM TELL") is the fourth of the charming restaurants of Saigon and certainly not necessarily fourth from the point of excellence. There are champions of each of this quartet. Even in Paris or Provence, the *Guillaume Tell* would be considered top flight. Service, cuisine, and atmosphere all commend it to you. Not terribly expensive.

The MAJESTIC HOTEL commands a magnificent view overlooking Saigon's river. It is in the center of the shopping and business districts. In the gloaming, at cocktail time, the *Majestic* sidewalk cafe is a riot of color, and an excellent place to watch the international passing parade. The *Majestic*'s roof top restaurant is delightful and adjoins an attractive panoramic

VIET NAM (cont.)—Saigon

bar overlooking the entire city and surrounding countryside. Vietnamese specialties served in the roof top restaurant should be ordered at least half a day before they are required. The *Majestic* also features à la carte Chinese and French dishes.

ARC-EN-CIEL, in **Cholon**, is a Chinese restaurant featuring both Pekingese and Cantonese menus. This restaurant is noted for the length of its menu with more than 900 dishes. Music.

The floating restaurant, MY CAHN, on the river near the *Club Nautique*, is romantically situated and offers a fine table.

PALAIS-DE-JADE, DONG KHANH and CHEONG NAM in **Cholon** are well known for the variety and excellence of their Chinese cuisine.

Vietnamese food is delicious. It may be sampled at the TOUR D'ARGENT next to the *Club Nautique*, and at the CON-GA-QUAY restaurant in *Thu-Duc*.

The night life situation in Saigon is uncertain due to the volatile political situation. As of going to press the *Moulin Rouge* and *La Galare* night clubs were operating and provide opportunity for dancing and occasional Vietnamese folklore dancing exhibitions. (Check locally for current status of after dark entertainment.)

CHAPTER 6

Your Orient Shopping Guide

Of the innumerable ecstasies that are the direct results and exhilarating by-products of foreign travel, none is more stimulating than that afforded by the opportunity to shop for foreign "treasures" in their native habitats.

In my European guidebook, *Aboard and Abroad,* I say, "The poets and philosophers have never proved conclusively to what degree distance lends enchantment to romance, but I can state categorically that where shopping is involved, the urge to buy in foreign lands multiplies magically in direct proportion to the distance from home. I am a good example to prove this point. It practically takes an Act of Congress to drag me into a domestic store, but . . . after all these years, I still pant, mentally, like a young lover as I approach my favorite foreign shopping centers.

"And why not? . . . *Souvenir* is the French word for 're-membrance' or 'memory.' This uninhibited desire of ours to bring home souvenirs is highly commendable. Your gifts will bring unbounded joy to others, and those purchases you retain will not only be decorative additions to your home, but will evoke glowing memories of delightful experiences abroad as long as you live."

331

I could have written the foregoing originally in behalf of the Orient with equal accuracy and enthusiasm.

A trip to the Far East will indeed fill the storehouse of your memories with a never ending series of happy events to be recalled with heartwarming fondness for years and years to come, as well as affording you an unparalleled shopping treat.

In addition to my numerous fascinating trips to glamorous Europe and the exotic Orient, I travel constantly and extensively within our continental limits which gives me the opportunity to visit with friends throughout the United States, many of whom are former Olson foreign tour members, zestful travelers and shoppers all.

When I visit in the homes of these friends, it always warms the cockles of my cardiac muscle to have them show me, with button-bursting pride, treasured mementoes acquired in **Hong Kong, Singapore, Tokyo,** or **Kyoto,** which souvenirs frequently are lovingly displayed in honored niches in their homes. It brings me great pleasure to hear a man say to his wife, "Darling, don't you remember that lovely afternoon when we bought this delightful cloisonné vase in **Kyoto?** What fun it was picking it out, and what joy it continues to bring us every day of our lives."

Each purchase selected with loving care will add immeasurably to the constantly recurring dividends you receive from your original investment in your trip to the ever exciting Orient.

The ingratiating fact of the Oriental shopping matter is that for purchases to be of lasting value to yourself or of immeasurable pride to the recipients of your gifts, the items need not be expensive. Quite on the contrary.

I frequently find myself savoring a two-dollar plaque or pagoda with as much relish as I enjoy a much more expensive print, *objet d'art,* or ornament.

The quality of the Oriental hand work is almost unbelievable. It is fashioned with infinite pains and untold patience, blended with the magic of age-old artistry. The quality of the merchandise available to be purchased and the endless variety of the shopping temptations that will be put before you in the Orient are incredible to behold.

The Orient is a vast intriguing shopping arcade with merchandise displayed so tantalizingly and so creatively as to instill in you an almost irrepressible urge to buy. Even a penurious, penny-pinching New England Yankee would find it virtually impossible to keep from "splurging" on some of these extraordinarily beautiful bargains. Through concentrated experience, I learned long ago that most things in life are expensive or inexpensive, desirable or undesirable, by comparison. This is particularly true of shopping in the Orient. So much has been written, and there has been so much conversation on this subject, however, that it is absolutely inevitable that a certain amount of tripe and calculated or innocent misinformation must of necessity have been disseminated.

As a student at *Purdue,* I worked in the kitchen of our fraternity house, serving meals to a group of ever voraciously hungry Phi Kappa Sigma Boilermakers. Our colored cook, Mrs. Henry, was a sagacious savant of the old school. She used to say, "Lawsy me, I just don't believe half of what I read and nothing of what I hear!"

To the foregoing, I can say only, "Amen," particularly in the realm of foreign travel. It is always the one-time tripper Cousin Charlie, or the once-to-the-Orient, once-to-**Europe** Aunt Agatha who knows every last detail of where you should go, what you should see, what you should buy, and where. These "mother's little helpers" will also tell you just what is, and what isn't, a bargain. Maybe!

I have always found that it pays to seek the advice of a professional whose continued well-being depends on being accurate and reliable. This is the best way to plan a trip, build a house, or draw up a contract. The shopping counsel contained in this chapter is unbiased and accurate.

From the foregoing, I do not wish to accentuate the negative. On the contrary, I am an eternal optimist who is quite certain that there is indeed a vast vat tumbling over with golden nuggets at the end of the rainbow, that every cloud, however externally dark, is lined with shimmering silver and that bargains abound the world over. Just don't be insipidly stupid. No one loves a real bargain more than I do, and the Orient abounds in real values. But there is nothing of worth that can be bought for an absolute pittance. Choose a house of quality for your shopping, get their best price, and you'll have a heart-warming bargain.

There is no question, for example, but that **Hong Kong** is the shoppers' paradise of the world today. But I must hasten to point out that even in this Valhalla of bargain seekers, vicuña coats are not given away with three S & H green stamps. Even in **Hong Kong,** you get what you pay for, even though Jack Paar, when he returned from his first trip there, left me with the television impression that a **Hong Kong** dressmaker paid him money to make his wife's gown for Jack Kennedy's inaugural ball. Could it be?

Even in this Far Eastern British Crown Colony, quality and price remain in a direct fixed ratio. Fortunately, that ratio is at a much lower level than we are accustomed to. Yes, you *can* have a man's suit made for twelve dollars in **Hong Kong,** but I don't think that anybody who is willing to spend six dollars and ninety-five cents for this guidebook would be happy with a twelve-dollar **Hong Kong** suit. The workmanship in such a garment is bound to be shoddy, and the material mediocre. No question about it.

Men's hand-tailored woolen suits of outstanding quality may be purchased for from fifty-five to sixty or seventy-five dollars. This includes the finest workmanship and the best of material. Such a suit, made by your favorite custom tailor in a big United States city, would cost you from a hundred and fifty to two hundred and fifty dollars. In **Hong Kong** men's fine silk suits, exquisitely tailored, will run between sixty and eighty-five dollars or about one-third of the Stateside price.

It is fairly safe to assume that a ratio similar to the above exists in regard to women's garments. Milady's **Hong Kong** price will be about one-half of what it would be for the same hand-tailored or ready-made garment at home.

The reason for this tremendous discrepancy should be immediately obvious. In **Hong Kong,** the labor is skilled, rapid, fastidious, and neat; it is also readily available at the lowest wage scale known in the civilized world. I would venture to say that the **Hong Kong** labor costs in a man's handmade suit do not exceed three dollars. Imagine it! The Chinese tailor, for all of his skill and aptitude, quite probably works at least four, if not five, days to earn as much as his American counterpart can earn easily in one hour.

Throughout the fine shopping areas of **Hong Kong,** you will see elaborately beaded sweaters and bags. These, as with countless other articles of clothing and general merchandise, represent tremendous bargains. Again the reason is obvious. The labor costs which would be prohibitive in many countries for hand beading are but a minute fraction in the Crown Colony.

But I beseech, implore, and entreat you: don't, I repeat don't, expect to buy a pair of thirty-five dollar shoes for a dollar ninety-eight cents, a twenty-five dollar handmade silk shirt for a dollar sixty-five, or a Christian Dior copy for six dollars and ninety-five cents. It just doesn't work that way . . . not even in **Hong Kong.**

One of the finest, and least heralded, bargains in the entire Orient is the Thai bronze tableware available in **Bangkok.** The gifts of this ultra-beautiful tableware which I have sent to various friends and relatives have evoked the most splendiferous ohs and ahs I have ever heard in my extensive travel experience.

Thai dolls are incredible. These exquisite numbers are decoratively attired in authentic period costumes, and, as dolls go, they might seem a bit expensive to you. They cost from seven to twenty-five or thirty dollars. However, you will realize what outstanding values they are when you see them.

Thai silk presents a real bargain. Unless you are a gemologist or have had extensive experience in buying precious stones, I would suggest that you keep yourself under a close check rein while traveling in the Orient. The pearls in **Japan** may of course be purchased with great confidence. Elsewhere, be careful!

Japan is a bulging warehouse of eye-popping bargains begging to be bought. **Singapore** shops are exotic and value packed. The **Philippines** and **South Viet Nam** both have much to tempt the traveling shopper.

When the five-hundred-dollar duty-free allowance for returning overseas visitors was reduced to one hundred dollars, foreign travelers let forth an agonized howl and gnashed their collective molars. Frankly, I disapproved of this move as being penny wise and pound foolish. But it is with us. Don't rush out to your nearest travel agent and cancel your trip abroad, however, because the duty-free allowance on your purchases is now less than the one-time liberal five hundred dollars. There are several facets that are important and pertinent which I will point out to you at this time. Please pay particular attention. One fact that is not generally understood is that the price at which you should declare your foreign purchases is that of a fair wholesale price. You are not obligated to declare your purchases at the retail cost that you were quoted and paid. This in itself is a big saving. Don't be misguided as many people are who feel that they have to carefully declare their purchases at exactly the price they paid. Secondly, there is the attractive, still operative, scheme whereby you may ship an unlimited number of duty-free gifts home to friends or relatives so long as each such gift does not exceed a fair wholesale price of ten dollars. This procedure is subject only to the limitation that not more than one package per day may be received by any one recipient. With prices and values being what they are in the Orient, you could very well complete your entire shopping list without exceeding the now reduced duty-free limit. If you take advantage of the duty-free shopping plan, be sure to remind the shopkeeper to mark each package carefully: "Unsolicited gift—value less than ten dollars." The ten-dollar gift packages shipped from the Orient, or any place else, need not be declared.

There is another important duty factor which is not generally understood: When you have made purchases which exceed your duty-free allowance, the least dutiable items among your purchases are lumped in the over one hundred dollar category. Many items that you might have purchased may be taxable at a rate of five or six per cent. The purchases which are taxable at more than fifteen per cent are rare. Should you exceed the one hundred dollar limit by four hundred dollars, for example, it would be well within the realm of possibility that your total duty would be thirty dollars or less.

If you are one who will spend two or three thousand dollars on your trip to the Orient and then spend days and weeks figuring out how to smuggle an extra package or two of cigarettes in order to save a nickel or a dime a package, I might point out to you you're quite human. 'Most everyone does. And if it galls you beyond expression to pay so much as ten dollars duty on your Orient shopping, that's only natural.

I have always been a fastidious advocate of carrying all of your purchases with you from abroad, and insofar as **Europe** is concerned I still am. In the Orient where so much of the travel is by plane, however, we must recognize that the weight limitations are such that it is utterly impossible to carry any but the tiniest purchases with you. I am pleased to report that the shipping services from the Orient are excellent, however. I have had the most comforting reports on the honesty, integrity, and efficiency of the good Oriental shop and store keepers, and have made numerous personal purchases which have been shipped to me either at my office or home which have arrived promptly and in perfect condition. There is an urgent word of caution which I trust you will heed in regard to such shipments: bring a good supply of personal or business cards with you with your home or business address clearly and completely engraved thereon. It is difficult (almost impossible) for most Orientals to read western style handwriting. If you fail to follow my advice and neglect to bring the cards with you, be sure, when inscribing your name and address, that you print this highly pertinent information in completely legible block letters. This is of the utmost importance.

It will take at least five weeks for shipments to reach the States from **Japan** or **Hong Kong** with shipping intervals of two months to ten weeks not being considered as unusual. The farther you go along, the longer the interval to allow for the surface shipments.

Costs for shipping small packages by ship are reasonable, with two or three dollars considered average to high for a good sized gift package from **Hong Kong** to **Chicago.**

There are several hints and suggestions that might prove worthwhile in your shopping daze. In the shopping arcade of **Tokyo's** *Imperial Hotel,* you will find an excellent package-wrapping service located catty corner from the *Imperial* branch of the *Japanese Post Office,* ten feet away. This outfit, *Odawara Shoten,* prepares packages with the utmost care and skill. I have had almost everything, including tourist pamphlets, films, collections of periodicals, books, and a variety of gifts, expertly wrapped there. Parcel post and airmail shipments may be posted there right on the spot. Fairly bulky packages may be shipped by air freight, which carries a rate of less than half of the air excess baggage charges. If you do not have too weighty packages and you desire to have them waiting on your return, send them by air. You'll be amazed how much you can ship by air for fifteen or twenty dollars. Lots.

Despite the fact that all good, reliable shops will efficiently prepare and promptly mail packages for you, you must be sure to make a careful note of each purchase as well as the date purchased and amount paid. Save *all* receipts.

The shops listed in this chapter are considered to be the soul of reliability. One of my associates or I have visited and carefully checked out each shop I have recommended. Elizabeth Kresler who is an inveterate international shopper has contributed generously to the shopping list. Vernon Brooks, Charles Dufresne, Matt Matisse, Chris O'Malley, and Matt Dillon have worked assiduously on this list. Mrs. Harriett Fox Grant who was formerly associated with me prior to her happy marriage has been generous in her shopping comments and recommendations. I have checked and counter-checked with that Orient expert, Harvey Mason, and with scores of discriminating friends and acquaintances who have shopped their way through the Orient. My good friends who are native to the Orient or have lived there long periods of time such as Joe Grace and Fritz Schmidt in **Tokyo,** Honesta Marcelo in **Manila,** Dick Banks who has lived all through the Orient, Kusa Panyarachun in **Bangkok,** Seth Clark in **Hong Kong,** and a wide variety of highly respected reliable additional associates and friends have all contributed most enthusiastically and accurately to the compilation of the shops that we have recommended.

Despite my extensive personal research and that of my friends and colleagues, I must hasten to caution you that we are made of flesh and blood as are the shopkeepers and store proprietors. We are all subject to human error. For example, we have in **Chicago** one of the finest department stores in the world. This emporium, despite its unquestioned excellence, is famous for its fantastic "bloopers." I remember a sad incident which developed when this particular deluxe department store sent furniture for an entire house to the *Board of Trade* office of the purchaser, while the bill was delivered to the empty house in the suburbs. This same store handled the recent re-decoration of my **Chicago** offices. They estimated that their furnishing and refurbishing job would be complete in from three to four weeks. It took five months! Unless you know me well, you can only take my word for it that such a state sends my blood pressure soaring higher than a rocket missile.

When you return from shopping in faraway places, patience is a great asset. Half a world and many centuries of educational and training differences separate you from the shop where you have made your purchases. Errors can and will arise. A vast majority of all the travelers who shop in the Orient are pleased with their results. I sincerely hope and believe that you will be, too. If you happen to be included in that small percentage to whom "something happens," be kind and considerate. Don't blow your stack, and *don't sue me.* My lawyer, John Dorgan, tells me I'm immune. Don't jump the gun and start frantically communicating with the hapless shopkeeper before a reasonable interval of time (ten weeks) has elapsed.

Bear in mind that packages shipped by surface mail from cities not on the regular ports of call of the transpacific lines, such as **Bangkok** or **Saigon,** must first be shipped, in bond, across other countries to reach a port where they can be placed on a ship.

There are few errors that can, or will, arise that a modicum of mutual trust and patience cannot iron out. Despite the speed of modern air mail, don't expect the same rapidity of reply from an Oriental shopkeeper that you would receive from your favorite hometown department store. The Oriental mind just doesn't work that way. It takes time. But in the end I am certain that for every dollar expended there will be that number of dollars' worth of merchandise received, plus the added pleasure of objects of rare beauty and worth that will enhance the memories of your wonderful trip.

Items shipped, other than the less than ten dollar gift packages, should be declared on the U.S. Customs form that you will fill out on arrival in the States—or en route on the homeward flight or voyage. Declare everything that has been acquired either accompanying you, to follow, or that has gone ahead. If you exceed your customs free quota, the authorities will select the least dutiable purchases on which to assess customs duty.

Most of the shops in the Orient are now of the fixed price variety (except in **Hong Kong** or **Singapore**), and you would no more haggle with them over a price than you would with *B. Altman* in **New York** or *I. Magnin* in **Los Angeles.** The price listed is usually *the* price and is to be paid. In most **Hong Kong** shops and the bazaar type of place, in **Singapore** for example, you may haggle, however, with effective results.

Be sure to remember that **Hawaii** is a state. You may send anything home by mail, air mail, or parcel post at domestic rates. There are no customs formalities involved, and nothing acquired in **Hawaii** needs to be declared. You will have numerous opportunities to acquire Oriental objects in **Hawaii** that may be shipped from there cheaply and expediently.

MY FAVORITE SHOPS

The CAMERA SHOP, ROYAL HAWAIIAN HOTEL, is one of the most amazingly efficient, cheerful little shops I have ever seen. Here you may have all types of film promptly developed or processed and may purchase just about any kind of camera, film, and accessory. If, by chance, you do not have time to photograph all of the wonders of Hawaii, don't fret. In this shop you will find all sorts of beautiful Kodachrome prints and transparencies as well as eight and sixteen millimeter colored moving picture film prints for sale which cover all

phases of **Hawaii** and Hawaiian life. Their shipping department is excellent. I highly recommend this shop.

The IMPERIAL HOTEL ARCADE, **Tokyo.** In the lower
level of the *Main Building,* you will find the most noteworthy
collection of shops in the Orient, if not in the world, under one
roof. To me, it is perfectly fascinating to loiter for hours win-
dow-shopping in this glamorous area where there are more
than twenty different high-class merchandising establishments
represented. The arcade group features cultured pearls, diamonds, silverware, Japanese paper, ivory, luggage, fabulous
mink, marten, and sables, bamboo stands, dressmaking and
pure silk fabrics, Oriental objects of art, silk shirts, pajamas,
neckties, cameras, lens, binoculars, porcelain, lacquerware, and
dolls.

In addition to the arcade of the *Imperial Hotel,* both the
Nikkatsu and the *Hotel New Japan* in **Tokyo** have wide selections in the groups of shops in their respective arcades.

I personally think it is lots and lots of fun to shop in the
arcades. There are those, however, who feel that to "go out
among them" and walk the streets or go by taxi to find their
shops and/or department stores is more fun. You have your
choice. Whatever you elect to do, on the following pages you
will find excellent lists of recommended stores and shops, as
well as shopping delights in the principal cities of the Orient.

YING TAI, LTD., 120 *Peninsula Hotel,* on the first
floor, and also on the first floor of the *Hong Kong Hilton,*
is my own very favorite **Hong Kong** tailor. Ying Tai and his
staff are a versatile team. They tailor exquisitely for both men
and women. This is a fabulous organization. Their skilled
aptitude is a joy to behold. Unlike most American tailors, Ying
Tai, in common with other Chinese custom tailors, seems to
"hit the fit on the button" on the very first try every time. On
my very first visit to Ying Tai, I ordered two topcoats and
two suits, had my measurements taken on Wednesday afternoon and the first fittings Thursday. The svelte garments (silk
suits and cashmere and vicuña coats) were finished on Friday.

Each garment fitted as well as the proverbial "paper on the wall." Ying Tai's collection of goods is most taste-appealing and includes Thai and Italian silks, woolens from Scotland, as well as ready-made famous-brand cashmere sweaters, plain or beaded. They make, and also have ready-made in stock, brocade evening coats, hunting jackets, and house coats which are breathtakingly beautiful. They also feature a superb selection of ladies' evening bags.

I am sure that there is no more thorough and polite service to be rendered any place than at Ying Tai's. Their quality is outstanding. It is my firm conviction that at Ying Tai's quality level, their prices can't be beat.

ASCOT CHANG COMPANY, 34 Kimberley Road, **Kowloon,** is a custom shirtmaker whose materials are excellent, choice great, and workmanship unexcelled. Shirts may be ordered one day and will be ready the next afternoon. Chang can either work to measure or to match a shirt which you leave with him. He will copy it to the finest tolerance. The Ascot Chang assortment of shirt fabrics is just short of fabulous. Here you save fifty to sixty-five per cent on comparable quality material and workmanship.

S. SAMRAN THAILAND COMPANY, LIMITED, 377/1 Petchburi Road. Magnificent bronze cutlery is one of the extraordinary specialties of **Thailand.** This artistic work is all done painstakingly by hand and includes all of the pieces that one would find in a fine silverware line, such as knives, butter knives, forks, salad forks, spoons, soup spoons, pickle forks, serving spoons, carving knives and forks, and ad infinitum. The exquisite ebony black handles are of polished buffalo horn or may be specially ordered alternatively with white ivory. The shiny black buffalo horn is much more complimentary to the bronze, however, and less expensive. The prices are unbelievably low. They range downward from seventy-five cents (our money) for the large serving knives and forks to as little as thirty-five or forty cents for the smaller items. In the *Samran* brochure, they say: "Like all excellent workmanship, *Samran*'s bronzeware has many imitators. But *Samran's* has never been equaled. Wherever you go today, Thai bronze means *Samran's*. The discriminating buyer, seeking beauty he can be proud of and dependability that is guaranteed, visits **Bangkok's** original bronze factory at *S. Samran Thailand,* for it is only at *Samran's* that you can be sure." To this, I can sincerely add a fervent "amen." *S. Samran* on bronze is like *sterling* on silver. It's the real McCoy. As Mr. Samran told me, "Money means little; it is soon gone. Reputation means everything; it lasts forever."

Other bronze items such as flower bowls, fruit trays, dessert plates, and Thai ceremonial bowls may also be purchased at *Samran's* in almost all sizes.

The *Samran* shop is small and not terribly prepossessing. Its work is fantastically beautiful. Their shipping service is punctilious. I can recommend *S. Samran Thailand Company, Limited,* without any mental equivocations whatsoever.

STATE OF HAWAII

Hawaii is especially noted for the following:

Hawaiian Clothing: Aloha shirts, beachwear, sportswear, Hawaiian dresses *(muumuu, holoku, holomuu, pakemuu),* grass skirts.

Hawaiian Food Specialties: *Kona* coffee, macadamia nuts, preserves and jellies, coconut chips and syrup, herbs.

Island Jewelry: Coral, pearls.

Island Woodcraft.

Woven Specialties: Woven *lauhala, tapa* cloth.

Island Perfumes.

Honolulu Shops

HAWAIIAN FOOD SPECIALTIES

FOODLAND—Ala Moana Center. A paradise for coconut chips, guava jelly, *Kona* coffee, *macadamia* nuts, and other Island products.

WING'S COFFEE COMPANY, LTD.—2228 Kalakaua Avenue *(Royal Hawaiian Market)* and 15 North Pauahi Street (downtown). All fine Hawaiian food specialties packed for

STATE OF HAWAII (cont.)—Honolulu

mailing. *Poha* preserves, vacuum-packed *Kona* coffee, Oriental herbs in abundance.

CHINESE TRADING COMPANY—31 North Pauahi Street. Amidst a wealth of local atmosphere an abundance of all sorts of condiments used in Oriental cooking wizardry as well as wicker ware and Oriental tableware.

HAWAIIAN DRESSES AND SPORTSWEAR

ELSIE DAS—2132 Kalakaua Avenue. Marvelous Hawaiian *muumuus* and Island dresses, available in beautiful materials from cotton to hand screened silks. Also casual separates, ready-made sportswear, handbags, jewelry, men's raw silk ties.

ELSIE KRASSAS—2225 Kalakaua Avenue. *Muumuus* again, with *holokus* a specialty (the ones with the train). Colorful hats contrived of *lauhala* and feathers. Feather leis for men's hats.

PAULINE LAKE—*Royal Hawaiian Hotel* (two shops). Striking fabrics a trademark for the wonderful Hawaiian dresses and sarongs made up here. Her saris are also gorgeous, and there's a fine gift assortment, too.

LIBERTY HOUSE—2314 Kalakaua Avenue. Gay selection of high fashion Hawaiian sportswear of all types. Also gift selections.

M. McINERNY—2269 Kalakaua Avenue. Sportswear of a more sedate variety, beachwear. The **Dynasty Shop** features brocaded and damask lingerie.

ROSS SUTHERLAND—2200 Kalakaua Avenue. Excellent resort and standard men's wear. Aloha and sports shirts. Marvelous beachwear.

WATUMULL STORES—2177 Kalakaua Avenue. Hawaiian wear, saris, batiks, sandals, and Indian crafts.

JEWELRY

GROSSMAN MOODY—2200 Kalakaua Avenue. Gems of Island design. Jade, pearls, crystal. Wonderful chests in which to hoard your purchases.

STATE OF HAWAII (cont.)—Honolulu

MAI FAI JEWELS—Ala Moana Center. Fine merchandise, large gift selection. Reasonable.

MERLE BOYER—824 Keeaumoku Street. Gold and silver work of a modern Hawaiian design, some fashioned in combination with dark Hawaiian wood (I refer to the eye-catching cuff links and earrings). Have a look, too, at the black coral.

MING'S—927 Fort Street, 2171 and 2325 Kalakaua Avenue, *Hawaiian Village Hotel*. Best known jeweler on the Islands. Fantastically beautiful ivory in island flower designs. Quality silver, coral, and jade pieces. Oriental art and antiques, too. *Ming's* also has a store in **Hilo**.

WICHMAN—2239 Kalakaua Avenue. All sorts of gorgeous pearls and precious gems. Branches in the *Reef* and *Royal Hawaiian Hotels*.

HAWAIIAN WOODCRAFT

BLAIR'S—Kalakaua Avenue and Lewers Road, workshop at 404 Ward Avenue (branches at the *Hawaiian Village* and *Reef Hotels*). World famed for island woods (most noted: *monkey pod* and *koa*). Items are cheaper at the workshop and it's interesting to watch the craftsmen at work.

HARRY'S CABINET AND CURIO FACTORY—332 Cooke Street. Visitors are welcome to tour and browse here any weekday. Items will be packed and shipped home if you wish.

HOUSE OF KALAI—1734 Mary Street, Kalihi-Kai. Worth a special visit because of the superior craftsmanship and reasonable prices.

SORENSON'S THE WOOD CARVER—985 Waimanu Street. Hardwood hand rubbed bowls and plates beautifully done. Also sculpted birds and fish—a wonderful gift idea, incidentally.

WOODROSE SHOP—2115 Kalakaua Avenue. Besides sculpted wooden bowls and other *monkey pod* and *koa* items, a fine selection of beautiful ceramics.

STATE OF HAWAII (cont.)—Honolulu

ORIENTAL OBJECTS

ROBERT ANSTETH, LTD.—2126 Kalakaua Avenue. Oriental furniture, screens, scrolls, bronzes, carvings. Japanese and Chinese lanterns. Rugs.

S. M. IIDA'S—8 South Beretania (downtown). Branch at *Ala Moana Center*. Everything, but everything, in Japanese wares from very expensive to downright cheap. Huge selection in the downtown store.

JOJI'S—1890 Kalakaua Avenue. Small and most select. Fine Japanese merchandise.

LACQUER SHOP—*Royal Hawaiian Hotel*. Oriental *objets d'art*. Antique lacquer and porcelain.

HAWAIIAN ART

THE GALLERY—*Hawaiian Village Hotel*. The best of the work of Island artists displayed (the exhibit changes from time to time to show new works). Browsers welcome.

GIMA'S GALLERY—*Ala Moana Center*. Excellent display of local art.

MISCELLANEOUS

AZURE KUOMO—*Royal Hawaiian Hotel*. Shop specializing in luxurious items for the man, woman, or child who has everything. Handloomed blankets, exquisite handmade infantwear, and an especially fine collection of maternity wear.

BAMBOO WINDOW—200 Ward Avenue. All kinds of "fruits of the loom"—wickers, bamboo curtains, *lauhala* products, mats, baskets, et cetera. The wind chimes, starting at two dollars, make appreciated gifts.

JOHN BRETON STORM ANTIQUE SHOP—1362 South Beretania Street. An antique shop that caters to the luxury trade.

BROWNY PERFUMES—1108 Auahi Street (factory). You're welcome to tour this perfume factory any weekday—

STATE OF HAWAII (cont.)—Honolulu

and you get a free sample on your tour of the fine perfume being made from local flowers (white ginger, *pikake, lani,* carnations, orchids—just to name a few).

CERAMICS HAWAII—1053 Kapahulu Avenue. Workshop and studio for island potters. The merchandise (lamp bases, tiles, ashtrays, light fixtures) is for sale.

GALLERY ASIEN—2119 Kalakaua Avenue. The world specialty shop of Harry Shupak. An Asian potpourri featuring graceful articles at reasonable prices.

INTERNATIONAL MARKET PLACE: Items of interest from all over the world, with emphasis on Polynesian specialties.

HONG KONG

Hong Kong is, without any question, the shopping paradise of the world. Here are bargains that will rend an old Scot's heart and displays so eye-appealing as to be wondrous in their richness. However great the bargains appear to be, I must call to your attention that practically without exception you will disappoint the shopkeeper if you do not bargain. If you find that every piece of merchandise in a shop is clearly labeled with a price tag, you may be fairly certain that this indeed is a fixed price store . . . but don't count on it implicitly. It is standard practice to make an offer well below the asking price and then reach a compromise "deal." Bargaining is an integral part of the merchandising system of Hong Kong. Whatever price is asked originally, you must demur. It is particularly true, if you are making several purchases, that you must insist on a quantity discount.

Comprehensive Certificate of Origin. Don't let this particular bit of international bureaucratic red tape "throw" you. Too much complicated gobbledygook has been written, and discussed, about Comprehensive Certificates and their intricacies. It's all very simple, really. To explain the situation in brief, the U. S. Treasury Department forbids that goods purchased in Hong Kong but made in Red China be brought into this coun-

HONG KONG (cont.)

try. Such commercial traffic is not permitted under any conditions. There are a limited number of certain other so-called Chinese type products which cannot be brought into the United States under any conditions, including antiques, Chinese type beverages (except wine for which Certificates are available), cashmere piece goods (Certificates are available for cashmere finished products), chinaware, Chinese type drugs and medicines (except *Tiger Balm*), hand paintings and scrolls of the Chinese type, and handmade lace and lace items. A Certificate of Origin merely guarantees that the item purchased was not made in Red China and that it may legally be brought into the States.

Merchandise which needs a Certificate of Origin to be permitted to be brought into the States includes: hardwood manufacture including furniture (which, incidentally, is a terrific bargain in Hong Kong), ivoryware, jade jewelry and unset jade stones, silk piece goods and silk garments, linen and cotton embroidered articles including handkerchiefs, blouses, tablecloths, Swatow work, and Chinese rugs made in Hong Kong. Most other merchandise may be brought home without special formalities.

What you must be careful to do is to ascertain if the store you have selected displays a Commerce and Industry Department registration for the issue of tourist Comprehensive Certificates of Origin. If you don't see one hanging on the wall, ask to see it. If this is not displayed or available, the shop will not be able to give you the Certificate, if required, and you will have difficulties when you return to the States. If you have any problems relative to the availability of a Certificate of Origin for any given item, you may contact the *Commerce and Industry Department* of the Hong Kong Government at the Fire Brigade Building, Connaught Road, Hong Kong, which is opposite the Vehicle Ferry on the **Victoria** side. The telephone number is 37198 or 20785.

There are hundreds, perhaps thousands, of tailors in Hong

HONG KONG (cont.)

Kong. Many of them are outstanding. The speed and dispatch with which fine garments are turned out by these skilled Hong Kong craftsmen is utterly fantastic. Bear in mind, however, that common sense must be used. Despite the fine work of these amazing people, if you order a suit, dress, or coat at six o'clock in the evening and expect to take a finished garment with you at nine in the morning, it can be done. It is not reasonable to expect, however, that such a garment will be as good as one on which there has been at least one or preferably two fittings . . . although I must confess that even an overnight job without a finished fitting will be as good as most American made clothes.

In reliable establishments, the selection of materials and fabrics is as wide as the world and as varied as its products are diverse. The Chinese tailors have an uncanny ability to help select a style that is becoming to a man or alluring to a woman.

Shoes, coats, dresses, and shirts are custom made specialties. The workmanship is superb, and the ability of the local craftsmen to create a new style for you or copy precisely your own model is almost eerie. Any of the tailors, shirtmakers, or custom shoemakers can copy an article even from a picture. They are utterly fantastic.

In Hong Kong stores and shops operated by Europeans are open until 5:30 P.M. on weekdays and until one P.M. on Saturdays. Chinese shops stay open much later and are open on Sunday.

Principal shopping areas are: in **Victoria**—*Gloucester Arcade, Central Building, Queen's Road Central, Des Voeux Road Central, Wyndham* and *Wellington Streets,* and in **Kowloon**— the *Ambassador Arcade, Hong Kong Hilton Arcade, Peninsula Hotel* (mezzanine floor), *Miramar Arcade, Mirador Arcade, Champagne Court Arcade, Nathan Road, Hankow Road, Canton Road, Carnarvon Road, Mody* and *Cameron Roads.*

I think you will be particularly attracted to the following reliable listing of Hong Kong shops and stores. For certain of the highly recommended shops, I am deeply grateful to my

HONG KONG (cont.)

friend Carl Kroch, the Chicago bookstore tycoon, and his charming sister Gretchen, Mrs. Charles L. Kelsch, of Hong Kong.

The following listings are alphabetical and are not separated into merchandise categories. The stores are of such excellence as to be impossible to "grade," and so many of them carry such a wide variety of merchandise as to defy cataloguing.

Hong Kong specialties include:

Jewels	Porcelains	Embroidered Articles
Curios	Tailoring	Christmas Cards
Brocades	Watches	English China
Laces	Cameras	Cashmere Sweaters (hand-beaded)
Ivories	Furniture	Cut Glass
Jades	Rugs	Sheffield Plate, Cutlery
Linens	Binoculars	

ADA LUM, Ground Floor, 142 Boundary Street, Kowloon. Also 1 Rutton Building, 11 Duddell Street, Hong Kong. Best known for just what you would think: Ada Lum dolls! Embroidery and appliqué also featured. Rather far from town.

ANDRE WATCH COMPANY, Astor Hotel Arcade, Carnarvon Road, Kowloon. Outstanding watches. *Andre* is the authorized agent in Hong Kong for *Patek Philippe* . . . enough said.

A. A. ANNEX, Miramar Hotel Arcade, Kowloon. Exquisite sweaters and purses.

ARTISTIC JEWELRY, 6 Cameron Road, Kowloon. Specialists in the Oriental arts, precious stones, diamonds, and jade.

ASCOT CHANG COMPANY, 34 Kimberley Road, Kowloon. My very favorite custom shirtmaker. See special write-up, page 343.

ASIA PHOTO SUPPLY, LTD., 10 Ice House Street, Hong Kong. Also a branch at 2A Humphrey's Avenue, Kowloon. Photo finishing and exceptional buys in cameras and camera supplies.

HONG KONG (cont.)

BENNY'S SHOE SHOP, 15A Cameron Road, Kowloon. Fashionable shoes in the latest styles. Outstanding workmanship. They can and will copy your own favorite style or create a new one for you.

BLUE SKY, 3 Carnarvon Road, Kowloon. One of the best shops for plain, beaded, and embroidered ladies' sweaters and gloves.

BONNIE'S, Miramar Hotel Arcade, Kowloon. Outstanding for beaded bags and sweaters.

BUDSON WATCH CO., Regent House, 86 Queen's Road Central, Hong Kong. *Budson* has virtually all of the agencies for the finest timepieces. Everything in watches.

CATHAY ARTS COMPANY, 2A Cameron Road, Kowloon. Handsome custom made furniture is a specialty. Fine values. Although the shipping charges on furniture sometimes exceed the Hong Kong cost, you will still have a huge saving when your furniture arrives in the States.

JIMMY CHEN & COMPANY, 12A Cameron Road, Kowloon. Men's tailoring at its best. The prices are commensurate with the fine quality and workmanship. A famous name.

CHOW'S JEWELRY, 34 Hankow Road, Kowloon. Exclusive agents for *Samran*'s bronzeware. If you don't get to **Thailand** and you want the finest values of the most unique and extraordinarily beautiful and serviceable tableware, stop by *Chow's Jewelry*. Their selection of *Samran* bronze cutlery is wonderful.

CHUN LOONG SANG PORCELAIN WARE, 122 Bonham Strand East, Hong Kong. Outstanding ceramics.

CINDERELLA SHOES, Miramar Arcade, Kowloon. Here one may have any shoe duplicated. If you buy silk garments, bring a swatch with you. *Cinderella* will match it for shoes.

BETTY CLEMO, 110/111 Peninsula Hotel. A gorgeous assortment. Custom tailoring and ready-to-wear clothing. Costume jewelry, fine silks, embroidered blouses.

DADLANI'S SILK STORE, Miramar Arcade, Kowloon. Lovely Indian fabrics.

HONG KONG (cont.)

DOREEN, 8D Humphrey's Avenue, Kowloon. Most everything for milady. Handbags, sweaters, gloves, beaded and embroidered articles. A wide selection of dresses and fabrics.

DYNASTY SALON (also known as MANDARIN TEXTILES, LTD.), Peninsula Hotel, Kowloon. A ready-to-wear shop that undertakes some custom tailoring of excellent quality. Brocades, lingerie, linens. The *Dynasty Salon* supplies quality merchandise to leading stores in the United States.

ECHO JEWELRY, 11 New Miramar Arcade, Kimberley Road, Kowloon. Fine jade, precious stones, and cultured pearls. A vast selection.

FALCONER'S, Alexandra House, Chater Road. This well-known reputable firm offers quality jewelry and gems with an emphasis on extraordinarily fine settings. Their jade is beautiful. Expensive.

FILMO DEPOT, LTD., 313-314 Marina House, Hong Kong. Everything for the shutterbug.

FRANCIA FASHIONS, 39A Kimberley Road, Kowloon. Excellent dressmaking with French detailing.

J. L. GEORGE, 3 Cameron Road, Kowloon. A lovely assortment of camphorwood chests, screens, and tables.

THE GOOD FRIEND, 14A Cameron Road, Kowloon. An interesting collection of art objects and jewelry.

GRENLEY'S, Alexander House, Des Voeux Road, Hong Kong. All sorts of British china, including *Royal Doulton, Wedgwood,* and *Spode.* The finest in cut glass, crystal, cutlery, and *Sheffield* plate.

GIGI, 3 Humphrey's Avenue, Kowloon. Among the very best of the Chinese custom shoemakers. The Chinese can duplicate any pair of shoes that you present to them.

HALLMARK TAILORING SHOP, 35 Cameron Road, Kowloon. Gene and Julia Loo offer every kind of fabric from the popular drip-dries to English silks and tweeds in the repertoire of their superb hand-tailored articles.

HARILELA'S, 32/34 Nathan Road, Kowloon, and corner of

HONG KONG (cont.)

Hankow and Middle Road, Kowloon. Well known for the quality workmanship of their tailoring. Also Indian saris, silks, and fine cashmeres. The displays are beautiful.

HENRY THE TAILOR, 37B Carnarvon Road, Kowloon. Excellent men's tailoring.

HONG KONG JADE CENTER, 20B Carnarvon Road, Kowloon. A well-known establishment that features custom-made settings. The specialty of the *Center*'s jewelry line is jade for which a Certificate of Origin is provided with each purchase. The workshop on the premises is open to visitors. Diamonds, star sapphires, pearls, emeralds, and other stones.

CHARLOTTE HORSTMANN, Suites 16/17, Marco Polo-Peninsula Court Hotel, Kowloon. The tailoring here is expensive, but the styling and workmanship are both exquisite. Charlotte offers her own designs. Also a selection of objects of art, fine furniture, costume jewelry, Bangkok silks, Siamese antiques, and temple rubbings. Highly recommended.

HUMPHREY'S ART FURNITURE CO., 1 Humphrey's Avenue, Kowloon. Lovely teakwood and camphorwood chests, coffee tables, and rosewood furniture.

JADE ASTOR JEWELRY COMPANY, Man Yee Building. Wonderful for jade. Ask for Winnie.

JOHNSON TAILORS, LTD., 60A Nathan Road, Kowloon (near the *Peninsula* and *Ambassador Hotels*). Beautifully detailed custom tailoring.

KANEBO SERVICE, LTD., 533 Central Building, Hong Kong. Silks, satins, taffeta, and pongee. Men's silk shirts and a choice of quality merchandise.

EILEEN KERSHAW LIMITED, 238 Peninsula Hotel, Kowloon. Eileen's prices are high, but her merchandise is extraordinarily good. Her selection is too wide to catalogue but includes costume jewelry, linens, brocades, rugs, and lovely accessories. Reliability is the keynote.

KODAK (Hong Kong) LTD., Ninth Floor, Shell House. All photographic supplies for still and moving picture cameras.

HONG KONG (cont.)

Ektachrome and Kodacolor processing as well as still prints and enlargements.

KOW HOO, 19/21 Hennessy Road, Hong Kong, and 134A Nathan Road, Kowloon. Men's shoes a specialty.

KOWLOON RATTANWARE COMPANY, 33 Hankow Road, Kowloon. All types of rattan ware including not only furniture but purses, trays, and miscellaneous items.

KUNG BROTHERS & CO., LTD., New Miramar Arcade and Hong Kong Hilton Arcade. Embroidery, watches, cameras, cultured pearls, jewelry, novelties, and gift items. The quality is wonderful.

LANE, CRAWFORD'S, Telephone House, Des Voeux Road, Hong Kong, and Miramar Arcade, Kowloon (two value-packed stores). *Lane, Crawford's* fabulous department stores are the exclusive Hong Kong agencies for *Mikimoto* cultured pearls and feature men's suit and shirt tailoring, jewelry of all kinds (available in custom settings), Oriental crafts, ladies' fashions, children's wear, shoes, stationery, toys, linens, and furniture. Additionally, there is an Elizabeth Arden beauty salon. A wide selection, indeed.

LE BEAU, Queen's Theater Building, Hong Kong, and Champagne Court, ground floor, Kowloon. Everything in intimate apparel for milady.

JAMES S. LEE AND CO., 225 Gloucester Road, Hong Kong, and Haiphong Mansion, Kowloon. The prices are moderate; the craftsmanship is outstanding. I think you will be particularly taken with the fine British woolens available for tailoring here. A fine assortment of cashmeres and perfumes also.

T. Y. LEE & CO., 229 Gloucester Road, Hong Kong. A full selection of fine jewelry but best known for jade, diamonds, and star sapphires.

LEE KEE BOOT & SHOE MAKER, LTD., 19 Hanyee Building, Hankow Road, Kowloon. Smart styles in men's and women's shoes.

HONG KONG (cont.)

LILLY SHOES, Miramar Arcade, Kowloon. The elegant footwear here is highly recommended.

S. Y. MA, 33A Hankow Road, Kowloon. A generous selection of fine furniture on which the most painstaking workmanship has been lavished. Also recommended for art objects.

MACKINTOSH'S, LTD., Alexandra House, Des Voeux Road, Hong Kong. Most noteworthy for British woolen ready-to-wear; argyles, sweaters, et cetera.

MILADY, 34 Ambassador Hotel—Far East Mansion Arcade, Kowloon. Simply fabulous Thai silk, beaded sweaters, handbags, readymade dresses and coats.

MOHAN'S LIMITED, 19A Hankow Road, Kowloon. Fine tailoring and a wide variety of outstanding merchandise.

NEE WUH TSENG, Ocean View Court, Mody Road, Kowloon. Distinctive teak, rosewood, and camphorwood furniture and furnishings.

NEW UNIVERSAL JEWELRY COMPANY, 8A Carnarvon Road, Kowloon (opposite the *Astor Hotel*). A reliable house with a vast selection of jewelry, including natural and cultured pearls, diamonds, jade, star rubies, other precious and semiprecious stones, and watches.

NORTH CHINA INDUSTRIES, 236 Nathan Road, Kowloon. Scintillating brocades.

OLD MARY SING SHUN COMPANY, 3-5 Chungking Arcade, Nathan Road, Kowloon. Teakwood and rosewood camphorwood-lined chests, furniture, bars, tables, as well as linens, curios, and watches. Lots of atmosphere.

ORIENTAL GEM EXCHANGE, LTD., No. 6 Champagne Court Arcade, Kimberley Road, Kowloon. A fine selection of precious stones, ivory, nielloware, and curios. Very reliable and well recommended.

ORIENTAL HANDWORK COMPANY, Wyndham Street, Hong Kong. Wonderful handkerchiefs. When you go there, ask for Diane.

PAGODA GIFT CENTER, Astor Hotel, Carnarvon Road,

HONG KONG (cont.)

Kowloon, and 31, Ground Floor, Far East Mansion, Middle Road, Kowloon. Beaded sweaters, brocades, Thai silk, hand-knit dresses, and ladies' tailoring.

PHOENIX, Room 213, Miramar Hotel, Kowloon. One of the best of Hong Kong's women's tailors.

PLAZA HOUSE, Far East Mansion, Kowloon (adjacent to the *Ambassador Hotel*). Famous for jewelry as well as ladies' and men's custom tailoring.

ROYAL JEWELRY, 104 Nathan Road, Kowloon. Both a wholesale and retail jewelry house, especially noted for diamonds, quality jewelry, and watches.

SHUI HWA WATCH COMPANY, 77 Queen's Road Central, Hong Kong, and 14 Miramar Hotel Arcade, Kimberley Road, Kowloon. Features Piaget ultra thin automatic watches. Outstanding quality.

SINAMEX JADE FACTORY, 19B Champagne Court, Kimberley Road, Kowloon. Excellent values in cut and polished jade and semiprecious stones.

M. SOONG, 25 Mody Road, Kowloon. This is an excellent address for chic women's clothing.

STANDARD CO., Alexandra House (ground floor), 22 Chater Road, Hong Kong. Specialists in fine gems and pearls.

STRENGTH AND COMPANY, 25A Cameron Road, Kowloon. A reliable store specializing in car-coats, raincoats, and ski jackets. Tremendous bargains.

SWATOW WENG LEE COMPANY, 52 Nathan Road, Kowloon. Unmentionables of the finest quality to make the feminine heart beat pitty-pat.

SWINDON BOOK SHOP, Mirador Mansion, 64 Nathan Road, Kowloon. A wide multilingual selection of tomes from which to choose.

TAILOR KO, Ground Floor, 88 Nathan Road, Kowloon. Truly outstanding tailor even among Hong Kong's exceptionally high level tailoring establishments.

HONG KONG (cont.)

TAI PING CARPET SALON (also known as HONG KONG CARPET MANUFACTURERS LIMITED), Middle Road, Kowloon. Beautifully executed Chinese rugs. This fine establishment is completely certified to provide you with a comprehensive Certificate of Origin for their excellent quality merchandise.

TAI SHUN JEWELRY COMPANY, 72 Queen's Road Central, Hong Kong. Such a wide variety of superb jewelry that just "window shopping" is a pleasure. Excellent values.

TANG'S & CO., 16 Carnarvon Road, Kowloon. Everything in the way of cameras, radios, binoculars, projectors . . . even typewriters. Fine developing, printing, and enlarging as well.

VAN ZIANG, 2 Carnarvon Road, Kowloon. This tailoring house comes highly recommended.

S. L. WANG & CO., 88 Nathan Road, Kowloon (Second Floor). Shirtmakers deluxe. Fine materials, excellent craftsmanship.

WELFARE HANDICRAFT SHOP, Salisbury Road, Kowloon. The wide variety of attractive, tempting souvenirs and gift items featured here are made by refugees. The prices are extraordinarily low and the quality high.

A. WHITE & COMPANY, 21J Hankow Road, Kowloon. *White*'s features everything in the field of cameras, transistor radios, tape recorders, field glasses, binoculars, and projectors.

WHITEAWAY, LAIDLAW & CO., LTD., 18/20 Connaught Road Central, Hong Kong. A top-flight department store offering a wide selection of British woolen clothing.

YEE CHEONG & COMPANY, 69 Granville Road, Kowloon. The finest in children's wear including hand-smocked dresses, appliqué, and "coolie" pajamas.

YING TAI, LTD., Peninsula Hotel, Kowloon, and Hong Kong Hilton Hotel, Victoria. My very favorite tailor. Absolutely tops for both men and women. Gift items deluxe. Superb for silks, brocades, lingerie, and sweaters, both beaded and plain. See special write-up, page 342.

HONG KONG (cont.)

WILLIAM YU & M. K. LOO, 112 Peninsula Hotel, Kowloon. The setting of this men's and women's tailoring shop is in the lap of luxury.

Y. WILLIAM YU AND FRANK L. CHAN, 30 Kimberley Road, Kowloon. Men's and women's tailors.

ZOU NAN, 5 Prat Avenue. Exclusive women's tailors at moderate prices.

JAPAN

In addition to the soft, lovely French word *souvenir,* used and understood around the globe to mean "something to remember . . . a gift," Germans use *das andenken,* the Spanish say *recuerdo* or *obsequio,* while in the Far East the Filipinos speak of *ala-ala,* the Chinese of *li-ping,* and ninety-three million Japanese use the expression *o-miyagi.*

When we think of shopping in the Orient, giddy visions of **Hong Kong,** the shopper's paradise, naturally spring to mind, but **Japan,** too, is a veritable treasure-trove of *o-miyagi,* or gifts, to give others or, stretching the point, gifts to yourself!

Japanese artisans have, through the centuries, turned their deft fingers, fertile artistic imaginations, and exquisite sense of impeccable taste to making wondrous big things and exquisitely perfect little things.

With limitless supplies of gold, silver, ivory, jade, pearl, lacquer, bamboo, glass, stone, crystal, brass, bronze, iron, wood, and clay with which to work, they have moulded, wrought, and shaped everything conceivable for the eye to admire and the soul to savor. Today, as in the past, these craftsmen are busily at work. You'll be fascinated by the ingenious, beautiful products of their creative minds and skillful hands.

All you need is this simple formula: have yen, will spend. The Japanese artists will do the rest.

Our word for it would be "taste," but the Japanese call it *shibui, wabi,* and *sabi,* a trinity of words that combine to mean the same thing. *Shibui* translates into refinement, balance, and

JAPAN (cont.)

definition. *Wabi,* another esoteric word, means quiet dignity and restraint in artistic creation, while *sabi* is elegant simplicity and quiet atmosphere of artistry. *Shibui, wabi,* and *sabi* are implicit in every work of the traditional artist and craftsman with which Japan abounds.

Treasured techniques and arts have been handed down from Japanese fathers to sons for generations as in few other lands. The priceless traits that make for skillful fabrication have also been inherited, together with the necessary qualities of patience, reflection, and the desire to spend tireless hours lingering over infinitely minute details. The skillful hands, agile minds, and artistic spirits of the modern Japanese are a natural evolution of the centuries of creative concentration and breeding to create things of beauty.

PEARLS are Japan's greatest gift to the shopping world. Their four main points are luster, shape, size, and color. A thick pearl layer is a feature of the cultured gems which provides the fine luster. Perfectly round pearls are considered best and are most in demand. "Drop" and "pear" shaped pearls are deemed inferior, though oddly shaped and uneven pearls, called "Baroques," can be put to good use for special purposes and effects. Complete half-sphere pearls, called "Mabe," popular for rings and earrings, are generally larger than the average round pearl.

A pearl's value is in direct proportion to its size and symmetry. Pink and white pearls are thought the most valuable, while the black, blue, gray, or golden ones are usually less valuable since they tend, eventually, to lose their luster.

Heat, acid, moisture, and some household chemicals can damage pearls, causing flaws to appear and luster to dull. To keep your pearls in perfect condition, take care to wipe them clean of perspiration and face powder before putting them away. Every now and then wash your necklace in warm water, using a bath soap followed by an application of a few drops of baby oil which will bring out the original luster. Necklace

JAPAN (cont.)

strings should be replaced at least once a year to prevent rotting and subsequent breakage.

Unstrung pearls, or pearls strung on an unknotted string, carry a duty of only a fraction of the finished necklaces.

CLOISONNÉ is a baked enamel called, in Japanese, *Shippo* to describe jewelry known in the Sanskrit as "Septa Retuna" or the "Seven Heavenly Treasures," representing gold, silver, emerald, agate, coral, crystal, and pearl. Cloisonné appreciation and ownership, once confined to the noble few, is now familiar to and beloved by the general public. The cloisonné process consists of baking colored enamel onto copper or silver objects, which are coated and baked a total of three times.

Opaque, translucent, and transparent enamels are used to achieve the desired artistic cloisonné effects; the clearer the enamel, the more the metal's luster is permitted to show through. The final cloisonné result is a beautifully shaped surface of varying coloration and lighting. "Pigeon's blood" is judged by many experts to be the finest, the most artistic, and most treasured type of cloisonné.

DAMASCENE, a complex technique of jewelry making which originated in the pre-Christian era in Damascus, was brought to Japan in A.D. 700. At present, the technique is practiced principally in **Kyoto.** Originally applied only to making Buddhist utensils, mirrors, warriors' helmets, and swords, damascene is now applied to inexpensive costume jewelry, letter openers, smoking articles, and decorative room pieces.

The damascene process involves numerous fine lines being chiselled with delicate instruments on a steel foundation and then inlaid with 24K gold and sterling silver. The surfaces are first corroded with nitric acid and rusted with ammonia chloride which process is halted by immersion in boiling green tea. Several layers of lacquer are next baked on the entire surface, followed by polishing the design with charcoal and then the final engraving and retouching.

LACQUERWARE, another of Japan's more famous products,

JAPAN (cont.)

known as *urushi* or *shikki,* was introduced more than two thousand years ago and has been used in home and ceremonial dining ever since. Lacquer bowls can be used for hot soups, tea, and foods, and can withstand the ravishing of acid, alkali, alcohol, heat, and an immense amount of everyday use. The quality of the sheen of the lacquered article, gold speckled on red, silver on brown, etc., is a fine indication of the quality; the brighter the surface, the better the product. Available in jewel boxes, cigarette cases, plates, platters, bowls, tea cups, saucers, and screens, lacquerware is now usually made with a metallic rather than a wooden base. Like so many other fine arts and crafts, lacquerware was introduced into Japan from China.

CARVED IVORY. One of the most fascinating art objects is the ivory figurine, some carved from half a billiard ball, others, in one piece, from the single tusk of an Indian elephant. Figures depict all kinds of people, animals, and scenes; they tell stories, record history, re-create legends, and portray historic personalities such as warriors, Buddhist saints, sages, and monarchs.

Ivory statues, some two feet or more in height, and little hand objects, called *ne-tsuke* by Japanese admirers, are often stained a light yellowish brown with the aid of special tools and needles. Ivory also carves into valued chess and checkers sets and accessories.

KIMONOS AND OBIS. Kimono literally means "wearing thing," but most of us westerners think of the word as signifying the beautiful Japanese ladies' formal and semi-formal robes. These garments may be both complicated and expensive, heavily brocaded and ornamented, for such formal occasions as weddings and funerals. But they also come in all qualities, types, and weights of cloth from silk down to rayon and other synthetic mixtures. Kimonos are available in almost all price categories. One can buy a heavy quilted kimono for winter, a light, flimsy, inexpensive one for summer, and they are avail-

JAPAN (cont.)

able for boys, girls, and tiny tots. Obis are the decorative sashes that hold the kimono in place; some are pre-tied, others must be hand manipulated . . . sometimes quite a job.

The Japanese display their wares with an inbred sense of artistic wizardry. Even in a simple fruit store, the owner has taken the trouble to make his goods shine, polishing each piece separately and lovingly.

Profusion is on every hand in Japan. Before buying, one must take care, search, ponder, and select.

Your choice of purchases in **Japan** is so considerable that I have taken the liberty of dividing them into categories. They are:

THE OLD RELIABLES

Antiques and Woodblock Prints
Cultured Pearls, Jade, and Ivory Carvings
Raw Silks, Brocades, and Damask
Kimonos and Obis
Cloisonné, Lacquerware, and Damascene
Pottery and Porcelainware
Wrought Iron Work
Stone, Paper, and Wood Products

SOMETHING NEW

Cameras, Optical Goods, and Binoculars
Transistor Radios, Record Players, and Portable Television Sets
Gold and Silver Inlay Articles
High-grade Luggage and Leather Goods
Tortoise Shellware, Bone China, and Chinaware
Hunting Rifles and Cutlery made by old swordmakers

FOR THE CHILDREN

Fabulous Dolls (representing, through hair styles, kimono styles, poses, and ornaments, each period of Japan's long history)
Delightful Toys and Paper Fans
Gay Kimonos and Happi Coats

JAPAN (cont.)

Rice-straw Slippers and Wooden Clogs

Ornaments—bone, crystal, coral, and tortoise shell

FOR THE HOUSE

Carved Wood Furniture and Bambooware

Washable Raw Silk Curtains

Coffee, End Tables, and Nests of Tables

Dining Room Screens—three to six panels

Place Sets and Napkins

THE UNEXPECTED

Japanese Furs (real buys, but watch the quality)

Wigs, Hairpieces, and Braids

Sendai Chests of brass-bound camphorwood

Mother-of-pearl Inlaid Chests of Drawers

Pictures Stitched in Silk Thread

Cuff Links made from old Samurai Sword Ornaments

ATTRACTIVE LITTLE EXTRA THINGS

Whistling Sake Bottles, Sake Bottles and Cups

Music Boxes, Bamboo Violins, and tuneful Cigarette Lighters

Paper Parasols and Rice Paper Stationery

Artificial Flowers and Bamboo Mats and Name Cards

Noh Play Masks

When you clear customs after your arrival in Japan, you will have appended to your Passport a "Record of Purchase of Commodities Tax Exempt for Export" form. Guard this assiduously; it will permit you to make purchases of a variety of items free of local tax in specially designated stores dealing with foreign tourists. You must present this form, and immigration registration card, on your departure from Japan, at which time you may be called upon to show your tax-free purchases. Pack accordingly.

Tax-free purchases, at a saving of from 18 to 50 per cent, include: pearls, precious metal items, articles for interior decoration, cloisonné, furs, woodblock prints, ceramic ware, personal

JAPAN (cont.)

ornaments, cameras, binoculars, telescopes, art objects covered or plated with precious metals, ivory figurines, lacquered metal articles used for smoking utensils, tortoise shell, and coral, dolls and ornaments, hunting guns, portable TV sets, radios, slide projectors, timepieces and toys. There are others.

For your convenience, I have compiled a list, at the end of this section, giving you all the tax-free stores in Japan as well as the members of the *Japan Souvenir Association*.

You need not slight the non-tax-free places completely, where proprietors often come down in price and offer good buys. Silks, for example, not on the tax-free list, are highly desirable and often may be bargained for profitably. It is, however, a safe bet to shop with members of the *Japan Souvenir Association*. These stores, where almost all articles in which you might be interested may be bought tax free upon presentation of your passport, have been designated by local revenue offices, and purchases made therein can be checked through customs quickly and easily at your port of departure.

The fascinating arcades are worthy of your attention. The best are located in **Tokyo** and **Kyoto**. The arcades in the *Tokyo Hilton Hotel, Imperial Hotel, Palace Hotel, Okura Hotel, New Japan Hotel, Nikkatsu Hotel,* the *Sukiyabashi Shopping Center,* and the two-story *International Arcade* near the *Imperial Hotel* are the best in **Tokyo,** and I think you will find the arcades in the *Miyako, Kyoto,* and *International Hotels* in **Kyoto** outstanding. The smaller arcades are attractive, too—such as those in the basement of the *Ginza Tokyu Hotel,* on the ground floor of the *Old Marunouchi Building* facing *Tokyo Central Station,* and at the *Tokyo International Airport.*

A visit to a great Japanese department store is an unusual experience. The best ones are on the *Ginza* and in the *Nihombashi* area. Others are located in the suburbs with which **Tokyo** abounds, like *Shinjuku, Ikebukuro,* and *Shibuya.* As I have said so often in these pages, the only thing really bizarre in Japan is the commonplace. The exotic is normal. Nowhere else

JAPAN (cont.)

in the world can one find so many strange happenings under one roof as in a Japanese department store. Here, for example, one may see Shinto nuptials, a flower arrangement ceremony, a tea ceremony, an exhibition of Chinese bone-rubbing paintings, a collective camera work exposition, or the ancient treasures of the Imperial household of Iran. These department stores are fantastic, complete with rooftop zoos, amusement parks, beer halls, and cosmopolitan scenic restaurants where other weddings are held. They sell everything from living-room furniture to lotus seeds, centipede oil, tinned steamed bees, and Japanese guitars made from catskin.

But don't let me create an image of Japanese department stores that might induce you to believe that these emporiums are not brilliant merchandising organizations as well as purveyors of the oddities mentioned above. Here one may see fashion shows comparable to the best in the west, brilliant clothing sections offering excellent western and Oriental garments, radio and television sections, magnificent furniture and housewear departments, plus all of the odds and ends of world-wide merchandising. And, since Japan is not a Christian nation, the "Departos" as the Japanese call them are open on Sundays!

Department store prices are fixed; they are not subject to bargaining, haggling, argumentation, or debate. English is spoken in most sections of all the larger department stores, and interpreters are on call in sections where a language barrier may arise. Interpreters may be readily identified by their pink buttons.

I want to share with you some superb Japanese shopping experiences in **Tokyo,** in the so-called *Kansai* area of **Kyoto, Osaka,** and **Kobe,** as well as other shopping gems here, there, and all around. Please remember that even much longer lists than those which follow could never begin to tell the whole shopping story of a nation such as Japan blessed with so many artisans, endowed with such great skills, and such glamorous products. These will serve you only as a preliminary guide;

JAPAN (cont.)

that's my only intent. Your own exploration can do the rest. Among my pets in **Tokyo** are:

The KORIN SILK MANSION, a gorgeous gallery for the display and sale of silk products, located in the former town residence of Prince and Princess Takamatsu (he is the younger brother of His Majesty Emperor Hirohito). The *Silk Mansion* sells the finest products of each of the major Japanese silk mills, with a handloom length selling for as little as $2.50 per meter (or $2.25 per yard)! Silk is not on the tax-free list, and, while one may do so elsewhere, one doesn't bargain at the *Silk Mansion*. There are prices here, however, to meet every taste, and all are outstanding values. Ask for Mr. Kawazoe, a dapper, silver-haired gentleman whose English is impeccable. You can enjoy a cup of tea or stroll through the magnificent gardens. Near Shiba Street at the Isarago bus stop, between A and B Avenues (phone 441-0113), the *Korin Silk Mansion* is open daily ten A.M. until five P.M.

K. UYEDA, *Imperial Arcade,* silversmiths and jewelers unexcelled, is **Tokyo's** oldest store. I'll always pay this elegant shop a return visit. It seems to sell just everything. Open ten A.M. until 6:30 P.M.

JAPAN SWORD, B Avenue and 12th Street (phone 431-0654, 2256 or 2271), features ancient and modern swords fitted with gold, jewels, and decorative metals. Besides the wonderful old blades that would make a samurai gasp, this place offers cutlery, much of it centuries old and marvelously wrought. There are hunting knives, carving sets, barbecue and steak knives, and jackknives, to name a few. You have but to ask to watch the manufacturing process. Open daily from nine A.M. to six P.M. and Sundays from nine A.M. to five P.M.

CIRO'S, heartily recommended and easy to find on F Avenue between 15th and the *Meiji Park* entrance, is a homemaker's dream come true. The happy profusion of folkcraft includes wrought iron lamps, old Sendai chests, soma ware, gold screens,

JAPAN (cont.)

bronze ornaments, and bamboo articles. Open from nine A.M. until six P.M. daily except Sundays and Japanese holidays.

ICHY'S, another fascinating shop, nearer the junction of F and 15th Street, is the home of wood carving, the *Noh* mask, and sculpturing.

The bulk of the ART GOODS SHOPPING CENTERS are located in an intriguing district known as *Azabu,* bounded by Mita and B Avenues, by 10th Street, and Avenues D and F. The shops are readily reached by cab, a ride of about 45¢ cost. The innumerable pleasing shops here deal in rare objects, wonderful works of ivory, jade, silk, cloisonné, lacquerware, pearl, bronze, brass, and iron. I suggest the following as being well stocked and reliable: NORITAKE CHINA (NITTO TOKI), phone 591-9376/7; TSUKAMOTO MASHIKO-WARE SHOP, phone 481-4567; TAKARA SHOKAI, phone 501-8712; OSHIRO, phone 501-2671/2; JAPANESE PAINTING CENTER, phone 501-9322; YANAGAWA ART STORE, phone 408-3325; YUSHIMA-SEIDO, phone 921-4606; ASAHI ART, D near 17th Street; KOTOBUKIYA, F near *Meiji Park* entrance; HAIBARA, W between Ginza and 10th Street, fabulous for paper and stationery in an old Dickensian World atmosphere; the KOCHUKYO ART GALLERY and the FUGENDO ART SHOP (in back of the *Takashimaya Department Store*); and the ROPPONGI GABO GALLERY, near Roppongi crossing, D and 15th Street These are only a few of many. I suggest you take an exploratory stroll up Mita, B, D, or F Avenues. See for yourself; you will find the time and effort worthwhile.

TAKUMI, 5th Street near *Shimbashi Station,* is impossible to beat for folkcraft, that which the Japanese call *min-gei,* or, actually, folk art that serves a modern purpose. *Mingei* designs often are hundreds of years old and are available in porcelain-ware, paper, metal, woodwork, silk, and cloth. The word *min-gei* means literally "to serve the people," and to fulfill this purpose the craftware must be within the means of the ordinary person. In *Takumi* one finds *imari*-ware, *bizen*-ware,

JAPAN (cont.)

and *kutani*-ware (fine porcelains), homely old iron kettles, paper ornaments, bamboo kitchen utensils, children's playthings . . . an unusual world of antiques. *Takumi* is a Diners Club member and is open daily from ten A.M. until seven P.M.

The IMPERIAL HOTEL ARCADE is one of my very favorites. There, in a group of stores, one can satisfy virtually every shopping dream without ever leaving the hotel. The other brilliant shopping arcades found in the *Palace, Okura, New Japan,* and *Nikkatsu Hotels* feature either the following shops or similar. Shopping in either the department stores or arcades is convenient, easy, and efficient. Only the most reliable shops are represented in the arcades. You may count implicitly on them, and include: MOH LONG's pure silk fabrics, raw silk, shantung, pongee, taffeta, faille, satin, and brocades. KOHRAI means fine millinery; MAYUYAMA is noted for art work, woodblock prints, and many tempting things; and TOYO PORCELAIN for what its name says. KITTY'S is the spot for unique *kokeshi* dolls, bambooware, and name cards; ASAHI SHOTEN for cultured pearls, jewelry, and ivory figurines; FUTABA for furs; and OKUBO BROTHERS for silverware, crystals, cloisonné, and lacquerware . . . and, of course, MIKIMOTO'S for pearls, pearls, pearls. At ODAWARA SHOTEN one finds a happy service: in addition to the profusion of fine Oriental *objets d'art,* they will pack, crate, and ship all you buy, from them or any other store, doing it wonderfully well, quickly, and reasonably. In the *Imperial Hotel Arcade,* other shops are: HODOTA (ivory), SUGA (photo shop), TORII (handbags), K. UEDA (fine arts and jewelry), CHIKYUDO (luggage), MIYAJIMA (florist), SAITO (drugs and toiletries), SATO (film service, transparencies, and cameras), MACHI (dressmaking), and OMIYA (shirts, pajamas, and neckties).

I think you'll find a cab ride to the AKIHABARA (electronics) and KANDA (books) districts of **Tokyo,** fifteen to twenty minutes, less than sixty cents, worthwhile.

JAPAN (cont.)

The AKIHABARA District is an area of a few blocks in the immediate vicinity of *Akihabara Station* (on the main *Yamate Loop Line,* a station away from *Ueno Station*) where there are small and big shops, many of them under a common series of roof extensions, separate ones off to one side, across the street, and around the corner, all dealing in electrical and electronic goods, at wholesale and special low prices which can be made even lower through bargaining. This area is the home of hi-fi, stereo, TV, transistor radios, household electronic devices, records, electronics for entertainment, tape recorders, players, and turntables.

In the KANDA District, Japan reproduces its version of the famed **Paris** *Left Bank* bookworld. Here one finds scores of students and endless stalls and shops crammed with reading matter . . . shop after shop after shop jam-packed with books, books, and more books, old and new, Japanese and western. As an added thrill (ugh), across the street from the volumes are **Tokyo's** native style pharmacies. These weird shops specialize in frogs' blood, powdered snake, crushed spiders, live newts, poultices of ants and flies, all of which are allegedly good for what, if anything, ails you.

Tokyo

PEARLS

Japan's best buy may be purchased at the following:

THE ARCADE SHOPS—listed previously. All good.

FUJI—Namiki-dori Street almost at Annex Avenue. This tax exempt store, closed on Sundays, cultivates its own pearls. Magnificent brooches, bracelets, necklaces, tie clasps, earrings, rings, and other pearl items.

KITAMURA—Sukiyabashi Shopping Center. No tax for visitors to Japan.

K. MIKIMOTO. A special word goes to *Mikimoto's,* probably Japan's most famous name. World renowned for pearls,

JAPAN (cont.)—Tokyo

famed also for other jewelry and silverware, *Mikimoto* is ubiquitous . . . on the Ginza between Z and Exchange, in the Imperial Hotel Arcade, in Osaka, Kobe, Kyoto . . . in a word, deservedly, almost everywhere.

YACHIYO PEARL—near Shirobasha, off Ginza between Annex and Z. Pearls and genuine gems. Open daily from ten A.M. to nine P.M.

TAKASHIMA—Ryokan Avenue near 15th Street, has its own cultivating farm in Sasebo, Kyushu. Open nine A.M. to five P.M. daily.

CLOISONNÉ

THE ARCADES

ANDO, Z between Ginza and 5th (phone 571-0888).

DAMASCENE

The finest damascene to be found in **Tokyo** may be purchased at AMITA, Second Floor, Sukiyabashi Shopping Center. (*Amita*'s headquarters are in **Kyoto,** home of modern damascene.) If you wish, you are welcome to come watch the complete fascinating damascene handwork process. Open daily from ten A.M. until nine P.M.

LACQUERWARE

THE ARCADES

KUROEYA—Ginza between W and Nihonbashi (phone 271-3356/7).

TAKAYAMA SANSHODO—one block from the corner of X and 15th (phone 671-1957).

IVORY

THE ARCADES

KITAGAWA IVORY CO.—Aoyama Akasaka, Minatoku (phone 401-7496).

JAPAN (cont.)—Tokyo

MAKINO IVORY—Yanakamachi, Daito-ku (phone 821-4787).

SUNAMOTO—opposite the Imperial Hotel Annex (phone 591-5610).

KIMONOS AND OBIS

THE ARCADES

K. HAYASHI—10th Street at T Avenue (phone 851-9247).

ICHI FUJI—three blocks to Kyobashi from Miharabashi crossing (phone 561-0959).

KYOTO SILK—near *Harajuku Station* (phone 401-2912).

TAKARA CO.—on Ryokan Avenue (phone 501-8712).

SILK GOODS

THE ARCADES

KANEBO—Ginza and St. Luke's Avenue (phone 561-8711). Sales outlet for the famed textile company. Bolts and bolts and bolts of every conceivable color and design, and on the top floor what a friend of mine aptly calls "Ladies' Land" . . . and no mistake about it. A battery of dress designers awaits you.

KAWAMURA—Ginza half a block from Utility Avenue.

MILDRED WARDER—at the entrance to the rear of the *American Embassy* (phone 431-7976). U.S. interior decorator and designer par excellence.

MINATO—on D Avenue between 10th and 15th Streets.

TATSUMURA TEXTILE—Second Floor, Mitsui Building, Hibiya.

KORIN SILK GALLERY—very special as already noted.

DEPARTMENT STORES IN TOKYO (the biggest and best)

DAIMARU—New Tokyo Station Building, 5th and X. Closed Thursdays. Open 10 to 6.

HANKYU—Z and 5th Street. Closed Mondays. Open 10 to 6.

KOMATSU—Ginza near Annex. Closed Thursdays. Open 10:30 to 6.

JAPAN (cont.)—Tokyo

MATSUYA—Ginza at Exchange. Closed Thursdays. Open 10 to 6.

MATSUZAKAYA—Ginza at Annex. Closed Thursdays. Open 10 to 6.

MITSUKOSHI—Nihonbashi. Closed Mondays. Open 10 to 6.

SHIROKIYA—Nihonbashi, W and Ginza. Closed Mondays. Open 10 to 6.

TAKASHIMAYA—Ginza, Nihonbashi. Closed Mondays. Open 10 to 6.

DEPARTMENT STORES IN TOKYO'S SUB-CITIES

TOKOKO—Shibuya. Closed Mondays. Open 10 to 6.

ISETAN—Shinjuku. Closed Mondays. Open 10 to 6.

SEIBU—Ikebukuro. Closed Thursdays. Open 10 to 6.

MATSUZAKAYA—Ueno. Closed Mondays. Open 10 to 5:30.

SOGO—*Yuraku-cho Station.* Closed Wednesdays. Open 10 to 6.

TAILORING (MEN AND WOMEN)

Perhaps you haven't been or aren't going to **Hong Kong,** or perhaps you've been there and didn't finish up. This need not be catastrophic. The following are excellent Japanese tailors:

BAROMON (Royal Hong Kong Tailor)—Room 409, Fukoku Building, A Avenue between the *Imperial Hotel* and *NHK Building.* This Hong Kong tailor transplanted to Japan caters to some of the best dressed men in the world. One may have two day tailoring service.

HENRY—New Japan Hotel. One of the world's best. Men's shirts and suits are his specialties.

JAMES S. LEE—Yoyogi between 30th and F. Fine cloth, good tailoring, for both men and women.

OXFORD—First Floor, San Shin Building, one block from the *Imperial Hotel,* Avenue A near Z. Hand tailoring for both ladies and men.

SMILEY HONG KONG CLOTHING—15th between D

JAPAN (cont.)—Tokyo

and F, in front of *Hardy Barracks*. Another Hong Kong tailor featuring quality workmanship, fine materials, and forty-eight hour service if required.

DOLLS

Among the most gracious, delightful dolls in all of the world are the Japanese. I have a vast collection of dolls from all over the world. My Japanese and Thai dolls always evince the most spectacular ohs and ahs. Although the very heartland of the doll manufacturing industry is **Kyoto,** there are several excellent shops in **Tokyo,** including:

KABUKIYA—Second Floor, Sukiyabashi Shopping Center (phone 571-8076).

YASUDA—a block off R Avenue between T and V (phone 661-6717).

YOSHITOKU CO. LTD.—3 Asakusabashi, 1-chome, Minato-ku (near *Asakusa Temple*). Most famous of all. The very best for dolls.

YOURS'—in front of the *Takarazuka Theater,* near the *Imperial Hotel* (phone 591-1211, extension 457).

MISCELLANEOUS

Here are just a few more shops which sell goods not yet covered:

JENA—Z between Ginza and 5th Street. For books and magazines, one of the few stores dealing exclusively with English publications. Professional works and Orientalia. Open from ten A.M. to ten P.M.

MATSUSHIMA—Ginza between St. Luke's and Exchange Avenues. The finest in cameras, binoculars, telescopes, optical goods, and accessories.

KATSUMIDO—on the Ginza. Cameras and all that pertains to them. Tops.

ORIENTAL BAZAAR—Yoyogi between F and 30th (phone 401-3933). One of Japan's largest art stores, featuring all kinds

JAPAN (cont.)—Tokyo

of curios and fine arts. Open daily from 9:30 A.M. to 6:30 P.M. throughout the year.

KIDDY LAND—Yoyogi between 30th and F (phone 401-6503). For dolls, dolls, dolls.

CHIKUSENDO-HONTEN—between X and W on 15th Street (phone 671-0750). For fans, lanterns, parasols, and post cards.

TSURUYA—on Ginza near Y Avenue (phone 561-4062). Fishing tackle.

SIBERIAN—First Floor, Fukoku Building, near 10th on A Avenue (phone 591-1776). Furs.

SHIMURA—Yoyogi between F and 30th (phone 401-6322). A complete stock of silk and gold screens, Shoji screens, butterfly paper, and lanterns.

ISHIKATSU—on F Avenue, two blocks down toward the *Meiji Park* entrance from 15th Street (phone 401-1677/2505/5938). The foremost stonecutters in all Japan. All types of stone lanterns, monuments, and garden pieces in artistic designs.

HUNTER—Sukiyabashi Shopping Center (phone 571-6272). All manner of records, Japanese and foreign, old and modern, *Kabuki, Koto* (harp), *samisen* (banjo), *Gagaku* (ancient court music), folk songs, and hit tunes. Open ten A.M. to nine P.M.

TANI SHIRTS—17th at D, next to the *Chinese Embassy* (phone 408-5566/7). First class high grade shirtmakers.

TOSHIBA GINZA STORE—5th near Utility (phone 571-7802). TV, transistor radios, all manner of electric-electronic items. Products of the world famous **Tokyo** *Shibaura Electric Company,* the "GE of Japan."

And for *ukiyo-e,* those celebrated "Floating Island" woodblock prints that James A. Michener wrote a whole wonderful book about, try these:

MATSUNAGA—Sukiyabashi Shopping Center (phone 571-7818).

KAIGADO—F between 15th and *Meiji Park* (phone 401-2059/7750).

JAPAN (cont.)—Tokyo

SAKAI—opposite the *Imperial Hotel* (phone 591-4678). The oldest store in Japan, founded by the owner's grandfather in 1784.

TAKAMIZAWA UKIYOE STORE—Annex Avenue at the *Ginza* (phone 571-6381).

S. WATANABE COLOR PRINT CO.—9 Ginza Nishi, 8-chome (a ten-minute walk from the *Imperial Hotel*). Outstanding wood-block prints.

Kyoto

Close rival to **Tokyo** in shopping pleasures is the grand old capital of feudal days, **Kyoto,** quite properly dubbed the "Paris of the Far East."

Kyoto's chief shopping areas are on *Shinmonzen* (New Gate) and *Furumonzen* (Old Gate) *Streets,* and *Nawate-cho* in the *Gion District,* near Japan's most famous *Geisha* quarter; along *Sanjo* and *Shijo Streets;* in the *Miyako, International,* and *Kyoto Hotels;* on *Kawaramachi* and, to a lesser extent, on *Karasuma-dori* and the maze of streets between these two.

Kyoto specializes in its own artistic finery. Its artisans live in their own districts, with the brocade people being in *Nisshi-jin* and the pottery makers along *Higashiyama-dori.* It is possible, and I would say highly desirable, to watch these consecrated souls at their daily loving tasks. They enjoy the attention, and you'll be thrilled, as I was, to be a party to the scene. Factory visits are enthusiastically encouraged and easy to arrange.

Silk-weaving, performed in the homes of the craftsmen themselves, dates back to the city's founding in 794 when the Imperial Family's demands for fine art and fabrics imported from Chinese artisans helped introduce new and improved methods of fabric making in Kyoto. Dyed fabrics known as *yuzen,* another Kyoto specialty, were first introduced to Japan from China by a wandering Buddhist priest who lived from 1696 until 1753.

Porcelainware produced in Kyoto is known collectively as

JAPAN (cont.)—Kyoto

the *kyoyaki, kiyomizu,* and *awata* types. Kyoto lacquerware is known for its quality and elegance.

Everything worthwhile is to be found in profusion in Kyoto: pearls, ivory, jade, jewelry, cloisonné, damascene, dolls, fans, bambooware, and silk.

Kyoto's "Big Nine," as they are called, are by now familiar names to you from their shops in Tokyo. They are AMITA, H. NISHIMURA, INABA, M. YAMAMOTO, KOSHIDA, KABUKIYA, MURAI, UCHIDA, and YOKOYAMA . . . and one must never forget the two greatest merchandising names in Japan, MIKIMOTO and YAMANAKA, the latter a wonderful art gallery with pre-Pacific War outlets in the States.

Among **Kyoto's** universally excellent stores, I especially recommend the following:

ANTIQUE AND MODERN ART GOODS

KATO & CO., LTD.—Shinmonzen Street, Higashiyama-ku. Bronze, brassware, curios.

R. KITA—256 Shinmonzen Street. Select *Imari* and *Kutani* ware; old obis.

S. OKUMURA & CO., LTD.—Shinmonzen Street. Bronze, brassware, fine art curios.

Y. TSURUKI (GION CO., LTD.)—Shinmonzen Street. Wood and ivory carvings are a specialty; also screens, scrolls, *Netsukes,* lacquerware and porcelain.

YAMANAKA & CO., 14 Sanjobo-cho, Awataguchi. Japanese and Chinese works of art, antiques, pearls and silks.

YOKOYAMA, INC.—Shinbashi-agaru, Nawate. Screen makers, art curios.

BOOKS

PERKINS ORIENTAL BOOKS—91 Higashi Tenno-cho, Okazaki, Sakyo-ku. This outstanding, unusual book haven reflects the character of scholarly P. D. Perkins, whose knowl-

JAPAN (cont.)—Kyoto
edge of books and Japan is prodigious. Books of virtually every type and kind, in various languages, are for sale.

CAMERAS AND BINOCULARS

MUTSUMIDO CO. LTD.—Shijo-Kawaramachi. Cameras, lenses, movies, binoculars.

SANJO SAKURAYA CAMERA SHOP—Kawaramachi, Sanjo-Minami. Distinguished cameras.

UEDA CAMERA SHOP—Sanjo Kawaramachi. Cameras, accessories, Sony radios.

CLOISONNÉ

INABA CLOISONNÉ CO.—Sanjo Shirakawabashi. Cloisonné and artistic enamel ware.

DAMASCENE

AMITA JEWELRY CORP.—Marutamachi, Kawaramachi. Damascene, silver, cultured pearls, rock crystal jewelry, and ivory carved ornaments.

FUJI FINE ARTS CO., LTD.—Shirakawabashi Sanjo. Damascene wares.

DEPARTMENT STORES

DAIMARU—Shijo-dori Takakura.
FUJII-DAIMARU—Shijo-dori Teramachi.
MARUBUTSU—In front of Kyoto Station.
TAKASHIMAYA—Shijo-dori Kawaramachi.

DOLLS

"ASHIDAYA" S. NAKAYAMA DOLL MFG. CO.—Shomen Dotemachi-sagaru. All kinds of dolls.

K. FUJII, 14 Nawate Street. Lovely costume dolls; curios and modern art.

KIMURA OOSHIDO CO., LTD.—Kiyomizu 1-chome. Clay and silk dolls; *Noh* masks.

JAPAN (cont.)—Kyoto

KOSHIN OHBAYASHI—88 Shimoshibamoto-cho, Shichiku. Japanese warrior models, swords.

TANAKAYA—Shijo Yanaginobamba. Kyoto dolls a specialty.

FANS

MIYAWAKI BAISEN-AN CO., LTD.—Rokkaku Tominokoji, Nakagyo-ku. Fans.

GIFTS

SAKURAIYA—Shinkyogoku, Sanjo-dori. Souvenir and gift items.

HAND BAGS

KATORIYA & CO., LTD.—580 Minami-gawa, Gionmachi. Hand bags, accessories.

M. YAMAMOTO & CO., LTD.—Furumonzen Street. Hand bags of the most deluxe sort.

LACQUERWARE

ASOBE—Takakura-Nishiiru, Shijo-dori. Beautiful lacquerware.

MIYAZAKI CO., LTD.—Ebisugawa Sakaimachi, Nakagyoku. Lacquerware, furniture, and wooden ware.

H. NISHIMURA'S LACQUER FACTORY—Okazaki Park (Nijo Street). Lacquerware.

JAPANESE LANTERNS

TSUJIKURA CO., LTD.—Kawaramachi Shijo-agaru. Wonderful lanterns and parasols.

PEARLS

MIKIMOTO PEARLS—261 Shinmonzen Street. Only the best.

PORCELAIN AND SATSUMA

KOSHIDA "SATSUMAYA"—Furumonzen Street. Satsuma and porcelain.

KOTOBUKI POTTERY MANUFACTURING CO.—260 Shinmonzen Street. Satsuma and porcelain. Don't miss their buttons and earrings.

KYOTO CERAMIC (KYOTO TOJIKI KAIKAN)—Gojo Higashi-Oji. Kyoto ceramics.

MANJUDO CO., LTD.—391 Higashi 3-chome. Special earthen products.

TACHIKICHI CO., LTD.—Shijo Tominokoji. Fine china and porcelain.

SILKS AND BROCADES

THE ASAHI TRADING CO., LTD.—Shinmachi-Nijo. Kimonos, happi coats, fine apparel.

"BROCADE" S. NISHIMURA & CO.—Furumonzen Street. Brocade materials, ready to wear.

FUJI EMBROIDERY CO., LTD.—Corner, Marutamachi Teromachi. Embroidery pictures, folding fans, and silk goods.

HAGOROMO & CO.—Shinmonzen Street. *Kanebo* silk materials and articles.

KANEBO SERVICE CO., LTD.—Shijo Kawaramachi. *Kanebo* silk goods.

MURAI & CO., LTD.—236 Shinmonzen Street. Kimonos, brocades, fans, embroideries.

T. NAKAMURA—372 Nawate Sanjo. Brocades, batiks, *Noren* curtains, hand bags.

ORI DONO TEXTILE GALLERY LTD.—Kawaramachi Nijo. Fuji silk and brocades.

TATSUMURA SILK MANSION—43-1 Shimogawara-cho, Nanzenji. Silks and silk goods.

JAPAN (cont.)—Kyoto

RELIGIOUS UTENSILS

KOBORI-BUTSUGU MANUFACTURING CO.—Higashi-honganji-mae, Karasuma-dori. Temple bells, wooden Buddha images, shrine furniture.

WOOD BLOCK PRINTS

MIKUMO WOOD BLOCK PRINT CO., LTD.—Shijo Street, Nakashinmichi. Hand prints, Christmas cards, dyed products.

THE RED LANTERN SHOP—236 Shinmonzen Street. Japanese prints.

UCHIDA WOODBLOCK PRINTING CO., LTD.—Maru-tamachi Street. Prints, cards.

UNSO-DO CO., LTD.—Nijo Teramachi. Prints, Christmas cards, frames.

SPECIAL NOTE: I believe the *Miyako Hotel Arcade* was especially designed to make Kyoto shopping a joy. Thirty-two of the finest shops and stores are represented in the *Arcade,* and in this one small area you can engage in one of the most satisfying shopping experiences to be had in this world. Don't fail to browse through these fine shops. The *Kyoto Hotel* and the *Kyoto International Hotel* also have appealing complete arcades in which shopping may be enjoyed at its best.

Beppu

COMMERCIAL MUSEUM. The *Commercial Museum* is both an exhibition hall to show off the creations of the area and a state-controlled retail store. The principal products of the area are bamboo, Japanese ceramics, and pottery, lacquerware, and hard boxwood ware.

The shops in the *Suginoi Hotel* display attractive merchandise in an inviting environment. Here, too, you will enjoy looking even if you do not buy.

JAPAN (cont.)

Kobe

Kobe's principal shopping area is the *Motomachi*. The following shops are recommended:

CAMERAS AND PHOTO SUPPLIES

NEW PEARL—in front of the Kobe *Daimaru Department Store*. All kinds of cameras.

YOSHIDA—57, 1-chome, Motomachi-dori. Cameras and accessories.

DAMASCENE

AMITA—Main Floor, Kobe International House. That famous name again.

DEPARTMENT STORES

DAIMARU—40 Akashicho, Ikuta-ku.
HANKYU—5, 4-chome, Kanocho, Ikuta-ku.
MITSUKOSHI—280, 6-chome, Motomachi-dori.
SOGO—23, 8-chome, Onoecho, Fukai-ku.

DRUGS AND MEDICINE

AMERICAN PHARMACY—36, 3-chome, Shimoyamate-dori, Ikuta-ku. Closed Sundays.

JAPANESE ART

PEONY—2-chome, Motomachi-dori.

FOLK CRAFTS

TAKUMI CRAFT SHOP—Main Floor, Kobe International House. Lovely handcrafts.

OPTICAL GOODS

MAOZEN—1-chome, Motomachi-dori. Kowa microscopes, binoculars.

JAPAN (cont.)—Kobe

PEARLS

KITAMURA PEARL—74, 2-chome, Motomachi-dori, Ikuta-ku.

K. MIKIMOTO, INC.—Main Floor, Kobe International House.

SATSUMA AND PORCELAIN

SOKO CHINA (HIROYOSHI TRADING CO.)—30, 3-chome, Shimoyamate-dori, Ikuta-ku.

SILKS AND BROCADES

KANEBO SANNOMIYA STORE—Main Floor, Kobe International House.

TATSUMURA TEXTILE COMPANY—Main Floor, Kobe International House.

Miyajima

Good shopping is found on *Miyajima,* the enchanting shrine island half an hour from **Hiroshima,** in a colorful area nearby the famous "floating" shrine. The local pottery is called *Miyajima-yaki.* The isle is justly proud of its unusual wood carvings; the bowls are cut the length of the grain, making not for concentric rings but rather for watermarkings or whorls like on moire taffeta.

Other good buys are salad bowls made of *zelkova* wood as well as tables, desks, and chairs. There is a curio store that sells *Hagi-yaki,* pottery from nearby Yamaguchi Prefecture. The antiques are good values. The principal Miyajima shops which I can recommend to you are:

HIRANO—A wood-carving establishment boasting of hardwood skillfully carved into a variety of objects, including

JAPAN (cont.)—Miyajima

pagodas, trays, and idols. The selection is great, and the prices are cheap.

There are two reliable antique shops: KIMURA, which offers extraordinary values in old prints and gold-inlaid boxes, trays, and other utilitarian and decorative pieces, and CHOSHI, which, while rich in antiquities, is a shop of the more popular priced variety.

Nagasaki

The main shopping thoroughfares of Nagasaki are: *Hama-machi*, *Shin-daika-dori*, and *Moto-kago-machi-dori*. These areas are always happily crowded with eager buyers inspecting and buying the specialties of the area which include tortoise shell ware, coral, delicate porcelain, enchanting embroidery, and accurate ship models. Such nationwide specialties as pearls are also on sale here. The tortoise shell ware of Nagasaki is particularly noteworthy and includes cuff links, cigarette cases, and spectacle frames.

Nagoya

Nagoya's main shopping street is the *Hirokojidori*, with recommended shops including:

CAMERAS

HIDAKAYA—7, 2-chome, Minami-Otsudori, Naka-ku.
MORI—2, 4-chome, Hirokoji, Naka-ku.

CHINAWARE

CHUO TOKI SHOKAI (NORITAKE CHINA)—2, 5-chome, Buheicho, Higashi-ku.

DAMASCENE

AMITA—Meitetsu International Shopping Center. Damascene and silver jewelry.

JAPAN (cont.)—Nagoya

DEPARTMENT STORES

MARUEI—4, 4-chome, Sakaemachi, Naka-ku. Closed Wednesdays.

MATSUZAKAYA—9, 2-chome, Minamiotsudori, Naka-ku. Closed Mondays.

MEITETSU—223, 1-chome, Sasajima-cho, Nakamura-ku. Closed Mondays.

ORIENTAL NAKAMURA—11, 6-chome, Sakaemachi, Naka-ku. Closed Mondays.

INTERNATIONAL SHOPPING CENTER

Located on the sixth floor of the *Meitetsu Department Store* and devoted solely to the sale of Japan's most attractive goods to foreign shoppers.

PEARLS

MIKIMOTO PEARLS—Meitetsu International Shopping Center, 6th floor, *Meitetsu Department Store.*

Nikko

S. KOBAYASHI TRADING CO., LTD., 910-1 Nikko, on Main Street not far from the *Kanaya Hotel,* is one of the finest art curio stores in Japan. Such a lovely, large, well-stocked store could well be a museum. One is graciously invited to browse. The main store lies about one hundred yards from the street, though a small sidewalk display window makes the store's presence known to passers-by. Among the wonderful merchandise available are genuine and imitation antiques, fine ivory carvings, ceramic ware, and a complete assortment of Japanese quality souvenirs. The management is completely honest and will authenticate all pieces as being either replicas of antiques, antiques, ivory carved from one piece or from several. Despite its air of ultra elegance, prices are not dear. Many fine souvenir bargains may be had for a few dollars, while quality items are available in profusion for less than ten dollars.

JAPAN (cont.)

Osaka

Osaka's most fascinating shopping area is the *Shinsai-bashi* area. The stores are excellent; the values are great. Here is an excellent list:

ANTIQUES AND ART

YOSHIKAWA, 17, 2-chome, Shinsaibashi-suji, Minami-ku.

BAGS

HASHIMOTO—21, Mitsudera-suji, Minami-ku.

CAMERAS AND PHOTO SUPPLIES

KAWAHARA—2 Umedacho, Kita-ku.

OPTON—Shin-Asahi Building, 22, 2-chome, Nakanoshima, Kita-ku.

TODOROKI—11, 1-chome, Shinsaibashi-suji, Minami-ku.

DEPARTMENT STORES

DAIMARU DEPARTMENT STORE—Shinsaibashi-suji, Minami-ku.

HANKYU DEPARTMENT STORE—Umeda, Kitaku.

HANSHIN DEPARTMENT STORE—Umeda, Kitaku.

KINTETSU ABENO DEPARTMENT STORE—Abeno, Abeno-ku.

MATSUZAKAYA DEPARTMENT STORE—Nipponbashi, Naniwa-ku.

SOGO DEPARTMENT STORE—Shinsaibashi-suji, Minami-ku.

TAKASHIMAYA DEPARTMENT STORE—Namba, Minami-ku, with a gift shop in the *Osaka Grand Hotel.*

DOLLS

KATSUMURA—53, 8-chome, Uehom-machi, Tennoji-ku.

JAPAN (cont.)—Osaka

LACQUERWARE

MASUDA—36, 2-chome, Shinsaibashi-suji, Minami-ku.

PEARLS

K. MIKIMOTO, INC.—First Floor, Shin-Osaka Building, 25, 1-chome, Dojima Hamadori, Kitaku.

SHOPPING CORNER

OSAKA INTERNATIONAL TRADE CENTER—First Floor, Osaka International Trade Center Building. Located in the heart of the city. Japan's most famous merchandising firms are featured. Highly recommended.

SILKS

KANEBO—First Floor, Minamikan Building. Kanebo silk products.

WOOD-BLOCK PRINTS

ASAHI GIFT CENTER—First Floor, Shin-Asahi Building.

Yokohama

Our shopping journey might well end at **Yokohama** from whence the great liners lift anchor. Yokohama has two main shopping areas: the *Isezaki-cho* area and the bustling, more modern *Motomachi* region. Both of these shopping areas have a great deal to offer. English is spoken, prices argued over, and a cup of tea enjoyed as the purchases are wrapped up. The smart boys down here even meet the big APL liners with rented limousines, trying to win their way into the hearts of the tourists newly treading Japanese soil before the shops and stores of **Tokyo** or **Kyoto** swallow them up.

Here are a few who won their way to my heart . . . and pocketbook:

JAPAN (cont.)—Yokohama

ARTS AND CRAFTS

ART—45, 4-chome, Tokiwacho (in front of the *Toho Theater* on Bashamichi Street). Screens, modern art, dolls, pearls.

CAMERAS AND PHOTO SUPPLIES

EASTERN—in front of the British Consulate near South Pier. Transistor radios, cameras, binoculars.

RETS SUN—35, 1-chome, Isezaki-cho. Cameras and binoculars. Developing, printing, and enlarging in three to six hours.

YOKOHAMA—24 Yamashitache. Cameras, binoculars, transistor radios.

IVORY

K. HODOTA—Silk Center Arcade, 1 Yamashitacho. Ivory carvings.

KIMONOS

SUN BROS.—70, 2-chome, Isezaki-cho; also Silk Center Arcade. Kimonos, happi coats, silk materials.

OPTICAL GOODS

KINSHODO—2-chome, Isezaki-cho; also Silk Center Arcade. Lenses, binoculars.

PEARLS AND JEWELRY

H. ONO—Motomachi Shopping Street. Cultured pearls and other precious gems.

K. MIKIMOTO—Silk Center Arcade.

T. OMORI PEARL—go straight from *NYK Building* past Honcho Crossing. Cultured pearls.

SILKS AND SILK PRODUCTS

OLYMPUS—8, 1-chome, Honcho. Material by the yard or by the piece. Shirts made to order.

JAPAN (cont.)—Yokohama

WATANUI—Silk Center Arcade. Brocades, satins, raw silk, finished articles.

SPECIAL NOTE: The SILK CENTER ARCADE, mentioned in the foregoing and located at the neck of *South Pier,* is simply marvelous. You will find representatives of Japan's most distinguished merchandisers firmly ensconced here. A shopper's paradise par excellence.

Hokkaido

A final word about *Ainu* handcraft products, the arts and wares of Japan's "hairy people," the original Caucasian inhabitants of the Japanese isles now penned up in the northly isle of *Hokkaido.* Carved bears and bark-cloth novelties are their primitive specialties. The cloth is uniquely woven from the inner fiber of the elm tree in a complexity of patterns and dyed with natural vegetable dyes. Good selections of these wares come easily at the western style *New Hokkai Hotel,* the *Marui Imai Department Store,* and the *Baihodo* folk crafts shop, all three on the main street, *Heiwa-dori,* in **Asahigawa City.** Other goods are available in **Sapporo** and **Hakodate** cities, at **Noboribetsu Hot Springs,** and at the two chief *Ainu* villages.

Now that you've finished shopping and you rummage around and find you've still got some loose yen, don't let it bother you. You don't *have* to spend it . . . no, not at all. Right up to the moment of your departure, you are entitled, legally and easily, to cash in up to one hundred dollars' worth of local currency; that's 36,000 yen. Thus your unspent coin of the realm can be reconverted into U.S. dollars for happy shopping elsewhere.

JAPAN (cont.)

JAPAN SOUVENIR ASSOCIATION STORES
(asterisk indicates TAX-FREE STORES)

Tokyo

* Amita Jewelry Corp., Tokyo Branch . . . Sukiyabashi Shopping Center, Ginza.
* Ando Cloisonné Co., Tokyo Branch . . . 4 Ginza 5-chome.
* Asahi Shoten . . . Imperial Hotel Arcade, Uchisaiwaicho.
* Cannon Camera Co., Inc., Ginza Service Center . . . 2 Ginza 6-chome.

  Iwata Glass Co., Ltd. . . . 29 Shinjuku 3-chome.

  Japan Sword Co., Ltd. . . . 80 Shiba Nishikubo Tomoecho, Minato-ku.

  Kanebo Service Co., Tokyo Store . . . 2 Ginza 3-chome.
* Kinjo Camera Co. . . . 2 Ginza 7-chome.
* Matoba & Co., Inc. . . . Nikkatsu Arcade, Yurakucho.
* Matsushima Opt. Co. . . . 2 Ginza 3-chome.
* Mayuyama & Co. . . . Imperial Hotel Arcade, Uchisaiwaicho.
* K. Mikimoto, Inc. . . . 2 Ginza 4-chome.
* Miura Camera Shop . . . Marunouchi Bldg., Marunouchi.

  "Noritake China" Nitto Toki Shokai . . . 29 Shiba Toranomon, Minato-ku.
* Odawara Shoten . . . Imperial Hotel Arcade, Uchisaiwaicho.
* Okubo Brothers . . . Imperial Hotel Arcade, Uchisaiwaicho.
* Soga Fur Co. . . . 2 Ginza 5-chome.

  Takumi Craft Shop . . . 3 Ginza Nishi 8-chome.
* K. Uyeda . . . Imperial Hotel Arcade, Uchisaiwaicho.
* S. Watanabe Color Print Co. . . . 9 Ginza Nishi 8-chome.

  Yamada Heiando . . 4 Edobashi 3-chome, Nihombashi, Chuo-ku.
* Yamaoka Fur Co. . . . 2 Ginza 8-chome.
* Yoshitoku Co., Ltd. . . . 3 Asakusabashi 1-chome, Taito-ku.

Kobe

* Amita Jewelry Corp., Kobe Branch. ⎫
* Imanishi Opt. Co.   ⎬ Kobe International House,
  Kanebo Service Co., Kobe Store   ⎪ Goko-dori 8-chome,
* K. Mikimoto, Inc., Kobe Store   ⎭ Fukiai-ku
* Hiroyoshi Trading Co., Ltd. . . . Shimoyamate-dori 3-chome.

JAPAN (cont.)

Kyoto

* Amita Jewelry Corp. Ltd. . . . Marutamachi Kawaramachi, Nishi-iru.

* Inaba Cloisonné Co. . . . Sanjo Shirakawabashi, Higashiyama-ku.

Kanebo Service Co., Kyoto Store . . . Kawaramachi Shijo, Naka-gyo-ku.

* O. Komai, Inc. . . . Shimmozen-dori, Higashiyama-ku.

Koshida Satsumaya . . . Furumonzen-dori Yamato-oji, Higashi-yama-ku.

* Mikumo Woodblock Print Co., Ltd. . . . Shijo Nakashimmichi Nishi-iru, Nakagyo-ku.

Murai & Co. . . . Shimmonzen-dori, Yamato-oji Higashi-iru, Higashiyama-ku.

H. Nishimura's Lacquer Factory . . . Okazaki Park (Nijo St.), Sakyo-ku.

"Brocade" S. Nishimura . . . Furumonzen-dori Motomachi, Higashiyama-ku.

* Ori-dono Textile Gallery, Ltd. . . . Kawaramachi Nijo, Nakagyo-ku.

Tatsumura Silk Mansion . . . Shimogawaracho Nanzenji, Sakyo-ku.

* Uchida Woodblock Printing Co., Ltd. . . . Marutamachi Kawara-machi Nishi-iru.

* Yamanaka & Co. . . . Awataguchi Sanjobo, Higashiyama-ku.

M. Yamamoto & Co., Ltd. . . . Furumonzen-dori Nawate, Hi-gashiyama-ku.

* Yokoyama, Inc. . . . Nawate Shimbashi Agaru, Higashiyama-ku.

Nagoya

* Ando Cloisonné Co. . . . 1 Minamiotsu-dori 3-chome, Naka-ku.

* Amita Jewelry Corp.
Hoya Glass Works, Ltd.
Iwata Glass Co., Ltd.
Kanebo Service Co.
Matsuzaki & Co.
* K. Mikimoto, Inc.

} Meitetsu International Shopping Center, 6th Floor, Meitetsu Dept. Store, Sasashimacho, Nakamura-ku.

JAPAN (cont.)—Nagoya

"Noritake China" Chuo Toki Shokai

Sango Toki Co., Ltd.

Sasaki Glass Mfg. Co., Ltd.

Tatsumura Textile Co., Ltd.

Yoshitoku Co., Ltd.

* Seiko Center

Meitetsu International Shopping Center, 6th Floor, Meitetsu Dept. Store, Sasashimacho, Nakamura-ku.

Nikko

* S. Kobayashi Trading Co., Ltd. . . . Nakahachiishi, Nikko.

Osaka

Hashimoto Service Shop . . . 21 Mitsuteracho, Mido-suji, Minami-ku.

* Kawahara Camera Store . . . 2 Umedacho, Kita-ku.

* K. Mikimoto, Inc., Osaka Store . . . Shin Osaka Bldg., 1 Hama-dori Dojima, Kita-ku.

Yokohama

* Acme Trading Co., Ltd. . . . 17 Nippon Odori, Naka-ku.

* Art Trading Co. . . . 45 Tokiwamachi 4-chome, Naka-ku.

Image Co., Ltd. . . . Silk Center, Yamashitacho, Naka-ku.

* Hakusui Ivory Co., Inc. . . . 18 Motomachi 1-chome, Naka-ku.

* K. Mikimoto, Inc., Yokohama Store . . . Silk Center, Yamashitacho, Naka-ku.

Watanui Silk . . . Silk Center, Yamashitacho, Naka-ku.

MACAO

MACAO is especially noted for the following:

Portuguese imports: Embroideries, tiles, ceramics, filigree work, port wines.

J. LEMOS—Avenida Almeida Ribeiro. This is the best place to buy the wines of **Portugal** at a terrific saving. The selection includes the finest ports and Madeiras.

ROSITA'S—Avenida Almeida Ribeiro. A wide selection of Portuguese gift specialties. Among the nicer items are lovely

MACAO (cont.)

silver filigree jewelry, laces and embroideries from *Madeira,* and some attractive ceramics. The prices on this merchandise are the best this side of **Lisbon.**

NOTE: If you count any stamp collectors among your **Ameri-** can friends, you'll want to take back some of the colorful Macanese stamps for their collections. Remember if you go to the post office to purchase them that you must pay there in the currency of **Macao; Hong Kong** dollars will not be accepted.

FEDERATION OF MALAYSIA

Almost everything that one may purchase elsewhere in the Orient may be had throughout **Malaysia,** while **Penang,** a free port, offers, as do **Singapore** and **Hong Kong,** goods from all over the world at prices generally lower than at their point of origin. There are watches from **Switzerland,** radios and optical goods from **Germany,** transistors from **Japan,** cameras from all countries, textiles from **America** and **Ireland,** silks from **India** and **China,** Chinese ivory and jade articles, Siamese and Indian ornaments, and Indonesian woodcarving.

Native specialties include:

Handmade Kelantan silverware
Malayan arts and crafts
Malayan batik for sarong material of brilliantly flowered designs in light blue, green, orange and red which is also attractive for men's sports shirts.
Kain Songket (Malayan brocade) is now made in five yard lengths suitable for western style evening gowns.
Superb hand loomed silver and gold embroidered sarong material
Pewter. As the leading producer of tin in the world, it is only natural that Malaya should be renowned for its pewter. When one remembers what skilled artists these patient, happy people are, it is easy to understand what lovely work can be done in making ash trays, cigarette boxes, tea sets, beer mugs, candlesticks, and other decorative pewter pieces.

FEDERATION OF MALAYSIA (cont.)

Except in the largest department stores, the shopkeeper of Malaya would be most unhappy if you failed to bargain with him over prices.

Kuala Lumpur

DYAL CHAND'S, 63-65 Batu Road, a department store displaying both men's and women's garments and fine fabrics.

GIAN SINGH'S, 13 Mountbatten Road, a department store featuring exquisite yard goods, rich fabrics, and excellent tailoring.

GLOBE SILK STORE, 55/57 Batu Road, a large department store best known for its outstanding fabrics.

MOGHAL'S, Bukit Bintang Road, with a show room in the *Federal Hotel*'s basement. An exclusive men's store featuring sports wear and fine tailoring.

PERAK DAN SUTERA, *Hotel Merlin,* Treacher Road, features Kelantan silver, costume jewelry, Malayan arts and crafts, and Indonesian and Malayan batik.

ROBINSON'S, the famous department store, in Mountbatten Road. Everything of quality.

SELANGOR PEWTER COMPANY, 219 Batu Road, offers Malaya's outstanding specialty.

TEIPING LACE COMPANY, 217 Batu Road, souvenirs of all kinds including silverware, linen, porcelain, pewter, and handicrafts.

IN GENERAL: Batu Road houses Indian style shops for selecting beautiful saris and *chollies; Petaling Street* is the principal Chinese shopping thoroughfare; while European style shops and the *Malayan Handicraft Center* are found in *Mountbatten Road.*

Penang

DANIEL'S JEWELERS, *Eastern & Oriental Hotel,* exquisite jewelry of the finest craftsmanship.

N. B. SIMON, 19 Penang Road, manufacturing jewelers

FEDERATION OF MALAYSIA (cont.)—Penang
who make and sell Malayan pewter, also Siamese jewelry, diamonds, pearls, and Kelantan silver.

IN GENERAL: The **Penang** shopping centers are: *Bishop Street, Beach Street, Penang Road, Campbell Street,* and *Kimberly Street.*

Don't hesitate to bargain.

THE PHILIPPINES

THE PHILIPPINES are especially noted for the following:

Handwoven Fabrics: *Piña, jusi, patadiong, ramie,* and *Ilocano* fashioned into women's dresses and blouses, men's clothing, table cloths, exquisite luncheon sets and cocktail napkins, lovely ladies' stoles, colorful draperies, rich bedspreads, fine handkerchiefs, and adorable infants' clothing.

Wood Carvings: Especially the skilled work of the Igorots.

Moro Brass Ware

Embroideries

Hardwood Products: Jet black *ḳamagong,* warm red-brown *narra,* Philippine mahogany known as *tanguile,* and the darkish red *dao* and *tindalo* woods are used in making salad and fruit bowls, salt and pepper shakers, bread trays, humidors, pipe racks, dinner plates, and even fine furniture.

Sea Shell and Mother-of-Pearl Products

Manila Hemp (*Abaca*) **Products:** Sandals, bags, and rugs.

Philippine Pottery, Rattan Ware, Bamboo, and Wicker Objects

Red and White Coral Ornaments

Reptile Products: Crocodile and snakeskin.

Native Dolls

Native Jewelry: Black coral, *Osmeña* pearls, *Mindanao* mother-of-pearl, antique gold and silver filigree.

Among the finest of the handwoven fabrics are:
PATADIONG, a soft, fine, cotton fabric, is used to make the colorful native women's costumes of the same name and is also a basic material for table cloths, tea sets, draperies, bed-spreads, and napkins.

THE PHILIPPINES (cont.)

PINA, a richly lustrous, gentle, ecru-colored cloth hand-woven from pineapple fibers, is used to make *barongs,* dinner sets, napkins, dresses, stoles, blouses, and draperies.

JUSI cloth, stronger than *piña,* is handwoven from raw silk and numbers among its uses men's *barongs,* ladies' stoles, dresses, and blouses.

ILOCANO, a hand loomed cotton cloth, strong but soft and attractive, is the basic material in dresses, place mats, napkins, draperies, and bedspreads.

RAMIE, machine woven from a Filipino type of flax, is considerably sturdier than cotton but is characterized by a linen-like texture. Its colors are rainbow-hued, and it's a popular fabric for the less expensive *barongs,* luncheon sets, dresses and shirts.

BAMBOO is woven into a soft lush fabric for drapes, blinds, and blankets.

The Ifugaos, one of the Igorot tribes, trace their *Luzon* mountain history back more than three thousand years. They have contributed generously to the arts and crafts of the Philippines. Igorot fabrics, hand loomed in the mountains north of **Baguio,** are sturdy and brilliantly hued. The ingenious Igorots are best known, however, for their wood carvings which are both richly decorative and highly utilitarian. The skillfully carved images of the Igorot gods are rather difficult to locate, but they are available for purchase.

The Muslims of *Mindanao* and *Sulu* in the southern reaches of the Philippines produce extraordinarily intricate hand work including cigarette boxes, vases, and percussion musical instruments.

The Manila shirt, known locally as the *barong tagalog* or more simply as the *barong,* is a unique specialty of the Philippines. These men's garments are beautifully embroidered, high necked, long sleeved shirts fashioned most generally from *piña* or *jusi* cloth, though *ramie* is also used. The exquisite *barongs*

THE PHILIPPINES (cont.)
are worn evenings in lieu of formal dinner clothes or shirt, tie, and business suit.

Filipino fabrics do not always react to conventional washing procedures as do your pet materials at home. Keep the instructions included with your local purchases; they may come in handy.

Bargaining is a favorite Filipino occupation. Fixed price tags will be prominently displayed in a few of the larger department stores and will, no doubt, make haggling futile, but don't hesitate to try. Elsewhere, however, you are bound to get clipped if you don't enter into the spirit of the occasion vigorously. Make a maximum offer of fifty per cent of the asking price. You may not succeed in securing the full generous fifty per cent discount you seek, but par for the course is a whopping forty per cent off. You're a sissy if you pay more.

Recommended Shops in Manila

DEPARTMENT STORES

AGUINALDO'S, 600 Echague. Imported and local goods, porcelain, glassware, costume jewelry, handbags, draperies, rugs, furniture, and men's accessories including a huge selection of *barong tagalogs*.

ESQUIRE BINGHAM, Escolta. A fine choice of native merchandise.

FRANCIS, 303 Dasmariñas. Particularly well known for imported fabrics, smart handbags, notions and novelties. Attractive women's and children's ready-to-wear section.

HEACOCK'S, 406-407 Dasmariñas. Imported handbags, luggage, lamps, jewelry, glassware, silverware, men's accessories, perfume, and watch repairs.

OCEANIC COMMERCIAL, 299 Escolta. Watches, clocks, jewelry, silverware, men's accessories, and a wide range of department store products.

THE PHILIPPINES (cont.)—Manila

OTHER MANILA SHOPS

ADRIANO'S, 1139 A. Mabini. Finest hardwood furniture, cabinets, chandeliers, cigarette boxes, and chests.

ALEXANDER'S SHOP, 1171 A. Mabini, Ermita. Hand embroidered and monogrammed articles, *jusi* and *piña* blouses, *ramie* tea sets, handbags, *barong* materials, and Baguio hand-woven shirts. Custom made men's *barongs* will be ready in 24 hours.

ALTOCRAFT, INC., Seaview and Guevara Avenues, San Juan, **Rizal** (near **Manila**). Magnificent display of native dolls. Worth a visit just to look. Don't miss it.

ANG TIBAY, 278 Escolta. Colorfully beaded slippers.

ARTE ESPAÑOL, 1311 M. H. del Pilar (near corner Padre Faura). Beautifully executed wrought iron articles including garden and interior furniture, chandeliers, and gate post lamps.

AURELIA'S, 1158 A. Mabini. A men's and women's shop featuring *barongs, patadiongs,* and western style clothes for both sexes. Souvenirs, Igorot carvings, and snakeskin handbags are specialties.

CHINA DRAWN WORK, 1048 M. H. del Pilar. Ivory carvings, enamel and silver bracelets, cuff links, pins, brass trays, teakwood, lacquered screens, and camphor chests.

CHINESE CANDLE STORE, 665 Ongpin (near corner Nueva Street). All kinds of beautiful ornamental candles.

CONCHITA SALVADOR'S. Don't be discouraged; you'll find it just off the *National Highway* in back of House No. 852—a sign points the way. Finest embroidered *piña* blouses and ladies' dresses, luncheon sets, handbags, and fine quality heavily embroidered tablecloths. Custom-made tablecloths take about three months, plus a month or so for shipping.

FREIXAS, 211 Carriedo. Spanish fans, veils, combs, dolls, and other Spanish imports.

GESLANI'S, 69 Echague Street. Here the versatility of native Philippine handicrafts is richly displayed.

THE PHILIPPINES (cont.)—Manila

HIGHLAND SHOP, 1505 A. Mabini. All of the fine hand-woven fabrics of the Philippines are available in ready-to-wear clothing or by the yard. Here you will also find an excellent section devoted to accessories.

HOUSE OF PUYAT, 190 Rodriguez Arias. Quality Philippine hardwood furniture.

JIM'S MERCHANDISING, 1128 A. Mabini. Embroidered *piña* and *jusi* handbags, place mats, mother-of-pearl products, and filigree jewelry are specialties. *Barongs* custom made in 24 hours.

LEPANTO CRAFTS, INC., 1505 A. Mabini. Exclusive outlet for *Lepanto* fabrics: skirts, neckties, shirts, guest towels, ladies' stoles, and natural banana fiber draperies. Igorot *ada-an* wood carvings, too.

LO HON MEN CO., 500 Isaac Pearl. Well made, attractive rattan furniture, bassinets, picnic baskets, bread and fruit baskets, and clothes hampers.

MANILA HOTEL "LA PLAZITA." A variety of specialty shops. Each one features choice merchandise. A bit expensive, but you are sure to be satisfied with anything you buy in these shops.

NEW YORKER, 1421 A. Mabini. Handpainted raffia skirts, hand embroidered *jusi* shirts, and handbags. Native *balintawaks* and *patadiongs;* try one on—they're cute.

PHILIPPINE EDUCATION CO., 1104 Castillejos (off Arlegui). This excellent book store has a fine souvenir department featuring quality woodenware, jewelry, coral, bamboo, pearls, and hemp items.

PHILIPPINE HOME CRAFTS AND GIFT SHOP, 1557 A. Mabini. Specializing in high-quality woodenware, bowls, fruit trays, candelabra, lamps, hemp, buri and bamboo draperies, and jewelry. Perhaps the finest array of native crafts and merchandise in Manila.

PRESCILLA'S GIFT SHOP, 1339 A. Mabini. Baguio carv-

THE PHILIPPINES (cont.)—Manila

ings, handbags, veils, shawls, luncheon sets, jackets, carvings, and jewelry.

RATTAN ART & DECORATIONS, INC., M. H. del Pilar and Padre Faura. Outstanding rattan furniture. You can arrange for shipping your purchases home.

SEGUNDINA C. VIZCARRA, 1039 A. Mabini. The hand embroidered *piña, jusi* and linen articles include cocktail, luncheon, and dinner sets, men's *barongs,* and women's blouses. Handbags, silver filigree jewelry, black coral and mother-of-pearl items, and woodenware.

SHELL-CRAFT & BUTTON CORP., 2885 Beata, Pandacan. Beautiful mother-of-pearl dishes, tableware, and pearl buttons. Wonderful shell items such as place mats, cigarette boxes, and hanging lanterns.

SWATOW DRAWN WORKS, 1060 Isaac Peral. Marvelous teakwood and camphor chests, porcelain ware, Chinese slippers, ladies' jackets and pajamas, *jusi* and *piña* cocktail sets, napkins, and handkerchiefs.

TESORO'S, 1353 A. Mabini (also *Manila Hotel Arcade*). A three floor paradise of Philippine merchandise: carved wood articles, fabrics, embroideries, slippers, raffia bags, and colorful native dolls.

TREASURE HOUSE, Dewey Boulevard. The corals and pearls of **Baguio** and *Mindanao* are much in evidence. A remarkable collection of quality jewelry of all kinds.

TRES CHIC, 1431 A. Mabini. As its name suggests, very smart. Custom made and ready-to-wear dresses. The decorative handpainted raffia skirts are adorable. Embroidered *piña* and *jusi* blouses a specialty. The imported yard goods are elegant.

SINGAPORE

Singapore, a duty-free port with no purchase or luxury taxes, affords the international traveler outstanding bargains.

Films can be purchased in Singapore cheaper than in **Chicago, San Francisco,** or **New York.** Fine linens, china and glassware

SINGAPORE (cont.)

from **Ireland, England,** and **Japan,** as well as local products, can be purchased at rare bargains. In Singapore one finds Indonesian batiks, Japanese and Indian silks, Chinese brocades, toys, and dolls from the world over. Here one may purchase Asiatic rugs, radios, tape recorders, watches, and furniture— anything that the mind can conceive and the soul desire may be had in Singapore—at a good price.

In Singapore, don't hesitate to bargain. Don't be overawed by the elegance or the lack thereof of the store surroundings. Bargain. You can always beat the asked price, I promise you.

Thai silk and bronze cutlery are as reasonable in Singapore as they are in their home country. Jewelry from the cheapest junk costume variety through the most exquisite precious stones as well as curios and antiques may be had at extraordinary bargains. Know your product, however, is always a good watch word in Singapore, as elsewhere.

Singapore shopkeepers usually speak English. You should have no linguistic barriers. Small shops are open daily, while the larger ones, including the department stores, are closed on Sunday and public holidays. Smaller shops are open from 8:00 A.M. to 8:00 P.M. or later, while the larger ones open at 9 A.M. and usually close at 5:00 P.M. except on Saturday when the closing hour is apt to be 1:00 P.M.

Don't miss *Change Alley,* between *Raffles Place* and the *Arcade.* This is the bargain hunter's paradise where one may purchase almost anything made anywhere in the world.

A bit later I shall list specific stores and shops but many items are best sought by "areas" which listing I will give you first. They are:

CARPETS of the finest quality are available from **India, Iran** (Persian), **China,** and **Great Britain.** They will be found principally in *Raffles Place, Battery Road, Stamford Road, Orchard Road, Tanglin Road,* and *Coleman Street.*

CAMERAS may be sought successfully in *Raffles Arcade,*

SINGAPORE (cont.)

Raffles Place, High Street, North Bridge Road, Cross Street, and *Middle Road.*

CURIOS and ANTIQUES abound in *Raffles Place, High Street, Coleman Street, Stamford Road, Battery Road, Orchard Road, Tanglin Road, Race Course Road,* and *Empress Place Kiosk.*

CLOTH and TEXTILES from all over the world which are available in the best department stores include Chinese brocades, Kelantan and Thai silk, Indonesian batik, Japanese fabrics, and Indian silks. These products can be found in *Raffles Arcade, Orchard Road, Tanglin Road, Arab Street, Empress Place Kiosk, Coleman Street, Chulia Street, High Street, North Bridge Road,* and *Serangoon Road.*

FURS, believe it or not, are a good bargain in Singapore and are found in *Raffles Place, Orchard Road,* and *Stamford Road.*

IVORY and JADE CARVINGS are sold in *Battery Road, Tanglin Road,* and *Orchard Road.*

GLASSWARE from the least expensive to the most decorative can be found in *Raffles Place, North Bridge Road, High Street, Orchard Road,* and *Collyer Quay.*

JEWELRY can best be found in *High Street, Orchard Road,* and *Raffles Place.*

RADIOS of all kinds from transistors through hi-fi and radio player recorders from the far corners of the world are available in *Orchard Road, North Bridge Road, Stamford Road, South Bridge Road* and *Selegie Road.*

SKINS such as snake and crocodile made into handbags, shoes, and belts can be found in *Stamford Road.*

TRAVEL LUGGAGE can be purchased amazingly inexpensively in *Raffles Place, Orchard Road, Circular Road,* and *South Bridge Road.*

WATCHES from **Switzerland,** the States, **Germany,** and other watchmaking centers are sold in *High Street, Raffles Place, Raffles Arcade, Change Alley, North Bridge Road,* and *South Bridge Road.*

SINGAPORE (cont.)

DRUG STORES and SPECIALTY SHOPS of all descriptions can be found in *Raffles Place.*

Specifically recommended stores, shops and department stores are:

JAPAN HOUSE DEPARTMENT STORE, 131 Middle Road. Best quality material. Exquisite tailoring. Custom made garments in 24 hours.

JOHN LITTLE & COMPANY, Raffles Place. An outstanding department store with a wide selection of merchandise.

ROBINSON'S, an air conditioned department store in Raffles Place, offers a large selection of merchandise, including clothing for men, women, and children, accessories, shoes, bags, dolls, toys, china, glassware and linens, to name a few. In *Robinson's* one will find a first class bar, a splendid restaurant, a beauty salon for women, and a barber shop.

The RAFFLES HOTEL ARCADE boasts of some fine shops, all of which are attractive and reliable and offer extraordinary fine values, included in which are:

CHANRAI'S, 81 High Street & Raffles Hotel. Men's suits, slacks, shoes, and cuff links.

CHINA TRADING COMPANY. Outstanding expensive Chinese curios, scrolls, porcelains, and carvings.

DORIS GEDDES' LITTLE SHOP, women's apparel of the best quality. Relatively expensive but the values are reassuring.

H. SENA, INC., *Raffles Hotel* and 48 High Street. Fine jewelry and silver.

Other recommended shops include:

A. I. COMPANY, Stamford Road. Shoes, slippers, and sandals.

AH CHUM, 61 Orchard Road. Fine men's tailoring.

ALLIED RADIO CORPORATION, 30 Circular Road, offers name-brand radios, tape recorders, and cameras at outstanding values.

AMIR & SONS, 276 Orchard Road. Beautiful carpets and rugs . . . Persian and Indian selections.

SINGAPORE (cont.)

ANTOINETTE, 324 Orchard Road. Thai silk and ladies' handbags, costume jewelry, stoles, and men's ties.

ARCADE TAILORING, 7 The Arcade. Ready-made suits, slacks and shirts, women's silk brocades, evening bags, dresses, scarves, blouses, and suit material. Rapid custom tailoring.

BAJAJ TEXTILES, Raffles Place. Incomparable Indian materials.

BATA SHOE COMPANY, The International Organization, North Bridge Road. Slippers, sandals, and shoes. Practical and cheap, but not excitingly styled.

BEHU, MEYER & COMPANY LTD., *Union Building,* Collyer Quay. Agfa cameras.

BUTTONS AND BOWS SHOP, Singapore Cold Storage Arcade, Orchard Road. Fine selection of Indian, Thai, Japanese, Chinese, and Pakistani merchandise.

CHEONG KEE & CO., 79 Hill Street. Art objects, curios.

CHINA ART HOUSE, 155 Orchard Road. Jewelry and Oriental art objects.

CHINA CRAFTS, 79 North Bridge Road. Chinese carpets, jades, ivory.

CHINA COMPANY, Battery Road. Rare porcelains, art objects.

DE SILVA, G. C., Raffles Place. Unusual and original design in fine jewelry.

DI SILVA LTD., B. P., 12-21 High Street. Imported watches, *Mikimoto* cultured pearls, jade, diamonds, souvenirs, and curios.

EASTMAN KODAK COMPANY, 135 Robinson Road. Excellent for your purchases and for fast film developing.

ELSIE MARY, 13 Battery Road. Haut couture. Finest ladies' fashions. Gorgeous brocades.

ESQUIRE, 86 High Street. Men's ready-to-wear, custom-made apparel, and accessories.

GIAN SINGH'S, Raffles Place. Exquisite Indian imports.

HANDLOOMS, 23 Race Course Road. Indian textiles, dress

SINGAPORE (cont.)

materials, stoles, bedspreads, towels, scarves, rugs, and raw silks.

HILDA'S, 90-A Orchard Road. Dresses and accessories, with custom-made garments available in 24 hours.

HONG SUNG, 309 Orchard Road. Antiques, ivory, jade, jewelry, and Peking carpets.

INDONESIAN ARTS AND CURIOS, 33 Tanglin Road. Indonesian and Malayan handicrafts.

KING & COMPANY, Raffles Place Arcade. Toys and sporting goods.

KONG ON TRADING COMPANY, Victoria Street. Art objects and jade.

LANKA JEWELERS, 20 Battery Road. Exquisite jewels and silver. Diamonds, precious stones, pearls, jade, watches, clocks, silverware, crystal ware, and cutlery.

HELEN B. LING, 97 Tanglin Road. Star of Siam silks, dresses, coats, fine woolens, antiques, ceramics, jewelry, lamps, and furniture.

MADELINE, LTD., 278 Orchard Road (next to *Prince's Restaurant*). Superbly fashioned gowns in brocades and silks.

MALAYA PHOTO STORE, 105 North Bridge Road. Outlet for Olympus Auto Eye. Fine values in photographic supplies, transistors, projectors, and binoculars.

MALAYAN ARTS AND CRAFTS SOCIETY SHOP, Empress Place. Authentic Malayan handicrafts including knives, brocades, woven straw mats, batiks, jewelry, basketware, and silver. Very inexpensive.

MALAYAN-JAVANESE ARTS AND CURIOS, 157 Orchard Road. Malayan and Indonesian arts and curios.

MIDDLE SHOP COMPANY, 60 Middle Road. Exotic sandals, slippers, and shoes.

MOON GATE, 278 Orchard Road. Furniture, silverware, jade, ceramics, jewelry, paintings, carpets, bronze, and ivory.

ORIENTAL CARPET PALACE, 295 Orchard Road. Persian and Indian carpets.

SINGAPORE (cont.)

ORIENT CRAFTS, 108 Orchard Road. Malayan and Indian imports.

PEKING LACE COMPANY, 66 North Bridge Road (near *Adelphi Hotel*). Chinese objects of art.

RAFFLES SILK STORE, 6 Raffles Place. Women's and men's tailoring in 24 hours. Woolens, silks, dacrons, brocades and batiks.

REX PHOTO SHOP, 2 Raffles Place. Rapid developing for all of your films.

ROLEX SALES AND SERVICE, Crosby House, 75 Robinson Road. Rolex watches.

SILVER CRAFT, Penang Lane. Silver and copper items.

C. K. TANG, Orchard Road. Oriental curios, textiles, and souvenirs. The prices are fixed. Don't bargain.

THAI CRAFT, 11 The Arcade (off Raffles Place). Dress and upholstery fabrics, stoles, scarves, evening bags, neckties, sport shirts, and slacks.

THAI SILK SHOP, Winchester Arcade. Fine imported materials.

TOWN & COUNTRY, Orchard Road, Ladies' and children's wear. Cosmetics, perfumes, and local costumes.

WASSAIMULL'S, High Street. Handbags and accessories.

YIP LEE WOH, Stamford Road. Reptile handbags, cases, and accessories.

TAIWAN *(Formosa)*

TAIWAN is especially noted for the following:

Bamboo-ware, Straw Mats, and Rice Paper Products
Ceramics and Lacquerware
Corals and Shells
Embroidery
Rugs and Carpets
Snakeskin Products
Dolls and Books
Wood Carvings

TAIWAN *(Formosa)* (cont.)

Here are a few of the stores I found of interest browsing about in the main shopping center of **Taipei:**

BOOKCASE SHOP, 180 Chung Shan North Road, Section II. Books and souvenirs.

CAVES BOOK COMPANY, 99 Chung Shan North Road, Section II. Oriental art and handicrafts.

CHARLIE'S CARVED FURNITURE STORE, 20 Chung Shan North Road opposite the *Marco Polo Hostel* of the U. S. Military Assistance Advisory Group. Tainan carved furniture and high-grade Taiwanese gifts.

CHINA ARTISTIC CARVED FURNITURE CO., LTD., 34 Chung Shan North Road, Section III. Outstanding values in magnificent furniture, specializing in inlays of brass, silver, soapstone, ox bone, and mother-of-pearl on perspectives of figures, landscapes, flowers, or animals. Ready-made or to order, your design may be copied or they will create patterns for you.

CHINA HOUSE STONE-CARVINGS, 30 Chung Shan North Road. Green jade, soapstone work, all kinds of fine stonework.

FONG PUU COMPANY, 35 Chungking Road South. Selected Taiwan tea.

LIBERTY RUG MANUFACTURING CO., LTD., 13 Chung Shan North Road. Lovely rugs.

LUCY BOOK STORE, 123 Chungking South Road, Section I, opposite the *Bank of Taiwan*. An excellent selection of books, excellent buys throughout Taiwan.

MADAME CHEN FURNITURE STUDIO, 36 Nanking East Road, Section I. An agglomeration of chests, furniture, wooden screens, et cetera. Also chinaware and fine porcelain.

MONARCH HANDICRAFTS, 91-2 Chung Shan North Road, Section II. The best in local products.

NEW TAIWAN PRODUCTS COMPANY, LTD. (also TAIWAN RUGS MANUFACTURING CO.), 82 Po-Ai Road. Oriental rugs, hand-knotted Tientsin rugs, and hooked rugs of wool, ramie flax, jute, and cotton.

TAIWAN *(Formosa)* (cont.)

PAO HO HONG, 83 Heng Yang Road. All sorts of carved coral items.

SWATOW DRAWN WORK COMPANY, 25 Chung Shan Road North. Exquisite embroideries.

TAIWAN GIFT SHOP, 59-3 Chung Shan North Road, Section II. For just what the name says: a wide variety of local specialties.

TAN CHIANG BOOK COMPANY, 135 Chungking South Road, Section I, opposite the *Bank of Taiwan*. Assorted interesting tomes.

NOTE: A word of advice, if I may—Look for the emblem of the *Taiwan Visitors Association*. These stores are all pledged to maintain the highest ethical standards in prices, shop conduct, and quality.

THAILAND

Thailand is especially noted for the following:

Bronzeware
Dolls
Jewelry: Princess rings, star sapphires, star rubies, and blue and white zircons.
Khon (Thai Classical Dancing) **Masks**
Lacquerware, Gilt Wood Carvings
Nielloware: Typical product of black and silver.
Silver
Thai Celadon (Ancient Pottery): Vases, tableware, ash trays, bowls.
Thai Handwoven Silks and Cottons
Wind Bells (Thai Temple Bells)
Curios

Bargaining in Thailand is not only accepted but is expected and is good fun. There are few fixed prices except in the very best shops, and even there a little haggling is in order. Be *extremely* cautious about buying expensive jewelry. If you don't know precious gems, don't make a large investment in them.

THAILAND (cont.)

Bangkok

Shopping arcades in the *Rama, Erawan,* and *Oriental Hotels* make shopping convenient and easy. In addition to the shops included in the following list, there are excellent shops in the *Rama Arcade,* including:

A. A. CO., LTD. Jewelry, gifts, and souvenirs.

DESIGN THAI SILK SHOP. Jacqueline Ayer designs Jim Thompson's silks into ladies' wear, men's jackets, neckties, and sports shirts.

RUBY JEWELRY. Fine jewelry and antique gold nielloware are featured.

THAI ARTS BOUTIQUES. Antiques, sculptures, paintings, wood carvings, furniture, rattanware, Thai silk and cotton, lamps, and lampshades are offered.

SILKS

BANGKOK SILK, 92/93 Patpong Road. Fine quality silks.

DEBANOM THAI SILK, 135 Gaysorn Road, Rajaprasong. Brocades, scarves, handbags, neckties, sport shirts. Original designs.

STAR OF SIAM, show rooms in the *Erawan* and *Oriental Hotels.* Beautiful silk dresses, coats, stoles, yard goods, and ties.

THAI SILK COMPANY, LTD. (Jim Thompson's), 311/6-7 Surawongse Road. Next door to *Swissair.* Expensive. Worth a visit, as Mr. Thompson has the largest selection in town.

JEWELRY, SILVERWARE, AND NIELLOWARE

AINSLIE'S JEWELERS, 1146 New Road, near the *General Post Office.* Good buys in star sapphires and princess rings. Modern and antique jewelry, quite reliable.

ALEX AND COMPANY, Oriental Avenue. Highly recommended; the best. All types of jewelry, silverware, nielloware, pearls, and antiques, with a large variety of bracelets, earrings, cigarette boxes, etc.

THAILAND (cont.)—Bangkok

THE 9 GEMS, Erawan Hotel Lobby. A good selection.

H. SENA, INC., 10 Oriental Avenue and *Erawan Hotel*. Fine quality jewelry, silverware, crystal, imported ceramics, watches, china, and platinum.

T. SENG & COMPANY, 15-19 Thipvaree Lane, Ban-Moh Road. Silver, gold, nielloware, bronze, gems, and Thai silk.

THAI NAKORN, near *Memorial Bridge*. Recommended.

THAI CELADON GIFT SHOP, Somchit Lane, near British Embassy. Featuring vases, water jars, lamp bases, embossed bowls, planters, dinnerware, and other Celadon pieces.

ZERNER, LTD., 68 Sathorn Road, showrooms in the *Rama* and *Oriental Hotels*. Specializes in fine stones with unusual made-to-order settings. Ask to see the cutting and polishing process of these jewels.

BRONZEWARE

S. SAMRAN THAILAND, 1245 New Road (in town) and the Workshop which is the preferred address located at 377/11 Petchburi Road. Bronze tableware is an excellent buy. The best in Thailand. See special write-up page 343.

R. THAI BRONZEMAKERS, *Erawan Hotel*. All types of bronze.

TEMPLE BELLS

THAI HOME INDUSTRIES, Oriental Avenue. Bronze and brass wind bells. Handicrafts from all parts of Thailand. Hand-woven fabrics of artistic design, lacquerware, wood carvings, Thai musical instruments, dolls, puppets, and *Khon* (Thai classical dance) masks.

ANTIQUES AND CURIOS

MONOGRAM, Erawan Hotel Arcade. Old paintings, objects of art, bronze Buddhas, Thai stone heads, and curios.

PENG SENG, 99 Nakorn Kasem/2nd Lane. Antiques and curios.

THAILAND (cont.)—Bangkok

RECORDINGS

TECK HUAT, 286 Nakorn Road. Recordings of Siamese music.

FILM PURCHASE AND PROCESSING

KODAK PRODUCTS DIVISION, The Borneo Company, LTD., Selom Road. Ektachrome, Kodachrome, and black-and-white film are generously available. Developing is done speedily.

DOLLS

Thai dolls are exquisite. The costumes are of the finest materials, ornate with gold and other precious metal brocade, and are authentic to the last detail. They are expensive, but worth it. An excellent place to buy these beautiful souvenirs is in the show room of the TOURIST ORGANIZATION OF THAILAND, Sri Ayudhya Road.

SHIPPING PURCHASES FROM BANGKOK. Principal purchases that I recommend you make in Thailand are bronzeware, temple (wind) bells, dolls, and silk.

Samran is completely reliable. Should you purchase your bronzeware from him, he can be relied on implicitly to ship efficiently (insured) precisely the merchandise that you have purchased.

One must bear in mind, however, that **Bangkok** is halfway around the world from the States. Parcels shipped by surface transportation will take from two to four months at a minimum to reach your home town. If you do have something shipped, therefore, don't be on needles and pins waiting for the express man to ring your door bell the day after you return home from your trip. Time and patience will conquer all.

Unless you are planning to start a Thai silk shop, whatever purchases you make in **Bangkok** should not be too voluminous to carry with you. Since shops other than *Samran* are not so

THAILAND (cont.)—Bangkok

skilled at handling shipments, I would recommend that any purchases that you wish to have sent from **Bangkok** should be turned over to the forwarding department of the *World Travel Service,* a company which is the soul of integrity and efficiency. Mr. Kusa Panyarachun, president of W.T.S. was educated in the States and has a dynamic personality. He has built one of the great travel organizations of the world. The *World Travel Service* will make shipments either by air freight or by surface cargo, but they do not handle parcel post packages. The small things that you might wish to ship should be packed snugly and sent through the post office, which has a branch in your hotel.

SOUTH VIET NAM

South Viet Nam is especially noted for the following:

Lacquerware
Ceramics and Pottery
Silver Work
Embroidery and Textiles
Vietnamese and Chinese Antiques
Brass and Bronzeware
Tortoise Shell Articles
Ivory

Saigon

CENTRAL MARKET, **Saigon.** All sorts of interesting miscellaneous merchandise.

HANDICRAFT DEVELOPMENT CENTER, 86 Tu Do Street, one block from the *Caravelle Hotel* (there is also a sales display counter at the *Saigon Airport*). Even for "just lookers" this exhibition of the native crafts of the Vietnamese is a must. Everything on display is for sale and for those who want the very best of the wares of Viet Nam at really bargain prices, this is the place to come. Highly recommended. Attractive shops of all kinds are to be found on Tu-Do and Le-Loi Streets.

SOUTH VIET NAM (cont.)—Saigon

THAI VAN BIEU, Duong Tu Do. Embroideries.

THANH LE, Duong Tu Do. The loveliest lacquerware you'll ever see.

Just a short distance from **Saigon** are the villages of **Thu-Dau-Mot** where an abundance of lacquerware may be purchased and **Bien-Hoa** especially recommended for your purchases of pottery and bronzeware. A visit to the handicraft centers will make a fine excursion trip and give you an opportunity to see the Vietnamese countryside.

CHAPTER 7

Holidays, Festivals, and Special Events

THE PEOPLE of the far side of the world embrace an amazing agglomeration of ethnological heritages, national customs, and religious tenets.

In the Orient one finds a few Christians, but most of the Asiatics are Buddhists, Shintoists, Moslems, or Hindus. Each of these solemn, deeply rooted religions places great importance on colorful ritualistic expression. The mass observance of anniversaries of important religious dates, the cleansing and purification ceremonies, the rites of driving out the evil spirits, and just plain joyous ecclesiastical celebrations are more numerous, by far, among the Far Eastern religions than in all our Christian faiths combined.

In addition to the church celebrations, other enthusiastic and colorful events are celebrated, none of which is more universally enjoyed than the *Chinese New Year* celebrated salubriously in the **Federation of Malaysia, Taiwan,** and **Hong Kong.**

In **Kyoto,** for example, never a week passes but what there is some fete, fair, festival, holiday, or special event. Throughout **Japan** the number and scope of the festivals are almost beyond our ability to comprehend. The Chinese, too, have seemingly countless special national events.

It is obviously impossible to attempt to list every special event that takes place, but since these occasions are of such great interest and engender so much local color, it is important that one traveling through the Orient should attend at least one of the host of fetes, fairs, festivals, or special events.

On the following pages I have listed many of the more important special events, the preparations for which are complex and frequently include entire villages, cities, or areas.

This list is accurate, though of necessity incomplete. Many of the holidays (particularly of Chinese origin) are calculated by the lunar calendar and will vary as much as a month or two from year to year. Others are of a fixed nature. After studying the listings, and having planned your trip, check with your travel agent as to the specific dates of the variable festivals, or drop me a note at One North La Salle Street, Chicago, and we will see that you have the exact information as to the festivals that might be celebrated during the course of your dream trip.

HOLIDAYS, FESTIVALS, SPECIAL EVENTS

CAMBODIA

January 1	NEW YEAR'S DAY—All offices and banks are closed.
April 13, 14 and 15	CAMBODIAN NEW YEAR—Three-day celebration observed throughout the country.
May 1	LABOR DAY—Festivities typical of May Day observances in the western world.
May 6	FESTIVAL OF THE CONSTITUTION —Patriotic commemoration in honor of Cambodia's constitution.
November 9	CAMBODIAN INDEPENDENCE DAY —Parades, parties, and fireworks add to the celebration.
December 10	RIGHTS OF MAN—A national holiday.
December 25	CHRISTMAS DAY—Happy and joyous gatherings throughout the country.

STATE OF HAWAII

January and/ or February	CHINESE NEW YEAR and NARCISSUS FESTIVAL. For seven days preceding and five days following the Chinese New Year's Day, there is colorful Chinese pageantry, a lantern parade, a queen contest and coronation, fireworks, and a narcissus (New Year flower of China) banquet.
Mid to Late March	KA PALAPALA Cultural Beauty Pageant at the *University of Hawaii*. Coeds representing Hawaii's seven principal nationalities take part in a beauty pageant and perform costumed dances and songs traditional to their respective homelands.

STATE OF HAWAII (cont.)

March and April	CHERRY BLOSSOM FESTIVAL. Celebrated by Japanese community in **Honolulu.** Parades, dancing, fireworks, musical programs, ceremonial tea, displays of *bonsai, bonseki,* and floral arrangements.
March 26	PRINCE KUHIO DAY. Typical Hawaiian holiday, honoring Jonah Kalanianaole Kuhio, Hawaii's first delegate to Congress. Pageantry, special events at resort hotels, Hawaiian chants, and musical tribute at the *Royal Mausoleum* in *Nuuanu Valley,* **Honolulu.**
March or April (Palm Sunday)	HAWAIIAN EASTER EGG SHOW. Runs approximately one week at *Ala Moana Pavilion,* **Honolulu.** Nearly 1,000 elaborately painted eggs, some in Hawaiian *tapa* design, are displayed.
March or April (Easter)	EASTER SUNDAY SUNRISE SERVICES (Interdenominational) at the *Punchbowl, National Memorial Cemetery of the Pacific,* **Honolulu.** Easter bonnet breakfasts and fashion parades at *Waikiki* resort hotels.
April 9	WESAK DAY (always observed on Sunday in **Honolulu**). Kimono-clad dancers perform ritual dances in honor of Buddha in *Kapiolani Park, Waikiki Beach.* Ceremonial sweet tea. Special programs in English and Japanese in Buddhist temples throughout Hawaii, open to visitors.
May 1	LEI DAY. Major celebration in **Honolulu** includes state-wide lei exhibits for prizes at *Waikiki Beach Park.* Lei Queen presides

STATE OF HAWAII (cont.)

	over free hula pageant. Festivities throughout the resort islands include the wearing and presenting of leis.
June 11	KAMEHAMEHA DAY. One of Hawaii's most colorful holidays honoring King Kamehameha I. Lavish parade in **Honolulu** features flower-trimmed floats, girls on horseback wearing long Hawaiian dresses and leis. Hawaiian pageantry, hulas, and *Holoku Ball,* open to public, with parade of old-time and modern Hawaiian formal dress.
Late June to Mid-July	FIFTIETH STATE FAIR—*Waikiki*. Entertainers, beauty contests, hula shows, exhibits of arts, crafts, produce, and livestock. Polynesian and Oriental food booths.
July 4	INDEPENDENCE DAY. Celebrated with fire works at *Waikiki Shell*. Outrigger canoe races, special water sports at *Waikiki Beach*.
July and August	BON ODORI. *Bon* dance season in Hawaii with dances every weekend during season. Kimono-dressed Japanese Buddhist dancers perform traditional dances of joy, circling lantern-lit towers. Visitors with kimonos welcome to join or watch ceremonies.
August (first two Sundays)	HULA FESTIVAL (on *Oahu*). Hundreds of costumed dancers—men, women, and children—to the accompaniment of ancient and modern Hawaiian instruments.
October (third week)	ALOHA WEEK on *Oahu Island*. This is the Mardi Gras of the *Pacific* and the larg-

STATE OF HAWAII (cont.)

est of Hawaii's many festivals. During this week, the schedule includes hula dances, parades, street dancing, Hawaiian and international pageantry, an inter-island outrigger canoe race, massed choral singing at *Waikiki Shell,* and special exhibits of early Hawaiiana at the *Bishop Museum.* An *Aloha Week* royal court in costumes of ancient Hawaii rules all events. A Waikiki *Hoolaulea* (street carnival) and luaus are all part of the fun. (Note: *Aloha Week* is celebrated three days preceding the *Oahu* date on *Molokai Island* and the week following on the islands of *Hawaii, Maui,* and *Kauai.*)

November   INTERNATIONAL SURFING CHAMPIONSHIPS—*Makaha Beach, Oahu.* Men, women, and children ride five- to twenty-foot waves in spectacular surfing competition.

December 4   BODHI DAY—Anniversary of the enlightenment of Buddha, which is said to have happened under a bodhi tree. There is a sunrise ceremony, Japanese ceremonial dance program, and traditional Buddhist rites open to the public.

December 31   NEW YEAR'S EVE—Fireworks display in **Honolulu.** Special international programs at resort hotels and night clubs on all of the islands.

NOTE: A HUKILAU (Polynesian fishing festival and native feast) takes place every fourth Sunday, except in December, at **Laie,** *Oahu,* a sixty-minute drive from *Waikiki Beach.*

HONG KONG

*January or February** — CHINESE NEW YEAR—The most impressive and important of the Chinese festivals, lasting from five to fifteen days. Celebration includes fireworks and colorful flower fairs. By tradition all debts must be paid on or before the last day of the year. The New Year greeting is *"Kung Hay Fat Choy,"* meaning "prosperity." Stores are closed from two to three days during the festivities.

*February or March** — LANTERN FESTIVAL—The official end of the *Chinese New Year* period. Lanterns are displayed throughout Hong Kong, and parties are held honoring Ts'ai Shen Yeh, the God of Wealth, in homes and stores.

*April or May** — CHING MING—*Ancestral Remembrance Day.* The Chinese populace make pilgrimages to the graves of their ancestors placing food and offerings for the dead.

April 21 — BIRTHDAY OF HER MAJESTY THE QUEEN—A national holiday in this British Crown Colony.

*Early May** — BIRTHDAY OF T'IEN HAU—The Queen of Heaven and Goddess of Fishermen and Boat People. Celebration includes processions to the twenty-four temples named after her, lion dances, and the boat people's pilgrimage to *Tai Miao Temple, Joss House Bay,* on the eastern approach to the harbor.

---

*The Chinese calendar is based on the orbiting of the moon, and therefore the dates vary from year to year.

HONG KONG (cont.)

Mid-May *   CHEUNG CHAU BUN FESTIVAL (generally referred to as the "Festival of the Bun Hills")—Signifying the annual atonement of the souls of all animals and fish whose lives have been taken during the year. Huge mounds of breakfast buns are erected, and there are processions of floats, Chinese opera shows, and lion dances on *Cheung Chau Island*. There is a mad scramble for the consecrated buns at the climax of this three day celebration.

May or June *   DRAGON BOAT FESTIVAL AND REGATTA—Commemorating the attempt to save the poet-statesman, Chu Yuen, who drowned on the fifth day of the fifth moon in the third century B.C. The boats of the various villages are assembled for inter-temple races, the most spectacular being those held at *Kennedy Town* and *Aberdeen*. There are special tourist excursions to witness the races.

Late July *   BIRTHDAY OF LU PAN, Master Builder. There are no public celebrations on this builders' holiday, but you might enjoy the interesting observances held at *Lu Pan Temple, Kennedy Town*.

Late August *   THE FEAST OF THE HUNGRY GHOSTS. According to Chinese superstition this is the period when ancestors return to earth to visit their descendants. All manner of paper effigies and other gifts are put

---

* The Chinese calendar is based on the orbiting of the moon, and therefore the dates vary from year to year.

HONG KONG (cont.)

out for them, and the stores are richly abundant with supplies for their use. The general celebration is accompanied by fireworks and the burning of joss sticks.

*August or September**	THE MAIDEN FESTIVAL—Celebration commemorating the meeting once a year of the shepherd and the weaver girl across the Milky Way which takes place according to custom on the seventh day of the seventh moon.
*Late September to Early October**	MOON OR MID-AUTUMN FESTIVAL —Special day set aside in worship of the Goddess of the Moon (the fifteenth day of the eighth moon). Lanterns of every description are aglow in restaurants and shops, and local bakeries feature yummy moon cakes.
Early October	BIRTHDAY OF CONFUCIUS. Rituals held at Confucian temples.
October-November	ANNUAL FESTIVAL OF THE ARTS. A monthlong presentation of exhibitions, concerts, folk dances, and dramatic performances.
*October or November**	CHUNG YEUNG FESTIVAL—Thousands of Chinese scramble up *Victoria Peak* hoping thus traditionally to avoid calamity during the coming year. Based on a two-thousand-year-old legend, this custom is followed on the ninth day of the ninth moon.

* The Chinese calendar is based on the orbiting of the moon, and therefore the dates vary from year to year.

HONG KONG (cont.)

December-January	**Annual Exhibition of Hong Kong Products** at which a complete range of manufactured products is displayed lasting for one month.

JAPAN

January 1-3	NEW YEAR CELEBRATION—For the first three days of the New Year, every home is gaily decorated with the national flag and a *"kado matsu,"* a pair of pine twig and bamboo stalk stands symbolizing good luck. Festivities include the exchanging of greetings, visits to shrines, and the wearing of traditional costumes. Almost all business activity ceases for nearly a week.
January 6	"DEZOME SHIKI"—Annual Firemen's Demonstration. After a parade of the fire brigades past the *Imperial Palace,* the demonstration takes place in front of the *Imperial Palace Plaza* and in the outer garden of the *Meiji Shrine,* **Tokyo.** The demonstration features spectacular acrobatic feats by the firemen atop their bamboo ladders.
January 15	ADULTS' DAY—National Holiday honoring those young men and women who have come of age and are now able to vote.
Mid-January	"HATSUBASHO" SUMO TOURNAMENT—The first of the six annual fifteen-day *"sumo"* (Japanese wrestling) tournaments opens at the *Kokugikan Arena, Asakusa Kuramae,* **Tokyo.**
Early February	"SETSUBUN"—Annual last day of winter celebration, involving the throwing about of

JAPAN (cont.)

beans thus customarily inviting the year's good fortune into the home and driving away misfortune. The festivities at *Hommonji Temple* in **Tokyo** and at *Narita Fudo Temple* in Chiba Prefecture are the most colorful.

Early February   LANTERN FESTIVAL—The *Kasuga Shrine,* **Nara,** is ablaze with the lights of over three thousand lanterns.

March 3   "HINA MATSURI"—Dolls' Festival. The finest dolls of each Japanese family are displayed in the home.

March 12   WATER-DRAWING FESTIVAL OF THE TODAIJI. Young Buddhist ascetics brandish twelve giant torches at the *Nigatsudo Hall* of the *Todaiji Temple,* **Nara,** in the evening. The religious folk scramble for the embers which are shaken off since these are believed to have magic power against evil. At two A.M., the *Omizu Tori* (water drawing) rites commence, accompanied by traditional Japanese music. This entire ceremony represents to the people of this area a harbinger of the coming spring.

Mid-March   The second annual fifteen-day "SUMO" TOURNAMENT begins in **Osaka.**

*Late March-April-   CHERRY BLOSSOM FESTIVAL SEA-
Early May*   SON—Differing slightly throughout Japan according to the type of tree, district, and weather conditions. Celebrations include dance-plays in the all-girl theaters of **Tokyo, Osaka,** and **Kyoto.**

JAPAN (cont.)

April 8	"HANA MATSURI" (Flower Festival)—Also honoring BUDDHA'S BIRTHDAY. Observed at all the Buddhist temples throughout Japan, some of which have a parade of children in festival costume.
Early to Late April	NAGASAKI KITE-FLYING CONTESTS—Held on the mountains surrounding the city. Fierce but good-natured competition among the contestants.
Mid-April	SANNO FESTIVAL—Held at the *Hie Shrine*, **Takayama**. The parade of floats is magnificent.
Mid-April to Early May	OSAKA INTERNATIONAL FESTIVAL—Japanese traditional stage arts; ballet, opera, and music of an international nature.
Mid-April to Early May	INTERNATIONAL MUSIC FESTIVAL—Held in the *Metropolitan Memorial Cultural Hall* of *Ueno Park*, **Tokyo**.
Mid-April to Early May	INTERNATIONAL TRADE FAIR—**Tokyo** or **Osaka** (held in these two cities in alternate years).
April 21-30	"MIBU KYOGEN"—13th century pantomime comedies are presented at the *Mibu Temple* in **Kyoto**.
April 29	BIRTHDAY OF THE EMPEROR—A National Holiday. This is one of the two days of the year (New Year's Day is the other) on which the public is permitted to enter the *Imperial Palace* grounds in **Tokyo**.
May 3	CONSTITUTION MEMORIAL DAY—A national holiday commemorating Japan's

JAPAN (cont.)

New Constitution put into effect on this date in 1947.

May 5   CHILDREN'S FESTIVAL—National Holiday for the boys and girls of Japan.

Mid-May through CORMORANT FISHING SEASON—On
Mid-October   the *Nagara River*, **Gifu.** Really cheating, since the fish are caught by trained cormorant birds rather than by the fishermen themselves.

Mid-May   The third annual fifteen-day "SUMO" TOURNAMENT commences at the *Kokugikan Arena, Asakusa Kuramae,* **Tokyo.**

May 15   "AOI MATSURI"—THE HOLLYHOCK FESTIVAL. Re-enactment of the feudal Imperial processions takes place from the old *Imperial Palace* to the *Shimogamo* and *Kamigamo Shrines,* **Kyoto.**

JAPAN (cont.)

May 16-18	SANJA FESTIVAL—*Asakusa Shrine,* **Tokyo.** Youths parade through the streets carrying portable shrines.
May 17	GRAND FESTIVAL OF TOSHOGU SHRINE, **Nikko**—Featuring a parade of over one thousand people dressed in feudal armor.
May 21	BOAT FESTIVAL at ARASHIYAMA— **Kyoto.** A gaily decorated fleet of Old World splendor proceeds down the *Oi River* in colorful pageantry.
June	PEIRON BOAT RACE—**Nagasaki.** Rowing race staged between ancient whaling vessels accompanied by the clatter of gongs and percussion instruments.
June 14	ANNUAL RICE PLANTING FESTIVAL—*Sumiyoshi Shrine,* **Osaka.** The transplanting of rice seedlings in the paddy field of the *Shrine* is performed by an even dozen beautiful girls. Traditional music is featured.
June 14-16	SANNO FESTIVAL OF THE HIE SHRINE—**Tokyo.** One of **Tokyo's** most fabulous festivals. The shrine palanquins are paraded through the downtown streets of the city amid much hilarity.
July 1	OPENING OF THE FUJI CLIMBING SEASON. The first of July marks the official opening of the season for climbing *Mt. Fuji* and other of the peaks of the *Northern* and *Southern Japan Alps.* This

JAPAN (cont.)

date also marks the formal opening of many of the major bathing resorts.

July 7

TANABATA (STAR) FESTIVAL—Annual observation of the uniting of Vega and Altair, two stars, who, according to legend, are lovers whom the King of Heaven allows to meet just once each year. Houses and streets throughout the country are festooned with gay streamers and papier mâché figures.

Mid-July

BON FESTIVAL or FEAST OF LANTERNS—Observation by Buddhist families in commemoration of their deceased who, or so the Buddhist tenet professes, revisit the earth during this time. The festival highlights include lantern-floating throughout Japan in miniature boats which supposedly carry back to heaven the spirits of the dead after their "visits" and the colorful *"Bon Odori"* dances performed in many of the cities (the one in **Nikko** is well worth traveling from the capital to attend).

Mid-July

FOURTH "SUMO" TOURNAMENT, of fifteen days' duration, commences in **Nagoya.**

July 16

MUSIC FESTIVAL OF ITSUKUSHIMA SHRINE—*Miyajima.* The procession of ornamented watercraft takes place with accompaniment of *gagaku* harmony.

July—Third Week

GION FESTIVAL—*Yasaka Shrine,* **Kyoto.** **Kyoto's** most spectacular summer fete deservedly of world prominence. Picturesque parades, much fun.

JAPAN (cont.)

July (third or fourth Saturday)	ANNUAL FIREWORKS DISPLAY—On the *Sumida River*, **Tokyo.**
August 16	ANNUAL MT. NYOIGADAKE BONFIRE—**Kyoto.** The lighting of a huge conflagration in memory of a legendary Buddhist deity who reputedly appeared on this mount surrounded by an incandescent halo.
September 14-16	TSURUGAOKA HACHIMANGU SHRINE FESTIVAL—**Kamakura.** Archery performed by riders garbed as samurai warriors is featured.
Late September	AUTUMNAL "SUMO" TOURNAMENT—*Kokugikan Arena, Asakusa Kuramae,* **Tokyo.** Fifteen more days of Japanese style wrestling.
October 22	"JIDAI MATSURI" (sometimes called the FESTIVAL OF ERAS)—*Heian Shrine,* **Kyoto.** In celebration of the founding of **Kyoto** in 794, the city's citizens parade in costumes typical of the various periods of **Kyoto's** fabulous history.
November 3	CULTURE DAY (National Holiday). Meetings to encourage Japan to honor its ancient cultural ways and espouse new culture. Persons who have made important progress in culture are decorated with the Order of Culture Merit.
November	"TORI-NO-ICHI" (COCK FAIR)—*Otori Shrine, Asakusa,* **Tokyo.** Shopping festival. Bamboo rakes for household shrines (said

JAPAN (cont.)

	to bring good luck) are featured at most shops.
Mid-November	FINAL ANNUAL "SUMO" TOURNAMENT—**Fukuoka.** Of fifteen days' duration.
November 23	LABOR THANKSGIVING DAY (National Holiday). Similar to our Thanksgiving celebration, as the Japanese people thank God for their yearly harvest.
December 1-26	KAOMISE KABUKI PLAYS—Top *Kabuki* performances at the *Minami-za Theater, Shijo,* **Kyoto.**
December 24	CHRISTMAS EVE BALLS—*Imperial Hotel* in **Tokyo** and other cosmopolitan social spots.
Late December	YEAR-END MARKETS—Observed in most of Japan's larger cities. New Year decorations for the country's religious edifices are purchased at this time.
December 31	OMISOKA, the "GRAND LAST DAY"— A family celebration when relatives gather to wait for the midnight clanging of the *Joya-no-Kane,* traditional 108 rings of the temple bells proclaiming the arrival of the New Year.

MACAO

January or February	CHINESE NEW YEAR—The most important of the Chinese holidays in Macao. Prior to the holiday itself, flowers, foods, toys, and religious articles are sold in shops and stalls. Don't miss the flower stalls in

MACAO (cont.)

front of the *Municipal Council Building* which are a particularly enchanting maze of color.

Mid-February to Early March (two days)

PROCESSION OF OUR LORD OF PASSOS—Two day religious festival marked by processions of worshippers who carry church statuary through the streets of the city from *St. Augustine Church* to the *Cathedral.*

Mid-April

GODDESS A-MA FESTIVAL—A three day festival honoring Neung Ma, the goddess for whom Macao was named. Fishermen gather at the *Temple of Ma-Kok-Miu* in her honor, and religious ceremonies, Macao musical fetes, and dramatic presentations are all included in the celebration.

May 13

PROCESSION OF OUR LADY OF FATIMA—The officials of the church lead the population of the city in this rich and colorful procession from the *Church of St. Domingo* to *Penha Chapel.*

June 10

PORTUGESE NATIONAL DAY— Marked by a military parade in the morning in front of *Government House* and an afternoon children's parade in *Camoens Gardens.*

Early November

THE MACAO GRAND PRIX—Annual auto races at the *Guia* circuit.

NOTE: Nearly all of the Chinese festivals listed under **Hong Kong** (pages 420-422) are observed with just as much festivity and ceremony in **Macao**. Please refer to the **Hong Kong** listings for the dates and events.

FEDERATION OF MALAYSIA

The Federation of Malaysia's three main racial groups, Malays, Chinese, and Indians, each have their own culture and background. Almost every day is some sort of a festival day in Malaysia. The following are the most universally celebrated.

January or February THAIPUSAM—A lavish, spectacular religious festival celebrated by the Hindus in honor of the birth of Lord Subramaniam. Penang's *Waterfall Temple* attracts masses of Hindus all day long, large numbers of them punctured with skewers penetrating their bodies. The night procession is one of great splendor. In **Kuala Lumpur** the Indian faithful who climb the 287 steps of the limestone cave-temple also have a variety of needles, pins and nails inserted through their skin.

January or February CHINESE NEW YEAR. As elsewhere in the world, this gala occasion is enthusiastically celebrated by the Chinese community. Everyone dresses up in his gayest raiment and visits everyone else, to the explosive chattering of snapping firecrackers. All of the Buddhist temples are filled to overflowing.

Late February CHOR SOO KONG'S BIRTHDAY. The celebration of this deity's naissance is particularly observed in **Penang** where the Chinese gather to pray at the *Snake Temple,* before which a unique theatrical performance takes place.

Late February or March BIRTHDAY OF THE JADE EMPEROR. Throughout Malaysia devout Chinese place

FEDERATION OF MALAYSIA (cont.)

whole roasted pigs and collections of fruit on specially constructed altars before their houses for the edification of the Jade Emperor. The birthday is celebrated by visiting at temples, particularly the *Th'nee Kong Thuah Temple* in **Penang.**

March

CHAP GOH MEH, another Chinese festival observed largely in **Penang,** sees gaily decorated automobiles carrying orchestras and individual musicians passing in gay procession.

March

CHINGAY—A Malayan-Chinese festival celebrated in **Penang** and **Johore Bahru.** The exuberant parades feature a mad agglomeration of music, flags, and floats.

March

HARI RAYA PUASA—Celebrated the first day of the tenth month of the Mohammedan calendar. The thanksgiving which takes place during *Hari Raya Puasa* and conviviality which accompanies it are the conclusion of a full month's fasting period.

March or April (Good Friday)

GOOD FRIDAY PROCESSION—Celebrated throughout the Federation. A particularly impressive parade takes place at *Bunga Raya* in **Malacca,** where a huge statue of Christ is carried to *St. Peter's Church.*

March or April (Easter)

EASTER SUNDAY—Another solemn day that is celebrated particularly in *Bunga Raya* with a procession to *St. Peter's.*

April

BIRTHDAY OF THE GODDESS OF MERCY—A Chinese holiday in which

FEDERATION OF MALAYSIA (cont.)

	theatrical performances are offered as displays of gratitude by the worshippers. The focal points of the worship and celebration are in **Kuala Lumpur, Malacca,** and **Penang.**
April or May	WESAK DAY—Celebration of Lord Buddha's birthday during which the temples observe special rites. The evening is the occasion of lantern parades throughout the Federation. In **Penang,** an illuminated image of Buddha is carried in the parade, while the procession at **Kuala Lumpur** terminates in the *Lake Gardens.*
June 29	FEAST OF ST. PETER—A festival of the fisherman particularly celebrated in *Banda Praya* in **Malacca** with ceremonies at the *Church of the Assumption.*
July to September	The most unusual special event of which I know. During this season the giant turtles emerge from the *South China Sea* to lay eggs on the east coast. Huge throngs gather to watch the arrival and ultimate departures of these denizens of the deep, eight and more feet in length.
August	MANDI SAFAR, the *National Bathing Festival*—Observed by the Muslims in **Malacca, Selangor** and **Penang.** The devout celebrate wearing gay costumes, riding in decorated carts, singing folk songs, dancing on the beaches, and by inundations in the water.
Late August	THE FESTIVAL OF THE HUNGRY GHOSTS. Gay celebrations take place in

FEDERATION OF MALAYSIA (cont.)

the market places throughout the Federation. Huge tables groan with masses of food offered to the deities. Paper clothing and joss money are consumed by fire as further offerings to the gods. Theatrical performances and puppet shows accompany the celebrations.

August 31 MERDEKA DAY *(Hari Kemerdekaan)*— A combination of our own Fourth of July and the Fourteenth of July, *Bastille Day,* of France. Malaysia's independence is celebrated with illuminated, decorated buildings, musical events, theatrical performances, and enthusiastic processions. In the nation's capital, **Kuala Lumpur,** the Malays, Chinese, and Indians combine to present songs and dances at an outdoor theater in the colorful *Lake Gardens.*

September 6-8 MARKET FESTIVAL, celebrated only in **Johore Bahru** by the Chinese. The market place is the scene of Chinese classic drama.

October FESTIVAL OF THE NINE EMPEROR GODS. The Chinese believers clamber up the more than 1,200 steps to *Kew Ong Yeah Temple* perched on *Paya Terubong Hill* in **Penang.** The parade commemorates the nine gods who ascended to heaven. Throughout Malaya, one sees mediums squatting on beds of sharp spikes with skewers piercing their cheeks. In **Kuala Lumpur** the fire-walking ceremony at *Kau Ong Yah Temple* is awesome.

FEDERATION OF MALAYSIA (cont.)

October 22   CHILDREN'S DAY IN KUALA LUM-
                PUR. 30,000 or more school children are
                entertained at *Merdeka Stadium* with bands,
                balloon displays, Malayan football, and dem-
                onstrations of motorcycle acrobatics. Other
                towns celebrate to a lesser degree.

October 28   THE BIRTHDAY OF THE SULTAN
                OF JOHORE—Celebrated with aquatic
                and athletic competitions and presentation
                of top-flight drama, opera, and concerts.

October or   DEEPAVALI—A Hindu ceremony cele-
November   brating the slaying of the mythological King
                Naragasura by Lord Krishna.

December 22 to ANNUAL TRADE FAIR—*New World
January 8   Park* in **George Town, Penang.**

December 25   CHRISTMAS DAY.

THE PHILIPPINES

January 1   NEW YEAR'S DAY.

January 6   THE FEAST OF THE THREE KINGS
                celebrates the end of the Christmas season
                with a Parade of the Three Kings in both
                Cebu and **Manila.**

January 9   FIESTA OF QUIAPO DISTRICT—**Ma-
                nila's** most colossal festival, inspired by
                the *Black Nazarene.* The devout descend in
                hordes on *Quiapo* for the offering of the
                traditional sacrifice which involves pulling
                a carriage bearing the centuries old image
                of the *Nazarene* en route to Calvary, while
                the entire district is encircled by candle-

THE PHILIPPINES (cont.)

	bearing faithful. The fiesta is preceded by nine days of concerts, theatrical performances, and amateur entertainment in front of the baroque church in which the image is enshrined.
Mid-January	NATIONAL BAND CONTEST in *Luneta Park,* **Manila,** in which bands from neighboring towns enter the competition.
January 21-22	FIESTA, **Cebu City**—In honor of the Santo Niño, patron saint of **Cebu.** It is believed that the saint's image was carried to the Philippines by Magellan. The *San Augustin Church* is the site of the *"pit senyor"* dance which is a combination of classic dancing and boogie-woogie during which the image of the saint is on display.
Late January	FIESTA—**Vigan,** Ilocos Sur. Vigan, the one truly Spanish town enduring in the Philippines today, celebrates its festival honoring San Pablo Apostol with a carnival atmosphere, cock-fights, theatrical performances and local entertainment.
First Harvest in January	PIPIGAN FESTIVAL—**Novaliches,** Rizal. During the *Pipigan,* crowds mass outside farmers' dwellings where the "pinipig" is roasted on an open fire and consumed with rice flakes which are made by beating newly harvested *malagkit.* The beating of the *malagkit* must be attuned to the tempo of the songs and folk dances.
February 1-3	TOWN FIESTA, **Silang,** Cavite, which honors its patroness.

THE PHILIPPINES (cont.)

February 11   OUR LADY OF LOURDES FETE,
                     Lourdes Church, Santa Mesa Heights,
                     Quezon City—A fiesta commemorating
                     the appearance of the apparition. It is cele-
                     brated with solemn rites in the morning
                     and afternoon and a gigantic parade of
                     penance in the evening.

March or April   HOLY WEEK—Celebrated everywhere in
                     the Philippines and accompanied by mag-
                     nificent church ceremonies, theatrical pro-
                     ductions and the chanting of the Passion.
                     The Holy Week ceremonies combine the
                     native traditions, the utterly bizarre ancient
                     rites, and events of great religious signifi-
                     cance. Passion plays are given throughout
                     the islands and are considered by the vil-
                     lagers to be one of their most important
                     activities of the year. Many of the Passion
                     plays take hours and hours to present.

March or April   GOOD FRIDAY is observed universally,
                     during which the flagellants are seen
                     staggering everywhere with bleeding backs
                     lacerated by the biting whips. The flagel-
                     lants, always a great attraction, are followed
                     by hordes of the devout who watch them
                     bathe in the sea at the end of their painful
                     journey. Throughout the countryside, fig-
                     ures garbed like Christ carry huge crosses
                     along the road and are flogged by men in
                     Roman military garb.

March or April   EASTER SUNDAY. The rituals in **Rizal,**
                     Cavite and **Bulacan** are particularly impres-
                     sive when, at dawn, separate processions

THE PHILIPPINES (cont.)

emanate from church doors, the one led by the image of the resurrected Christ, while the second procession is following the veiled image of Mary. The processions come together in the town plaza under a specially constructed garland of flowers from which hangs a papier-mâché heart enveloping a little girl garbed as an angel singing "Alleluja" as she is lowered through the chorus of angels to remove the veil from the Virgin.

April

APRIL WEEK is to **Baguio** what *June Week* is to *West Point*. The graduation rites for the *Philippine Military Academy* take place to the accompaniment of parades, reviews, athletic events, and great festivity.

April 28

TOWN FIESTA—**Hagonor**, Bulacan. The street decorations are the most magnificent imaginable taking more than two months to prepare.

May 1

LABOR DAY features a tremendous torch parade in **Manila's** *Luneta Park*.

May 1-31

FLORES DE MAYO—A church ceremony of an entire month's duration, during which children, always dressed in white, present flowers, in the church, to the Queen of May.

May 15

CARABAO (Water Buffalo) FESTIVAL takes place in many towns and villages during which the water buffalo, gaily bedecked with flowers, are marched through the streets to the local church where they are blessed.

THE PHILIPPINES (cont.)

May 17-19	FIESTA, **Obando,** Bulacan, which honors the town's three patron saints, is particularly devoted to the women desiring to be blessed with children, who perform interminable dances between the patio and the church's altar during which time they beseech the saints for aid in becoming mothers.
May 31	SANTA CRUZ DE MAYO is countrywide and considered to be the most gorgeous of the festivals of the land. This festival began as a religious fete to commemorate the finding of the Cross, but now there are many other traditions which have grown around *Santa Cruz de Mayo.* The costumes are outlandish, some portraying religious and historical events, others depicting completely illusory characters. The *Santa Cruz de Mayo* parade is followed by a *"pabatin"* in which a large bamboo trellis has been bedecked with all sorts of goodies designed to bring joy to the hearts of the kiddies. The band plays, the bamboo trellis is lowered within reach of the youngsters, the band plays faster, the children gather in the sweets, and great gay disorder reigns.
June 17	FREEDOM DAY—Celebrated with band concerts, parades, fireworks, athletic events, formal parties, church services, and great outpourings of national enthusiasm.
June 19	DR. JOSE P. RIZAL'S BIRTHDAY—A national holiday.
June 24	ST. JOHN'S DAY, Fiesta in **San Juan,** Rizal—Commemorated by a religious pro-

THE PHILIPPINES (cont.)

cession during which hilarity prevails with passers-by being doused with water to, theoretically at least, re-enact the baptism ceremony.

June 29 FLUVIAL FESTIVAL, **Apalit,** Pampanga, honors St. Peter and St. Paul. A water procession, a relic of the Spanish occupation, features the image of St. Peter borne up and down the *Pampanga River.*

July 6 BOCAWE RIVER FESTIVAL. Lighted river boats form a colorful procession near **Manila.** The significance is religious.

July 29 TOWN FIESTA—**Pateros,** Rizal. There are parades and river processions as well as street dancing.

August 19 BIRTHDAY OF THE LATE PRESIDENT MANUEL QUEZON—A national holiday. An impressive military parade takes place in **Quezon City.**

August 19-20 FIESTA, **Lucban,** Quezon—Feasts galore and colorful processions.

August 26 CRY OF BALINTAWAK DAY—Honoring the 1896 rebellion against Spain. The focal points of the celebration are around special monuments in **Balintawak, Quezon City,** and **Caloocan,** Rizal. There are parades, great displays of flowers, and special programs honoring these national heroes.

August 31 BIRTHDAY OF THE LATE PRESIDENT RAMON MAGSAYSAY—A national holiday.

THE PHILIPPINES (cont.)

September 10	SUNDUAN FESTIVAL—**La Huerta, Parañaque,** Rizal. 100 gorgeous gals in bright gowns are accompanied by 100 beaus carrying parasols matching the fashion gowns. There are brass bands and fireworks.
September 17	FEAST OF OUR LADY OF PENA-FRANCIA—**Bicolandia's** largest festival, in **Naga,** Camarines Sur. The *Naga River* is literally choked with magnificently adorned barges.
November 10	FIESTA, **Cavite City,** is characterized by the night procession on *Manila Bay* to *Cabuco Beach Caridad.*
November 15	PHILIPPINE-AMERICAN DAY—Celebrated in all of the big cities with impressive parades.
December 8-9	FIESTA, **Taal,** Batangas, features a waterborne procession on the *Pansipit River.*
December 16 to January 6	The 22-DAY CHRISTMAS CELEBRATION is universally celebrated. The religious ceremony takes place with 4:00 A.M. masses. A great joyous expression pours forth during this three-week span as church bells gaily clatter, the roadside stalls sell all of the native specialties, the streets are gaily decorated, and there are serenades and carols.
December 24	The CHRISTMAS LANTERN FESTIVAL, **San Fernando,** Pampanga, is a contest to determine the most elegant and largest lantern in the land.

THE PHILIPPINES (cont.)

December 24 CHRISTMAS EVE ceremonies include the *"panunuluyan,"* a Tagalog fete which includes characters who, posing as Joseph and the Virgin Mary seeking shelter, knock on doors throughout the towns and are followed by groups of faithful, singing carols. Shelter is always found shortly before midnight.

December 24 MALACANANG CHRISTMAS FESTIVAL, **Manila**—The underprivileged children come to the *Presidential Palace* where they are given gifts in an impressive candle-lit ceremony.

December 30 RIZAL DAY—Marking the moment of infamy when Dr. Jose P. Rizal was executed in 1896.

December 31 NEW YEAR'S EVE is celebrated much like almost everywhere else throughout the civilized world, with bands, lanterns, cannons, firecrackers, parades, private parties, and impressive ceremonies.

SINGAPORE

January 1 NEW YEAR'S DAY—Celebrated throughout the island. The harbor off *Clifford Pier* is the scene of a water carnival, sea sports, and small craft competitions.

January or February THAIPUSAM is particularly celebrated at the *Chettiar Hindu Temple* on *Tank Road.* This universal Hindu holy day sees the devout arrive at the temple in semi-trances,

SINGAPORE (cont.)

	their skin punctured by nails, spikes, and other sharp objects thought to bring forgiveness for their sins.
January or February	CHINESE NEW YEAR—An occasion of great celebration, including the ubiquitous firecrackers, great feasting, and solemn exchanges of family visits.
March	HARI RAYA PUASA—Commemorating the termination of the Ramadan month of fasting. The Muslims gaily bedeck themselves in native costumes and exchange visits.
Early April	The ANNUAL SINGAPORE FLOWER SHOW—*Happy World Stadium*. This three-day event is bursting with the colors of tropical shrubs, flowers and plants.
April or May	WESAK DAY—Commemorating the birth, death, and enlightenment of Lord Buddha. The Buddhists rally in the center of the city before beginning the great procession with highly decorated, illuminated floats.
May 1	LABOR DAY—A national holiday.
May or June	HARI RAYA HAJI—Celebrated by the Malays in Singapore commemorating the pilgrimage to Mecca. The day is dedicated to prayers and gatherings in the mosques.
June 3	NATIONAL DAY—Celebrating the granting of self-government to Singapore. The festivities last for an entire week throughout the island.

SINGAPORE (cont.)

August 1	A public holiday.
August	MANDI SAFAR—Malay festival of the beaches celebrated by the cleansing of the bodies, throughout the day and night, on all the beaches of the island.
August or September	MOHAMMED'S BIRTHDAY—Celebrated by all of the Muslims with ritualistic ceremonies and parades. Public and private buildings are gaily decorated and illuminated.
Late August	THE FEAST OF THE HUNGRY GHOSTS (also called *All Souls' Day*). In Singapore, the *Feast of the Hungry Ghosts* is a particularly fruitful one for photographers. Exotic paper religious objects are displayed, and tables are filled with food for both returning ancestors and the deities.
Late September to Early October	MOON FESTIVAL—A day on which all restaurants and shops are emblazoned with a variety of colored lights. Moon cakes are baked and sold almost everywhere in Singapore, being seen not only in all bake shops but at the sidewalk stalls as well.
Early October	ANNUAL ORCHID SHOW—An unbelievably wide variety of beautiful blooms is on display.
October or November	DEEPAVALI—The *Festival of Lights*. This is the day on which Lord Krishna slew the oppressive King Naragasura and freed the people from the bondage of the tyrant. Firecrackers explode and lights twinkle.

SINGAPORE (cont.)

December 22	WINTER SOLSTICE—Celebrating the festival of the shortest day of the year.
December 25	CHRISTMAS DAY.

TAIWAN *(Formosa)*

January 1	NEW YEAR'S DAY—A legal holiday.
January or February	CHINESE NEW YEAR. This festival is particularly impressive in Taiwan, with celebrations going on for a minimum of three days with all business having ground to a dead stop. During this feasting and festivity, gambling parties are legally observed among friends. Jillions of firecrackers create a sub-atomic chain reaction.
February or March	LANTERN FESTIVAL—The official termination of the New Year holiday when gay lanterns in odd designs and shapes may be purchased at all shops. In the evening the streets are aglow with the lights of the lanterns.
May	BUDDHA BATHING FESTIVAL honors Buddha's birth during which fete water is doused on Buddha images before they are paraded through the streets of all of the towns, villages, and hamlets of Taiwan. Special prayers are offered in the Buddhist temples on the island.
May or June	DRAGON BOAT FESTIVAL marks the anniversary of the death of Chu Yuen, reputedly China's greatest poet. He committed suicide in the year 221 B.C. in the *Milo*

TAIWAN *(Formosa)* (cont.)

River. Fishermen unsuccessfully attempted to thwart his self-destruction. Now the fishermen each year bedeck their boats with dragons' heads and tails and compete in races. Each temple is represented by a team of fishermen. The *Tamsui River* is the sundown site of the **Taipei** boat races.

Late August   GHOST FESTIVAL *("The Feast of the Hungry Ghosts"* or *"All Souls' Day").* Celebrated as in **Hong Kong, Singapore** and **Malaya.**

Late September   MID-AUTUMN, or MOON, FESTIVAL. See **Hong Kong** write-up.

Late September   CONFUCIUS' BIRTHDAY—A most solemn event. The Confucian feather dance is performed in a temple outside **Taipei.**

October 10   The DOUBLE TENTH DAY commemorates the 1911 birth of the Republic of China. The festivities include military reviews, rallies of the people, great sporting events, and private programs.

October 25   TAIWAN RESTORATION DAY honors the reclamation of **Formosa** by **China** in 1945, 50 years after the Japanese had occupied the island.

November 12   BIRTHDAY OF DR. SUN YAT-SEN, founder of the Republic of China—A national holiday.

THAILAND

January 1   NEW YEAR. Ceremonies are held at the *Phra Mane Ground* in front of the *Grand*

THAILAND (cont.)

Palace along with games and amusements. Food stalls are set up and special film shows and dance dramas are held. The New Year is also celebrated by the Thai Buddhists with much pomp at the temples. Saffron-robed monks receive alms, bells are tolled, and gongs are sounded.

About February   MAKHA BUJA FESTIVAL. The season for making pilgrimages to *Phra Buddha Baht (Foot Print Shrine), Phra Chai (Buddha's Shadow* on the side of a hill), *Phra Taen Sila Art,* west of **Uttaradit,** and *Phra Taen Dong Rang,* north of **Rajburi.**

April 6   CHAKRI DAY. The *Pantheon* in the *Royal Palace* grounds at **Bangkok** is opened to the public. Clad in their Sunday best, the people come with flowers, incense and carrying tapers to place blooms at the statues of the eight kings of the present dynasty.

Mid-April   SONGKRAN FESTIVAL. Formerly a religious fete, this festival now involves much merrymaking. Images of Buddha are bathed with water as a mark of veneration. In the villages, this rite is apt to become a war of friendly combat between the sexes. At Court, the King receives a ceremonial bath in accordance with the ancient royal rite. *Songkran* actually marks the beginning of the new year according to the Maha Sakaraj calendar (now practically out of use in Thailand). In **Bangkok** this festival is also highlighted by a kite-flying contest in which the biggest and most original are

THAILAND (cont.)

	honored. These kite contests are held at *Phra Mane Ground*.
Mid-April	KO PRA SAI—The rite of building sand *chedis* within the temple precincts. For each grain of sand carried to the temple, one of the smaller sins is supposed to be atoned for, and in the process the temple grounds are provided with fresh clean sand.
Early May	VISAKHA BUJA—Festival commemorating Buddha's birth, enlightenment, and "passing into Nirvana" (union with God). The feast lasts for three days during which time the people flock to the temples for the reading of the holy scriptures during the day, and at night the temples are illuminated by paper lanterns and candle processions.
May, June, and July	BUAT NAK (ordination to the priesthood). Actually, it makes no difference when this takes place just so long as it is not during Lent. In Thailand it is considered proper that every young man enter the priesthood at the age of twenty-one for religious training and to gain knowledge of Buddhism in general. He need only stay for a short time.
July–September	BUDDHIST LENT (PARNSA). Lent begins in July and lasts for three months. During that time members of the brotherhood of the orange robe are prohibited from passing the night outside the cloister to which they belong. Entering Lent is known

THAILAND (cont.)

as *"Khao Parnsa."* The faithful then visit the temples, often bearing gifts for the monks.

August 12

HER MAJESTY'S BIRTHDAY—A national holiday.

Mid-October

ORK PARNSA (Lent expires), and the "SART" festival is celebrated. Friends exchange sweets, but this is for the most part a family celebration. *Ork Parnsa* is followed by competitive canoe racing on the river and canals between teams of boys and girls amid much gaiety.

October 23

CHULALONGKORN DAY. A ceremony is performed in commemoration of King Chulalongkorn at the king's equestrian statue which stands on the plaza in front of the *Parliament House (Throne Hall)*. The people bring floral wreaths and incense as tokens of their love and adoration.

Late October

TOD KATHIN—The annual offering of gifts to the Buddhist monks (mostly new saffron robes), observed all over the country. Most elaborate of the countrywide processions is the *Royal Procession* in **Bangkok** with golden barges rowed down the river to the *Temple of the Dawn*.

Late October

PHU KHAO THONG *(Golden Mount)* FAIR in **Bangkok** lasts for three days. The base of the chedi crowning the tree clad brick mountain is wrapped in red cloth, and thousands of pilgrims climb the stairs to worship the relics of the Buddha en-

THAILAND (cont.)

shrined within. At the foot of the mount and in the surrounding streets, all kinds of toys, sweets, and cakes are sold in booths. There are modern film shows, Siamese shadow plays, and popular and classical dance dramas. A similar fair is held at the same time at **Nakorn Pathom.**

Late October and Early November   PHRA-CHEDI-KLANG-NAM (a beautiful *chedi* on an island in the river opposite the town of **Paknam**). Annual boat race and pilgrimage to this temple island. Large crowds of people come by boat, rail, and car from **Bangkok** and environs.

Late October or November   LOY KRATHONG—"To float a leaf cup" . . . Festival of the floating lights in leaf cups. Held the night of the full moon. In the *"krathong"* besides a candle and one or more incense sticks is usually a small coin and sometimes a mouthful of betel. The people carry one or two to the water's edge, light the candle and incense and set them adrift. This symbolizes the floating away of one's sins and troubles.

November to May   CLASSICAL DANCE SEASON at the *Fine Arts Department Theatre,* **Bangkok.**

December 5   BIRTHDAY OF THE KING OF THAILAND. This National Day is celebrated with religious ceremonies, and official receptions; royal family and officials gather in the *Throne Hall.*

December 10   CONSTITUTION DAY.

THAILAND (cont.)

All Year   THAI-STYLE BOXING at *Rajadamnoen Stadium* in **Bangkok** on Tuesdays, Thursdays, and Sundays. On Saturdays at *Lumpini Stadium*.

All Year   CLASSICAL DANCING and SIAMESE FENCING nearly every day at the *Fine Arts Department, Buddhai Suwan School of Fencing,* or the *Phakavali Institute of Dance and Music*.

VIET NAM

January or February   "TET"—The lunar New Year. This is one of Viet Nam's most spectacular celebrations and includes the exchanging of gifts, illumination of public buildings, noisy parades in the streets of **Saigon,** and especially in **Cholon City,** with huge cavorting dragons, and the exploding of firecrackers.

March   TRUNG SISTERS' ANNIVERSARY and WOMEN'S DAY. This colorful celebration commemorating two Vietnamese heroines is highlighted by a parade with horses and elephants as the special attraction, an evening torchlight parade, and the annual presentation of awards to the outstanding women of the year. This falls on the sixth day of the second lunar month.

April or May   BUDDHA'S BIRTHDAY—Religious services and processions are held in and around the various temples and pagodas. Buddha's birthday falls on the eighth day of the fourth lunar month.

VIET NAM (cont.)

May 1	LABOR DAY—A holiday throughout Viet Nam.
May or June	CORPUS CHRISTI—A procession of Viet Nam's Christian population takes place around the *Basilica* of **Saigon** late in the afternoon.
Mid- to Late August	FEAST OF THE WANDERING GHOSTS—Observed particularly in the rural areas in the offering of food and gifts in front of homes and temples to be utilized by the nomadic souls of the forgotten dead. The offerings are by custom supposed to cause the ghosts to protect their households from evil.
Early September to Late March	BIG GAME HUNTING SEASON.
September or October	MID-AUTUMN or CHILDREN'S FESTIVAL—A school holiday and day of gaiety for Vietnamese children marked by competitive unicorn dances and parades. This festival is celebrated on the fifteenth day of the eighth lunar month.
September or October	MARSHAL TRAN-HUNG DAO'S BIRTHDAY—Observed as NAVY DAY on the twentieth day of the eighth lunar month. Services are held at the *Marshal's Temple* in **Saigon** along with a large parade of naval units.
October	SAIGON INTERNATIONAL FAIR AND EXHIBITION.

VIET NAM (cont.)

October 26   CONSTITUTION DAY (also called NA-
                    TIONAL DAY)—The Vietnamese equiv-
                    alent of our Fourth of July. The celebration
                    features a military parade, motor scooter
                    and bicycle races, the evening illumination
                    of public buildings, and a torchlight parade
                    in **Saigon.**

CHAPTER 8

Helpful Hints

"You have before you the most fascinating and unforgettable travel experiences of your lifetime. Travel with an open mind. Be thrilled, not provoked, with things that are different. Don't be a 'home towner.' People throughout the world are well familiar with the Hollywood impressions of America. They will be amazingly unimpressed with your tales of the bigness of America and the wealth of your fellow Americans. You can, indeed, be an ambassador of good will while traveling abroad. You can do as much as Foreign Aid dollars and the combined work of diplomats and statesmen by being your own genial, wonderful, natural self. Seek and be thrilled with the highways and byways that have been wonderful travel experiences for many centuries before America was discovered. People in ancient lands are proud of their historical background, of their heritage, and of their countries. They are by nature likable, friendly, and hospitable people. They will welcome you with open arms if you will only give them a chance. Please do."

The above words, directly from my heart, were written originally for my best-selling European guidebook, *Aboard and Abroad,* and say succinctly that which I feel deeply.

The following pages contain a potpourri of nuggets of

travel trivia which, individually and collectively, should prove helpful and interesting to beginners, as well as to experienced Orient travelers.

ADDRESSING MESSAGES TO PORTS OF EMBARKA-TION. Should you wish to send a bon voyage letter, telegram, or gift to a friend or relative sailing or flying from the West Coast, the address in the first instance needs only to include the name of the passenger, the name of the ship, the pier number, the class in which the passenger is traveling, the sailing date, and, most important of all, the port city: **Los Angeles, San Francisco, San Diego, Portland,** or **Seattle.** Should the lucky voyager be leaving by air, one has but to send the wire, or letter, in care of the airline at the proper airport, giving, if possible, the flight number, the hour of departure, and the date of departure.

BON VOYAGE GIFTS. Friends and relatives of departing foreign travelers have long since established the pleasant custom of sending bon voyage gifts. Such offerings can best be placed in two categories: (1) those given before the travelers leave home and (2) those received at the port of departure.

There is something to be said for both procedures.

Here are a few helpful hints on the subject:

If the travelers are proceeding by air, don't send a gift to the airport. A wire, yes. But a gift, definitely no. The baggage problem at a busy airport is too complex to confound it with the acquisition of a new possession.

For the voyager departing by ship, the traditional gifts are flowers; wine, champagne or other alcoholic bottled goods; candy; and fruit. I implore you on bended knee, however, not to succumb to the temptation to send a gorgeous basket of fruit to a ship; no other gesture I can think of so nearly emulates the carrying of coals to Newcastle. Most transpacific ocean liners carry as much fruit as one can find in California and Florida combined. And it's free to passengers. Don't send fruit.

FLOWERS MAKE THE BEST GIFT. They add a bright cheery note to a stateroom, usually last a long time, and are something that persons about to embark on a voyage would not normally think to buy themselves.

Flowers may be sent by wire, which I have found a reliable procedure, or they may be purchased in a florist shop in the port city of embarkation. I think the latter plan is preferable because you can drop a note to the florist of your choice and enclose your own card. There is something much more personal and heartwarming about a gift accompanied by a card in the handwriting of the donor. Should you wish a contact for bon voyage flowers in **San Francisco,** I can heartily recommend Podesta Baldocci, florists, whose address is 224 Grant Avenue (phone Sutter 1-6200).

CHAMPAGNE, WINE or a bottle of any other of your traveling friend's favorite beverage makes a festive present.

A gift of alcoholic beverage may be handled through the steamship line or through a store in the port city of departure. The latter procedure is more pleasant, I think, since a store will provide a gaily wrapped package, while on the ship the wine steward or barman will merely hand over the bottle(s). In **San Francisco,** for wine and spirits I can recommend the City of Paris Department Store, Union Square and Stonestown, and the White House Department Store of San Francisco, Sutter and Grant Avenue.

CANDY, too, makes an excellent parting remembrance, particularly if delivered to the ship. In **San Francisco,** either of the aforementioned department stores will handle such deliveries.

A PASSPORT CASE, embossed in gold letters, may be purchased in department stores, specialty shops, and leather stores. $15.00 to $25.00 will buy an excellent leather case. The leatherette variety may be purchased much less expensively.

A "MY TRIP ABROAD" record book, particularly for more youthful travelers, is always well received. These books may serve as a combination diary and notebook for the trip.

FOUNTAIN PENS AND PENCILS. Even notorious "non-writers" become glib when traveling and invariably will either keep a record of experiences or send post cards and letters.

Then, too, there are innumerable forms to be filled out. A standard pen and pencil set makes a fine gift, but a ballpoint pen, with at least one refill, is even much better because of the problem which high altitudes present for pens filled with liquid ink.

TRAVELING CLOCK. A compact traveling alarm clock, the folding leather variety, is an invaluable adjunct to the traveler's wardrobe. Be sure that the one you buy has a luminous dial and that the alarm has a strident voice.

GUIDEBOOKS. I have prepared an excellent bibliography for the Orient traveler which appears on pages 48–50. One or more of these volumes will make a most welcome gift. Travelers, whether proceeding by ship or air, have much more time to read en route than they have at home. Guidebooks, handbooks of travel, fiction, historical novels, and biographies with Oriental settings are excellent choices.

MAPS. A set of city and area maps of the countries to be visited is usually well received.

AIRMAIL. Because of the horrendous distances separating us from the Orient, the use of airmail is almost obligatory to avoid insurmountable delays. Surface mail "just won't catch up." Airmail is currently being delivered in principal cities in the Orient on the third, fourth, or fifth day on the calendar after posting in the States. Because of crossing the International Date Line, this actually means that the mail arrives in the Orient 48 to 96 hours after it leaves "Home Town, U.S.A." The foregoing is particularly true of **Tokyo, Hong Kong, Singapore, Manila,** and **Bangkok,** with slightly longer elapsed time necessary for **Osaka, Kobe, Kyoto, Sapporo, Siem Reap, Saigon, Kuala Lumpur,** or Baguio.

AIRMAIL RATES FOR LETTERS AND LETTER PACKAGES. The airmail rates for letters and letter packages to **Cambodia, Hong Kong, Japan, Macao, Federation of Malaysia,** the **Philippines, Taiwan** *(Formosa),* **Thailand,** and **Viet Nam** are 25¢ per each half ounce or fraction thereof. Merchandise is prohibited in letters or letter packages to **Japan** and **Taiwan** *(Formosa).*

AIRMAIL RATES FOR ARTICLES OTHER THAN LETTERS, POST CARDS, AND PARCEL POST. Such things as printed matter and samples of merchandise may be sent by air to **Cambodia, Hong Kong, Japan, Macao, Malaysia,** the **Philippines, Thailand,** and **Viet Nam** at the rate of 50¢ for the first two ounces and 30¢ for each additional two ounces.

INTERNATIONAL AIR PARCEL POST. Should one have occasion to send packages abroad, one may do so by air parcel post which is a good deal cheaper than airmail. The rates that I shall quote here are from the United States to the countries involved. The air parcel post rates from these countries to the United States are not necessarily exactly the same but will be comparable. To **Hong Kong,** air parcel post costs $1.68 for the first four ounces and 79¢ for each subsequent four ounces. To **Japan,** the rate for the first four ounces is $1.39 and 50¢ for each succeeding four ounces. To **Macao,** the first four ounces cost $2.04 and each subsequent four ounces 79¢; to **Malaysia,** the first four ounces cost $2.05 and each subsequent four ounces 90¢; to the **Philippines,** the first four ounces cost $1.93 and each subsequent four ounces 74¢; to **Thailand,** $2.08 will pay for the first four ounces and 74¢ for each additional four ounces, while to **Viet Nam,** the first four ounces cost $2.09 and each subsequent four ounces 82¢. Parcels sent to **Japan, Malaysia,** and **Cambodia** may be insured. To **Hong Kong, Japan, Macao, Viet Nam, Thailand,** and **Malaysia,** the weight limit is 22 pounds per package and to the **Philippines,** a maximum of 44 pounds. To send international air parcel post packages from the States requires a Custom Declaration Form 2966, Dispatch Note 2972, and a parcel post sticker Form 2922 must be attached to each parcel.

PARCEL POST RATES BY SEA (AND OTHER SURFACE TRANSPORTATION) to addressees in the United States from:

Weight of Parcel	Tokyo $(U.S.)	Taipei $(U.S.)	Hong Kong $(U.S.)	Manila $(U.S.)	Bang- kok $(U.S.)	Saigon $(U.S.)
1 kg. (2.2 lbs.)	0.72	0.75	1.08	0.39	1.20	1.29
2 kgs. (4.4 lbs.)	1.28	1.12	1.50	0.57	2.15	2.23
3 kgs. (6.6 lbs.)	1.76	1.50	1.50	0.75	2.15	2.23
4 kgs. (8.8 lbs.)	2.33	1.87	1.92	0.93	3.33	3.20
5 kgs. (11.0 lbs.)	2.82	2.25	1.92	1.23	3.33	3.20
6 kgs. (13.2 lbs.)	3.61	2.62	3.50	1.41	5.51	6.03
7 kgs. (15.4 lbs.)	4.10	3.00	3.50	1.59	5.51	6.03
8 kgs. (17.6 lbs.)	4.58	3.37	3.50	1.77	5.51	6.03
9 kgs. (19.8 lbs.)	5.07	3.75	3.50	1.95	5.51	6.03
10 kgs. (22.0 lbs.)	5.56	4.12	3.50	2.13	5.51	6.03

INTERNATIONAL TELEPHONE CALLS are wonderful. It is comforting to know that, though half a world apart, a conversation with home is as easily accomplished as picking up the phone. Transpacific telephone connections from most Oriental cities to the States may be made rapidly. It is almost as routine to call the North American Continent from **Tokyo** and **Hong Kong** as it is to call from **Chicago** to **Cleveland**— and easier than it usually is to complete a call to **New York** from the Windy City. On most overseas calls, the voice is heard with crystal clarity at both ends of the conversation.

The following reasonable rates are quoted for three minutes and are subject to the usual tax:

NEW YORK and CHICAGO to HONOLULU

Day—Station to Station	$ 7.50
Day—Person to Person	10.50
Night—Station to Station	6.75
Night—Person to Person	8.25

Additional Rate:
$2.50 each additional minute during the day.
$2.25 each additional minute during the night.

LOS ANGELES to HONOLULU

Day—Station to Station	$6.00
Day—Person to Person	9.00
Night—Station to Station	5.25
Night—Person to Person	8.25

Additional Rate:

$2.00 each additional minute during the day.

$1.75 each additional minute during the night.

ANYWHERE in the U.S. to JAPAN, MANILA, SINGAPORE

Weekday rate (day or night)	$12.00
Sunday rate (day or night)	9.00

ANYWHERE in the U.S. to HONG KONG

$12.00 ($4.00 each additional minute)

ANYWHERE in the U.S. to BANGKOK

$15.00 ($5.00 each additional minute)

ANYWHERE in the U.S. to SAIGON

$12.00 ($4.00 each additional minute)

CABLEGRAMS. Messages may be sent abroad either "fast" or "deferred," with the former being delivered promptly, usually within three hours, while the deferred cables are usually received the next morning. In ascertaining the whereabouts of your friend or loved one to whom you are sending a cable or telephoning, be sure to refer to the chart on page 487 showing the time differential between your home town and the Orient, where "today is frequently tomorrow." When it is twelve o'clock Sunday noon in **Tokyo,** it is nine P.M. Saturday night in **Chicago.** When cabling from the Orient, a deferred message, having been sent "overnight," will arrive the morning that it is sent, while a fast cable from **New York** filed at three P.M. won't be delivered until after breakfast the next day. Peculiar, isn't it?

In cablegrams, not only the address and signature count toward the total number of words to be paid for in a message but the designation of the type of telegram (which must be included) takes one word: either "Deferred" or "Fast." Be brief. If you expect to be cabling frequently to your home or office, establish a cable address which, for a small fee, may be filed with Western Union and will obviate the use of the full name and address. My Chicago cable address is, for example, Oltrav, Chicago, two words instead of the expensive eight or nine which would have to be used to include my complete name and address.

The following table of rates gives the cable charges for each type of service from anywhere in the United States to

HONG KONG:	FAST:	$ .27 per word
	DEF.:	$2.97 for first 22 words, 13½¢ each additional word
TOKYO:	FAST:	$ .34 per word
	DEF.:	$3.74 for first 22 words, 17¢ each additional word
HONOLULU:	FAST:	$ .21 per word
	DEF.:	$2.31 for first 22 words, 10½¢ each additional word
BOMBAY:	FAST:	$ .27 per word
	DEF.:	$2.97 for first 22 words, 13½¢ each additional word
SAIGON:	FAST:	$ .34 per word
	DEF.:	$3.74 for first 22 words, 17¢ each additional word
SINGAPORE:	FAST:	$ .27 per word
	DEF.:	$2.97 for first 22 words, 13½¢ each additional word
MANILA:	FAST:	$ .34 per word
	DEF.:	$3.74 for first 22 words, 17¢ each additional word
BANGKOK:	FAST:	$ .34 per word
	DEF.:	$3.74 for first 22 words, 17¢ each additional word

RADIOGRAMS may be sent to or from ships at sea. The address in this type of message should include only the name of the person for whom the message is intended and the steamship. The radio company sometimes wishes to know from which port the ship departed, in which direction it is sailing, and on what ocean it is plying. Radiograms, like cablegrams, are charged for on the basis of the total number of words including address, description (one word) of type of message, and signature.

INFORMATION OFFICES. Several of the Far East foreign governments (as well as our state of Hawaii) maintain offices in the United States to disseminate attractive literature and information on the wonders of their countries (or state). They are helpful in every conceivable way to potential visitors, travel agents, and even armchair travelers desiring information on their section of the world. Most of these agencies provide moving picture films for travel agents and colorful posters to anyone who requests them. As in all other forms of endeavor, some of these offices are much better and more helpful than others.

HONG KONG TOURIST ASSOCIATION. During the course of my long, pleasant association in the travel business, I have dealt with real professionals in the field of government tourist offices such as the fine people of the *French Government Tourist Office,* the *British Travel Association,* the *Danish Government Tourist Office,* and others of the absolutely superb top flight European bureaus, but I have never seen a service to exceed the magnificence of the *Hong Kong Tourist Association.* They are absolutely tops. As one will find listed below, there are two H.K.T.A. information centres in **Hong Kong,** plus their executive offices, and three offices in the United States. Anything that one might wish to have in the way of information on shopping, customs regulations, restaurants, materials, business connections, or clubs will be quickly and cheerfully handed over or briskly transmitted by the *Hong Kong Tourist Information Offices* whose addresses are:

Chicago (2)—10 North La Salle Street—ST 2-5835
New York (22)—501 Madison Avenue—PL 2-5660
San Francisco—291 Geary Street—YU 6-2858
Hong Kong—1 East Wing, *Peninsula Hotel,* Kowloon—69201
   or
Hong Kong—*Star Ferry Concourse,* Hong Kong—20969
Hong Kong (Executive Office)—Caroline Mansions, 4 Yung
   Ping Road, Hong Kong—776211

The JAPANESE NATIONAL TOURIST ASSOCIATION is, to the best of my knowledge, the largest and best-equipped of the foreign government tourist organizations representing the Asiatic countries on the North American continent. In addition to masses of colorful free material, JNTA offers at a very small cost an extensive library of books describing the principal cities and islands of Japan with other volumes covering all phases of Japanese life, art, architecture, culture, history, and customs of the country. The JNTA moving pictures are sublime.

Mr. Kazuo "Howard" Iwata, currently director of JNTA in New York, is one of Japan's most Americanized individuals, a human dynamo ably representing his country. Other JNTA offices and personnel are outstanding, ever on their toes to be helpful.

The *Japanese National Tourist Association* offices are located as follows:

Chicago (1)—333 North Michigan Avenue—332-3975
Honolulu (15)—109 Kaiulani Avenue—99-1036
New York (20)—45 Rockefeller Plaza—PL 7-5640
San Francisco—651 Market Street—EX 2-6640
Tokyo—1 Marunouchi—231-1855

PATA is an association made up of a mélange of members whose corporate and national interests are deeply rooted in the Orient. Hotels, tour, travel and sightseeing organizations, steamships and airlines, and state and government bureaus have banded together to promote travel to the *Pacific* area. They have done a magnificent job.

The *Pacific Area Travel Association* (PATA) office is located at:

San Francisco (8)—153 Kearny Street—YU 6-4646

OTHER PACIFIC AREA AND FAR EAST TOURIST INFORMATION BUREAUS are located as follows:

CAMBODIA

Department of Tourism
   Phnom Penh—Phlauv Preah Bat Sisowath

HAWAII

Hawaii Visitors Bureau
   Chicago (11)—400 North Michigan Avenue—WH 4-6694
   Honolulu (15)—2051 Kalakaua Avenue *(Waikiki)*—9-2211
or
2285 Kalakaua Avenue
   New York—609 Fifth Avenue—PL 9-3655
   San Francisco—212 Stockton Street—GA 1-6626

FEDERATION OF MALAYSIA

Malaysia Department of Tourism
   San Francisco—58 Sutter Street
Malaysian Embassy, Information Section
   Washington, D.C. (8)—2401 Massachusetts Avenue, N.W.—AD 4-7600
Department of Tourism
   Kuala Lumpur, Federation of Malaysia—P.O. Box 328—K.L. 89837

THE PHILIPPINES

Philippine Travel & Information Office
   San Francisco (8)—212 Stockton Street—GA 1-0179
   New York (17)—535 Fifth Avenue

The Board of Travel and Tourist Industry
        and
The Philippine Tourist and Travel Association
   Manila—*Travel Center,* Shurdut Bldg., *Intramuros,* **Manila**

SINGAPORE *(Malaysia)*

Tourist Section, Ministry of Culture
   Singapore (1)—P.O. Box 484
The Singapore Tourist Association
   Singapore—Tourist Information Center (next to *Adelphi Hotel*)

TAIWAN *(Formosa)*

Taiwan Visitors Association
   Taipei—21 Chung Shan North Road, Section 3.
Taiwan Visitors Association
   Burbank, California—3411 Tulare Avenue—VI 9-6336
Chinese News Service
   New York (20)—30 Rockefeller Plaza

THAILAND

Office of Public Relations Attaché, Royal Thai Embassy
   Washington, D.C.—2490 Tracy Place, N.W.—NO 7-8395
Tourist Organization of Thailand
   Bangkok—Mansion 2, Rajdamnern Avenue—24641

PORTUGAL (For **Macao**)

Casa de Portugal
   New York (22)—447 Madison Avenue—PL 5-9806

STEAMSHIPS AND AIRLINES operating to and through the *Pacific* are excellent sources for printed material or miscellaneous information on the Orient. The *American President Lines* produces two fine publications, "Orient Holiday" and "Travel Guide to the Orient and Around the World," covering not only all phases of their services but including excellent geographical and historical vignettes and helpful information for the traveler. The *Japan Air Lines, Air France*, BOAC, *Pan American*, and other airlines serving the far side of the world all have prepared colorful and informative publications that are available to travelers and their agents. Some of these publications are given away; others, such as *Pan American*'s "New Horizons," are for sale. The latter is a compendium of capsule facts on virtually every country sufficiently large to own an airport. The cost of "New Horizons" is $2.00 a copy.

The ASIAN TRAVEL MANUAL, compiled and edited for travel agents by William Neal Connor, is an amazing work. This hefty, well organized 8½ x 11 inch loose leaf publication contains hundreds of pages crammed with practical information on world travel. The cost is $45.00, plus nominal revision charges, and is worth every penny of it. I heartily recommend the *Asian Travel Manual* for travel agents.

VISAS, FOREIGN CONSULATES AND EMBASSIES. In Chapter One I have outlined the situation in regard to visas for the Oriental countries and recommended that you work with your travel agent in securing this documentation. He will handle these time consuming, annoying chores for you either personally or through a visa securing service.

If, however, you are the rugged individualist type who insists on doing everything for himself, you will need the addresses of the consulates who can provide you with the visa forms and requirements. They are as follows:

FAR EAST CONSULATES AND EMBASSIES IN THE UNITED STATES

BRITISH (for Hong Kong)

Atlanta (3)	422 Hurt Bldg.	JA 4-2691
Baltimore (2)	Keyser Bldg.	SA 7-1082
Boston (16)	2610 John Hancock Bldg.	LI 2-2810
Chicago (4)	200 S. Michigan Ave.	WE 9-5166
Cleveland (43)	1828 Illuminating Bldg.	MA 1-7674

Denver (2)	607 Colorado Bldg.	AC 2-2729
Detroit (26)	1865 Guardian Bldg.	WO 2-4776
Honolulu	Alexander Young Bldg.	5-6185
Houston (4)	3103 Fannin St.	JA 6-1441
Kansas City (6)	922 Walnut St.	GR 1-1644
Los Angeles (13)	448 S. Hill St.	MA 6-4411
Miami	723 Ingraham Bldg.	FR 3-0844
Mobile	350 St. Joseph St.	HE 3-8402
New Orleans (12)	403 Int'l. Trade Mart	JA 2-5152
New York (16)	630 Fifth Ave.	CI 6-6300
Norfolk	Nat'l. Bank of Commerce Bldg.	MA 7-1934
Philadelphia (7)	12 S. 12th St.	WA 5-2430
Portland	715 Lewis Bldg.	CA 7-5669
St. Louis (3)	1221 Locust St.	MA 1-4689
St. Paul (1)	1st Nat'l. Bank Bldg.	CA 2-2551
San Francisco (15)	2516 Pacific Ave.	FI 6-3033
Seattle	1805 Exchange Bldg.	MA 4-2990
*Washington, D.C.	3100 Massachusetts Ave.	HO 2-1340

CAMBODIA

| Washington, D.C. | 4500 16th St., N.W. | RA 3-8500 |

JAPAN

Chicago (11)	520 N. Michigan Ave.	MI 2-1959
Honolulu	1742 Nuuanu Ave.	6-2226
Los Angeles (14)	510 W. Sixth St.	MA 3-4168
New Orleans	411 Int'l. Trade Mart	EX 2101
New York (22)	235 East 42nd Street	YU 6-1600
Portland	632 American Bank Bldg.	CA 2-9903
San Francisco (4)	346 California St.	YU 2-0780
Seattle (4)	520 Union Pacific Bldg.	MA 2-8522
*Washington, D.C.	2514 Massachusetts Ave., N.W.	AD 4-2269

---

* Embassies

FEDERATION OF MALAYSIA

*Washington, D.C.   2401 Massachusetts Ave., N.W.

PHILIPPINES

Chicago (6)	201 N. Wells St.	DE 2-6458
Honolulu	2433 Nuuanu Ave.	50-1878
Los Angeles	448 S. Hill St.	MA 6-2369
New Orleans	124 Camp St.	TU 2755
New York (1)	350 Fifth Ave.	LO 5-1420
San Francisco	World Trade Center	YU 2-3271
Seattle	1721 Smith Tower Bldg.	SE 6268
*Washington, D.C.	1617 Massachusetts Ave., N.W.	HO 2-1400

PORTUGAL (for Macao)

Boston	31 Commonwealth Ave.	KE 6-8740
Houston	2202 Nance St.	
Los Angeles	724 S. Spring St.	
New Orleans	808 Queen & Crescent Bldg.	
New York	630 Fifth Ave.	CI 6-4580
Philadelphia	521 Bourse Bldg.	
San Francisco	3298 Washington St.	FI 6-3400
*Washington, D.C.	2125 Kalorama Rd., N.W.	

TAIWAN *(Formosa)*

Chicago	205 W. Wacker Drive	FR 2-1284
Honolulu	1634 Makiki	97-7285
Houston	4808 Austin St.	JA 2-1177
Los Angeles	448 S. Hill St.	MA 9-3369
New York	30 Rockefeller Plaza	CI 6-3403
San Francisco	551 Montgomery St.	DO 2-7680
Seattle	607 Third Ave.	MU 4586
Washington, D.C.	2311 Massachusetts Ave., N.W.	NO 7-9000

* Embassies

THAILAND

Detroit	201 W. Fort St.	
Los Angeles (14)	530 West Sixth St.	VA 9807
Miami	600 Brickell Ave.	
Philadelphia	7836 Montgomery Ave., Elkins Park	ME 5-2018
Richmond, Va. (19)	Mutual Bldg.	
San Francisco (4)	405 Montgomery St.	GA 1-8630
*Washington, D.C.	2490 Tracy Place, N.W.	NO 7-8395

VIET NAM

Washington, D.C.	2251 R St., N.W.	AD 4-3301

UNITED STATES EMBASSIES AND CONSULATES IN THE FAR EAST

We can all be proud of the overwhelming majority of our State Department representatives abroad (*The Ugly American* notwithstanding). Many of my friends, associates, clients, and I have had numerous occasions in the past three decades to call on the staffs of our Embassies and Consulates in far-off lands. In each such instance, an emergency, of one degree or another, was involved. Never have these gracious, intelligent, and well-trained people failed to rise to the occasion. Whether the need has arisen from illness or accident, loss of passport or funds, flood, fire, or other catastrophe, the Embassy and Consular representatives have been towers of strength and thoroughly sympathetic. The following addresses are important ones for you. Our Embassies and Consulates are located:

---

* Embassies

JAPAN

Tokyo—American Embassy, Annex No. 1—2 Aoi-cho, Akasaka, Minato Ku

Yokohama—American Consulate General—6 Yamashita-cho Naka-ku

Nagoya—American Consulate—16 4-chome, Kuwana-machi, Naka-ku

Kobe-Osaka—American Consulate General—10 Kano-cho 6-chome, Ikuta-ku

There are no American consular officials in **Kyoto, Beppu,** or **Hiroshima.**

THAILAND

Bangkok—American Embassy—Krung Thep

CAMBODIA

Phnom Penh—American Embassy—16 Oknha Chan Nak

VIET NAM

Saigon—American Embassy—(no street address necessary)

BRITISH CROWN COLONY

Hong Kong—American Consulate General—(no street address necessary)

REPUBLIC OF THE PHILIPPINES

Manila—American Embassy—(no street address necessary)
Baguio—No American Consular service

FEDERATION OF MALAYSIA

Kuala Lumpur—American Embassy—*Magnet House*, Campbell Road

Penang—American Consulate—1 Church Street Ghaut

Singapore—American Consulate General—(no street address necessary)

BRITISH AND AMERICAN EQUIVALENTS

These words and phrases may be helpful to you in **Hong Kong**:

British	*American*
Biscuits	Crackers or cookies
Bonnet (automobile)	Hood (automobile)
Bowler (hat)	Derby (hat)
Braces	Suspenders
Cheerio	Hello or so long
Cheers	Skol, here's to you, or down the hatch
Chemists	Drug store
Chips	French fries
Crisps	Potato chips
Diversion	Detour
Drapers	Dry goods store
Elementary School	Grammar School
Fly over	Over-pass
Frock	Dress
Geyser	Water heater
Holiday	Vacation
Knock me up	Pick me up (usually early A.M.)
Leg pulling	Kidding
Lift	Elevator
Petrol	Gasoline
Pram	Baby buggy
Private School	Public School
Queue up	To form a line
Return Ticket	Round-trip ticket
Round about	Traffic circle
Screw (variable)	Salary or wage
Single Ticket	One-way ticket
Skimmer or boater	Straw hat
Sweets	Candy
Tram	Street car
Trunk Call	Long Distance Call
Tube or Underground	Subway
Waistcoat	Vest

PRONUNCIATION. JAL, the Japan Air Lines, puts out an excellent booklet entitled "Parlez vous Japanese?" It's interesting and informative. Those of you who travel on this excellent airline will have access to this helpful pamphlet without cost. I will make a few simple observations apropos of this problem which, if either carefully noted or perused in passing, should stand you in good stead.

In Japanese each syllable is pronounced. In almost every instance, particularly with common names, there is no special emphasis given to any syllable. They all go marching forward to individual expression without favor.

One of the two most popular controversial words is the ill-fated town of **Hiroshima.** Some Johnny-come-lately linguists have a tendency to pronounce it H'roash'ima with the heavy accent on the *roash.* Railroad conductors, train porters, travel agents, and men in the street, however, pronounce it He-row-she-ma, with equal care and attention being given to articulating each of the four syllables.

The other controversial word is the one which describes the delightful Japanese specialty, sukiyaki. Almost without exception restaurateurs, hotel men, men and women in the street, and those dining with chopsticks pronounce each syllable, and it comes out sook-ee-ahk-ee, again giving no special care or attention or bestowing any merits on any one syllable. However, one of the most distinguished of the hoteliers of the world, Mr. Inumaru, and his protégé Kawana, manager of the *Miyako Hotel* in **Kyoto,** both pronounce this delectable dish ski-ahk-ee with quite a punch to both the *ski* and the *ahk.* If you just stick with the four syllable pronunciation, sook-ee-ahk-ee, everyone will know what you mean, and you'll get in no trouble.

The other great dining specialty, tempura, is quite simple as well. It is merely tem-poor-a, all syllables receiving equal attention. **Beppu** is merely Bep-poo, pronouncing both syllables as one does in Kobe which is pronounced Coe (like the college in Iowa) bay. **Kyoto** is a simple three syllable word pronounced Key-oh-toe. Strangely enough, the Japanese themselves have a slight tendency to slur on the pronunciation of **Tokyo** which we make into three separate syllables: Toe-key-oh. There is no mistaking their pronunciation, but they have a tendency to make it a two syllable word: Toe-keyo, hitting the "key" just a little hard. I presume this is one of the exceptions which prove the rule of pronouncing every syllable. Osaka is Oh-sah-kah, each syllable individually pronounced. **Miyanoshita** can be cumbersome but not if you pronounce each syllable. It comes out as follows: Mee-ann-oh-sheet-ah . . . simple.

Thailand, of course, is pronounced Tie-land, and the inhabitants are called Thais, pronounced Ties. **Thailand,** incidentally, means "happy land," and I can assure you it is one of the happiest lands I've ever seen. Curiously enough, the language barrier is less severe in **Thailand** than it is in **Japan.** Apparently, English is more readily picked up by the Thais, and many of the waiters, bus boys, maids, and taxi drivers understand a considerable amount of our jargon and don't do too badly with their own pronunciation. In **Japan,** however, outside of the big hotels, there is a very definite linguistic barrier. It is a very wise idea when you leave your hotel to be sure that you have a card on which is written in Japanese the name of the hotel. By all means have the door man write the name of the shop to which you are proceeding or the place of entertainment or wherever. Japanese taxi drivers just don't parlez Anglais . . . not a word.

In **The Philippines,** of course, English is spoken and is the basic tongue. In **Singapore,** there is no linguistic problem. In **Cambodia** you will probably not stay long enough to run into a linguistic barrier, and in **Viet Nam** most of the Vietnamese speak French and a number speak English. The torrid little charmer of **Siem Reap** is easily handled pronunciation-wise. It is merely See-em-reap, just as you would tell somebody to go out to the fields to watch the reapers in action. **Saigon** is an old favorite that I'm sure everyone is familiar with; namely, Sighgon. Johore is quite easy with a hard "j" pronounced Joe-hoar with no emphasis on either syllable. Hit them both.

BEAUTY PARLORS AND BARBER SHOPS are covered in Chapter 1.

MASSEUR AND MASSEUSE. Many travelers find periodic massage beneficial. If you have never enjoyed the relaxing luxury of an expertly applied massage, you may wish to do so while traveling in the Orient. Apart from the "treatments" in **Japan's** Turkish and hot spring baths in the resort areas, which are quite different, massage is available in the beauty salons for women or in one's hotel room in almost every city that you will visit. Appointments for a massage may be made (for men or women) merely by speaking with someone at the hotel's information or front desk. All the good hotels maintain direct contact with individuals skilled in the most scientific massage methods.

A GUIDEBOOK'S FORMAT. Writing a guidebook has many of the same pitfalls as managing an office building, a professional baseball team, or coaching a prominent big time football team. In this field, one's work is subject to the critical perusal of large numbers of readers whose opinions do not necessarily coincide with the author's and whose knowledge and experience are all too frequently scant. I have found from long, if not bitter, experience that it is not always possible to please everyone—although I now have some gimmicks on that subject, too. The most controversial element of a good guidebook is its make-up. Some of my readers, including my sophisticated friends, the itchy-footed Everett and Ralph Michaels, insist that everything pertaining to one city or country should be in one section of the book. It is their opinion that, when speaking of **Tokyo,** I should include not only the geographical and historical vignettes but also the restaurants, hotels, shopping, local customs, etc.

There are others, more numerous if not as erudite, who feel that my preparing separate chapters on restaurants, hotels, shopping, helpful hints, et cetera, makes the reader's job easier. Obviously I belong to this latter school of thought.

TIPPING. Whatever format is followed, there are certain important subjects on which it is worthwhile to be redundant. Tipping is one of these areas. In several other sections of this Olson brainchild, I have mentioned how I, and the locals, feel about tipping. Here is a brief review:

Japan is the last world bastion holding out against the universal tipping custom, and she, I believe, is fighting a losing battle. To date, almost without exception, Japanese hoteliers and restaurateurs, who include 10% for gratuities in the bill, are fiercely opposed to guests passing out gratuities to their employees. In many of the good hotels and restaurants, a tip, even if graciously proffered, will be refused. And in the 1960's at that! Unbelievable.

I have always been anxious to express my appreciation to maids, room service employees, restaurant waiters and waitresses, bellboys, porters, and others in Japanese hotels as well as elsewhere. Without exception, my offered gratuities have been pleasantly and politely, but firmly, refused. I have stopped trying. Taxi drivers in **Japan** are, for the most part, not yet up to the idea of tipping. They neither expect a tip nor will they always accept one if extended. Beauticians and barbers, on the other hand, have caught on. They like the custom and will not pass up a tip—large or small. Old **Tokyo** residents, however, sense that the tide is turning, but it will be a while yet before *all* taxi drivers, bus boys, and headwaiters will have succumbed to the outstretched palm.

In other countries, tipping is a normally accepted practice. Bear in mind, please, that in ALL of the countries, **Japan** included, a service gratuity (usually 10% or more) has been placed on your restaurant, bar, and hotel bill. The foregoing is almost always true. You can check the bills to be sure.

Except in **Japan,** the desk clerk may be tipped, as well as maids, bellboys, door men, waiters and headwaiters.

Americans, except for that minute group of one-tenth of one per cent of our unbelievably mean fellow countrymen whose ancestors must have been smuggled across the *Atlantic* under the barnacles of the *Mayflower,* always overtip.

In the Orient, it is much easier than it is elsewhere to tip too much because the wage scale is so much lower than any place else in which we are used to traveling.

Forty U.S. dollars a month is a large salary for a working-man in the Orient. Workers in **Hong Kong** who earn a dollar a day are "hot shots." Should you give a dinner party and leave a $5.00 tip, it would be the equivalent of adding four days' pay to the waiter's salary for serving just one meal to one table.

I have ever been welcomed back every place I have ever been because I have treated everyone with whom I have done business, and who has served me, generously and with consideration. Overtipping with me is almost a specialized extracurricular activity. Therefore, in this department, "Do as I say, fool, not as I do!"

DRIVE TO THE LEFT is the order of the day in **Japan, Hong Kong, Thailand, Singapore** and **Malaysia.** In **Hawaii,** the **Philippines, Viet Nam,** and **Cambodia,** the traffic flows to the right.

FILMS. One need not carry film from home for the entire journey around the Orient, since all types and categories may be purchased in quantity in **Hawaii** at Mainland prices and in **Hong Kong** and **Singapore** at prices considerably lower than at home. For films in **Hong Kong,** I can particularly recommend the *Filmo Depot Ltd.,* Marina House, headed by my friend, Mr. H. Corra. Here one not only may buy films, cameras, and supplies, but the *Filmo Depot* has the largest library of exposed film for sale of any company in the world. Should you wish an 8 or 16 mm. Kodachrome record of your journey through the Orient, Mr. Corra and his staff can offer you most reasonably a film sequence of your entire trip. Fascinating film on other sections of the world is also available. In **Hawaii** fine color reproductions of the islands are for sale at reputable camera and Kodak supply stores. The store in the *Royal Hawaiian Hotel* has a particularly well-stocked film library.

KODACHROME FILM is virtually impossible to secure in **Japan.** Ektachrome is available in great quantities, but Kodachrome film in **Japan** is as hard to find as a speakeasy in Evanston, Illinois. Strange though it may seem, however, Kodachrome film can now (since 1963) be processed in **Japan.**

AIR MAILING FILMS HOME for processing may be handled efficiently and reasonably. Films carry the relatively inexpensive rate of airmail printed matter.

PACKING SERVICE. Packing is an art in the Orient. I have never received packages from any other place that were so deftly put together as those sent from **Singapore, Thailand, Hong Kong,** and **Japan.** The Orientals do a simply marvelous wrapping job. My one real complaint about Europe is that the one thing you can be sure of is that, during the course of any season, packages will arrive in the States in bad condition. It is possible, of course, that this *can* happen from the Orient, but from the Far East it is the exception rather than the rule. Each of the good shopkeepers can be counted on implicitly to pack his merchandise well for shipping.

There are special packing services that are available, the best of which is in the Arcade of the original wing of **Tokyo's** *Imperial Hotel* opposite the *Imperial's* Branch Post Office. The *World Travel Service* in **Bangkok** offers an excellent packaging and shipping service. Here one may have almost anything at all efficiently packaged. Wherever possible, avoid shipping by freight. Freight packages or crates invariably necessitate a freight broker at the point of entry whose fees must be adequate to cover the time and services rendered but which charges frequently get completely out of proportion to the value of the merchandise. I have seen freight forwarding house bills of $48.00 to $50.00 on a $35.00 shipment, which just doesn't make sense. Freight brokers may be called upon and their services charged to you without your knowledge.

"HEALTH HINTS FOR THE TROPICS" is an excellent copyrighted booklet published by the *American Society of Tropical Medicine and Hygiene.* Its fourth edition appeared in 1960. The following pertinent excerpts from this fine publication will, I am confident, be of interest:

"It is well for travelers to the tropics to be neither too romantic nor too cynical about their destination. . . . Let it be emphasized right at the start that life can be safe, comfortable, and pleasant under most tropical conditions. There is no need for undue apprehension or concern because the conditions encountered may be new or unknown to the traveler. Tropical diseases in general are well understood, are preventable, are for the most part susceptible to cure by modern methods, and are not the mysterious maladies or unknown fevers so often referred to in popular fiction.

"In the tropics, as elsewhere, if proper attention is given to personal hygiene and certain elementary safeguards, there is remarkably little reason why health should be jeopardized. To get along well in the tropics, it is necessary to be alert and intelligent enough to follow the simple rules of hygiene, to cultivate certain health habits, to take a few extra sanitary precautions, having to do chiefly with the preparation of food, purification of water, and protection from the bites of insects. . . . The prospective traveler should acquire reliable and specific knowledge of the tropical area to be visited and take the time to make careful plans.

"Travelers with a history of motion sickness are advised to take Marezine (cyclizine hydrochloride) 50 mg. one half hour before departure. Children 6-10: 25 mg. Children under 6: 12½ mg. This dose may be repeated before meals as required. Bonamine (meclizine), Dramamine (dimenhydrinate), or Phenergan (promethazine) may also be used in appropriate doses."

SEA OR AIR SICKNESS can now really be relegated to the dim and distant past. There is no reason why anyone, however squeamish, need suffer the slightest discomfort either while in the air or on the water. The original seasick preventatives were originated for the amphibious forces, and were quite effective, but the progress made in this field since the war is astounding. While your own doctor can best advise you on this subject, pursuant to the paragraph above, I have known a number of travelers who have reported excellent results with both Marezine and Bonamine.

DOCTORS and good hospitals are generously available throughout the Orient. For routine medical requirements, consult your hotel information desk, tour conductor, or travel representative. For serious accident or physical disorder, particularly one requiring surgery, be sure to check with the American Embassy or Consular Service, which can give you excellent advice and be solicitously helpful.

LAUNDRY AND DRY CLEANING SERVICES are superb in all good hotels in the Orient. See Chapter 1.

NEWSPAPERS in the English language may be purchased in all of the large cities covered in this guidebook. The principal English language newspapers in Japan are the *Japan Times,* the *Asahi Evening News,* the *English Mainichi,* and the *Yomiuri News.* Movies, plays, and operas; local fetes, fairs, and festivals; and other events likely to be of special interest to American visitors will be found in these papers.

TRANSISTOR RADIOS are good fun. If you don't bring one along, don't fret; they may be had cheaply throughout the Orient, especially in **Japan, Hong Kong,** and **Singapore.** Two observations in this department are apropos: (1) DO NOT USE YOUR TRANSISTOR RADIO EN ROUTE IN AN AIRCRAFT. It has now been established that use of electronic devices in aircraft in flight has a detrimental effect on the plane's instruments. (2) Many of the hotels in which you will stay are equipped with radio and/or television sets, although I still like to have a transistor radio with me.

ELECTRIC IRONS are really superfluous travel baggage these days. What with nylon, orlon, and dacron to provide wrinkle proof garments and all hotels providing such rapid and inexpensive pressing services, it is scarcely worthwhile to lug even a streamlined travel iron around such great distances. Should you elect to carry an iron, however, be sure that it is a genuine travel iron, able to handle variable voltage, amperage, and cycles. In the Orient there is a variation from 110 to 220 volts, and the amperage and kilocycle variation is even greater. Adaptor plugs are required in various foreign countries in order to plug the implement into the different electrical outlets.

INTERNATIONAL CREDIT CARDS. A number of restaurants, hotels, and shops in the Orient recognize one or more of the international credit cards. Whether or not you wish to use one of these "on the cuff Open Sesames" depends on your own personality and character. I have always been of the "pay now, travel later" school of thought. It irks me no end to have bills popping up two to five months after I have enjoyed an experience. This always puts a flaw in an otherwise perfect memory. I can tell you without fear of contradiction that the bills, when they ultimately arrive, will always be much larger than you remembered them. This is true even when the bills are submitted accurately and the foreign exchange figured correctly.

From my own experience I have found that while bills from the credit card institutions are normally correct they can always bear a certain amount of close perusal.

These companies process mountains of accounts in dollars, francs, yen, lire, Malayan Straits and Hong Kong dollars, pesetas, pesos, marks, kroner, pounds, and bahts, to name a few. Even dealing with U.S. dollars, errors can creep in, but with the foreign element entering into the picture, there are not only the hazards of the normal overburdened routine involved but also the complexities of varying foreign exchanges and in many instances unfamiliar types of Oriental and other alien billing. If you carry traveler's checks and your own checkbook, I think that you will get by quite nicely without the credit cards.

MILITARY GRAVES IN THE PACIFIC. The *American Battle Monuments Commission,* Washington 25, D.C., has a list of graves in the *Pacific* area. Should your trip include such a sad mission, you may write to this Commission for information on the exact locations of cemeteries and specific graves. There are large United States military cemeteries in **Honolulu** and at *Fort McKinley* in **Manila.**

JAPANESE LIKE TO BE CALLED JUST THAT. They are not at all happy with the terms "Nipponese," "Japs," or "Nips."

CAUCASIAN and ASIAN normally are thought to be more descriptive and certainly more polite words than white versus yellow.

HOUSES OF WORSHIP. Protestant and Catholic churches and Jewish synagogues are numerous throughout the Orient. With the exception of **Siem Reap,** which is too small to be so endowed, each community covered in this guidebook will have a church of your choice in which to worship. I have refrained from listing these churches because they are so plentiful. Your tour conductor, travel agent, or hotel information desk will be glad to give you detailed instructions as to how to reach your house of worship.

The ABACUS is an amazing arithmetical calculator which originated eons ago in China. Its complicated use is largely limited to the Chinese. One sees a lot of the abacus in **Hong Kong, Taiwan,** and to a lesser degree in the Chinese sections of the other Oriental cities. Based on the logarithmic principle, the abacus is a small oblong frame supporting a series of thin metal fingers each of which is a sliding surface for a handful of oval wooden counters which are flicked up and down by rapidly calculating Chinese. The clatter of the counters is as characteristic of Chinese sections as the cacophony of the mah-jongg players. Mutuel clerks at the race track, tellers in the banks, cashiers in stores and restaurants, and vendors in the street all solve their daily mathematical problems with the abacus.

The SOROBAN, the Japanese version of the abacus, enables the skilled user to compute faster than an adding machine or an electric comptometer. It is curious that the Chinese and Japanese, who are both very clever in mathematics, should, from habit, use the abacus and the soroban for even the simplest "2 plus 2" problems as well as to solve the most complex of multi-plication figures.

SINGAPORE IS NO LONGER A BRITISH CROWN COLONY. **Hong Kong** is. Mail to the latter should be addressed "**Hong Kong,** British Crown Colony." Parenthetically, after **Hong Kong,** one can mention either "**Kowloon**" or "**Victoria**" as the case might be. It expedites matters.

Singapore mail can be addressed simply to "**Singapore.**" Since **Singapore** has now joined the **Federation of Malaysia,** it would not be amiss to address mail to "**Singapore, Malaysia**" or "**Singapore, Federation of Malaysia.**" The mail won't be lost in any event.

HAWAII, being a state, carries the same mail rate as does every other state in the Union. This is true of airmail, first class, and special delivery.

HOME VISIT PROGRAM. In Denmark, the "Meet the Danes" program has become both famous and popular. This well conceived idea is taking root in the Orient, particularly in **Japan.** The best organized is the *"Kyoto Home Visit Program"* through which it is possible to visit in a private home to participate in a tea ceremony and enjoy an absorbing two hours or so with a fascinating family in their native habitat. The *Bureau of Tourist Industry* in **Kyoto,** phone 3-1936, or the *Kyoto Trade and Tourist Association,* **Tokyo,** phone 231-3750, can make the necessary arrangements. Your travel agent or the hotel information desk will be happy to assist you should you desire to participate. If you accept such an invitation, you must stay at least 2 hours and observe the amenities of international courtesy which, in **Japan,** calls for the guest to bring gifts. If you do not bear such gifts, you will be welcome but not considered a very thoughtful visitor. Boxes of candy, wine, or even hard liquor are quite acceptable as home visit gifts.

GIGOLOS, professional dancing partners for women, do not exist in the Orient. In the Far East, one finds multiple thousands of cute, curvacious, avidly eager hostesses to assist the male brute to enjoy himself, but a similar service is not rendered to our own delectably pampered fair sex.

MORAL VALUES. One cannot generalize on the morals of an entire country. I have found that it is difficult to pinpoint moral patterns within one city of the United States, let alone within a whole country. Sections of **Chicago,** for example, are the epitome of propriety, while other parts of the city and immediate suburbs are licentious, embracing immoral dives, slot machines, bookie joints, and more.

It is obvious, therefore, when I am asked about the moral tone of the Orient that there is no such thing as a general answer. One thing for certain is that prostitution is now illegal in **Japan.** But isn't it most everywhere? Before being banned, the better hotels in **Japan** had a naive way of handling the prostitution situation: A gentleman could bring a lady to his room any time during the day or evening that he chose. If the lady was in the room after midnight, however, she could not leave alone until morning. Accompanied, yes. Unaccompanied, no. The situation now? What's the situation in America? It depends!

There is little, if any, question but that the Oriental mind looks upon the male-female relationship rather differently than does the westerner.

It seems to me that in the Orient there are many more gals on the loose than there are in either Europe or America. This is not a statistical fact, merely an educated guess.

But I know that I need not remind anyone thoughtful enough to read this book that good manners, a reflection of good breeding, are as universally respected in the Orient as they are elsewhere in the world. The women of **Japan, Taiwan, Hong Kong, Singapore,** or other Far Eastern countries are as worthy of your respect and courtesy as are women elsewhere in the world. We Americans have a fantastic habit of generalizing and have embarrassed each other on numerous occasions by assuming that all girls in various corners of the world are "on the make" and that they all are to be had for the asking, with or without a price. To the best of my knowledge, such a situation exists no place.

INTERNATIONAL TIME ZONES. If, after having crossed the International Date Line a half dozen or more times, you still don't know what has taken place, don't worry. Neither does anybody else. A curious state of confusion exists not only with neophyte travelers but with professional travel people including at least one ship captain that I know. Time and again, I have asked business friends in **Honolulu,** "What day and time is it in **Tokyo** now?" and have been met with only blank looks. I have asked travel agents, tour operators, correspondents, and business people in **Tokyo, Singapore,** and **Bangkok,** "What day and what time is it in **Chicago** now?" Most of them don't even know what day it is, let alone the hour.

To illustrate the complexity of the situation, here is how I personally ascertain the day and time in **Chicago** when I am in **Tokyo:** I first look at the time in **Tokyo,** let us say it is eight o'clock in the morning. I then add half a day (twelve hours), making it eight P.M., and subtract three hours, making it five P.M., and then subtract twenty-four hours, making it five o'clock the night before, which is correct. You need not drop me a note and point out how primerish this is and that the process could be cut short. I know that it can. I also know that every time I use a short cut I err. So does most everybody else. The foregoing works.

I have compiled an accurate table which will save you from fussing with my "arithmeticler." A word or two of explanation about what happens on crossing the International Date Line might be of some interest and conceivably of some help. The popular misconception is that, on crossing the International Date Line, one loses or gains 24 hours, depending on the direction of the voyage. Nothing could be farther from the truth. The world's relative time is computed from precise basic time at **Greenwich, England,** just down the *River Thames* from **London.** Assuming that all of the following places are on standard (as opposed to daylight) time, we will find that **New York** is five hours behind Greenwich Time; **Chicago,** six hours; **Denver,** seven hours; **San Francisco,** eight hours; and **Honolulu,** ten hours in arrears of Greenwich Time. By the time the International Date Line is reached, roughly half a day has already been "lost."

If this subject interests you, take the time to study the table below. If you do, you will find that it is not always true that "when it's today in **Chicago,** it's tomorrow in **Tokyo.**" When it's one minute after midnight Sunday morning in **Chicago,** it is also Sunday in **Tokyo,** being one minute after three p.m. there. Obviously there are nine hours each day during which **Chicago** and **Tokyo** share the same day and date.

The following table is subject to slight variations during the period of daylight saving time but will never be more than an hour off:

WHAT TIME IS IT?

When it's 6:00 p.m. Monday in **Chicago,** it is:

Monday	*Tuesday*	
7:00 p.m.		in New York
Midnight		in London
5:00 p.m.		in Denver
4:00 p.m.		in San Francisco
2:00 p.m.		in Honolulu
	9:00 a.m.	in Tokyo
	8:00 a.m.	in Hong Kong
	8:00 a.m.	in Macao
	8:00 a.m.	in Manila
	8:00 a.m.	in Taiwan
	7:30 a.m.	in Singapore
	7:30 a.m.	in Malaya
	7:30 a.m.	in Indonesia
	7:00 a.m.	in Thailand
	7:00 a.m.	in Viet Nam
	7:00 a.m.	in Cambodia

WHAT TIME IS IT?

When it's 12:00 noon Monday in **Tokyo,** it is:

Monday	*Sunday*	
10:00 A.M.		in Cambodia
10:00 A.M.		in Thailand
10:00 A.M.		in Viet Nam
10:30 A.M.		in Malaya
10:30 A.M.		in Singapore
10:30 A.M.		in Indonesia
11:00 A.M.		in Manila
11:00 A.M.		in Hong Kong
11:00 A.M.		in Macao
11:00 A.M.		in Taiwan
	5:00 P.M.	in Honolulu
	7:00 P.M.	in San Francisco
	8:00 P.M.	in Denver
	9:00 P.M.	in Chicago
	10:00 P.M.	in New York
3:00 A.M.		in London

"PORTABLE CLOTHESLINE." Many department, specialty, and variety stores carry elastic clotheslines with adaptable

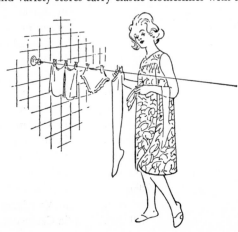

snapper end clamps. This gadget is a blessing and may be strung either in the bathroom or bedroom to accommodate your drip-dries or other laundry. A word of caution: The funniest mishap that I have heard of in the past several years happened recently to one of our young tour members in Brussels. She had delayed doing her laundry for a week or more and after lunch one fine day undertook to launder her slips, bras, panties, hose, and what-have-you. The amount of clothes to be hung up was too great to be accommodated in the bathroom; hence she strung the elastic line from the top of the window, which was open, to the buffer knob on top of the door. Having completed the chore of hanging all her unmentionables on the line stretched across the room, she lay down to enjoy a well earned nap. Her room-mate, not knowing the state of the laundry-filled bedroom, elected to return and, on opening the door, the elastic clothes-line became a colossal slingshot hurling all the clothes out the window. She shrieked. The girls stood helplessly by as this collection of personal female attire fluttered down to the *Boulevard Albert Max*. Don't let this happen to you.

SOAP is provided by the hotels in the Orient. If you have a favorite brand, you'd better either carry a few bars along or start seeking out the local pharmacies and beauty parlors on arrival in the Orient. The distribution of French and American soap is quite good in the Orient. Very likely you can find just the brand your heart desires, particularly in the larger cities.

TOILET—JAPANESE STYLE. It is delicate to discuss and difficult to describe the Japanese-style toilet. This device is entirely foreign to anything within our civilized experience. In our prim, sheltered western society, it is considered bad taste to discuss such earthy subjects publicly. I shall do so delicately. The object in question is a sausage-slender ceramic device, a mere slit, virtually flush with the floor, the use of which would take years of acrobatic practice to master.

You need not be required to use the Japanese variety. In railroad trains, you will find a door marked "Toilet—Japanese Style" at one end of the car, while at the other end is a facility labeled "Toilet—Western Style." No problem. You will be in an awkward position, however, should you choose an old-style Japanese inn, where only the floor-level variety is available. Most inns, however, now have at least one or two western style rooms with corresponding facilities.

The BIDET, a kidney-shaped enamel lavatory piece, is not as generally found in the Orient as it is in Europe, but it is not unknown in Asia. The bidet is not a baby bath, nor was it designed as a place to wash hose or filmy undies. The bidet was primarily designed to aid and abet feminine hygiene although its use now has been enlarged to include other functions such as being used as a launderette by visiting Americans.

TOILET PAPER. The European variety of toilet tissue is a riot. I have often said that European toilet paper is like wax paper on one side and sandpaper on the other and does not perform the function of either. In the Orient it is different. You may not find your own favorite brand of soft downy tissue, but the texture is sufficiently firm and soft to eliminate the necessity of your wishing to carry rolls of this cumbersome commodity with you.

WATER. What would we do without it? Because of its important role in our daily dietary habits, great care should be exercised in ascertaining whether or not water is potable. One encounters no problem whatsoever traveling through the Orient insofar as water is concerned if the traveler only uses a fraction of a modicum of good sense. It is a sane and sensible precaution to inquire at each new place of entry as to whether or not the tap water is good to drink. If not, the management of the hotel—if it is good enough to be in this book—will provide bottled water for the room and will have bottled still and mineral water as well as soft drinks in the bar and restaurant. In **Japan, Singapore, Malaya,** and in the better places in **South Viet Nam,** the water, generally speaking, is quite reliable. Elsewhere (except **Hawaii,** of course, where the water supply is pure) you will wish to take the precaution of ordering bottled water.

FRUIT provides one of the eating joys of traveling in the Orient. Almost all the fruits known to us are available and there are many local varieties that are sure to please our taste buds. The fruit is quite safe in all reputable places. Normal precautions should be taken. If it's peelable, peel it. If not, wash it.

COFFEE. This brew should give you no trouble. It seems paradoxical that as remote as the Orient is they should have extremely palatable coffee. In **Hawaii,** not only do they have all of the brands with which we are familiar on the mainland but also the unusually tasty *Kona* coffee. In **Japan,** the **Philippines, Singapore, Thailand, Cambodia, Viet Nam, Hong Kong,** and **Macao,** the coffee is of the American type. Occasionally, as in **Viet Nam,** this happy situation is curious, since this country was originally a part of Indochina, which was ruled by the French. Despite the fact that I am a grade one Francophile, the only thing I cannot tolerate in **France** is the coffee. There I take tea for breakfast, and for luncheon and dinner I choose either a concentrated coffee from home or French coffee diluted with three parts of hot water to one of the local version of coffee. In **Viet Nam,** however, the coffee is "stateside style."

CIGARS AND CIGARETTES. In **Japan,** American cigars and cigarettes are now generally available at leading hotels and department stores. Cigars are still not overly plentiful but cigarettes (plain, filter, or menthol) are on sale, even though not all brands are always to be had. In the other countries, "smokes" are relatively plentiful and not too expensive.

SHOES. Be prepared to take them off. Throughout the Orient and particularly in **Japan,** there are many places where it is either polite or obligatory to remove one's foot covering. In all Japanese homes, inns, and restaurants (operated Japanese style), one is expected to remove his shoes at the entrance where light slippers are available. (Men will appreciate a pair of easy-to-remove loafers to be worn when traveling throughout the Orient.) It is definitely expected that as one enters a Japanese bedroom the slippers will be left at the entrance. There are various shrines and temples in each of the countries in which one's shoes must be left at the entrance. The local guides will give adequate notice of any public buildings in which one's shoes should not be worn.

ROBES FOR GUESTS. In Japanese inns and in hotels that are operated partially as a Japanese inn (such as the *Suginoi* in **Beppu**), one will find all-purpose Japanese robes in the room. One may wear these to the thermal baths, to dinner, on the streets, or lounging, as one's fancy dictates. On the first effort, one will no doubt seek the help of the maid in donning the paraphernalia as the Japanese kimono is a complex outfit consisting of two bulky garments and sash which must be handled properly if one doesn't wish to appear as though emerging from a night in a haystack.

EYEGLASSES. If you wear glasses, be sure to bring your lens prescription with you. Such prescriptions can be filled readily almost everywhere that you go. In **Japan**, for example, your prescription can be filled in a matter of two hours or so. Rapid and efficient service is available elsewhere.

INSURANCE. Assure yourself of peace of mind while traveling by carrying adequate baggage, health, and accident insurance. Your travel agent will be pleased to issue your insurance policies. When insuring luggage and personal effects, be sure that you take out adequate coverage. Unless one stops to think about it, or is familiar with such insurance, it is easy to err. For example, if you carry $300.00 worth of insurance and lose a $250.00 item, you will not have any chance of recovering $250.00. If your luggage and personal effects with which you are traveling can be evaluated at $1,200.00 and you are covered with a $300.00 insurance policy, you are only one-fourth covered. Therefore, in losing something valued at $250.00, you may, at a maximum, recover only $62.50. Carry plenty of insurance. Everyone's traveling effects are much more valuable than he realizes. While the loss of luggage is extremely rare, it is always possible to lose individual items. Insurance provides a desired peace of mind factor and I repeat: "Get plenty of insurance" . . . and don't forget health and accident insurance as well. Many all-coverage home insurance policies now cover personal effects while traveling. Be sure to check to see if yours does.

RESTRICTED ITEMS. In traveling from country to country, the customs officials are usually on the lookout for tobacco and alcoholic beverages and do not object to your carrying with you the purchases you have made while traveling provided you intend to bring these items home.

Into **Japan** one may bring, for example, 300 cigarettes, 50 cigars, some pipe tobacco, and six bottles of alcoholic beverage. Almost all of the other countries permit visitors to bring in at least one quart of alcoholic beverage and from 100 to 300 cigarettes, 50 cigars and some pipe tobacco. The **South Viet Nam** regulations are the most strict, although I have never noted any effort to police the regulations there. For whatever it may be worth, the **South Viet Nam** customs laws permit the visitor to carry into the country only one, opened, bottle of alcoholic beverage and one opened pack of cigarettes.

U.S. CUSTOMS. The duty-free exemption on articles acquired abroad for returning United States citizens and residents
is $100.00 per person. Such duty-free purchases must be suit-
able for household or personal use, or as souvenirs or curios if
intended for personal use, or as gifts to others.

One must not deduct the $100.00 allowance from the declara-
tion being made. This will be done by the customs officials. In
addition to the $100.00 per person duty-free custom allowance,
one may mail any number of gift packages from abroad provided that the value of each such package is less than $10.00.
These gift packages may be sent from any country and must
be marked "Unsolicited Gift—Value Less than $10.00" and
provided that not more than one such duty-free package is
received by any one person per day. Gifts that have been mailed
in the less than $10.00 category should not be declared upon
one's return. These items do not count against the penurious
$100.00 allowance.

DECLARATION FORM (U.S. CUSTOMS). On your re-
turn to the States, the purser of your westbound ship or plane
will hand you the necessary United States Customs form.
Returning by ship you will go through customs at your point
of debarkation on the mainland: **San Francisco, Long Beach,**
or **Los Angeles.** Returning by air, if you are aboard a plane with
a regularly scheduled stop at **Honolulu,** you will probably pass
through customs in our island paradise. Since January 1, 1964,
oral declarations have been sufficient for purchases abroad totaling $100 or less. The returning passenger has merely to fill out
a simple 8¼ x 4¼-inch card giving his name, ship or flight
number, address, and the date. Articles acquired abroad in excess of the one-hundred-dollar duty-free exemption must be item-
ized. It is a wise precaution to secure receipted bills for all of
your purchases. Keep them as a record. I personally have found
that customs officials for the most part are not at all interested
in these receipts and are quite content to allow you to list your
purchases at the fair wholesale price rather than the retail
price which you paid. It is well, notwithstanding, to have the

receipts in case they are called for. If there is any controversy as to the reasonable value of an article acquired abroad, either by outright purchase or as a gift, the customs offices each have an appraiser on hand to fix a fair price on any item in question. It seems to me that the customs service thinks that all Americans are suckers and pay too much for what they buy because, on scanning their appraisal list, every item I have noted has been evaluated far below the normal retail price charged abroad.

TRAVELER'S CHECKS cost but little and are highly recommended for carrying your funds while traveling. The amount of spending money that you wish to take along will depend a great deal on what advance arrangements you have made for your travels. If you are, as I hope, on a prepaid plan which takes care of all necessary traveling expenses, including hotel bills, meals, transportation, transfers, and sightseeing, you will be required to carry funds only for shopping and miscellaneous spending money. If, on the other hand, you are to pay hotels, meals, sightseeing, transfers, local transportation, tips, taxes, and other expenses, the amount of ready cash you will need can be prodigious. In the event that you are carrying reasonably large sums, you should buy $50 and $100 checks (the latter is the largest available) for the most part. Whatever the amount, however, be sure to have some $10 traveler's checks (the lowest denominations) and a supply of one-dollar bills. The smaller denomination checks are helpful should you have some last-minute small souvenir shopping, post cards, or a small bill at the concierge desk to settle. The dollar bills are particularly helpful for last-minute tipping or stamp purchase after the coin of the realm has been exhausted. Dollars can be used almost any place you travel. They can be helpful when traveling between countries when you might not have the currency of the country to which you are proceeding. At this time, a few dollar bills will take care of mineral water, wine, a meal on the train, and the station porter's tip.

FOREIGN EXCHANGE. This widely discussed, sometimes

complex, subject need not baffle you at all. It isn't necessary to memorize or even understand every last facet of foreign exchange. Carry this book with you and refer to the following pages whenever a problem arises. People the world over are generally honest. Some must be watched very carefully, but as a reliable rule of thumb deal only with high-class reputable people and don't worry. Becoming familiar with foreign currencies and customs is all part of the fun of traveling. You will be delighted handling all sorts of queer-sounding, odd-looking foreign money. You will, of course, wish to have at least a superficial acquaintance with the coins, bills, and values of the exchange media with which you will be confronted.

Cash your dollars or traveler's checks at reliable places such as the cash desk of your good hotel, a recognized bank, or official exchange bureau.

The BLACK MARKET is a negligible factor in the Orient. Outside the country, Japanese yen may be purchased at a five to ten per cent better rate than within the country, where the legal rate is 360 yen to the dollar. In the States one may get as many as 388 yen to the dollar. **Hong Kong** dollars vary slightly from day to day from the normally accepted standard of $5.70 H.K. to the U.S. dollar. One may sometimes get as many as $6 H.K. to the U.S. dollar, but this is through legal, accepted channels, with no black market being involved.

In **Viet Nam,** the legal commercial exchange rate is 35 piastres to the U.S. dollar, but there is a special tourist rate which is just twice as generous—allowing 70 piastres to the U.S. dollar, which special tourist rate varies slightly from time to time, but it is both legal and official.

In **Cambodia,** on the other hand, the black market rate is really the only effective one. Officially there are 35 riels to the dollar, while unofficially one may secure 75 riels to the dollar in one of the "free ports" such as **Singapore** or **Hong Kong,** or even in **Saigon. Cambodia** exercises a fairly rigid currency control, and, if you are paying your own expenses as you go along, a certain amount of legal exchange must be secured at the *Grand Hotel,* the only place in **Siem Reap,** for example, that dollars or traveler's checks may be converted to riels. Unless yours is an abnormal case, you will probably be staying in **Siem Reap** only for a day or less and the amount of riels required will be negligible since there is little shopping.

If you would feel happier about it, you may purchase a small amount of currency of each of the countries to be visited in advance. This procedure provides the advantage of permitting you to familiarize yourself with the pieces of money, but it is, I must say, a bit of a nuisance to keep and carry these coins or little bills around the Orient in anticipation of spending them later. All of the airports offer official exchange banks readily at hand to convert your traveler's checks, dollars, or other currencies to the local currencies. Should you wish to wait to convert your money until you get to your hotel, you can always use a dollar bill or two for tips or other needs at the airport or station.

Money markets throughout the world are volatile. The revaluation of our own United States currency which, while not anticipated, could always take place or the revaluation of any of the currencies of the countries treated in this book could render one or more of the following tables inaccurate. When prepared, the tables listed herein were in apple-pie order and reliable. Before departure, have a word with your travel agent, however, to inquire if there have been any basis revaluations recently in the foreign exchange picture.

CAMBODIA

The official rate of Cambodian riels to the dollar is thirty-five to one. There is, however, such an "open" black market of seventy-five to one that I have used both these rates in the table below. One hundred sen equal one riel. Only four hundred riels may be taken into Cambodia (this rule is strictly adhered to).

Cambodian to			U.S. to Cambodian		Cambodian
	U.S. (35)	U.S. (75)		bodian (35)	bodian (75)
Sen	**Cents**	**Cents**	**Cents**	**Sen**	**Sen**
10	.2857¢	.133¢	1¢	35	75
25	.71425¢	.3325¢		**Riels**	**Riels**
50	1.4285¢	.665¢	5¢	1.75	3.75
Riels			10¢	3.5	7.5
1	2.857¢	1.33¢	25¢	8.75	18.75
5	14.285¢	6.65¢	50¢	17.5	37.5
10	28.57¢	13.30¢			
25	71.425¢	33.25¢	**Dollars**		
	Dollars		$1.00	35	75
50	$1.4285	66.5¢	$5.00	175	375
		Dollars	$10.00	350	750
100	$2.857	$1.33	$20.00	700	1,500
500	$14.285	$6.65	$50.00	1,750	3,750
1,000	$28.57	$13.30	$100.00	3,500	7,500
5,000	$142.85	$66.50	$1,000.00	35,000	75,000

HONG KONG

Although the official rate is 5.70 Hong Kong dollars to the
United States dollar, currency control exists in name only in
the Crown Colony and the open market rate fluctuates between
HK$5.70 and HK$6.00 to US$1.00. For an easy approxima-
tion of prices on your shopping sprees here, you can figure
about six Hong Kong dollars to each United States dollar.
(There are times when, on the free market, the rate is something less than HK$5.70 to US$1.00.) There are one hundred
Hong Kong cents to each Hong Kong dollar. Banknotes are
in the denominations of five, ten, one hundred, and five hundred Hong Kong dollars. In my conversion table below, I have
used the rate of 5.75 Hong Kong dollars to our dollar which
is a bit better than the official rate and probably a trifle worse
than you will actually get.

Hong Kong to U.S.		U.S. to Hong Kong	
HK Cents	**Cents**	**Cents**	**HK Cents**
1	⅙¢	1¢	5¾
5	⅞¢	5¢	28¾
10	1¾¢	10¢	57½
25	4.35¢		**HK Dollars**
50	8.7¢	25¢	1.435
HK Dollars		50¢	2.875
1	17.4¢	**Dollars**	
5	87¢	$1.00	5.75
	Dollars	$5.00	28.75
10	$1.74	$10.00	57.50
20	$3.48	$20.00	115.00
50	$8.70	$50.00	287.50
100	$17.40	$100.00	575.00
500	$87.00	$500.00	2875.00

NOTE: As mentioned above, there are no limitations on currency that may be taken into or out of Hong Kong. Nonetheless, no gold bullion may be taken in or out of Hong Kong without a permit. Since carrying gold bullion about has never been one of my major packing problems, I almost neglected to mention this, but please take note if it concerns you.

JAPAN

In Japan, you'll have lots of fun with the monetary "coin of the realm," the yen. The official rate is 360 yen to the dollar, which means that each yen is worth approximately (very) one-third of a penny. There are one hundred sen in each yen, but for your purchases this of course will have no significance as this unit is no longer used in the purchase of merchandise. Yen banknotes come in denominations of one hundred, five hundred, one thousand, five thousand, and ten thousand, and there are yen coins of one (aluminum), five (brass), ten (copper), fifty (silver-like), and one hundred. Although there is no limit to the amount of paper money you may take into Japan, if it amounts to more than the equivalent of five hundred dollars, it must be declared. On your departure, any yen you may still have on hand can be reconverted (only one reconversion transaction permitted) up to a limit of thirty-six thousand yen —one hundred dollars. Yen may be purchased at your home-town bank at the rate of about 388 yen to the dollar. There is a fairly constant black market yen rate of about four hundred fifteen to the dollar, but I hasten to emphasize that for the American tourist this does not exist. Stay out of trouble and change your money at the official rate.

Japanese to U.S.		*U.S. to Japanese*	
Yen	**Cents**	**Cents**	**Yen**
1	.28¢	1¢	3.6
5	1.4¢	5¢	18
10	2.8¢	10¢	36
50	14¢	25¢	90
100	28¢	50¢	180
200	56¢	**Dollars**	
	Dollars	$1.00	360
500	$1.39	$5.00	1,800
1,000	$2.78	$10.00	3,600
2,000	$5.56	$20.00	7,200
5,000	$13.89	$50.00	18,000
10,000	$27.78	$100.00	36,000

MACAO

The official unit of currency in Macao is the pataca, with one hundred avos equalling one pataca. The official rate of patacas to the dollar is 5.70, exactly the same as Hong Kong dollars, but here, too, a free market exists. The pataca and the Hong Kong dollar usually move together, so that you may expect to get the same number of patacas as you would Hong Kong dollars for each of your dollars. Both Hong Kong dollars and patacas are in circulation and may be used for your purchases throughout Macao with one exception: the post office. Remember it's patacas only there and Hong Kong currency will not be accepted in payment. In the conversion table below, I have used the official rate of 5.70 patacas to the dollar.

Macao to U.S.			U.S. to Macao	
Avos	**Cents**		**Cents**	**Avos**
1	⅙¢		1¢	5.70
5	⅞¢		5¢	28.55
10	1¾¢		10¢	57.0
25	4⅜¢			**Patacas**
50	8¾¢		25¢	1.4275
Patacas			50¢	2.855
1	17½¢		**Dollars**	
5	87½¢		$1.00	5.70
	Dollars		$5.00	28.55
10	$1.75		$10.00	57.00
20	$3.50		$20.00	114.20
50	$8.75		$50.00	285.50
100	$17.50		$100.00	570.00
500	$87.50		$500.00	2855.00

THE PHILIPPINES

For many years, the official rate of Philippine pesos to United States dollars was firmly fixed at two to one by legislation. This unrealistic rate, however, together with all currency control, has now been abolished. On the free exchange market, the rate varies but has been figured in the following table at 3.20 Philippine pesos to the dollar. One hundred centavos equal one peso. If you have been longing to have lots of "folding money," you are going to be delighted with the situation here, since all of the currency is in banknotes from five centavos on up. A word of warning: if you're planning on doing any exploring outside of Manila, you'd better have your Philippine pesos handy because in the rural areas it is extremely difficult, and sometimes impossible, to get your foreign currency or traveler's checks changed.

Philippine to U.S.		*U.S. to Philippine*	
Centavos	**Cents**	**Cents**	**Centavos**
5	1.56¢	1¢	3.2
10	3.12¢	5¢	16
25	7.8¢	10¢	32
50	15.6¢	25¢	80
Pesos			**Pesos**
1	31.2¢	50¢	1.60
	Dollars	**Dollars**	
5	$1.56	$1.00	3.20
10	$3.12	$5.00	16
20	$6.24	$10.00	32
50	$15.60	$20.00	64
100	$31.20	$50.00	160
500	$156.00	$100.00	320
1,000	$312.00	$500.00	1600

SINGAPORE AND MALAYSIA

The Malaysian dollar, formerly called the Straits or Singapore dollar, is regarded as legal tender throughout Malaysia (Malaya, Singapore, North Borneo, and Sarawak) and Brunei. There are one hundred cents in each Malaysian dollar, and the official rate is 3.06 to the United States dollar. There is a limit of one hundred Malaysian dollars upon entering and leaving Singapore.

Singapore to U.S.		*U.S. to Singapore*	
M. Cents	**Cents**	**Cents**	**M. Cents**
1	⅓¢	1¢	3.06
5	1.645¢	5¢	15.3
10	3.29¢	10¢	30.6
25	8.225¢	25¢	76.5
50	16.45¢		**M. Dollars**
M. Dollars		50¢	1.53
1	32.9¢	**Dollars**	
	Dollars	$1.00	3.06
5	$1.645	$5.00	15.30

Singapore to U.S.		U.S. to Singapore	
M. Dollars	**Dollars**	**Dollars**	**M. Dollars**
10	$3.29	$10.00	30.60
20	$6.58	$20.00	61.20
50	$16.45	$50.00	153.00
100	$32.90	$100.00	306.00

TAIWAN

Have you always wanted to be a dollar millionaire? While still not easy, it is 40 times less difficult in Taiwan than in the United States since there are now 40 new Taiwan dollars (written N.T. 40) to each American dollar.

As one would expect, there are 100 Taiwan (or Formosa) cents to the N.T. dollar.

In case you happen to have your pockets bulging with gold or silver bullion, you will not be disturbed on your arrival in Taiwan but it must be declared as must any other foreign exchange you might have on your person including U.S. dollars, Hong Kong dollars, Japanese yen, or any other currency.

N.T. 500 dollars only may be brought into the country.

Taiwan to U.S.		U.S. to Taiwan	
Cents	**Cents**	**Cents**	**Dollars (N.T.)**
10	.250¢	10¢	4.00
25	.627¢	25¢	10.00
50	1.25¢	50¢	20.00
Dollars (N.T.)		**Dollars**	
1	2.5¢	$1.00	40.00
5	12.5¢	$5.00	200.00
10	25¢	$10.00	400.00
	Dollars	$25.00	1,000.00
50	$1.25	$50.00	2,000.00
100	$2.50	$100.00	4,000.00
400	$10.00	$500.00	20,000.00
500	$12.50	$1,000.00	40,000.00
1,000	$25.00		

THAILAND

The currency regulations in Thailand are just about the strictest to be found in the Asian countries. Only one hundred forty dollars in United States currency may be taken into the country, although the amount of dollars in traveler's checks or letters of credit is not limited. The official monetary unit is the baht or tical which you will hear referred to as the "tic." The rate is 20.75 baht to the dollar. Hence, the old cliché: "A Thai tical is worth an American nickel." Each baht is equal to one hundred satang. Baht banknotes are in the denominations of one (blue), five (dark purple), ten (reddish-brown), twenty (green), and one hundred (red), and there are coins of five, ten, twenty-five, fifty, and one hundred satang. In Hong Kong's free money market, it is possible to purchase baht at the rate of approximately twenty-two to the dollar, but remember if you do that only five hundred baht may be taken into or out of Thailand.

Thai to U.S.		*U.S. to Thai*	
Satang	**Cents**	**Cents**	**Satang**
5	¼ ¢	1¢	20.75
10	½ ¢		**Baht (Tical)**
25	1.205¢	5¢	1.0375
50	2.4095¢	10¢	2.075
Baht (Tical)		25¢	5.1875
1	4.819¢	50¢	10.375
5	24.1¢	**Dollars**	
10	48.19¢	$1.00	20.75
20	96.38¢	$5.00	103.75
	Dollars	$10.00	207.5
100	$4.82	$20.00	415
200	$9.64	$50.00	1,037.5
		$100.00	2,075

VIET NAM

Although the official rate is thirty-five Vietnamese piastres to the United States dollar, the government has made available to the American tourist a special "tourist rate" of seventy-three piastres—also called "dông"—to the dollar. One hundred Vietnamese cents equal one piastre. Only four hundred piastres may be taken into Viet Nam. Upon presentation of the proper Currency Control Certificate, you may convert any remaining piastres you may have on hand to dollars upon your departure from the country.

Vietnamese to U. S.		*U. S. to Vietnamese*	
Cents	**Cents**	**Cents**	**Cents**
5	.0685¢	1¢	73
10	.137¢		**Piastres**
25	.3425¢	5¢	3.65
50	.685¢	10¢	7.3
Piastres		25¢	18.25
1	1.37¢	50¢	36.5
5	6.85¢	**Dollars**	
10	13.7¢	$1.00	73
25	34.25¢	$5.00	365
50	68.5¢	$10.00	730
	Dollars	$20.00	1,460
100	$1.37	$50.00	3,650
500	$6.85	$100.00	7,300
1,000	$13.70		
5,000	$68.50		

SUGGESTIONS FOR MAKING GOOD PICTURES

I have been fortunate in having had the opportunity to make colorful pictorial records of scores of trips abroad, in all parts of the world.

The Orient is a particularly fertile field for the photographer —professional or amateur. In this vivid area the light is brilliant, the inanimate objects and products of nature are unique and colorful, while the people with their varied customs and costumes are priceless models—almost always available for the asking.

Take either your still or moving picture camera with you . . . or both. I favor movies, but many experienced travelers and photographers do extremely well with stills.

By all means whether they be still or moving, be sure that yours are color pictures. Black-and-white pictures just cannot begin to do justice to the Oriental array of colors, which virtually explode before your lens.

Taking passably good pictures seems simple enough, but I have seen horrible miscarriages of photographic justice in my years in the travel business. Some folks just don't use good sense when shooting pictures. It is amazing to me how some people can be so successful in their chosen field and how utterly inept they are in other lines of endeavor, particularly photography.

Here are a few simple procedures to follow to help make your pictures lasting mementos to be exhibited with pride.

If you are a moving picture photographer, don't, I repeat, DON'T "pan." More film is spoiled through moving the camera to encompass a large scene than from any other single source . . . including poor light. Let all the motion come through the lens, not from your hands or your tripod.

Frame all of your pictures with some nearby object, preferably a colorful one. If the scene to be taken is a distant one, try to shoot it through an opening in some trees, through an arch, from under a tree with branches hanging down, or with other foreground material to give the picture depth and added interest.

Don't try to economize on your film. Too short shots can be deadly on the eyes of the viewers. Make it a rule to count slowly to at least seven for any given scene. If there is considerable action and/or interest, a slow count of ten is not too much.

It has been my experience that—whether you travel completely independently, on a preplanned independent trip, or on a conducted tour—if your plans have been made well, you will have adequate time to take pictures to your heart's content.

As mentioned in Chapter Six and elsewhere, unusually attractive bargains may be had in the purchase of film in Singapore, Penang, and Hong Kong. In these three "free ports" you may purchase any type of film cheaper than you can buy it in your home town. Kodachrome film is difficult to secure in Japan.

If for any reason your pictures do not turn out to your satisfaction, you may purchase a complete record of your trip through my good friends in **Hong Kong,** the *Filmo Depot Ltd.* Their films are taken by experts and edited with the sure hand of a professional.

Your finished film effort, for my basic recommended trip, should be some 2,000 feet of movie film, which means that you will probably wish to shoot about 2,500 feet of 16 millimeter, or correspondingly less for 8 mm. cameras. And for stills, a minimum of 350 to 400 slides.

Roger Hynes, my close associate, and I have put together the following scenario suggestions in our film "Around the Orient with Olson" which has been unusually successful. These are the shots we took. They will do a good job for you, too.

SCENARIO SUGGESTIONS

CAMBODIA

Angkor Thom

Approach and Gate
Bayon Temple: Front view: close-up of bas-reliefs, and close-up of "4 faces"
Brass Tower
The *Royal Palace*
The *Terrace of the Leper King*

CAMBODIA (cont.)

Phnom Bakheng (Between **Angkor Thom** and *Angkor Wat*)

Stone lion, ladder steps, and views from top

Preah Khan, in the jungle's embrace, and **Ta Prohm,** also unclaimed from the jungle

Angkor Wat

Views from distance, across moat
Entrance to causeway
Shots from causeway
Interior court views

Siem Reap

Scenes along river
Grand Hotel d'Angkor

HAWAII (OAHU)

Honolulu

Airport: plane, with *Diamond Head* in background. Lei ceremony on arrival
Dock: ship arriving. Lei ceremony
Royal Mausoleum grounds
Iolani Palace-Judiciary Building, King Kamehameha statue
Aloha Tower
Stevenson's grass hut and *Waioli Tea Room*
Pacific National Cemetery (Punchbowl Crater)

Waikiki

Beach scenes with *Diamond Head* in background
Surf rider—catamarans and canoes
Kalakaua Avenue (near *International Market Place*)
International Market Place
University of Hawaii campus
Kapiolani Park—Sunday band concert—hula dancers

HAWAII (OAHU) (cont.)

Around the Island

Kahaluu: coral gardens; posed pictures with picturesque natives; and the *Sacred Falls*

Laie: the *Mormon Temple* grounds

Nuuanu Pali: the view from the cliff; close-up of gorgeous flowers

HONG KONG and MACAO

Victoria

Victoria and *Victoria Peak* from harbor and from **Kowloon** (view from roof restaurant of *Ambassador Hotel* particularly effective)

Star Ferry: loading and unloading; "melting pot" scenes of mixed races

Walla-wallas (water taxis) from *Star Ferry*

Advertising sampans from *Star Ferry*

Rickshaws in action

The *Peak Tramway:* shots of **Victoria,** the harbor and **Kowloon** while ascending or descending

Victoria Peak: panoramic vista from the top

Tiger Balm Gardens: entrance, statuary, and gardens

Hong Kong Hotel–Repulse Bay, beach and nearby apartments

Aberdeen

General panoramic view of the floating homes with close-up of two or three of them

Views along *Quay:* scurrying coolies; colorful costumes; stacks of drying fish

Floating restaurant: shots of sampan crossing; the restaurant from the sampan; choosing fish and having your choice lifted out of tank; interior of restaurant

HONG KONG and MACAO (cont.)

Happy Valley

From hill in background
Hong Kong Race Track
Soccer and cricket grounds

West Point, Morlo-Gai, and Ladder Streets

You can't miss a marvelous sequence in these colorful Chinese areas: outdoor shops, food stalls, barbers, and people, people, people (too bad you can't photograph the sounds)

Kowloon and Victoria

Typhoon Shelters
Harbor tour by boat

Kowloon

Peninsula and *Ambassador Hotels*
Views along Nathan Road
Castle Peak: Dragon Inn or *Luk Yuen Resort; Castle Peak Bay* from *Castle Peak*

Yuen Long

Typical market city: markets; *Hakka* (the strangers) in native costumes

Kam Tin

The old *Walled City:* walls; street scene

Tai Po

Water folk in junks and sampans
Red China border: locals will pose
Amah's Rock

Shatin Heights and Valley

HONG KONG and MACAO (cont.)

MACAO

Cathedral of Sao Paula
Kam Yung Temple
The Barrier Gate
Panoramic view of city, harbor and nearby islands

JAPAN

Tokyo

The *National Diet Building*
Tokyo Tower, three views: (1) from distance of about a quarter of a mile with *Mt. Fuji* in the background (which is difficult to capture because of haze and/or clouds); (2) a "straight-up" view; and (3) human interest shots around base of visitors gawking in open-mouthed amazement
Ueno Park: garden scenes replete with flowers, rocks, and water; kids and grownups in typical postures; youngsters on the Monorail; and view of the Zoo
Tsukiji Fish Market
Geisha and rickshaws at *twilight* in the Shimbashi-Geisha District; *night* in the neon-lit Ginza area. Be sure to use night film. The *Hattori Building* corner is particularly color-ful and animated; an *evening* shot along Namiki Dori, in the carbaret-bar area of Nishi Ginza
Ginza by day—from fixed position, and in motion from automobile or streetcar
The *Imperial Palace:* with swans from Germany floating gracefully in the moat in the foreground; the *Palace* itself taken from high up in the *Palace Hotel;* and the impressive walls. "Shoot" the nearby office building line-up from a point immediately in front of the *Imperial Palace* including A Avenue and the Marunouchi district. This makes an ex-cellent night shot
The *"Red Gate"* and gardens of *Tokyo University*
The façade of the *Kabukiza Theater*

JAPAN (cont.)—Tokyo

Meiji Shrine: Meiji outer gardens; *Torii* gate

The interior of a *Sumo* wrestling ring—with the human pachyderms in action

Korakuen Baseball Stadium—in action

The *Tokyo National Athletic Stadium*—setting for the Olympics in 1964

One of the justly famed gardens: *Happo-en, Chinzanso, Korakuen,* or *Shinjuku* (try *Chinzanso*'s famous Mongolian barbecue while there)

Imperial Hotel, sign on old part. *Palace Hotel* from across *Imperial Palace* moat

Asakusa Amusement Quarter: red and green demons at entrance; surging crowds; novelty shops; stalls; and refreshment stands (very colorful); incense stick brazier in front of the *Shrine;* the *Shrine;* and the *Pagoda*

Red street telephones in action

Yokohama

Port of Yokohama—ships at anchor

Kamakura

The Big Buddha

Hakone Area

Hotels: *Fujiya* gardens and pool; view across pool to *Mount Fuji* and general mountain panorama from *Hotel Kowaki-en Great Hell* (Hot Springs)

Views from the "10 Province" Pass

"Double" view of *Mt. Fuji*—actual image and a reflected one in *Lake Hakone* (known alternatively as *Lake Ashi* and the *Lake of the Reeds—Reed Lake*)

Mt. Fuji from *Long-Tailed Pass*

Golf course

JAPAN (cont.)

Inland Sea

Views leaving **Osaka** and/or **Kobe**
Deck scenes of Japanese students
Scenes on the bridge with pretty girls (lots of them always available)
Island scenery and seascapes en route
Approach to **Beppu**

Beppu

"Bathers" buried in hot sand
Monkeys *(Mt. Takasaki)* being fed. Try to catch them stealing peanuts and tangerines.
Kanko Volcano
Tatsumaki—"Old Faithful"
Chi-no-ike (Pond of Blood)
Main street in town (shoot toward the sea)

Kyoto

Geisha girls en route to work
Philosopher's Garden; *Moss Temple*
Temple of the 1,001 Buddhist Warriors
Sanjo Bridge
Street scenes of a local holiday or fete day
A scene depicting hand manufacture of lacquerware or porcelain
Shinogyoku Street scenes
Ponto-cho Street amusement area
Old Imperial Palace
Nijo Detached Palace
Katsura imperial villa and garden
Nijo Castle, including Japanese water garden
The *Kinkakuji Temple* (Golden Pavilion) across pond getting full reflection in the water
The *Nishi Honganji Temple* (architecturally probably the

JAPAN (cont.)—Kyoto

best Buddhist temple in Japan)
The *Ginkakuji Temple* (Silver Pavilion)
The *Heian Shrine* (gardens to the rear are exquisite)
The *Chion-in Temple* and garden
The *Sanju-Sangen-do Temple*
The *Kiyomizu Temple* and nearby *Five-Storied Pagoda* (Yasaka)
Zen gardens of the *Saihoji Temple* (also known as the *Moss Temple*)

Nara

Deer in *Nara Park*—try to "shoot" someone (preferably young Japanese girls) feeding the "little deers"
The Great Daibutsu Buddha in *Todaiji Temple*
Sarusawa Pond. Shoot the *Kofukuji Temple* and its five-storied pagoda across the pond and through the willows. This is a photographic gem.
The 13-foot *Bronze Lantern* before the *Todaiji Temple*
The *Kasuga* (Vermilion) *Shrine*
Stone lantern approach to the *Kasuga-Wakamiya Shrine*
Dreamland (Japan's answer to *Disneyland*)—Mississippi paddle steamer; miniature railway; jungle settings; and feudal castles

Osaka

Panoramic view of city, including river from top of *Osaka Grand Hotel* or the *Alaska Restaurant.* Street scenes at night (emphasize neon signs)
Osaka Castle—outside and views from top

Takarazuka

Takarazuka All Girls Opera—on stage, in action
Amusement Park (porpoises and monkeys in action)

JAPAN (cont.)

Hiroshima

Ruins of *Industrial Exposition Hall* (hypo center of A-bomb explosion)
Peace Boulevard
Peace Bridge
Peace Tower—A-bomb Museum
Panorama from *Hijiyama Hill*

Miyajima (Itsukushima—or Shrine Island)

The *"Floating" Shrine* through its "floating" *torii*—from the water
The *Pagoda*
Street scene in town

Nagasaki

View of port from *Kazagushira Hill*
The terraced residential section
Peace Park statue
Madame Butterfly's house

Lake Chuzenji District

Hairpin turns (get 3 sharp curves at one shot from about the 24th bend)
The *Kegon Waterfall* from point adjacent to its base
Boats on *Lake Chuzenji*
The cavorting captive trout in the nearby fishery

Nikko

The verdant entrance to the *Nikko Kanko Hotel*
The *Toshogu Shrine*
The *Rinnoji Temple*
The ornate *Yomeimon Gate* (Gate of Sunlight)
The red lacquer *Five-Storied Pagoda*
The *Sacred Stable* decorated with the "see no evil, hear no

JAPAN (cont.)—Nikko

evil, speak no evil" monkeys

The façade of the *Sacred Palanquin House*

The *Karamon* (Chinese) *Gate*

The *Mausoleum*, with its decorative *Sleeping Cat*

The rapids of the *Daiya River* near the *Toshogu shrines*

The *Kegon* waterfalls in the *Nikko National Park*

THE PHILIPPINES

Manila

Escolta street scene: be sure to get *jeepneys*, horse-drawn *calesas*, and modern cars as well as the exteriors of the stores and shops

Manila Bay at sunset from near *Manila Hotel*

Sweep of Dewey Boulevard; *Luneta Park* and *Dr. Rizal* monument

American Embassy

Jai Alai Fronton (exterior)

Malacana Palace (gardens and residence)

Ruins of *Intramuros*

University of Santo Tomás

Forbes Park residential quarter

Memorial to the Unknown Soldier

Ships at anchor in north and south port districts

Manila Hotel (general view—and outdoor terrace and pool)

Manila to Tagaytay Ridge:

Fishing village street scenes with boats at anchor in harbor; *Las Piñas Church* with its bamboo organ; fruit, flower and produce markets which line the road; colorful native houses on stilts; *Taal Vista Lodge:* grounds and gardens; *Taal Volcano; Taal Lake;* and the smoldering Valley

Baguio

Military academy

Burnham Park and *Mansion House* grounds

THE PHILIPPINES (cont.)

Banaue (in Ifugao)

Rice terraces

FEDERATION OF MALAYSIA

Singapore

Change Alley
Trishaws on the move
The race track
The *Great World Amusement Park*
Botanical Gardens (flowers and monkeys being fed)
The *Singapore River:* sampans, junks, and busy water life
Tiger Balm Gardens
Views along Nicoll Highway: the Esplanade; *Cenotaph;*
Queen Elizabeth Walk; the harbor
The *Assembly House; St. Andrew's Cathedral,* and *Municipal Building*
Fort Canning Hill
Raffles Place
Eating stalls in Beach Road
Bukit Timah Nature Reserve
Siang Lim Sian Si Temple
The *Holy Sultan Mosque*
The *Gap* (at sunset)
Residential areas
Nanyang University
Malay village (Geylang)
Chinatown open-air markets

Johore Bahru

Town Hall
Istana Besar
The Mosque

TAIWAN (Formosa)

Taipei and Environs

One of the Five Gates

The *Martyrs Shrine*

The *Lung Shan Temple*

Confucius Temple

Botanical Gardens

Presidential Square

Chen Huang Temple

The Zoo

Chilung: the beach

Chihnan Temple: photograph the "1,000 steps"

Mount Ta Tun: take a panoramic view from *Yangming Shan* (Grass Mountain) of **Taipei**

Wulai: aboriginal dancers, barefoot girls perform near the springs of the Cataract

Kuanyin Shan (Mount Goddess of Mercy). Flaming forests in the fall silhouette the temple

Pakuashan (Central Taiwan)

The world's largest statue of Buddha

THAILAND

Bangkok

Grand Palace and *Wat Phra Keo* (still pictures only within the grounds—no movies)

Wat Arun (Temple of the Dawn). Excellent views are to be had from the river

Wat Po (Temple of the Reclining Buddha). Exterior and interior views; the Bhodi Tree (on the grounds)

Wat Benchamabopit (Marble Temple). Get diving kids on boat landing

Wat Sraket

Wat Rajaprodist

Saffron-robed monks in temples, on streets, and in parks

THAILAND (cont.)—Bangkok

Rajadamnoen Avenue: street scenes; public buildings; light posts; Thai boxers—there is enough light here to photograph indoors

Jim Thompson's Thai house

Kite flying

Saranrom Garden

Snake Farm

Dusit Zoo (royal white elephant)

Fehukao Thong (Golden Mount)

Lumpini Park

The *Throne Hall*

The *klongs* (canals) and floating markets (go early in the morning); native houses; bathing and swimming in the *klongs*

VIET NAM

Saigon

Tu Do Street in late afternoon with emphasis on pretty girls in their *ao dai* costumes

Hotel Majestic Street Cafe at cocktail hour

View up and down river from rooftop *Dining Terrace* of the *Majestic Hotel*

View overlooking square and cathedral from *Caravelle Hotel Roof Terrace*

View across square toward *Caravelle Hotel*

Colorful trees and flowers in *Botanical Garden*

Central Market

Flower Market

Independence Palace through gates and from busy street leading to *Palace*

Tomb and *Temple* of Marshal Le Van Duyet

Street scenes in **Cholon:** pedicabs and busy traffic

PART II

CHAPTER 9

Cambodia

THE KINGDOM of **Cambodia,** snuggled cosily between **Thailand, Laos,** and **Viet Nam,** has, at its southern extremity, access to the *Gulf of Thailand* (formerly the *Gulf of Siam*) and, ultimately, the *South China Sea*. Its capital is **Phnom Penh,** while its most fascinating city is **Siem Reap.** Physically, the Cambodians resemble their neighbors to the west, the Thais, more than the Vietnamese, who live immediately to their east. The men are tall, the women rather short, and both are dark brown with ebony black hair and wear the *langouti* (loincloth) which the men supplement with a short jacket and the women with a scarf or a long clinging robe draped about the body. Many sophisticated travelers consider the Cambodians, Thais, and Vietnamese among the most physically attractive people in the world. None of the other man-made wonders of the world are so unique, amazing, or utterly prepossessing as **Angkor Thom** and *Angkor Wat*.

HISTORICALLY one cannot give the Southeast Asians high marks for keeping or preserving accurate archives. We know, of course, that in 1863 France took over Cambodia as a protectorate and that this tiny kingdom has been independent since 1953. What little is known of the early history of the region has come from chiseled writings and sculptures found in the *Ang-*

kor ruins, old letters written by Asiatic traders, legends handed down through generations, and from the histories of other Asiatic countries which mention **Kambuja (Cambodia).** It can be readily understood how little the world knew of the wondrous *Angkor* area when one realizes that every last vestige of a remarkable civilization was swallowed up by the almost impenetrable jungle and "lost" for more than five centuries. There was no knowledge either in the western world or in most of Asia that the mighty Khmer empire had ever flourished, or was, subsequently, being devoured by the jungle's vegetation. Because of its proximity to **Thailand,** then known as **Siam,** frequent incursions took place between the two countries, with evidences of Siamese domination of Cambodia and vice versa.

It is believed that **Kambuja** was a flourishing kingdom ruled by Hindus of Indian origin in the first century. The early ruling dynasties, though relatively obscure, are thought to have been continuous until the emergence of the Khmer dynasty which had its origin circa 500, came to a glorious peak early in the 9th century, and flourished until the 15th century.

King Jayavarman II was the founding genius of the long line of Khmer kings who were to become the most avid builders of any monarchs in the world. Never has a succession of sovereigns created such regal architectural splendors as did the Khmers. The scintillating luxury in which the nobility lived and the comfort in which the people existed had not previously been known in tropical areas. It is questionable if, even today, many Asians live as well as did the 9th to 15th century Kambujans. It was the same Jayavarman II who founded the king-god cult known as the *Deva Raja* in which he pledged to keep his people free from all alien subjugation. Jayavarman II's sanctification as God-King was ceremonialized by the Brahman high priests dedicated to the Hindu god Siva.

Because of the incredible fertility and favorable position of this land, Jayavarman II, in his ever perspicacious way, foresaw the possibility of harvesting sufficient farm products, raising enough cattle, and catching enough fish in this one limited

area to feed all of the Kambujans who, in later reigns, numbered over one million. He was firm in his conviction that he
was establishing a kingdom that would forever remain completely independent of all neighboring lands. It was his fervent
desire to establish a never ending line of monarchs who would
rule free people living in peace and comfort subsisting entirely
on the production of their own land and waterways. Subsequent Khmer monarchs were, like Jayavarman II, equally intent on agricultural self-sufficiency and acutely aware of the
efficient utilization of water. Nowhere in the world outside
of Kambuja was there then such an intricate complexity of
waterways; natural rivers and lakes were skillfully worked
into the grand plan interspersed with canals, irrigation ditches,
reservoirs, artificial lakes, pools, and ponds.

It is believed that the original capital established by Jayavarman II was near the present **Angkor Thom,** while later kings
used four other sites as their Kambujan capitals before King
Yasovarman I established his seat of government on the present
site of **Angkor Thom** toward the end of the 9th century.

Angkor in the Cambodian language means "city," while
Vat in the native tongue means "temple" and is pronounced
Wat; hence the accepted spelling is *Angkor Wat. Thom* means
"big" or "great." Angkor, the city and royal residence, was all
three—great, big, and the capital; hence **Angkor Thom.**

Early Khmer rulers were Hindus, and the decorative motif
of many of the temples and palaces fell under this religious
influence. During the 12th century construction of the astounding *Angkor Wat,* Suryavarman II was converted to Buddhism,
which religion prevailed thereafter in Kambuja. While previous
Khmer rulers had dedicated their temples to Siva, *Angkor Wat*
was dedicated to Vishnu, the god of Suryavarman's personal
choice.

Jayavarman VII was the Khmer ruler during the apogee
of *Angkor's* architectural orgy. Lavish stories documented
by Queen Indra Devi in *Angkor's* carved panels and also
the Sanskrit records indicate that no less than several thousand

decorators and builders were constantly kept busy under Jaya-varman VII in continuing the breathtaking construction which included, among others, the *Bayon Temple.*

Precise reasons for the mass departure from this magnificent area have been sought from Queen Indra Devi's inscriptions and other documents throughout Asia. Fortunately, enough material has now become available to throw considerable light on the subject. The Khmers' commendable concern for the safety and well-being of their people is well known. Late in the one hundred year Siamese War which began in the 14th century, the Khmers suffered a series of stinging defeats which no doubt led the King to believe that *Angkor* was no longer militarily tenable. Whatever the reasons, *Angkor* was entirely deserted toward the mid-15th century. After the exodus from *Angkor,* the next known Cambodian capital was **Lovek,** suc-ceeded by **Oudong,** which was followed by **Phnom Penh,** the present capital.

In attempting to write of *Angkor,* one is faced with a vir-tually impossible descriptive task. Before my first visit to this superlative set of ruins, I had read everything on which I could cast my eyes as to the location, background, history, and phys-ical properties of the setting, but to no avail. When I arrived in **Siem Reap,** a wide spot in the jungle 196 miles from **Phnom Penh** and 262 miles from **Bangkok,** I was as unprepared for what awaited me as though I had never heard the name *Ang-kor.* This is not astounding, really, as those of us from the western world have little conception of Asia's people, places, or things. The Orient lies a vast distance from us, and we have no ethnical or historical ties with this section of the globe. Europe on the other hand is the homeland of our race, and few American cities or communities are without first- or second-generation citizens of European ancestry. My own mother and father were born in Sweden; our next-door neighbors were born in Italy. Many of my friends and associates either were born abroad or have parents or grandparents who were. Europe is an open book; the Orient is both mysterious and incomprehensible. Even jungles are unknown entities to those of us who have not flown over, or been through, the moss-matted forests in whose dense foliage monkeys scurry, birds cry, insects hum, animals slink, and reptiles slither.

When *Angkor* was deserted in the 15th century, it was completely lost to the tangled jungle until 1861 when the French naturalist, Henri Mouhot, literally stumbled on it. He had actually come to Asia on another mission but had heard so many tales of these "God created" wonders that he made a search for the ruins which, with the aid of local guides, he found . . . though not, as popularly believed, completely by accident. It is almost impossible to imagine the fierce fertility engendered by this soft climate, rich soil, brilliant sunshine, and more than adequate rain. The clinging moss, entangling vines, and huge leafy trees completely enshrouded the shrines, temples, and palaces for more than four hundred years.

The work of clearing *Angkor*'s principal structures from the jungle has progressed for more than a century. *Angkor Wat* has been denuded of its forestation and largely restored to its original state of being. Some temples, homes, hospitals, palaces, rest houses, and public buildings have been partially cleared and restored. Others have been left captives of the jungle. Through the centuries, the silk-cotton, banyan, and other great trees grew through many of the buildings and strangled others. Roots of some of these arboreal monsters are eight to ten feet in diameter and have traversed, penetrated, or strangled sturdy foundations and huge walls. Sinuous vines have clambered through buildings in wild profusion.

To restore the structures, the vegetation in some instances was hacked away, but in many others whole sections of the buildings were taken apart, freed of their gnawing captors, and rebuilt stone by stone.

Many of *Angkor*'s edifices were built in pyramid-like style, rising from terraced platforms. These buildings were enclosed by moats and irrigation canals which emptied into elegant lakes. The bas-relief carvings are of Hindu, Buddhist, and other deities. Others depict the everyday life of the rulers and their people.

With the exception of its capital, **Phnom Penh,** Cambodia today is still largely primitive jungle country. In the days of the Khmers, the natives who were not housed within the confines of **Angkor Thom** lived in thatched roof huts built on stilts to keep them high and dry in the rainy season. The Cambodians were then, as now, largely fishermen and agriculturists, with rice being the principal produce. Today many Cambodians are concentrated around the long lake, *Tonle Sap,* which stretches from near **Siem Reap** to a point not far distant from **Phnom Penh.**

The Khmers built a labyrinth of irrigation ditches and extensive canals which stretched from *Tonle Sap,* an unorthodox lake, which body of water cooperates with the *Mekong River* to create a completely unusual situation: during the dry season, all waters flow from the lake to the canals, ditches, and countryside, while during the wet season, all waters flow *to* the lake, their courses having been reversed.

HOTELS in Cambodia are adequate. The best hotel in **Siem Reap,** the *Grand Hotel d'Angkor,* a gleaming white edifice on the edge of the city, is under new management (1961) and, while an old hotel, has a certain air about it. All rooms have private bath, but by all means do try to arrange to reserve in advance a room with window box air conditioning. The hotel is not centrally cooled, but a number of rooms are equipped with reasonably efficient window boxes.

FOOD. There are a number of interesting facets to the operation of the *Grand Hotel.* As a French establishment, one would expect a Continental breakfast would be served. Nothing could be further from the truth. The breakfasts are both large and good. *Grand Hotel* lunches and dinners are more than adequate.

The *Grand Hotel Bar-Lounge* is an intriguing page from Somerset Maugham, with huge fans lazily wafting air overhead and French-speaking Oriental barmen concocting American drinks. The transportation of supplies to **Siem Reap** must be a kingsize problem. This does not deter the *Grand Hotel* management. Without any question, the bar of the *Grand Hotel* is one of the best stocked outside of a populous metropolitan area. One may order, and be served, Tavel Rosé, Pouilly-Fuisse, or dozens of other wines, your favorite champagne, Dubonnet, Coca-Cola, Pepsi-Cola, Seven Up, Tuborg or Muenchener beer from Denmark or Germany, chianti wine from Italy, Scotch, bourbon, or rye whisky, Gordon's or House of Lords gin, Perrier or Canada Dry sparkling water, and, for variety, ice cold watermelon.

The *Hotel de la Paix,* the *Grand*'s annex in town, is a bit depressing. The *Auberge des Ruines,* facing the road running along the moat in front of *Angkor Wat,* is new and air conditioned, but it reminds me of a not too attractive motel.

If you are unable to secure reservations at any of the foregoing three hotels, which is possible since the demand is great and the number of rooms not nearly adequate, don't spend the night in **Siem Reap.**

There are two excellent hotels in **Phnom Penh.** The new Swiss-managed *Monorom,* with more than half of its rooms air conditioned, boasts a roof terrace for dinner dancing. The *Hotel Le Royal,* set amid a large lovely plot of ground with a swimming pool, has all air conditioned rooms.

HYGIENE. One will not wish to drink Cambodia's tap water, but since all types of soft drinks and bottled water are on hand in profusion, this should not prove a hardship. The *Grand Hotel* serves my favorite Evian water bottled in France.

Angkor Wat is four and one-quarter miles, by good road, from the *Grand Hotel.* **Angkor Thom** is a mile farther along. I urge that you leave *Angkor Wat* for last, however, though you must bypass it en route to *Phnom Bakheng,* **Angkor Thom,** *Preah Khan, Pre Rup, Ta Prohm,* and the other wonders of the area. *Angkor Wat* is to be seen to best advantage in the late afternoon.

PHNOM BAKHENG. After passing *Angkor Wat* and

shortly before reaching **Angkor Thom,** the approach to *Phnom Bakheng* will be heralded by two handsome stone lions not far from the road. This mountain temple, so named because it is on *Angkor*'s highest point, was built by Yasovarman I and is reached by the noted almost vertical "ladder steps"—the most steeply inclined steps in all *Angkor*. In his heyday as monarch, Yasovarman I could stride to the terrace of this magnificent temple and overlook the river, moat, canals, and reservoirs as well as a jungle of wooden huts on stilts lining the waterways. The climb today is arduous but the view over the surrounding countryside is more than worth the effort. If you are under doctor's orders, by all means don't attempt this climb.

ANGKOR THOM, originally named *Yasodharapura,* is a perfectly square walled city surrounded by a moat and entered by five highly ornate gates: the *Gate of the Dead, Gate of Victory, North Gate, West Gate,* and *South Gate.* Each causeway approaching the gates over the moat is lined with a profusion of grotesque statues seven to ten feet in height portraying demons and animals with weird animal, human, and demon faces. The most striking features of the five identical gates are the huge statues which surmount them consisting of four faces whose huge expanses, facing to the four principal compass points, are in relaxed repose with eyes closed and a touch of a smile tugging at the lips and cheeks.

Jayavarman VII, the most ambitious of the building kings, rebuilt **Angkor Thom** after he had driven out the invading Chams. To insure the safety of the city, he had the now renowned double walls built.

The bewitching BAYON TEMPLE in the geometric center of **Angkor Thom** was built in the form of a Greek cross surrounded by a vast outer gallery. In a remarkable state of preservation, the *Bayon* is one of the weirdest monuments erected by the Khmer kings, with a central sanctuary, circular in shape, having a chapel at each end and twelve radiating chapels all supported by a massive base. The chapels formed the foundation for the forest of towers rising 150 feet above the ground in an amazing agglomeration of stone. The *Bayon,* with its double surrounding galleries, contains carvings of more than 11,000 human figures and animal shapes in sculptured bas-reliefs.

In a remote way, the temple is reminiscent of the Egyptian pyramids, though much more fantastic, containing a complex of chapels, cut-up galleries, meditation sanctuaries, and art galleries. Its center tower is emblazoned with four Brobdingnagian faces of solid gold, facing the immutable horizon, surmounting 172 lesser faces, themselves six and one-half feet high, smiling down from 43 ornate towers. The *Bayon Temple* was erected to house the protecting holy spirits; it is, therefore, reasonable to assume that the four principal gold faces depict four of the god kings whose handsome faces are of smiling mien, strong and endowed with a look of regal grandeur. The bas-relief panels in the long galleries portray the life lived in the time of the Khmers including fishermen pursuing their daily chores, warriors fighting battles on land and sea, hunters stalking their prey in the forests, scenes in the market place, plodding elephants, clambering monkeys, and game cocks fighting ferociously.

The BRASS TOWER *(Baphuon),* built by King Udayadityavarman II in the 11th century, to the north and west of the *Bayon,* is another enormous temple following the pyramid motif. This monumental temple 450 yards long and 150 yards wide was used by artists to practice bas-relief work, which came out very well indeed. *Baphuon* was a temple of the Royal God.

PHIMEANAKAS, just north of *Baphuon* and south of the *Royal Palace,* was the smallest of the **Angkor Thom** pyramid-temples. An early legend referred to the *Phimeanakas* as a palace inhabited by an evil serpent which the king not only visited but paid homage to. Not so. The apparent truth of the matter is that *Phimeanakas,* erected as a temple, remained so.

The ROYAL PALACE, overlooking the *Leper King's Terrace, Elephant Terrace, Royal Plaza,* and the *Twelve Stone Towers,* was so terraced as to command an imposing view over the *Royal Plaza* in which gorgeous unbelievable entertainment was presented for the monarch and his court, including fireworks, dancing girls by the thousands, circuses, and athletic events. Within the palace, life was lived on a fabulous scale. The royal family owned thousands of slaves and lived in incredible splendor. The public rooms were lavishly gilded and bejeweled, with the private quarters being equally sumptuous. Lavish swimming pools and ornate baths were everywhere. The populace must have been immaculate, as well they should be, as neither men nor women were clothed above the waist except with sparkling precious jewels.

The TERRACE OF THE ELEPHANTS, an entertainment and audience hall, is annexed to the *Palace,* though facing it. More than one thousand feet long and forty-five feet wide, much of the remaining wall is ornamented with lumbering pachyderms either in hunting postures or engaged in eating lotus plants.

The TERRACE OF THE LEPER KING is most unusual, its wall being decorated with six, sometimes seven, bas-relief rows. The motif of these carvings deals with kings in full battle array surrounded by their court and courtesans in ceremonial parade. The lower part of the wall is concerned with fish and marine life which has led historians to believe the carved panel was the original western foundation of a huge lake which quite probably was destroyed by Jayavarman VII when he built the *Terrace of the Elephants.*

BANTEAY SREI, the *Temple of Women,* fifteen miles from the protecting walls of **Angkor Thom,** believed to be the largest built in the era of the Khmers, has been completely reclaimed from the jungle and is rich in overly ornate carvings in its red sandstone. Here one may see bosomy dancing girls, demons, animals, deities, and combinations of reproductions of the real, the human, and the combined unreal and inhuman. It is believed that *Banteay Srei* was constructed by Jayavarman V in the late 10th century. The temple is reached over bumpy roads by Jeep or land rover.

Leaving the north gate of **Angkor Thom** and proceeding northeast, one arrives at PREAH KHAN, built by Jayavarman VII, which is one of the area's largest monuments. Its moats are approximately half a mile from those of **Angkor Thom.** Much of *Preah Khan* is still in the embrace of the jungle but it presents an interesting object for one's attention because the temple is jungle locked.

Proceeding east one passes NEAK PEAN, a monumental sanctuary from the era of Jayavarman VII, and further on, TA SOM, an unusual example of brick construction whose arches are gracefully tiered.

Farther south and east is MEBON, a temple erected on an island in the center of *Baray Lake,* artificially created by the Khmer Yacoverman.

PRE RUP is another pyramidal monument, the central terrace of which is a square rising about fifty feet above the surrounding countryside.

SRAH SRANG, south of the road leading from *Pre Rup* to *Ta Prohm,* is a placid body of water one-half mile long by a quarter mile wide which never dries up even in the midst of a drought. The ruins of a wooden pavilion may be seen on the island in *Srah Srang.*

TA PROHM has not been reclaimed from the jungle. Roots, trunks, and even branches flare through the temple in smothering profusion. There are vines and mosses. In some instances, the vegetation acts as a wedge prying the temple apart and in others as a vise to encompass it. Paths have been cleared, and *Ta Prohm* may be visited in relative ease. Carved inscriptions in *Ta Prohm* delineate the statistics of the daily life in *Ta Prohm,* where thousands of priests, women dancers, and ordinary citizens resided. Your guide, from the inscriptions, can tell you how many fish, how much rice and flour, and how many cattle were devoured there each day.

BANTEAY KDEI, adjacent to the *Srah Srang,* is a simple temple which for inexplicable reasons was never completely overgrown by vegetation. Monks apparently lived on long after the non-ecclesiastical personnel had fled.

Other temples on the so-called "small circuit" are TA KEO, the work of Suryavarman I, which, had it been finished, would have been the first temple constructed entirely in sandstone, but because of inexperience with this type of building material, it was never completed. CHAU SAY TEVODA and THOM-MANOM are believed to have been built by Suryavarman II in the early 12th century.

ANGKOR WAT, the grandest and most magnificent of the temples of the world, built by Suryavarman II between A.D. 1112 and 1182, is an edifice of absolutely awesome proportions. The entire circumference is guarded by a moat, 627 feet wide, which forms a perfect rectangle. Between the moat and the temple is a great wall forming an inner rectangle one mile in length on each side. From the bridge spanning the moat to the west, the causeway stretches 420 yards to the temple's steps at the front entrance. The causeway's entrance is decorated by three pretentious minaret-like domes, each of sufficient stature to completely dominate an ordinary temple.

The entire structure, its colonnades and causeways, are of sandstone and laterite blocks rubbed to a state of such unblemished perfection as to enable them to be perfectly fitted one to another.

Unlike Christian temples, *Angkor Wat* (the "city temple") was erected not as a place of mass worship but as a sanctuary for the gods and as a funeral temple for the kings. It was here that the kings were cremated, their ashes interred, and from where the god kings left to take their places on *Mt. Maru,* the Cambodian version of *Mt. Olympus,* the earthly home of the gods, which *Angkor Wat* symbolizes.

In dedicating *Angkor Wat* to the Brahman god, Vishnu, whose statue will be found in the central tower at its lower extremity, Suryavarman II could not overlook himself as God King and shares "top billing" with Vishnu in the deification of *Angkor Wat.*

Each of the temple's four corners is guarded by a turret-like tower. The interior of the temple is a series of galleries, walls and areas within walls, sharply inclined steps, and breathtaking bas-relief façades. The galleries are joined to the shrine by covered passages.

The temple spreads over an area of more than five hundred acres. Its three tiers rise to a height of 212 feet, while the principal sanctuary stands on a base 42 feet in height, rising 132 feet therefrom. *Angkor Wat*'s triple terraced galleries surround cruciform courts. The temple is crowned by five lotus bud towers.

I recommend that you drive around the circumference of *Angkor Wat* to view its beauty from a distance before making your late afternoon entrance over the moat and causeway from the west, when the glorious temple will be softly floodlit by the gentle afternoon sun. As one approaches the temple, its sheer beauty and exciting size become more pronounced with each step.

One sees virtually every type of human activity carved on the walls and pillars in bas-relief, but the dominant motif is of the deities.

The south gallery is the most fascinating. Here, in the 900 yard long cloister, are illustrated legends in vivid carving, the most illuminating of which are two panels devoted to Surya-varman. One panel portrays the monarch holding an audience before a large group of priests, prostrate subjects, and war-riors, while the other depicts the king either off to war or in a warlike parade astride an elephant and accompanied by his generals and court.

The eastern gallery features marine denizens in a sea of milk, deities, and huge men.

In addition to *Angkor Wat,* the *Bayon Temple,* and others mentioned in the foregoing, there are some 45 Hindu and Buddhist temples in *Angkor.*

SIEM REAP, a village of less than 6,000 inhabitants, retains much of the flavor of native life in the time of the Khmers. Except for a scattering of relatively modern houses in the heart of town, the inhabitants lead a primitive life, living in stilted native type huts. As one follows the road that winds along the banks of the *Siem Reap River,* the Cambodians may be seen at their daily tasks of rice husking, dough making, house building, washing and bathing in the river. If one goes on to *Lake Tonle Sap,* one will see the natives busily engaged in fishing. **Siem Reap** has been largely hacked out of the jungle, and were it not for its famous *Angkor* neighbors would have little to offer the visitor. The *Central Market Place* and a few bazaar-type shops will help make an after-dinner stroll pleasant.

PHNOM PENH, Cambodia's capital, is a busy city with a population of more than 500,000 located on the *Tonle Sap* and *Mekong Rivers.* Founded in the late 14th century, the city has been the nation's permanent capital for about one hundred years.

As a former French stronghold, **Phnom Penh** exudes French provincial atmosphere. While not as scintillating as **Saigon, Phnom Penh** is another bit of France transplanted.

During the rainy season, the *Mekong River* becomes so swollen as to cause the *Tonle Sap River* to reverse its course and literally run uphill. From **Phnom Penh** to *Lake Tonle Sap*, the area becomes completely inundated with water.

The ROYAL PALACE is noted for its silver pagoda, while the *Jayavarman VII Museum* is known for its Art School.

One of **Phnom Penh's** great theatrical attractions is the girl company of Royal Cambodian dancers.

A VISA is required for Cambodia. Should your advance plans not have included a visit to Cambodia and you did not secure a visa before leaving home, there need be no problem. You may secure a tourist visa, good for three months, in **Bangkok,** Thailand; **Saigon,** South Viet Nam; **New Delhi,** India; or at other Cambodian governmental headquarters.

THE APPROACH. There are flights each morning from **Bangkok** to **Siem Reap** which planes return late in the afternoon. Several planes a week fly from **Saigon** to **Phnom Penh, Siem Reap,** and **Bangkok** and return the next day. *Royal Air Cambodge,* piloted by Frenchmen, flies DC-3's. *Air Vietnam* and *Thai Airways* also serve Cambodia. (N.B. For the duration of the present diplomatic crisis the foregoing is not applicable. Cambodia is virtually isolated from foreign visitors. Check with your travel agent before attempting to include Cambodia in your itinerary.)

CLIMATE. The rainy season begins in May and continues to October. From November through April, there is little if any rain, and the days are very hot.

A mosquito repellent may prove a worthwhile addition to your travel accessories for your **Siem Reap** visit. On each of the past several times that I have been there, I have neither seen nor heard any of the pesky little creatures. Chris O'Malley and Matt Dillon, my friends and travel associates, on the other hand, on their most recent visit to **Siem Reap** attracted the pests in droves. Better be prepared just in case!

ELEPHANTS. Have you always wanted to ride an elephant? Well, if so, **Siem Reap** is the place. Your travel man or the hotel concierge can arrange just such an experience for you . . . free! And don't be afraid.

LANGUAGE. Local inhabitants have their own native tongue, but almost all of the hotel and trades people speak French and English.

DURATION OF STAY. Because of **Siem Reap's** heat, I suggest flying there from **Bangkok** in the morning and, as soon as your luggage has been stowed in the *Grand Hotel,* that you continue on to visit *Phnom Bakheng,* **Angkor Thom,** and the other wonders of that incredible area. Return to the hotel for luncheon and take a siesta until 3:30 or 4:00 P.M. You will then have adequate time to visit and admire the glories of *Angkor Wat* to your heart's content in the cool of the late afternoon. Stay for dinner, and the night, and fly on the next morning to **Phnom Penh** or **Saigon.** (When flights again are normal.)

When flights permit, it is a good idea to arrive in **Siem Reap** in the morning from **Bangkok** and fly back again late in the afternoon. There is much to recommend this plan, but it has one serious disadvantage. In order to catch the return plane, one must emerge from luncheon during the hottest period of the day to continue the most important segment of the sightseeing in *Angkor Wat.*

If in **Siem Reap** you don't expect much in the way of creature comforts, you are quite apt to be pleasantly surprised. It's not at all bad, really . . . and the memories will live forever.

Under normal conditions, the *World Travel Service of Bangkok,* one of the best and most efficient travel organizations I have ever known, maintains a resident manager in **Siem Reap,** with headquarters in the *Grand Hotel d'Angkor.* If you are not on a tour and have not made previous arrangements to visit

Siem Reap from **Bangkok,** by all means call at the offices of the *World Travel Service.* They operate splendid one- and two-day tours to **Siem Reap.**

Apart from their other services, the *World Travel Service* airport man at **Siem Reap** will smooth your way rapidly and painlessly through Immigration and Customs; otherwise, the paper work involved in Cambodia can be voluminous and annoying. With *World Travel Service,* you can relax and enjoy yourself. All will go smoothly with a minimum of effort expended on your part.

As of going to press with this edition the political situation in Cambodia precluded visiting this gemlike country. It is hoped that before this volume's ink is dry that the situation will have cleared and the foregoing will all be of practical value.

CHAPTER 10

Hawaii

ON MARCH 12, 1959, the U.S. House of Representatives passed **Hawaii's** *Act of Statehood*, the first step toward making these incomparably beautiful islands the fiftieth and only truly tropical state of the union.

Hawaii, a chain of idyllic Pacific islands of breathtaking beauty, takes its name from the largest of the group. The flower laden, softly scented islands, seven of which are inhabited, are, in order of size: *Hawaii, Maui, Oahu, Kauai, Molokai, Lanai,* and *Niihau.*

CLIMATE. The Islands' mean temperatures range from 71 degrees in winter to 78 degrees in summer, with winter's low temperature seldom dropping below 65 degrees and summer's high almost never exceeding 85 degrees. There are virtually no seasons, no excessive heat even in the lowest altitudes, and no cold weather. This permanently balmy weather can be simply and accurately described as "just perfect." Even in December and January, the nearest approach to a rainy season, one can expect some precipitation only every other day.

Hawaii's almost indescribable scenery is noteworthy for its paint pot panoramic features, unspoiled primeval forests, palm bordered golden sand beaches, massive mysterious mountains,

540

active volcanoes, deep cleft green valleys, plunging waterfalls, grassy plains, magnificent flowers, and shrubs . . . some of which are unique in the world. Hawaii's extravagant natural wonders are so numerous as to become almost commonplace.

HAWAIIAN ATTIRE. My comments relative to shipboard clothing largely apply to daytime garb in Hawaii. You can let your sartorial imagination run wild. The sky is the limit. You name it. Daytime wear is decidedly informal, if not bizarre. Men wear rainbow-hued sport shirts—called Aloha shirts in this corner of the world—and shorts or slacks. The gals wear shorts, bermuda or shorter, halters, blouses, or *muumuus,* or slacks, and slippers, sandals, or bare feet. For dinner, however, be sure to inquire in advance the custom of the dining establishment you have elected to frequent. The *Monarch Room* of the *Royal Hawaiian, Canlis' Charcoal Broiler, Michele's,* and other top flight establishments require that men wear ties and jackets and that women be properly dressed according to standards established in cooler climes. In many other good restaurants, the dinner hour is not at all formal.

The foregoing applies to *Waikiki* where almost all of the visitors to *Oahu* are quartered. In downtown **Honolulu**, businessmen wear jackets, cotton or silk shirts, and neckties to their offices. Should a man appear in a downtown **Honolulu** restaurant for luncheon wearing a sports (Aloha) shirt, he will be served courteously.

On the neighboring islands, the clothing situation is, if possible, more informal than on *Oahu.*

Tours and cruises must play an important part in your first trip to the Islands. It is essential that you place yourself in the hands of a travel expert and follow an intelligent pre-planned program of seeing the Islands. There are scores of excellent, packaged group tours among which will be one or more to fit your needs. Even though you elect to travel independently through the Islands, I urge that you do so under the auspices of a good travel agent or operator with itinerary and reservations all pre-established. This type of plan is called a D.I.T. (Domestic Independent Trip).

If you have followed my sagacious advice, you will have: (1) made all your Hawaiian plans and reservations before leaving home, (2) will be on a good tour having the time of your life, (3) will be gaily traveling on a pre-arranged D.I.T., or (4) will at least have asked your local agent for the name of his representative in **Honolulu**. If through some slip-up you have failed to establish an Hawaiian travel contact, I can recommend *All Travel, Inc.* at 2354 Kalakaua Avenue, Honolulu, Hawaii, phone 934-971. My old friend Sandy Allen, longtime Cleveland, Ohio, resident, is *All Travel's* president and general manager.

In my opinion, one should, at a minimum, take the one day trip around *Oahu* and a six day tour of *Maui* (one night), *Hawaii* (three days and two nights), and *Kauai* (two days and two nights), returning to **Honolulu** on the afternoon of the sixth day. Such a trip, tax included, on the basis of sharing a double room, is about $250, with a single room costing some $40 more. It's worth it.

POPULATION. The ethnic make-up of the polyglot population of the Islands is even more intriguing than their history and natural wonders. Here the allegedly irreconcilable twain of East and West have completely and successfully merged in a manner unknown elsewhere. 650,000 U.S. citizens of various races and creeds work and live side by side in perfect harmony. 13,000 handsome citizens can claim pure Hawaiian descent.

The successful fusion of the Islands' varied racial elements is due chiefly to the natural and unaffected warmhearted hospitality of the Hawaiians themselves, a character trait that has endured since the days of the early Anglo-Saxon settlers.

Hawaii's international racial blending has produced a large group of strikingly attractive people whose good looks are universally admired.

The Hawaiians' innate kindheartedness, unalloyed desire to please, and natural instinct for beauty result from their perfect climate, the ease in obtaining life's necessities, and the natural splendor of their surroundings.

Because of centuries of cross-breeding and the basic unreliability of such intimate statistics, an accurate breakdown of the population by races is impossible. The following carefully compiled list may be considered as a reasonably good approximation of the Islanders' origins, however.

13,000 pure Hawaiians	80,000 Filipinos
110,000 of Hawaiian descent	14,000 Puerto Ricans
170,000 native-born Americans, British, Dutch, Portuguese, French, Irish, Spanish, Scandinavians, and others.	12,000 Koreans
	3,500 of American Negro descent
	40,000 Chinese
	210,000 Japanese

HOTELS AND RESTAURANTS are magnificent and, except at extraordinary peak periods or during special conventions, adequate. Not only does *Waikiki* pride itself on as fine a collection of hostelries as one could dare dream of, but the neighboring islands also boast of superbly sumptuous hotels, inns, and cottages. Hotel dining rooms are universally splendid, and a wide variety of outstanding restaurants invite your patronage.

HAWAII'S HISTORY, prior to the 10th century, is veiled in obscurity, but it is known that during the 10th and 11th centuries relays of skillful Asiatic seafarers sailed great distances over uncharted seas from the south *Pacific* area, reaching the archipelago to find the Islands a pluperfect paradise. The travelers, prepared for every eventuality, arrived in great double-hulled sailing canoes, bringing with them fowl and domestic animals, young fertile women for the propagation of their race, and seeds, not only for all the basic foods indigenous to their native islands but also for fruit and coconut trees.

The early Hawaiians were a warlike lot, being expert swimmers, fond of sport, music, and dancing. The hula, so popular with today's visitors, is of ancient origin, originally performed during the early Hawaiians' sacred rites. The founding

Hawaiians soon established a primitive feudal system of government on a definitive class basis under chiefs and important warriors who fought to retain their ruling positions over the communities of farmers and fishermen.

The settlers had no knowledge of the use of metals which necessitated their utter reliance on wood, stone, bones, and teeth for fashioning weapons and household utensils.

Although fruit, fowl, vegetables, and some meat were available, fishing remained the Islanders' staple source of food supply for many years. Because the mild climate required only the crudest form of shelter, the original domestic architecture was primitive.

Modern Hawaiian history, as far as the outside world is concerned, began on January 18, 1778, when the renowned globe-girdling Captain James Cook in his flag ship *"Resolution"* accompanied by the *"Discovery"* sighted the northern islands of *Kauai, Niihau,* and *Oahu.* He named these the *Sandwich Islands* after Lord Sandwich of the British Admiralty under whose auspices the two-ship expedition sailed. Cook toured the islands briefly, then sailed off to explore the northern *Pacific,* returning eleven months later to discover the remaining archipelago islands.

After coasting about off southern *Hawaii,* Cook's ships dropped anchor in *Kealakekua Bay,* where thousands of natives, who had watched his great ships with amazement, massed to greet him, believing him the reincarnation of Lono, God of All Nature, Welfare, and Peace. Like the Arab tribes of the East, the Hawaiians regarded welcoming strangers as a sacred obligation. All went well at first, the British provisioning their ships, exchanging gifts with the local chiefs, and sailing safely away.

Bad weather, unfortunately, was to prove Cook's undoing. Two weeks after his departure, he was obliged to return to the bay for repairs. The original amicable relations with the friendly natives soon deteriorated and became strained over the theft of some ship's tools and a long-boat which was burned in

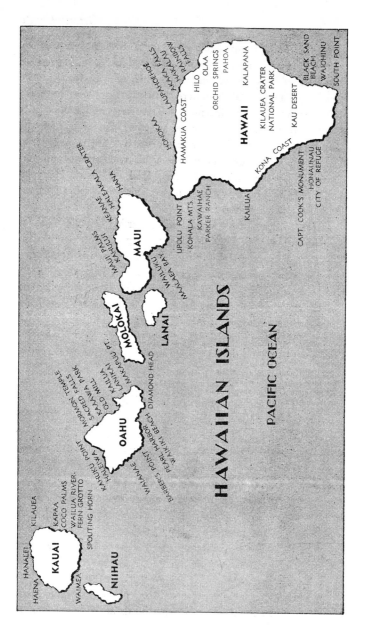

HAWAIIAN ISLANDS

PACIFIC OCEAN

KAUAI
HANALEI
HAENA
KILAJEA
KAPAA
COCO PALMS
WAILUA RIVER·
FERN GROTTO
SPOUTING HORN
WAIMEA

NIIHAU

OAHU
KAHUKU POINT
MORMON TEMPLE
SACRED PARK
KAYAYA FALLS
OLD TIMU
KAILUA
LANIKAI
MAKAPUU PT.
DIAMOND HEAD
WAIKIKI BEACH
PEARL HARBOR
BARBERS POINT
WAIANAE

MOLOKAI

LANAI

MAUI
MAUI PALMS
IAO FALLS
KAHULUI
KEANAE
HALEAKALA CRATER
HANA
WAILUKU
WAILUA BAY
MAHAEA BAY

HAWAII
LAUPAHOEHOE FALLS
AKAKAAU
RAINBOW
FALLS
HONOKAA
HILO
OLAA
ORCHID SPRINGS
PAHOA
HAMAKUA COAST
KALAPANA
KILAUEA CRATER
NATIONAL PARK
KAU DESERT
BLACK SAND
BEACH
WAIOHINU
SOUTH POINT
KONA COAST
UPOLU POINT
KOHALA MTS
KAWAIHAE
PARKER RANCH
KAILUA
CAPT COOK'S MONUMENT
HONAUNAU
CITY OF REFUGE

order to extract the precious nails larcenously. On February 14, 1779, Cook came ashore with an armed party of marines in an attempt to seize the paramount chief and his family to be held as hostages until the pilfered British articles were returned. This show of force incensed the natives; hundreds hastily armed themselves with crude weapons and menaced the sailors who hastily withdrew to the beach to try to re-embark. At this point, Cook, cut off from his companions and surrounded by the furious Islanders, fired his pistol. His men followed suit. During the mad melee which followed, Cook was clubbed and stabbed to death.

Even in death the Islanders still regarded Captain Cook as something very special if no longer as a god. They stripped his flesh from his bones, distributing it among the local chiefs.

The fatal incident was followed by retaliatory action by Cook's crew. The ships bombarded the island severely, and several days of fierce fighting ensued. Eventually the remaining portions of the unfortunate Captain's skeleton were returned to the British for burial at sea.

The HAWAIIAN KINGS. One of Cook's island visitors on board his flag ship was a young warrior named Kamehameha, who was to become the founder of a dynasty that ruled Hawaii for a full century. Kamehameha had been deeply impressed with the wonders of Cook's ships, particularly their powerful steel guns and methods of navigation. This same Kamehameha, to gain a commanding personal position, soon plunged the Islands into internal wars and, in 1795, after the bloody battle of *Nuuanu Pali,* gained the mastery of the island of *Oahu.* By 1810, he ruled over the entire archipelago.

To develop the natural resources of his nation and modernize its methods, the new king called on foreign adventurers and traders for assistance including the Britishers, John Young and George Vancouver. As time went on, American traders were included in the list of the king's advisors.

Kamehameha became an able, wise ruler encouraging trade with foreigners, with the result that goods never before seen by the Hawaiians poured into the Islands. The king, succumbing in 1819, was buried in a secret spot, presumably a cave, which has never been found. His son, Kamehameha II, ruled Hawaii with the aid of the Dowager Queen. Together they put down the vicious practice of the old pagan rites and eliminated the "tabu" system which had been particularly onerous to women who were forbidden many privileges accorded the males. At this crucial point in Hawaiian history, 1820, missionaries arrived in fast clipper ships from New England.

Missionaries, it developed, were to have a profound effect on the Islands, their welfare, religion, and economy. The religious newcomers proved to be even greater traders than teachers of Christianity, some of their descendants being the chief landowners in Hawaii today. The first crusading arrivals were Congregationalists, the Roman Catholics arrived in 1827, with the Mormons coming in 1850.

Kamehameha III succeeded to the throne June 6, 1825, with Kaahumanu acting as regent during his infancy, ruling until 1854. When the American influence was in its ascendancy, one of the missionaries became a cabinet minister and another a royal advisor to the king. From 1843 to 1851, a period of political and national unrest existed during which the great powers—France, Britain, and the United States—jockeyed to gain a firm foothold in the Polynesian kingdom. In July of 1843, Lord Paulet, a British naval captain, actually seized supreme power from the king, which he retained for several months.

King Kamehameha IV, 1854-1863, nephew of Kamehameha III, and his Queen were both descended from the Englishman, John Young. In their reign, British interests again became temporarily dominant, with the Episcopalian Church becoming recognized officially as the state religion. The missionaries had wasted no time in introducing educational centers, building schools, and encouraging persons of all ages to learn English and study Christianity. The indolent but docile and kindly Islanders had at first resented covering their fine physiques in hideous western clothes but eventually adopted the covered up *muumuu* after considerable pressure from the religious whites. Now, more than a century later, this shapeless form of dress has become fashionable among women visitors to Hawaii for both street and beach wear and has even been adopted for casual wear on the mainland.

The Islands' enormous industrial increase necessitated imported labor, the origin of racial integration in the islands. Chinese workers first arrived in 1852, with the Japanese coming in 1868. Between 1878 and 1914, the Portuguese, Spaniards, Russians, Germans, and others descended on the archipelago.

In 1874, King Kalakaua, who ruled until 1891, became the first Hawaiian king to visit the United States which resulted in a treaty further binding American interests to those of Hawaii. Unfortunately, Kalakaua attempted to revive the absolute monarchy with all its old abuses, causing a revolution to break out in 1887, the same year that the United States secured *Pearl Harbor,* which now famous installation was not put to use as a naval base until thirteen years later. The king suffered a crushing defeat, and, though not deposed, his powers became limited and democratic.

In 1891, the King's sister, Liliuokalani, ascended the throne but, like her brother, tried to practice autocratic methods. She succeeded no better than her brother and was deposed, a republic being established under Sanford B. Dole, an American by descent. In August, 1898, the deteriorating political situation necessitated the occupation of *Pearl Harbor* by the United States. We annexed Hawaii later the same year.

The 1900 census put the population of the Islands at 154,000 persons. On July 4, 1960, Hawaii became the fiftieth state of the union with a population of 630,000 citizens.

THE ISLAND OF OAHU

Oahu Island, appropriately named "The Gathering Place," is the third largest of the Hawaiian group with an area of 604 square miles and an ever-growing population of over 500,000

(1961), the majority of whom are centered in and around **Honolulu,** the capital.

The island contains two magnificent massive mountain chains, startling coastal scenery, placid plateaus supporting pineapple and sugar cane plantations, first class roads which snake through virgin forests, great cliffs, and tropical beaches of unparalleled beauty.

The numerous excellent tours arranged around the island cover over one hundred miles and take a full day to complete. Tourists can enjoy a luncheon break at some renowned beauty spot, a great favorite being the *Crouching Lion Inn* at *Kaaawa* whose name is derived from a nearby rock formation towering above the sea in the shape of the king of beasts.

HONOLULU AND ITS ENVIRONS. Hawaii's ever-growing capital metropolis represents the all embracing spirit of the Islands, whose traditional welcome "Aloha" means love, friendship, and good fellowship. **Honolulu** is a city of warm welcome, colorfully displayed on the arrival and departure of ships and planes at the famed harbor and teeming *International Airport.* The waterfront and airport form an exciting backdrop for the gay carnival atmosphere of arrival and departure days, with brilliantly colored floral leis being placed on the shoulders of arriving and departing visitors.

The famous passenger liners are welcomed by diving boys, pretty curvacious girls, and the celebrated *Royal Hawaiian Band.* Intense excitement and friendship prevail on the crowded wharf as the sleek ships dock on brilliant sun-splashed mornings.

Honolulu is a modern city dotted with skyscrapers, magnificent hotels, successful business firms, modern schools, fine churches, bustling docks, a busy air terminal, parks, a noisy *Chinatown,* and one of the world's most famous naval bases.

DIAMOND HEAD. What the *Eiffel Tower* is to **Paris,** the *Coliseum* to **Rome,** the *Rock* to **Gibraltar,** and the *Tower* to **London,** *Diamond Head* is to **Honolulu.** Not only is it a renowned landmark but a statuesque thing of incredible beauty.

An extinct volcano once called *Leahi Hill,* "The Forehead of

Ahi Fish," it was later known as *Diamond Point, Yellow Hill,* and *Conical Mountain.*

Diamond Head, which takes its now accepted name from the shimmering calcite crystals which British sailors once mistook for diamonds, dominates *Waikiki* and **Honolulu** and acts as a splendiferous backdrop for both. Seven hundred sixty-one feet in height, *Diamond Head's* perimeter spreads more than four thousand awesome feet. The mountain, owned by the United States Government, covers close to 750 acres.

Although *Diamond Head* resembles *Gibraltar* only insofar as they are both "trade marks," nonetheless during World War II *Diamond Head* played a role comparable to that of its Mediterranean counterpart, with the mountain literally being hollowed out to serve as a base for gun mounts, command posts, communication headquarters, and mess facilities for large personnel units.

From the sea, from the air, from the beaches, the towns, the mountains or the plateaus, from wherever one views the loveliness of this distinctive mountain, it reflects a shimmering picture of iridescent beauty.

WAIKIKI is the best known, most chic, ultra smart, and at the same time publicly popular beach in the world. The fun, romance, and adventure of the ages is embodied in the mental image of the shimmering white sands of *Waikiki.*

"How beautiful to do nothing . . . and afterwards to rest up" goes a legendary Hawaiian proverb. And I know of no place where doing nothing beautifully can be enjoyed to such a consummate degree of ultimate pleasure as at *Waikiki.*

Though *Waikiki* and *Waikiki Beach* are two separate, though tangent, entities, one invariably thinks first of the beach and surf before the terra firma. To be reasonably logical, I shall discuss the beach first.

There are those who would say that there are finer beaches even in Hawaii than *Waikiki* and many others who would point out the excellence of beaches in other sections of the world. The simple fact of the matter is, however, there is no finer place to loaf, laze, sun, surf, bathe, yacht, catamaran, or canoe than at *Waikiki*. The sands are indeed soft and white, the sun is ubiquitous, and the water never below seventy degrees—frequently comfortably higher. The reef near the shore protects the area from annoying, even dangerous, currents and produces waves on schedule to enhance the pleasure of all forms of surfing.

The crescent shape of *Waikiki* stretches from a point opposite the *Hawaiian Village* near the *Yacht Harbor* past the *Reef Hotel*, the *Halekulani Hotel*, the *Outrigger Canoe Club*, the *Queen's Surf*, the famous *Royal Hawaiian*, the *Moana* and *Surf Rider Hotels*, the *Aquarium*, and the *Natatorium* to the shadows of *Diamond Head*.

"Surfing," "surf board riding," and "surf riding" may be used interchangeably to describe the principal native water sport, performed locally with consummate skill. Few if any of us from the mainland ever attain the lithesome grace of those who have grown up in the Islands and who can stand so easily and confidently while being borne shoreward at speeds up to forty miles per hour. Native surfers can easily stand on their heads, sit down, lie down, carry passengers piggyback, or place a long distance telephone call while riding the breakers.

Surf canoeing is zestful and exhilarating fun which can be enjoyed in outrigger canoes, available for hire reasonably at the intake of one's breath. The outrigger is a well positioned pontoon which serves as a buoyancy strut, like using a three wheel bicycle instead of a two wheeler, but there the simile ends because the outrigger skims the surf with a speed equal to any of the craft propelled by waves. Catamarans are in essence huge, sailed, outrigger canoes.

Surf boards, outrigger canoes, and catamarans are so readily for hire as to make it inexpedient to list the sources here. On the beach just look and you will find a boat anxiously waiting to be hired.

The ALA WAI is a canal which separates *Waikiki* from metropolitan **Honolulu,** other business districts, and residential areas.

KALAKAUA AVENUE is *Waikiki's* main thoroughfare initially running roughly parallel to the Beach, but the farther west one travels, the farther it is from the ocean. On Kalakaua Avenue, one finds an exciting cross section of the world's goods and services, smart, expensive shops and restaurants that are a delight to the senses, as well as inexpensive "five-and-ten" type souvenir shops, popular priced stores, fine coffee shops, and medium priced restaurants. Something is available for everybody in this highly ornamented, richly colored "boulevard of dreams."

The INTERNATIONAL MARKET PLACE, almost across the street from the *Royal Hawaiian Hotel* grounds, is the pulse beat of the heart of *Waikiki,* bounded by the *Waikiki Theater,* the *Princess Kaiulani Hotel,* and catercorner across from the *Moana* and *Surf Rider Hotels,* not far from the *Post Office.* The *International Market Place,* also mentioned in the "Dining Out Chapter," is an agglomeration of shopping outlets for all types of souvenirs, substantial products, an art gallery, and dining center for either hot dogs and hamburgers or in an international epicurean setting with cuisine and prices to match. Here there is music, dancing, and entertainment. Stroll around; you will see someone you know, I am sure, and be intrigued with the international flavor of the atmosphere. The *Visitor's Information Center* (not to be confused with the *Hawaii Visitors Bureau* on the other side of Kalakaua Avenue) will give you any and all information you might require on what's what and who's who in the *International Market Place*.

An exciting drive takes one down Kalakaua Avenue to Ala Moana Boulevard past the *Yacht Club* and the great Honolulu marine *Harbor* to the heart of downtown **Honolulu.**

The UNIVERSITY OF HAWAII, situated in the *Manoa Valley* surrounded by hundreds of varieties of trees, is gaily bedecked with flowers. The passing parade of students is of outstanding interest. I know of no other university setting where one may see such gay attire and such utter informality or such a blending of racial strains in the world. Marine biology and tropical agriculture are featured courses of instruction.

The WAIKIKI AQUARIUM, on Kalakaua Avenue, west of *Kapiolani Park* facing the ocean at *Waikiki,* is a fascinating attraction for visitors, containing a collection of brilliantly hued and varied tropical fish viewed through great glass tanks. The *Aquarium* has a special large pool for seals and aquatic mammals.

KAPIOLANI PARK is a typical tropical park spilling over with gay colors and verdant greenery. At the extremity of Kalakaua Avenue, *Kapiolani Park* is the setting for the Sunday afternoon concerts of the *Royal Hawaiian Band.* The HONOLULU ZOO is a part of *Kapiolani Park.* On Tuesday and Thursday mornings except in the early "winter months," *Kodak Hawaii* puts on colorful authentic hula shows near the *Natatorium* in the park. Here photographers may chronicle the slow, sensuous Hawaiian hula or the rat-a-tat Tahitian hula in specially selected surroundings, grass hut backdrop and all. Individual "shots" of the dancing beauties may be made after the public show. The park has an attractive well used golf driving range.

WAIKIKI SHELL is the summer home of the *Honolulu Symphony Orchestra.*

Honolulu's CHINATOWN is, as one might expect in such a cosmopolitan setting, a substantial one. The Honolulu *Chinese Chamber of Commerce* arranges *Chinatown* shopping tours which include an excellent typical Chinese luncheon.

The ARCHIVES OF HAWAII, within the *Iolani Palace* grounds, contain the most complete and fascinating souvenirs of Hawaii's history including photographs, books, prints, documents, treaties, and relics.

The QUEEN EMMA MUSEUM was the summer home of the famed wife of Kamehameha IV which has now been put in order by the Daughters of Hawaii. It is a show place for the Queen's regal remembrances of Old Hawaii. Among other of the *Museum's* historic settings is the *Edinburgh Room* in which, in 1869, the Duke of Edinburgh was entertained.

SEA LIFE PARK, at Makapuu Point, 13 miles from Waikiki, is the largest exhibit of marine life in the world. Open daily, except Monday, from 10 A.M. to 6 P.M. Performances are held every 45 minutes. Admission $2.30 for adults and $1.15 for children 7 to 12 years of age. Children under 7 free.

The ROYAL MAUSOLEUM, the final resting place of most of the Kamehameha dynasty rulers, is impressive in its simplicity. The *Royal Chapel* is paneled with native wood and tastefully decorated with stained glass windows. The grounds are handsomely adorned with royal palm trees.

BISHOP MUSEUM was founded in 1889 in memoriam to the Hawaiian Princess Bernice Pauahi by her husband, Charles Reed Bishop, a descendant of one of the early missionaries and a member of one of the island's most important families. The building's grim exterior belies its fabulous exhibits chronicling the history of Hawaii from the earliest pagan days to present times. Here articles illustrating every facet of Hawaii's history may be seen including war drums, articles used in human sacrifice, outrigger canoes, and rare examples of venerable Polynesian and Hawaiian antiques. The intricately fashioned feather capes and cloaks seen in the *Museum* were once worn by great chieftains, and some are of the greatest rarity, containing feathers from long extinct birds.

IOLANI PALACE, completed at great cost in 1882, is the only edifice in the United States to contain a genuine royal *Throne Room,* and now houses the Hawaii State Legislature whose Senate and House of Representatives debate in the erstwhile *Dining* and *Throne Rooms* respectively. King Kalakaua and his sister, Queen Liliuokalani, were the only Hawaiian monarchs to live here. The *Palace* façade is semi-early Victorian, the interior being ornate with rich Hawaiian woods, gilded crystal chandeliers from Europe, large mirrors on the walls, and numerous historical paintings in the halls and salons. The Governor makes his office in the Monarch's erstwhile bedroom.

The JUDICIARY BUILDING, facing *Iolani Palace,* was the kingdom's original parliament building. The contemporary courtroom was at one time a chamber of the Island's noblemen. The great gold-leaf statue of King Kamehameha I, heroic in size and imaginative in design, stands before the *Judiciary Building* in full view of *Iolani Palace.*

The CIVIC CENTER includes the *City Hall, Post Office, Library,* and other public buildings.

The GOVERNOR'S RESIDENCE, *Washington Place,* a stone's throw from *Iolani Palace* on Beretania Street, is a colonial style house, the former residence of the last Queen of Hawaii, Liliuokalani, who lived here until her death in 1917.

GOLF COURSES on *Oahu* are good and plentiful. The private courses are *Waialae Country Club, Moanalua Country Club, Oahu Country Club, Mid-Pacific Country Club,* and the *International Country Club.* Except for *Oahu,* visiting golfers are welcomed on the payment of the greens fees. The *Oahu Country Club* is limited to members and their invited guests. Two of the military courses, *Leilehua* and *Wahiawa,* are open to the public. The municipal courses, *Ala Wai, Kahuku,* and *Pali,* are also open to the public.

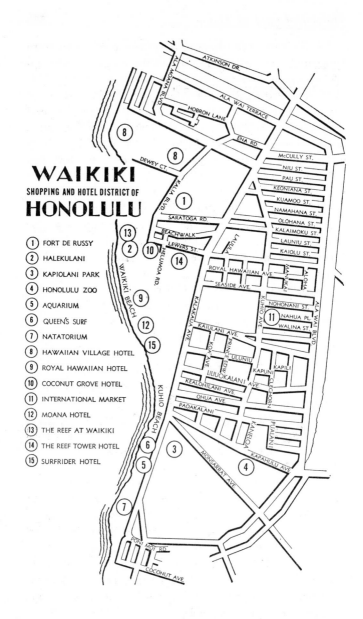

WAIKIKI
SHOPPING AND HOTEL DISTRICT OF
HONOLULU

1. FORT DE RUSSY
2. HALEKULANI
3. KAPIOLANI PARK
4. HONOLULU ZOO
5. AQUARIUM
6. QUEEN'S SURF
7. NATATORIUM
8. HAWAIIAN VILLAGE HOTEL
9. ROYAL HAWAIIAN HOTEL
10. COCONUT GROVE HOTEL
11. INTERNATIONAL MARKET
12. MOANA HOTEL
13. THE REEF AT WAIKIKI
14. THE REEF TOWER HOTEL
15. SURFRIDER HOTEL

The ALOHA TOWER, located near Pier Nine in downtown **Honolulu,** is one of the first landmarks seen by passengers approaching *Honolulu Harbor.* From the *Tower's* tenth floor observation vantage point, a sweeping panorama is obtained.

The INTERNATIONAL AIRPORT, largest and most important airport in the *Pacific* east of **Tokyo,** knows no customs difficulties for U.S. citizens on arriving from or returning to the mainland. Customs formalities take place here for passengers arriving from the Orient, New Zealand, or Australia. Although a less carnival-like atmosphere prevails for arrivals by air, one does see charming Hawaiian girls with leis and kisses to welcome lucky travelers.

The HONOLULU ACADEMY OF ARTS is a modern, artistic building with excellently arranged salons containing displays of early American, British, Renaissance, and Oriental art. The *Academy* is also the cultural scene of plays, concerts, lectures, and musical productions.

PEARL HARBOR provides visitors one of the most interesting and popular excursions on the island. Numerous tour and travel services offer three hour trips daily, by yacht or catamaran, around this historic *Harbor.* The tour costs from $6.66 to $9.99, depending on the vessel selected for the excursion. A free tour is available through the U.S. Navy by advance reservation.

The "run" from *Honolulu Harbor* to *Pearl Harbor* in a smart sightseeing craft is filled with scenic interest. An impressive view of *Waikiki* and *Diamond Head* is obtained astern when leaving **Honolulu,** while the busy *International Airport* is to starboard.

The water circuit of the huge *Harbor* includes *Hickam Field* and *Ford Island.* In *Battleship Row* one sees the hull, largely submerged, of the mighty though tragic *Arizona* in which the bodies of 1,200 men are entombed. Each morning and evening the Stars and Stripes are raised and lowered above the *Arizona's* hulk which remains on the Navy's active duty list in perpetuity. Cameras may not be used while in *Pearl Harbor.*

ROBERT LOUIS STEVENSON'S GRASS HUT, presented

to the author by Princess Kaiulani, is now in the *Manoa Valley* grounds of the celebrated *Waioli Tea Room,* although it was originally elsewhere in **Honolulu** when Stevenson lived in it.

TRIPLER HOSPITAL is acknowledged to be the largest, most up-to-date, and best equipped military hospital in the world. The nine story building has a roof garden, library, gymnasium, swimming pool, shops, large restaurant, and private broadcasting station.

The PACIFIC NATIONAL MEMORIAL CEMETERY in *Punchbowl Crater* overlooking **Honolulu** and *Honolulu Harbor* is one of the most impressive sights I have ever seen. Exquisite good taste has been used in laying out this resting place of our World War II and Korean war dead. It is a moving experience to walk or drive slowly through this sedately impressive war memorial. Ernie Pyle rests here.

TENNENT ART FOUNDATION is snugly located below the *Punchbowl* in a picturesque garden. The hours when the *Art Foundation* is open are infrequent. Should your interest in art be such that you would like to see the best collection of Hawaii's outstanding artist, Madge Tennent, call for an appointment. The collection may be seen at almost any reasonable hour.

PINEAPPLE CANNERY. One really hasn't been to Hawaii if he or she has not visited at least one pineapple plantation and cannery. The local tour companies all regularly operate excursions to the canneries.

A tour around *Oahu* includes the following:

KAILUA AND LANIKAI are now suburban residential sections on *Kailua Bay*'s sandy shores. Once the island's capital, home of mighty monarchs, and the island's most populated area, these communities now see their businessmen set off each morning for **Honolulu** almost fifteen miles away and return to their refreshing shores each evening.

The BLOW HOLE, a natural phenomenon located at *Koko Head* east of *Maunalua Bay,* is caused by the sea being forced through a narrow lava tube. The water's pressure results in a geyser shooting upwards to a considerable height.

MAKAPUU LIGHTHOUSE on *Makapuu Point,* a short distance farther on, is the first beacon seen by air and sea travelers as they approach the island from the Pacific Coast. *Makapuu's* beam extends fifty luminous miles to sea. From here, one's view encompasses *Waimanalo Bay* and *Rabbit Island.*

RABBIT ISLAND, not far from *Makapuu Point,* is known as a modern aviary. The singing of its birds can, under favorable conditions, be heard on *Oahu.* Some say the island took its name from the droves of *lapin* reputed to have lived here at one time. More probably, however, the name comes from the shape of the island, resembling, remotely at least, a bunny.

The CORAL GARDENS OF KANEOHE BAY, enticingly beautiful marine designs of fantastic coral formations on the bottom of the sea, can be seen clearly through the crystal clear water. An excursion to the *Coral Gardens* in a glass bottom boat lasts less than an hour and costs $2.50 for adults and $1.00 for children.

The KANEOHE YACHT CLUB overlooks the bay. The old town of **Kaneohe** is now developing into a smart suburban area.

The MARINE AIR STATION on the estuary was the first landmark for the approaching Japanese aircraft flying toward *Pearl Harbor* on December 7, 1941.

KAHANA BAY, a romantic spot once the site of an original Hawaiian settlement, is commemorated by the islanders in their nostalgic song, "Beautiful Kahana." The early settlers gathered taro and fruit, while their seafood was provided by the bay and fresh water streams.

NUUANU PALI is one of the world's most historic and fabulous beauty spots, a sheer cliff, some seven miles from the capital. This precipitous drop of 1,200 feet was the dramatic setting of the last stand of the hapless defenders of the island against King Kamehameha's army. Here the unfortunate resisting forces, unable to cut their way through the king's forces or escape by other means, were forced over the precipice to be dashed to pieces in the gorge below. The view from *Nuuanu Pali,* one of the world's finest, embraces a vast panorama of colorful mountain vistas and great plains extending to the distant sea.

KAHALUU, a village five miles north of the *Coral Gardens* on *Kaneohe Bay,* contains the *House of Coral* and a Hawaiian perfume "factory." The former is a well stocked gift shop featuring local produce, island curios, antiques, and Polynesian articles, while in the perfume laboratory visitors can examine or purchase exotic Hawaiian scents.

KAAAWA is the site of the already mentioned *Crouching Lion Inn.*

The SACRED FALLS is located in a jagged ravine 2,500 feet deep at *Hauula,* where, at the beginning of the *Kaliuwaa Valley,* sizzling waters plunge over a one hundred foot drop into a pool popular with bathing enthusiasts.

LAIE, some miles further on, is best known for the *Mormon Center* surrounding its lavish *Temple* set amidst gorgeously colored landscaped gardens and approached by a series of spectacularly terraced pools. Guides are available to conduct visitors through the grounds.

The industrious settlement is largely made up of descendants of the original hardy Salt Lake City missionaries who were among the first settlers to promote sugar plantations.

The *Polynesian Cultural Center,* located adjacent to the *Mormon Temple,* includes six authentic Polynesian villages inhabited by the peoples of Tonga, Tahiti, Samoa, Fiji, and Hawaii, and New Zealand Maoris. Open from 9 A.M. to 5 P.M. daily.

Laie is also noted for its monthly fishing festival featuring hula dancing and a colorful succulent feast.

WAIMEA VALLEY penetrates the *Koolau Range* some two and one-half miles inland. This section is known for its religious historical background, having been the site of countless ancient temples.

WAIALUA PLANTATION, off the *Kamehameha Highway*

above **Haleiwa,** is remarkable for its efficiency of operation and the happy economic state enjoyed by the workers who are in virtual partnership with the management. The plantation virtually climbs up the mountainsides, its brightly colored fruit adding a showy mass to the local setting.

WAHIAWA, a city built on the plateau of an extinct volcano between the *Waianae* and *Koolau* mountain ranges, is the residential section of the area's pineapple plantation workers and the shopping center and gathering place for those living in and around the nearby *Schofield Barracks.*

MOUNT KAALA, 4,000 feet, highest peak in the *Waianae Mountains,* towers over this area.

KAENA POINT lighthouse is on the extreme westerly cape of *Oahu,* which lonely area is inhabited chiefly by fishermen of Japanese descent. It was here that the mythical Maui made his unsuccessful efforts to unite, physically, the islands of *Oahu* and *Maui.*

THE ISLAND OF HAWAII

Hawaii, the Orchid Island, is the largest of the Hawaiian chain with an area of 4,030 square miles, being 92 miles in length from its extreme northerly point, *Upolu,* to the southerly tip of *South Point,* and 75 miles across from *Keahole Light* south of *Makole Point* to *Kumukahi Point* to the east. The most easterly and southerly of the group, *Hawaii,* which is adorned with millions of blooms of more than 20,000 different varieties and species of orchids, is almost twice as large as the combined area of all the other islands.

Hawaii is a paradise for bathing by day or moonlight, skin diving, deep sea fishing, hiking, and picturesque motoring.

Pele, Goddess of Fire, is paramount in the lives and minds of all of the Islanders, particularly Hawaiians who, understandably, still half believe in her actual physical presence.

Hawaii need not rely exclusively on the wonders of her mountains and scenic masterpieces because the island also abounds in historic associations, rich cattle ranches, and abundant sugar plantations.

HILO, the island's capital, seat of the local government, and center of all business and shopping, is the only town on the island of *Hawaii* with a population as numerous as 20,000, being a small scale modern city with fine hotels, restaurants, shops, churches, an important seaport, and a busy airport linking it with daily flights to the other islands.

Hilo, meaning "New Moon," the shape of the city facing the scenic crescent shaped bay, has suffered two disastrous tidal waves, the first in 1946, followed by another in 1960. On both occasions extensive property damage was accompanied by considerable loss of life. Though few evidences of the most recent tragedy are visible today, rebuilding is not yet complete. **Hilo** is known for its parks and gardens richly ornamented with orchids. The most popular of these parks was LILIUOKALANI (not yet fully repaired), a lovely Japanese garden opposite *Coconut Island,* while KONG'S FLORAL GARDENS are most attractive, with Oriental bridges, pools, a Japanese tea house, and a profusion of orchids which can be purchased by visitors. This island's capital, the world center for the orchid business, has two golf links, a municipal course and the *Hilo Country Club* outside the city.

COMMERCIAL GARDENS, well worth visiting, include *Mauna Loa Orchids* on Kamehameha Avenue, *Jewel Box Gardens* on Manona Street, *Oda'a Flowers* on Hinano Street, and *Hirose Nursery* on Josephine Lane.

Hilo's fully sheltered harbor has excellent facilities for handling all types of cargo with the emphasis being on the rapid and efficient loading of bulk sugar.

The NAHA STONE on the lawn of the *Hilo County Library* is said to have been the criterion for aspirants to the throne. To lift it was to qualify for the monarchy. Kamehameha as a young man did manhandle it easily. Try it!

The RAINBOW FALLS one mile due north of the city afford a photogenic excursion from **Hilo.** The *Falls,* which should be visited during the morning light when the sun reflected from the vapor rising from the *Falls* assures a lovely display of changing rainbow hues, are formed by the *Wailuku River* cascading over a high volcanic ledge.

The HAWAII NATIONAL PARK area which reaches from the sea to the top of *Mauna Loa* includes an extraordinary volcanic region with ancient lava deserts, gigantic fern forests, plunging waterfalls, green valleys, magnificent flowers, and glowing tropical scenery. The drive from **Hilo** to the rim of *Kilauea Crater* in the *Park* is 35 miles.

The *Park,* just over 300 square miles in area, is maintained by the *National Park Service,* its volcanic research being conducted by the U.S. Geological Survey.

THE VOLCANO HOUSE AND CRATERS. One has scarcely left the tropical forests when *Volcano House Hotel,* built on the rim of *Kilauea Crater* about 4,000 feet above sea level, is reached. From here there are magnificent views of the crater and *Mauna Loa,* whose gradual slope belies its towering high altitude of 13,680 feet. Tropical life is intermingled with the unique lava tubes remaining from former eruptions. The tubes were caused by the cooling condensation of the glowing lava while flowing down the mountainsides. The streaming masses eventually solidified into hollow tubes large enough for visitors to enter. Some of these tubes extend down the mountainside for many miles, the longest and most spectacular being the *Thurston Tube* snaking down twenty miles before terminating in cultivated land. *Thurston's* entrance is covered with tropical vegetation.

Visitors need not worry about dangers from the volcano when staying at *Volcano House.* This comfortable hotel is promptly closed if the *National Park* experts, constantly watching the Fire Goddess' habits, detect any signs of possible serious eruptions.

Among the local marvels is a walk from *Volcano House* to the BIRD PARK, an extraordinary natural aviary which consists of an oasis in the midst of lava flows where the birds, whose singing is distinctly heard, feed on plants and tall trees bearing the lehua blossoms. Be *sure* to wear stout shoes if you decide to take the rugged hike from *Volcano House.*

At LITTLE KILAUEA, steam still issues from vents in the ground. Here one can see the ponderous course of the lava flow of the 1959 eruptions.

HALEMAUMAU *(The Fire Pit)* is the most fabulous spectacle in the *Park* and one of the world's few active volcano craters that can be approached in absolute safety. The crater, over 3,000 feet in diameter, is about 800 feet deep, which depth varies according to the condition of the seething, belching, burping cauldron below.

The MUSEUM, small but interesting, near *Volcano House* includes a collection of volcanic exhibits.

Color movies awesomely depicting former eruptions are shown daily at 9:30 A.M. and 1:30 P.M. in the theater of the *Volcanic Observatory.*

MOUNTS MAUNA LOA and KILAUEA, the sputtering, smoking, active colorful volcanoes, are *Hawaii*'s most spectacular showpieces. *Mauna Loa,* 13,680 feet, is the world's most effusive erupter.

MAUNA KEA, a dormant volcano whose crest is 13,800 feet above sea level, is the highest land mass on earth, six spectacular miles from giddy top to crustaceous sea bottom, topping *Mount Everest* by more than two thousand feet. *Mauna Kea,* like the active *Mauna Loa,* is crowned with snow during the winter months.

Recent notable eruptions of the two active volcanoes are as follows: *Mauna Loa:* 1935, during which United States military aircraft were obliged to drop bombs to divert the deadly flow of lava from engulfing the capital city of **Hilo,** and 1942, when the aerial action had to be repeated. Later eruptions took place in 1949 and 1950.

Kilauea: This lower crater of the main mass is particularly active, churning violently and puffing ominously most of the time. The years 1952, 1954, and 1955 witnessed its red hot outpourings, with the latest eruptions taking place on November 15, 1959 and January 13, 1960, the latter of which inflicted great damage to crops and houses; but, fortunately, there were no lives lost, the local inhabitants having had plenty of warning. These fantastic pyrotechnic spectacles were witnessed by thousands of tourists, some of whom even flew over the craters as the deadly barrage of molten rock and glowing lava burst forth.

In 1790 Chief Keoua, King Kamehameha I's most powerful enemy, and his army were caught by a violent eruption about five miles south of *Kilauea Crater* where thousands of his men were trapped in the burning lava. The footprints of the fleeing troops can be clearly seen in the now hardened lava.

TOURING THE ISLAND

Conducted tours of *Hawaii,* like on the other islands, are excellent. Tours begin either on arrival at *Kailua Airport* on the historic *Kona Coast,* which I believe is preferable, or at **Hilo.**

The KONA DISTRICT on the island's south shore is known for the production of its celebrated coffee, the excellence of its deep sea fishing, and for its connections with the island's pagan days.

The following are the *Kona Coast* high spots:

KAILUA-KONA, in the shadow of *Mount Hualalai,* one of *Hawaii's* historic settings, was the seat of the great King Kamehameha I's government. Kamehameha, born on *Hawaii* in the village of **Kohala,** succumbed in **Kailua.** The deluxe *King Kamehameha Hotel* is built on the site of his palace, some remains of which can still be seen. An ancient pagan temple near **Kailua,** over two hundred years old when Kamehameha rebuilt it, is an interesting echo of the Great One's day. A palace built at **Kailua** by the famous Hawaiian nobleman, John Adams, when Governor of *Hawaii Island* over a hundred years ago, became the seaside residence of the gay monarch, Kalakaua (1874-1891), who somewhat resembled England's

"Merry Monarch," Charles II. Here he wined, dined, and danced and was entertained by a veritable bevy of pretty women. The building is now a museum containing old articles once belonging to Hawaiian kings and queens including Queen Kapiolani's peacock-feathered hat in which she appeared at Queen Victoria's court at Windsor. The pagan pieces found in the museum include instruments for killing enemies by "wishing" them to death, a favorite implement of the witch doctors.

CITY OF REFUGE, about twenty miles from **Kailua,** was a legendary place of sanctuary for those persons fleeing their enemies, wordly problems, or their furious chiefs. This haven, also an ancient sanctuary for violators of "tabu," includes the remains of two temples in a sylvan park-like setting close to the fishing village of HONAUNAU. The temple area contains massive stone walls and altars for pagan rites. Little is known about the *City of Refuge,* but guides relish showing visitors a "sacrificial altar rock" which they avow was used for human sacrifices, which, if genuine, would cast doubt on the spot having been a reliable haven, though it could have been that some of the refugees' crimes were too heinous even for the **Kailua** priesthood to stomach!

UPPER HONAUNAU is the site of one of the island's earliest Catholic churches, bizarrely decorated with inaccurately depicted Biblical murals.

KEALAKEKUA, on the bay fourteen miles south of **Kailua,** was the dramatic and historic spot where Captain Cook lost his life at the hands of the angry natives. On every hand one sees relics of the explorer including *Captain Cook's Monument,* surrounded by palm trees, and a cannon from his flagship, both of which overlook the spot where he was struck down.

A fishing village, a few miles north along the coast on *Kealakekua Bay,* was the birthplace of King Kamehameha III (1833-1854). The *"Royal Slide,"* where the king indulged in a popular and dangerous type of tobogganing, is in the hills above the village. In this local version of the sport, tobogganers coast precariously on a great leaf called a *ti* rather than on a western style sled.

Deep sea fishing is good off all the islands, but particularly so off the *Kona Coast* whose waters teem with fighting game fish such as giant marlin, weighing from 500 to well over 800 pounds, white albacore of some 250 to 350 pounds, mackerel of king-size dimensions, and the deadly barracuda. Information regarding this sport may be secured at the *Kona Inn,* headquarters of the fishing business, where gear and tackle will be provided. Modern well equipped cabin cruisers are available for hire from the *Kailua-Kona* wharf.

Kailua to Hilo via the Hamakua Coast

Having explored the *Kona Coast,* the tours which begin their itinerary in **Kona** proceed on the second day over attractively situated Highway 19 to **Hilo** via **Waimea** (**Kamuela**) and the beautiful *Hamakua Coast* (tours starting in **Hilo** merely reverse the days). The tour route skirts the base of the 8,269-foot extinct volcano *Mount Hualalai,* then continues to the slopes of *Mauna Kea* to **Waimea** and the famous *Parker Cattle Ranch. Mauna Kea* is a sportsman's happy hunting ground, with hiking, climbing, shooting, and skiing. There is a variety of birds and game for the sportsman's gun including

pheasant, quail, partridge, wild sheep, boars, and goats. Hunters' base camps are located at levels between 8,000 and 9,000
feet above sea level.

WAIMEA, JOHN PARKER, and the PARKER RANCH.
The *Parker Ranch,* said to be the second largest in the U.S.A.,
covers an area of some 262,000 acres and is stocked with huge
herds of cattle, horses, and sheep. The ranch is the success story
(so far overlooked by Hollywood) of a fabulous American,
John Parker, who in his youth escaped from a British trading
vessel during the Anglo-American War of 1812. His ship was
lying close enough off the *Kohala Peninsula* to enable Parker
to swim ashore. In those days, white men were a much admired
rarity among the Hawaiians, and Parker made friends with the
great Kamehameha I, obtaining from the king the rights to
trade and breed cattle over the entire *Waimea Plateau* area. He
founded his vast herds of white-faced cattle from animals originally brought to the Islands by Captain George Vancouver in
1792. The present owner is a descendant of John Parker, who
married a highborn Hawaiian girl while on a visit to the island of *Maui.*

This countryside reminds one of the American West, with
Hawaiian cowboys driving cattle and ten-gallon-hatted horse-
men riding about on the ranching business. The Hawaiians
were originally initiated into horsemanship, roping, and corral-
ling cattle in 1831 by Mexican cowboys of Spanish descent imported for this purpose.

From **Waimea** one follows Highway 25 to the *Kohala Peninsula* whose history is associated with the great King Kamehameha who was born at **Kohala** near the scenic *Pololu Valley.*
Here one sees the original of the heroic statue of Kamehameha
which was lost at sea off the *Falkland Islands* while being
shipped from Italy and was recovered two years later. A duplicate of this statue stands in **Honolulu** before the *Judiciary
Building,* facing the *Iolani Palace.*

The *Pololu Valley* once was the site of old Hawaiian temples, the ruins of which may still be seen. To visit the scenic

splendors of the *Valley,* the descent must be made on mule back, arrangements for which may be made at the *Waimea Ranch Hotel.* The *Valley* scenery is truly stupendous, with the road passing over and under great cliffs towering above and looming beneath the highway.

The final fifty miles to **Hilo** is along the scenic *Hamakua Coast.*

The AKAKA FALLS, not far from the highway, provide the most magnificent water display on the island, plunging giddily over a 425 foot vertical drop in a cloud of mist and spray. Nearby one finds a parking place for cars and a lookout from which to view the falls, the neighboring tropical plant life, flowering shrubs, and rich brilliant vegetation.

The BLACK SAND BEACHES OF KALAPANA AND KAIMU are the best known, though not *Hawaii*'s only, black beaches formed by volcanic ash of past centuries. The ebony sands, soft and powdery to the touch, have a beautiful backdrop of green-leafed trees, giant ferns, and tropical foliage. The contrasting white crested waves thundering onto the midnight dark sands with the azure blue sea beyond present an unforgettable picture. Although swimming in this area is considered dangerous, experts enjoy it. The *Kalapana-Kaimu* area is linked to **Hilo,** 37 miles away, by an excellent highway.

THE ISLAND OF MAUI

MAUI, between *Hawaii* and *Molokai,* known as the "Valley Island," is second largest of the Hawaiian Islands. Twenty-five miles from north to south and thirty-eight from east to west, it has an area of 728 square miles with a population of about 40,000. The principal town, **Wailuku** (population 8,000), is seventy miles distant from **Honolulu.** The island is composed of two mountainous areas of volatile volcanic origin divided by an isthmus seven miles wide.

Maui is an island of scenic serenity, steeped in mythology, with an exciting romantic and historical background. Mythology explains the island's birth this way: mythical half-god Maui,

Hawaii's first fire maker and most ardent fisherman of all time, netted the island from the sea depths, then pushed up the sky to make room for the trees and mountains. Not yet satisfied, he seized the sun and held it captive until it had agreed to slow down its pace in the heavens, thus enabling him to have longer hours for his favorite sport of fishing.

Maui has the largest dormant volcanic crater in the world, *Mount Haleakala,* "House of the Sun," which thrusts its craggy summit 10,032 feet into the crystal clear blue *Pacific* skies.

The island scenery is magnificent, with spectacular coastlines, soft sand beaches, rugged cliffs, and deep sylvan valleys bursting with tropical foliage and trees. *Maui* is popular with hikers, bathers, skin divers, horseback riders, and picnickers. It is easily accessible from **Honolulu** by plane in forty minutes, with thirteen flights per day operating to *Kahului Airport.* There is also a daily flight from **Honolulu** to **Hana** with a short stop at **Kahului.** *Maui* is included in almost all of the inter-island tours.

TOURING THE ISLAND

WAILUKU, the island's tiny capital with a population of about 7,000, lies on the *Isthmus* near the port city of **Kahului** at the head of the *Iao Valley* and is the hub from which good roads emanate in all directions, an excellent center from which to tour the island. It is a cheerful town in which the four star attraction to visitors is the *Museum* containing historical objects of old Hawaiian civilization from very early times to the beginning of the 19th century, native wood furniture, and ancient tribal drawings known as *"petroglyphs."*

IAO VALLEY, one of the most popular and interesting spots on the island, was the scene of the disastrous 1790 defeat of the Mauian warriors who, trapped in the narrow valley by Kamehameha, were slaughtered almost en masse, their bloody bodies damming the stream.

KEPANIWAI ("The Damming of the Waters") PUBLIC PARK, close to the valley, has as its most spectacular object

the freak volcanic monolith, the *Iao Needle,* rising almost vertically 1,200 feet above the valley's plush floor. By moonlight, at sunset or sunrise, the great rock is an unforgettable sight.

KAHULUI, *Maui*'s main sea and air port with a population of 4,500, has become famous as the most up-to-date example of model town planning in the Islands where attractive houses with colorful gardens have been made available to householders at comparatively low costs. The residential area is already graced with more than 1,000 modern homes, while as many more are being planned and built. The patio shopping center is decorated with a central fountain. The lanai shops are outstanding examples of architectural beauty. The Hawaiian Commercial Sugar Company, which works the largest cane sugar plantation in the United States, has financed the housing scheme. The Company's headquarters, open to inspection, are located two miles southeast of town, while the island's principal airport is two miles due east of **Kahului.** There are excellent hotels, two of which, the *Maui Palms* and the *Maui Hukilau,* both opened in 1960, are luxurious.

The showy drive from **Kahului** or **Wailuku** to **Lahaina** has a plethora of rugged scenic effects. Fine views of the mountains are enjoyed as one travels due south across the neck of the *Isthmus* to **Maalaea,** an attractive fishing village on a placid bay across which can be seen the tiny islands of *Lanai* and *Kahoolawe.*

From *Maalaea Bay,* the highway, carved out of the great cliffs, skirts the thundering sea until it reaches lovely **Lahaina.**

LAHAINA, Hawaii's ancient capital, reeks with romance. Located on *Maui's* leeward southwest coast, **Lahaina** is snugly sheltered from the trade winds and in its roadstead once anchored the Pacific's greatest whaling fleet and units of the United States fleet. The first Hawaiian missionaries arrived in **Lahaina** in 1831, and although it is today a quiet little colonial-type town, **Lahaina** was once the most revered spot on the Islands, a hallowed royal burial ground. In *Wainee Cemetery* rest Queens Keopuolani and Kalakua, wives of Kamehameha I; King Kaumualii, the last of the Kauaian kings; high officials; and powerful chiefs. Queen Keopuolani was the mother of two kings, Kamehameha II and Kamehameha III.

The town's most exciting period followed the removal of the capital to **Honolulu** when, from 1840 to 1865, it became the center of the Pacific whaling industry, its harbor a forest of masts from hundreds of ships bobbing at anchor. Women swarmed the port, and night found the streets and bars ringing with the raucous shouts and lusty songs of sailors, fights and brawls springing up everywhere. The old *Pioneer Inn* was the favorite haunt of whaling skippers and crews enjoying the hectic pleasures of life ashore.

The fervent Boston missionaries arrived on the island in 1831 and soon thereafter were to become the natural enemies of the free living, fun loving whaling community. The missionaries' war against the violence and immorality of the whalers has been dramatically portrayed in James Michener's incomparable novel, *Hawaii.* The old *Pioneer Inn,* overlooking the once crowded roadstead, still stands as a reminder of those lusty days, being a contemporary show place of the town.

LAHAINALUNA SCHOOL is one of the oldest active schools in the U.S.A., having been established by the missionaries in 1831.

The giant banyan tree, the largest in Hawaii, has stood in the center of the town more than one hundred years. It spreads almost an acre of shade.

HALEAKALA CRATER, 10,032 feet above sea level, is one of nature's marvels and *Maui*'s principal point of tourist interest. The extinct volcano's rim, 22 miles in circumference, towers almost 3,000 feet over its fabulous floor and some 10,000 feet above the so-called "Bottomless Pit" formed by a volcanic tube or shaft, thrusting downward to an as yet unexplored point near sea level. The crater's floor is over seven miles long and two miles wide, containing a lake, desert, other smaller craters, forests, meadows, and fruit bushes.

The HALEAKALA NATIONAL PARK, included until 1961 as part of the *Hawaii National Park*, is readily reached by an excellent road, bordered by verdant sugar cane plantations, from **Wailuku, Kahului, Hana, Keanae,** and **Paia.** En route to the summit, the road from the west passes through the *Kula* region, where, at an altitude a mile above sea level, one finds the secluded tiny rustic *Kula Lodge.* Here in an idyllic setting one may enjoy a cool drink, dine comfortably, or find lodging for the night.

The HALEAKALA CRATER OBSERVATORY, overlooking the many-hued abyss below, is forty miles by road from **Wailuku,** 22 miles as the albatross flies. Unless you are a first cousin to a mountain goat or the ultra rugged outdoor type, I would suggest that you absorb the eerie beauty of this nature's monster by field glass or telescope from the comfort and safety of the *Observatory,* from which vantage lookout one's vision also encompasses the panoramic splendor of all of *Maui* and, under favorable conditions, the neighboring islands as well. The view of nearby *Koolau Gap* is particularly worthwhile.

A not inconsiderable role in the gay color ensemble of the crater is played by the rare silversword plants which are to be seen everywhere. These natural phenomena, whose sword-like leaves resemble porcupine quills, shimmer in the sunlight like freshly polished silver. The blossoms, which bloom but once, are brilliant scarlet and soft buffed brown.

At the *Silversword Inn,* 6,800 feet above sea level, or nearby *Haleakala Lodge,* run by the *Park Service* and headquarters of the Rangers, one can make arrangements for a one-, two-, or three-day guided tour to the floor of the crater either in the saddle or on foot, with overnight stops being made in comfortable camps maintained by the *Park Service.*

HANA AND ITS ENVIRONS. Even in Hawaii where natural beauty is considered commonplace, **Hana** and its surroundings are outstandingly lovely. The 55 miles of scenic highway from **Wailuku** skirts past colorful coastal scenery indented with tiny, picturesque fishing settlements unchanged by time. The road twists and winds through no less than 33 dense, tropically foliaged, deep ravines, past misting waterfalls cascading over sheer drops and through leafy forests. Here one sees the *ape* plant whose leaves are larger than a man.

For those whose time is limited, **Hana** can be reached by plane in only twenty minutes from **Kahului. Hana's** airport is located on the coast between **Hana** and **Hamoa** close to the two most perfect bathing beaches on *Maui.*

HANA, *Hana Valley,* and the surrounding area, once a sugar plantation and now a cattle ranch and hotel resort property owned and operated by Mr. Paul Fagan, who is largely responsible for the economic well-being of the native populace, are delightful in every way. Fagan's ultra chic and luxurious, though informal, *Hotel Hana Maui* attracts discriminating, well-heeled guests who enjoy riding, hunting, fishing, surf pleasures, native entertainment, picnicking at its finest, plates for true gourmets, impeccable service, and personal attention par excellence. The hotel's opulent public rooms, magnificently appointed sleeping rooms, smart cottages, and vast ranch combine to make this one of the world's most desirable resort areas. Surf swimming is at its most rugged best at the nearby soft sand beach of **Hamoa,** while the gentle harbor-side beach offers a cordial invitation to the neophytes of the surf.

In addition to its superb setting, **Hana** has hallowed historical associations, being the site of a fierce battle between the great Napoleon-like King and the hapless defenders of *Maui.* Vestiges of the fray can still be found.

HANA BAY, where Captain Cook anchored in 1778, has important religious connotations. Helio, an Hawaiian converted to Roman Catholicism, became a celebrated preacher in 1850 and is buried close to the shore at **Wailua** on the slopes of *Haleakala.*

It is said that Kamehameha's hulking favorite and adored queen, Kaahumanu, was born in an obscure cave near here.

The WAILUA FALLS cascade from high on *Haleakala's* slopes, while the *Seven Sacred Pools of Kipahulu* flow into one another at different levels to form a favorite basin for fresh water bathers.

Hana remains relatively aloof from outside unrest and influences and is populated with a higher percentage of pure Hawaiian stock than any other place on *Maui.* **Hana's** climate rivals that of *Kula's* slopes, being blessed with year-round temperatures between seventy and eighty degrees.

KAANAPALI area, on *Maui's* northwesterly tip, has blossomed into one of the island's most glorious resort areas. The sea here is at its most scintillating aquamarine best, with beaches vast and white. There are water sports galore, fishing, and golfing. The luxurious *Sheraton-Maui* and *Royal Lahaina* hotels have already captured an enthusiastic coterie of followers. The *Kaanapali Beach* hotel is expected to be equally popular.

THE ISLAND OF KAUAI

KAUAI, the "Garden Isle," is a 555 square mile tropical arborium, whose vegetation, trees, flowers, and other natural attractions have been fully exploited by the film industry in the famous "Sadie Thompson," "Pagan Love Song," "South Pacific," and other Technicolor epics produced on the island.

Kauai, most northerly of the Hawaiian Islands and adjacent to *Oahu,* is fourth in size among the group, circular in shape with a diameter of 33 miles and a population of 30,000 persons. Here a legend is told similar to Erin's pixie tales. *Kauai's* Menehunes, mythical "Little People," are much like their Irish counterparts. According to Hawaiian lore, the island's first inhabitants are said to have been a mere two feet high. The Menehunes carried out prodigious building operations such as erecting stone walls, excavating great ponds for fish, and creating lasting works, many of which are still in evidence today. Archaeologists have pointed out perspicaciously that Hawaiians, who followed the Menehunes chronologically, for one reason or another never learned to build with stones or even to cut them properly for construction. The nebulous Menehunes, like the prodigious pixies, carried out all of their work at night, for, or so the legends tell us, unless they finished their ambitious tasks before daylight, they themselves would turn to stone.

To unromantic non-believers, there is an obvious explanation which places these busy builders in the realm of reality; namely, the very early Polynesian settlers were indeed wee people in contrast to the statuesque, magnificently built and handsome Hawaiian Polynesians who eventually invaded *Kauai* and whose descendants claim the ancestry of highborn Tahitians, which family tree stepladder is upheld by the definite similarity of the two languages.

Geologically, the island is a huge extinct volcano cast up when the main archipelago mass was borne from the ocean depths. All of the island's settlements are on, or not far from, the ocean's shores. The mountains culminate in the heights of *Mounts Waialeale* and *Kawaikini* at 5,080 and 5,170 feet altitude respectively. *Kauai* owes its splendid foliage and ultra green aspect to the watery swampland between the *Waialeale* and *Kawaikini* peaks which humid area is annotated on many maps as the "wettest spot on earth," with the average rainfall being almost forty inches per month. This overly fulsome precipitation permits *Kauai* to boast of being the only Hawaiian island indented with rivers of sufficient size and depth to be considered navigable.

Historically, the islanders proudly and accurately claim to have remained unconquered by the Great King, though it took a wily ruse to bring about this happy situation. In 1810, *Kauai's* last ruler, the wise King Kaumualii, cleverly avoided the inevitable deadly defeat by acknowledging himself a vassal of Kamehameha, even though one invasion attempt had already failed thanks to a violent storm having scattered Kamehameha's canoes.

Kaumualii was almost as profound a character as was his overlord, being beloved by his people and popular with all who met or traded with him, including the Great King. On the latter's death, Kamehameha's son had the audacity to kidnap Kaumualii and carry him off to *Oahu* where Kamehameha's redoubtable widow, and erstwhile favorite queen, proceeded to marry both the hostage and his son. Wow!

The island's industries, in order of economic importance, are sugar, pineapples, and rice, with *Kauai's* first successful sugar plantation having been inaugurated at **Koloa** by an American named Ladd in 1835. He started with only twelve acres of land. The twenty-seven contemporary sugar plantations spread, octopus-like, over more than 220,000 acres.

Among *Kauai's* principal points of interest are:

LIHUE, the island's pleasant little capital with a population of 4,000 inhabitants, containing typical local civic buildings, a main street, bank, hospital, and several churches, but chiefly notable for having one of the largest producing sugar mills in Hawaii. The island's airport is on the edge of **Lihue.**

NAWILIWILI HARBOR, the busy port of **Lihue,** is capable of handling large vessels. Nearby are *Kalapaki Beach* and the luxurious *Kauai Surf Hotel.*

MENEHUNE FISH POND. This sensational artificial pond, one mile from **Lihue,** the work of the legendary Menehunes, is as mysterious as it is fascinating. The pond's four foot thick walls are built of hewn stone, accurately laid to a point about six feet above the pond's surface. Legend relates that the "Little People" massed shoulder to shoulder in a great human chain stretching miles over hill and dale to a quarry where other Menehunes excavated and prepared the stones which were passed from hand to hand until they reached the pond where the masons built the dam. The Menehunes worked like fury since there was absolutely no time to waste if they were to beat the dawn ossification deadline. The work was completed in time, but, alas, the "Little People's" Queen and her brother tarried too long one night admiring the finished masterpieces, and the first rays of the roseate dawn caused the royal brother and sister to turn to stone. Today two large regal-looking stones overlook the pond.

KOLOA, a famous old town southwest of **Lihue,** was, as previously pointed out, the site of the first sugar mill on the island. On the lawn outside of the plantation office, one can see a small German locomotive which dates from 1881, the first engine in Hawaii to have replaced oxen drawn transportation. Roman Catholic missionaries arrived in **Koloa** in 1841 and built their church, which still stands, in 1856.

SPOUTING HORN consists of a seaside hole in a lava tube which periodically jettisons a column of spray, sometimes shooting up over 100 feet in height, the varying altitudes of the salt water geysers being governed by the constantly changing tidal forces. After each eruption, watchers hear a deep sighing sound which in reality is a natural phenomenon produced, as a hollow echo, by air being forced through another hole. The Hawaiians insist, however, that the sound is from a dragon who was trapped eons ago and has remained there ever since.

The nearby attractive *Polynesia Inn,* with cottage apartments, faces the beach.

HANAPEPE, or BABY-MAKING, VALLEY is a velvety green tropical indentation set off by red cliffs which derived its nickname in ancient times from the fact that Hawaiian women, hitherto unable to produce children, visited the valley with amazingly successful results, or so it is said! From here fine views of the great *Waimea Canyon,* nine miles to the northwest, can be obtained.

WAIMEA, an ultramodern plantation town overlooking *Waimea Canyon* on the river of the same name, was the scene of Captain Cook's first landing in Hawaii on January 15, 1778. Early in the 19th century, the then flourishing sandalwood export trade was centered in **Waimea,** but the industry was short-lived. Avaricious traders and chiefs "on the make" leveled the island's sandalwood trees, making no provisions for their reforestation.

I have mentioned in passing the kidnapping of King Kaumualii. This dastardly act took place in 1821 while Kaumualii was visiting his overlord, Kamehameha II, in the latter's royal yacht which was anchored in *Waimea Bay.* Kamehameha II arranged the kidnapping, set the trap, and in due course sent the King and his son back to *Oahu* as hostages, where, it will be remembered, the redoubtable dowager Queen Kaahumanu, who weighed in at three hundred pounds, married both father and son.

The *Waimea Foreign Church,* completed in 1854, was sponsored by the abducted King's wife, Queen Kapule, another three hundred pound beauty. Loss of her husband drove this lady into becoming a fanatical Christian.

Waimea was another home of the legendary Menehunes.

WAIMEA CANYON is a curious natural cleft known as the "Grand Canyon of the Pacific" and is usually the fitting dramatic finale for the first day of a tour of the island.

The view of the Canyon from the *Puu Ka Pele Lookout* bedazzles the sightseer as he looks down and across the great mile wide gorge splashed with magnificent shifting colors which change according to the time of day. Early in the day, pastels are particularly noteworthy in the gorge, while in the afternoon one sees an unforgettable spectacle of brilliant rainbow hues, ten miles of sheer, massive, paint pot colored cliffs. *Waimea Canyon* is as utterly unspoiled as was ancient Hawaii before

Captain Cook first gazed on *Kauai*'s green clad tropical beaches.

From *Kokee,* the summer resort plateau, the road continues a further three miles to terminate at KALALAU LOOKOUT, which, if possible, is even more awe-inspiring than *Puu Ka Pele.* Here the ground falls away 4,000 feet to the tropical valley below, providing a view which can only be described as fabulous.

From the rugged NA PALI CLIFFS, ahead of the *Lookout,* one senses almost, rather than hears, the thunderous Pacific breaking in spray on this desolate coast.

WAILUA, center of the island's old royalty, located at the mouth of the *Wailua River,* is easily reached by car. From here one may embark on the three mile cruise to the famous *Fern Grotto,* a most rewarding river trip. The old original *King's Highway* on which the Kauaian Kings were carried by their royal staff lest their sacred feet touch the ground crosses the bridge from which the river boats start their sightseeing journeys. The modern boat trip is a delight to the eye, with the river banks being covered with hyacinths, hau trees, and pili grass. Passengers can go ashore when the boat reaches a point close to the *Fern Grotto* and nearby *Wailua Waterfalls.* The grotto's entrance is almost completely obscured by masses of gigantic, graceful maidenhead ferns hanging from the overhead cliff.

HOLO-HOLO-KU HEIAU, one of the most renowned pagan temples in Hawaii, is dedicated to the ominous god Ku whose worship entailed human sacrifices. The temple was restored before the Second World War and is an almost perfect example of the ancient Hawaiian *Heiau,* with the sacrificial altar being inside the precincts. The temple is near a royal coconut grove, the *King's Highway,* and the deluxe *Coco Palms Resort Hotel.*

The site of the *Sacred Birth Stones,* near the temple, was the scene of elaborate ceremonies connected with royal births.

POIPU BEACH area, at **Koloa** on the southern tip of the island, 20 minutes by car from the airport, is nestled in a secluded ocean cove. Here one finds the famed Kimball family's *Waiohai Hotel,* consisting of a luxurious main house and a series of charming one- and two-story guest houses, the soon to be opened *Sheraton-Kauai Hotel,* and the popular *Hyatt House.*

KILAUEA, a plantation village, is celebrated for its lighthouse with the largest reflector of its kind in the world.

HANALEI is one of the most scenic sections in Hawaii. The views from the *Lookout* toward both the sea and land are breathtaking. The *Hanalei River* is beneath the *Lookout,* while **Hanalei** itself is a peaceful settlement in which is found an interesting old *Mission House* built in 1840, closely resembling both inside and out a New England home. In direct contrast to the Christian atmosphere is the fact that **Hanalei** was the headquarters of the pagan goddess, Laka. Hula dancing, of which Laka was the patron, is said to have originated here.

HAENA and its three mysterious caves are close to the great *Na Pali Cliffs.* It was here that the *Bali Hai* sequence of "South Pacific" was shot and that Pele, Goddess of Fire, made her home. It is said that the pyromaniacal deity fell in love with a handsome chieftain from Haena, but being unable to make any progress with him, sent for her beautiful sister, Laka, to come from the big island to persuade the object of her adoration to come to Pele in her headquarters in the *Kilauea Volcano.* Sad to say, the sister failed to seduce the young chieftain.

The MANINIHOLO DRY CAVE is supposed to have been dug by the Menehunes.

The WAIKAPALAE and the WAIKANALOA WET CAVES are particularly popular with today's bathers who enjoy the crystal clear waters and the romantic atmosphere, especially so since these caverns were Laka's hideout while she was attempting to capture the chieftain's heart for her sister, Pele.

THE ISLAND OF MOLOKAI

MOLOKAI, the "Friendly Isle," fifth in size of the archipelago group, is only 25 miles from *Oahu,* with a mere half hour separating **Honolulu's** *International Airport* and *Molokai's*

Hoolehuia Airport. Molokai, the most untouched and natural of the major islands, accords a charming reception to visitors, notable even among the cordial Hawaiians. In the early decades of this century, *Molokai* was known as the "Lonely Isle" because of the original population of 6,000 or more, less than 1,000 Molokaians remained.

Before 1834, the islanders lived comfortably, growing taro, keeping poultry and livestock, and fishing off the prolific *Penguin Bank*. Between 1834 and 1919, the natives gradually abandoned their lands, migrating to other islands where greater opportunity knocked appealingly at their doors. This sad state of affairs again was altered by the advent in *Molokai* of the pineapple industry. The years from 1920 to 1935 saw the number of inhabitants grow from 1,000 to 6,675, which numbers have now slipped back a bit, with approximately 5,000 friendly people living on *Molokai*.

The island was formed by three separate volcanic eruptions during different eons of time, which have produced three distinctly different areas varying widely from one another. One upheaval created the eastern part culminating in *Mount Kamakou, Molokai*'s highest point of 4,970 feet above sea level; another formed the western part, with *Mount Puu Nana* at 1,381 feet; and finally the last eruption created the northern peninsula of *Kalaupapa* with its magnificent towering cliffs shooting up nearly 3,000 feet straight from the sea.

Molokai is the island to explore for those who would enjoy a glimpse of what Hawaii and its inhabitants used to be. Here the greater part of the people are either purebred Hawaiians or at least fifty per cent so. The island's exports are principally pineapples and cattle, the latter originally having been made up exclusively of Longhorns introduced in 1840 by a German ranching pioneer, but Herefords were introduced in 1923 and now predominate.

There is some flaw to be found in almost every Eden. In *Molokai* the shortcoming is the distressing water scarcity. The island has to rely exclusively on springs and wells for its fresh water. *Molokai,* with an area of 260 square miles, is 37 miles long at its extreme points by 10 miles wide. The present population will undoubtedly increase when irrigation is improved. **Kaunakakai,** the little capital, has some 1,000 inhabitants, but market days see the greater part of the island's population in town.

The Hawaiian Homes Act of 1921 was the reason for the great increase of the predominantly Hawaiian population. The Act provided that 40-acre lots on *Molokai* were to be allocated free to homesteaders with a minimum of fifty per cent of pure Hawaiian blood, and the island was also granted funds and administrative help for roadmaking and improving the vital water supply situation. These projects are not yet complete, although in 1961 a five-mile water tunnel for irrigation purposes was completed. A partial antidote to *Molokai's* arid plight has been the planting of algaroba trees which need very little water. These trees have flourished and proved invaluable for cattle.

KAUNAKAKAI, the tiny capital, *Molokai's* sole city, town, or village, somewhat resembling a frontier town in the days of America's early West, is the best base from which to explore the island. The cosy *Seaside Inn,* beautifully situated on the beach, is at present the island's only hotel, although another resort hotel is being prepared on the *Cooke Ranch* on high ground north of the town. The *Seaside Inn's* owners and proprietors, Mr. and Mrs. Henry Pali, are among the island's greatest assets, being indispensable to tourists and sports lovers. They hire out taxis, drive-yourself cars, and arrange guides and provide equipment for hunting, climbing, and fishing.

Game is abundant, particularly wild deer which were brought here by the Duke of Edinburgh in 1869. There are also wild boar and game birds.

PENGUIN BANK, a submarine shelf, located off the island's southwest shores, extending for nearly 30 miles, is a great cliff whose edge rises steeply 3,600 feet from the ocean floor to a point some 200 feet beneath the water's surface. The bank is a fisherman's paradise having provided the staple diet for olden day Hawaiians and is still an important source of food supply.

The GEORGE P. COOKE RANCH, comprising a spacious main lodge and adjacent bungalows, is being readied as a luxury resort hotel complete with tennis courts and swimming pool. The Cookes are descendants of early missionaries.

PINEAPPLE INDUSTRY. The same road that leads to the *Cooke Ranch* passes the pineapple plantations of Libby, McNeill and Libby, the California Packing Corporation, and the Pacific Pineapple Company. The first two companies were started in 1923 and 1927, and the latter in 1947. Although a great island asset, the opportunities in the pineapple business have encouraged the islanders either to sell their homesteads to the companies, or themselves to go to work in the business, or both. These results have not been beneficial to the Homestead Act.

The KALAUPAPA PENINSULA AND SETTLEMENT is a tongue of land jutting three miles into the Pacific, three and one-half miles across its base, containing some of the finest scenery on the *Pali Coast*. Apart from its scenery, *Kalaupapa* is internationally famous for its *Hansen's Disease Settlement*, the scene of the work of the brave Belgian priest, Father Damien, among the early lepers of the island. This terrible disease with all its grim associations is now practically a thing of the past. If treated in its early stages, leprosy is perfectly curable. The stigma, horror, and old-fashioned disgrace of leprosy, encouraged by religious tradition, are fortunately dying out. The invaluable sulfone drugs are to leprosy what penicillin has become to a score of other hitherto dangerous and almost incurable ailments.

Father Damien came to *Kalaupapa* in 1864 with a group of dedicated and devoted helpers. They pledged their lives to improving the appalling conditions that existed in the settlement. King Kamehameha V had merely allocated the peninsula as a place of life imprisonment for the unfortunate patients. *Kalaupapa* is virtually inaccessible by land, being cut off from the rest of the island by great volcanic cliffs 2,000 feet high, which make travel difficult but provide a modern scenic wonder. Within this natural prison, the unfortunates lingered until death mercifully put an end to them. Father Damien eventually contracted the disease and succumbed, the martyr of *Kalaupapa*.

In 1936, the Belgian King Leopold's request for the return of Damien's body was granted, and the priest was reburied in the Church of St. Jacques at **Louvain** near his birthplace.

In 1864, the whole peninsula was barren and windswept, but in later years many trees were planted to protect the settlement buildings. The patients now number a mere handful, for successful cures have yearly reduced the number to a negligible quantity. The remaining *Kalaupapa* patients live in separate cottages and have a school, movies, athletics, dancing, organized picnics, and outings, with three churches—Episcopalian, Roman Catholic, and Mormon—being represented.

Kalaupapa has its own airfield, a tranquil landing ground overlooking the blue *Pacific*. Visitors arriving by air are exposed to a splendid view of the settlement, *Molokai Lighthouse,* and the crater on whose summit stands an 18 foot white cross, a fitting symbol to Father Damien and those who assisted him.

THE ISLAND OF LANAI

LANAI, sixth in size of the islands, just off *Maui*'s coast, is a "big business" island despite its small 90,000 acre area, 14,000 of which are entirely given over to pineapple production. The island is an extinct volcano, stretching a mere thirteen miles from east to west and slightly less from north to south. Minute *Lanai*'s area is but 140 square miles, with a population of only 2,400 persons.

KAUMALAPAU, 60 miles from **Honolulu,** is the island's port from which the pineapple crop is exported, with **Lanai City,** the capital, located in the center of the island on a 1,400 foot plateau. *Lanai*'s present fertile and prosperous condition is entirely due to the pineapple trade. In 1792, when Captain

Vancouver, the celebrated seaman and explorer, sailed past *Lanai*'s shores, he noted that the "naked appearance of the island seems thinly covered with shriveled grass in a scorched state."

This early nakedness caused the ancient Hawaiians to regard *Lanai* as being haunted by evil spirits, no effort being made to settle there for a thousand years after the other islands were thriving. Legend relates that the unpleasant son of a *Maui* King was banished to *Lanai* by his father, where the terrible child proved too much for the evil spirits who fled the island.

In 1854, the Mormons arrived, bent on colonization, but ten years later their leader, Walter M. Gibson, quarreled with his church and was excommunicated. By 1890, the island was once more desolate and uninhabited. Gibson's daughter inherited this white elephant, and her efforts to grow sugar cane failed due to shortage of water. Later the Baldwin Brothers took over, and they in turn sold out to the Dole Hawaiian Pineapple Company, Ltd. for the handsome sum of $1,100,000.00, a fabulous sum for those days, but the Company recouped the original purchase price plus a profit within two years.

Modern *Lanai* is a reflection of the Hawaiian Pineapple Company, the world's greatest producers of the fruit, who converted a wilderness into a thriving community with every known amenity for the workers.

LANAI CITY is a small capital but it is the most modern and best serviced community in the *Pacific,* its excellent facilities, like everything else on the island, being due to the bounty of the Hawaiian Pineapple Company. The town, mainly populated by some 2,000 of the firm's workers, is 1,400 feet above sea level on a beautiful plateau at the base of *Mount Lanaihale.*

The Company has built good roads, and the water is plentiful, being pumped from wells and springs, or piped from the hills. The pineapple fields are irrigated in case of drought, and erosion has been overcome by introducing pine plantations and planting thousands of acres in grass. The only inn, the *Lanai Hotel,* is small but comfortable.

KANNOLU VILLAGE, one of several existing deserted old Hawaiian villages, once teeming with life, was popular with King Kamehameha I, who used it as a holiday center.

The northern coast is picturesque and a favorite with "beach-combers," both amateur and professional. Many ships have come to grief off this shore line, and fascinating salvage material is always being collected by the islanders and their visitors.

THE ISLAND OF NIIHAU

NIIHAU, smallest of all the main inhabited islands, lies less than twenty miles southwest of *Kauai* and is 18 miles long by six miles wide, with an area of 72 square miles. It is 1,281 feet above sea level at its highest point. The population of only 230 is 100% Hawaiian stock. The island is privately owned and protected. No visitors except the invited personal friends of the owners or the islanders themselves can land.

In 1863, a widow, Mrs. Elizabeth Sinclair, and her family left Scotland to winter in Hawaii. In **Honolulu** they became friends of King Kamehameha IV who sold *Niihau* to Mrs. Sinclair. The Robinsons, descendants of Mrs. Sinclair, now own the island.

The inhabitants of this tiny stronghold of Old Hawaii are the only citizens in the island group who still speak the original tongue and very little, if any, English. The children are taught basic English in the small school, but directly lessons are over, they revert to pure Hawaiian.

Niihau is unique in other respects. The only connections with the outside world are a boat service for mail and supplies. *Niihau* possesses no port; hence, landing spots, which are at the mercy of weather conditions, are specified in advance.

The islanders are intensely religious. Sunday being physically and mentally a day of rest, the entire population attends a long-drawn-out church service.

The Niihauans breed sheep, keep pigs, raise shorthorn **cattle,** catch wild turkeys and peacocks, and keep bees. There are a few horses on the island. Since World War II, contact with the outside world has been kept up with radio facilities installed by American troops; until then, the islanders used the ancient method of lighting beacon fires on high ground.

The island's greatest excitement came on December 7, 1941, when a Japanese pilot ran out of fuel after bombing *Pearl Harbor* and landed on *Niihau*. Although seriously wounded by three of the Japanese's bullets, a huge Hawaiian, one Benjamin Kanahele, seized the Japanese and crushed his head against a stone wall. For this, Benjamin received the Medal of Merit and Purple Heart.

CHAPTER 11

Hong Kong and Macao

HONG KONG

SUPERLATIVES must of necessity flow freely when describing most areas in the Far East. To attempt to paint a mental picture of **Hong Kong** one must employ the most vivid of colorfully descriptive words, picturesque expressions, and sentences bulging with imagery that simply must be exaggerated . . . but aren't.

The approach to this tiny, exciting, and exquisitely beautiful British Crown Colony is impressive to all visitors whether they arrive by sea or by air, but for pure unadulterated pageantry the approach from the sea is unique.

The ruffled surface of **Hong Kong's** azure blue harbor waters is always agog with a seething pandemonium of marine activity. No traveler can fail to be indelibly impressed with the sights that greet his eyes as his ship leaves the *South China Sea* to enter Hong Kong's almost landlocked *Victoria Harbor*. High sterned junks will catch one's eye. These curious, ancient water-going workhorses will be in evidence everywhere with their odd batwing sails billowing and their low bows busy with Chinese coolie crews, all dressed in identical baggy pants and conical straw hats just as their ancestors who handled these same vessels through the centuries. There will be colorful

sampans and other ancient Oriental craft in vivid contrast to
the huge gleaming ships of the western world that anchor in
the harbor or tie up at **Kowloon's** piers. Canopied craft will
move unevenly out of the ship's course, while tiny single
oared rowboats operated by Chinese women standing in the
stern carrying babies piggyback will dodge in and out among
the myriad of harbor craft. There will be *walla-wallas,* the water
taxi motorboats, cruising about at great speed, smart pleasure
yachts, and busy ferryboats with their polyglot passenger lists
scurrying between the *Star Ferry Terminals* on either side of
the harbor, and ponderous car ferries laden with passenger
vehicles, sightseeing motor coaches, and heavy-duty lorries.

Breathtakingly beautiful *Hong Kong Island,* with the Colony's capital city **Victoria,** is to the left of the approaching vessels. The gleaming white buildings and skyscrapers of the city
rising from the water's edge are silhouetted majestically by the
glorious backdrop of *Victoria Peak,* highest point on the island,
which towers to an almost vertical 1,805 feet above the bay.
Directly facing **Victoria** across the cobalt blue harbor waters
are the *Kowloon Peninsula,* the city of **Kowloon,** and the main
docking terminus for ocean-going liners. The fantastic harbor,
which covers an area of more than sixteen square miles, averages from one to three miles across, with its entrance through
the *Lyemun Pass* being the narrowest point, only 880 yards
in width. The harbor is of great depth, and the mightiest liners
from the world's greatest shipyards may comfortably be accommodated in this picturesque roadstead.

Travelers approaching the never-never land from the air will
also be awed by the scene of indescribable beauty below,
encompassing the steep hills of the *Kowloon* mainland, intricately terraced fields, the ruggedly indented coast line, and
the ship jammed harbor. As the mammoth airliner swooshes
into *Kai Tak Airport,* the visitor will already be imbued with
the magnificence of the setting.

By night, the area is a tracery of dancing lights, a romantic
picture of lasting loveliness.

HISTORICAL BACKGROUND. **Hong Kong,** meaning "Isle of Fragrant Waters," was, according to local lore, founded on a prophecy. In A.D. 1100, a scholarly Cantonese seeking a "lucky" grave site came upon a stone near *Hong Kong Island* inscribed with the following:

"Across the waters when 'tis dark a million lights shall glow,
    And in their paths ten thousand ships go passing to and
    fro . . ."

Nothing could be written today that could better describe the contemporary aerial view of *Hong Kong Island* and *Kowloon.*

Hong Kong, lying in the *South China Sea* just south of the Tropic of Cancer, is the generic name given to the entire British Crown Colony which includes *Hong Kong Island,* measuring 29 square miles and having as its principal city **Victoria;** *Kowloon Peninsula;* the *New Territories,* by far the largest area of the colony; *Lantao,* a large island, half again as big as *Hong Kong Island,* which is just now being developed as a result of the government's aggressive water conservation policy involving construction of the huge *Shek Pik* reservoir and the planting of myriads of trees; *Lamma,* a sleepy island to the seaward of *Hong Kong Island,* whose fisherfolk follow the centuries-old skills of their ancestors; *Cheung Chau* or *Dumbbell Island,* so called for its two elevated extremities with the narrow stretch of flat land in between; and several hundred other smaller uninhabited islands.

The *Kowloon Peninsula,* on the China mainland, derives its name, which in Chinese means "nine dragons," from another ancient tale. The legend insists that the boy emperor Ti Ping, the last of the Sung dynasty, was in frightened flight from the fierce Mongol tribes that had devastated North China, when, in a vision, he was informed he would know his new home when he arrived at a setting where nine dragons met. When he reached the area known today as *Kowloon,* he learned from local villagers that the mountains looming purple in the background were called dragons. There was only one fallacy: Ti

Ping could locate only eight hills and he was looking for nine dragons. This didn't phase the natives. They pointed out that in Chinese mythology emperors are frequently portrayed as dragons. He made the ninth. Hence, the name *Kowloon*.

The LOCAL SETTING. For those who have not visited the British Crown Colony, it is difficult to describe accurately the nomenclature of the Hong Kong area. To simplify the situation, however, there are only four basic names you must remember: *Hong Kong, Victoria, Kowloon* and the *New Territories*. The complications stem from the fact that Hong Kong is the name that describes three things: (1) the entire Crown Colony, (2) the most central and populated island of the group, and (3) **Victoria City.** (One frequently hears in **Kowloon** I'm going over to **Hong Kong** for dinner." What the person means is he is going to the city of **Victoria** on *Hong Kong Island* to dine, at *P.G. (Parisian Grill)* for example.)

Kowloon is both a city and a peninsula, and the *New Territories,* to be described later, are not new at all, having been leased in 1898.

The heart of *Hong Kong Island* is **Victoria** (city), more simply and generally called **Hong Kong.** Here one finds the old-style British administrative buildings side by shoulder with great gleaming skyscrapers and huge, teeming, new ultrasmart hotels. It is a throbbing downtown business area directly opposite **Kowloon** to which it is linked by the *Star Ferry* which shuttles across the harbor in five minutes' time.

On *Hong Kong,* one finds in addition to the airline and steamship offices, travel agencies, large business firms, smart shops, fine restaurants, busy hotels, the Chinatown section of *Wanchai* (Suzie Wong's home district), *Victoria Peak,* the ladder streets, *West Point, Kennedy Town, Central District, Aberdeen, Happy Valley, Deep Water Bay, Repulse Bay, Stanley,* and *Shek-o.*

Kowloon is a burgeoning city with its famous *Nathan Road, Canton Road, Salisbury Road, Haiphong Road,* the *Whitfield Barracks,* the *Navy Repair Basin,* and a jillion or more shops, hotels, and neon signs that brighten the Oriental night skies as brightly as those above Broadway.

The *New Territories* include the picturesque little towns of **Shatin**, *Shatin Heights* and *Valley*, **Kam Tin, Yuen Long, Lo Wu** on the China border, and others which I shall describe later.

CLIMATE. Despite Hong Kong's being located in a sub-tropical area, the weather during much of the year is cool and comfortable. The winter months from October to March are dry, sunny, and clear. Temperatures are moderate but not cold. In March and April, the humidity increases, and the temperature rises slightly. By May, there are foggy days, clouds in the sky, and more humidity. Summer begins toward mid-May and continues to mid-September with daytime temperatures varying from eighty to ninety degrees Fahrenheit or slightly higher. It is during these months that the rain may be expected, sometimes in torrential quantities, which is, of course, a happy situation. Hong Kong has no rivers, lakes, or other source of water, and it is on the summer rains that the local populace depends for the year round supply of water. By mid-September, the temperature and the humidity have dropped sharply, and autumn, the most glorious time of the year, begins. September, October, and November are simply delightful in every way, with moderate temperatures and the most unbelievably blue skies.

MODERN HISTORY. The modern history of Hong Kong dates from 1841, when **China** ceded the island of *Hong Kong* to the British, who have an amazing aptitude for losing battles and winning wars and for muddling through to victory despite their all too frequent ineptitudes.

In 1842, the then British Foreign Secretary, Lord Palmerston, in speaking of Hong Kong's future, said, "It seems obvious that Hong Kong will never be a mart for trade." He was much less sagacious than the forecast of the future inscribed on the stone discovered by the Cantonese scholar, for now, in the 1960's,

HONG KONG

WYLIE RD.

GASCOIGNE RD.

CHATHAM RD.

JORDAN RD.

AUSTIN RD.

OBSERVATORY RD.

KIMBERLY RD.

GRANVILLE RD.

CAMERON RD.

NATHAN RD.

PRAT AVE.

MODY ROAD

CANTON RD.

HAI PHONG RD.

LOCK RD.

HANKOW RD.

ASHLEY RD.

MIDDLE ROAD

PEKING RD.

SALISBURY RD.

KOWLOON PENINSULA

N
E
W
S

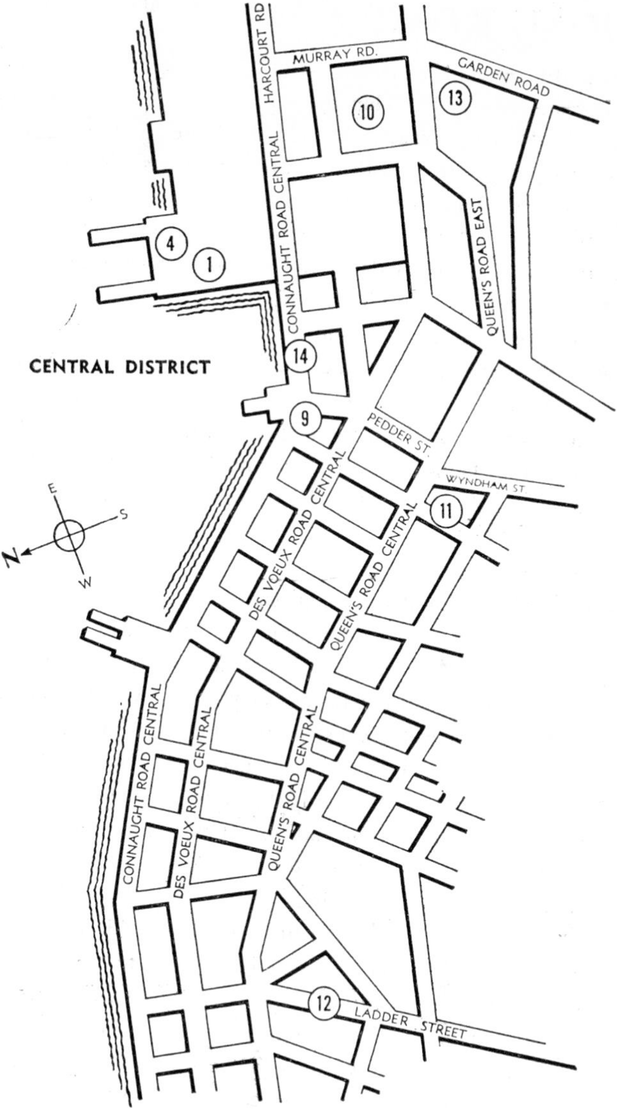

CENTRAL DISTRICT

HARCOURT RD

MURRAY RD.

GARDEN ROAD

CONNAUGHT ROAD CENTRAL

QUEEN'S ROAD EAST

PEDDER ST.

WYNDHAM ST

DES VOEUX ROAD CENTRAL

QUEEN'S ROAD CENTRAL

CONNAUGHT ROAD CENTRAL

DES VOEUX ROAD CENTRAL

QUEEN'S ROAD CENTRAL

LADDER STREET

⑩ ⑬ ④ ① ⑭ ⑨ ⑪ ⑫

N E S W

"across these waters a million lights *do* glow, and more than ten thousand ships go passing to and fro."

The British had been trading with **China** for about one hundred years prior to 1841, but the experience had been frustrating. The Manchu dynasty despised the "foreign devils" and, though willing to trade with them, put every possible difficulty and humiliation in their paths. Not only was the commerce carried out in a most discouraging atmosphere, but bloodthirsty pirates roamed the area and all too frequently captured the British ships and murdered their crews.

Affairs between Chinese and British authorities reached a crucial point in 1839 when the so-called "Opium War" broke out. All trading activities ground to a halt. As a result of the British victories over the Chinese fleet and the blockade of the *Canton River,* Hong Kong was captured and ceded, in perpetuity, to the British by the *Treaty of Nanking* which was consummated in 1842.

Two curiosities developed as a result of the treaty. The Chinese Imperial Court knew nothing of the arrangement, and only because the official who negotiated it was a member of the Royal Family was his head kept from the executioner's sword. Captain Charles Elliot, the Royal Navy officer who had dealt with the Chinese, was dismissed from the Navy for having accepted such a worthless piece of property.

It is true, of course, that the island seemed to have little to recommend it, being barren and almost waterless, and, as ill fate would decree, it suffered two typhoons in its first year as a member of the British Empire.

But the harbor is one of the finest in the world, and soon the traders' faith in its fantastic potentiality began to be justified. In 1860, the *Kowloon Peninsula* and *Stonecutters Island* were ceded to Britain, again in perpetuity.

The words "in perpetuity" used in the foregoing should be read with care. Barring war or seizure, these are British forever. Not so, however, with the *New Territories,* the large island of

Lantao, and numerous smaller ones which were leased from China in 1898 for a period of 99 years.

The *New Territories,* which now are being expanded and rapidly exploited, are of approximately 365 square miles. *Hong Kong Island* is only 29 square miles, the territory of *Kowloon*—permanently ceded to Britain—is 3½ square miles, and *Stonecutters Island* just a flyspeck in the *South China Sea.*

It is a matter of some sober conjecture what will transpire in 1997 when the present lease runs out, particularly in view of the peculiar political philosophy of the present "landlords."

There has been no further acquisition of Hong Kong real estate since 1898 other than by reclamation from the sea.

The POPULATION. The official census of 1961, the first taken in thirty years, showed Hong Kong's population to be 3,139,709 broken down as follows: *Kowloon,* 1,588,825; *Hong Kong Island,* 1,005,041; *New Territories,* 409,945; and the water population, those living on the 21,292 sampans and junks scattered over Hong Kong's territorial waters including the *Typhoon Shelters* and *Aberdeen,* was 135,898.

The overwhelming majority, more than ninety-nine per cent, of the Colony's residents are Chinese. It must be noted briefly that there are almost as many different types of Chinese as there are types of Europeans. Hong Kong's majority is made up largely of South Chinese, but there are others residing in Hong Kong from Shanghai, North China, the Coastal provinces, and West China who possess greatly different physical characteristics, and whose eating habits, customs, and costumes are not at all like those of the South Chinese. The balance of the less than one per cent of the population is made up primarily of British, Americans, Portuguese, Indians, Filipinos, French, Dutch, Japanese, and Italians.

The ancient inhabitants who occupied the area prior to the 18th century must of necessity be thought of as Hong Kong's only real natives, just as the Indians are our only basic native inhabitants.

The "water people," known as *Tanka* and *Hok Lo,* are

nomads who make up the 135,898 members of the floating population, spending their entire lives from birth through adolescence, marriage, senility, to death on their sampans and junks.

There are also the Cantonese *Punti,* or native people, and the unusually garbed *Hakka,* or "strangers," who do much of the farming in the *New Territories.* I shall mention them later.

On *Hong Kong Island* and in *Kowloon,* the population density is a tightly packed two thousand persons per acre.

A SHOPPER'S EDEN. Were it not for its sparkling beauty, teeming masses of seething humanity, its unique setting on the brink of **Red China** and its geographical situation within a few miles distance of an Oriental world with walled villages, ancient rice growing farms, and its justly earned fame as an epicurean paradise, Hong Kong would still be the most alluring magnet in the world because of the magnificence of its shopping.

Almost all of the shopping details are thoroughly covered in Chapter Six, but I would be remiss in describing Hong Kong were I not to devote a few paragraphs to the mass mania that has swept the world known as, "Let's go shopping in Hong Kong."

I know of no item of merchandise that cannot be purchased cheaper in Hong Kong than in the country of its origin. There are a number of reasons for this amazingly happy situation. Hong Kong is a free port. Except for alcohol and tobacco, there are no import taxes, export taxes, or purchase taxes. Goods such as Swiss watches; German and Japanese cameras; Italian, Siamese, and Indian silks; French perfumes; English leather and woolens; and American raw materials are shipped to Hong Kong in great quantities either for sale in its natural state or for processing. But that is only part of the story. The taxes paid by stores, shops, and Hong Kong business people are the lowest, by far, in the civilized world. Personal income taxes run from $2\frac{1}{2}\%$ to 25% maximum on gross earnings, while business profits are taxed at a flat $12\frac{1}{2}\%$ after a basic deduction of the first HK $1,400 of profit. What a paradise! Some countries subsidize export prices in order to profit on foreign exchange, which means that some goods are sold to Hong Kong merchants considerably cheaper than wholesale prices in their own country. The labor cost in Hong Kong is much cheaper, by comparison, than in many other countries. The cost of doing business in Hong Kong represents a smaller percentage of what it costs a businessman to operate elsewhere. The merchant's profit markup here can be much less than elsewhere and still see him prosper. Cotton woven in our own South and shipped to Hong Kong can be converted into fine custom-made shirts for much less than they can be made in New York, Chicago, or San Francisco. Thus, whether one seeks handmade beaded sweaters, dresses, suits, coats, furs, carved ivory chess sets, jade, jewelry, objects of art, brocades, furniture, rosewood or teakwood chests, or lacquered screens, one can buy cheaper in Hong Kong.

One can get a real bargain in a Chinese sailing junk with auxiliary motor, which, believe it or not, well-heeled Americans are beginning to purchase. Just what I've always needed on *Lake Michigan!* Why not?

There are more than one thousand factories in Hong Kong making shoes, handbags, briefcases and luggage, toys, rugs, and embroidered linens in addition to all of the artisans engaged in making all of the fine handwork that is available.

As mentioned in Chapter Six, and worthy of reiteration here, be sure that you deal with reputable merchants. I have compiled accurate lists for your guidance, and additional information can be secured from the *Hong Kong Tourist Association*. While our Customs men frequently do not request it, the regulations require that you receive a comprehensive *Certificate of Origin* issued by the Hong Kong government on Chinese types of goods purchased in Hong Kong (no goods made in Communist China can be brought into the U.S.). Don't do a back flip over this. The whole process is simple. Read about it in Chapter Six, but do business with established merchants and you won't have to worry.

Since I am only a junior type of genius, I cannot hope to be able to forecast what the political savants in Washington will ultimately do with the duty-free allowance which was precipitously reduced to $100 in the early days of the New Frontier. It will probably be raised shortly. In the meantime, however, I can assure you that anything you purchase in Hong Kong can be brought into the States, duty paid on it, and still afford you a king-sized bargain.

A GOURMET'S DELIGHT. Hong Kong is famous for the variety of its international cuisine. It is universally admitted to have restaurants which serve the best Chinese food anywhere. There are North China and Peking cuisines, East and South Chinese menus, Cantonese food and Indian dishes, English, Russian, French, German, Imperial Russian, Italian, and Scandinavian plates . . . all just out of this world. That's all there is to it. I have given complete details as to the specific types of cuisine and the restaurants that serve them in Chapter Five.

CLOTHING. During December, January, and February, the climate is a bit chilly, with the average temperature being sixty-three degrees. Normal Midwest fall clothing with a light topcoat will be comfortable. The balance of the year lightweight tropical clothing will be in order. Except during the warmest and most humid summer months, a man will be comfortable with a light sports jacket, sports shirt or shirt with tie, and slacks during the day. In almost all good restaurants, one will wish to wear a tie and jacket for lunch or dinner. The gals can be guided accordingly.

LOCAL TRANSPORTATION. Local transportation is bountiful, rapidly efficient, and cheap. Taxi rates begin at 17¢ U.S. for the first mile and 14¢ U.S. for each succeeding mile in *Kowloon,* while on the *Island of Hong Kong* the rates begin at 25¢ for the first mile and are about 17¢ U.S. a mile for each mile thereafter. The buses which remind you for all the world of the bright red and green London omnibuses cost only H.K. 20¢ for almost all distances both in *Hong Kong* and on the *Peninsula.* Imagine . . . less than 4¢ U.S. On *Hong Kong*

Island, there are a large number of British type streetcars which charge the same fares as the buses.

Rickshaws are romantic. This is the only place in the world where they still exist. The cost is about 17¢ U.S. for each five minutes of use. Hong Kong traffic makes the use of these ancient vehicles, however colorful, risky as a form of transport.

The *Peak Tram,* an efficient funicular sightseeing railway which clambers up the side of *Victoria Peak,* costs 10¢ U.S.

The *Star Ferry* is a fantastic institution. These incredible, modern, convenient, and comfortable vessels ply back and forth between *Kowloon* and *Hong Kong* in five minutes each direction. Last year they carried almost 150,000,000 passengers across *Victoria Harbor.* The population of Hong Kong is only three million souls, remember? The *Star Ferry* is very easily located. In *Kowloon* it is a long stone's throw from the *Peninsula* and *Ambassador Hotels,* catercorner across from the police headquarters and adjacent to the intersection of *Canton* and *Salisbury Roads.* The new *Star Ferry Terminal* on the island is between *Queen's Pier* and *Blake Pier* adjacent to the brand new *City Hall* opposite the *Supreme Court Building.*

The *Star Ferry* operates every few minutes in each direction from very early in the morning until very late at night. Don't hesitate to try the ferry. There is no language barrier. It's fun. The fare is H.K. 20¢ each way.

The *walla-wallas,* water taxi motorboats, can be hired for trips across the harbor, around the harbor, or for longer trips. For simply crossing the harbor, a water taxi, holding eight passengers, can be hired for H.K. $3.00 (U.S. 50¢). For longer trips around the harbor, the cost is U.S. 67¢ per boat for each half hour. The water taxis operate all night.

DRIVE YOURSELF CARS are now available. If you have a valid driver's license from your home state or an International Driver's License, you may hire a car at rates which begin at approximately $10 per day, or about U.S. $70 per week. Hong Kong traffic is left hand drive, however, and the pace is frantic. You can do much better in private cars with chauffeurs, taxis, or rickshaws. Believe me. Don't try to drive.

TIPPING is a universally regarded Hong Kong custom. Any sane or sensible rule for tipping that would apply in Europe or in the United States will guide you here. Ten to fifteen per cent is normal. You'll get remarkably good service.

LANGUAGE AND RELIGION. The Chinese Cantonese dialect is heard most widely in Hong Kong, though English is the official language. Almost all businessmen, many servants, taxi drivers, and others speak English in one form or another.

The religions range from Buddhism, Taoism, and other Oriental religions which predominate to Christian denominations, particularly the Anglicans and Roman Catholics. All Christian holidays are observed. Numbered among the Christian denominations which have churches in Hong Kong are the following: Anglican, Assembly of God, Baptist, Christian and Missionary Alliance, Christian Science, Church of Christ, Church of Jesus Christ of Latter Day Saints, English Methodist, Gospel Hall Brethren, Lutheran including American, English, and Missouri Synod, Greek Orthodox, Roman Catholic, and Seventh Day Adventist. There are two interdenominational and one Jewish synagogue.

CLUBS AND SOCIETIES. There are a number of Hong Kong clubs and societies in which a visitor might be interested including the *American Club, American Women's Association of Hong Kong,* the *American University Club of Hong Kong,* the *Correspondents Club, Hong Kong Junior Chamber of Commerce, Jewish Recreational Club, Lions Club of Hong Kong and Kowloon, Rotary Clubs of Hong Kong Island East and Hong Kong Island West,* the *YMCA,* and *YWCA.*

The REFUGEE PROBLEM. The mass immigration of refugees from **Red China,** while creating a horrendous, virtually insoluble, problem, is not unprecedented in Hong Kong's history. Thousands came to Hong Kong during the *Taiping Rebellion* in the 1850's, many came following the inauguration of the Chinese republic in 1911, while scores of thousands more entered the British Crown Colony in 1937 when **Japan** invaded **China.** Thus, the influx of refugees who have poured into Hong Kong since the termination of the four-year Japanese occupation of Hong Kong during World War II is not a new experience for the Crown Colony, merely a much bigger one. In May of 1962, spurred by intolerable living conditions and near famine in Red China, the number of pathetic refugees attempting to resettle in Hong Kong became so great that reluctantly the authorities were forced to turn them back.

Prior to the spring of 1962, all ilks entered Hong Kong. The total number of human souls received in Hong Kong numbered in the millions. These people fled their native land without a penny and without resources other than the clothes on their backs. It is inevitable that in such a tiny area as Hong Kong immediate housing could not be readily made available for all who arrived. One will see scores of thousands of refugees in Hong Kong actually living in caves and in makeshift huts. It must be pointed out that this was not a problem of Hong Kong's making, but Hong Kong has tackled the messy situation with courage and vision. Between 1954 and 1959, more than 300,000 refugees were resettled in government-built housing. By the fall of 1960, new settlement rehousing for an average of

3,000 refugees was being opened every ten days, which represents a monumental undertaking. These resettlement houses are great modern multiple-apartment dwellings. Because of the utter cleanliness of their habits, the Chinese are constantly washing their clothing and household effects. Such a brilliant mélange of multi-hued fabrics has probably never before hung from balconies and windows anywhere in the world. Many too many people must of necessity live in limited areas to get them off the streets and out of squalid huts. How many more Chinese seeking refuge can be absorbed in already overcrowded Hong Kong is problematical.

It is a significant and curious commentary that in order for the officials of Hong Kong to feed the destitute Chinese refugees they must buy much of the food from **Red China.**

GOVERNMENT. Hong Kong is a British Crown Colony governed under a constitution set forth in documents known as "Letters Patent," which provides for a governor, an executive council, and a legislative council. The royal instructions transmitted to the governor by the British Secretary of State for the Colonies describe the membership of the executive and legislative councils. The Common Law and Statutes of England as they existed in 1843 form the basic legal system of Hong Kong.

HOTELS. Fortunately, a building boom in hotels has eased the erstwhile acute shortage of housing facilities for visitors to the Crown Colony. The grand old *Peninsula,* one of the regal establishments of the world, the *Marco Polo-Peninsula Court,* the new *Ambassador,* the *President, Miramar,* and *Park* head the list of topflight establishments in **Kowloon,** and the magnificent *Mandarin* and *Hilton Hotels* in **Victoria** head the list in Hong Kong. I have covered the situation thoroughly in Chapter Four, but I must reiterate here that if you have the good sense to request a reservation early, you will be able to live as comfortably in Hong Kong as anywhere in the world. The first class and luxury hotels are fully air conditioned.

GUIDES. The Hong Kong licensed guides are among the

best in the world. To become a guide registered with the *Hong Kong Tourist Association,* a candidate must pass a written and oral test, must speak fluent English, have a good education, be of good character, and possessed of intelligence. When licensed, the guide will be given an identification card which he must carry at all times and a badge which must be worn when on duty. Here is a special word of caution: don't, and I repeat *don't,* choose a guide from the street; don't be in a position where you let yourself be picked up by a street guide. Such a sloppy procedure is completely unnecessary, as good guides are available through all the leading travel agencies. The "hustlers" who work the streets are almost certain to be unreliable . . . or much worse.

Hong Kong is a well-policed area. Traffic policemen are majestically and strategically placed on miniature pagodas at key intersections. With the exception of officers, each policeman wears a numbered shoulder patch. If the patch is red, it indicates that the policeman speaks English.

DURATION OF STAY. "How long shall I stay in Hong Kong?" The best answer I can give to that one is "longer than you had intended." I have never met or known of anyone who was ready to leave Hong Kong when his planned stay had come to an end. The *Hong Kong Tourist Association* has kept accurate statistics which show that whereas as recently as four years ago the average stay in Hong Kong was three and one-half days, it is now seven days. This is an average stay. It must be remembered that there are certain cruise ships that stop only one, two, or at the maximum three days, which means that for those who are on a free schedule the average Hong Kong stay must be closer to ten days. My suggestion is that nine to ten days would be the minimum that you should plan to remain in Hong Kong. You will be busy as a beaver every minute even if you stay ten days. Two weeks is not too long.

PRINCIPAL POINTS OF INTEREST

Hong Kong Island

VICTORIA—CENTRAL DISTRICT. The city of **Victoria** is the economic core and heart beat of the Colony. It is situated on the north shore directly opposite the *Kowloon Peninsula,* five minutes by ferry or water taxi over the blue waters of the famous harbor. Architecturally, the city is a happy mélange of dignified old-style western-type buildings, soaring modern sky-scrapers, broad boulevards, and narrow busy "ladder" streets rising from the crowded waterfront toward the peak. Here, jammed like sardines, Chinese merchants and their customers haggle under brilliantly blazoned vertically painted signs. **Victoria's** business section, much of it reclaimed from the harbor, represents the modern western world with its buses, trams, limousines, taxis, snarled traffic, and businessmen in dignified business suits. The eastern touch is added to the *Central District* by the rickshaws scooting through traffic, the slender hipped women in their intriguing *cheongsams,* and other Chinese costumes of all types.

In **Victoria's** *Central District,* one finds the names of internationally famous firms such as the renowned house of *Jardine,*

Matheson, while the area between *Des Voeux Road Central* and *Queen's Road Central* is dominated by the massive modern impressive buildings of the *Hong Kong and Shanghai Banking Corporation.* Nearby rises the seventeen-story *Bank of China,* clearinghouse and financial listening post for Red China, the *Hong Kong Hilton* and *Mandarin Hotels.* In this area one finds most of the chic shops and restaurants, the Supreme Court building, and Chinese shops dealing in gold, jewelry, precious gems, Oriental crafts, furnishings, paintings, ivory, and foodstuffs.

VICTORIA PEAK rises precipitously in majestic glory from the waterfront to its sheer dominating height of 1,805 feet. From its summit, the view over **Victoria,** the harbor, the hills of *Kowloon, Repulse Bay,* and the entire area forms a delightful panoramic vista. On a clear day, one may see Communist China brooding in the distance.

The *Peak Tramway,* actually a funicular railway, will whisk one effortlessly to the peak in ten minutes' time. The ride is exciting. The gradients are so steeply banked that passengers have the optical illusion that the passing houses, erected on the steep hillside, are leaning at impossible angles and are on the verge of tumbling down the slopes. The ozone on the *Peak* is refreshing; its temperature is always ten to fifteen degrees cooler than in the city. There is a cafe at the top to refresh the body while the spirit is being satiated with the splendored view. One *must* visit *Victoria Peak* twice: by day and by night. As spectacular and soul satisfying as is the daytime vista, the romance of the setting at night is indescribable. The flashing neon signs of **Kowloon** and **Victoria,** the bobbing lights of the ships in the harbor, the mysterious subdued lights on the junks and sampans in the typhoon harbors and at *Aberdeen,* the headlights of the cars skirting the island and traversing the thoroughfares of **Kowloon** combine to emblazon an unforgettable mental image.

Victoria Peak is the plush, lush residential section of Hong Kong's elite. The homes are beautiful and delightfully landscaped with velvet pad lawns and gardens ablaze with color.

The TIGER BALM GARDENS are situated above *North Point* at the top of *Tai Hang Road*. Everything that I have said about the *Tiger Balm Gardens* in **Singapore** can be repeated here. Certainly one is never neutral in reaction to these fantastic collections. They are either revolting or startlingly attractive. Here, as in **Singapore,** the project was conceived and designed by the brothers Aw Boon Haw and Aw Boon Par. Aw Boon Haw was the fabulous rags-to-riches Chinese character who parlayed an idea for a patent medicine into a multimillion-dollar operation. Of his numerous medicines, the best known is *Tiger Balm,* an ointment that is good for everything from flat feet and fallen arches to skin diseases, falling hair, tummy ache, and more personal problems. Skeptical westerners are apt to think of these medicines as purely quack concoctions. I have intelligent acquaintances, however, who swear by *Tiger Balm.* Whatever the merit of the product, the brothers Aw Boon Haw and Aw Boon Par became financiers, philanthropists, and solid citizens whose business empire embraced newspapers, insurance, and the gamut of successful international undertakings spread ubiquitously through Southeast Asia. Whatever their merits or demerits, one could no more leave Hong Kong without seeing *Tiger Balm Gardens* than leave **Niagara** without seeing the *Falls*. The *Gardens* have been constructed on a series of spectacular terraces containing weird grottos, fantastic temples, nightmarish statues of animals including elephants, dragons, monkeys, tigers, ad infinitum. Everything has been painted in bright colors—garish reds, blues, purples, with gleaming white interspersing the vivid coloration of the setting. A seven-story white pagoda, approached by a great flight of steps, dominates the scene. A statue dedicated to the brothers is inscribed as follows:

"Dedicated to the memory of Aw Boon Par who dreamt of the Future, the Present, and learnt eternal truths from the Past, and to the continuance of those sparkling gems of Charity and Good Will of Aw Boon Haw."

Members of the Aw family live in the mansion on the grounds. It is not open to the general public, but arrangements can be made to enter and I have visited it on several occasions. The edifice contains invaluable collections of jade, objects of art, wood carved treasures, and antiques.

REPULSE BAY, on the south side of the island, may be reached comfortably in twenty minutes by car from **Victoria.** The beautiful bay, enclosed on three sides by green hills, takes its name from the British battleship *H.M.S. Repulse* which was responsible for ridding this section of the world of the bloodthirsty pirates who practiced their nefarious deeds during the mid-18th century. The crescent-shaped bay is blessed with soft white sand washed by incredibly blue waters. The deluxe *Hong Kong Hotel–Repulse Bay,* one of the finest in the Far East, looms over the beach and gardens and is the center of the popular bathing resort area. If one plans to come for a swim at *Repulse Bay,* a lunch on the terrace of the lovely hotel must be part of your excursion. Luncheon here is a delightful experience any day but particularly so on Sunday when a special buffet is served. The beaches of the bay are always busy with visitors sunning and bathing. Facilities are available for locker rental at the *Sea View Beach House,* and, if necessary, you may rent a bathing suit. There are other local facilities for changing clothes; a tea room, bar, and restaurant are all adjacent to the beach. Smart new apartment buildings are being constructed on the heights overlooking the water. Nearby is *Eucliff,* the fabulous mansion of Eu Tong Sen, another of the great Chinese millionaires who enjoyed building things. Since he was an ardent admirer of British and European ways and things, he had his house built as a replica of a medieval English castle filled with arms, armor, and antique furnishings. One has to enjoy the structure from the outside, however, as it is not open to the public.

DEEP WATER BAY, situated on the same inlet as *Repulse Bay,* commands a view almost equally beautiful. The *Deep Water Bay* area, which has a fine nine hole golf course belonging to the *Royal Hong Kong Golf Club,* is an attractive, popular, and smart residential area.

STANLEY, fast becoming a smart suburban residential area, possesses an excellent beach and is the site of the tragic *Hong Kong Prison,* known alternatively as *Stanley Prison.* It is Hong Kong's only prison for men and is vividly etched in the minds of thousands of British and their allies who spent the dreadful days of World War II interned here by the Japanese.

SHEK-O, at the extreme eastern and southern tip of the island, is a seaside village boasting of an excellent beach. Bath houses are not available but tents may be rented inexpensively.

ABERDEEN, on the south shore of *Hong Kong Island,* is the floating home of thousands of the *Tanka* and *Hok Lo,* the Chinese water people who live their entire lives in junks and sampans. The area is a vast forest of spars and canopies. Thousands of these junks, sampans, and miniature houseboat-type craft are huddled together in slumlike squalor. These boats are jammed so close together that one can walk for great distances crossing deck after deck littered with cooking utensils and all of the accoutrements necessary for life's maintenance. The washing flaps in the breeze above deck. The inhabitants of this watery nested jungle are fisher folk. When the men are out to sea, many of the women supplement the family income by transporting visitors from the quayside to the famed and colorful floating restaurants offshore. For several miles the waterfront is lined with great piles of drying fish.

The *Sea Palace* and *Tai Pak* floating restaurants are garishly decorated by day and brilliantly illuminated at night. One simply cannot visit Hong Kong without taking either lunch or dinner, preferably both, at one of the floating restaurants. It is an epicurean experience unlike any other. When the visitor arrives at the dockside sea approach to the *Sea Palace* or *Tai Pak,* the scene is a busy one. Sampans swarm about ready to whisk one across the several hundred yards to the restaurants. The boats are manned by women, frequently having with them their patient well-behaved children who play in the boat's bottom. The floating restaurants are two-story establishments with scores of *mah-jongg* players clackety-clacking the ivory pieces on the main deck. Each restaurant has its own reservoir stocked with fish from which you may choose your meal. The Chinese cuisine served here is replete with Oriental dishes prepared in Cantonese style.

The shoreside village is a typically crowded Chinese community, with each of the buildings sporting colorful perpendicular signs. The hills back of *Aberdeen* are excellent vantage points from which to view and photograph the melting pot setting of *Aberdeen,* which was at one time a pirates' lair.

POSSESSION POINT, on *Hollywood Road,* is the site of the first landing of British on Hong Kong from the *H.M.S. Sulphur* on January 26, 1841.

SHAUKIWAN, on the northern shore of the eastern tip of the island, is dominated by large apartment and office buildings. The indented harbor was at one time a pirates' sanctuary and is today crowded with junks and sampans in which many more of the Colony's water people live.

HAPPY VALLEY is the site of the *Hong Kong Race Track*. As a long-time devotee of the turf, I have visited race tracks in a score or more countries. Hong Kong's is the most unusual course I have ever seen. The *Club House* is seven stories tall and served by tiers of efficient lifts. Within the *Jockey Club* are a number of private clubs. To have access to the *Club House* area, one must either belong to the *Royal Hong Kong Jockey Club* or be a bona fide guest of a member, but to enter the hallowed precincts of the private clubs one must be a member of the *Hong Kong Club,* the *Chinese Club,* or one of a dozen or more with premises in this building. Visitors may now enjoy guest membership for the club enclosure. Your travel agent can arrange it. Requests must be made at least two weeks before a Saturday race, however.

Each of the clubs has its own bar, buffet, restaurant, and terrace. Each has its own mutuel windows. The first race is run at 11:30, the second at noon, the third at 12:30, with the horses for the fourth race going to the post at 1:00, after which time out is taken for tiffin (lunch). One may choose a cold buffet, hot lunch, or a combination of the two. Racing is resumed at 2:30. The Chinese are avid gamblers. The grandstand and open areas are always packed to capacity. The track is turf, and after each race Chinese women of the *Hakka* strain clad in black costumes with lace fringed hats and armed with tampers circle the track smoothing down the turf which has been disturbed by the horses' hoofs. All of the jockeys are gentlemen jockeys, many being business and professional men in town. The horses are Australian ponies. The betting is of the totalizator variety with a huge "tote" board recording every bet made. Each of the parimutuel clerks has an abacus board with which to rapidly figure the amounts due lucky betters.

Racing begins in October and continues through May.

WONG NEI CHUNG GAP is the arterial passage from the island's north to south side. It proceeds from **Victoria's** *Central District,* passes *Happy Valley,* interlaces swank residential areas, and carries on to *Repulse* and *Deep Water Bays.*

POKFULAM, near the western extremity of the south shore, is noted for the dairy farms of *Dairy Farm, Ltd.,* one of the island's show places; the huge *Queen Mary Hospital;* and *Hong Kong University.* The Chinese cemeteries located here are distinguished by their "armchair" graves.

WEST POINT is Old China in a modern world. The congestion is unbelievable, with hundreds of people jammed in each house or apartment and rooftops used by scores of other inhabitants. It is here that the ever-present noises of Chinese areas rise to their crescendo. Street shops, artisans at work, narrow streets teeming with people, children riding piggyback on their mothers, open-air laundries with the multicolored wash streaming from windows on bamboo poles, street hairdressers, and open-air food stalls are blended into the *West Point* picture.

MAN MO MIU, over one hundred years old, is the oldest Chinese temple in Hong Kong. It is rich in color and may be photographed. Nearby is a ladder street giving access to:

MORLO-GAI, the incredible "Thieves Market." The variety of items for sale in this ladder street bargain center is actually endless. Whatever the asking price, your first offer must be at least ninety per cent below it. Since you are not an Oriental, the odds are extremely good that you will pay more than you should for any purchase you make. Even so, good values are to be had . . . but at *Morlo-Gai, be careful.*

TYTAM RESERVOIR, not far from *Fort Lyemun,* which guards the eastern entrance to *Victoria Harbor,* is the vital rain water storage bin for Hong Kong's water supply. Don't drink the water from the tap, however . . . and it might be well to limit your vegetable consumption to those that have been cooked.

LADDER STREETS, rising from *Queen's Road,* are characteristic of Hong Kong and only Hong Kong. They are, to the American mind, as Chinese as *cheongsams* and rice. These almost perpendicular streets, consisting of steep stairways, lead up to *Lower Lascar Row,* commonly known as "Cat Street." The thoroughfare bearing the name "Ladder Street" is not well known locally, as it is somewhat off the beaten path and few

visitors find it. The ladder streets collectively are found in the
Wanchai and *Sai Ying Pun Districts,* crowded Chinese quarters
which were featured in "The World of Suzie Wong" (her hotel
is in *Wanchai*). You must climb up one ladder street to its top,
which will be on the lower portion of *Victoria Peak,* walk a
block to the next ladder street, and walk down again. If not
the full distance, do try at least to cross one or more of the
intersecting lane-like streets. Here, too, you will see every conceivable type of open-air stall for food (which I wouldn't
sample if I were you), handcraft, daily necessities, books and
magazines of all descriptions. These districts are indescribably
crowded and oozing over with the sights, smells, and sounds of
the Orient.

ADVERTISING SAMPANS. From time to time, you will
see gaily bedecked sampans from whose masts and spars and
on whose deckhouses may be seen colorful signs, all in Chinese.
These are advertising sampans to call native products to the
attention of the ferryboat riders.

NORTH POINT, below *Tiger Balm Gardens,* is inhabited
largely by Northern Chinese, from which fact it gets its local
nickname of "Little Shanghai."

TYPHOON SHELTERS. There are extensive typhoon shelters both in *Hong Kong* and *Kowloon.* The former is called
the *Causeway Bay Typhoon Shelter,* while the latter, *Yaumati,*
is by far the larger and better known. Built to protect shipping
from the ravages of the monsoons and typhoons, both are inhabited by thousands of water folk. *Yaumati* seemed to me far
more attractive as a marine home than *Aberdeen.* The water
is deep, and the boats are all afloat both at high and low tide,
which isn't true at *Aberdeen.* The atmosphere seems much
healthier and the boats much cleaner. Here at *Yaumati* there
are waterborne schools, churches, restaurants, and supply centers. These people are more prosperous and seem to live a
pleasant life. There is even a floating red light district.

The HONG KONG TOURIST ASSOCIATION is one of
the most active and intelligently operated tourist associations

with which I have ever come in contact. Its executive director, Major Harry F. Stanley, makes his headquarters in the executive offices at *Caroline Mansions,* 4 Yun Ping Road. The telephone number is 776211-5. The association operates information centres in the *Peninsula Hotel,* Number One East Wing, phone number 69201, and in the Hong Kong *Star Ferry Concourse* where the phone number is 20969. Membership in the *Hong Kong Tourist Association* includes international passenger carriers, travel agents, hotels, shops, restaurants, publishers, night clubs, tailors, and virtually all types of business people. It is a wise precaution to look for the insignia of membership in the *Hong Kong Tourist Association* when one shops. If you have any problems while in *Hong Kong* or are seeking information not contained herein, by all means communicate with the *Hong Kong Tourist Association.* You can be sure of being cordially and graciously treated, and will be given accurate, impartial, and unbiased information. I heartily recommend the *Hong Kong Tourist Association.* "Around and About Hong Kong" is the official guidebook of the *Hong Kong Tourist Association.* It is free, excellent, and contains much valuable information to help you best utilize your time in Hong Kong, including priceless information on shops, restaurants, transportation, and the like.

Kowloon and the New Territories

KOWLOON, only 3½ square miles in area, is the Colony's principal shopping center. Here are located not only the retail shops but workshops and factories, many of which may be visited. From transistor radios to Chinese junks, everything is available in **Kowloon.** At one time almost all of the wonderful hotels were to be found in **Kowloon,** city of the nine dragons. There are now more topflight hotels here than ever before, but **Victoria** is pressing for leadership in the prestige level luxury hotel field. Once a walled and fortified city, **Kowloon** today is bright and modern though still possessed of narrow Chinese streets and houses, relics of its ancient historic past.

NATHAN ROAD bisects **Kowloon.** This principal thoroughfare, which runs past the *Peninsula* and *Ambassador Hotels,*
is broad and beautiful, reminiscent of a European or high class
American boulevard. As it passes the *Whitfield Barracks* and
Parade Grounds, it takes on a lower class commercial aspect.
If one is a camera addict, be sure to get some night Kodachrome film and drive along *Nathan Road* after dark. One's
lens will be rewarded with the greatest concentration of agglomerated neon colors outside of Broadway or the Ginza.

The Hong Kong terminus of the *Kowloon–Canton Railway*
from which a train enters **Red China** each day is located in
front of the *Police Headquarters* virtually next door to the
Peninsula and *Ambassador Hotels.* SALISBURY ROAD, adjacent to the railway, connects the lower end of the *Kowloon
Peninsula* from east to west. To the west, CANTON ROAD
parallels the harbor and passes the *Hong Kong* and *Kowloon
Wharves* and the *Godown.* A stroll from the *Peninsula Hotel*
along *Salisbury Road* and up *Canton Road* presents a mem-

orable marine panorama. At the docks I have seen the ships of as many as fifteen nations represented, great and small. One may stroll as far as the *Yaumati Car Ferry* and the *Typhoon Shelter* beyond. Though it's rather a long walk, one can then turn right to *Nathan Road* and return to the starting point. I hasten to caution you: it's quite a long walk if you are not an intrepid stroller, about an hour and a half at a brisk pace . . . but worth it.

Chatham Road runs along the eastern end of the peninsula and leads to the modern installation at *Kai Tak Airport.*

Kowloon is the starting point for a visit to Old World China: The NEW TERRITORIES. An excellent road, 56 miles in length, permits a fascinating circular tour which may easily be accomplished in five hours.

Before leaving the city, one must stop to view one or another of the resettlement estates which have been constructed by the Hong Kong authorities for the miserable refugees from Red China. Unless it might have been the tenement slums of the lower East Side of New York, the population concentration in the resettlement estates is the greatest the world has ever known. But by such positive action as the building of these multiple apartment dwellings, eight, nine, and ten stories high, many of the pitiful creatures' lives have been saved. The *New Territories* include the Colony's industrial belt, resort areas, sand beaches, systematically terraced rice paddy fields, and small farmsteads.

The *New Territories* present a true picture of the Chinese peasants in their native habitat. These agricultural workers, in spite of their primitive farm implements and ancient methods of tilling and irrigation, unchanged for centuries, have overcome the most difficult terrain and have succeeded in growing verdant crops of rice, sugar cane, a variety of vegetables, and ginger root.

Everywhere in the *New Territories* there are additional evidences of Old China . . . slant roof villages, timeworn walled cities, soaring Buddhist pagodas, and mystical gardens.

As we enter the *New Territories,* our first view is of:

TSUN WAN, an excellent example of the Colony's industrial growth. This was originally a small country fishing village, but, thanks to a reclamation project and economic expansion, it is now a manufacturing area producing silks, textiles, and fabrics.

CASTLE PEAK, some ten miles beyond *Tsun Wan,* is on a two-thousand-foot bluff overlooking *Castle Peak Bay,* a busy body of water with bobbing junks and sampans. The *Dragon's Inn* and *Luk Yuen* resort, both attractive and colorful rest stops, are on *Castle Peak. Luk Yuen* possesses two ponds, one large enough to accommodate rowboats.

TSING SHAN MONASTERY, erected on the steep mountainside, is surrounded by pine and eucalyptus trees. Its 15th-century grotto contains relics which the local Chinese believe to be the bones of a dragon which emerged from the sea centuries ago.

YUEN LONG, a busy colorful market place with a population of more than 30,000, has a main street said to be typical of any South China rural community. Here one sees the greatest concentration of the *Hakka,* or strangers, who work the farms of the *New Territories.* Their costumes are black, the hats enormous. If time permits, you will want to spend a half an hour or so strolling through the village taking pictures of the produce markets and the interesting gatherings of natives.

The Communist China border is quite unprepossessing. From a hilltop surmounted by the *Lok Ma Chau Police Station,* one may look across the *Shum Chun River* to **China** beyond.

KAM TIN is an ancient, though grubby, walled and moated village which is typical of the remote districts of China. Watchtowers guard the village corners, and its moat is spanned by an earthen bridge. The villagers are direct descendants of the original *Puntis* who live their narrow lives much as their ancestors have for more than a thousand years. Within the walls is a shrine dedicated to the god of land. The approach to *Kam*

Tin is through ornate iron gates which made history in 1899. When the *New Territories* were taken over by the British, the villagers, unaware of an official occupation, became alarmed at the troop movements nearby, retired behind their walls, and locking the gates, refused to open them. The British had no alternative. The soldiers stormed the village, and as a souvenir the British governor appropriated the ornamental gates. On his retirement, he took them back to Britain. In 1924, however, the villagers petitioned for their return, and a year later they were brought back and, with suitable ceremony, replaced.

In the nearby fields, the farmers can be seen at work with their ancient plows drawn by oxen and "irrigation" being effected by harnessed humans. The natives fill the sprinkling cans, attach them to yokes over their shoulders, and dogtrot through the fields spreading the precious water.

FAN LING, a farming community and market center, is set in picturesque surroundings comprised of gently rolling green hills and peaceful valleys. Only a few miles distant, to the north, lies the boundary of Red China. Near the town are the two eighteen hole golf courses of the *Royal Hong Kong Golf Club* and the British troops' recreation center.

TAI PO, a market town on the *Kowloon-Canton Railway* facing *Tolo Harbor* where, like *Aberdeen, Stanley,* and the *Typhoon Shelters,* there is a concentration of water folk. The road from **Tai Po** to **Kowloon** passes through the most scenic section of the *New Territories*.

The SHATIN VALLEY is known for its scenic splendor and numerous shrines and monasteries. The most important of the religious edifices is the *Monastery of Sailam* with its ancestral hall enshrined to the goddess of grace. The hilltop chapel of *Tao Fong Shan* is unusual and equally interesting, built by the Scandinavian Mission to enable Buddhists to study Christianity. The chapel has a Buddhist-type altar, but is surmounted by a crucifix instead of Buddha's image. The *Shatin Palace* floating restaurant, moored at **Shatin,** is comparable to the *Tai Pak* and *Sea Palace* at Aberdeen.

The 10,000 BUDDHA MONASTERY is quite new, and its temple contains if not ten thousand at least several thousand small Buddhas. There is a pagoda, several large Buddhas, and statues of Wai Toa, god of protection, and Koon Yum, goddess of mercy.

AMAH'S ROCK resembles a woman's figure atop the hill opposite the *Sailam Monastery*. The Chinese call this natural figure *Mong Fu Kwai*, or "Hoping Husband Returns." The sad but charming 13th-century legend relates the following: An imperial officer with a lovely young wife was recalled by the emperor then at war in Canton. The army was defeated, but the wife learned that her husband had survived and would return. Time passed, a son was born, and the mother's resources were running out, so she was obliged to seek work as a wood cutter. Despite her chores, each day she climbed the hill with her child to watch for her husband's return. At long last, she spied him hurrying up the hill, and as they embraced she fainted with emotion and soon died from the shock. The rock on which she had stood so long watching for her husband was transformed into a woman's shape, remaining forever looking toward Canton.

Tai Mo Shan, or "Big Hat Mountain," is the highest peak in the area, 3,140 feet, and derives its name from the fact that its summit is generally hidden by a thin layer of white clouds.

The route continues through the RICE VALLEY, lying at the apex of the bay, to SHATIN HILLS on which the *Shatin Heights Hotel* is perched. Luncheon may be taken comfortably at the *Shatin Heights Hotel* or four miles farther along on the terrace of the *Carlton Hotel* overlooking **Kowloon,** the harbor, and *Hong Kong Island.*

RED CHINA is, particularly for the *New Territories,* the host of the British Crown Colony. This tenantship presents a most unusual arrangement. The Crown Colony's lease of the *New Territories* will expire in 1997, a relatively few years hence. What will happen then will of course be determined by the ultimate fate of communism in China. On the other hand, it might then, as it does now, serve the purpose of the Communist bosses to have contact with the outside world through the medium of Hong Kong. During both World Wars I and II, all the warring factions felt it worthwhile to permit Switzerland to remain neutral. Though Hong Kong was brutally occupied by the Japanese in World War II, the Red Chinese have never seen fit to gobble up this island paradise. Perhaps they never will, for here they own a big bank, operate stores and shops, and have a built-in listening post to the world.

ENTERTAINMENT IN HONG KONG

CINEMA THEATERS are popular in Hong Kong. The Chinese are avid film fans and the bloodier and more sensational the scripts, the better they like them. As of 1962, there were 52 cinemas in Hong Kong divided as follows: Cantonese, 26; American-European, 18; Mandarin, 6; and Japanese, 2. Hong Kong's two most luxurious and up-to-date theaters are the *Queen's* and *London.*

CHINESE OPERA. No Hong Kong visitor should miss attending a Chinese Cantonese grand opera. These fascinating entertainments unfortunately are all too few and far between. Their performances are well advertised and may be seen at the following theaters where reservations are advisable:

KO SHING—117 Queen's Road West—Hong Kong 4-8883
TAI PING—421 Queen's Road West—Hong Kong
CENTRAL THEATRE—270 Queen's Road Central—Hong Kong 4-9013
LAI CHI KOK—Lai Chi Kok Amusement Park—Kowloon

It is not necessary to understand the background or words of the players to appreciate this expressive form of genuine Chinese art. Chinese opera is of ancient origin dating back to the T'ang dynasty of A.D. 618–906, and was embellished and improved during the famous Ming dynasty of the 15th and 16th centuries. The artists' costumes are well worth seeing. They are magnificent in color, embroidery, and material. The facial make-up is elaborate and carries great significance insofar as the character the actor represents is concerned. The orchestra of about a dozen musicians is hidden in the wings and is a curiosity in itself. There is no conductor or musical score. The timing, rhythm, correct measure, and punctuations are led by wooden clappers and leather drums. The singing, more directly tied to the action and movements of the artists than in western opera, adds emphasis to each movement, including the overly extravagant facial expressions. Scenery and static stage background are scanty in order that the audience may concentrate on the actors whose affected use of symbolic expressions and gestures conveys the dramatic story. Gestures must represent the actions of closing imaginary doors, drinking from invisible cups, climbing nonexistent stairs, and eating food that is not there. The actions of the Chinese opera are quite similar to Shakespearean plays of England's 16th century. Everything in the Chinese opera is carried out with great dignity; nobody hurries through his part. As mentioned, make-up is of the greatest importance, since each character must have a different face . . . cunning, sly characters have white faces, a faithful wife is made up in red, a quick-tempered but valorous warrior is made up in black and white. Each type of character has a different "face."

PLAYS. Usually the plays presented in Hong Kong have a historical background and seem interminable. They last for hours at a time, sometimes even being continued the following week. Audiences arrive armed with food and refreshments.

RECREATION AND SPORTS. In addition to swimming, one may expect to see cricket matches, football games, and British style bowling. There are golf, tennis, shooting, and fishing in the Colony. Hong Kong's private clubs have, in recent years, relaxed their rigid barriers and made visitors welcome. One can play tennis, bridge or golf at one or another of the clubs through arrangements made by the Hong Kong Tourist Association. The *Royal Hong Kong Golf Club* has three challenging courses awaiting you, all you need is a letter from your club secretary.

WATER TOURS. There are excellent water tours embracing *Hong Kong Island, Kowloon,* and the *New Territories* which are well organized by *Hong Kong Water Tours* and others. This is a must in your Hong Kong sightseeing. The island tours include the *Yaumati Typhoon Shelter,* the harbor, *Repulse Bay,* the *Wanchai* waterfront including Suzie Wong's hotel, and luncheon at one of the floating restaurants at *Aberdeen.*

CHEONGSAM is not just the slit dress that many Chinese girls wear; it is also a native institution. This sheath-like, form-fitting, high necked garment holds great fascination . . . for men at least. Slits vary from a few inches above the knee to within gasping proximity of the hips. Fortunately, Chinese girls and women have figures that enhance the loveliness of this dress. One sees the *cheongsam* in all of the better and higher class areas. They are not worn by peasants. Ladies of light virtue and born aristocrats may be seen in the native costume. It is said that inconspicuous zippers are sometimes built into the "slits" and that as the fancy dictates the slit may be lengthened or shortened to fit the occasion.

MACAO

Macao, separated from **Hong Kong** by only forty miles of sparkling blue water, is the oldest European settlement on the **China** mainland. Founded in 1557, it is set against green hills and the swirling waters of the *Pearl River* estuary.

Curiously enough, though completely surrounded by **Red China,** the Communists have never interfered with the affairs of this unique colony. It was here in 1844 that the first treaty between **China** and the **United States** was signed.

The old city is a study of contrasts between stately European architecture and the lacy Chinese counterpart. Much of the city retains its atmosphere of 17th-century **Portugal** imbued with Chinese culture and traditions.

The province comprises **Macao City** and two small islands, *Taipa* and *Coloane*. Provincial law requires that every structure be painted every two years. The resultant blaze of color is an eye-clashing mixture of the Latin and the Oriental, much as is **Macao's** food and way of life. Chinese, Portuguese, and American style dishes are served in the restaurants.

I heartily urge that you make a visit, however brief, to **Macao** from **Hong Kong**. Don't check out of your **Hong Kong** hotel. One may fly to **Macao** in a matter of minutes in a twin engine *Piaggio* P-136 amphibian airplane or alternatively make the journey in a matter of three hours each way in one of three vessels: the *Tai Loy*, the *Fat Shan*, or the *Tak Shing*. All of these ships are comfortable and have some air conditioned cabins. Travel first class. Check locally on the schedules. They change from week to week. The *S.S. Macao*, carrying 1,400 passengers has been renovated at great expense and makes two round trips daily between **Hong Kong** and **Macao**. Running time is two hours each way. Food and drinks are served aboard the **Macao** ships. The new hydrofoil service whisks one between **Hong Kong** and **Macao** in a thrilling seventy minutes. Accommodations are limited; be sure you have a confirmed hydrofoil reservation if you choose this mode of transportation.

There is a twenty-minute ferry service between **Macao City** and *Taipa*, and one between *Taipa* and *Coloane* which takes fifteen minutes.

The POPULATION includes some 200,000 of whom only 3,500 are Portuguese. The Chinese and Europeans live side by side in complete harmony. On the islands, ten thousand busy workers make firecrackers which are one of the chief exports of the colony. Incense sticks are manufactured here and used locally. Fireworks in **Macao** are used to celebrate most every festive occasion including weddings, births, ship launchings, and public holidays.

SHOPPING and GAMBLING are **Macao's** twin attractions. Along the *Avenida Almeida Ribeiro,* Portuguese porcelains, earthenware, embroideries, filigree work, perfumes, wines and liqueurs, jewelry, and Indian silks are all for sale. Off the *Avenida* in twisting Chinese alleys are food stalls, herb shops, fortunetellers, and professional letter writers.

But the real business of Macao is gambling. The principal games now being played are *"Ku Sik"* and *fan-tan*. The first is played with three dice, and bets are made on any number from four to seventeen, high and low, three of a kind, and the turn of a single die.

In *fan-tan,* the croupier plunges a rice bowl upside down on a pile of buttons. Bets are placed on the side of a square marked from one to four. The croupier lifts the bowl and starts counting the buttons with a bamboo sliver four at a time. The remainder determines the winner . . . four, three, two, or one.

It is an interesting sidelight of this game that the moment the croupier spills the pile of buttons regular devotees call out what the remainder will be. They are never wrong. Their ears are carefully attuned. Many a visitor who has placed a bet has been surprised to have somebody tap him on the shoulder and tell him that he has won or lost before the croupier has even begun counting.

The storied *Hotel Central,* once the gay gambling center, has been closed and its place taken by the lavish new European-type casino which, embracing a hotel, restaurant and other amusements, features the above-mentioned games of chance plus roulette, *chemin de fer,* and baccara. Greyhound racing has recently been introduced in Macao. American citizens may not gamble in Communist-controlled casinos.

The CATHEDRAL OF SAO PAULO, built in 1602 and destroyed by fire in 1835, is still resplendent though all that remains is the façade. From the top of the stairs approaching the *Cathedral,* a fine view of the old city is obtained. *Sao Paulo* was built by Christian Japanese artists, and it was considered a masterpiece of Christian interpretation in Oriental context.

KAM YUNG TEMPLE was the site of the signing of the 1844 treaty between **China** and the **United States.** It has three great courts containing figures of Buddha, his disciples, and the goddesses of purity and mercy. The latter are surrounded by gilded statues of saints, one of which is no less than the famous explorer and adventurer, Marco Polo. How he managed to get into this sacred company remains a mystery. In the temple garden is a stone table on which the famous treaty was signed by Cushing and the Chinese viceroy. It was also in this temple that Doctor Sun Yat-sen, father of the Chinese Republic, founded the *Kuomintang* which led to the Chinese Revolution and the downfall of the Manchu dynasty.

The OLD PROTESTANT CEMETERY is of interest. The tombstones in this old burial ground, originated by the British East India Company in 1821, bear the names of famous daring pioneers and adventurers now long forgotten.

GARDEN AND GROTTO OF CAMOENS. On a hillside close to the *Cemetery* is an attractive old 18th-century garden and house once belonging to the East India Company. In the garden is an unusual grotto (or cave) containing a statue of Portugal's most famous poet, Luiz Vaz de Camoens, who was a great traveler and one of the first Portuguese to arrive in **Macao.** Most of Camoens' epic poem "The Lusiads" was written in this garden which is now a public park.

The BARRIER GATE divides **Macao** from **Red China,** and through it comes much of **Macao's** food supply.

Ma Kok Miu, the *Temple of Ah Ma,* and *Lin Fung Miu* are among the Chinese temples of interest.

Match manufacturing is another of the industries of **Macao.** If you have seen matches made in **Jonkoping, Sweden,** a big surprise awaits you in **Macao.** They are made differently here. One may visit a local match factory.

In **Macao,** one may use American dollars, Hong Kong dollars, or purchase the local coin of the realm, the pataca, which in turn is divided into one hundred avos. As noted elsewhere, a Portuguese visa is necessary to visit **Macao.** It may be obtained at the Portuguese Consulate in **Hong Kong.**

CHAPTER 12

Japan

THIS INCREDIBLY SCENIC COUNTRY, outstanding for its hospitality, ancient culture, and strident modernism, awaits the western visitor with open arms.

No other nation, great or small, having suffered such a catastrophic defeat, has ever made such an astonishing industrial and financial recovery as has **Japan.** With amazing rapidity, the Japanese have overcome stupendous postwar difficulties and have adopted the habits and the manners of their victors with an almost alarming fervor, yet retained much of their own ancient way, fascinating customs, traditions, and background.

Japan is a country of majestic mountains and towering hills with a rich variety of magnificent and ever changing scenery that will ever delight the eye. Fast mountain rivers, lovely tumbling waterfalls, and innumerable placid lakes of unsurpassed beauty alternate pleasingly with fertile farming areas nestled between rugged mountain ranges.

Fujiyama, one of the world's most renowned and breathtaking mountains, powdered nine months a year with a conical crest of virgin snow, is visible from **Tokyo** on clear days. This external symbol of Japan is only a fleeting hour and a half by rail from the capital.

During the idyllic Japanese spring which lasts from March to May, the high temperatures reach 70 degrees, and the entire land is then lush with gorgeous flowers and blossoms beginning early in the season with brilliant plum blossoms followed by apricot and orange blooms decorating the countryside and reaching an unrivaled horticultural crescendo in April when the country is bedecked with the splendor of the blooming cherry blossoms. No other land in the world is so bounteously blessed by nature with an aesthetic saturation of unrivaled hues as is Japan with its seemingly infinite variety of flaming maples, gorgeous azaleas, tranquil lotus blossoms, and golden chrysanthemums. When the Japanese islands burst into their annual spring, summer, and fall riots of color, there is presented to the visitor a panorama of rainbow shades worth traveling the world over to see.

GEOGRAPHICAL BACKGROUND. Japan is composed of four major islands consisting of 46 prefectures, or provinces: to the north, the little known *Hokkaido* (30,334 square miles); *Honshu* (88,968 square miles), the largest and best known which includes *Mount Fuji (Fujiyama),* **Tokyo,** the capital, **Kyoto,** the ancient capital, **Yokohama, Kobe, Osaka,** and **Hiroshima;** the *Isle of Shikoku* (7,280 square miles); and the most southerly island of *Kyushu,* embracing **Beppu, Hakata,** and the ill-fated **Nagasaki,** atom-bombed old original Dutch trading fort and home of the legendary *"Madame Butterfly."* There are innumerable other small islets, extending off the Japanese coast in the north *Pacific*. The undulating coast line of the four main islands exceeds 16,000 scenic miles.

The country is punctuated with thermal hot springs reputedly of great medicinal value and thriving spas set in inviting Japanese gardens. The coast line, deeply indented and rugged, has hundreds of pine-clad islets of rare and exotic charm.

THE CLIMATE. One may not generalize about the climate or the seasonal temperatures of Japan. A considerable distance is traversed from the northern tip of *Hokkaido* to the most

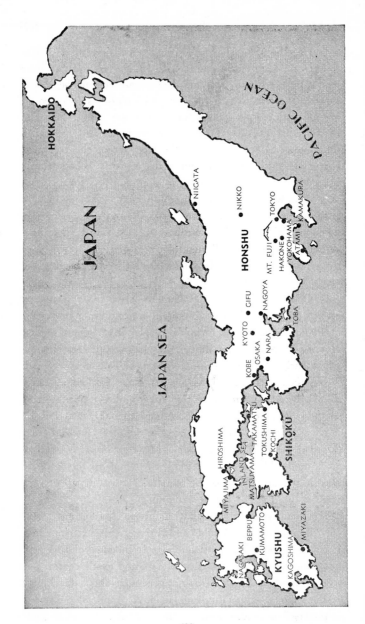

southern point on *Kyushu,* and the weather understandably varies between these two extremities.

The islands of *Honshu, Shikoku,* and *Kyushu* might be compared, temperature-wise, to **New York City, Chicago,** or **Paris, France.** On *Honshu,* which embraces **Tokyo, Yokohama,** and **Kyoto,** the daily winter mean temperature is approximately 38 degrees Fahrenheit, while the summer days average 77 degrees, with high temperatures ranging to 90 degrees and above. The spring and fall seasons are quite moderate, with the average daytime temperature ranging from 60 to 65 degrees or more. In southern *Kyushu* the winters are Japan's warmest, but the summers are about the same as in central *Honshu. Kyushu's* **Kagoshima,** for example, has an average winter daytime temperature of a moderate 45 degrees Fahrenheit, but in the summer the days seldom are hotter than in **Tokyo,** with the fall days averaging 66 degrees.

Hokkaido's northerly position, however, causes its climate to vary considerably from the other islands. **Sapporo,** the capital, has an average January daytime temperature of 20 degrees Fahrenheit. In the summer **Sapporo's** high thermometer reading seldom goes above 70 degrees, while the average is 67.5 degrees. Spring days in the north average 42 degrees and in the fall it's warmer, with an average of 50 degrees. *Hokkaido's* summer days are normally crisp, clear, and dry.

With the exception of *Hokkaido,* June frequently sees the Japanese islands visited by the gentle *nyubai,* a misty rain which leaves the atmosphere dripping with humidity. The rains are usually dried up by mid-July, but the heat lingers on until early or mid-September. A typhoon or two will normally threaten the islands in the late summer or early fall, but the full force of these heavy blows can generally be counted on to be dissipated elsewhere.

There are generous seasonal snowfalls in *Hokkaido* and northern *Honshu,* but in the central and southern sections what little snow does fall seldom lasts long enough to be enjoyed. **Tokyo** generally has one big snowfall a season, in late

February—often it is a pip! No snow at all has fallen on **Tokyo** during the past several winters, which have been surprisingly mild.

Climatically Japan is at the acme of its perfection during the spring and fall, with winter having much to recommend it as a travel season. From late March through May and late September through December the islands are graced with magnificent floral coloration, the skies are radiantly blue, and the days are usually clear, crisp, and devoid of humidity. The winter sparkles with urban gaiety, while the ski resorts beckon to the sports enthusiasts. This season, though it can be frigid, is usually blessed with both blue skies and bright sun. All forms of winter sports are available in the mountain hamlets, with modern ski lifts aiding and abetting the gay throngs who crowd the runs. Ice skating is a popular sport enjoyed on many lakes, ponds, and artificial outdoor and indoor rinks. Should your visit to Japan be in the winter, bring along a fur coat, overcoat, or topcoat and you'll be comfortable and happy. In June one needs a raincoat and umbrella, and, until mid-September, light tropical weight clothing. During the summer months city hotels and restaurants are generously air conditioned, and nature has provided natural acclimatization to *Hokkaido* and the mountain resorts.

TRADITIONS, CUSTOMS, AND BACKGROUND. No other country in the world can exceed Japan's gracious age-old traditions, countless art treasures, or historic and exotic mementoes. Despite their craze for western modernity, the Japanese have preserved and basically revere their legends and unique customs. It is this colorful and fascinating combination of East and West which delights the visitor.

The TEA CEREMONY. The ancient tea ceremony, *Cha-no-yu,* has been a continuous integral and aesthetic part of the Japanese daily life since the 9th century.

Inevitably you will be exposed to one or more tea ceremonies during your visit to Japan, but you will not be expected to know how to follow all of the rituals about which I am about

to tell you in connection with this highly stylized performance. When the tea ceremony is performed for overseas visitors,
great latitude in etiquette is permitted.

In A.D. 805, tea was introduced to Japan from **China** by a
Buddhist priest and was first planted on *Mount Hiei* in the
vicinity of **Kyoto.** Today tea is one of Japan's important national products.

The consumption of this stimulant was originally a highly
regarded part of the religious ceremonies. Then, as now, the
aesthetic qualities of the tea ceremony were considered a contribution to an artistic way of life.

Apart from its religious significance, the Buddhist priests
drank tea to relieve their weariness during prolonged periods
of solitude. They, and the laymen, long clung to the belief that
tea was of considerable medicinal value, particularly as an
antidote to the adverse effect of encroaching years on the eyes,
though other curative attributes were also credited to this brew.

The rituals of the tea service were religiously adhered to
and participated in exclusively by priests and aristocrats for six
centuries. They placed great faith in the tea ceremony for in-
ducing serenity of mind and cultivating good manners. Today

the tea ceremony is universally observed by all Japanese—particularly the wealthier class, who go to great pains and expense to continue the aesthetic cultivation of the art.

There are two well-known traditional tea ceremony schools: *Ura-senke* and *Omote-senke*. The rituals vary with the calendar and the alma mater of the host.

The following description deals with the ceremony as traditionally observed in private homes for invited guests. In public tea rooms, the basic concepts are followed, but, of necessity, there are variations.

The etiquette is extremely confining, with five guests being the specified number for the home ceremony. They gather in the *yoritsuki* (waiting room) which is contiguous with the tea room in which the traditional matting is found. The arrangements of the room are significant, and the Japanese guests understand that they are obliged to make suitable complimentary remarks relative to the accoutrements. To fail to do so would be considered a serious faux pas and would deeply offend the host.

When the guests have assembled, the host enters and, after the traditional ceremonial bow, silently goes into the tea room, the signal that all is ready. The head guest initiates the act of purification, which includes the cleansing of the mouth and hands, and then the guests proceed to the tea room, minus shoes, of course. The ceremonial room is reached through a twenty foot typical garden walk *(roji)* so designed as to make complete the detachment from the rude, crude outside world and to establish the necessary aura of peaceful tranquility. The *roji* is not of any specific design but usually will be a combination of the handiwork of man and the endowments of nature. A pond, small bridge, stone lantern, dwarf trees, and other decorative arrangements may be a part of the *roji*.

The alcove to the tea room *(tokonoma)* is adorned with a scroll which the guests must gaze upon with rapturous awe from their kneeling position on a mat just in front of the alcove. Then begins a period of general adulation of the decorations and furnishings.

After proper exclamations of surprise and admiration of the incense burner usually located in a nearby niche, the *kaiseki,* the introductory meal, considered to be of great significance, is served. The host places the dishes before the guests, each of whom has his own separate tray and service. This food is not considered a dinner at all but merely a prelude to the tea service. Etiquette dictates that each morsel so served must be consumed. The host carries the trays himself but carefully abstains from consuming the food with his guests. After the food has vanished, the ceremony continues with the guests placing their various empty bowls, dishes, and trays together, the host himself carrying them ceremoniously from the room. The sweets are then served, and in due course the lead guest shepherds the others into the *naka-dachi,* a mid-waiting room.

After a respectable interval, a soft gong signal is sounded. The tea ceremonial is almost ready to begin . . . but not, however, until after the hands have been washed again and the mouths re-rinsed. Then the guests return to the tea room where a complete rearrangement has been made in their absence. There are now flowers in place of the scroll.

The ceremonial tea *(koi-cha)* is thick, almost gooey. After hot water has been added to this paste-like substance, it is vigorously stirred with a bamboo whiskbroom-like device into a consistency not at all unlike a cream soup. After the tea has attained its proper consistency, the bowl is placed before the lead guest who then performs his carefully rehearsed ritual. He must first follow the ancient and modern tradition of the bow (yes, again!), which he does with great gusto before grasping the bowl firmly in his left hand, being careful to employ his right hand as a guide, to assay his first delicate taste. He must savor this sip with obvious pleasure and permit a suitable pause to ensue before exclaiming, in most flattering terms, that the aroma and palate titillating qualities of the tea are of the finest. But this it not all. He must then, normally, continue and take two more sips before relinquishing the bowl to the second guest, who repeats the performance and then puts the bowl in circulation for the completion of its rounds. Research has not informed me whether or not such a horrendous catastrophe as dropping the bowl has ever taken place and if so what the consequences were. I would presume that this would call for hara-kiri at least.

As each guest has his go at the bowl, it is carefully wiped with *kaishi,* a paper prepared especially for this chore. It is incumbent upon the head guest to request permission to scrutinize the tea bowl, the tea caddy, and the bamboo spoon. Permission is always granted, and each of the guests may express his delight at these artistic heirlooms. After the main ceremony has been completed, *usu-cha,* so-called "thin" tea or tea as we know it, is generally served. This tea "chaser" is presented with only a modicum of ritual.

Centuries of tradition and years of habitual tea ceremonies no doubt have cultivated the Japanese taste for the ceremonial tea. I personally find it to be rather bitter, though the sweets served just before the guests drink have a tendency to make it more palatable, and the thin variety served later introduces a sweeter, more desirable, lasting taste.

By the time the thin tea has been finished, several hours will have passed since the party assembled. We would find such a process physically tiresome and mentally debilitating. Not so with the Japanese guests. They have been invited, of course, because they are known to each other and to the host and also because they are adherents to the art of the tea ceremony.

Carefully studied conversation plays an important role during the formalities of the tea service, with the subjects discussed covering a wide range. No scandal, please.

When the ceremonies at long last have run their seemingly endless course, the guests again (ad infinitum) bow profusely and leave. Etiquette requires that the next day each guest should either call in person to express his delight at the ceremony or write a "bread and butter" note promptly.

A number of the ancient tea houses are still in existence. You would find a visit to one of them to be of interest. As one might expect, many of them are in **Kyoto,** including the *Ginka-kuji,* a National Treasure, known alternatively and perhaps more popularly as *The Silver Pavilion.* This was the home base of Shuko, originator in the 15th century of the tea ceremony as it is known today. In the *Detached Palace* at **Kyoto** is the *Shokin-tei,* laid out by another of the great personalities of the tea ceremony, Kobori Enshu, of the late 16th and early 17th centuries. *Koho-an* and *Shinju-an* are also in **Kyoto,** as is *Myoki-an,* a National Treasure, former home of Sen-no Rikyu, the celebrated 16th-century tea cultist.

The ancient *Rokuso-an* is in the *National Museum* in **Tokyo.**

It is much more fun to participate in the tea ceremony seated on the mats, as do the Japanese. It is now so arranged, however, that foreign guests may participate in these rituals seated more comfortably. The *Sado-Kaikan* in **Tokyo,** among others, has a private tea room furnished in western style.

I am particularly fond of **Tokyo's** delightful *Happoen Garden* where the tea ceremonial is practiced.

The GEISHA. Japan and *Geisha* are virtually synonymous words, even for those who have never visited the country. Most foreigners, though understandably curious, are entirely ignorant of the precise functions of, or the true position held by, these dainty, colorful, fragile young women, made famous in the west through the operatic strains of *"Madame Butterfly."* *Geisha* means "accomplished person," which, with additional complexities, is precisely what they are.

The *Geisha* play an intrinsic role in the social and economic drama of Japan. Whether or not these carefully trained creatures are to be considered prostitutes depends largely on one's point of view. The Japanese do not consider them as such. Most Americans, unfamiliar with Japan and the *Geisha,* would.

They represent the ancient culture and ritualistic Japanese symbolism of the art of pleasing. The *Geisha* interpretation of what constitutes good fun and mellow relaxation pleases Japanese gentlemen but is a world apart from the westerner's ideas on the subject. The word *"Geisha,"* incidentally, is always used in the singular.

I must point out that the beauteous hostesses who swarm through the night clubs and cafes of the land are not *Geisha* at all but only resemble the "accomplished person" in her crudest form. The hostesses have not had the training for the complicated profession which is the last echo of the manners and customs of feudalism and privilege.

Her thorough training provides the *Geisha* with innumerable skills and a considerable knowledge which permits her to put her male client completely at ease. Of her many responsibilities, none is more important to the *Geisha* than to help her benefactors forget their business frustrations, domestic troubles, and worrisome details, which under her tender guidance seem to evaporate. She creates an illusion of "all's well with the world," however transitory and illusory this sense of well-being may be.

To the visitor, the *Geisha* appear merely as pretty, artificial, showpieces, entrancing the guests with their winning smiles, manners, and graceful bows, to disappear when the party is over. The well-heeled Japanese male regards them quite differently, however. His idea of a perfect evening begins with a drink, a visit to his favorite Turkish bath, and a palate-pleasing dinner, served with *sake* or rice wine, consumed while being amused by a beautiful *Geisha's* singing, dancing, playing music or games. The *Geisha* gracefully presides with consummate skill over each of these pleasures.

It is quite customary for *Geisha* to parade under adopted names which normally are as exotic as their profession.

Everyone who visits Japan should regard a visit to a *Geisha* tea house, restaurant, or special *Geisha* party house as a "must." Japanese men never take their wives, or their female friends, to such *Geisha* entertainment. These affairs, however, can be arranged for American men and women without difficulty or embarrassment.

There are a number of *Geisha* houses to be found in *Tsukiji,* the canal area adjacent to the Ginza; *Shimbashi,* near the lower Ginza; and *Akasaka,* in the entertainment district, as well as in other surrounding districts bordering central **Tokyo.** They are also scattered throughout Japan and are easy to find. Your local travel representative will be delighted to arrange a *Geisha* party for you and your friends. For a lark, I'm sure that a good time will be had by both the *Geisha* and their guests should you choose to enjoy such an evening. I might mention that *Geisha* entertainment varies considerably, from their stilted dancing and singing to hilarious songs and games depicting incidents in baseball games, alpine climbing, or nautical adventure. The various "Tokyo By Night" tours invariably include an hour or so in a *Geisha* house.

Historically, *Geisha* are trained as assiduously and thoroughly as are ballet dancers, thoroughbred horses, or dental technicians. **Kyoto** is the center of *Geisha* training, and the girls are considered to be the glory of that city. Preliminary training begins as early as the age of nine. In olden times, it was not unusual for girls to be placed in *Geisha* houses as bonded apprentices shortly after their training began. Now the neophyte must have attained her 15th birthday before she can enter a *Geisha* house, and while she does obligate herself to return money expended in her behalf for her training, clothes, and accoutrements, she is no longer considered to be in a state of modern peonage. Many girls look forward zestfully to becoming *Geisha* if for no other reason than that this profession, considered locally to be honorable, enables her to escape from brutally strict family supervision and to elude domestic or factory slavery as the wonders of the outside world unfold before her delighted eyes. Curiously enough, even today most respectable Japanese females cannot share the emancipated life of European or American women. Most are still bound by tradition despite the increasing availability of higher education.

The basic *Geisha* training is geared to make the girls good companions in every way. Not only must they become consummately skilled in the ways of the theater, music, dancing, and other forms of entertainment, but they are trained in recitation, elocution, and the performance of the tea and flower ceremonies. In the modern curriculum of *Geisha* training, arithmetic and at least an elementary course in English are usually given. Unless it is a rare *Geisha*, you will learn when you visit with one, however, that their knowledge of English is at best completely rudimentary.

When she turns 15, the girl aspiring to become a *Geisha* in **Kyoto** enters one of the houses owned by a successful retired *Geisha* and as soon as she has progressed well in her training and is considered ready, she will have the opportunity to perform in the *Kaburenjo Theater*, in the *Gion Quarter*, the extraordinarily colorful *Miyako Odori*, known as the "Cherry Dance," performed from the first of April until the middle of May. Others of the young *Geisha* will have their opportunity to appear in public at the *Kamogawa Odori*, also in **Kyoto**, performed from mid-April until mid-May.

The girls—called *"maiko"*—are considered to be apprentices until they have attained their 21st birthday. They are, however, permitted to entertain in restaurants and in *Geisha* houses with the full-fledged *Geisha* and start earning money shortly after they have entered into their apprenticeship arrangement. This is fortunate since to be launched into the profession of the "accomplished person" is quite expensive. The silk kimonos are frightfully dear, costing a minimum of $150 to $200 and more. The basic standard piece of equipment of all the *Geisha* is the ivory and catskin *samisen* which was originally introduced from **China** at least four centuries ago. It is a beautiful lutelike musical instrument which follows her wherever she goes and accompanies her songs. It is taken for granted that the *Geisha* will have an elaborate wardrobe which includes jewelry, combs, special wigs, and traditional accessories, all of which are not inexpensive.

The ritualistic movements we consider to be rather artificial, including the graded bows, are an integral part of her repertoire. The *maiko* also learns the art of flattery which must be tempered with subtlety according to the type of guest or guests she is hired to entertain.

The elegant *Geisha* quite probably will be the last bastion of antiquity to stand up to the rapidly encroaching western customs, which since the war have been substituted for many of the ancient, delightful Japanese traditions. These highly skilled, carefully trained creatures abound in contemporary Tokyo, Kyoto, Osaka, and the other principal cities, and there are many more in training, although the number of trainees, or apprentices, is less now than before the war and shows no sign of increasing.

As I mentioned above, *Geisha* are not prostitutes per se. They do not normally enter into an arrangement for one evening in return for a sum of money. They are human, however, living a life in close proximity to attractive, rich men, and are continuously tempted. In fact, the old *"Madame Butterfly"* theme is not far from real life. The *Geisha* is well aware that her charms cannot last and that she must first accumulate considerable income to pay off her apprenticeship and the investment in her wardrobe and accessories. She is also all too aware that she must put aside something for her old age. Some wed and marry very well indeed. These marriages are considered just as natural as we consider marriages of our own screen stars. Other *Geisha* enter into relationships and arrangements with well off, sometimes elderly admirers, called "patrons," who sometimes wait a long time for a *Geisha's* exclusive favors. Whatever the deal, everything to do with the *Geisha* is conducted with decorum and good taste. The law of supply and demand operates in this league as elsewhere. The higher the class of the *Geisha* and the more famous she has become, the harder and more expensive it is to obtain her favors. It is curious that the successful male contender adds to his own social prestige and admiration of his fellow men in direct ratio to his *Geisha's* attainments. Curious, isn't it? It is not unusual for such successful women to become the mistresses of men in the highest positions in business and government.

TRANSPORTATION. The magic carpet of international air travel has brought this incomparably beautiful and interesting country to the doorstep of the western world. The traveler may now fly directly to **Tokyo** from our West Coast in less than 12 hours' flying time. For those who prefer a more leisurely method of travel, many transpacific luxury liners will fill their requirements. The pleasant invigorating sea journey from the United States Pacific Coast takes about 15 days via **Hawaii,** ten or eleven days over the direct Great Circle route.

RAIL TRANSPORTATION. Japan's railway system, inaugurated in 1872, is not only the newest but one of the most efficient in the civilized world. When the first steam-powered train chug-chugged from **Tokyo** to **Yokohama,** it was a momentous occasion dignified by the deity-like presence of the great Emperor Meiji and his court entourage, all dressed up in their ceremonial best. The advent of this new magnificent mode of travel brought with it unbounded happiness to the Japanese. Inland highway transportation even now is not good; then, it was atrocious. Favorite resort areas, remote cross-country destinations, and even neighboring cities could then be reached only by means of tortuous travel on foot or, for the rich, in palanquins (or *kago*) toted by surefooted serfs. Later the palanquins disappeared only to be replaced by rickshaws and, subsequently, by horse-drawn vehicles. It was not unusual for journeys to consume painstaking weeks.

The development of Japan's contemporary rail system represents extraordinary accomplishments of advanced engineering. The rights of way include tunnels, bridges, and viaducts which are, proportionately, the most numerous in the world.

The government's *Japanese National Railways* (JNR) system, which owns the major through lines interlacing the principal islands with their ribbons of steel, operates with the utmost in speed, regularity, and reliability.

Many of the myriad panting interurban trains and some of the remote rural lines are privately owned.

On its through lines, the JNR offers its passengers a choice of two classes in equipment which is new, fresh, modern, and generally a joy to behold. The reclining seats are comfortable, and the train attendants render perfect service. The express trains are divided into three categories: the elite *"limited,"* the popular *"ordinary,"* and the workaday *"semi."* The swank *limited express* service names its trains with such charming titles as *Swallow, Pigeon, Sea Gull, Echo,* and *Sea Breeze.*

The *limited expresses,* which operate south to **Fukuoka** and **Nagasaki** via **Nagoya, Kyoto, Osaka,** and **Kobe** and north to **Aomori,** are each provided with one, and one only, fourteen-seat parlor car equipped with luxurious swivel, armchair-type seats. Since the demand for parlor car seats is great and the supply limited, one immediately asks why there are not more parlor cars. I don't know. Frankly, first class is so good I see no particular need for parlor cars at all.

Tea and light snacks are served in the parlor car, and, in addition to the dining car service, green-clad girls constantly circulate through all the cars dispensing, at very reasonable prices, a wide variety of food and refreshments. In the morning one may have tea, wafers, and cake and, a bit later, tangerines, boxes of candy, and cake. Ice cream, milk, coffee, tea, and soft drinks are also dispensed.

One may telephone from the parlor cars of the *limited express* trains in addition to listening to the public address system, music, or individual radios tuned to NHK-1 and NHK-2. These two government radio stations cater to two different tastes: the former is on a more elevated level, while the latter is devoted to popular listening.

In first class, each coach is equipped with a courteous "car boy" who will stow your wraps and hand baggage in the overhead rack and your heavy luggage in a special end-of-the-car compartment. He is constantly tidying up his car, sweeping and mopping to insure hygienic cleanliness. The dining car is always number six in the *express* trains, while in the *limited express* trains it is usually number five.

Dining car meals, as in Europe, are served at fixed hours, with advance reservations necessary. On a well-filled train, there may be as many as five sittings with forty minutes allotted for each service. The first luncheon sitting is at eleven A.M., the next one at 11:40, with succeeding sittings continuing at 12:20, 1:00, and 1:40. It is normally not necessary to go to the dining car to make your mealtime reservation, but if you board a train other than at its point of origin, you most likely will have missed the opportunity to make your reservation in your own car, and I suggest a trip to the diner for this purpose. The steward and a helper will pass through the entire train soon after its departure to arrange reservations and also to take your luncheon or dinner order. Unlike European diners, in Japan there is a choice for each course. The main dish usually includes a choice of steak, chicken, chop, or cutlet. Japanese and western style meals are offered on a table d'hôte basis and are more than adequate. Like almost any place else in the world, neither the service nor food quality is constant on all trains every day. I had a tenderloin steak on the train between **Beppu** and **Hiroshima,** for example, which was simply delicious. It was done to a state of epicurean perfection, juicy and delectable, as tender as one could ever desire. The next day on the very same train I ordered the same dish. It was mediocre, though not bad. Dining car meals include soup, meat or fowl, potatoes, cooked vegetable, salad, and dessert. There normally is a choice of bread and butter or rice as a "side dish." Meal prices vary from just over a dollar to approximately three dollars.

The dining car wine list is all encompassing, offering the would-be imbiber brandy, bourbon, Canadian or Scotch whisky, gin, beer, stout, and *sake*. Manhattan, martini, and Gibson cocktails are available, as are gin fizz, Cinzano, and vermouth. Imported Medoc and St. Emilien wines are listed for sale but are not always available. A Scotch and soda will cost about a dollar, while Japanese beer sells for about 50 cents for a large bottle (four table-size glasses).

The steward, who, incidentally, just might be a stewardess, will speak English understandably. Meals are served by cute little girls in emerald green costumes enhanced by pert white aprons, collars, and cuffs. Their white headbands accentuate their pretty softly dark complexions. These gals, like all other Japanese, are antiseptically bright and shining clean. They are refreshing to see. Service is rapid and efficient.

All of the principal routes are electrified, permitting high speed rail service at its best. The 12-car *express* from **Tokyo** to **Osaka,** the fastest in Japan, covers the three hundred and thirty-nine miles in an amazing (virtually unbelievable) *three* hours. This special *express* operates at hourly intervals. *Limited express* trains, making the run in about four hours, depart frequently.

The Japanese railway business is stupendous. Nowhere else either in Europe or America have I ever seen such a constant state of quantitatively concentrated train riders. The coaches bulge with their human freight from early morning to late at night. Towns with strange names, many of which I had never previously heard mentioned, have beehive busy stations with four or more platforms, each continuously crowded with avid travelers. Despite the linguistic barrier, which is formidable, one need not experience too great difficulty in negotiating through-train trips on the main lines, as all signs in the stations, on the platforms, and in the trains are in both Japanese and English.

I heartily recommend that you confine your rail adventures to the *express* and *limited express* trains or, if you are ultra-adventuresome—or as a last resort if no other tickets are available—to the *semi-express* service. I'm afraid that you would find the going rather rough, virtually impossible, on the *local* and *commuter* trains. I have a friend who lives in suburban **Tokyo** and commutes 20 miles each way daily. He tells me that during the last three and a half years he has yet to find a seat.

I have been in the main **Kobe** station at a time when four trains were being loaded simultaneously, each of them with a dozen or more coaches. Two were through trains and two were bright reddish-yellow *suburban* trains. **Kobe,** incidentally, is served by the nationalized through-train service and by two very important private suburban lines. On the **Kyoto-Osaka** suburban service, each coach boasts of a television set which is constantly in use.

Principal distances from **Tokyo** covered by the *Japan National Railways* are as follows:

Atami	66	Miles
Beppu	765.5	"
Mount Fuji area	68	" (approx.)
Hakata (Fukuoka)	1,409.5	"
Hiroshima	557.5	"
Kamakura	31	"
Kobe	364	"
Kyoto	325.5	"
Miyanoshita (via Odawara)	60	"
Nagoya	228	"
Nara	308.5	"
Nikko	91.5	"
Odawara	50.5	"
Osaka	339	"
Sapporo	705.5	"
Yokohama	19	"

On the long runs from **Tokyo** to **Fukuoka** and **Aomori,** excellent sleeping cars are used which include both roomettes and the upper-lower berth sleeping arrangements. Tall American men have a bit of a problem as the berths are somewhat short.

The *Romance Train*. This all-reserved-seat, completely articulated train runs between **Tokyo's** *Shinjuku Station* and *Yumoto Station* in the *Hakone National Park*. Beautiful in appearance, excellent in its facilities, and speedy in its operation, this popular train is used by happy weekenders, honeymooners, all varieties of Japanese, and their overseas visitors.

The supplemental fees for riding the *express* trains vary

according to the distance traveled. For example, the supplement from **Tokyo** to **Hakata (Fukuoka)** is $5.00, while from **Tokyo** to **Kyoto** and **Kobe,** a lesser distance, the charge is the same. On the *ordinary express* trains, the fee up to 300 kilometers (186 miles) is $1.22, while for distances over 300 kilometers, the fee is $1.84.

Tour groups of 15 or more in number are subject to discounts of at least 20 per cent depending on the group's size. Operators should secure a "Tourist Party Certificate" obtainable in advance from the *Japanese Consular Corps,* or in Japan on arrival of the group from the *Ministry of Transportation (Tourist Industry Bureau),* or from the entry examiner at the port of entry.

On the *semi-express* trains where both reserved and unreserved reclining seats are available, the supplemental fee is 70 cents irrespective of the distance traveled. On the *limited* and *ordinary express* trains, reservations are *de rigueur.* Even should you travel on a *semi-express* train, I would recommend that you make a reservation.

In the *limited* and *semi-express* trains, intercom speakers are employed to make bilingual announcements as well as to soothe the travelers with soft music. The name of, and time of arrival at, the next town is announced shortly after the departure from each preceding station. Passengers may receive telegrams at stations included on their itinerary. Such messages will be handed to the conductor by the stationmaster, the recipient's name called over the train loud-speaker, and the message promptly delivered.

As a supplementary aid to the train's internal announcements, each station is provided with a public address system. As trains roll in, a sonorous voice repetitiously intones the name of the station. If by chance you had missed the announcement in the train, and should you fail to see the name on the station platform where it is written in large western letters and in two styles of bold Japanese characters, you have but to listen. The pronouncement over the local loud-speaker is so clear even to our ears that you should not be carried beyond your anticipated destination, even if you try!

The platforms are generously endowed with shops and strolling vendors. Even in my favorite **Italy,** the station vending activity takes a remote back seat to the Japanese variety.

Most stations will have two, three, or more kiosks which dispense souvenirs, toys and games, newspapers, magazines, candy, cake, soft drinks, beer, and even hard liquor.

The mobile vendors dispense a variety of fruit and beverages plus complete Japanese style box lunches, chopsticks included.

The platforms are also equipped with stone or marble wash troughs. A half dozen or more "wash-ups" are available to freshen up from your journey. Comfort stations are present, but not always of the western style.

The Japanese trains run on rapid operating schedules. Stops are often unbelievably brief. On the *express* and *limited express* train schedules, most stations merit only a one minute halt. Even for the big cities a two minute stop is considered lengthy. **Kyoto,** for example, rates only a two minute stop on the *express* train schedules. Precisely two minutes after its arrival, an *express* train will be on its way irrespective of whether or not all passengers and baggage are aboard. Step lively.

Traveling Americans find the principal problem caused by this rapid scheduling arises from carrying too much cumbersome luggage. It will be helpful to your porter and car boy, as well as certainly saving you the possible ultimate embarrassment of traveling without luggage, if you would personally carry as much of your small gear aboard as possible. If the porter has to cope with all your niffs and naffs, your big luggage, and care for other passengers, time will just not permit him to complete his chores. There is nothing that inspires such a devastating feeling as to be standing by the window gazing helplessly outward as you see your pet suitcase fading lonesomely away on a receding station platform.

I have ever followed the policy of "do as I say, fool, not as I do." I advocate traveling lightly. Even when traveling in the

Orient, however, I must of necessity have two suitcases which are supplemented by one or two cameras, a briefcase, and a portable dictating machine. On a recent trip to Japan, a friend came aboard to assist me with my miscellaneous packages. In the ensuing confusion of departure, the train pulled out with him still in the coach. Fortunately, the next stop was less than an hour away. Time, tide, and Japanese trains wait for no man!

There is another point of remarkable Japanese efficiency which we could do well to emulate at home. Each station platform is clearly marked with the numbers 1 through 13 to correspond with the train coach numbers, indicating where the entrance to each coach will be when the train stops. For example, if you are holding reservations for coach number four, you seek out that number on the platform. You will find that the numeral four will be exactly in the middle of coach number four when the train arrives and that the front and rear doors will be precisely where their positions are marked on the concrete. Boarding passengers patiently queue up at their indicated car positions so that as soon as the detraining passengers have been disgorged, the incoming passengers may ascend quickly and efficiently.

The INLAND SEA. One of the very delightful journeys that you may take in Japan is on the *Inland Sea*. The setting is colorful and picturesque, and the voyage on the simply magnificent ships will be a memorable experience. You must be certain to select only one of the new ships, the *Kurenai Maru, Kohaku Maru,* or *Murasaki Maru,* which ply between **Osaka, Kobe, Takamatsu, Matsuyama,** and **Beppu.** The older *Inland Sea* ships are simply not up to our standards.

After a great deal of study and thought, I would recommend that you board one of the three new vessels either at **Osaka or Kobe** for the daylight trip to **Beppu.** (The daylight trip may also be made from **Beppu** to **Osaka/Kobe** in a new ship.) The departure time from **Osaka** is 7:20 in the morning, and you arrive at **Beppu** at 8:30 at night. The ship is equipped with modern staterooms, a beautiful dining room, delightful lounges, ship to shore telephone, radio, and television. There is adequate deck space and a bar which serves soft and hard drinks. Don't book passage on the *Inland Sea* without being absolutely certain that the voyage will be undertaken in one of the above-mentioned new ships.

It is very wise to make a reservation for one of the staterooms. The early hour of departure from either **Osaka or Kobe** means that you will probably wish to come aboard, have breakfast, and enjoy the sights of the two harbors and the busy traffic at the head of the *Inland Sea*. You can rest for a leisurely period and then come out on deck to see the beautiful islands and sea traffic that is an important part of the passing parade of the *Inland Sea*.

DOMESTIC AIRLINES. *JAL,* the famous transpacific carrier, also operates a network of domestic services. Cities served by *JAL* include **Tokyo, Osaka-Kobe, Fukuoka,** and **Sapporo** *(Hokkaido).* The *All-Nippon Airways, Fuji Airways,* and other domestic airlines also service **Sapporo, Misawa,** and **Sendai,** as well as **Kanazawa, Nagoya, Osaka, Fukuoka,** *Hachijo Island,* **Takamatsu, Kochi, Yonago, Iwakuni, Kokura, Kagoshima, Kumamoto, Miyazaki,** and **Omura.**

ROAD TRAVEL. The only outward manifestation of backwardness in the Japanese transportation picture is the lack of adequate cross-country arterial highway systems. Roads are not yet up to those of other lands. Don't plan to drive cross country without carefully checking the availability of adequate roads. New arterial highways are being built rapidly. A new 4-lane highway links **Kyoto** to the **Koke–Osaka** industrial area. For the first time in Japanese history this road permits a speed limit of 62.5 miles an hour with a minimum speed of 32.5 miles an hour. The new *Hakone Skyline Toll Highway* and the *Mt. Fuji* toll road were opened in 1964. Work is being rushed on a toll highway connecting **Tokyo** with **Nagoya.** This "Tomei Highway" will be completed by 1968 with segments opening when ready.

Japan is a left hand drive country both in the cities and rural areas. Watch carefully for cars coming from the "wrong direction."

OTHER WATER FERRY SERVICES. In addition to the extensive *Inland Sea* water routes, there are various other excellent services throughout the islands. Hydrofoils now operate between **Nagoya** and **Toba** (Mikimoto's *Pearl Island*) and between **Osaka/Kobe** and **Takamatsu**.

Hokkaido, the northernmost major "home" island, is connected with its sister island, *Honshu*, by a series of sea services.

There are important connections from **Tokyo** to the fine resorts on the *Izu Peninsula*. Daily services operate between **Tokyo** and **Atami** via *Oshima Island* with a stop at **Ito**, as well as between **Tokyo** and **Shimoda**. There are coastal services along the peninsula serving almost all the towns and villages and *Hatsushima (Island)* as well. The small coastal steamers are still not recommended as a method by which to tour, as the boats are, frankly, primitive and not up to international standards. It is still better to visit the *Izu Peninsula* by rail. There is now a rail line that extends to **Shimoda** on the tip of the *Peninsula* from **Tokyo** and **Atami**.

POPULATION AND HISTORY. Ninety-nine million Japanese live in an area slightly smaller than California, but though the population continues to increase, thanks to wise government control the birth rate has been reduced from an alarming 28.1 per thousand in 1950 to a moderate 18.0 per thousand in 1960. During the last five years, Japan's capital income has increased by a generous 40 per cent, her exports by a whopping 80 per cent.

The family bowl of rice continues by popular choice to be the nation's main food, even though the Japanese are enjoying an unprecedented prosperity. The improvement in their over-all standard of living is incredible. In recent years, the national well-being has been greatly abetted by continuous favorable harvests, but the rapidly growing population requires ever-increasing room for more general farming and additional rice crops. Because only one-sixth of the tiny country is capable of food production, large-scale reclamation of land from the sea has become a vital necessity. Dramatic examples of this work are the dykes in northwest *Kyushu* which cut off the bay east of Isahaya to produce 1,800 acres of fertile farmland and the draining of Japan's second largest lake, *Hachiro Gata,* in northwest *Honshu,* an area covering 42,000 arable acres from which vast quantities of additional rice may be harvested each year.

For the visitor to understand and appreciate the complex character of the Japanese, a brief glimpse into the nation's past is necessary. Among the earliest known inhabitants were Caucasian migrants who moved into the country via Siberia and the *Kurile Islands.* These people, known as the *Ainus,* were Japan's aborigines. Several thousand descendants of these primitive people can still be seen on northerly *Hokkaido Island,* although a pure aborigine, or *Ainu,* is rare today after generations of intermarriage. The main ethnological roots of Japan, however, sprang from rugged Mongoloid stock via Korea, with additional ancestral rootlets of mild Malayan, Indonesian, and soft Polynesian peoples.

Throughout her early history, Japan has been swayed and influenced by the once-great Chinese Empire, a nation far older than Japan, whose ancient and brilliant culture was famous throughout the world long before the birth of Christ. Japan's earliest written record, dated A.D. 712, states that Jimmu Tenno, grandson of the Sun Goddess, ascended the throne as first Emperor of Japan in 660 B.C. All succeeding emperors traced their line back to that date and automatically became gods, to be revered and worshipped by the masses. This unhealthy tradition was actively practiced until the nation's final defeat in World War II. Curiously enough, the practice of this pagan symbolism was even more seriously insisted upon when Japan was first opened up to western influences *after* the historic arrival of Commodore Matthew Perry in 1853.

For some time, Japan was actually ruled by ruthless feudal lords who, with their loyal followers called *samurai,* kept the Emperors "on the shelf," in the background, while outwardly proclaiming them as absolute monarchs. Occasionally, the Emperor became a mere puppet to be ruled by a Regent who in turn was ruled by a war lord called a *Shogun.* On other occasions, strong Emperors arose to rule autocratically on their own. Japan's first international relations were with **Korea** and **China.** Priests and scholars from these countries introduced Buddhism into Japan, a religion which has flourished side by side with the Shinto cult, even mixing with it, until today we find millions of Japanese who follow the tenets of both religions.

An omnipotent feudal society organized a policy of national isolation, a form of early but even more violent Fascism and the theory of race superiority than was practiced in Hitler's **Germany** or Mussolini's **Italy.** During the 16th century, the Portuguese began trading in the Far East using nearby **Macao** as the base of their operations and thus brought Japan to the attention of the western world for the first time. St. Francis Xavier introduced Christianity to the country, and by the end of the 16th century many Catholic churches were built to be used by more than 300,000 worshippers. It isn't true, of course, but there *seem* to be as many Christian churches in Japan today as there are in America. In 1592, Hideyoshi Toyotomi, a great "Taiko" of humble origin, successfully invaded **Korea.** This "Napoleon of Japan" disliked the Christians, but fortunately he died in 1598 before his harsh anti-Christian edicts could be carried out. His power passed to one of his generals, Iyeyasu, who moved his seat of government to **Edo** (now **Tokyo**), the nation's present capital. At first this leader favored the Christians. He even tolerated a few foreigners including the English adventurer William Adams, who became an advisor of the Shogun. By 1614, however, the oppressed Christians were again being persecuted, so much so that in 1637 they rose up in righteous rebellion at **Shimabara,** a town east of **Nagasaki.** They were aided to a small degree by other, non-Christian, elements who had been infuriated by the insufferably harsh rule and intolerable taxation. After months of bloody but brave opposition, the rebellion was squelched. Thousands of Christians and their supporters had been killed in battle or tortured and then executed. As the Roman emperors had learned centuries earlier, however, Christianity is a hardy religion, particularly under oppression. The sect went underground in **Nagasaki** for 220 years. The faith was handed down from generation to generation, finally reappearing to be officially recognized. Christianity then developed rapidly, and a great church was built in **Nagasaki,** seating more than 6,000 people. It was one of the marvels of *Kyushu,* though sadly it was destroyed by the second atom bomb which was dropped on August 9, 1945. Today the ruins of the church remain as a perpetual reminder of the horrors of atomic warfare.

Commodore Perry arrived in Japan in 1853, and the first American consulate was opened at **Shimoda** in 1856. The treaty which was signed between the United States and Japan in 1854 led to the eventual downfall of feudal power. A Japanese constitution was accepted by the great Emperor Meiji, who opened up the nation to western influences and expanded international trade and domestic industry.

The old chestnut "out of the frying pan into the fire" might well be applied to the era that followed Japanese feudalism. Shintoism formerly had been based on respectful nature worship, from the Sun to the Emperor, then down through all natural phenomena, beautiful, awe-inspiring, or humble, such as mountains, gardens, trees, and even reptiles and insects. Now the religion mainly assumed deification of the Emperor's person, whose omnipotence was necessary to insure the unswerving devotion of the masses. An increased respect for the Shinto priesthood also ensued which was marked by punctilious personal ceremonial behavior in the daily lives of the people.

Thus was born that Japanese fanaticism which endured right up to the national disillusionment at the end of World War II. From early childhood, boys and girls were constantly reminded that happiness in the next world was easily obtained by dying for the Imperial god. They were told that they themselves would become divine in the next world, though to a lesser degree, of course, than the Emperor. The male youth of Japan was indoctrinated with a brutal militarism, more violent, even, than that practiced in the rigid Prussian armies half a world away. The fanatic national outlook reached its heady height in the 1942–45 era, when our forces in the *Pacific,* **Burma,** and **Malaya** were puzzled by the enemies' astonishing battle zeal and fanatical courage, later returning on the eve of Japan's total defeat with the astounding *kamikaze* airmen, who joyfully committed suicide dives onto Allied warships. Such impractical behavior not only insured their own divinity but the destruction of their enemies.

The Emperor moved from **Kyoto** to **Tokyo** in 1868, which once again made **Tokyo** the nation's capital. The Japanese are great emulators and access to western influence planted in them the seed of desire to copy the Great Powers in all things, particularly those of a military nature. Strong Japanese naval forces were built following the British pattern, while their army was organized along Prussian lines.

In 1894 and 1895, Japan moved toward external military expansion. She defeated **China** and in 1895 seized the *Isle of Taiwan (Formosa)* and attacked Russia's Far Eastern possessions, crushing the Imperial Czarist navy by defeating important units of the Far Eastern Fleet in the great battle near *Tsushima Island* while the balance of the Russian navy was either scuttled or bottled up at *Port Arthur.* In so doing, such advanced weapons as mines and torpedoes were used. The conquests of **Korea** and **Manchuria** were rousing successes. From then on, Japan became the most modern and powerful industrial nation in Asia. Her military force was second to none in the Far East.

The year 1941 heralded the attack on *Pearl Harbor* as well as the utter subjection of **Burma, Singapore,** and **Hong Kong,** but Japan's ultimate defeat by the Allies, and her formal surrender to General MacArthur on September 2, 1945, shattered her hopes of aggrandizement and world conquest.

On March 20, 1953, Japan ratified the peace treaty with the United States that restored her full sovereignty. Once all fear of the conquerors had subsided, MacArthur's democratic indoctrination was fervently seized upon by the Japanese. As occurs in most old countries where there has been no time to assimilate gradually the democratic principles and concepts, the violent change from subjection to freedom of thought and action left the people breathless and over-eager to throw all inhibitions to the winds. But democracy, as western nations understand it, is still only skin-deep in Japan. Fortunately, the best of the old culture remains—the charming manners, the courtesy, the delightful old social customs, and the exquisite beauty of the country itself.

The Japanese had fought with fanatical zeal and lost every-thing. When the war was over, they bowed to the victors with an equally determined Eastern stoicism. General MacArthur's psychological appreciation of the people, his regal bearing, dapper mien, and utter disregard of personal danger singularly impressed all classes of Japanese society. Many of his orders and reforms which struck at thousands of years of deeply entrenched emotions, cliques, habits, and customs were not always understood or appreciated. The shattering change from an ancient and established order of life to that of a new and unheard-of order frequently caused resentment and confusion. But the over-all feelings toward a conqueror who had behaved with such lofty magnanimity of purpose and selfless determina-tion, unparalleled in the world's history, gained MacArthur universal, if sometimes grudging, admiration and respect.

At MacArthur's instigation, Emperor Hirohito went on the air to address the nation for the second time (the first was the Emperor's address to the Japanese nation announcing Japan's surrender), proclaiming that he was an ordinary human po-tentate and not a god. Thus the 1,300-year myth of his ances-tors' godliness was exploded in a few unprecedented minutes. The peace treaty prohibited Japan from maintaining armed forces, but in 1954 new legislation provided for a small Japanese military, naval, and air "defense force" whose strength is now about 180,000 men.

The Japanese have learned through the centuries to adjust

themselves to new circumstances. Perhaps this attitude comes easier to nations unaccustomed to generations of democratic institutions. They have adjusted themselves to frequent and sometimes terrible earthquakes, life under cruel autocratic war lords, the horrors of the last conflict, and now to the influence of the west, with its obvious advantages but also its drawbacks. In country places, western visitors may sometimes find themselves being closely observed, even surreptitiously stared at or whispered about. But the Japanese are the world's most expressively polite people. Bowing is a symbol of their mutual respect. The depth of the bow expresses the degree of their respect. They bow gracefully from the waist when they greet you and when they take leave of you. Old men, young boys, matronly women, and pretty girls all bow, as do waiters, bellhops, taxi drivers, and lovely hostesses in night clubs. It is done in homes, hotels, stations, department stores, elevators, restaurants, tea houses, trains, and on the streets. They all bow to one another. Recently, in the waiting room at **Tokyo's** *Haneda Airport* I saw two couples bow to each other for at least 12 minutes. With this ceremonial bending from the waist goes a smile and murmured greeting. When Japanese stare or whisper, no rudeness is intended. It is an intense interest, a vast curiosity about all foreigners, particularly Americans. Everyone wants to understand English, although, apart from interpreters and persons in direct contact with visitors, their efforts are not always too successful. This desire to please is the natural result of wanting to make foreigners feel "at home" and happy. Japan is bending over backwards to welcome the tourist. Everybody wants to please, it seems—bellhops, waiters, shop assistants, beautiful hostesses —and we must not forget the charming, dainty *Geisha*. Visitors will have the vacation of their lives in Japan. Believe me!

JAPANESE SPORTS

The Japanese are as avidly enthusiastic in the pursuit of a well-rounded athletic program as are we Americans. They are zestfully partisan spectators, and despite their smaller stature (generally), they are skilled and adroit sports performers. They excel in many body contact competitions as well as in individual and team sports.

The Japanese have embraced all of our games and competitions. The only minor exception is that, as in **England** and on the Continent, soccer is more popular in Japan than is our form of football.

In addition to all of the games we know well, there are several sports that are completely native to Japan: one is *judo* (*jujitsu*) and another *sumo,* a most curious form of wrestling. The following brief descriptions will enable you to feel at home in this corner of the Japanese athletic world.

JUDO (JUJITSU). This art of hand-to-hand and body-to-body combat is not, by our standards, so much a competitive athletic endeavor as it is a form of developing physical fitness, a pastime rather than a métier of competition. Many men and women take up *judo* merely to perfect their own personal self-defense. Unlike *sumo* which has a hoary history, *judo* is relatively modern, having been practiced in its present form for less than 100 years. The now famous founder of **Tokyo's** *Kodokan* (*Judo Hall*), J. Kano, not only devised the modern concepts of the art but perfected its fine points and taught it so enthusiastically over such a widespread area that today it is one of the best known of the physical arts of the world.

Judo is not an aggressive activity; on the contrary, it is a form of skilled self-defense. The more perfected practitioners of *jujitsu* needn't put their own muscular power to work at all. Instead, they convert the energy and offensive aggressiveness of the opponent to the defender's advantage. It is because of this capitalization of the weakness of the defender that a tiny individual can overcome a most powerful adversary with ease. A well-trained woman may readily conquer a strong man. The three facets of *judo* are known as *Nage-waza, Katame-waza,* and *Atemi-waza,* which, interpreted into our language, mean: (1) the ability to throw the opponent heavily to the ground; (2) the placing of the adversary in such a position by virtue of well-learned holds that he is completely immobilized; and, finally (3) inflicting blows with the hand, fist, knee or foot in such strategic areas as to completely immobilize the adversary.

Because this sport (when not practiced in actual self-defense) is on a purely friendly basis, one of the fundamental instructions given to the neophyte followers of *jujitsu* is in the rapid resuscitation of an unconscious adversary.

There is quite probably no other form of athletics that is available to such a vast segment of the population and is so well rounded in imparting bodily fitness and physical perfection to its proponents.

During the *jujitsu* games, the participants are garbed in typical two-piece *judo* costumes consisting of specially designed coats and pants which strangely enough are pure white with a belt of contrasting color. The players are carefully graded according to experience and ultimate skill, the classifications being indicated by a different colored belt for each grade, of which there are 10. It seems to me to be something of an oddity that so many elderly Japanese excel in a sport in which such physical violence is so heavily emphasized. Athletics in Japan are not usually coeducational, but this is not true of *judo;* a number of lady experts take part. In **Tokyo's** *Kodokan,* there are special rooms in which the gals perform. The *Kodokan* training periods are open to the public, and spectators appear in droves each afternoon. A number of **Tokyo's** American colony and trainees from abroad have taken up *judo,* and they may be seen daily working on the *Kodokan's* mats. Though it is an entirely Japanese innovation, *judo* is not completely unknown in America and Europe where there are schools which teach this sport. In Japan, the sport comes to its annual peak in the autumn when leading experts participate in the *Kodokan's* All-Japan Meet.

SUMO. This curious sport, with its colorful rituals and much grimacing, groaning, grunting, and posturing, can be most baffling to the uninitiated.

Semi-religious in its expression, *sumo* has been practiced since time immemorial. Because of its ascetic symbolism, the ring's canopy is representative of the ancient Shinto shrine; the posts which act as the shrine's columns are adorned with colossal red, white, green, and blue tassels. The *sumo* ring, not unlike our boxing dais, is raised for better visibility and covered by the aforementioned canopy. The ring covering is cushioned with loose sand, with its edges supported by heavy sand bags.

The physical appearance of the wrestlers is fantastically unique. They wear their hair long, fastened tightly on the top of the head in a topknot, and, apart from an almost negligible loincloth, their enormous glistening brown bodies are stark naked.

Just as in *jujitsu,* the *sumo* wrestlers are very carefully rated and placed in specially designated categories to keep the competition on an even keel while the wrestlers are being fattened up like turkeys for Thanksgiving dinner. It is the supercolossal, fatso type of *sumo* gladiator who attracts the most interested following and for whom the crowds shout. These well-padded pachyderms are the only gargantuan species of Japanese. The wrestlers are out of all proportion to the populace. Most of the *sumo* experts tip the scales at over 200 pounds, and some are as heavy as 300 pounds. Despite this excessive avoirdupois, they are highly muscular and extraordinarily dexterous. The skilled professionals are known as *maku-no-uchi,* which, translated, means "within the curtain," while the less skilled are known as *maku-shita*—"outside the curtain." Matches are always planned either inside or outside the curtain, never between.

To get a match started, the adversaries proceed ponderously to the platform where they salute each other ceremoniously, are introduced to the audience, and then stalk to their corners. One of the colorful ceremonies of the match is the sprinkling of the ring with salt to purify the area and drive away the evil spirits. Another ritual is the washing of the mouth with water that is stored in small vats in each corner.

The competitors advance toward one another glaring ominously. The starting stance consists of the two obese characters each squatting before the other. The hands must be clenched and touching the ground as they each avidly await the opportunity for the onslaught. This is the period of greatest frustration for the spectators. It seems each second that big things are about to happen, but this is usually not so. False starts can follow one upon the other ad nauseam. The ancient rules specify that both contestants must launch themselves into combat simultaneously. If not, it is considered a false start and the whole rigamarole of mouth rinsing, salt sprinkling, glowering, and padding about must begin all over again. It was once not considered unusual for the contestants to enter into a series of false starts for an hour or more. The more recent rules, however, make it obligatory for the contestants to make a simultaneous rise not more than five minutes after the first squat.

When the ponderous action begins, the two leviathans envelop one another with their cleaver-like hands, log-like arms, and sinuous legs. Their enormous bellies are mashed together.

To the Japanese, much of the enjoyment of the contests revolves around the preliminaries. Unfortunately from the viewer's standpoint, once the contest has been entered, it seldom proceeds for more than a minute. The victory is won when the opponent is hurled to the ground with any part of his body, other than his feet, coming in contact with the mat. The other condition of victory is that the loser either be forcefully ejected from the ring, or step out of the combat zone accidentally.

Once started, the action proceeds so rapidly and violently that the referee can, and sometimes does, err. As in America, the crowd is quick to voice its displeasure against the referee's decision. The participant who has been ruled against may appeal the original decision to the four officials who line the ringside for this purpose. Their decision is final.

Six annual *sumo* championship tournaments, held in the winter, spring, summer and fall in **Tokyo, Osaka** and elsewhere, evoke near-national hysteria. In the *sumo* arenas, always bursting with avid spectators, one sits in ancient Japanese style, shoes off and squatting on mats. The more elite seats consist of square cushions on the mats, each large enough for four persons. Each day for a fortnight the onlookers dig in for hours on end. Many bring their meals with them, while others buy them from the local vendors. National champions, who are as highly idolized in Japan as are football, basketball, baseball, and boxing heroes in this country or bull fighters in **Spain,** soccer and cricket participants in **England,** or road racers in **France** and **Italy,** receive large cash prizes as well as a symbolic national pennant.

All of the seemingly endless matches of the *sumo* tournaments are telecast, as are scores of lesser contests throughout the year. No self-respecting bar dares to be without a TV set on which to view these competitions and the baseball games. If I have failed to give you all the inside highlights of *sumo,* I am sure that your favorite Japanese barkeep will, though I believe that the foregoing is sufficiently clear and complete to take you out of the neophyte *sumo* spectator class.

SWIMMING. The inhabitants of an island nation would, quite naturally, be expected to become expertly adept at swimming, and the Japanese have, indeed, since times of antiquity, been a nation of fish-like swimmers. Of all of the sports in which these people are skilled, they have come closer to dominating world swimming competition than any other field. The Japanese swim as much for pleasure as they train assiduously for championship proficiency. The crawl stroke, which we long ago adopted and which is variously believed to have originated in either **Australia** and/or America, was used in Japan early in this century, long before it was generally adopted throughout the world.

As early as 1924, the Japanese Olympic team made a creditable showing in the **Paris** Olympics, and by 1932 the Japanese were beginning to garner Olympic gold medals. In the Berlin games of 1936, the Japanese swimmers were victorious in seven of the eleven competitive events in which they participated. The big time calibre of the Japanese swimmers declined momentarily in the immediate postwar era, but by 1956 they were "back in the swim" and by 1960 had again returned to Olympic championship contention in the **Rome** games.

Japan's islands are literally oozing with swimming pools, lakes, beaches, and swimming stadiums.

BASEBALL is as much of a national mania in Japan as it is here in the land of Abner Doubleday, its founding father. Not only is the sport of tremendous spectator interest and highly partisan at both the amateur and professional levels, but youngsters literally grow up with a baseball bat in their hands. From early spring until late fall, the radio waves and television screens are alive with the crisp crack of the bat and the thud of the ball in Japanese gloves.

Hardly had Doubleday invented the game in America before it was introduced to Japan, in 1873, where it was first played at the *Kaisei School*. By the roaring twenties, an enthusiastic university baseball league was functioning with round robin games being held in the spring and fall before tremendous throngs of highly agitated spectators. The *Yale-Harvard* classics of the Japanese university league are the *Waseda* versus *Keio* baseball games, which draw a packed stadium full every time they clash.

The two professional baseball leagues include teams representing all of the major metropolitan areas of Japan.

The Japanese have learned the game well and provide all its inherent local color. To watch a game in Japan is just like watching a game in America including the pre-game warmup sessions, pepper parties, infield practice, and all of the other amenities which are observed exactly as we know them. The only slight difference between our and their version that I have discerned is in the playing field itself. Grass doesn't always seem to grow where desired in Japan, and the entire infield of the Japanese diamond can be pretty bare.

The professional World Series is held in the fall, when the national interest is colossal. Both **Tokyo** and **Osaka** have stadiums seating from 55,000 to 85,000 spectators. Ball parks seating 40,000 spectators are commonplace.

SOFTBALL. Not to be outdone, Japan also has a huge, fervent coterie of softball adherents. Their ball, made of a type of congealed gum, is somewhat different from ours, which is no longer very soft. The Japanese, who claim to have invented "soft baseball," designed it for Little Leaguers, but it is now played by everyone, young and old, on virtually every piece of vacant ground in Japan. It is estimated that well over 1,000,000 amateur softball players are in active competition, although there are no professional teams.

TENNIS enjoys about the same degree of prominence in Japan, where it has been played since the 19th century, as it does in America. Japanese teams have been participating at **Wimbledon, Forest Hills,** and the *Stade Roland Garros* for at least four decades. They have had Davis Cup teams since 1921. The Japanese are expert shotmakers and cover the court with the nimbleness of frightened fawns, but their lack of height mitigates against them in professional and international amateur competition, where, nevertheless, they always make a good showing. The All-Japan Tennis Championships and the Inter-

Collegiate meets are well attended. There are tennis clubs in all of the principal cities of Japan.

TABLE TENNIS is much more popular in Japan than it is in the States. It was introduced there in the early 1920's, and not only do Japanese of all ages play and play well, but Japanese teams have done extraordinarily well in world competition. They won the World Table Tennis Meet in 1952. Most Japanese hotels and *ryokan* (inns) have tables which are always in use. The ardent players are as good as they are enthusiastic. The unique "pen grip" way of holding the paddle is used when the Japanese play.

FOOTBALL. The Japanese are versatile in their adaptation of this game, playing soccer, rugby, and American football, but of the three, only soccer has ever really caught on. There seems to be a slight current resurgence of interest in the American variety but nothing to compare with our interest in the pig-skin sport. Generally speaking, football in its various forms is played at the amateur level.

GOLF. The royal and ancient game of **St. Andrews** is enthusiastically participated in by many Japanese. Proportionately, its two hundred courses are considerably less than in many other countries, but those Japanese who play the game play it extraordinarily well. The professionals are highly proficient, and many amateurs hit the ball far and true. They are exceptionally good putters.

The courses, of which there are a dozen in the **Tokyo** metropolitan area, are maintained in excellent condition. The putting surfaces are magnificent. There are both public and private courses. The resort courses are run as private clubs, but playing facilities are available to the hotel guests. Guest cards may be arranged at most courses throughout Japan. By all means, if you plan to play, bring your own golf shoes. Playing golf is now considered a solid status symbol, and most company executives hold memberships in private golf courses.

SKIING. Skiing is a great sport in Japan enthusiastically participated in by millions of sparkly-eyed, cheeks-aglow Japanese.

The season is a lengthy one, lasting from December to late March in the *Central Honshu Alps*, while on *Hokkaido* and in the high areas of northern *Honshu*, it continues until as late as mid-May and sometimes, in the *Alps*, into the early summer months.

Japan's ski slopes are so well graded as to care for the veriest tyro out for the first time and the expert who has proved his mettle at **St. Moritz, Davos, Megeve,** *Gross Gloeckner,* **Sweden** and **Norway.** The runs are fine, but the social amenities after skiing at the lodges are not of the same caliber.

Modern western style hotels, Japanese inns, and reasonable hostels are strewn throughout each winter sports area.

There is, in Japan, the added delight, found nowhere else, of plunging into a steaming indoor or outdoor hot spring pool and enjoying a soul-satisfying thermal soak after a hard day of jumping, slaloming, and cross-country skiing. Mineral waters soothe one's aching muscles and keep one fit for another bout on the trail the next morning.

Theodor von Lerch, an Austro-Hungarian military officer, is responsible for skiing in Japan, bringing this sport to the island in 1910 and remaining to help develop the sport in *Hokkaido* and in northern *Honshu*'s **Niigata.** Twelve years later Japan held its first national championship ski meet at **Otaru** on *Hokkaido,* and in 1928 sent its first fully proficient team to the Winter Olympics, where Japanese skiers and jumpers have participated regularly ever since, except during the war years. They have shown increased skill each time out. The best of Japan's competitors is Chiharu "Chick" Igaya, master slalom contestant, who was graduated from Dartmouth just a few years ago.

Lifts and ropeways are plentiful. And best of all, despite the mass popularity of the sport with the outdoor-minded Japanese men and women, the slopes are seldom too crowded except for weekends and national holidays.

Almost all of the ski areas are conveniently located to **Tokyo,** being from two to ten hours away by train. The resorts on the island of *Hokkaido* are the exception, but even there the trails and slopes can be reached by *JAL* jets flying in less than two hours from the capital city to **Sapporo.**

The best of Japan's skiing is found: (1) on *Mt. Fuji's* lower snow-clad slopes and adjacent vicinities; in the *Nikko National Park,* especially near *Lake Yumoto,* a hot spring paradise; (2) in the *Echigo-Yuzawa* district, largest in Japan; (3) in the *Joetsu* district in the waist of *Honshu;* (4) in the northern Japan *Alps* of *Mts. Shirouma, Tateyama,* and *Norikura;* (5) on the *Sugadaira* and *Myoko Plateaus* (with the fine *Akakura Hotel* offering the best accommodation); (6) *Mt. Ibuki* in the *Kansai* district (one of the nation's best slalom grounds); (7) the *Zao* region near **Sendai** in the *Tohoku* district (tops in downhill and cross-country skiing alike, in the "Frosted Fairyland Forest" area especially); (8) near **Kyoto** at **Makino;** (9) near **Sapporo,** *Hokkaido Island,* or *Mt. Kannabe* in the *Kansai, Mt. Sankaku* and *Mt. Arai;* (10) at **Goshiki Spa** (eight hours from **Tokyo's** *Ueno Station* in Yamagata Prefecture); (11) best of all, from the visitor's viewpoint, the fabulous area near **Hoppo, Yudanaka,** and **Shiga Heights.** This latter, reached by train and *weasel* (a tracked jeep-like snow vehicle equipped with tank treads) in eight hours from **Tokyo,** offers the fashionable, château-like *Shiga Heights Hotel* which provides twin French and Japanese cuisines, a roaring pine-knot fireplace, and superb mineral baths. The *Heights,* whose season runs from mid-December to late March, is a broad, spa-dotted terrain, with ski lifts, fine powdered snow such as skiers revel in finding, and unrivaled slopes in white birch and pine tree atmosphere.

SKATING. Skiing's sister sport is enormously popular with the rank and file of Japanese. Lakes and frozen indoor and outdoor rinks provide ample opportunity for those who enjoy participating in this health stimulating pastime. In **Tokyo,** the *Korakuen* and *Tokyo Skating Rinks* are both readily accessible.

HORSE RACING. The "sport of kings" thrives but has not yet reached the crescendo that it has in America. Weekend and holiday racing is particularly popular, with 12 races being featured on Sundays and 11 on Saturdays and national holidays. The first race is normally contested at 11 A.M., with time out later for lunch. The *Japanese Derby* is held at **Fuchu City** in **Tokyo,** the most famous of Japan's racecourses, and attracts a great deal of attention. Racing takes place from early spring until late fall. Consult the English language newspapers for details of dates and starting times.

HORSEMANSHIP. This exclusive sport is nevertheless one of colorful interest should you be in Japan in July. On the eleventh and twelfth, the *Nomaoi Matsuri* is observed near *Haranomachi Station,* approximately 180 miles from **Tokyo.** During this incredible display of horsemanship, simulated samurai warriors ride in the full war panoply of the Middle Ages replete with streaming banners. This spectacle is worth traveling a long distance to see.

BOXING. The manly art of fisticuffs is largely participated in by students. Since World War II, there has been a growing interest shown in boxing, but to date there are no internationally famous bouts that might attract your attention except in the fly through featherweights. There have been a dozen world title fights staged since 1951 in **Tokyo** and **Osaka.** From one emerged Japan's first titleholder, flyweight Yoshio Shirai. He was managed by an American professor from Nebraska!

BASKETBALL. Despite the diminutive size of the Japanese, they are amazingly skillful, fast basketball players. High school and college teams are springing up throughout Japan, and representatives of these leagues have participated throughout the Far East as well as in the recent Olympic Games in **Rome,** where the American five eliminated the Japanese team. There is no professional basketball.

ROWING and YACHTING. Neither of these pastimes has become ingrained in the Japanese. Sailing on the lakes and at sea resorts has of recent years become moderately popular, and some wealthy Japanese own yachts. There are a few sailing and speedboat races held during the summer months. The four principal **Tokyo** motorboat racecourses are *Edogawa, Heiwa-jima, Tamagawa,* and *Toda.*

CYCLING. This two-wheeled sport has about the same relative popularity in Japan that it does in America, with nothing of the fervor of the European regard for this form of competition or local exercise. The principal bicycle racing takes place at the *Korakuen* and *Keiokaku Race Tracks.* Motorcycle racing takes place at the course called *Oi Race.*

TRACK and FIELD SPORTS. The Japanese have enjoyed a great recent renaissance of interest in track and field participation and spectatorship. Almost everywhere you go in Japan, you will see lads of all ages practicing their sprinting or distance running, high jumping, pole vaulting, javelin throwing, or shot-putting. The zeal with which the Japanese are approaching the 1964 Olympic Games is sure to give further impetus to this already mushrooming sport. There are now vast stadiums which, however large, will be expanded for the **Tokyo** Olympic Games. Japan has had half a dozen world's champions in the past.

MOUNTAINEERING. Mass mountain climbing is native to Japan. From the first of July until mid-August, *Mount Fuji* is assaulted by hundreds of thousands of huffing and puffing mountaineers. As described elsewhere, the ascent of *Fuji* may be made from four principal points along well-defined trails which are lined with temples and stone rest houses stocked with simple food and light refreshments. In addition to the *Mount Fuji* ascent, hordes of ambitious mountaineers wend their weary way to other dizzy heights. Mountaineering should not be confused with mountain climbing as we think of it in other lands where the rugged faces of mountains are challenged laboriously niche by handmade niche, with hardy climbers clinging precariously to rugged raw stone, bound to one another by stout cords. That type of mountain climbing does exist in Japan, but, by and large, the Japanese variety of mountaineering—that of following well-defined routes—though less dangerous, is available to the masses.

HUNTING is another sport that each year sees increasing throngs of avid Japanese sportsmen stalking their favorite prey. The Japanese variety of hunting is much more arduous than our western style. Because the prey is usually found in remote Alpine areas which are far from any ready access by vehicle, much toilsome marching on foot is considered as part of the fun. The Japanese think nothing of traversing 20 or more miles during the course of the day's hunting. The open season on birds throughout Japan is from the first of November until the fifteenth of January. The quarry includes pheasant, quail, partridge, wild geese, et cetera. The wild game season in *Hokkaido* is from the middle of November until the end of January, elsewhere from December 15th to January 31st. Among the beasts to be hunted are wild boar, bears, fox, marten, squirrels, and rabbits. Hunting licenses, readily obtainable for about ten dollars, must be secured.

FISHING, where the finned creatures constitute a basic ingredient of the national diet, is a fine art. Professional fishing is carried on in a great scale, while fishing for sport attracts innumerable Japanese devotees of Isaak Walton. American sportsmen will no doubt be most attracted to angling for rainbow and brook trout, but in addition to the fresh water variety, there is great excitement to be had by going out to sea for the deep salt water sport.

CORMORANT FISHING. In addition to lake, stream, and deep-sea fishing, there is cormorant fishing, the most unique form of fishing in the world. The cormorant is an unusual bird about the size of a large goose whose prey in the *Nagara River,* at **Gifu,** 20 miles north of **Nagoya,** is the tasty *ayu,* or river trout. Cormorant fishing begins in May and continues through mid-October. Should you wish to enjoy cormorant fishing as a spectator, you may make all arrangements at **Gifu,** or through your travel representative in **Tokyo** or **Nagoya.** Cormorant fishing takes place each evening except during occasional muddy water weather or at the full moon when the cormorant fishing is postponed for the night. Should you become a part of this

exciting scene, you will find it both stimulating and fascinating. Guests may view the sport from public barges or private houseboats. I will describe the procedure for the latter. On arrival in **Gifu** spectators proceed to a Japanese inn near the river where, after tea is served by lovely waitresses, one changes into a Japanese kimono and *getas* (wooden clogs). The boat is prepared for you, with *Geisha* girls, Japanese robed waitresses, two polemen dressed only in union suits, well-stocked bar, a picnic table laden with sandwiches, assorted hors d'oeuvres, fish, fruit, and dainty delicacies.

Rope pullers sturdily implanted in the river's bed pull the visitor's craft smoothly into the wide stream, like Volga boatmen. The craft is then poled upstream about a mile and a half and parked, stern ashore, parallel to a hundred or so other barges and launches. The occupants of the other craft will range from fellow Americans to entire clans of Japanese out on a gay holiday. As they wait, the spectators may be heard as they join in communal singing and chanting all up and down the river. At sunset a bedecked barge floats down forming a stage for a group of dancing girls *(odoriko)* performing for the entertainment of the watchers to the strains of Victrola music. As the last rays of the setting sun blend with the rapidly dimming sky, a fireworks exhibit from midstream blazons forth. The cormorant fishing boats then start upstream preparatory to the downstream fishing run.

Each fishing boat contains three to four fishermen. The master, who stands in the bow, is attired in the traditional grass skirt and helmet. With consummate skill, he controls a dozen cormorants, each tethered on a 10-foot line, who paddle energetically about the boat. Skillfully and avidly they watch for their prey. On occasions, a further four to six cormorants are controlled by another man stationed farther aft in the boat. Another man tends the decoy fire which is aflame in an iron cradle which projects from the forward gunwale. One man devotes his attention and energies to steering the boat. The schools of *ayu* are attracted to the decoy fire like pitiful moths to a scorching light. The fish begin to rise to the surface, a signal for the cormorants, who take great delight in their job, to plunge gracefully beneath the waters and return to the surface with captive fish in their gullets. To get the fish involves a bit of high level trickery. Each cormorant's neck is tethered by a loose metal ring or a cord in such a way that he cannot possibly swallow a fish of normal size, but must retain his catch until his neck becomes so heavy with fish that he is unable to steer himself and flounders about out of control, which state is usually attained with 4 fish weighing about one and a half pounds. When this unbalanced state is attained, the birds are hauled into the boat and the fish are forcefully ejected from their necks. The whole exciting business then starts all over again.

By assiduously applying themselves to the task at hand, the cormorants can catch incredible numbers of *ayu* during the course of an evening. The most startling and amazing feature of the whole gizmo is that the birds, instead of becoming completely frustrated by being unable to swallow the fish, show every stupid form of continuous interest throughout the catch and eagerly recommence after each performance.

The fishermen who owe their livelihood to these underwater beagles hold them in the highest regard. The initial cormorant training is said to be relatively simple. After a fortnight or so of preliminary instruction, the birds are considered sufficiently tame to be permitted to swim in company with the working cormorants to accustom them to their future chores. Once put "in harness," the cormorants can work for almost five years before being honorably retired. Each team of cormorants has a captain, a highly experienced bird who keeps his subordinates in order and insures that there is no poaching on each other's preserves. The cormorants are native to northern *Honshu*. It is customary to bag them in the winter and train them in the spring. In early summer, the birds, ready to serve their apprenticeship, are brought to **Gifu** and sold to the natives.

BOWLING is still in its infancy in Japan, but the sport is becoming extremely popular, particularly with Japan's younger set. The *Tokyo Bowling Center,* in the outer gardens of the *Meiji Shrine,* is new, modern, and popular. *Brunswick* has a contract with a prominent Japanese trading house, *Mitsui,* and fine alleys are mushrooming.

HOT TOWELS. One ingratiating Japanese custom to which you will not only become accustomed but I believe ultimately enamored of is the one of serving piping hot towels on any and almost every occasion. *O-shibori,* the Japanese call them.

If you flew to the Orient via *Japan Air Lines,* you will have had an early indoctrination into this refreshing ritual. (Other air carriers have also adopted this excellent custom.) The towels are served tightly rolled in little wicker baskets. When steamingly unrolled, they are used to wipe your face and hands, a hygienic as well as stimulating process. This procedure is repeated before all Japanese style meals, in railroad trains, in cabarets, cafes, and bars.

MASSAGE. The Japanese are devotees of health rituals, and many of them enjoy a daily massage. This custom has spilled over to include foreign visitors, if they so desire. In almost every Japanese hotel or inn, a masseur is available for a man, and a masseuse for a woman, with little or no advance notice. Many of Japan's blind population learn this trade for a source of revenue. You have but to tell the desk clerk the hour you desire the attention. The massage usually takes about an hour and costs about a dollar.

TURKISH BATHS. The Japanese version of the Turkish bath is something that I'm sure the Turks never dreamed would evolve from this most famed of the specialties of their native land.

As I have said elsewhere and reiterate here, the only thing that amazes the visitor to the Land of the Rising Sun, or should, is the normal. The abnormal you must almost take for granted.

The Japanese Turkish bath stands unique in the world's offerings of the unusual and bizarre.

There are close to 100 Turkish bath establishments in **Tokyo** alone, plus a generous sprinkling throughout the rest of Japan. The one that I know best is the *Ginza Turkish Bath* at 7, 1-chome, Ginza. Ralph Michaels likes the *Elysee;* every male has his favorite. Take your pick. The fantastic, amazing Turkish bath procedure is as follows:

When you enter the small foyer from the street, you are confronted with a small, pleasant lounge and desk not unlike that of a quiet, small hotel. You pay the fee of about $2.50 and may, if you wish, choose from a variety of refreshments before proceeding to the business at hand.

You will be directed to an intimate private room, and when you arrive you will be greeted by a young, pretty, well-proportioned Japanese girl clad in scant shorts and brief bra, who will immediately drop to her knees so as to undo your shoelaces and remove your shoes. She will provide you with a pair of slippers. You then step up into a room which is the upper half of a split-level duo-compartment arrangement in which you will find a dressing table equipped with various and sundry ointments, liniments, powders, and other massage accessories, and a massage table. In the far, lower half of the room is located the old-fashioned wooden steam box, fitted with a foam rubber seat and equipped with removable top side slabs into which a circle has been cut just large enough for your neck. Your head protrudes. Adjacent to the Turkish bath is a deep rectangular sunken bath which penetrates to a depth of about three and a half feet. The water is scalding hot. Additionally, there is to be found a shower bath, hot and cold running water hydrants, and a minute stool, beside which are three gaily colored water bowls each with a capacity of about two quarts. Various soaps and lathers are scattered about.

Once having crossed the threshold and having had one's shoes removed, the performance begins. Without the slightest show of personal reaction or embarrassment, the attendant proceeds to divest her client of his coat, trousers, necktie, shirt, socks, et al. Each garment is meticulously cared for. The trousers, shirt, and jacket are placed on hangers and the underthings in a specially prepared wicker basket. When totally "prepared," the client is led to the steam cubicle, seated on the foam rubber cushions, and the top fitted snugly into place. The sizzling steam is then turned on. For the next quarter of an hour or so, as the 190-degree humid heat commences, perspiration oozes from the client, and "Toots" gently massages the troubled brow with cool towels. In due course, the steam is turned off, the cover removed, and the client directed to the steaming sunken tile bath. As the client leaves the sunken bath, he is directed to a tiny wooden stool, particularly minute for one of Olson's avoirdupois. Once seated, the attendant bestows on her client a thorough cleansing process which includes a vigorous stem to stern scrubbing. She omits nothing. I must say that, despite her youth and attractiveness, the ministrations are as impersonal as such an intimate process can be. Included in the personal attentions are a "close shave," manicure, and even hair trim, if needed or desired. When the scouring is completed, the next step is the rubbing table. The massage, professionally rendered, is refreshing and relaxing.

To the very best of my knowledge, there is no "hanky-panky" in the better Turkish baths although this does exist in the questionable ones. Despite the intimacy of the occasion, no personal relationship is either encouraged or permitted.

There are establishments for the ladies which are also popular and well attended.

I think you will find the experience of a Japanese Turkish bath stimulating physically and fascinating as another international travel adventure.

Other recommended Turkish baths in **Tokyo** are:

CHIKYU KAIKAN—In front of the *Shinjuku Koma Theater*. Open one P.M. to midnight.
RIKI'S TURKISH BATH CENTER—at *Riki's Sport Center* in *Shibuya*.
Open ten A.M. to two A.M.
SANTE—441, 1-chome, *Nishiokubo Shinjuku*.
Open one P.M. to one A.M.
TOKYO ONSEN—*Ginza,* 6-chome. (Annex at 3rd **Lane**) (Japan's first and most famous).
Open noon to midnight.

Kobe:

TORUKO ONSEN—Shimoyamate-dori, 2-chome.

Kyoto:

MIMATSU—Shin-Kyogoku, Shijo Agaru.

Osaka:

TORUKO CENTER—14 Kuroemon-cho, Minami-ku.

PUBLIC TELEPHONES. Though my friend, Dale F. Castle, of Illinois Bell Telephone will dispute it, many countries of the world are well ahead of us in the convenient and efficient use of the telephone. Throughout Japan, streetside and cafe telephones are almost as abundant as pigeons in *St. Mark's Square*. These brightly painted red instruments are found on tables in sidewalk cafes, in convenient niches along the street, and almost every place that wires can conceivably be strung. I doubt that the average visitor is going to be urgently pressed to use a street telephone, but it's fun to watch the Japanese in animated conversation. Teen-agers use them extensively.

The COMPLICATED ADDRESS SYSTEM. The bewildering complexity of the Japanese address system—or, more accurately, lack thereof—is almost inexplicable, and certainly, to us, incomprehensible. The confusing agglomeration of numbers, names and descriptive expletives has, as I will explain on the next several pages, significant, even imperative, meaning to the Japanese. To us, the uninitiated westerners, the multiple pyramiding, sometimes seemingly redundant, names and numbers in an address are gibberish.

For your peace of mind and guidance in following the maps in this guidebook, I have, in listing addresses and describing locations, followed the western style of designation. I believe this will prove helpful to my readers; it will, however, mean nothing to Japanese taxi drivers . . . believe me.

In order not to compound a natural confusion on the subject, I have purposely refrained from using complete addresses throughout this book. As I have explained elsewhere, taxi drivers, policemen, and others outside your hotel upon whom you might be dependent for directions will neither read nor understand Anglicized Japanese. But the solution to the address problem is surprisingly simple. Any hotel which I have recommended will, before you leave for your shopping expedition, dining adventure, or evening out, have skilled helpers on hand to provide you with specially prepared cards inscribed with the complete Japanese style address of your destination or series of destinations. Don't venture forth without proper address documentation. You're almost certain to get lost if you do.

You will note when you read English language periodicals in Japan that from the maze of names and numbers in every address you can select something that of itself resembles an American address, such as Avenue A and 10th Street, F and Yoyogi intersections, or the corner of 11th and Y. You will love the simplicity of such appellations, but unfortunately, even now, this American style almost never means anything to anybody but you and me.

Until recently the Japanese didn't name their streets. Avenue A, for example, to you and me is quite simple. It runs past the *Imperial Hotel*. It passes the *Nikkatsu Hotel* and is adjacent to the *Imperial Palace*, but even a principal thoroughfare such as this has previously been unnamed.

In the somewhat nebulous future, this helter-skelter situation *may* be somewhat alleviated. Members of the American colony in Japan have intrepidly assailed those in authority and begged them to do something about naming the streets, particularly the principal ones. Paul Aurell, a long-time resident of Japan and fluent in the native tongue, is one of the prime movers to bring order out of chaos. Thus the Japanese authorities are naming some principal avenues, but only the tourists pay any attention to the new system. The Japanese blithely have nothing to do with the new policy and can only understand where a foreign visitor wishes to go if the directions are written in Japanese.

In many addresses, you will see **Tokyo** written "Tokyo-*to*." The *"to"* in this case means "metropolis." **Tokyo** is the only *"to"* in Japan. **Osaka** addresses will be written "Osaka-*fu*" and **Kyoto,** "Kyoto-*fu*." *"Fu"* means "a populated place" and ranks between *"to"* and *"shi."* Just as **Tokyo** is the only *"to,"* **Osaka** and **Kyoto** are the only *"fu's."* *"Fu,"* as *"ken,"* described below, can also mean "prefecture." *"Shi"* means "city." *"Machi"* means "town," while *"mura"* designates a village.

The larger units such as metropolis, city, town, and village are not numerous. Other terms include *"Ku,"* which you see all the time and which means the ward of a city or town. One of the most common terms which, just to complicate the issue, may be spelled in any one of three ways—*"cho,"* *"chome,"* or *"cho-me"* (pronounced cho-meh)—means block. *"Banchi"* designates the number on the street. *"Machi"* on the one hand designates a part of a town; on the other hand, it can and does refer to a street even though the usually accepted words for street are *"michi"* and *"dori."* To further muddle up the situation, *"dori"* may be pronounced alternatively *"tori."*

To add another bizarre element to this already boiling witch's cauldron, we must bear in mind that by our standards Japanese do things backwards. They write their surname first and then their given name, and list their addresses with what we would call the last part first and, as logically as day follows night, the first part last.

To illustrate: one may live at 1013 W Street, N.W., Washington 6, D.C., U.S.A. This we would understand. The Japanese equivalent would be as follows: U.S.A., D.C., 6, Washington, N.W., 1013 W Street, then the name—Jones, William. Or thereabouts. To transcribe this into Japanese, a sensible ordinary address would be: Tokyo-to, Shibuya-ku, 6-Chome, 15 Banchi, Apartment 28, and then the name; which, translated into reasonable English, means that the individual abides in Apartment 28, No. 15, Sixth Block, Shibuya Ward, Tokyo metropolis. I'm not at all certain that this is even simple to the Japanese. Maybe.

Let's take a look at a good business address. This might be, to a Japanese reading it his way, Kanagawa Ken, Yokohama Shi, Naka-ku, Motomachi, 3-Chome, Ichi-Banchi, and then the name. Translated again, this means that the gentleman's place of business is located at No. 1, Third Block, Moto town, Naka-ward, Yokohama City, and, yes, another factor: *"ken"* means prefecture, of which there are forty-six in Japan's major four home islands. In other words, starting out with "Kanagawa *Ken*" means that it is the Kanagawa Prefecture (state).

"Chiho" refers to a region of which there are seven. *"Chiho"* can also be roughly considered "territory" referring to a district like our former "Arizona Territory."

An occasional address will include the word *"bashi,"* sometimes pronounced *"hashi"* which means "bridge." This is to give the visitor, his chauffeur, or taxi driver a further clue as to the locale.

To the best of my knowledge, **New York City** is the only town, village, city or metropolis in the United States in which street numbers do not give you a clue as to the location of the address. Number One Fifth Avenue is practically in Greenwich Village, while Number One Park Avenue is a considerable distance uptown even though the streets are parallel. 500 Fifth Avenue is at the corner of 42nd Street, while a block over on Vanderbilt Avenue the number is 52, for example. Broadway and 42nd Street carries a Broadway number in the two thousands. I have never found a Manhattan taxi driver who had a formula for locating addresses other than by a thorough knowledge of local lore.

We shouldn't be so completely impatient with the Japanese numbering system when in our own country we are, in our largest city, equally numerically illogical. The Japanese have gone us one better, however, except in **Boston** where, I understand, houses in certain old sections are numbered according to the same curious procedure followed in designating all Japanese dwellings. The ground for the first house built in a given area, for example, was No. 1, the second was No. 2, and the third No. 3, even though they might be relatively widely separated. In due course after an area was built up, it was not unusual to have No. 1 adjacent to No. 17 which in turn abutted on No. 34. There could be two or more houses on Ground Number 10, for example. That was well and good, particularly after the local postman, coach drivers, and visiting guests were sufficiently instructed into the intricacies of locating the edifice. But we must not forget that Japan has known, among other things, wars, fires, floods, earthquakes, tidal waves, and innumerable "acts of God." Houses have tumbled, been blown down, burned and been bombed. It is not inconceivable that House No. 3 succumbed to a tremor and when rebuilt of course could not have its original number but must take the next free number in line, perhaps No. 167. When No. 7 was blown down and rebuilt, it conceivably reappeared as No. 206. In the meantime, there were lapses in the rules, and there were duplications in numbering. In some areas, it is not unusual to find a dozen or more houses all bearing the same number—55, for instance. Imagine the utter consternation to be seeking Mr. Suzuki (the Smith, Jones, or Brown of Japan) at No. 55!

Hotels catering to American visitors, the department stores, restaurants, and night clubs employ English-speaking personnel who can readily write the full and proper address of well-known establishments for you. It is not inconceivable, however, that you will be invited out for dinner. Many Americans have Japanese friends or friends of friends who will be honored to have you in their home for dinner, tea, or even cocktails. It is your host who must give you the directions for finding his house. I implore you on bended knees if you are invited out: there is no detail too minor or minute to plot out on a map beforehand. Be sure that your host writes absolutely explicit instructions including the name and description of a gas station or tobacco shop on the corner, the bridge on which you turn left, the trolley tracks a hundred yards down the road, and/or any and all identifying marks. As I have mentioned under *"Helpful Hints"* and in the shopping section, Kodachrome moving picture film is still not easy to get in Japan. Not long ago, after the cute little gal at the *Imperial Hotel* information desk had telephoned a number of camera shops in **Tokyo** for me, she located a shop carrying the desired film and very graciously wrote the complex address of the little shop on a card which I held in my hand and guarded assiduously even after the taxi driver had perused it, first with an abstract look and then with a gleam of recognition. The driver kept referring to it every few blocks. I'm sure we only drove about seven miles out of our way before finally locating the much sought after establishment.

If you go out to be entertained and arrive at your host's house less than thirty minutes late, he will be both enormously pleased and gratified that his directions were so unusually good. Such is the Japanese address system.

SCHOOL CUSTOMS. You may be interested to know that

Japanese grammar school kids carry their books in a knapsack-like arrangement over both shoulders with straps on their backs, kids in junior high school carry their books on one hip with a white strap crisscross over the far shoulder, and college students carry their books in briefcases like businessmen.

Isn't that just something?

JAPANESE STUDENT GROUP TRAVEL. One of Japan's most interesting and familiar sights is that of masses of students, both boys and girls, touring their country in organized groups. The authorities have wisely decreed that, as part of their school curriculum, Japanese youngsters, from as early an age as possible, must see and study their beautiful, historic land. School groups down to kindergarten level are always on the march. Bands of uniformed boys, with shiny bangs and girls with brief incipient pigtails, may be seen daily in motor coaches, on trains or ships, sightseeing in historic buildings, or avidly absorbing the natural beauty of the country.

On Sundays children not on tour may be seen in the city streets and parks sketching in groups. They all wear badges which give their names in case they get lost, rain hats, school bags, and school emblems.

If the old saying, "As the twig is bent, so grows the tree" is accurately prophetic, the Japanese must ultimately become the world's most proficient travelers. The Japanese are their own best tourists, and touring in groups is the normal method of traveling. It is amazing to see so many children traveling and sightseeing with so very few teachers. The groups are always in perfect response, exhibiting automatic obedience, with the young individuals suppressing their own interests to those of the group, which approach has long been a behavior characteristic in Japanese society.

Many inns, which give special student group rates, lay quilt after quilt on the floors of large airy rooms onto which the youngsters pile happily. It is a unique experience to wander into a public bath in some remote rural hostelry and find scores of giggling, happily babbling boys and girls soaping up *outside* the bath. They will quite probably turn out to be members of a school group on an outing.

It does one's heart good to see these joyous youngsters trotting along the highways and up the mountain trails, or sitting down and listening to a "live" or recorded explanation of a shrine or historical monument or capturing lovely scenes on sketch pads. The youngsters, who always seem to be enjoying themselves, are natural, friendly and pleasantly curious. They are hopelessly addicted shutterbugs and will be thrilled if you will permit them to photograph you with their group. I have also found that students adore being photographed. If you are seeking local color for your lens, invite a few students to enter the range of your camera; they'll acquiesce with alacrity.

KAMIKAZE. The derivation of this name, which we think of in terms of World War II suicide bombers, is of interest. *Kamikaze* means "divine wind." Some centuries ago, on two different occasions, the Mongolians attempted to invade Japan. Each time, as they were preparing to assault the shores, a typhoon roared down on them and sank all of their ships. Because of this fortuitous happenstance, the Japanese prayed at the *Great Buddha Shrine* of **Kamakura,** near **Tokyo,** and other such sites for the "divine wind" which had saved them. In World War II, when the United States naval forces were rebuilt and the tide of battle went against the Japanese, they prayed for such a "divine wind" to eliminate our ships. When it didn't come and when more prosaic bombing patterns failed to do the job, they recruited the suicide bomber corps (one-way trips) to attempt to make their own divine wind. Hence . . . *kamikaze.*

RELIGIONS IN JAPAN. One of the oddest facets of Japanese life which seems incomprehensible to the stranger is the curious approach to religion.

The Japanese just don't seem to take religion seriously. Except for Japanese Christians, there is no set day for worship such as Sunday for Christians, no holy day like Saturday for the Jews, and no orderly schedule for going to the temples and shrines, the equivalent of our churches, synagogues, tabernacles, or cathedrals. The shrines and temples seem more like places for sightseeing and enjoying annual festivals than for contemplation, prayer, meditation, or organized worship. Briefly put, religion in Japan seems disorganized, a thing apart from rather than the center of life, thought and deed.

This curious Japanese lack of concentrated religious manifestation is due to the inherent differences between Buddhism and Shintoism on one hand and Christianity on the other. Neither Shintoism nor Buddhism is now a militant religion. They make no recourse to evangelism nor do they attempt to sell themselves.

In Japan it is entirely possible for a family to have faith in all three religions. In the same household one may find the *Butsudan* (the family altar); the less elaborately carved and painted but intricately assembled *Kami-Dana,* the "God Shelf" of Shinto belief; and a picture of Christ, a crucifix or some artifice of Christian belief. A Japanese sees no inconsistency in revering his ancestors in the Shinto way, continuing his traditional national belief in the precepts of Buddhism, and still worshipping in his Sunday best at the Christian church of his selection. If pressed, he might explain he seeks a way of life from the best of all three, a synthesis of religious experience. Perhaps he is right. Certainly to his way of thought there is nothing illogical in his ascetic behavior.

BUDDHISM, which, briefly, is the worship of multiple deities and idols, was first known in Japan in A.D. 552, being imported from **Korea.** Shortly after that, Buddhist interest was further aroused in Japan by the advent of nuns, priests, images, carvings, temple artisans, and architects. By the late 6th century, thanks to the great Prince Shotoku, Buddhism had become of paramount importance. Shotoku was to Buddhism in Japan what King Asoka was to India or what the Roman Emperor Constantine was to Christianity. The prince made Buddhism the court faith, and under him construction of religious edifices thrived. He was a true prince of the faith.

Buddhism's deep faith, far too complex to discuss in these

brief pages, is primarily of Chinese origin, having been transmitted to Japan by the avenue of **Korea.** It has been called a basic philosophy by the Japanese.

The *Heian Period* (794-1185) saw the celebrated national figures, Dengyo-Daishi and Kobo-Daishi, helping to develop the Japanese form of the religion, but Buddhism became engulfed in corruption, secularism, and even bitter fratricidal warfare, as sect after sect multiplied; but later, strife was diminished and Buddhism was returned to its quiet beginnings. Today some 42,540,325 Buddhists, according to latest official reckoning, adhere to 12 major sects and numerous smaller splinter sects. They belong to at least 105,000 temples. Buddhism is frequently called the religion of death and of the future. Whatever the beliefs of the deceased, almost all Japanese funerals are held under Buddhist auspices.

The SHINTO religion is one of nationalism and primitivism whose adherents worship nature and ancestors alike. *Amaterasu-Omikami* ("Great Heaven-Shining-Goddess") is the deity of the Sun, and Japan is the "Rising Sun" nation. Under this legendary figure, created at the dawn of Japanese history, is the pantheon of eight million gods and goddesses, constantly being added to at a personal or familial level. In Shintoism, faith lies in the Japanese gods of mountains, rivers, lakes, oceans, winds, fires, ancestors, great men, and close relations alike.

Originally Shinto offered neither theology nor ethics, basing itself on this precept: "Follow the genuine impulses of your heart." Elements of Confucianism entered later. The notions of the hierarchy of loyalty—of wife to husband, son to father, younger people to older ones, serfs to lords, and finally (as World War II showed so tragically) subjects to Emperor—is the fundamental belief of Shinto.

Shinto, seized upon by the ultranationalistic militarists to sanctify their actions, tumbled into temporary eclipse with Japan's utter defeat in the Pacific War. The fact that the Emperor, head of the Shinto faith, renounced his deity was another telling blow, and the sects fell into discredit during the confused postwar nightmare of struggling from war's ruins. Shintoism was, in many ways, outlawed during the seven year U. S. Military Occupation. Though not actually legislated out of existence, it was seriously circumscribed by edict and attitude alike.

The revival came swiftly, however, and the Shinto worship, consisting primarily of obeisances, offerings and prayers, abetted by deep-rooted beliefs, Japanese love of pageantry, ceremony, tradition, and the colorful annual and semiannual festivals, is once more of great significance. It is difficult, if not impossible, to determine the actual numbers of Shinto sect adherents, but one can note that as of latest official reckoning there were more than 90,000 shrines with over 15,000 priests. There are at least 70 million Japanese who follow Shintoism.

Shinto priests officiate at non-Shinto religious ceremonies, particularly at births and weddings, and play an important part in dedicating new buildings. Modern hotels, department stores, and office buildings frequently display the sign of Shinto, the *torii* gate, on their roofs.

CHRISTIANITY in Japan was in the early days, from 1549 to 1638, confined to Roman Catholicism when the Spanish and Portuguese missionaries were very active. The renowned crusader at that time was none other than the great Francis Xavier, who was later to become a saint. Before the missionaries were expelled, some 300,000 Japanese were converted, including high ranking generals and court ladies. The original ban on Christian teaching and practice was instituted by Hideyoshi, Japan's so-called "Napoleon." Even harsher edicts were later put into operation as a result of the 1637 *Shimabara Rebellion* near **Nagasaki.** The Christian faith once introduced was never completely wiped out, however, and grew defiantly, particularly in *Kyushu,* ever a Christian stronghold, always predominantly Catholic.

Protestant missions began their work in 1859, but great obstacles were met, which were not overcome until the overthrow of the Shogunate and the demise of the feudal system in

1868. By 1873 Christianity was flourishing, with missionaries carrying on their conversions, teaching, preaching, writing, and building with official sanction. In the same year those Christians who had been banished came back from exile and were restored to their places in their original communities.

Another boon to the Christian faithful was the translation of the Bible into Japanese. The printing of the Old Testament in Japanese characters took place in 1879, while the New Testament had been completed in 1876. An ecstasy of reform which rolled over the islands in the late 19th century was inspired by the desire to modernize, Europeanize, and grow great, and gave added impetus to the headway of the Christian doctrines.

Christianity was badly hurt by the wave of frantic nationalism that engulfed the nation in the years leading up to Japan's fatal entry into the Second World War. Today, with the original Constitution promulgated in 1889 and the New Constitution of postwar vintage both granting full freedom of religion, and with the influence of the west now great again, Christianity has had an upturn. Nonetheless, it must be noted that of Japan's 93.5 millions, only a slender handful—around 600,000 people—are considered, by themselves and their churches, to be professing Christians.

CREMATION. Today almost all Japanese of all religions and faiths are cremated. Buddhist priests preside at the majority of Japanese funerals. If the deceased is, as are so many Japanese, a believer in both faiths, Shinto priests wearing white robes, black high-crowned bonnets, and waving the sacred *sakaki* tree branches often assist in the services.

The Buddhist priests read or chant in mournful singsong fashion the ancient *sutras* (scriptures). Cremation, no doubt adopted by the Japanese because of acute lack of land space, is something that would be indecent, even outrageously blasphemous, in the eyes of the more Buddhist-minded Thais and Burmese.

In the *Kasoba,* the cremation building, rather unpalatable practices, to the western mind, are observed. The corpse is reduced to ash quickly, but charred bones are picked from the ash by chopsticks and kept as remembrances of the departed until burial ceremonies are performed. Ashes are deposited in urns and taken to the family altar, which is highly polished black lacquer, trimmed and embossed with gold or gold leaf, and found in an honored part of the house.

The ashes in Shinto rites rest in a small urn on the *Kami-Dana,* the "God Shelf," in front of a replica of a Shinto shrine, complete with *torii* gate, sacred *sakaki* branches with the *nusa* tied on, and traditional offerings of food and drink.

Cremation is currently widely practiced in both urban and rural circles, as a result of which cemeteries as we know them are not the commonplace sight in Japan that they are in the west. They are found only in odd clusters in areas that appear otherwise unusable, such as on hillocks, knolls rising out of paddyland, and in remote, forlorn sections of the towns. Certain exceptions exist to the foregoing, such as in the case of the famed *Tama Cemetery* where many Imperial people lie buried, after having been cremated. There are two exceptionally beautiful **Tokyo-to** burying grounds: *Koganei* in the outskirts and *Aoyama* in the capital's heart. Both places are much frequented in the spring and fall when they are generously endowed with cherry blossoms and tinted maple foliage.

One can easily spot a funeral in Japan. The house or store of the departed is set off with black and white striped curtains and large blown-up pictures of the deceased, edged across top left- and right-hand corners with black cloth bands, often of velvet. Crowds of quiet-faced mourners gather including relatives and friends, the men being attired in morning coats and striped trousers or black family-crested kimonos. The women wear severely shaded, black and white crested kimonos.

TOKYO

Tokyo, the world's most populous metropolis with some 10 million inhabitants, is a huge, sprawling, bright light, boom town city that has become an international magnet attracting, like steel filings, masses of new residents and overseas visitors.

Many Japanese vividly remember the rain of death and destruction that was poured on **Tokyo** from the skies in 1944-45, while others, less numerous, can reflect back to that dreadful noon of September 1, 1923, when the earth shuddered sickeningly and fires raced through the capital's matchbox houses, swallowing up half of **Tokyo** and much of **Yokohama** in a sea of flames. After World War II, much of **Tokyo** was rebuilt in ferro-concrete, cement, and stone, but the great bulk of the population, though working in modern buildings, still dwells in traditional paper and bamboo wood houses.

Tokyo is not an old city, as world history is reckoned, dating back only to the end of the 12th century when the place was merely a settlement on the great *Musashi* plain. Under its ancient name of **Edo** ("Estuary"), **Tokyo** became Japan's imperial capital in 1868, while the modern city was until recently only a group of unconnected farm hamlets and villages including the sub-areas of *Shinjuku, Shibuya, Ikebukuro, Gotanda, Shinagawa,* and *Meguro* which are within the radius of the Imperial shadow cast from the palace, home of the Imperial Family since the *Meiji Restoration.*

The center of national administration, education, culture, finance, politics, entertainment, and the arts, **Tokyo** is intersected by the sluggish *Sumida River* that flows to *Tokyo Bay* from the *Great Kwanto* rice plain granary.

Tokyo, called, in Japan, **Tokyo-to** (metropolis), covers 796.5 square miles in which more than 10% of the nation's total population resides.

A bustling modern capital with marble-fronted office buildings, great metropolitan dailies, international conventions, a Japan baseball world series, the largest airport in Asia, an Olympic site, a National Diet, and more modern industry than any other city of Japan save for **Osaka, Tokyo** lives partly in the dream world of the past including rickshaws, *Geisha* tea houses, public baths where men and women are sometimes only vaguely separated, flower arrangement schools that are the leaf

CENTRAL TOKYO

1. YASUKUNI SHRINE
2. KORAKUEN GARDEN
3. NATIONAL DIET BLDG.
4. MEIJI MEMORIAL GALLERY
5. KABUKI-ZA THEATER
6. ST. LUKE'S HOSPITAL
7. NISHI-HONGAN-JI TEMPLE
8. TOGEKI THEATER
9. EMBUJO THEATER
10. GINZA TOKYU HOTEL
11. TAKARAZUKA THEATER
12. NIKKATSU HOTEL
13. OKURA HOTEL
14. SHIBA PARK
15. PALACE HOTEL
16. IMPERIAL HOTEL
17. U. S. EMBASSY
18. ZOJOJI TEMPLE
19. TOKYO TOWER
20. IMPERIAL PALACE
21. HIBIYA PARK
22. CANADIAN EMBASSY
23. TAKASHIMAYA DEPT. STORE
24. NICHIGEKI THEATER

690

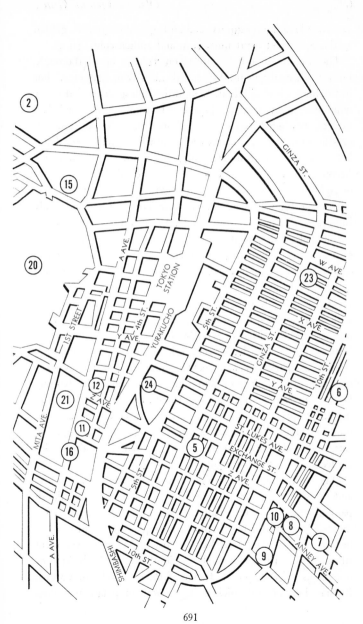

and twig breath of antiquity, and an Imperial court with golden carriages, ancient court musicians, and annual court games.

The kimono is seen less today on **Tokyo's** broad thorough-fares and shambling mud-spattered alleys than heretofore, but in the homes it is different. Behind the sliding doors and paper windows, many modern Japanese tycoons, professional ball players, bewigged *Geisha,* schoolboys, research workers, impressionist painters, and seductive, plucked eyebrowed dance hall girls shed their street clothes for kimonos, lay quilts for sleeping on the rice thatch mat floors, store their bedding out of sight in the daytime, dine on traditional rice, raw fish and bean paste soup, prepare special New Year's dishes and study calligraphy, *sumi-e* painting, and other olden-day arts.

But **Tokyo,** despite its haunting sense of the past, is a city of exuberant entertainment, nude chorus lines, neon lights, night baseball, all-night coffee shops, self-service elevators, supermarkets, wine stewards in French-style bistros, department stores, rooftop golf driving ranges, hamburger joints and policemen on night patrol rousing lovers in the parks. In **Tokyo** one can find blood banks, body-building classes, ancient archery instruction, Turkish baths, centipede oil cures for rheumatism, drunks on park benches, cocktail hour sirens, subway exits spewing forth millions of commuters daily, monorails, bathing beauty contests, fashion shows, traditional *kabuki* and *Noh* drama, puppet shows, all-girl operas, incense-burning ceremonies, cherry blossom festivals, temples dedicated to dogs and cats, and Buddhist masses for worn-out needles, children's discarded dolls and pet chipmunks.

One can eat squid, lotus roots, roasted sparrows (head, claws and all), raw lobster, embryonic eggs on a stick, cuttlefish painted with soy sauce, blowfish, mud eel, mock turtle, fermented bean curd, bamboo shoots, and quail's eggs, or one can be served with American ham or bacon and eggs, succulent sirloin steak, rib roast of beef, Southern fried chicken or marvelous *filet mignon,* Italian *fettucine* and minestrone, Russian borscht and chicken Kiev, German potato pancakes,

Chinese bird's-nest soup, French sole *bonne femme,* British mutton chops, Korean barbecued beef strips, Turkish delight, Polish *bliny,* Jewish pastrami, bagels, and lox, Scandinavian smorgasbord, or sophisticated sea food à la Prunier.

One sees fish-tailed Cadillacs in **Tokyo** as well as farmers in pantaloons and traditional *hachimaki* (sweat towel knotted about their brows).

In **Tokyo** one still sees scores of thousands of people wearing the hideous gauze mouth and nose masks to "keep off the colds"—a reminder of a custom that started during the worldwide flu epidemic of 1919 and still flourishes. One hears the soft footfall of the rickshaw boy, and listens to the cry of the night noodle vendor, the dawn bean curd salesman and the everyday call of the man who sells goldfish, bamboo ware, and fruits.

The old ways live again on the *Sumida River,* during the great *"Kawabiraki"* July firework displays and again, in mid-August, during the *"Toro Nagashi,"* river festival dedicated to the spirits of the dead when one can hear the tinkle of *Geisha* music and the cries of the floating minstrels every evening.

Tokyo is a busy but friendly city where one will find Christian churches, Jewish synagogues, Buddhist temples, Shinto shrines, and Moslem mosques as well as U. S. banks and business firms, drugstores, restaurants, stores, and shops. I promise, you will not get lonesome, bored or homesick in **Tokyo.** Never.

Tokyo is the off-to-one-corner tomb of the famed 47 Ronin, the *Shrine of Departed Souls,* and the temple to the memory of all the nation's war dead. **Tokyo** is smart restaurants and chic night clubs, as well as the dim bar-filled alleys of *Shinjuku* and the cabaret and supper club area of *Nishi Ginza* where lovelies ply customers with food and drink for a price.

Tokyo is the hordes of well-wishers flocking to the *Imperial Palace Plaza* on New Year's Day to greet the Emperor across *Ni-ju Bridge,* the tricky acrobatics of Japan's skilled firemen performing on the *Imperial Plaza,* the temple priests at *Setsubun* tossing beans to the crowds on "Devil Expelling" Day and the advent of His Majesty in the *Diet Building,* reading the rescript that puts that august legislative body in session.

Outside, but nearby, to the southwest lie **Yokohama;** the old feudal city of **Kamakura** with its celebrated *Buddha;* **Atami** and the spa-studded peninsula of *Izu;* the *Fuji Five Lakes,* and the grape and crystal country around **Kofu City.** To the northeast lie **Nikko,** and the hot springs beyond, while across *Tokyo Bay* lies the fast developing *Chiba,* with its fertile green countryside sloping down to fishing hamlets, open beaches, and summer resorts. The mountains are filled with hot springs, mountain rivers crowded with trout, temples on mountain tops reached by cablecars and ropeways, reservoirs, a network of golf courses, and near-virgin wilderness for skier, mountain climber, hunter, and outdoor adventurer. To the north-northeast lies Gumma Prefecture with 64 registered mineral springs, Japan's top skiing country, a vast hunting paradise, and off to one side under volcanic *Mt. Asama,* the nation's great summer abode, **Karuizawa.**

Tokyo inside, **Tokyo** outside, the city is never far from the countryside and even in the country there is a hint of the wonderful metropolis not far off.

It seems trite to say **Tokyo** is Japan, but it is more right than trite.

One's drive from the mammoth *Haneda International Airport* or **Yokohama's** docks to downtown **Tokyo** may prove to be a sharp initial scenic disappointment after your great expectations and happy arrival experiences, but the efficiency and courtesy of the airport or dock officials in handling customs and passport formalities are in pleasant contrast to that of our own frequently fouled up bureaucratic health, customs, and immigration procedures. In **Tokyo,** the whole affair, with rare exceptions, is over in a few minutes.

In no time the visitor finds himself in an airport limousine, private car, or taxi en route to his hotel, threading its way through the densest traffic in all of the world. As recently as 1964, the journey from the airport to the *Imperial Hotel* took as long as one hour and a half during the rush hour or three quarters of an hour to an hour in non-"traffic peak" hours. The opening of the new **Tokyo–Haneda** (*International Airport*) expressway has greatly reduced the driving time, but one must still allow about an hour for the journey. The long-heralded monorail from the airport to central **Tokyo** is scheduled to begin operations as this edition goes to press and will make the trip between these two points in an incredibly short 15 minutes. Hold your hat!

This gigantic city, whose expanding population already exceeds 10,000,000, and whose metropolitan area embraces 14,000,000 souls, spreads its tentacles in a seemingly endless series of drab two-story buildings, cheek by jowl with impressive modern steel-and-concrete office buildings and hotels. Unless one looks for it, there appears to be little sign of the appalling devastation from wartime air attacks. It is well to remember that **Tokyo** had suffered incredible damage by fires and earthquakes centuries before World War II. **Tokyo** was almost completely ruined by fires in 1601, 1657, and in 1772. The 1923 earthquake, too, was one of the worst in history. Buildings that survived that tragedy are rare and shown virtually as historic monuments. Obviously, therefore, with only a few exceptions, there are really no ancient buildings remaining in the city. As for the destructive effects of the war, the principal and precise pattern bombing which took place from March to May of 1945 caused more total destruction to **Tokyo** (though not as much percentagewise) than did the atomic bomb attack on **Hiroshima,** *a fact not realized by most people.*

The immense task of rebuilding the world's largest city can best be expressed by the fact that during 1961 alone more than $600,000,000 worth of new buildings were constructed. Stone, concrete, and steel structures still spring up like mushrooms almost overnight. The streets and boulevards of **Tokyo** are an astonishing agglomeration of East and West. This vast metropolis is truly a churning "melting pot."

The GINZA district stretching from *Kyobashi Bridge* to *Shimbashi Bridge* is much more than a commercial street, gay boulevard, business district, entertainment center, or a shopping neighborhood. It is a mélange of each of the foregoing—a vibrant, pulsating symbol of modern Japan; by night the central *Ginza* rivals the glitter of *Broadway,* the sparkle of *Piccadilly Circus, State Street*'s gaiety, and the joie de vivre of *Montmartre;* Christmas Eve on the *Ginza* outsparkles New Year's Eve on *Times Square.* In physical aesthetic beauty, it can never rival *Fifth Avenue,* the *Rue de Rivoli* or *Michigan Boulevard,* but it does serve as an equally entrancing shopping center.

But to me the *Ginza*'s bars, night clubs, shops, department stores, office buildings, restaurants, and coffee houses constitute only a backdrop for the indescribably colorful passing parade which courses through this thoroughfare in never-ending teeming, exotic excitement. One may be entranced with a greater variety of interesting, contrasting costumes and nationalities in 10 minutes on the *Ginza* than in months, even years, of travel most any place else in the world. I have found the gaily colored kimono with the contrasting wide obi sashes which the girls wear to be as fascinating a costume as is to be found in the world today. And on the *Ginza* the visitor will see many of them as well as a scattering of the equally traditional but more subdued kimono, sash, and sandal garb of the older women. But, alas, you will also see countless teen-age gals dashing about in "American traditional" costumes—blue jeans and sneakers, while the teen-age boys dart in and out of traffic wearing tattered slacks and highly decorated sweat or T shirts.

It is not at all unusual to see females of all ages on the *Ginza* in smart, well-tailored, western style suits and dresses, who figuratively rub shoulders with men in turbans and flowing robes and other women in enchanting saris. There will be girls, or women, carrying babies on their backs in *Ombu* fashion, while the gaudy *Geisha* will catch the eye. The Buddhists and Shinto priests, businessmen, and tourists from far continents add to the *Ginza*'s luster. There are unobtrusive prostitutes slouching in doorways, and beggars in the alleys. The students always seem to appear in groups. At night there is no diminution of the *Ginza*'s pedestrian activities. Take a stroll, join the *"gim bura"* as the Japanese put it, enjoy the blatant vivacity of the heart of **Tokyo's** entertainment world.

The *Ginza* by day or the *Ginza* by night—it's always exciting, and the traffic indescribably chaotic. Streetcars clanging their bells, young men on motor bikes in crash helmets, trousered girls sitting behind them, roar past to the next traffic stop, and the taxis, frequently called *"kamikazes,"* driven at a furious speed as they dart in and out of this maelstrom of vehicles.

The *Ginza* (now officially known as *Ginza dori* or *Chuodori*) is not only a street but is the name given to a large, lustrous area.

AVENUE Z (now officially known as *Harumidori*) pierces the heart of downtown **Tokyo** at right angles to the *Ginza,* at the intersection of which is found a branch of the famous *Mitsukoshi Department Store*. This frantic street is lined with business buildings, shops, stores, coffee houses, theaters, restaurants, and hotels, including the vast *Nikkatsu Hotel* and office building. Z crosses busy Avenue A and is ultimately surrounded by the finery of *Hibiya Park* on one side and the *Imperial Pal-*

ace. At the main intersection of the *Ginza* and Avenue Z one finds a huge glowing cylindrical glass structure called the "Dream Center" exhibiting Mitsubishi products.

TENTH STREET forms an almost perfect circle with the *Imperial Palace* at its hub. Within its embrace are the main downtown points of interest, and at its outer extremity are the *Hotel New Japan*, the *Little Club*, the *Okura Hotel*, and the *American Embassy*.

AVENUE A is a broad, tree-lined boulevard that enters **Tokyo's** heartland past the Brobdingnagian *Tokyo Tower*, *Shiba* and *Hibiya Parks*, the *Imperial Hotel* and *Imperial Palace*. On it is the renowned *Dai Ichi Building*, General Mac-Arthur's headquarters, many modern office buildings, the new luxurious *Palace Hotel*, and *Marunouchi*.

1ST AVENUE for a short distance parallels Avenue A, passes lovely gardens and swings along the *Imperial Palace* moat to be concentric with 10th Street.

The MARUNOUCHI QUARTER. Just as the *Ginza* is the shopping and amusement center of the city, the *Marunouchi*, in the most westernized section of the city, is the hub of **Tokyo's** commercial activities. More than 100 modern western style buildings contain governmental organizations, foreign embassies, diplomatic offices, big business firms, banks, department stores, and hotels. The vast *Otemachi Building*, largest in **Tokyo** and the entire Orient, completed in 1958, itself covers 27 acres in area and floor space combined in the north end of *Marunouchi*.

The eight-storied *Marunouchi Building*, with hundreds of business offices, stores, and restaurants, is said to be used by more than 100,000 persons daily. Opposite is the eight-storied *New Marunouchi Building* occupied by still more stores, restaurants, and banks.

Three- and four-storied old red-brick buildings, symmetrical in design and reminiscent of Great Britain, are found among the ultrasmart, modern *Marunouchi* structures.

About 350 years ago, this section of **Tokyo** was reclaimed from the sea to provide land for the mansions of the aristocracy.

During the Imperial *Meiji Restoration* in 1868, these "tenants" were replaced by government offices and barracks. In 1873, a fire destroyed the *Quarter,* and for 20 years the district was abandoned to grass and weeds. Reconstruction was planned and carried out by the British architect, Dr. Josiah Condor, who, with a staff of Japanese architects, built new brick buildings once known as "One Block of London." Among these are Japan's first "western style" buildings and thus of architectural interest, but unfortunately they are being destroyed and replaced by modern buildings to make more space for busy **Tokyo.**

SHOPS, STORES, AND ARCADES. All are covered in Chapter Six. In passing, it is of interest to note, however, that in **Tokyo** there is to be purchased every conceivable object obtainable in America or Europe in addition to exotic articles rarely seen elsewhere by most western visitors. There are lacquer boxes, beautifully decorated in black, scarlet, and gold; wigs for women generally and *Geisha* specifically; pharmacies, unique to Japan, with reptiles preserved in spirits, mummified snakes and lizards, and ancient cures for almost every ailment. The older Japanese generation still often relies on these age-old traditional cures. Perhaps the most unusual goods, at least to western eyes, are displayed in the shops offering centuries-old dwarf plants and twisted, gnarled trees. Delightful, tiny Japanese miniature gardens, complete with lake, bridges, trees, and figures typical of the *Willow Pattern* design, so famous throughout the world, will entice the passing visitor.

The large and lovely Japanese department stores, as modern as any in America, have their own gardens, amusement parks for children, escalators and elevators, fresh beautiful displays of merchandise, pet shops, restaurants and coffee shops, bakery departments, private theaters, and an artistic beauty of layout. Although a complete shopping list will be found in Chapter Six, some of the better known department stores and arcade shops selling specialties are noted here. The *Tatsumura* and *Kanebo* stores are noted for silk kimonos. The *Mitsukoshi,* one of the biggest, offers domestic and imported goods; the *Toyoko* features the *Munekata Gallery* selling prints by world-famous Japanese artists, including Shiko Munekata. Beautiful things can be bought in the arcades in the *Imperial,* the *Nikkatsu, New Japan,* and *Palace Hotels.* Here, as in most other stores and shops, the Japanese waive the 16 per cent Commodity Tax on various goods purchased by overseas visitors, the items including cameras, cultured pearls, furs, binoculars (a particularly good buy), and ivory. Goods in the larger department stores are sold at fixed prices plain to see, but, although the Japanese are not as prone to heavy bargaining with customers as are some other Asian nations, small merchants consider a little haggling necessary to "save face."

No longer is it taken for granted that the Japanese manufacture only cheap, mass-produced goods. Today the Japanese accent is on quality, the only way to contend with and outdo, if possible, the western markets. Japanese precision goods now available are at an all-time high. Such articles as cameras, transistor radios, and both color and black-and-white TV sets can compare with the best that the west has to offer. Optical instruments are also of a high order and very, very cheap. But the days of only copying other countries' goods are over. The Japanese have invented their own industrial methods, techniques, and mechanical refinements.

The nation's industrial production is vast and its standards of living are high. There are now more than six and a half million TV sets in Japan, many of them color sets. The majority of the radios and TV's blaring forth are produced in the capital. Japan's rapid rise from the poverty and ruin of 1945 has been phenomenal. The burgeoning of the world-renowned Sony Corporation of **Tokyo** is a typical example of what has been accomplished industrially. In 1945 a tiny group of determined men founded this successful company with a capitalization of only $500. After successfully making magnetic tape recorders, they turned to the tiny transistor radios with which they hit the jack pot. Their very first model sold one million sets; the latest models are selling like the proverbial house afire. In 1946 Sony employed a mere 35 workers. Today it has thousands of employees. Then, its sales were in the hundreds of dollars. Today its sales are measured in tens of millions of dollars. This is but one of many fabulous Japanese postwar success stories.

COFFEE HOUSES . . . TEA ROOMS. Japanese cities of all sizes feature coffee and tea rooms in a big way. These range from tiny holes in the wall to plush, mammoth, magnificent establishments, of which **Tokyo** boasts a total of at least five thousand. Some occupy several floors in modern steel-and-chromium buildings and feature several orchestras, while others are small, dimly lit, intimate but comfortable dens much patronized by Japanese youth. These young men and women sit in entranced silence listening to hi-fi music, American jazz, light opera, or the classics of Bach, Mozart, Beethoven, or Brahms. For the first time in Japanese history, women can enjoy themselves in public on almost equal terms with the lordly male, their presence being a startling revelation of the changing face of modern Japan.

Most tea and coffee houses are known for some special musical attraction, such as swing or light opera music, rock 'n' roll, popular crooner type singers, or even for beautiful waitresses. But most important is that the visitor can enjoy a whole evening with a cup of tea or coffee costing about 30 cents and be left alone to enjoy himself as long as he wishes.

TOKYO BY NIGHT. As darkness falls, the great, straggling, garish city comes into its own. The *Ginza* becomes a fabulous spectacle, lit up by furiously flashing neon signs advertising a thousand wares, its sidewalks a multi-colored stream of gay, laughing crowds. **Tokyo,** furiously business-bent by day, now plunges into every form of nocturnal revelry to meet every type of taste. **Tokyo's** night life is the most concentrated in the world.

There are all kinds of theatrical entertainment: undress "girlie" shows, night club cabarets, and the traditional *Kabuki,* feudal dramas of Old Japan. The famous, gorgeously costumed all-girl *Takarazuka* musical company has one unit which plays in **Tokyo** in its own vast theater, formerly, during the "occupation era," called the *Ernie Pyle Theater* (opposite the side doors of the *Imperial*). At the *Nichigeki Theater* and the *Asakusa Kokusai,* all-girl Japanese spectacles are staged with fully costumed girls.

The "STRIP." A few comments here on strip shows and how they have affected the Japanese: For centuries mixed public bathing including unrelated men, women, and children as well as family groups has been common in Japan. Nudity, as such, meant nothing. The young and old, male and female, innocently shared the relaxing joy of the almost scalding water. Western ideas are, of course, entirely different. The American occupation of Japan impressed on the Japanese the strange western regard for nudity as something daring and exciting when applied to pretty women. The army left, but the western tourists began to arrive. To "give the visitor what he wants" means good business and has been carried out wholeheartedly—in the better places with excellent taste. The chief and unbelievable result of this new type of entertainment is that the Japanese male who previously couldn't have cared less about naked women has now climbed on the American bandwagon and stands in line to spend money to see what traditionally could be viewed free. Sex is advertised blatantly. Nudity is commercialized in public. There is not only no false modesty, there is none.

BARS. There are possibly more than 25,000 bars in **Tokyo,** but this may be a conservative estimate. All the narrow lanes and streets leading from the *Ginza* are lined with them, while at *Asakusa* and in the *Shimbashi Station* area, they number hundreds more. Most are small and nearly all are serviced by attractive young girls, either behind the bar or acting as hostesses.

MOVIE THEATERS abound in Japan. The marquees are gay in shimmering neon proclaiming the horrors or the delights of the cinema of the moment. Colorful billboards throughout the city extol the virtues or the excitements of the current movies. Our western cowboy pictures are enormously popular with the younger Japanese audiences. American and foreign films normally retain the English or foreign dialogue with Japanese subtitles. This, incidentally, is not true of Japanese TV. I have seen Dennis the Menace talking fluent Japanese, and it was a riot. A number of Continental motion picture films are shown, and here, too, the French, Italian, or Hungarian dialogue is frequently retained with Japanese subtitles, although the dubbing-in of Japanese dialogue is proving more popular to Japanese TV viewers.

CABARETS and SUPPER SHOWS. The extracurricular activities of the Japanese play such an important role in their day-to-day life that, while cabarets, restaurants, and night clubs are covered in greater detail in another chapter, a word here may not be amiss. There are all types, classes, and dimensions of night life establishments in **Tokyo.** Many of them have sparkling dance bands, excellent cuisine, and magnificent floor shows. Others are lowdown and earthy. High class or low-brow, nearly all have hostesses who, young, seductive, and beautiful, descend on the lonely male like lovely birds of prey.

The better night clubs, bars, and restaurants are scattered about the city, but the less "high class" types of clubs and bars are massed in and around the *Ginza, Asakusa,* and other heavy traffic sectors of the city.

ASAKUSA. By night, this brash large amusement center, in the uptown heart of **Tokyo,** is a "jumping" dervish. Its bars, coffee houses, restaurants, cinema houses, and small theaters are thronged nightly with crowds of thrill seekers, erotic and otherwise. The *Kokusai Theater* is renowned for its spectacular musical shows. The pinball parlors *(pachinko)* have become a postwar craze with Japanese youth. Naughty burlesque strip shows are staged in tiny basement theaters in which the audiences are jam-packed like perspiring sardines.

THE GODDESS OF MERCY TEMPLE, *Asakusa Kannon*, incongruously enough, is located amid all this raucousness. This much venerated building, known also as the *Sensoji Temple,* was rebuilt in 1955 to replace the former 17th-century *Hall, Gate,* and beautiful 100-foot *Pagoda* which were all destroyed during the war. Legend relates that the petite statue of Kannon, a 1.8-inch golden image now enshrined in the *Main Hall,* was accidentally netted by a fisherman on the local *Sumida River.* The lane leading to the temple is lined with a wide variety of shops, in an area known as *"nakamise,"* where cookies, cakes, candies, and other refreshments are prepared before your eyes. Trinket stores abound.

KABUKI PERFORMANCES are presented at several theaters which feature this amazing form of drama. The best known are the *Kabuki-za, Ginza-Higashi,* near the intersection of 10th and Z, the *Yomiuri Hall,* on the seventh floor of *Yomiuri Kaikan,* next to the *Yurakucho Station,* and the *Shimbashi Embujo.* This strange medieval performance will tax your credulity, but it's awesome to see. The pace is at times slow and stately, and then violent and dramatic. For hours on end the gorgeously dressed characters perform to enthusiastic Japanese audiences, many of whom are dressed in their brilliant national costume, the kimono, as if to wrest the magnificent past from a drab

present. Manifest throughout the basic motifs are the age-old conflicts and tragedy pertaining to life's eternal concern with love, adultery, and death. The story of the *"Forty-Seven Ronin,"* or feudal knights, is the favorite *Kabuki* plot. Although most audiences have witnessed this production scores of times, it invariably drives them to frenzied appreciation. This dramatization of an historic event depicts the most famous example of gory guts-spilling hara-kiri in Japanese history. The overlord of the *"Forty-Seven Ronin"* had been grievously wronged by a yet higher lord and committed the even more serious grievous offense of flashing his blade in his superior's castle yard. As a result, he was obliged to die by his own sword in the traditional hara-kiri style. This dreadful demise made the overlord's followers *Ronin,* or *samurai* without a master, which, in the curious ancient Japanese feudal code, was considered a further insult. One winter night the furious *Ronin* burst into the higher lord's castle, beheaded him, and mercilessly killed his followers. This example of heroic revenge transformed the *Ronin* into national heroes, causing the Shogun generously, by prevailing standards, to permit them in time-honored fashion to commit hara-kiri too. Although the Emperor, Shogun, and the court sympathized with these men since they were loyal to their master, the Shogun was unable to condone their deed since it constituted a threat to the authority of the court in the form of future uprisings if he forgave their act. Side by side, the *Ronin* now lie in the courtyard of the *Sengakuji Temple* in **Tokyo**. There are "afternoon" and evening performances at the *Kabuki* theaters, usually at eleven A.M. and four P.M.

NOH. Another form of ancient native Japanese drama is known as *Noh,* and was originated especially and exclusively for noblemen, as contrasted with *Kabuki* which was created and preserved as entertainment for all the people. To say *Noh* drags is to put it mildly. *Noh,* a more peculiar, more uncanny form of art than *Kabuki,* was created during the 14th century. The dialogue is short and staccato, occasionally accompanied by ancient Japanese musical instruments. The western mind is quite capable of grasping the exciting essentials of *Kabuki* but can only regard *Noh* as a kind of dull, symbolic fantasy. The male *Noh* actors play the female parts just as in *Kabuki.* The 14th-century court language used in *Noh* is so hard to follow that even the majority of Japanese audiences are incapable of understanding it. The ability of the audience to understand the dialogue is further hampered by the traditional speaking habits of the characters, who rumble, whine, or cry out in falsetto accents, according to the actor's interpretation of his male or female role. The beautifully contrived masks which are often worn add to the incongruity of the scenes. Actors begin their training for *Noh* in their childhood and are normally not adept until they have attained at least their thirtieth birthday. Present-day audiences are not the noblemen for whom the *Noh* was intended but representatives of the masses who come to the theater ready to make a night of it, often bringing sandwiches with them to be consumed during the acts. Others purchase food on the premises. Check locally for performance times; they're odd.

BALLET and MUSIC. Western ballet, a type of entertainment very popular with the Japanese, is performed by foreign troupes who visit **Tokyo** quite regularly. There are some local ballet companies, but the figures of the Japanese just do not lend themselves to this western art.

Four symphony orchestras in the capital, during the season, present a series of well-attended concerts. The most important of these groups is the *Tokyo Philharmonic Orchestra* which performs on the radio under the name of *"N.H.K."*

OPERA has long been popular in Japan, but its development was interrupted during the Pacific war. It now flourishes again. The present craze for music of all types is largely due to our American influence and the growth in popularity of radio and television. The radio features music of all types. Musical education in the schools and universities has progressed recently by leaps and bounds. The NISSEI THEATER, facing *Hibiya Park,* was opened in 1963 and is one of the world's finest opera houses.

UENO PARK *(Way-No Park)*. For generations, Japan has had an enormous influence on western art. The people of all classes have an extraordinary instinct for the expression of beauty in all its forms. Examples of this national flair include the expert arranging of flowers, the growing of dwarf trees, the faultless simplicity of interior decorating, and landscape gardening. **Tokyo** can boast a splendid cultural background, revived after the destruction of war. The center of Japanese art is located in and around *Ueno Park,* which contains:

The TOKYO NATIONAL MUSEUM is a huge building containing diverse collections of sculpture, carvings, textile art, armor, ceramics, early paintings from the 18th and 19th centuries, prints, 17th and 19th century lacquerwork, and calligraphy. These treasures are housed in buildings covering an area of more than four acres.

The NATIONAL MUSEUM OF WESTERN ART, erected in 1959, is a three-storied reinforced concrete structure built to house the famous *Matsukata Collection* of western sculpture and paintings collected by the late owner.

The NATIONAL SCIENCE MUSEUM, opened in 1928,

contains a vast collection of exhibits in the field of botany, physics, chemistry, and astronomy.

The ZOOLOGICAL GARDENS is a menagerie, generously stocked with both birds and animals, open throughout the year. Many of the animals, foreign and domestic, are seen roaming in their native habitats. One of the unusual attractions of the *Gardens,* particularly for children, is the monorail on which two streamlined coaches are whisked along for a distance of some 360 yards—a forerunner of bigger things to come in **Tokyo.** A full-fledged monorail is planned in the not too distant future to carry passengers from downtown **Tokyo** to the *Haneda Airport.* Mr. Tetsuzo Inumaru, president of the *Imperial Hotel,* is head of the projected full-scale monorail project which, when completed, will cut the time for the journey from downtown **Tokyo** to the airport to fifteen minutes.

SHINOBAZU POND, a shimmering body of water over a quarter of a mile in circumference, situated near the *Zoological Gardens,* affords fine opportunities to row or paddle, while picturesque promenades may be made around the shores and through the surrounding gardens.

TOSHOGU SHRINE, also near the *Ueno Zoological Gardens,* dates back to 1626 and honors the wicked Iyeyasu Tokugawa, persecutor of the Christians. Overly ornate, it contains original letters of the Tokugawa and other exhibits of antiquity.

The TRANSPORTATION MUSEUM, near the *Mansei-bashi Bridge,* contains thousands of exhibits including Japan's "Number One Locomotive" made in 1871 by the Vulcan Foundry Company of Lancashire, England, a fascinating relic. This engine pioneered the *Tokyo-Yokohama Line* in 1872. Another locomotive on display was manufactured by an American firm, in Pittsburgh, for the *Hokkaido Railway.*

The FOLKCRAFT MUSEUM at **Komaba,** half an hour by electric train from **Tokyo,** houses highly interesting examples of Japanese arts and folkcraft. The museum is small but worthwhile.

The IMPERIAL PALACE. In 1868 the great Emperor Meiji transferred the Imperial Court from **Kyoto** to **Tokyo.** Meiji, father of modern Japan, converted the site of the Shogun's palace to the Imperial residence, originally a maze of austere, sedate buildings surrounded by walls and moats. These buildings were largely destroyed during the Pacific war. Although the Emperor's "godliness" no longer exists, no other modern monarch lives in such complete privacy as this unusual *Palace* affords. In actual fact, there is no single structure in these stately grounds which we would consider a palace as such. Rather, a modern residence has been rebuilt which is, in fact, a series of modest low-built buildings occupied by the Emperor and his democratized family, buildings and gardens which remain invisible to the outer world. The original *Palace* structures are being replaced and will be used for official functions.

The *Palace* and its considerable grounds are situated in the heart of downtown **Tokyo,** near *Tokyo Station, Marunouchi,* the *Palace* and *Imperial Hotels.* The area, known simply as the *Imperial Palace,* is surrounded by powerfully built inclined walls composed of colossal blocks of masonry of different sizes dotted with periodic corner towers. One may glimpse the tops of twisted pine trees over the walls. The inner enclosure, covering an area of 250 acres, is surrounded by a linked series of tranquil, willow-fringed, beautiful old moats crossed by occasional bridges, the best known of which is the *Niju-bashi* or *"Double Bridge."* The front wing of the *Palace* is protected by a heavy gateway. The *Daimyo,* as the feudal lords were known, lived in the outer gardens beyond the front moat. The public is permitted to visit the *Imperial Palace* on only two days during the year: the first is on the occasion of the New Year's Festival, January second, and the second is on the Emperor's birthday, April twenty-ninth. At other times, would-be visitors can get only as far as the open space in front of the first bridge. Special permission can be obtained to see the inner garden area of the *Palace,* but this garden is of no special interest.

Understandably, the Emperor's popularity declined drastically after the war. Even today, some of the younger generation of Japan view him with marked indifference approaching disillusionment. However, the marriage of Crown Prince Akihito to the pretty commoner, Michiko Shoda, and the subsequent birth of an heir, Prince Hiro, has done much to dispel this postwar antipathy. This is particularly true of the older generation, and even the younger folks are showing signs of greater affection for the royal family.

The renaissance of the Imperial family's popularity was clearly demonstrated during the New Year's Festival of 1961 when throngs crowded the *Palace* grounds to the extent of more than 170,000.

NATIONAL DIET BUILDING. This great seat of Parliament, on *Kasumigaseki Hill,* is one of Japan's loftiest structures, surmounted by a ponderous central tower 215 feet in height. The 390-room *Diet* and *Tower* are of gleaming white granite and rugged concrete. Begun in 1918, the *National Diet Building* took 18 years to build at the then staggering cost of 26,000,000 yen. It is a matter of national pride that only domestic materials were used in building the *Diet.* One half of the building contains the 450-seat House of Councillors, the other half the

House of Representatives with 460 seats. The combined *Visitors' Galleries* of both Houses can accommodate a total of over 1,700 persons. Foreigners may arrange a visit to the *Diet* through the Japanese Government Information Office.

The TOKYO CENTRAL STATION, transportation nerve center of all Japan, is situated close to the *Ministry of Transport,* the main headquarters of the *Japan Travel Bureau,* the *Kokusai Kanko Hotel,* and other offices connected with the travel industry.

The NIHOMBASHI BRIDGE AREA was formerly considered the center of **Tokyo.** The *Bridge* was the point used as the base from which to calculate distances to all points in Japan in the 17th century. *Nihombashi* is the northern continuation of the *Ginza,* **Tokyo's** fashionable downtown shopping district. *Nihombashi* runs into *Ginza* and *Shimbashi,* and the three succeeding links of *Nihombashi, Ginza,* and *Shimbashi Street* combine to become one of the busiest and most enticing of the arterial units of the capital. In the center of the city, through which these thoroughfares cut, we find many fine restaurants, shops, and important department stores including *Takashimaya, Shirokiya,* and *Mitsukoshi.* William Adams, an English sailor, the first Englishman to settle in Japan, originally lived in an obscure street near *Nihombashi Bridge.* A monument marking the site of Adams' home was dedicated in 1930. It is inscribed: "In memory of William Adams, known as Miura Anjin, the first Englishman to settle in Japan, coming as pilot on board the *Charity* in 1600, who resided in a mansion built on this spot, who instructed Ieyasu, the first Tokugawa Shogun, on gunnery, geography, mathematics, et cetera, rendering valuable services in foreign affairs, and who married a Japanese lady, Miss Magome, and died on May 16th, 1620, at the age of forty-five years."

The CENTRAL WHOLESALE MARKET is one of the world's largest produce enterprises where wholesale marketing in fowl, fish, shellfish, fruit, meat, and vegetables takes place.

In SHIBA PARK we find the historic Buddhist *Zojoji*

Temple, seat of the local *Jodo* sect, and the beautiful, much admired two-storied red lacquer *Sammon,* or *Tower Gate,* which was built in 1605 and has survived every disaster since. The *Temple* houses more than 200 rare historical relics. This diverse and popular park possesses a swimming pool, athletic grounds, golf driving range, apricot trees, and flowering shrubberies.

TOKYO TOWER, the world's tallest steel structure rises near *Shiba Park.* It soars majestically over **Tokyo** and the surrounding area. Just as the *Eiffel Tower* is the aesthetic symbol of **Paris,** so *Tokyo Tower* is rapidly becoming the symbol of the Japanese capital. The construction and silhouettes of the *Eiffel* and *Tokyo Towers* are quite similar, though the Japanese counterpart rises to a spectacular 1,092 feet, more than 100 feet higher than its ethereal Parisian twin. The *Eiffel Tower* is largely decorative, while the Tokyo version, built in 1958, is highly utilitarian, being used for the broadcasting of multi-purpose TV and radio programs. Two observation platforms, located at 390 and 738 foot elevations, may be reached by elevator. The view from the upper platform is majestic. At the tower's base is a tall *Modern Science Museum* exhibiting the most recent achievements in electronics. Also at the base are amusement rooms, shops, snack bars, and tea rooms.

SENGAKUJI TEMPLE is famous for being the place of interment of the *Forty-Seven Ronin,* who rest in rigid adherence to the military rank they held in life. The tomb of Oishi Yoshio is roofed over. Next to his niche is the resting place of the lord of *Ako.* Beside the path leading to the burial court is a traditional well. One of the temple buildings contains interesting mementos of the *Forty-Seven Ronin.*

ZEMPUKUJI TEMPLE (near *Juban*) is of historical significance to Americans because it was used as a residence, in 1859, by Townsend Harris, our first Minister to Japan, and as the United States Legation. The temple buildings, dating from the 9th century, have been victims of numerous conflagrations. Most recently constructed since 1945, they are now particularly sacred to the Japanese. Ancient documents of Kobo-Daishi from 1,100 years ago are preserved in the *Temple* as are sacred carvings and pictures. A mammoth gingko tree, considered to be **Tokyo's** largest, most ancient, and most interesting relic, is in the alluring gardens.

AKASAKA DETACHED PALACE. Among the crazy-quilt bedlam of **Tokyo** architecture, this fine French Louis Quatorze palace, designed on the plan of a miniature *Versailles,* is of particular interest. Near *Yotsuya Station,* it is a most luxurious regal structure, formerly the Dowager Empress' residence. Among its famous guests was the then Prince of Wales (now the Duke of Windsor). The two-story *Palace,* almost impervious to fire and earthquakes, is rich with granite and imported marble. The *Egyptian Room, Hall of the Feathered Robe* (ballroom), and *Hall of the Flowers and Birds* contain famous paintings by French and Japanese artists. This *Palace* is now used as a library and is open to the public. The gardens in the rear are a popular spot in the summer.

MEIJI SHRINE. This is a visitor's "must." Don't miss it, please. The whole vast area is lovely, and, apart from its historical connotations, the gardens, athletic facilities, and general décor are inviting and spectacular in themselves. Before the war, this shrine was the holy objective of one of Japan's great pilgrimages and is still visited by large, respectful crowds which are particularly dense during the three-day annual festival from November first through November third. Erected to the memory of the Emperor Meiji, one of Japan's greatest rulers, the original shrine was partially destroyed by bombs on April 1, 1945. This disaster helped to destroy the nation's faith in Imperial divinity. Until then, the populace had firmly and steadfastly believed that both the *Imperial Palace* and the *Meiji Shrine* were immune from enemy attack, even though all other homes and structures might be reduced to ashes.

The original shrine, completed in 1925, comprised an *Outer Garden, Memorial Picture Gallery,* the *Meiji Memorial Hall, Inner Garden,* and the *Shrine* itself. Reconstruction was ultimately completed in October of 1958.

Outer Garden (120 acres). This area, laid out as a beautiful public park, includes the 56,000-seat athletic stadium, the 60,000-seat baseball park, two vast swimming pools, a huge auditorium, and a Rugby football ground.

The *Memorial Picture Gallery,* consecrated to the memory of Emperor Meiji and his wife, represents an excellent blend of modern and traditional Japanese architecture. It contains oil paintings by famous artists and Japanese style pictures depicting the lives of the Emperor and his wife. The oil paintings depicting the life of the Emperor are huge and to some foreign tourists resemble calendar art, but they do serve to educate the people in from the farms.

Meiji Memorial Hall, separated from the *Outer Garden* by a streetcar line, was once a segment of the *Aoyama Palace.* Here, in 1882, the Emperor and all his Court assembled to hear profound discussions on the proposed Constitution. The *Hall,* with a seating capacity of 600, contains a stage and wide screen for movies, but is perhaps best known for its colorful weddings.

The *Inner Garden.* This lovely park and garden, covering approximately 180 acres, is one of the beloved sights of **Tokyo,** bedecked as it is with 120,000 trees and shrubs presented by people from all over the nation. The *Inner Garden* contains the finest iris display in the city, with close to 100 varieties of this beautiful flower. The water lilies bloom at the same time as the iris in June and early July.

The *sanctuary* is approached by a broad walk spanned by four great 13th-century red *torii* gates. The second *torii* from the main entrance is 40 feet high with huge supporting pillars. These *torii* gates, found at entrances to all Shinto shrines, are symbolic representations of the mysterious entrance, or womb, of life.

HIBIYA PARK, laid out in 1903 and covering more than 40 acres, is the oldest western style park in Japan. Here feudal family bailiwicks stood and warriors paraded. The *Hibiya* wisteria and azaleas are exquisite in the spring, while the chrysanthemums draw innumerable enchanted visitors during the autumn. Scores of all kinds of trees adorn the park among which are some decorative dogwoods sent from America as a "bread and butter" thank you in return for the gift of Japanese cherry trees which now grace our nation's capital. Buildings around or near the park include the *Nippon Kangyo Bank, N.H.K. Building, Imperial Hotel, Sanshin Building,* the *Metropolitan Police Board,* the *Supreme Court* and other major government edifices.

The N.H.K. BUILDING, situated south of *Hibiya Park,* is the ultramodern "Radio City" of **Tokyo.** N.H.K. stands for *Nippon Hoso Kyokai,* the government broadcasting station.

The Shinto YASUKUNI SHRINE is the memorial to those who have fallen in all the nation's wars. A colossal granite *torii* stands at the southern entrance. The beautiful cherry trees in the shrine precincts bloom in early April. Impressive stone lanterns abound in the outer precincts, while a great bronze *torii* guards the path to the shrine.

The KORAKUEN GARDEN was formerly the property of the lords of Mito, members of a branch of the great Tokugawa Shogunate family. The garden, dating from the early 17th century, was originally planned by Mitsukuni Mito, an expert and patron of the Chinese arts. The Hindu goddess, Benten, is commemorated on an island in the beautiful lake. The charming stone bridge is named *"Full Moon Bridge."* The *Korakuen Baseball Stadium,* seating 34,000 spectators, adjoins the gardens. Ski-jumping competitions are held here during the winter—on artificial snow.

The NATIONAL EDUCATION PARK OF NATURE, situated near *Meguro Station,* covers some 50 acres of inviting forest land extending over the whole of 2-chome, Shirogane-dai-machi at *Minato.* Title to the grounds was transferred from the Imperial Household to the State after World War II and was offered to the public in 1949. The park is covered with shrubs and centuries-old evergreen oaks of the various types which once surrounded ancient **Tokyo.**

TOKYO UNIVERSITY. Attendance at *Tokyo University,* a government institution, is not only an educational experience but also is considered to be an automatic stamp of genius on aspirants so fortunate as to be accepted for membership in the student body. So fervent is the zeal of young men to enter this almost hallowed seat of higher education that each year a number of would-be students commit suicide because they have failed the entrance examination.

The buildings and campus accommodating the 16,000 students cover 125 acres which were once the property of the Maeda feudal family. The *Akamon,* or "Red Gate," remains as a solitary reminder of the days of antiquity. The library is one of the most famous in the Far East. The landscaped garden is also noteworthy.

The BOTANICAL GARDENS of *Tokyo University* are

graced with ancient trees. When, in 1890, Emperor Taisho was Crown Prince, he planted some trees here which today constitute one of the garden's showplaces. Facing the garden is the *Tokyo Educational University,* a teachers college.

The GOKOKUJI TEMPLE, dating back to the 17th century, for almost 100 years has been a final resting place of the Imperial Family and other distinguished Japanese of noble birth. The amber-colored Kannon goddess reigns over the temple. The 20 omnipresent stone lanterns are magnificent replicas done by the finest lantern craftsmen. Be sure to visit the *Main Hall* and the *Gekkoden Hall.* They are among the most important of the Japanese Cultural Properties.

KAMATA *(Umeyashiki)* is worthy of a visit. Here is to be found a famous Japanese apricot garden with ancient trees of great beauty where the Emperor Meiji and his leading advisors frequently met in a peaceful pastoral setting.

DENENCHOFU is one of Tokyo's more enchanting suburbs. In a city already noted for its entrancing gardens, this is outstanding. Here are the residences of topflight business executives from **Tokyo** and **Yokohama.** The homes are particularly alluring by virtue of their settings as well as their interesting old architectural features. Many of the walled estates exude an atmosphere of dignified charm. This engaging area can well be favorably compared to the best of Long Island, Westchester County, Beverly Hills, or Chicago's plush North Shore.

The MOHAMMEDAN MOSQUE is one of only two Mohammedan mosques in all Japan. The other is at **Kobe.**

The exquisite APRICOT GARDEN OF KUJI is a great attraction throughout the year, but in the early spring when the blossoms are in full bloom, it presents a sight of unparalleled beauty. In addition to its own lovely charm, the *Apricot Garden* is situated on the peach tree-studded banks of the *Tama River* about one and a half hours by rail from **Tokyo.**

INTERNATIONAL CHRISTIAN UNIVERSITY seeks to indoctrinate students of Japan and foreign countries in world democracy. Standard university courses are also taught, many in English.

TAMA CEMETERY, the final resting place of many of the nation's great military leaders, diplomats, and statesmen, resembles an inviting public park. It is readily accessible from downtown **Tokyo.**

RIKUGIEN GARDEN. Of the many reasons that I am so anxious that you should travel through Japan in the spring or fall, one of the most compelling is that you should see the many Japanese gardens in their full glory. The *Rikugien Garden,* north of *Tokyo University,* was laid out between 1688 and 1704. It is considered to be one of the finest landscape gardens in **Tokyo** and, like most of the fine parks and gardens of **Tokyo,** was formerly the estate of a feudal lord.

NICOLAI CATHEDRAL, as are most Greek Orthodox churches, is possessed of a statuesque beauty. Situated on the summit of *Surugadai Hill* overlooking a section of **Tokyo,** the dome and the belfry are 114 feet and 123 feet high respectively. The present structure is a renovation of the original building.

The SILK GALLERY. Japan has always been justly famed for the richness and the quality of her silks. This gallery, both a museum and commercial outlet, displays and sells the finest of Japan's most celebrated product. There are nine alluring halls exhibiting the beautiful silk fabrics which are for sale, as well as others where ancient Japanese silk fabrics of fabulous quality are on display. Open ten A.M. to five P.M. daily except on stock-taking day, usually the 25th of each month.

KODOKAN JUDO HALL. Have you always felt that your life was incomplete without taking up the art of *judo?* If so, your every wish can be fulfilled. It is within your province to become skillfully adept at this renowned Japanese art of self-defense. *Kodokan Judo Hall,* believe it or not, is used daily by hundreds of foreign students of all ages who practice and take lessons. This establishment, founded in 1882, contains more than 500 practice mats as well as seats for 2,000 spectators. The registration fees, as well as the charges for individual instruction, are amazingly inexpensive—a mere pittance. You will of course require the proper costuming. Don't worry. For five or six dollars you can get the complete set of garments. In Japan prices of costumes and clothing vary according to size, a practical arrangement, indeed. (For a more complete description of *judo,* see write-up under Sports.)

WASEDA UNIVERSITY, near *Takatanobaba Station,* founded in 1882, is probably Japan's outstanding privately endowed school. Its enrollment, including various branches, exceeds 25,000 students. Visitors from the United States will be interested in the *Okuma Memorial Auditorium*'s chimes which are American made.

WASEDA'S TSUBOUCHI MEMORIAL THEATER MUSEUM, unique in the Orient, was constructed in 1928. This theatrical museum was named after Dr. Shoyo Tsubouchi (1859-1935), who attained eminence as a dramatist and as a translator of Shakespeare. Within the museum are voluminous mementos of both the Japanese and foreign theater.

TOKYO TRANSPORTATION

There are two things that must be said in favor of Tokyo public transportation. It is frightfully enthusiastic and there is a great deal of it. Unfortunately, it is also inadequate.

TAXIS are numerous, efficient, and, as taxis go, quite comfortable. They may be found cruising about the city, at hotel stands, and railroad and air terminals. Despite the large number of cabs, Tokyo is no different from Paris, New York, or Chicago should the weather turn bad. Cabs then are hard to get. In inclement weather, I would suggest that you order a taxi in advance of your anticipated need. Basic fares are quite inexpensive with the original "flag pull" being between 70 and 100 yen (20 to 30 cents), depending on the size and type of taxi, some of which, incidentally, are imported cars, while others are of the local variety. The original charge covers the first two kilometers (1.28 miles). The additional charges are 20 yen (six cents) for each quarter kilometer. You may hire a taxi by the hour, a good idea if you're going to have protracted waiting periods at a remote restaurant or shopping.

The language barrier between cab riders and the drivers is formidable, a problem further complicated by the fact that, with the possible exception of the words *"Imperial Hotel,"* not one taxi driver in a thousand can recognize the English version, written or oral, of a Japanese name for a street, shop, department store, restaurant, hotel, or night club. The following is, I realize, redundantly repetitious but I must reiterate: Unless you enjoy chaotic frustration, it is of utmost importance that, before you leave your hotel, you have someone at the information desk write, in Japanese, the name of your destinations in the order in which you expect to visit them, together with a card of your hotel written in Japanese to insure your safe and speedy return. The alternative, particularly if you're going to visit just one place, is to have the door man, who will probably speak some English, instruct the driver where to go, how long to wait, and where to take you next. There are interpreters in all of the department stores and in some of the shops. All of the restaurants and night clubs that are included in this guide-book will have someone on hand who speaks English sufficiently well to take your order and direct your taxi from their establishment to your next destination.

PRIVATE CAR HIRE. Excellent private cars with chauffeurs are available. These should be arranged either in advance, through your home-town travel agency, or on the spot, through your travel agent's local representative or the information desk of your hotel. The rates vary according to the size and age of the car, distance to be traversed, and time involved. If you are not on a tour, I suggest you do your sightseeing by private car with individual guide.

NEW TOKYO HIGHWAYS were opened in 1964 to help ease the flow of Olympic Games traffic. There are 56 miles of new highways, 43 miles of newly widened roads, 8 new four-lane freeways, 8 loop and 9 radial highways. The old snail's pace of traffic has been slightly speeded by this construction.

SIGHTSEEING ARRANGEMENTS. I am a dyed-in-the-wool devotee of careful planning. I loathe and detest slipshod traveling. Not for a minute could I agree that it is either more fun or half as efficient to travel through the Orient, through Europe, or any place else abroad with a "do it yourself" kit, following a devil-may-care potluck program. If you are wise, you will arrange your complete sightseeing program before you leave the States, or failing that, you will no doubt have an established contact with the Japanese representative of your local travel agent or his tour operator. If you *are* on a potluck basis, however, I feel it my duty to explain some of the arrangements that are available.

The *Shin Nippon Kanko Company* operates an extraordinarily efficient service for sightseers in vehicles known as the "Pigeon Bus." These Pigeon Bus tours vary in length but have one thing in common: they ALL start from the north entrance of *Tokyo Station*. In addition to the embarkation from *Tokyo Station,* each of the Pigeon Bus tours calls for and deposits sightseers at the *Imperial Hotel*. Each motor coach is accompanied by an attractive young Japanese girl guide who performs her duties with evident pleasure, but don't be cross if you feel that your guide's English is not up to par. It is a matter of linguistic fact that almost all Japanese who learned their native language first can never, ever, speak English completely fluently without messing up almost beyond recognition every "l" and "r" and "b" and "v" that comes along. This might be disputed on both sides of the *Pacific,* but it is an incontrovertible fact.

The Pigeon Bus guides are good and their English spoken as well as any you're going to encounter. In addition to the comprehensive program of seeing Tokyo and its environs, the program includes shopping tours on Wednesdays and Saturdays and night tours which have proven extraordinarily popular. The Gray Line tours, by day or by night, are excellent. If you have not had the opportunity for a *Geisha* evening, by all means try a Tokyo By Night tour which will include an hour or more of this "so different" entertainment.

The *Japan Travel Bureau* offers a series of excellent day and night sightseeing tours in **Tokyo** and all other Japanese cities. *J.T.B.* is an amazingly efficient organization. Its programs may be purchased with confidence.

ELECTRIC TRAMWAYS (interurban service). The electric interurban services are quite efficient and connect **Tokyo** with **Yokohama** and **Odawara**. Unlike the railroad trains, the interurbans have only one class.

As I have noted elsewhere, the language barrier in Japan is a real one. If your stay in **Tokyo** is to be brief, and you have not had the opportunity to indoctrinate yourself in rudimentary Japanese (who can?) and are not able, confidently, to convey your wants and needs accurately in thoroughly understandable sign language or mental telepathy, I would recommend that you confine your local transportation vehicles to private cars and taxis. Just for the fun of it, however, ask your travel agency to provide you with a guide for a few hours of public transportation exploration. Under his shepherding, try the subway or a streetcar, but particularly ride an electric train. It's exciting. It is best, however, to avoid public transportation during rush hours. In the mad crush you could lose your guide and never get off the train!

ELECTRIC TRAINS

Yamate Loop Line: This elevated electric line runs completely around **Tokyo** in a much larger way but not unlike the original Chicago Loop. A section of the *Yamate Loop* passes through the center of the city and connects with the residential section. It has convenient connections with other electric lines enabling the long-suffering passengers to connect with *Tokyo Station, Shimbashi Station,* and **Yokohama,** as well as farther to the west and east to **Yoyogi** and **Chiba** respectively. The fares are amazingly inexpensive on both the subways and the

Loop electric trains. As in **London,** the fares are based on a zone system. You pay for the length of your ride.

The *Yamate Belt Line* completely encircles **Tokyo** proper via *Tokyo Station, Yurakucho, Shimbashi, Shinagawa, Shibuya, Shinjuku, Ikebukuro, Nippori, Ueno, Akihabara,* and many other city districts.

The *Chuo Line* connects **Tokyo** with *Asakawa* via *Shinjuku.* During the rush hours, the service is of the express variety, while during the rest of the day quite ordinary service prevails.

The *Keihin-Tohoku Line* is a very busy and important line which connects **Yokohama** *(Sakuragi-cho)* with **Omiya,** in Saitama Prefecture, via *Shinagawa, Shimbashi, Yurakucho,* **Tokyo,** and *Ueno.*

The *Yokosuka Line,* which provides an extremely rapid service, has its extremities in **Tokyo** and *Kurihama* in Kanagawa Prefecture. Intermediate stops are made at *Shimbashi, Shinagawa,* **Yokohama, Kamakura,** and **Yokosuka.**

The *Sobu Line* provides service between **Ochanomizu** and **Chiba.**

The *Joban Line* runs between *Ueno* and *Toride.*

STREETCARS

As previously mentioned, visitors are not particularly advised to make use, unaccompanied by a Japanese, of public buses and/or streetcars. The signs and the directions are quite sure to prove confusing and particularly during the rush hours this method of transportation is extraordinarily crowded. You would, of course, not be received with intended discourtesy but are sure to be bumped about as indeed are the Japanese, since there is no time or space for manners.

SUBWAYS

Tokyo's subterranean area is intertwined with an amazingly efficient network of underground electric subway lines, four in number, with a fifth under construction. The expanding population balloon has shot upwards with such a jet spurt that even the far-sighted city planners are being hard put to keep the transportation facilities on a relatively equal plane with the daily increasing requirements. Each of the four existing lines, *Ginza, Marunouchi, Ogikubo,* and *Hibiya,* is being rapidly expanded simultaneously with the building of the fifth line. The equipment varies from good, on the older lines, to "the best in the world" on the newer lines. Trains operate every $2\frac{1}{2}$ minutes during the rush hours and every four to six minutes during the more quiet periods. The stations are efficient and for the most part attractive. Some have restaurants and shops.

The *Ginza Line,* the oldest of the four systems, operates from *Shibuya* to *Asakusa.* It encompasses a total distance of just less than nine miles, from end to end, covered in approximately 30 minutes. Important areas serviced include the *Ginza, Ueno, Shibuya, Shimbashi, Asakusa,* hotel, theater, and shopping districts. The *Ginza Line* also connects with the *Marunouchi Line* at *Akasaka-Mitsuke* and with the trains of the *Japanese National Railways* at *Shibuya, Kanda,* and *Ueno* and to the *Isezaki Line* of the *Tobu Railways* at *Asakusa.*

The *Marunouchi Line,* a postwar effort of the *Teito Rapid Transit Authority,* operates from *Ikebukuro* to *Shinjuku,* a distance of approximately 10 miles, passing under the **Tokyo** metropolitan area in a U shape. It serves the educational centers, government office buildings, the *National Diet,* the *Korakuen Baseball Stadium,* and *Tokyo Station.* Connections are made with the *Ginza Line,* the *Yamate Loop,* and various lines of the *Japanese National Railways,* the *Seibu Railway,* the *Odakyu* and *Keio* lines.

The *Ogikubo Line* operates its main line from *Shinjuku* (terminus of the *Marunouchi Line*) to *Shin Nakano,* with a branch line from *Nakano Sakabe* to *Nakano Fushimicho,* serving, for the first time, the new metropolitan residential districts and connecting with the J.N.R. *Chuo Line.* Frequently trains of the *Marunouchi Line* continue over the *Ogikubo Line* to *Shin Nakano.*

The *Hibiya Line,* which was finally completed in 1964, proceeds from *Kita Senju* to *Naka-Meguro,* thus serving the principal points in the heart of the city as well as nearby outlying points and connecting with various lines of the *Japanese National Railways,* the *Tobu Railway Line,* the *Tokyu Express Railway Line,* the *Seibu Line,* the *Yamate Line,* and the *Marunouchi Line.*

EXCURSIONS FROM TOKYO

Yokohama

YOKOHAMA, a great seaport, frequently called "The Gateway to Japan," is 20 miles southwest of the capital on *Tokyo Bay.* Both **Tokyo** and **Yokohama** have become so vast and sprawling, however, that, as one drives between them, it is virtually impossible to discern whether one is in the seaport, the capital, or the suburbs of one or the other. The last time I drove to **Tokyo** after luncheon at the harbor view *Terrace Restaurant* of **Yokohama's** *Silk Hotel,* it took an agonizing hour and 30 minutes to buck the cumbersome traffic to the *Imperial Hotel.* There are frequent trains, however, on several lines, which cover the distance between the hearts of the two cities in 30 minutes or so.

Should you travel to Japan by ship, a most pleasant prospect, you will reach **Yokohama** through memorable *Tokyo Bay* after having viewed **Tokyo** as it looms impressively over the bow or over the starboard quarter. If your arrival should be so perfectly timed as to be in the atmospheric crystal clarity of the early morning hours, I implore that you hie yourself from your comfy bed to enjoy a view of unparalleled splendor, when, as it emerges from the haze, the entrancing oft-white cone of *Mount Fuji* is tinted a roseate hue by the first flaming fingers of the newly-emerged sun.

Until 1859, **Yokohama** exerted no influence as a world port, nor was it even significant as a Japanese entity, but in that year a tiny trickle, soon to be a roaring torrent, of trade with the outside world began. A century ago this sleepy fishing village

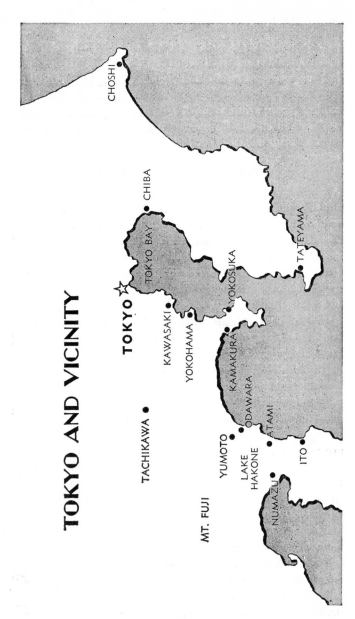

TOKYO AND VICINITY

CHOSHI

CHIBA

TOKYO BAY

TATEYAMA

TOKYO

YOKOSUKA

KAWASAKI

YOKOHAMA

KAMAKURA

TACHIKAWA

ODAWARA

ATAMI

YUMOTO

LAKE
HAKONE

ITO

MT. FUJI

NUMAZU

had but a handful of houses and fewer than 500 inhabitants.

In 1853, Commodore Perry steamed into *Uraga Harbor,* in the van of his shiny black fleet, carrying with him a letter bearing the seal and the signature of the President of the United States proposing trade treaties between the two countries. This portentous document, presented to Emperor Komei, resulted, within five years, in treaties which laid a lasting foundation for the international exchange of commerce and industry which has flourished for more than a century.

At that time foreigners were almost unknown and consequently little-trusted by the Japanese. The treaty specified that a section of nearby **Kanagawa** should be set apart for foreign settlers and that their safety and well-being would be guaranteed by the Imperial Japanese authorities. The Japanese authorities shortly afterward chose **Yokohama** as the foreign settlement instead of **Kanagawa.** Between 1854 and 1859, similar treaties and commercial grants of privilege were negotiated between Japan and **Great Britain, Russia,** and **The Netherlands,** which, combined with Japanese pacts with the **United States,** assured **Yokohama's** future as a renowned port. Voila! Japan emerged from her cocoon to become a world power.

Yokohama's population mushroomed more rapidly than rabbits in a hutch. In three short decades from 1859, the number of her inhabitants spiraled several hundredfold to more than 120,000 in 1889, and her harbor bulged romantically with ships flying the colorful ensigns of nations in the far corners of the earth.

The most appalling and devastating earthquake in history struck Japan at noon, September 1, 1923. This great disaster leveled **Yokohama** more effectively than the A-bombs subsequently destroyed **Hiroshima** and **Nagasaki.** But the Japanese are inured to disaster. With their usual fantastic resilience, the citizens of **Yokohama** rebuilt the city, their number attaining an amazing 850,000 persons by 1938. Some 22 years after the great disaster of 1923, **Yokohama** again, in 1945, was overtaken by destruction. This time the harbor was horribly devastated and the city almost completely gutted by bombs. By 1950, **Yokohama** had already bounced back with zealous fervor with close to a million inhabitants. The **Yokohama** of today, with a population of 1.4 million, is the number five city of the nation whose port handles 25 per cent of all of Japan's foreign trade. It is also an important industrial center for steel and heavy industry.

Because of **Yokohama's** proximity to its great neighbor, it is overshadowed as a center of sophisticated pleasure and cultural importance but is blessed with delightful parks, gorgeous gardens, and attractive shopping areas which, though less well known than **Tokyo's** fabulous *Ginza,* are fully as animated and exciting. The shops and department stores bulge with enticing merchandise. Particularly during the late afternoon hours, the shopping centers swarm with bargain-hunters from every nation. Sailors from their ships and foreign visitors speaking every tongue known to the Tower of Babel make frequent sorties to the **Yokohama** shops which, together with their specialties, are listed in Chapter Six.

Visit as many of the following places as your time allows.

YAMASHITA-CHO is the brilliant, hustling, and dynamic center of various diplomatic headquarters and most of the important office buildings.

The BUND, overlooking the harbor, is flanked by *Yamashita Park* on one side and modern office buildings on the other.

In YAMATE-CHO, the homes on the hill are reminiscent of those found in the finest residential sections throughout the world.

NOGEYAMA PARK, **Yokohama's** largest, clings to the side of a lovely hill from which excellent views of the harbor and city are to be enjoyed. This typical Japanese landscaped area is graced with a children's playground, an open-air theater, an entertainment hall, a large swimming pool, and a zoo. Influential Japanese have built lovely residential quarters near the park.

The CHINESE QUARTER is fascinating and noisy as are

Chinese quarters the world over. Chinese food there is of good quality with reasonable rates.

The NEGISHI RACE COURSE, the oldest in Japan, was founded in 1868 for the equine pleasure and wagering activities of the American and British residents. Horse racing no longer is practiced here, the infield now being a nine-hole golf course. The *Yokohama Nursery Company,* near the race course at *Karasawa,* is open to the public. If time permits, it is really worth a visit to see the gnarled dwarf trees.

SANKEIEN GARDEN, on *Tokyo Bay,* covers 47 engagingly beautiful acres. It is privately owned and contains historic buildings transported to **Yokohama** from remote sections of the country, each typical of its own locale. The "Spring Waiting House" (the *Taishunken*), an Important Cultural Property, as are many other of the garden's treasures, was removed from a village near **Nikko,** where its fame was enhanced by a visit paid to it there by General Grant in 1879. The 500-year-old *Pagoda* once stood at **Kamo** in Kyoto Prefecture.

HASSEI-DEN, near the *Sankeien Garden,* celebrates the priests Shinran and Nichiren, and Christ, Socrates, Confucius, Prince Shotoku, Kobo-Daishi, and Shakamuni, who are known, in **Yokohama** at least, as the "Eight Sages of the World." They are enshrined in the octagonal *Hassei-den* in niches surrounding the mirror believed locally to represent and portray the entire universe.

OFUNA, 11 miles from **Yokohama,** is best known as the "Hollywood of Japan," for it is here that we find the studios of one of the great cinema companies. The ubiquitous cherry trees along the banks of the *Kashio River* are particularly worthy of note during their fleeting season. It is hardly worth visiting at any other time.

KAMAKURA, 12 miles from **Yokohama** and 32 miles from **Tokyo,** is readily accessible from the capital by car or electric rail. It is noted as the site of one of Japan's most famous Buddhas, the *Kamakura Daibutsu (Great Buddha),* as an historic city of venerable tradition, as a favorite residential suburb for

commuters who reach downtown **Tokyo** in less than an hour
by rail, and also as a renowned resort possessed of innumerable
inviting beaches stretching for miles along the shores of the
sparkling *Sagami Bay,* separated from *Tokyo Bay* by the *Miura
Peninsula.*

Kamakura enjoys a favorable climate enhanced by its proximity to the warm sea currents. Its station is a beehive of activity at all times, particularly during the warm months when
happy vacationers come in droves to descend on the sandy bay
beaches, protected on three sides by verdant, undulating hills.

The contrasting ancient and modern city, bursting with art
works of incalculable value and breath-taking religious structures, was the one-time seat of the Shogunate government.
Yoritomo, a brilliant military leader of the 12th century, was
called Shogun (generalissimo), which appellation, quite naturally, was the result of Imperial decree. It was he who established the military government of **Kamakura.** In **Kamakura**
you will most probably be primarily interested in the *Great
Buddha,* but here, as in **Nara** and **Kyoto,** there is a plethora of
shrines and temples, all of which are centrally located and easily
reached one from the other by a short drive or easy walk. Good
"sights" in **Kamakura** include the *Tsurugaoka Hachimangu
Shrine,* the *Kamakura Art Museum,* the *Tomb of Yoritomo,*
the *Kamakuragu Shrine,* the *Kenchoji Temple,* the *Engakuji
Temple,* the *Hase Kannon Temple,* and *Katase.*

The *Kamakura Daibutsu (Great Buddha)* is one of the remarkable wonders of Japan. This colossal figure of the Buddhist divinity, Amida, sits serenely within the grounds of
Kotokuin Temple. It was twice housed in cavernous sheds, the
first of which was leveled by the elements in 1369. The replacement fared no better, succumbing to another devastating storm
and tidal wave in 1495. With calm majesty, the *Buddha* sat out
both disasters, coming through virtually unscathed. It now reposes peacefully exposed to the elements with no covering of
any kind. This impressive figure, more than 40 feet high on
its pedestal, has a face almost eight feet long and eyes three

feet five inches wide. It weighs more than 100 tons. Visitors may use the interior staircase to climb to the shoulders of the *Buddha.*

The bronze *Buddha* is the work of the sculptor, Ono Goroemon, who imparted to its face a sloe-eyed attitude of complete religious repose. The Buddhist religion considers the position of the hands with fingers touching and palms up to be the sign of unswerving belief and fidelity. Goroemon, of course, imparted to the *Great Buddha* just such a pose. The *Buddha* at **Nara** is much larger, the largest in Japan, but not as fine a work of art as we find here in **Kamakura** in the *Daibutsu.*

The TSURUGAOKA HACHIMANGU SHRINE is second only to the *Great Buddha* as **Kamakura's** most fascinating attraction. Azaleas, shrubs, pine, and cherry trees add a floral magnificence to this shrine which is particularly noted for its association with Japanese legends.

Hachimangu traces its origin, at a different location, to the year 1063 and a continuous existence on its present site since 1191. The present buildings were constructed in 1828, but the sculpturing, symmetry of design, and vivid decorative scheme follow the style of the *Momoyama Period,* which flourished in the 16th century.

Within the confines of the shrine are a huge *torii,* various secondary shrines, a huge gingko tree, and ancient mementos of war, many of which have been declared Important Cultural Properties. Each year, on September 15th, and 16th, mounted *Samurai* take part in an exhibition of target-shooting. The lotus ponds, made almost 900 years ago, are a blaze of blooms in late July and early August.

The KAMAKURA ART MUSEUM houses many valuable Important Cultural Properties of the 12th century. These art exhibits are of great value and compelling interest. There are also modern art exhibitions held here on a permanent basis. Open daily except December 28th through 31st.

The TOMB OF YORITOMO will be found on a gentle slope near the *Hachimangu Shrine* and the *Yokohama National University.* The celebrated Shogun is interred in such a way that his resting place, dominated by a unique, hoary five-foot pagoda, continuously views his earthly abode.

The ZUISENJI TEMPLE is best known for its 13th-century garden designed and executed by Soseki, a gifted priest, as a replica of a *Kamakura Period Zen garden.* Typical of this horticultural design, trees, stones, and water are beautifully blended for breath-taking effect. From the grounds dotted with apricot and maple trees, one commands an impressive panoramic view of **Kamakura** on one hand and the majestic *Mount Fuji* and the *Hakone* mountain range on the other.

The HASE KANNON TEMPLE, more formally called *Hasedera Temple,* is best known for its image, eleven-faced, of the Goddess of Mercy, Kannon, of whom one hears so much in Japan. There is a legend, told and retold so frequently as to be believed almost universally, that the **Kamakura** *Kannon* is carved from the same camphor log as is the **Nara** *Kannon.* The legend indicates that the **Kamakura** *Kannon* was cast into the sea at **Osaka** with the supplication that divine intervention should occur in behalf of seamen wherever the image should come ashore. The image was beached a decade and a half later at **Kamakura,** where it is properly honored in the *Hasedera Temple.*

INAMURAGASAKI POINT is another **Kamakura** locale labeled officially as a "Place of Historical Importance." I have previously mentioned the derivation of the name *"Kamikaze"* as applied to suicide bombers in World War II as stemming from the divine wind which, on two historic occasions, wrecked invading amphibious forces just as they seemed on the verge of success in invading Japan. *Inamuragasaki Point* has to do with another poignant legend, that of a 14th-century general, Nitta Yoshisada, who reputedly threw his golden sword into the relentless waters of the bay imploring the god of the sea to reverse the tide. The general, of course, was frantically endeavoring to rid the waters of the enemy's ships. A miracle took place, the water rushed out, the enemy fled in panic, and the loyal forces of Japan triumphed.

THE UKIYOE ART MUSEUM is privately owned by the celebrated architect Hirose and contains more than 5,000 works of art. Open 9 A.M. to 4 P.M. on Saturdays and Sundays only.

BEACHES. The best known of the **Kamakura** beaches are *Yuigahama* and *Shichiriga-hama.* As early as the 12th century, the Shoguns were using these beaches for equestrian and bow and arrow competitions. Should you be in **Tokyo** in midsummer, be on the alert for an announcement of the beach carnival at **Kamakura** (the dates vary from year to year). Tremendous crowds attend, and a gaudy carnival atmosphere permeates the area, with bands, beauty contests, and all the hoopla of Atlantic City. From these beaches, one may enjoy a view across the water to *Mount Fuji* and the islands of *Enoshima* and, from some vantage points, *Oshima.*

The NICHIREN TEMPLES, four in number, may be traced to the 13th-century furiously intolerant priest, Nichiren, who established the Buddhist sect bearing his name. He may or may not have sat on a stone near the railway station of **Kama-**

kura to preach to his followers, but a rock will be pointed out to you there as having served this purpose.

The KAMAKURA TEN-EN PARK is a paradise of cherry, apricot, and maple trees whose natural beauty is enhanced by blooming plants which provide a profusion of color from early spring until late fall.

KAMAKURAYAMA is the mountainous residential section of **Kamakura**. Very attractive homes are found here, and one has "arrived" if he can claim a summer resort abode in these green hills.

I believe that the foregoing includes adequate coverage of the **Kamakura** temples, but should you be particularly keen on the subject, I can point out that other important religious edifices in the immediate vicinity are the *Gokurakuji Temple,* the *Kamakuragu Shrine,* the *Kakuonji Temple,* the *Jomyoji Temple,* the *Hokaiji Temple,* the *Ennoji Temple,* the *Engakuji Temple,* the *Jochiji Temple,* the *Tokeiji Temple,* the *Jufukuji Temple,* the *Eishoji Temple,* and the *Kenchoji Temple.*

The Miura Peninsula

KATASE, FUJISAWA, and the COASTAL RESORTS. Japan is not noted for the excellence of its highways, but, for a distance of at least 25 miles, a splendid road parallels the coast line, with excellent opportunities for the traveler to enjoy the scenic sunning and bathing beaches of the entire *Enoshima-Kugenuma* district, called locally the "Miami Beach of Japan."

In the 13th century, Kublai Khan sent his envoys to the *Miura Peninsula* to seek largesse by force, but instead of succeeding, the envoys lost their heads to the sword at **Katase,** which, with its sister city, **Fujisawa City,** lies directly opposite *Enoshima Island.* In this area we also find the "miracle mile," where Nichiren, the cantankerous priest about whom we have spoken previously, was about to be beheaded when the executioner's sword inexplicably broke slap-dab in half. A commemorative stone in the grounds of the *Ryukoji Temple* marks the spot of this incredible event.

On the peninsula, there is an excellent golf course at **Fujisawa,** while other beach and residential towns are Zushi and **Hayama,** combinations of wealthy residential suburbia and summer resorts. The *National Railways* operate a sea house on the beach from July 1 to August 31. The establishment, designed mostly for Japanese, contains swimming pools, shower rooms, a vast area of lockers, and a huge snack bar.

The *Miura Peninsula* is dominated by *Ogusu Hill,* with an altitude of 793 feet, from which there is a splendid view of *Tokyo* and *Sagami Bays,* of *Fuji* in the distance, and of the entire peninsula.

YOKOSUKA, once an important naval base, now again pulses with marine activity. There are two excellent twin ports, **Nagaura** and **Yokosuka.** The great *Marine Museum* is located in the revered grounded flagship of Admiral Togo's fleet that humbled the Imperial Russian navy in the Russo-Japanese War of 1904-1905. *Tsukayama Park* is perhaps best known for the tomb of Captain William Adams, the first Englishman to settle in Japan, about whom I have written in the section under **Tokyo.**

KURIHAMA, not far from the center of **Yokosuka,** is best known as the site where Commodore Perry delivered the President's letter to the emissary of the Tokugawa Shogun in 1853. On the monument which commemorates this event is carved: "This monument commemorates the first arrival of Commodore Perry, Ambassador from the United States of America, who landed at this place July 14, 1853. Erected July 14, 1901, by America's Friend Association."

ENOSHIMA ISLAND is readily reached via a toll bridge from **Katase.** If you are in the area and have a car at your disposal, you will find this a little "picture island" bursting with local color. The *Amusement Park* is jumping with activity. The steel observation tower houses an elevator which carries visitors to the lighthouse above. The *Marineland* specializes in large denizens of the deep including whales and porpoises. The *Benten Caves,* eerie in their 360-foot depth, may be visited in an atmosphere not unlike that of the *Catacombs* of **Rome**. The visitors are given tapers, and if one perseveres to the far end of the caves, he will be rewarded with a view of the image of Benten, one of the seven deities of good luck.

OSHIMA ISLAND, 30 miles offshore, may be clearly seen from the heights of *Enoshima*.

The Izu Peninsula

The *Izu Peninsula*, jutting 40 miles into the Pacific Ocean, is considered the "Riviera of Japan." *"Yu-Izu,"* meaning "Hot Water—Gush Out," was the historical name for the peninsula. The *"yu"* was dropped, but the implication is clear. The area, which abounds in hot springs, is silhouetted by its back drop, the *Hakone* mountain range.

ATAMI, a busy, popular resort city with more than 50,000 inhabitants, lies on the sea 64 miles from **Tokyo**, 47 miles from **Yokohama,** and 23 miles from **Miyanoshita**. Climate is **Atami's** most persuasive ally. Summers usually find the thermometer here to be at least 10 degrees cooler than in **Tokyo**. During the winter it is normally eight to 10 degrees warmer than in the capital. The *Tokai Steamship Company* operates daily between **Tokyo** and **Atami** directly, via *Oshima Island,* or calling at **Ito**. The one-way journey takes between 9 and 13 hours, depending on the routing. A hydrofoil service is operated between *Enoshima* (the Picture Island) and **Atami** and **Ito**. There are four daily round trips between the latter two resorts.

The **Atami** hot springs bubble with an endless variety of indoor and out-of-doors baths ranging from the ultra-modest to inlaid mosaic splendor. These baths are kept perpetually filled with invigorating water from the nearby springs, rich in sulphur, manganese, and/or iron content of reputed therapeutic qualities. The temperature of the springs and baths varies from tepid to that which we would consider to be so scalding as to poach the westerner's thin skin.

The Japanese male is not quick to include his wife and family in his urban extracurricular recreation plans, but for the seaside vacations this order sometimes changes. He frequently packs up his wife, his family, and even his friends and takes them to the seashore or to a hot spring spa. The *Izu Peninsula* is particularly popular, where hordes of Japanese, most of them *en famille,* relax in splendid surroundings.

Most of the local inns have their own pools, from warm through tepid to practically boiling hot, where mixed communal bathing is sometimes in order.

One of the world's most unusual hotels, the *Kan-ichi,* is located at **Atami.** I have described it in Chapter Four, but it is so unusual that I think I should mention that the entire top floor, which is circular, revolves slowly but continuously in such a manner as to give guests on this floor the opportunity to enjoy the panoramic vista of the town, the mountains, the sea, and the beaches, all from the same room. This idea is so clever that I am recommending it to my friends in Europe, particularly on *Lake Lucerne, Lake Como* and on the *French Riviera.* How lovely it would be there to have every room on the water, at least part of the time. The *Atami Fujiya Hotel* can be recommended as a place to stay. There are also other suitable western style hotels and Japanese inns, and some which are a combination of both. Generally speaking, inn arrangements in **Atami** are fine for the Japanese tourist, and hotels and inns cater to the tastes of this trade rather than to the small number of foreign tourists who include stops here. **Atami** attracts the honeymooners, who visit there as we do Niagara Falls.

A motorboat trip can be made from **Atami** to *Hatsushima Island.* The speedboat covers the seven miles in approximately one hour. The natives of *Hatsushima Island,* eking out their existence by fishing and farming, enjoy an economic state that seems to be midway between a socialistic society and the *kibbutz* of **Israel.** The population of the island is fixed at 300 adults. The arable land of the island is distributed equally among them and the produce divided according to the needs of the family. The earnings on products sold are placed in a common pool. So as not to disrupt this perfect arithmetical balance, the natives have conceived an ultra-practical plan. When the population increases beyond 300, as it must as a natural result of birds, bees, and time, lots are drawn and the unlucky ones in excess of the 300 must leave the island.

The drive from **Atami** to *Hakone* via the *Jukkoku Pass* is spectacularly endowed with exquisite scenery. From the top of the pass, one may ascend in a cable car to view *Mount Fuji* in all of its scenic splendor. The crystal clear azure-blue placid waters of *Lake Hakone* mirror the reflection of *Mount Fuji* to form a picture of unforgettable beauty. A day's drive about the peninsula is worthwhile if you have extra time available. A feature of the west coast of the peninsula is the vivid contrasts of seaside scenery comparable to the *Italian* and *French Rivieras* coupled with the varied views of *Mount Fuji* that play peekaboo as one weaves in and out of the inlets.

Japan's hottest spring, the *Oyu,* the "Great Hot Water," has an incredible history. Originally, *Oyu* was a geyser, but the disruptive earthquake of 1923 quenched its spouting activity once and for all. The Japanese have such a cute way of combining fables and mythology with real life. According to mythology, *Oyu* arose from the sea with lethal effect on the marine life and devastating effect on the economic activities of the fishermen. A Buddhist priest saved the situation in A.D. 749, however. His powerful prayers were answered, and the geyser promptly proceeded to install itself in its present position. *Voilà!* I am told by an authoritative source, though I'm still a doubting Thomas, that *Oyu's* temperature is a plus-boiling, constant two hundred and twenty-six degrees Fahrenheit. *Oyu* quite understandably provides piping-hot water to local commercial establishments, one of which is near the spring and boasts of a hot water swimming pool.

Waters which include various mineral ingredients or deposits are, the world over, considered curatives for various ailments from mental anxiety to impotency. At **Atami,** the waters allegedly will, if bathed in, cure rheumatism, skin diseases, and nervous disorders, while, if taken internally, it is said that they will alleviate chronic diseases of the digestive organs as well as simple constipation.

Because of its happy geographical location, the horticultural life on the *Izu Peninsula* awakens earlier in the spring and is prolonged each fall. Cherry blossoms may be seen here at least six weeks, and frequently two months, before other places in the central *Honshu* area. On the *Tanna Pass Road,* hundreds of apricot trees will delight you when in bloom from late December until February. En route to the apricot orchards, within the grounds of the *Kinomiya Shrine,* one may view one of the largest camphor trees in the country. Its circumference at its largest point is more than 51 feet. You will recall my talking about the theatrical museum in **Tokyo** founded by Shoyo Tsubouchi. He lived in **Atami,** and his home may be visited.

IZUSAN SPA is to all intents and purposes a part of the city of **Atami.** The nine hole golf course is small but inviting. The shrine on the hill is of the 9th century, and the *Sagamiya Inn* has particularly invigorating private baths as well as a large hot water swimming pool which allegedly holds a thousand bathers at a time. Inns, to attract Japanese patrons, often go a bit overboard in their advertising statements.

ITO and KAWANA. These two important spas, about an hour's motoring beyond **Atami,** are collectively the golfing center of the *Izu Peninsula.* There are two picturesque 18-hole courses each at **Ito** and **Kawana.** The hot springs, almost a thousand in number, serve the homes, inns, and public baths. So curative is the water of this area that mythology has it that the wounded boars of antiquity bathed here to soothe their aches and pains.

The shallow JONOIKE POND, near *Ito Station,* is literally alive with churning fish.

The priest Nichiren really got around in this area. The *Butsugenji Temple* is ornamented with a painting which he executed while once incarcerated here during his turbulent life.

The ubiquitous Englishman Adams also made his presence well known in this area. Another monument is erected to him at the spot where he had the shipyard in which he built the first Japanese ocean liner along western lines early in the 17th century.

SHUNZENJI SPA, established in the 9th century, in consort with **Ito** and **Atami**, is a leading resort of the *Peninsula.* Its most unusual hot spring is *Tokko-no-yu* (Priest's Scepter Hot Spring). Not to be outdone by a feat of Moses, an 8th-century Buddhist priest selected a rock which he struck with his rod. At the blow hot water rushed forth. The spring, not large, may be used by only a few persons at a time for bathing purposes. The nearby *Asahi Waterfall* cascades into the *Kano River.* From the summit of *Mount Daruma,* a breathtaking vista of *Mount Fuji* is available.

NIRAYAMA SPA is small, known more for its historical landmarks than for its springs.

YUGASHIMA SPA and MOUNT AMAGI combine to form a lovely sylvan area seven and a half miles from **Shuzenji.** The *Joren Waterfall* blends beautifully into the floral picture. *Mount Amagi* is 3,690 feet in altitude. The area is cluttered with extinct volcanoes and verdant with cherry trees, azaleas, and other horticultural gems.

SHIMODA, at the base of the *Peninsula,* is a bustling seaport of more than passing interest to American visitors. The first consular site of the United States in Japan was established here by Townsend Harris, who unfurled the American flag for the first time in Japan on September 4, 1856.

Harris decided almost immediately that **Shimoda** was too remote and generally unsuitable as a consular port. He never presented his credentials to the government but instead, after some 19th-century bureaucratic red tape, moved to **Tokyo** on November 3, 1857, to become the first diplomat from the outside world recognized in what was then called **Edo.** His consulate, in the interim between landing at **Shimoda** and moving to **Tokyo,** was in the small *Gyokusenji Temple* in *Hamazaki Village* on the hill overlooking **Shimoda.** A stone tablet marks the spot in the temple grounds where Harris raised "the first Consular flag ever seen in this Empire." The inscription on the plaque is from his diary. A nearby wooden tablet will captivate your fancy. This commemorates the first cow to be killed in Japan for human consumption. Need I point out that it was erected by the eternally grateful butchers of **Tokyo.** This tablet bears the following inscription: "This monument erected by the butchers of Tokyo in 1931 marks the spot where the first cow in Japan was slaughtered for human consumption." Though the cow was never sacred in Japan as it is in **India,** all cattle were so highly prized for both their transportation and agricultural chores that their slaughter for food was never considered. When Harris and his party requested beef to eat, the Japanese were shocked.

Among the Harris mementoes in the temple, perhaps the most interesting is a laboriously inscribed eight volume diary which gives in great detail the minute by minute activities of Harris and his party each day that they were at **Shimoda.**

The KUROFUNE MATSURI *(Black Ship Festival),* since 1934 one of the major festivals of the *Peninsula,* is celebrated in **Shimoda** either in late spring or summer honoring Perry's arrival in Japan. The date varies each year. The American ambassador normally attends this commemorative event.

Fuji-Hakone-Izu National Park

Readily accessible from **Tokyo** by car, motor coach or train, this area is the garden spot of Japan. No more spectacular settings, scenic wonders, or horticultural displays are to be found than in the *Fuji-Hakone-Izu National Park,* all surmounted by the most perfectly formed mountain in the world. The combined park area covers some 235,000 acres.

It is not unusual to hear or speak of the *"Hakone National Park,"* the *"Izu National Park,"* or the *"Fuji National Park."* Though basically incorrect, the use of individual titles for each area is more definitive since the "tri-park" area lies within the districts of *Fuji, Hakone,* and *Izu.*

MOUNT FUJI, a majestic 12,397 feet, making it Japan's

highest peak, is undoubtedly the most frequently reproduced of the natural wonders of the world. It is photographed, painted, drawn, and sketched again and again. *Fujiyama*'s unbelievable symmetry and white-capped crown are familiar to people the world over.

Mount Fuji had been regarded through the centuries as a Shinto symbol, a deification continuing until late in World War II when, just as the emperor god was unable to ward off the bombs which drenched **Tokyo,** *Fujiyama* couldn't save the holy shrines from destruction, thereby actually "losing face" within Japan because of this frailty. Still held in high esteem, though, by almost all Japanese and climbed by thousands of pilgrims each year, *Fujiyama* is indeed the national mountain of Japan and a magnet to draw visitors from all over the world.

Mount Fuji is colossal. That's all there is to it. Everything associated with it is spectacular. At its vast base there are shimmering lakes, cascading waterfalls, verdant virgin forests, exquisite Alpine vegetation, and colorful plants and flowers. The *National Park* may be easily reached by rail or road from **Tokyo, Yokohama,** and their environs.

The HAKONE DISTRICT, between *Mount Fuji* and the *Izu Peninsula,* is one of Japan's most spectacular districts. There is substantial evidence that the entire district is the crater of a once active volcano. *Hakone* encompasses towns, villages, and resorts of commanding interest and is dotted with numerous other heroic mountains which add zest to the scenery. There are three mountains with peaks which tower to more than 3,500 feet: *Twin Mountain (Futago),* 3,580 feet; *Pony Peak (Koma),* 4,355 feet; and *God Mountain (Kamiyama),* 4,720 feet. These and the other mountains have, at one time or another, been actively volcanic and even today there are many points to indicate that great natural forces are still present beneath the surface. Everywhere that we cast our eyes, we see traces of sulphurous fumes and steam clouds which spurt forth from the crevices within the earth. One of the most dominant displays of nature's subterranean power may be found at *Owakidani,* the "Valley of Greater Boiling," where the trapped heat, under perpetual pressure, comes gushing through the earth to inundate the mountain gorge with aromatic traces of sulphur. Elsewhere these subterranean forces are close enough to the earth's surface to permit tiny eruptions to be created by any minor disturbance such as a puncture by a high heel.

Everywhere in the *Hakone District* steaming hot springs gurgle or spurt from the ground to be viewed in awe, or, in many instances, harnessed for commercial purposes. They are captured by manmade devices and piped into conduits, tanks, and cisterns. **Yumoto, Miyanoshita, Sengokuhara,** and **Gora,** among others in the district, have no need for hot water boilers. Their homes, hotel guest rooms, mineral baths, and swimming pools are supplied directly from the springs of the area. Because of its great beauty and multitude of natural phenomena, the *Hakone District* is extraordinarily popular throughout the year both with the Japanese and their overseas guests.

HAKONE HOT SPRINGS. While the hot springs are seemingly endless, there are traditionally a dozen hot spring resorts known as the "Twelve Spas of Hakone": **Ashinoyu, Dogashima, Gora, Kiga, Kowakidani, Miyanoshita** (in the heart of the *Hakone District*), **Sengokuhara, Sokokura, Tono-sawa, Ubako, Yumoto,** and **Yunohanazawa. Miyanoshita** is my very favorite . . . it has everything. **Yumoto** is the oldest of the established spa areas; **Gora** and **Sengokuhara** are extremely popular. I am also particularly fond of **Kowakidani,** near which is that "out of this world" modern but warmly hospitable hotel, *Kowaki-en.*

MIYANOSHITA SPA. **Miyanoshita Spa,** located 1,377 feet above sea level, may be used ideally as a hub for any and all of the scenic, picturesque trips in *Hakone.* The roads in all directions are excellent, and the walks are a joy of picturesque loveliness. Despite its feeling of utter isolation from the mundane outer world, **Miyanoshita,** idyllically set in scenic splendor, is only 45 miles from **Yokohama,** 65 miles from **Tokyo** and 54 miles from **Tokyo's** *Haneda International Airport.* The *Fujiya Hotel,* described in detail in Chapter Four, is charming. One of Japan's most sporting golf courses is the *Fujiya's Sengoku Golf Course* at **Sengokuhara,** five miles from the hotel.

My very favorite excursion to the *Hakone* mountains from **Miyanoshita** is via *Big Hell,* a gaping craggy gorge from whence boiling water and pungent gases continuously emanate. The excursion continues via *Long Tail Pass* for the base-to-summit view of *Mount Fuji* and thence to *Lake Hakone* for an exhilarating launch trip on the azure blue waters before returning to **Miyanoshita** by car.

Mount Sengen, 2,630 feet above sea level, is immediately to the rear of the *Fujiya Hotel.* Facing the *Fujiya* is *Mount Myojo* of 3,030 feet altitude. Many veteran travelers are of the opinion that the view from *Mount Myojo* is the finest in Japan, affording a vast panoramic view of all of *Hakone,* including the incomparable *Mount Fuji* with its unparalleled valleys, passes, and gorges. From *Mount Myojo,* the views to **Odawara,** *Sagami Bay,* the island of *Oshima,* and the glistening *Sakawa River* are magnificent. We Americans, unlike most Japanese, are not devoted hikers. Alpine enthusiasts estimate that one may climb to the summit of *Mount Sengen* in an hour from the *Fujiya Hotel* and that a sturdy walker can reach the heights of *Mount Myojo* in an hour and a half's climb. For them, yes. For us? No!

The **Miyanoshita** hot springs, of 186 degrees Fahrenheit, are considered to be extraordinarily beneficial to the health, and provide the hot running water to the rooms in the *Fujiya Hotel* as well as to the several public mineral baths in the other hotels. While the baths are considered curative, they need not be shunned if physical aid is not required. It is stated locally, as a matter of fact, that "the baths are beneficial in case of rheumatism, and nervous troubles, as well as renowned as a complexion beautifier." The water, named *Taiko-yu,* classified as saline, may be taken internally for the abatement of disorders of the liver and digestive tract. It is recommended for gargling in case of larynx and nose troubles. You couldn't do better at a county fair. The swimming pool is fed by mountain streams and is quite *cold* in summer.

Other highly recommended motor tours of exploration from **Miyanoshita** include visits to **Miyagino, Kowakidani** (be sure to stop at the *Kowaki-en Hotel* for at least a look-see), **Sengokuhara, Umijiri,** *Lake Ashi,* **Moto-Hakone, Ashinoyu, Sounzan, Ubako,** and the *Fuji Five Lakes.* A spectacular 20 to 35 mile trip including most of the foregoing can be made easily in half a day.

DOGASHIMA SPA, snugly nestled just below **Miyanoshita,** provides the vigorous hiker a walk of somewhat less than a quarter of an hour via a path balanced on the bank of a verdant ravine filled with pine forests and cascading waterfalls. The *Hayakawa River* lends scenic enchantment to **Dogashima,** whose hot spring is the same type as that of **Miyanoshita.** Should you not be an enthusiastic walker, fear not; an excellent cable car will carry you from **Miyanoshita** to **Dogashima** and back, or you may ride up and walk down, returning in complete comfort.

GORA SPA, two miles from **Miyanoshita** at the lower extremity of the cable car line to **Sounzan,** is perched 2,585 feet above sea level with a view encompassing the *Hayakawa River, Mount Myojin, Mount Myojo,* and other photogenic mountains. The *Hakone Art Museum,* situated at **Gora Spa,** is open daily May through November. The saline sulphur thermal water carried here by pipe from *Owakidani* is considered particularly efficacious for rheumatic and gynecopathic ailments. The view from the *Gora Hotel,* overlooking *Gora Gorge,* is greatly enhanced in cherry blossom time. The guardians of the *Gora Gorge* hot spring swimming pool still look with favor on the old order of things . . . nude mixed bathing does occur.

SENGOKUHARA SPA is the multiple name for four resorts which are *Motoyu, Hyoseki, Kamiyu,* and *Shimoyu.* This area is not only extraordinarily picturesque, on the heavily wooded incline of *Mount Daigatake,* but is a golfer's paradise. The *Sengoku Golf Course* has previously been mentioned as the club of the *Fujiya Hotel* of **Miyanoshita.** In addition there are the challenging courses of the *Dai Hakone* and *Hakone Country Clubs,* both of 18 holes. The **Sengokuhara** mineral waters are distributed commercially from *Owakidani* (Valley of Greater Boiling). The peripheral limits of **Sengokuhara** are unusual even for such an area, being bounded on the west by the *Sengokuhara Plain* covered with an eerie growth of pampas grass, on the north and west by sheltering mountains including *Mount Kintoki,* and on the south by the oft mentioned *Lake Ashi.* Just beyond *Lake Ashi,* a short drive from **Sengokuhara Spa,** is the *Otome (Maiden's) Pass.* From here, on a pleasant day, the view of *Mount Fuji* is unparalleled, while other magnificent panoramas may be enjoyed from *Mount Futago* and *Mount Koma,* the latter being reached by cable car. On *Koma's* peak is a hotel which has an indoor skating rink. Another spellbinding view of *Mount Fuji* may be obtained from *Nagao (Long Tail) Pass,* less than four miles from **Sengokuhara Spa.** Although *Otome Pass* is only a mile and a half from **Sengokuhara,** it is reached by such a zigzag route as to seem a much greater distance. **Sengokuhara** sweet corn, in season, is utterly delicious and popular even in **Tokyo.**

KOWAKIDANI SPA (Valley of Lesser Boiling) has not been given a mild "nickname" because of any lack of heat in its steam wells or saline-sulphur springs. On the contrary, its scorching steam geysers of 180 degrees Fahrenheit spout to 100 feet or more propelled by tremendous internal pressure. *Kowakidani,* also known as "Little Hell," is just over two miles from **Miyanoshita** near the road to *Lake Ashi.* The modern *Hotel Kowaki-en,* with its 18 hole *Ashinoko Country Club,* tennis courts, and swimming pool, is nearby. Cherry trees and azaleas abound in the **Kowakidani Spa** area. *Owakidani* (Valley of Greater Boiling), on the toll road from **Sounzan** to **Umijiri,** has so many saline-sulphurous hot springs that its waters are passed along by pipe to neighboring spas, sort of a Japanese version of "carrying coals to Newcastle."

ASHINOYU SPA, 2,900 feet above sea level on *Mount*

Koma, is midway between **Kowakidani Spa** and *Lake Ashi,* and features sulphurous springs. *Mount Futago, Mount Koma,* and *Mount Kamiyama* form rugged backdrops for **Ashinoyu.** If, contrary to good sense, you just absolutely must climb a mountain, all three of these are readily available for your conquest. I would suggest, however, that you follow the new roadway to a point midway up *Mount Koma* where a comfortable cable car will whisk you to the peak. An excellent 18 hole golf course *(Yunohana)* is found near **Ashinoyu.**

YUMOTO SPA is the first to greet one arriving, as many visitors do, from **Odawara. Yumoto's** altitude is scarcely more than 495 feet above sea level, but this most venerable of the *Hakone* spa resorts is busy because of its position at the "end of the line" of the *Odakyu Railway* from **Tokyo** and **Yokohama.** The electric rail ride from **Tokyo** takes about one hour and 40 minutes, and the continuing motor trip to **Yumoto Spa,** four miles away, consumes less than a quarter of an hour. **Yumoto's** thermal hot springs are said to be helpful for skin diseases, rheumatism, and nervous disorders, and the majestic waterfalls, *Tamadare* and *Hatsuhana,* are spectacularly situated above the *Crystal Screen. Jizo,* the children's deity, carved in the 8th century from raw rock, is enshrined as an image near the tumbling waters of *Hatsuhana.* The *Sounji* and *Shoganji Temples* are superbly set in scenic surroundings nearby. These temples are beautifully executed, rich in background, and bursting with historical legends eager to be told. If time permits, do try to visit one or another of these splendid shrines. If you do, be sure to have your guide tell you about the founder, Hojo Soun, and the blood and thunder saga of the **Soga** brothers. (No alliterative pun intended.)

TONOSAWA SPA, like **Dogashima,** is patiently poised over the rushing waters of the *Hayakawa River.* Less than a mile from **Yumoto,** the thermal waters of **Tonosawa** are the same as those of its sister spa.

LAKE ASHI (LAKE OF THE REEDS or LAKE HAKONE). The multiple nomenclature of this famous and entrancing mountain lake is confusing. The Japanese usually refer to it as *Lake Ashi* while most Americans think of it as *Lake Hakone*. It is referred to alternatively as "Lake of the Reeds," which is the English meaning of the term *Ashinoko,* as it is called by the Japanese. These are all one and the same fascinating body of water on whose glassy surface the image of *Mount Fuji* is frequently discernible, particularly in the early morning hours. A well-planned tour of the area will include a boat ride on *Lake Ashi* which may be taken from **Hakone-machi, Moto-Hakone,** or **Umijiri.** Excellent circle trips are available. One arrives at the lake-side by car, and boards an excursion launch for a scenic ride, then proceeds by cable car, and is met later by one's original motor vehicle. The fishing here is excellent, particularly for trout and black bass. Small boats may be rented for this purpose. The best spots for photographers to capture the reflection of *Mount Fuji* reflected in *Lake Ashi* are from the *Hakone Hotel* and the Japanese Cedar Tree Avenue (a part of the *Tokaido Highway*). In the fall, the "flaming forests" of maples of the area are magnets for thousands of visitors who have found that *Lake Ashi* provides a magnificent "platform" from which to view the "foliage on fire."

HAKONE-MACHI, though not one of the original 12 hot spring spas, may be considered *Lake Ashi*'s principal resort. The approach from **Moto-Hakone** is via an ostentatious, twisting road lined by a double row of venerable cedar trees. In France, the ancient *auberge* was an overnight stopping point for horse-drawn coaches while the *relais* was a restaurant for the coach passengers located at a point where the horses were changed. In historic Japan the stopping points for the horsedrawn vehicles were known as "post stations." There were great barriers set up between sections of the country at which all travelers had to descend from their vehicles to present their passports to the bureaucratic officials and state the object of their trip. Since photography was not yet invented, detailed passport descriptions had to suffice for positive identification. **Hakone-machi** is important historically not only as having been a distinguished post station of the 53 on the *Tokaido Highway* from **Edo** (**Tokyo**), but as a barrier town as well. Just east of town is a monument which indicates the spot where the barrier stood. At one time the *Tokaido Highway* saw the great nobles of the Tokugawa Shogunate proceeding in regal splendor with their retinues between the capital and their castles and estates.

There is a direct road from **Hakone-machi** to **Atami**, the seaside hot springs resort on the *Izu Peninsula,* which passes through the spectacular *Hakone Pass* and over the *Jukkoku Pass.*

The HAKONE MUSEUM across from the *Hakone Hotel* displays mementoes of the *Hakone Barrier,* including original descriptive passports, seals of feudal lords, old firearms, and coins.

Fishing, boating, and bathing constitute the main pleasure pursuits at **Hakone-machi.** The splendid *Hakone Hotel,* a little old but very friendly, under the same direction as the *Fujiya Hotel* at **Miyanoshita,** has both western and Japanese style rooms. The dining room is open to transients.

MOTO-HAKONE, a point of embarkation for the boat excursions on the lake, is on the east shore of *Lake Ashi,* seven miles from **Miyanoshita** and one mile from **Hakone-machi.** It is a mountain crossroads with the highways from **Hakone-machi, Yumoto, Miyanoshita,** and **Umijiri** converging here.

The HAKONE SHRINE, a quarter of a mile from **Moto-Hakone,** is a large 8th-century shrine on the side of a hill heavily shaded by maple trees. *Hakone Gongen,* as the shrine is more generally known, dedicated to three of the Shinto gods, was the hideaway for Yoritomo Minamoto when he was defeated near **Odawara** in the 12th century. There is a blood and guts fable in connection with *Hakone Gongen.* Should your travels take you here, the local guide will tell you the story. I wouldn't want to spoil it for you. July 31st and August 1st are the dates of the *Hakone Gongen* annual festival. Many of the sacred ceremonies, performed in the lake, are participated in not only by the priests but the parishioners and visitors from the entire area. The services are dedicated to the nine-headed dragon, considered locally to be the spirit of *Lake Ashi*. On the night of July 31st the lake presents a fairyland-like scene alive with floating lanterns.

Mount Fuji and the Five Lakes

MOUNT FUJI, known alternatively as FUJIYAMA or FUJI-SAN, rises to a graceful cone 12,397 feet above sea level. Its vast base and gentle slopes are adorned with glorious forests, shimmering lakes, and smart resorts. Though *Fuji* "lost face" during the war when its man-endowed deification failed to ward off the bombs of the enemy, the fact is not altered that, even now, *Fuji* is not considered as a mere mountain by the majority of the Japanese but as a national symbol. Even sophisticated travelers are unanimous in their belief that the world has little to offer that can exceed the glorious peak which is at times mysteriously enshrouded in clouds, at others reflected in the multicolored rays of a setting sun or in the morning's first light when the snow is tinged in a roseate hue. And in season its base and slopes are a mass of the vivid hues of cherry blossoms, azaleas, and chrysanthemums.

Fuji seems to hold a great deal of that which *Mount Olympus* once held for the ancient Greeks, a mysterious and spiritual fascination for all those who gaze upon it. Not only does the mountain offer its own superb scenic attraction but its environs are also endowed with year-round attractions both in scenic splendors and refreshing recreational facilities.

I shall not go into detail relative to climbing the peak. Tens of thousands of Japanese do climb it, but for the uninitiated and for those of us who have grown soft driving to the corner supermarket such a strain on the cardiac muscle is a bit too great. Should you, against my advice, insist on making this uphill hike, you may get complete details anywhere in the area for the clearly defined paths to the summit. I recommend that you follow the excellent motor roads which encircle the entire mountain and skirt the extraordinarily lovely five lakes that bathe the base. Cars and buses can now go up to the fifth station. The hiking routes commence at **Fuji-Yoshida** on the north or at **Gotemba** on the east. Should one elect to make the climb on foot: whichever of the paths to the summit is selected, there will be 10 rest-shelter huts along the route of climb, in which one may change clothing, buy or consume carried vittles, seek solace, or sleep for the night alongside other hikers on the thatched floor, as the case might be. The easiest of the departure points is from **Fuji-Yoshida City.** The motor route around the mountain extends for 100 miles.

Mount Fuji is a long extinct volcano, its last eruption taking place more than two centuries ago, though a faint vaporous finger still may occasionally stretch heavenward as a last reminder of the latent lava power of this smouldering giant. *Mount Fuji*'s crater is awesomely impressive, with a diameter of almost 2,000 feet. The bottom of the crater is some 730 feet below its rim. The circumference at the bottom is 222 feet.

The view from *Fujiyama* on a clear day is monumental, and to reach the summit at sunrise is the goal of all hikers. The panoramic sweep encompasses all the Japanese mountains, much of Japan itself, and miles and miles out into the blue *Pacific*. Two Shinto shrines and a meteorological observatory are on the summit as are two cold springs known as *"Sparkling Gold"* and *"Sparkling Silver,"* respectively. The crest for nine months has its mantle of snow, though summer midday temperatures there are well above freezing. *Sai-no-Kawara* is an area at the top where stones repose in religious postures.

Not to be outdone by their western friends, particularly those of us from Chicago, the summit frequently is littered with sandals, bottles, empty cartons, and snack refuse. Fortunately, none of this is discernible from below to mar the otherwise unblemished beauty of the mighty mountain. In the wintertime, the slopes are covered from top to bottom with a gentle blanket of snow.

Dr. Frederick Starr of Chicago is perhaps the best remembered of the foreign *Fuji* worshippers, having climbed to the summit numerous times. A monument commemorates his local Alpine activities.

In the immediate vicinity of *Mount Fuji* during the summer months, there are sites for fine fishing, boating, swimming, and camping. During the fall the duck and pheasant shooting is most rewarding, and in the wintertime there are exhilarating skiing and skating opportunities.

The FIVE LAKES, *Yamanaka, Kawaguchi, Saiko, Shoji,* and *Motosu,* themselves comprise a resort area at the north base of *Mount Fuji. Saiko* is also known as *Nishi-no-umi.* The mountain lakes' altitudes vary from *Kawaguchi's* 2,700 feet to *Yamanaka's* more than 3,200 feet.

LAKE YAMANAKA combines the distinction of being the largest lake in area, the highest in altitude, and the shallowest. Because of its altitude, the summers are soothingly cool, with an average daytime temperature of 68 degrees Fahrenheit. The championship *Fuji Golf Links* are located near the lake.

Yamanaka's Lake Festival is celebrated July 30th, when hundreds of lighted lanterns may be seen serenely drifting on the lake.

The woods that border the shores are heavily populated with singing birds for whom hundreds of tiny houses have been built. On the far shore of the lake facing *Fujiyama,* the Japanese enjoy the hike up *Mount Ishiwari,* 4,635 feet in altitude, from which the views are excellent. The *Fuji New Grand* and the *Yamanaka Hotels,* in the immediate vicinity, provide both western and Japanese style accommodations. The *Oshino Hakkai* springs are located a few miles north of the lake.

LAKE KAWAGUCHI, number two in size, is, as a resort, equally popular during each of the four seasons. From here, also, an excellent inverted view of *Mount Fuji* may be had. When, in winter's frigid months, *Kawaguchi's* waters are deeply frozen, the surface is transformed into a vast platform for hordes of avid, hardy ice fishermen. *Cormorant Isle,* rising from the crystal clear waters of the lake, is renowned for its shrine to the goddess Benten. The *Fuji View Hotel* is highly recommended.

FUNATSU, the best known of the resort villages, offers accommodation in several Japanese inns while the *Fuji-View Hotel* is a short distance from the lake. August 5th is the date of *Funatsu's* annual *Lantern Fete,* colorfully complete with fireworks.

LAKE SAIKO is favorably known to Isaak Walton's devotees for its unusually fine trout fishing. Of its several scenic attractions, the densely forested area known as the "Sea of Trees" *(Jukai)* is most spectacular. The vista from *Maple Hill (Momijidai)* is pleasing at all times. In the fall, the foliage is most vivid. The most ominously spectacular of the caves to be found here is the *Fuji Wind Cave (Fuji Fuketsu),* one of Japan's "Natural Treasures," situated in the *Jukai* forest at an altitude of approximately 3,700 feet. Because of its height above sea level, the cave is constantly in a state of near deep freeze.

LAKE SHOJI, the tiniest of the lakes, is intimately enshrouded by heavily wooded mountains. Its open side, as one would expect, faces *Mount Fuji. Panorama Hill (Mount Eboshidake),* looming 4,150 feet above and to the west of the lake, provides an excellent dais from which to enjoy the area's splendors.

LAKE MOTOSU, at the western flank of the group, is by far the deepest of the lakes and rarely freezes over. Its trout fishing is particularly rewarding in the spring and fall.

FUJI-YOSHIDA City is the northern takeoff for *Mount Fuji* climbers. Its most spectacular annual event, the *Fire Festival* of the *Sengen Shrine,* takes place on August 26. On festival night, scores of huge bonfires are lighted in the city. Simultaneously, scores of rest-hut keepers on the *Fuji* paths light up companion fires which form a flaring picture in the darkness. Throngs crowd the streets and form a procession bearing a portable *Mount Fuji* shrine to the *Sengen Shrine,* an ancient custom. Originally, this was the time for group prayer begging the gods to spare them from the deadly lava from ancient *Fuji* eruptions.

The wild azaleas which bloom high on *Mount Fuji* in June paint a picture of ethereal beauty best enjoyed from **Fuji-Yoshida City.** Both the azalea area and the *"yama-no-kami-no-fuji"* (wisteria of the mountain gods) are designated as Natural Treatures by the government.

SHIRAITO *(Fall of the White Threads)* is a gracefully spectacular waterfall of vast width. To the west of *Mount Fuji,* near *Lake Motosu,* I think it is well worth viewing.

MATSUSHIMA, northeast of **Tokyo** on the *Pacific Ocean,* is only an hour's drive from **Sendai City,** four hours by train from the capital. This "Pine-clad Island" constitutes—with *Ama-no-Hashidate ("The Bridge of Heaven")* close to **Kyoto,** and *Itsukushima ("Shrine Island")* at *Miyajima* in the *Inland Sea*—one of Japan's classic "Scenic Trio."

Matsushima's sights can be pleasantly absorbed in a day's time. The ferry from **Shiogama** plies leisurely among the pine-dotted islands of *Matsushima Bay.* On land, one may see *Matsushima Park* and the "Four Grand Sights": *Tomi-yama ("Rich Mountain"); Otakamori ("Great Falcon Woods"); Katsura-shima ("Cinnamon Island")* with its attractive bathing beach; and *Tamon-zan ("All-Hearing Sacred Mountain"). Yogasaki Promontory* is another area with a series of pleasing land and seascape views.

Other worthwhile local sights include *"Fan Valley"* and the caves of *"Male Island." Zuiganji Temple,* decorated with a verdant avenue of cedars, is noted for its deep *Hosshin's Cave.* Its Momoyama style buildings, designed in the 17th century, are Important Cultural Properties. The *Kanrantei,* a 16th-century cliffside abode of a onetime feudal lord of the area, is filled with priceless screens by the master Kano Sanraku himself.

SADO ISLAND, near **Niigata** in the *Japan Sea,* home of the famed maidens who sing the plaintive *Okesa* ballads and dance on the hard-packed sands, is an island of gold and silver mines, showy with camellia trees, and historically known as a place of exile—an Oriental *St. Helena* or *Elba* —of famous men in feudal times. *Sado,* readily reached by *All-*

Nippon Airways in a two-hour flight from **Tokyo** or, more lengthy but far more scenic, by express train to **Niigata** (through the *Great Kanto* rice bowl, the hot spring and ski resort studded *Central Mountain* range, and Japan's great *Yuzawa Tunnel*) followed by a two-and-a-half-hour luxury liner ride to **Ryotsu** port, is an eye-filling spot to delight the traveler.

Brooding *Mt. Kimpoku,* site of *Kuroki Gosho ("The Palace of the Unhewn Timbers")* towers over *Lake Kamo* while in a hut at *Komponji Temple,* in **Izumi,** "God's Angry Man," the priest Nichiren, lived while in exile. Four spectacular waterfalls spew forth on *Sado.*

The *Sado Kanko Hotel* at **Aikawa,** 16 miles and 45 minutes by taxi from the main port of entry, is as nice as can be expected in such a remote area. The two vest-pocket cruise ships, the *"Yumeji Maru"* and the *"Namiki Maru,"* which serve *Sado* are air conditioned and steam heated, as required, have some private cabins, and offer the voyager all the maritime comforts.

Nikko and Nikko National Park

NIKKO, **Nara,** and **Kyoto** are Japan's show places of the quintessence of man's artistic and architectural expression. Many Japanese, adoring the wonders of their country, urge that visitors savor the beauties of **Nikko** only after having seen all of the other treasures of these aesthetic islands. "If one sees **Nikko** first," they say, "everything else will seem like an anti-climax."

My charming friend, Ethel Einstein of Baltimore, one of America's most discriminating travelers, adores **Nikko,** placing it in the top echelon of her list of the world's treasure houses. Such praise is praise indeed.

Nikko's manmade glories and natural splendors combine to offer one a most rewarding day's sightseeing. Fortunately this ancient city and many splendored *National Park* are virtually suburbs of **Tokyo** 91 miles away. Several railroads connect the

two areas. I personally prefer the speedy, smart, ultramodern
private electric line which departs from the capital's *Asakusa
Station.* Making the run in less than two hours each way, one
may leave **Tokyo** circa 9 A.M., visit the shrines and temples before lunch, dine at the delightful *Kanaya Hotel,* ascend to the
crystal clear atmosphere of the *Lake Chuzenji* area for an afternoon enjoying the heaven-on-earth scenery, and yet return comfortably to **Tokyo** in time to freshen up for a late dinner, or,
if one's fancy dictates, overnight may be spent at the enchanting
château-like *Nikko Kanko Hotel* overlooking the lake or in
Nikko at the famed *Kanaya Hotel* adjacent to the shrines.

NIKKO NATIONAL PARK, of which **Nikko City** is the
hub, is a mélange of mountains, lakes, rivers, waterfalls, hot
springs, hot spring spas, hotels, inns, mausoleums, and shrines.
The unbelievably beautiful *Toshogu Shrine,* the breathtakingly
spectacular mile high *Lake Chuzenji,* **Yumoto Spa** on *Lake
Yunoko,* and the *Kegon Fall,* one of the largest and certainly
one of the most ostentatiously showy waterfalls in the Far East,
are among the best known attractions of this area.

Crystal clear streams punctuate *Nikko's* fields which are
aglow with flowers from early spring to late fall. During the

latter season, the ancient forests of pine, maple, and beech are a riotous multitude of blazing colors.

In the year 1624, the great Shogun Iemitsu Tokugawa conscripted a large corps of architects, artisans, designers, and workers to build the shrines, temples, bridges, pagodas, and gates of *Nikko*. They were dedicated to his grandfather, Iyeyasu Tokugawa, the first Shogun of the Tokugawa dynasty. The result was so incredibly marvelous that from the 17th century onward, without exception, visitors have been awed by the splendors of nature so happily blended with the artistic creative products of the genius of man.

Here, as in *Hakone National Park,* outdoor sports including fishing, sailing, camping, mountain climbing, skiing, and tobogganing predominate. If it is done outdoors, *Nikko* offers it generously.

A considerable segment of the roadway leading to *Nikko* is lined with an awesome display of Japanese cedars, or cryptomerias. More than 15,000 of these spectacular trees were planted in the 17th century at the time of the construction of the *Nikko Shrine* as a gift to Iemitsu Tokugawa by a nobleman who had fallen on evil days. This hard-luck lord was not able to compete with his rich rivals in gifts to the shrine but he had a stroke of genius and donated these trees which have now flourished for something over 300 years.

The *Nikko National Park* is surrounded by four principal prefectures: Tochigi, Gumma, Fukushima, and Niigata. Of such great national importance are the various objects of the *Nikko National Park* that almost without exception they are, by national decree, either National Treasures or Important Cultural Properties.

NIKKO CITY, which I shall describe here, and *Inner Nikko,* which I shall describe later, are both integral parts of *Nikko National Park*. **Nikko City** is the pulse beat of the national park and, from east to west, lies virtually in its center. From the *Nikko Station,* a mile-long sloping street descends to the river, the sacred bridge, and to the western section beyond which includes the hallowed mausoleums, sacred Shinto shrines, and Buddhist temples. **Nikko City** embraces *Toshogu,* the most famous of the shrines, as well as *Futaarasan Shrine, Rinnoji Temple,* and the *Daiyuin Mausoleum.*

The TOSHOGU SHRINE (Iyeyasu's Mausoleum) is noteworthy because of its great age, the magnificent artistry of the buildings, the splendor of the trees within the grounds, and the enormous richness of the gold leaf and other decorative designs which adorn the shrine and its companion buildings. After Iyeyasu Tokugawa, founder of the Tokugawa Shogunate, died in 1616 at the ripe old age of 74, his ashes were interred in the *Toshogu Shrine* in 1617, having been originally interred at **Kunozan.** The third Shogun, Iemitsu, thought the mausoleum so small that in 1624 he ordered it rebuilt in its present awesome proportions of grandeur. Thousands of the finest craftsmen, artisans, and humble workers toiled here for more than a decade. It was all completed in 1636.

Iyeyasu Tokugawa, as many lesser men today, was both a Buddhist and a follower of Shintoism. His ashes are consecrated per the concepts of Buddhism, while his spirit has been hallowed in the Shinto manner. The huge stone *torii* gate represents the Shinto element while the five-storied pagoda is Buddhist.

Yoritomo Minamoto, propounder of the feudal system, and Hideyoshi Toyotomi are spiritually enshrined in this national mausoleum monument as associate gods at a lesser level.

On May 17th and 18th and October 17th one may see the festival processions in all their ancient color and glory. There has been some indication that the festival days may be extended due to their popularity.

This shrine is indeed a happy blending of the architectural precepts of both the Buddhist and Shinto religions. In addition to the pagoda, the belfry and drum tower are Buddhist, while the Oratory, the Sacred Cistern and the aforementioned *torii* gate are Shinto, all within a limited area.

The RINNOJI TEMPLE *(Four-Dragons Temple),* itself an Important Cultural Property, should share with the *Toshogu*

Shrine equal billing in the *Nikko* production. *Shihonryuji,* the *Four-Dragons Temple,* was founded on this site in the 8th century by the great priest, Shodo-shonin. Early in the 9th century, by Imperial decree, the temple's name was changed to *Mangan-ji* and in 814 the area was named NIKKO. In 1655 the temple's title became *Rinnoji.* Both Buddhism and Shintoism were the official religions of *Rinnoji* until 1877 when they were divorced by law.

More than 100 *Rinnoji Temple* buildings were leveled by fire in 1684, but all have since been rebuilt. Lying midway between the *Mihashi Bridge* and the *Nikko Bridge* on one side and the five-storied pagoda on the other, it was at one time the temporary residence of General U. S. Grant. *Rinnoji Temple,* a most enchanting example of Buddhist architecture, contains tablets of all members of the Imperial Family and carries the Imperial chrysanthemum crest on its door. The *main hall,* the largest building in *Nikko,* contains the thousand handed Kannon, Amida, and the horse-headed Kannon. Each of these three great images is approximately 27 feet in height.

The YOMEIMON, *"Gate of Sunlight,"* a stunningly attractive gate to the shrine, is reached by a flight of stairs which open on the most magnificent of all of the hand-wrought works of art in Japan. The *Gate of Sunlight* is also known as the *"Twilight Gate"* and the *"Gate of Dreams."* Its intricate carving and brilliant coloration gives the *Yomeimon* a fabulous appearance.

The FIVE-STORIED PAGODA, 100-plus feet of brilliant red lacquerwork tempered with ocher-colored doors, lies at one apex of a more or less equilateral triangle between *Rinnoji Temple* and *Toshogu Shrine.* The 12 signs of the zodiac are carved on its walls in brilliant color. The five roofs represent the earth's five elements: earth, water, fire, wind, and heaven.

The SACRED STABLE follows the old superstitious belief that decorative, colorful monkeys carved on stables will guard the horses from contagious diseases. We find carved on the walls here the famous "hear no evil, speak no evil, see no evil" trio of monkeys. Scores of other monkeys are to be found throughout the *Sacred Stable* area. It was here that the Emperor's famed white horse used to be quartered.

The SACRED PALANQUIN HOUSE, adjoining the *Yomeimon Gate* just west of the *Karamon Gate,* is the consecrated warehouse for the portable sacred shrines, three in number, which play an important role in the *Nikko Festival.* The palanquins are dedicated to Iyeyasu Tokugawa, Hideyoshi Toyotomi and Yoritomo Minamoto. When these movable images are carried in the impressive procession, they are so ponderous they require 50 or more sturdy men to lift each one. This sacred building is adorned with bird and flower friezes of magnificent color. Heroic-sized Buddhist angels are painted on the ceiling.

KAGURADEN *(Sacred Dance Stage)* and UPPER SHRINE OFFICE. Within the inner court, there are several other noteworthy buildings. The *Sacred Dance Stage* is the only *Nikko* structure to exude, even slightly, a tinge of western style. The *Upper Shrine Office,* facing the *Sacred Dance Stage,* was formerly an incense hall for prayer recitals. Its columns, brackets, and friezes are intricately carved with contrasting fish and flowers.

The KARAMON GATE *(Chinese Gate),* a National Treasure, though somewhat smaller than the superbly attractive

Yomeimon Gate, is almost as fantastically beautiful. The front gable of the gate is decorated with a bronze carving of a mythological beast, while the east and west gables are covered with fierce dragons. A Chinese emperor and his followers are depicted in wooden statues. The door jambs are adorned in bold relief with Japanese apricots and bamboos, while the panels are carved with water and mountain birds, chrysanthemums, peonies, and more apricots. A harp-playing figure is on the ceiling, while Chinese celebrities have been carved amid the fruit and flowers. Only priests may pass through the *Karamon Gate.*

The ORATORY *(Haiden),* immediately adjacent to the *Karamon Gate,* is in essence another *hall* contiguous with the *main hall,* both of which are surrounded by a *sacred fence,* and together form the shrine's principal edifices. Once you have passed through the gate into the area between the *Karamon* and the *Oratory,* you must replace your shoes with slippers which will be supplied to you. The *Oratory* is composed of three parts all lavish with friezes and lintels splendidly carved with pheasants, phoenixes, dragons, pine trees, bamboo, Japanese apricots, and other incongruous but highly decorative objects. The dark blue background of the ceiling is superimposed with a dragon. The spirit of the deity in the rear of the *Oratory* is represented by the *Sacred Mirror,* two feet six inches in diameter.

The MAIN HALL *(Honden),* as previously noted, is, with the *Oratory,* surrounded by the *Tamagaki,* the Sacred Fence. The *Oratory* is three copperplated steps above the passage chamber known as the *Stone Room,* while the *Honden* is another five steps up. The ends of the *Honden's* rafters are carved with phoenixes, while the rest of the decorative scheme parallels that of the *Oratory,* of which it is, in fact, a continuation. Within the *Main Hall,* behind a paneled door, is the *Inner Sanctum,* comprised of the *Outer, Inner,* and *Innermost Chambers.* In the latter, surrounded by many wonderful works of craftsmanship, is the magnificent *Gokuden Shrine,* resplendent in gold lacquer, in which one finds the shrines of the spirits of Iyeyasu, Hideyoshi, and Yoritomo. While the deities of these personalities are enshrined here, none of these mysterious, beautiful, complicated, superb structures holds the ashes of Iyeyasu himself. He is interred in:

The MAUSOLEUM, reached readily from the terraced area separating the *Yomeimon* and *Karamon Gates.* The gate outside the *Mausoleum* is famous for the small cat known as *Nemuri-neko* sleeping in a bed of peonies. The highly embellished *Sakashitamon Gate* will next attract your attention. At the top of the 200 steps is a bronze *torii* flanked by a sacred *storehouse* and an *oratory,* preceded by a bronze *gate* and followed by the pagoda-shaped *tomb,* 11 feet high. Before the *tomb* are a bronze vase and an incense burner, while bronze beasts stand guard at the *gate* to fend off evil spirits. In 1683, an earthquake severely damaged the original tombstone which was replaced by the present one shortly thereafter. At the peak of the shogun's power, entrance was denied to the inner precincts to all visitors, including the privileged, except during the *Festival,* when the laymen were permitted beyond the *Sakashitamon Gate.* At other times, this area was open only to the priests, the shogun himself, his deputy, and his messengers.

The FUTAARASAN SHRINE, west of the *Sacred Palanquin House* and east of the *Yashamon Gate,* is not far from the *Toshogu Shrine.* This Shinto shrine houses the deity Omamuchi-no-Mikoto, his consort, and child. It was this trio who were believed to have brought happy economic days to the nation more than a thousand years ago. The entrance is guarded by a great bronze *torii,* 22 feet high. The lacquered *Chinese Gate* is behind the *Oratory,* while within *Futaarasan* is the *Main Shrine (Honden).* The antique bronze lantern, known as the *Goblin Lantern,* situated at a corner of the *Sacred Fence,* is seven feet high. According to the legend, the lantern, at night, turned into a goblin, and on one occasion was attacked and wounded by a group of samurai warriors. To this day, sword marks may be seen on the metal. The ancient umbrella pine outside the *Oratory* was planted in the 8th century. A divine three-trunked Japanese cedar stands near the holy water basin.

The DAIYUIN MAUSOLEUM, next in importance only to that of the *Toshogu Shrine,* dedicated to Iyeyasu Tokugawa, is the resting place of Iemitsu Tokugawa, the third Tokugawan shogun and founder of *Nikko's* glory. The *mausoleum* is situated on a secluded hill between the *Yashamon Gate* and *Futaarasan Shrine.* It was built with the thought that his resting place was not to be less splendid than his grandfather's, and it does indeed glitter with gold and other beautiful embellishments, though everything is on a rather smaller scale than the *Toshogu Shrine.* To reach the *Daiyuin Mausoleum,* visitors pass through four gates, the first of which is particularly richly decorated with gold carvings.

The ceiling, supported by 12 pillars, is ornamented with a 17th century painted dragon. The impressive granite cistern is viewed before proceeding up a flight of 21 steps lined with numerous stone lanterns. The second two-story gate, known as the *Nitemmon,* is covered with Buddhist deities and the Gods of Thunder and Wind. The middle court, where we find the *Belfry* and the *Drum Tower,* is reached by an additional flight of stone steps. The *Peony,* or *Third Gate,* is highly gilded. The fourth, and last, *Chinese Gate* is highly ornate with thick gold leaf.

The *Oratory* and the *Main Shrine,* not to be confused with the *Oratory* and the *Main Shrine* of the *Toshogu Shrine,* are also of great beauty and possessed of magnificent carvings and friezes. Carved flowers, animals, and birds, as well as gilded ornamentation, play an important role in both the *Oratory* and the *Main Shrine.* There are also a tortoise-shell lantern from Holland, ancient musical instruments, and bronze stork candlesticks. In the *Main Shrine* is a brilliantly lacquered wood carved figure of Iemitsu, three feet in height. The tiny gate leading to the innermost court is of pure Ming dynasty Chinese architecture. The *tomb,* of cast bronze, is reached by several steps leading up, first, from the *Oratory* to the *Sanctuary* and then to the *tomb*, which is similar to that of Iyeyasu.

The principal entrance to the area is over the *Nikko Bridge* parallel to the extraordinarily beautiful *Sacred Bridge (Mihashi)*. The latter, known alternatively as *Shinkyo (Divine Bridge)*, is not open to the public but is used only on festive and cere-monial days for sacred processions. It was here that the Priest Shodo of the late 8th and early 9th centuries forded the turbulent river mounted on two churning serpents. He was attempting to attain the heights of *Mount Nantai*. The present *Sacred Bridge* was built in 1907 as a duplicate of the original constructed in 1636. It is of red lacquer, metal, and gilt, with its stone supports resembling *torii* gates.

On crossing the *Nikko Bridge,* approaching *Rinnoji Temple,* the first of the great objects of the area which we pass is the *Sojourning-hall, Otabisho.* The three-storied *pagoda,* the *Hongu Shrine,* and the *Shihonryuji Temple* will be seen on the ascent to the shrines before reaching the *Rinnoji Temple* and the *Abbot's Palace.* Other important objects in the area are the *Sambutsudo* and the *Treasure Museum.*

The foregoing shrines, temples, palaces, pagodas, gates, mu-seums, and sacred objects lie on a gentle hill north of the *River Daiya* and to the west of the *River Inari* snuggled in an idyllic setting of venerable Japanese cedars.

The NIKKO BOTANICAL GARDEN, featuring a large collection of Alpine flowers, covers a vast area of more than 33 acres. The garden is famous for the *gamman-ga-fuchi deep,* where the *Daiya River* waters pound relentlessly against the craggy rocks to form a series of falls.

The NIKKO NATIONAL PARK MUSEUM includes sci-entific, natural, and geological displays native to the *Nikko National Park*.

The HOSO-O SKATING RINK (the most spectacular in the Orient) covers more than three acres. The site of hockey and skating competitions, it is open to the public by day and night.

NIKKO'S FESTIVALS. There are three *Nikko* festivals, held on May 17, October 17, and from August 1st to August 7th, though the May festival is the one normally known as *Nikko's Festival*. The October festival is a much smaller replica of that which is held in May. If you should be in Japan in the spring, by all means do try to trace your steps to *Nikko* on the seventeenth of May to see a most colorful and unforgettable spectacle. A thousand men dressed as samurai, accompanied by priests, march to the *Sacred Palanquin House* where they shoulder the massive portable shrines which include those commemorating Iyeyasu, Hideyoshi, and Yoritomo to carry them in a gorgeous parade to the *Sojourning-hall*. Weird ancient music accompanies the performance of the sacred dance and the offerings of the pilgrims. Each of the actors is garbed in traditional gaily colored costumes. After the rituals at the *Sojourning-hall*, the shrines are returned in holy procession to the *Sacred Palanquin House*. The August first to seventh festival sees thousands of pilgrims climbing the ruggedly steep 8,197 foot *Mount Nantai*. The pilgrims who attain the summit have performed a creditable athletic feat as well as religious pilgrimage. During another festival, the pilgrims climb the summit of *Mount Nantai* from the twentieth to the twenty-second of September.

During the ascent, the white-clad pilgrims pay homage at the three different shrines along the route. The pilgrimage is preceded by mass bathing in the lake, and the exodus begins shortly after midnight in order that the climbers, who are aided by Alpine sticks and tiny lanterns, may reach the top in time to see the glories of nature as the sun unfurls its first bursting rays.

The *Rinnoji Temple Festivals* are held on January 2 and June 2, the former being known as the *Gohanshiki* or *"Rice Ceremony."* In ancient times the pilgrimage was climaxed by the consuming of great bowls of rice, considered to be offerings of the deities. The priests, armed with massive sticks, saw to it that none passed up so much as a grain of rice, thereby offending the gods. The June festival, known as the *"Longevity*

Dance," is performed before the *Sambutsudo* by priests ornately garbed and carrying swords and fans.

Lake Chuzenji and District

Lake Chuzenji, poised at an alpine altitude of 4,194 feet above sea level, is situated 11 miles from **Nikko City.** The *lake,* the ethereal *Kegon Fall,* the surrounding mountains, and pastoral scenes of incredible beauty comprise a pleasant natural climax to the complicated architectural achievements of the *Nikko* shrines.

Lake Chuzenji may be reached from **Nikko** by a curvacious motor road which follows the *Daiya River* a great part of the way. It passes numerous shrines, dense woods, and cascading waterfalls. Towering mountains dominate the drive. The *"Irohazaka"* drive is one of the most spectacularly steep series of hairpin turns that my eyes have ever seen. Many of the 28 well-trimmed turns are of 180 degrees. The ascent is sharp and breathtaking. The roads are well constructed and completely safe.

The *Wind Cave* to the right of the road is believed to shelter a divine spirit that blew great gusts of wind from the cave's mouth, but the phenomenon probably can be naturally explained as erupting volcanic gases. The road, higher up, pierces a great gorge to attain *Sword Peak,* a vantage point from which the *Hoto* and *Hannya Waterfalls* may be viewed. These falls are surrounded by great masses of maple trees which are brilliant in their autumn garb. The high spot of the road is **Odaira,** from which one descends only slightly to **Chuzenji,** *Lake Chuzenji,* and the *Kegon Waterfall.*

From the *Irohazaka* hairpin turns the road straightens out for *Lake Chuzenji.* The approach is made even more spectacular by the sudden emergence of the lacy-like loveliness of *Kegon Fall.* Excellent motor coaches and private cars are available for this trip. An alternative routing is to proceed by electric car from *Nikko Station* to **Umagaeshi** to board a cable car across the *Daiya River* to **Akechidaira** for a connection for the short motor ride past *Kegon Fall* to **Chuzenji** and its lake.

Should you elect to proceed to *Lake Chuzenji* by electric and cable car, I heartily recommend that you pause at **Akechidaira** to take the aerial ropeway to the summit of *Tembodai,* a justly renowned lookout point. This aerial ropeway will afford you a more soul-stirring ride than even the **Umagaeshi** cable car. From *Tembodai,* the panoramic vista embraces *Lake Chuzenji,* the *Kegon Waterfall,* and the surrounding peaks.

LAKE CHUZENJI is, as previously noted, at a great altitude and is also possessed of a great depth which imparts to its waters an unbelievably rich blue coloration. The lake stretches in placid splendor four miles in length with the widest point being just under two miles. Because of its altitude, the summer temperature of the lake area seldom exceeds 80 degrees Fahrenheit. The *Lake Chuzenji* area, as a result of its proximity to **Tokyo** and its favorable climate, is a favorite summer resort. However, there are cherry blossoms in profusion which lend luscious coloration in the springtime, and the masses of maples light up the hillsides with their fantastic flaming fall colors. Anglers—lake and stream—will be interested to know that *Lake Chuzenji* is literally alive with salmon, trout, eels, and carp. If you wish, you may rent a boat and fishing tackle to have a "go" at them. Be sure to get a license, which you can do with assistance from any of the local hotels or at the nearby trout hatchery. Fishing is permitted from May 20th to September 20th. In the summer, chartered sightseeing motorboats abound on the lake; in the winter the skiing and skating in the area are excellent.

The KEGON WATERFALL is one of the great natural attractions of Japan. This splendid mass of water, which thunders 330 feet to the craggy receptacle below, is an unforgettable wispy spectacle adorned with soft silver spray at all times. *Kegon Fall* is fed from *Lake Chuzenji,* first emerging in a stream for over a quarter of a mile before it tumbles over the lava cliff to become *Kegon Waterfall.* The main waterfall is enhanced by the 12 little falls known as *Ju-ni-taki* which are formed by underground seepage from the lake. Should you visit the area in the wintertime, you will be greeted by the spectacle of *Kegon Waterfall* transformed into great ethereal ice fingers, the only discernible movement being tiny spatterings from the minor falls. I heartily recommend that you descend in the elevator which may be boarded at the **Chuzenji** bus stop. An awesome view of the falls may be had from the bottom of the crater.

MORE SHRINES. Perhaps your urge to see shrines will have been satiated in the *Toshogu-Nikko* area below. However, there are two in the **Chuzenji** vicinity: (1) *Futaarasan Chugushi*, roofed in copper tiles, which snuggles at the base of *Mount Nantai*. Its varnished pillars and walls are incredibly colorful. (2) The *Tachiki-Kannon*, near the *Lakeside Hotel*, presents an image of the Thousand-handed Kannon carved of wood more than 800 years ago.

NIKKO-YUMOTO SPA and LAKE YUNOKO. **Nikko-Yumoto Spa,** 19 miles from *Nikko Station* and eight miles from **Chuzenji,** on the shore of *Lake Yunoko*, is held in the embrace of three rugged mountains. If you are seeking a fishing license, you will find the *Government Trout Hatchery* on the *Chuzenji-Nikko-Yumoto Road*. This highway also passes the *Dragon's Head Cascade*, an inviting waterfall. Farther along, you will be able to view the lacy *Yudaki Waterfall* cascading down a precipitous 335 foot drop. The woods of the spa encroach the water's edge. The climate and fishing are similar to that of *Chuzenji*. The frozen waters of the lake are popular with skaters. Skiing expeditions are organized from the spa.

The *Nikko Mountains* are most impressive and beautiful. *Mount Shirane*, 8,507 feet, is the highest. *Mount Nantai* is the most famous. Other peaks climb to more than 6,000 feet and are bedecked with shrines on or near their summits.

SENJU-GA-HARA is a great swampland west and north of *Lake Chuzenji* which abounds in Alpine flora. A mythical battle took place here between two serpents.

INNER NIKKO (OKU-NIKKO) lies in the western rug-gedly mountainous district of *Nikko National Park.* Well known for its variety of mountains, swamps, flora, and spas, it is particularly popular with the Japanese.

KINUGAWA SPA and KAWAJI SPA are connected by the spectacular *Ryuo-Kyo Gorge.* They are old and popular with the Japanese. The neighborhood is noted for its hot springs, rushing torrential rivers, and streams.

SHIOBARA SPA and the NASU SPA contain 18 hot spring resorts. **Yumoto Spa** is the best known of the *Nasu* group. The *Nasu Golf Course,* of championship calibre, just outside of **Yumoto Spa** lies in a superb setting. The *Nikko Country Club,* just outside **Nikko City,** has an 18 hole course covering a pro-digious 7,000-plus yards of extremely challenging golf.

The Boso Peninsula

The *Boso Peninsula,* immediately south and east of **Tokyo,** is surrounded by *Tokyo Bay* and the *Pacific Ocean.* Because of its unusually high agricultural yield and the fruits of the sea caught by its fishermen, it is frequently known as **Tokyo's** "kitchen." Its beaches beckon summer vacationers. The penin-sula is largely in Chiba Prefecture, and **Chiba City** on the bay at the northwest juncture of the peninsula is connected with the capital by train. The service is fast and frequent. A diesel rail-way line passes around the peninsula whose shrines and temples are a focal point for innumerable pilgrims.

CHIBA, a city of more than 100,000 population, is the ad-ministrative and educational center of the prefecture, which is endowed with numerous bathing beaches. Its fish market is a beehive of activity.

CHOSHI, a commercial and tourist city, is two and a half hours from **Tokyo** by train. From **Choshi,** the fishermen sail far out to sea for tuna, mackerel, and sardines. Agriculturally, soy sauce is an important **Choshi** product. The **Choshi** area and the *Kasumigaura Lagoon* afford excellent winter duck hunting. The lower reaches of the *Tone River,* on which **Choshi** is located, are noted for their scenic beauty, while pine groves outline **Choshi's** bounteous beaches where the delightful *Isoya Hotel* is located.

CAPE INUBO, reached rapidly by electric rail from **Choshi,** is noteworthy for its lighthouse, towering over the waters, which may be visited. The beacon is a homing light for trans-pacific vessels. The seascapes here are worth the trip.

NARITA, the site of the chief shrine and the religious center of the *Boso Peninsula,* is reached in an hour from **Tokyo** by limited express trains of the *Keisei Electric Railway.* The *Shinshoji Temple,* originally built near **Narita,** was moved to its present site in 1705. Hordes of pilgrims descend on **Narita** during the non-agricultural producing months. The area has hosts of legends, and the temple is jam-packed with historic treasures such as a famous sword donated by the emperor early in the 10th century. The high priest Kancho used this sword, and the image of *Fudo,* to crush an ominous rebellion in 940. The image Kancho used to perform his miracle, known as *Fudo,* is legendarily a wave cutter, carved from a ship's oar. The story is that the deity appeared during a horrendous storm, and, with a single sweep of his sword, tamed the onrushing waves. In the shrine is a self-portrait of the famous 9th-century statesman, Michizane, which he executed while in exile in *Kyushu.*

KARUIZAWA, Japan's dapper summer resort, 90 miles from **Tokyo,** is the Japanese Hobe Sound, Bar Harbor, Newport and the Hamptons rolled in one. It is beautifully tucked away, on a high upland meadow, surrounded by a shroud of mountains, one of which is the still smoking volcanic *Mt. Asama.*

This quaint resort village is still something of a foreign enclave to which diplomats, newsmen, businessmen, and Japanese statesmen repair to escape the sultry heat of Japan's cities and also to enjoy the flame-hued fall months. **Karuizawa** is reached from **Tokyo** in less than three hours by fleet, crack express train, in about four hours by car over good, if truck-filled, roads, and only 50 minutes from **Tokyo's** heart by newly established helicopter service.

Karuizawa, 3,049 cool feet above the heat-holding *Kanto Plain,* maintains a temperature rarely hotter than 80 degrees Fahrenheit by day even when one is being simultaneously cooked at over 90 degrees F. in **Tokyo.** Nights are so cool, even in July and August, that a blanket feels good as does the fire in the fireplace with which most mountain-type western style villas are equipped.

Activities are abundant. There are three fine golf courses, a dozen tennis courts, trout fishing streams, a neighborhood filled with hot springs, bicycle and hiking trails which penetrate the silver birch, bamboo and piney woodlands. There are horseback riding, boating on *Swan Lake,* swimming in mountain pools, and that best of summer activities, relaxing and enjoying the view on one's own front porch as evening falls.

A wintertime town of 14,000 people, **Karuizawa** expands in the summer to nearly 45,000 when the police force balloons from seven regulars to 40 deputies in July and August. In winter there are hunting, snowshoeing, ice fishing, skiing, and skating.

The hotels here are paced by the grand *Mampei Hotel,* old fashioned in service and courtesy, but offering sparklingly up-to-date bedrooms, public rooms, and cuisine. The best inn, the *Tsuruya,* run by the town's active mayor, Mr. Sato, is on the *"Machi"*—the colorful shop-filled main street.

Ever popular, **Karuizawa** has become even more so since Crown Prince Akihito met his commoner bride, the present Princess Michiko, on the tennis courts here.

Karuizawa, a World War II refugee camp for diplomats trapped in Japan by the outbreak of hostilities, is known for its international cuisine. Local restaurants, open from June 15 to September 15, specialize in Chinese, French, Russian, Italian, Japanese, and Korean style cooking.

Other places of interest in the enchanting neighborhood are *Kusatsu,* the oldest, hottest hot spring in Japan, *Kose* and

Manza spas, the azalea meadows, the horse-grazing country of the *Asama Bokujo,* and the three Myogi jagged mountain peaks: *"White Cloud," "Golden Cock,"* and *"Golden Cave."* Several hundred years ago at *Oninooshidashi,* the "Devil Rock-Throwing-Out Spot," the volcanic eruptions of *Mt. Asama* made a Pompeii and a Herculaneum of several small Japanese villages. The lovely waterfalls at *Ryu-gaeri* ("Dragon Return Cascade") and *Tsurudamari* ("Storks Assembling Place") attract many visitors. There are attractive summer colonies at neighboring **Kita Karuizawa** and **Sen-ga-taki.**

THE REST OF JAPAN

Japanese Alps

KAMIKOCHI, known locally as the "Shangri-La" of Japan, is a hidden Alpine retreat, buried in the *Kamikochi Valley,* 5,000 feet above sea level filled with radioactive hot springs gushing in the shadows of soaring, snow-capped peaks. **Kamikochi** is eight to nine hours from **Tokyo** by express train and bus or taxi.

The area's great Swiss chalet-type inn, the *Kamikochi Imperial,* is under the same T. Inumaru's management as the *Imperial* in **Tokyo** and is open during most of July and August. From the hewn-timbered, stone-faced *Kamikochi Imperial* one may wander down to man-made, crystal clear *Taisho-ike,* as it is called by the Japanese after the Emperor Taisho, filled with lifeless birch trees, across *Kappa* ("River-Sprite") *Bridge* to the fishing, boating and canoeing area, or descend by convenient footpath to the neighboring hot springs including *Shirahone* and *Nakanoyu.*

Kamikochi is briskly cool even during the muggiest of summer days elsewhere in Japan. The view of nearby *"Spear Peak"* and other pinnacles of the *Japanese Alps* is excellent.

The JAPAN ALPS soar through *Honshu,* the principal Japanese island, at its thickest point. This region was literally "discovered" by two Englishmen, William Gowland, an engineer and outdoors enthusiast, and The Reverend Walter Weston, who later became known as the "Father of the Alps."

The *Alps* are known as the *Southern Alps, Central Alps,* and *Northern Alps* depending on their location. Peaks in all Alpine ranges tower upwards from 7,000 to 12,000 feet while the *Northern* range has more than 100 giants that touch the sky above 6,500 feet, 40 of which are over 8,000 feet in altitude. The Alpine monsters include *Akaishi, Shirane, Koma* (or *Kai-ga-take*), *Kiso-Koma-ga-take, Yari, Ontake, Norikura, Tsurugi, Shirouma, Otenjo, Harinoki,* and *Tateyama.*

The *Japanese Alps* are vastly popular with increasing numbers of ambitious mountain climbers who flock from all walks of life and all areas of Japan to challenge the year around ice-filled and snow-topped peaks. This is so dangerous that many young lives are lost each climbing season. One of the most famous Alpine sights is the so-called *"Ginza of the Alps,"* a lengthy, treacherous footpath carved along the saddle between two lofty peaks which harried climbers negotiate gingerly while "roped up" and moving slowly, hand over hand, using pitons and iron chains linked to iron hooks embedded in the granite.

The area teems with hot springs, splendid ski resorts, alpine flora, fauna, and breathtaking views.

You know my philosophy about mountaineering. Unless you are a professional or highly skilled amateur, don't indulge. If you choose to ignore my sagacious advice, watch out, equip yourself well, hire guides, get in shape, and study the always difficult, sometimes murderous terrain. Just like the other, older, more familiar Alps in Europe, Japanese mountain climbing is for experts, not for the casual freshman climber.

Hiroshima

It is a fervent wish, almost a religious desire on my part, that every man, woman, and child in the world could visit Hiroshima. There would never be another war were this wish fulfilled.

...e city is perhaps the most important spot in the nation: the "peace city" of Japan, risen phoenix-like from ashes and death.

At eight A.M. on August sixth, 1945, a warm pleasant day, office workers and troops were still surreptitiously picking up some of the thousands of leaflets dropped by our Air Force the previous day warning the population to evacuate the city. Those so engaged had to be careful, for the military authorities had issued orders that nobody was either to retrieve or read the leaflets. At 8:15 A.M. there was an appalling blast followed by blinding light. The one-megaton bomb, the first such awesome death-dealing device ever employed, had exploded at 1,800 feet directly over the center of the city—a miniature sun about 70 feet in diameter with an inferno-like temperature of 540,000 degrees Fahrenheit.

For your macabre information and sober reflection, **Hiroshima** was a city of 400,000 inhabitants. Over 142,000 men, women, and children were instantly killed, 100,000 were maimed and injured, and 58,000 survived unscathed. (These are the figures used in **Hiroshima,** and while they do not coincide exactly with ours, they are awesomely illustrative of the tragedy.) Many of the mercilessly burned inhabitants sought surcease by hurling their baked bodies into the river. It was boiling! Among the dead were two divisions of Japanese troops. Although this bomb was less than one-fiftieth the power of the modern hydrogen bomb of today, **Hiroshima** was virtually destroyed.

My friend, Fred Okuma, is an example. On that fateful "A Day," he was, by the grace of providence, on a train en route from **Hiroshima** to **Osaka.** His wife and 17-year-old son were in the garden of their home six miles from the **Hiroshima** hypo center at the time of the A-bomb's frightful explosion.

At the terrifying moment of the blast, Fred's train was 26 miles from his home town. When the mushroom cloud spiraled lethally aloft, he and his fellow travelers were understandably confused by the nature of the A cloud. Not having had previous experience with this type of total warfare, they knew not what carnage that awesome symbol portended.

He and his fellow travelers continued to **Osaka** where word greeted them that **Hiroshima** had been totally devastated by an entirely new type of bomb.

He was frantic to return at once but was unable to do so for a week. On the seventh day, he started back. The journey was a long, tedious chore. He alternately hitchhiked short rides between farms and plodded wearily by foot. Finally, eight desperate days after the blast, he arrived at his home. To his unmitigated joy, he not only found his wife and son alive and apparently in good health but his home was relatively unscathed. His wife told him that, apart from a tremendous heat wave that passed over them shortly after the A blast, they had felt little reaction to the bomb. The noise had been stupefying and the terror of the populace devastating, but they survived.

A few days later, on "A blast day" plus 19, he and his wife were having their morning tea together. She looked at Fred and said, "I'm going to die." Fred said, "You're kidding." She bowed, collapsed, and died.

Like many of the apparent "survivors," she had been afflicted with leukemia of the blood. Their son died six days later.

Because of his early return, Fred suffered from latent radiation and was hospitalized seven agonizing months.

Fred, incidentally, is disaster prone. His parents had moved to San Francisco, and as a lad he went through the fearful San Francisco earthquake in which he lost his parents. Subsequently he lost his wife and son in the first A blast of modern "civilization."

When, several days later, silence fell on the city, the Japanese and the world in general believed that it would be 75 years at least before **Hiroshima** could become habitable again. There were many who believed that the soil had been rendered sterile and would never again bear fruit or vegetables. This belief was partly due to the fantastic radiation "ghost shadows" of people and other objects found printed on the surface of solid concrete and/or granite. Photographs of these grisly reminders of the holocaust can be seen in the *Memorial Museum*. Two years later **Hiroshima** was on its way to recovery.

Hiroshima has now been rebuilt. Of the original city, the shells of only 13 buildings remained after the blast. Even they were completely gutted and were later torn down. The remains of only one has been left intact as a grim reminder of the tragedy: the *Industrial Exposition Hall,* with its now famous, or infamous, dome. So nearly as scientific experts can determine, this *Hall* is the precise "hypo center" of the A-bomb, directly below the explosion which burst at approximately 1,800 feet. The *Hall* is now a pitiful shell of a concrete building with the tangled mass of the steel dome remaining as an eternal symbol of the futility of conflict. The dome is a "drive and a mashie niblick shot" from the modern big league *Hiroshima ball park* with a seating capacity of 36,500. The hypo center stands near a lovely park in which bloom plants and scarlet flowers, proving that vegetation did soon reappear on the scene of desolation.

The rebuilding of the city was not beautifully done. *Peace Boulevard* and the *Peace Bridge* are symbolic but not captivatingly charming. Notwithstanding, **Hiroshima** has an attraction all of its own. Already this new city of 420,000 looks ancient and antiquated. Were it not for its association with "the" bomb and the fact that it is the steppingstone to *Miyajima,* an Old World island of utter charm and of much historic significance, **Hiroshima** would scarcely warrant a visit. As it is, however, I heartily recommend that you include it in your Japanese itinerary. You will reflect on it for years to come. And you will never forget the *Shinto Shrine* on *Miyajima.* It is fascinating beyond expression.

Hiroshima lies at the head of *Hiroshima Bay.* **Ujina, Hiroshima's** busy port, 3.7 miles from the heart of the city, but a part of it, is reached by car or train.

The *August Sixth Festival* has become the most impressive and important event in **Hiroshima.** Under the arch of the *Memorial Cenotaph* is a stone box on which is carved in Eng-

lish and Japanese: "Repose Thou in Peace. We Shall Ne
Make That Mistake Again." Inside the box (opened each A
gust sixth) are the names of almost all the scores of thousands
of victims.

The *Peace Tower* includes the *A-Bomb Museum* with tragic
exhibits of the disaster and photographs of the devastated city
and many of the victims.

Hijiyama Hill is the site of a huge radiation research center
where skilled Japanese and Americans strive to determine the
ultimate effects of atomic radiation. Scores of thousands of persons have been examined to date. The view from the hill over
the city, harbor, and *Miyajima* in the distance is exciting.

Hondori is Hiroshima's most important street.

The old *Hiroshima feudal castle* was obliterated in the A-
bomb blast, but the moat and grounds have been converted into
a sports area.

MIYAJIMA or ITSUKUSHIMA *("Shrine Island")*. This
beautiful island, an hour from Hiroshima by car and ferry,
should definitely be considered an absolute "must" on your trip
to Japan. The island is venerated by the Japanese who endeavor
to visit it at least once during their lives.

The *"Floating Shrine."* This Shinto shrine is of ancient
origin, with its existence recorded as early as A.D. 811. The
buildings have been reconstructed several times in their history
and consist of the main and subsidiary shrines connected by
outdoor galleries over 600 feet in length. The corridor of the
main shrine contains ancient armor and Buddhist sutra scrolls.

At high tide one has the impression that the shrine, including
its huge camphorwood *torii* 170 yards from shore, is gracefully
floating on the still blue water, a romantic illusion which is
dispelled when the water recedes leaving the mud flats exposed
to view.

A *Noh* stage has been erected over the water. In the *Morning Prayer Room* one may see a variety of old exhibits and
models of festival ships almost exactly similar to those still used
during the summer festival. The arched bridge (to the west)

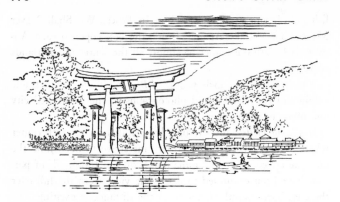

depicts the sacred *Bridge of Heaven.* The stone *torii* overlooking the lake is of 1905 vintage.

Senjo-Kaku, an old building known as the *Hall of a Thousand Mats,* is to the left of the shrine.

Shinto priests perform the sacred *Kagura Dance* on a wide camphorwood floor of the shrine which performance can be enjoyed by visitors on payment of a small fee. The performers of the fantastic outdoor ceremonial *Bugaku Ritual* wear magnificent costumes and ferocious masks formerly used by warriors to terrify their enemies. The *Bugaku* dance was performed originally only for the nobility, while the *Kagura* was for the masses.

A curious display of thousands of rice scoops hanging near the shrine originated from a superstitious "play on words." Troops headed for the Russo-Japanese War prayed here for victory and left their scoops as an offering to the gods. The words *"meshi-toru"* have the dual meaning of "rice taking" and "to conquer." The *Treasure Hall* houses thousands of valuable displays and treasures. The ancient *Deganji Temple,* built in A.D. 802, is held in sacred awe as the repository of the Buddha statue and the statues of his disciples.

Quite apart from *Shrine Island, Miyajima* is a most beautiful summer resort. During the month of April, a forest-full of cherry blossoms are in bloom, while during the summer, the island's temperature is moderate. No dogs are permitted to run loose on *Miyajima* because of the tame deer that roam there. Until the *Meiji Restoration,* neither births nor deaths were permitted, by regulation, on the island! Even today, funerals have to be carried out on the opposite shore.

One of the island's most beautiful spots is *Momiji-dani (Maple Valley),* a park-like area on a hillside saturated with scores of maple trees. Here one finds several charming *ryokan* (inns) and tea houses set in lovely and peaceful surroundings. *Mt. Misen* caps the heights of the island. One may ascend the summit by a ropeway and if the weather is fair, I urge that you do. From here several islands in the *Inland Sea,* **Hiroshima,** and the rest of *Miyajima* are spread out in magnificent array. A three and a half hour tour around *Miyajima* can be made in the *National Railway* steam launch or the *Matsudai Motorboat Company's* launch.

Nagoya

Nagoya's 1,600,000 inhabitants make it Japan's third largest city, and it is chiefly important as a thriving industrial center. **Nagoya,** 227 miles from **Tokyo,** 163 miles from **Atami,** 92 miles from **Kyoto,** and 119 miles from **Osaka,** enjoys a fine subway system. By *limited express* train one may be sped from the capital to **Nagoya** in less than four hours while the flying time is just over an hour.

This ultramodern metropolis has several excellent department stores, many fine shops, western style hotels and restaurants, theaters, movies, dance halls, museums, botanical gardens, and a zoo. The 18 hole golf course at nearby **Wago,** where a local member will be delighted to arrange guest privileges for you, is a good one. The *Nagoya Horse Race Course* is impressive. The *Baseball Park* seats 30,000, and the *Athletic Grounds* have accommodations for 50,000 spectators. **Nagoya,** bombed on May 14, 1945, has been completely rebuilt and continues to expand rapidly. Its wide main thoroughfares and prosperous business and shopping areas attest to the rapidity of its growth.

Nagoya's versatile manufacturing activities include heavy industry and the manufacture of textiles and toys. For more than seven centuries, **Nagoya** has been noted for its porcelain manufacture, pottery, and delicate cloisonné ware. The secret of the complex process for making cloisonné has been jealously guarded by local craftsmen for countless scores of years, fathers having passed along the carefully guarded formula to their sons for generations. Cloisonné coloring is as unique as is its opalescent glowing effect.

The city emerged from an original group of lordly fortresses and mansions in a manner much similar to the evolution of the British and Continental European medieval towns. The great Iyeyasu Tokugawa enriched the city early in the 17th century when he constructed one of Japan's most formidable castles for his son, Yoshinao. In 1882, the city became a commercial cotton-spinning center as well as an important hub in the watch and clock industry.

When Iyeyasu Tokugawa had NAGOYA CASTLE constructed in 1612, he paid no heed whatsoever to the cost or labor involved. The *donjon* (main tower) was surmounted by two solid gold dolphins, one of which was shipped halfway around the world in 1873 to be exhibited in Vienna. Disaster overtook the steamship carrying it back home. The vessel was sunk off the coast of Japan, the golden statue plunging to the ocean floor where it lay for six months until salvaged and returned to its perch high above the castle. Alas, the dolphins and the castle were destroyed during the 1945 air raid. In 1957, the restoration of the castle was begun and was completed as a museum in 1959—a duplicate, dolphins included, of the original. The original moat with its masonry walls and three turrets remains intact. The original doors and ceiling panels were stored in the hills during the war and are now on display in the new castle. They are well worth half an hour of your time when visiting the castle.

In and around the city one finds numerous shrines, the most important being the very sacred *Atsuta Shrine,* near *Atsuta*

Station, containing a sacred sword. Rebuilt in Japan's postwar construction era after 1945, *Atsuta's* annual festival is June 21.

HIGASHIYAMA PARK, its *Botanical Gardens* and *Zoo* are worthy of a visit if time permits. The animals roam without restriction in full view of the spectators, while within the park one finds impressive concrete reproductions of prehistoric animals.

TOKUGAWA ART MUSEUM, about a mile and a half east of *Nagoya Castle* and a former royal residence of the Tokugawa lords, contains a remarkable collection of armor, helmets, swords, and other historic treasures. The literary efforts of a number of former emperors are on view.

The NITTAIJI TEMPLE, on *Kakuozan Hill,* is a Thai-Japanese place of worship built in 1904. Located near *Higashiyama Park,* the temple grounds include a massive collection of gorgeous cherry trees and azalea plants. The King of Thailand presented the temple with a golden image of Buddha in 1900.

The KISO RAPIDS nearby may be "shot" comfortably in a specially constructed boat. The experience is as scenic as it is spectacular.

GIFU, like its neighbor **Nagoya,** grew from the lordly residences of antiquity. During the 16th and early 17th centuries, **Gifu's** history was stormy and hectic. It was taken by Iyeyasu's forces in 1610, but by 1891 a large thriving city had been built, only to be destroyed by an earthquake and its attendant conflagration. It was quickly rebuilt. Today it is a flourishing, attractive business city in the shadows of *Mount Inaba* bordering on the *Nobi Plain.* This city's most important interest to visitors, however, arises from its activity in regard to cormorant fishing, which unique Japanese procedure I have described under "Japanese Sports."

Industrially, **Gifu,** which is 246 miles from **Tokyo** and 19 miles from **Nagoya,** produces textiles, Japanese lanterns, paper umbrellas, and colorful fans. **Gifu** paper lanterns of fragile quality are on sale all over Japan during the summer months. They are extremely lovely and popular.

Ise-Shima National Park

ISE-SHIMA NATIONAL PARK houses the oldest Shinto shrines in Japan and is the home of the cultured pearl industry. The new "Asamayama Skyline" tollway skirts the "roof" of the *Ise-Shima National Park*. Linking the grand shrines of *Ise* with **Toba** city, the skyline drive affords motorists panoramic vistas of *Ise* plain, *Ise Bay, Toba Bay,* and the mountains of Shima.

ISE CITY (*Ise Jingu* in Japanese), the station for the *Jingu* shrines, is 73 miles from **Nagoya,** 295 miles from **Tokyo,** 109 miles from **Osaka,** and 84 miles from **Kyoto.** The *Ise-Shima National Park* encompasses close to 130,000 acres including all of Shima Province, the offshore islands, and a segment of Ise Province. Apart from its famous shrines, the *Shima Peninsula* is an incredibly scenic area, embracing the attractive resorts and bays of *Gokasho, Ago,* and *Matoya.*

The OUTER SHRINE *(Geku)* is dedicated to the goddess of farms. *The Inner,* or *Sun Goddess, Shrine* is especially interesting. As one approaches under the first *torii,* near an attractive bridge, one views a marvelous collection of ancient Japanese cedars and timeworn buildings, including the *Anzaisho,* an Imperial Rest House for the emperor to use when visiting the shrines. The enormous camphor tree is a local showpiece. It is at these shrines that the Emperor of Japan worships.

The route to the second *torii* takes one past additional buildings and offices to the main outer shrine, surrounded by four classical fences. The *Ise Shrines* are among the holiest and the most sacred in Japan, and perhaps the holiest of all. Within these handsome off-beat woods and paths, one finds shrines that are delightful in their extreme simplicity. Common courtesy dictates that visitors should remove their hats when standing before the shrines. The wood used in the construction of these shrines, gates, and rails is unpainted and has few metal ornaments. The 11-acre *Sacred Park* is highly rural in aspect.

The INNER SHRINE (NAIKU) is reached by crossing the

Ujibashi Bridge. Visitors and natives alike, having passed under the first *torii,* proceed to the banks of the *Isuzu River* to cleanse their mouth and hands before visiting the shrine. A secluded path, about a quarter of a mile long, leads past the second *torii* through the magnificent row of venerable Japanese cedars to the buildings of the *Naiku.* Before these simple temples, everyone stands momentarily at attention, bows, and claps his hands twice. The sword, mirror, and jewels, treasured and sacred to Shintoism, are enshrined within the *Naiku.* The mirror has been enshrined at *Geku* for close to two thousand years. The Shinto creed is basically one of simplicity, an excellent reason for the aesthetic wooden shrine buildings. It is an ancient tradition that this shrine shelter should be demolished every two decades and a new one built to replace it near its former site. The fifty-ninth razing took place in the fall of 1953.

FUTAMI-GA-URA, four miles from *Iseshi,* is a pleasant, relaxing resort with several excellent Japanese style inns set among soothing pine trees. These front on a fine seaboard promenade which hugs the coast of *Ise Bay.* Two of the best known of these attractive inns are the *Asahikan* and the *Futamikan,* which, though Japanese, are not strangers to western guests. Two historic rocks lying close to the shore, known as the *"Wedded Rocks,"* are associated with a charming and semi-religious ceremony which records their similarity to Izanagi and Izanami, legendary creators of Japan. On the fifth of January each year, a strong hemp rope that connects the two rocks is ostentatiously replaced, the ceremony being watched by crowds of onlookers. The "groom," the larger of the two rocks, bears a *torii* on its summit.

TOBA, a resort town and a departure point for short sea trips around the nearby pine clad islands, is connected with *Kashikojima Island* on *Ago Bay,* 15 miles away, by electric railway. The *Shima Kanko Hotel* on the island offers both western and Japanese style rooms. An excellent road connects Toba with Futami and *Kashikojima. Pearl Island* in *Ago Bay* is famous for its cultured pearl industry, particularly for the

Mikimoto Cultured Pearl Farm which owns the pearl centers in this area as well as in its five adjacent bays.

A BRIEF HISTORY OF THE CULTURED PEARL IN-DUSTRY. The story of the fabulously successful House of Mikimoto constitutes a fascinating drama which, surprisingly, has been overlooked by the usually perspicacious Hollywood moguls. Kokichi Mikimoto, grandiose grandfather of the present owner, was born in *Toba* in 1858, the son of a noodle tycoon. The then young Mikimoto had other ideas than being economically entwined by noodles, however palatable. He began, instead, to experiment with oysters to force them, aided by superimposed irritants, to produce pearls to order. European scientists previously had failed in similar efforts because of their inability to introduce the irritant without either killing the oyster or failing to affect it at all. Though the odds were heavily against him, young Mikimoto persevered. In 1888, he set up his *Toba* headquarters on *Ago Bay,* but, alas, in January of 1893, a disastrous sea water pestilence killed off most of the experimental oysters and ruined the efforts of his hard work. But, undaunted by his disappointments, he continued his experiments, aided by his indefatigable wife. He was laughed at or, worse, pitied by most of his friends, but in July, 1893, the tide turned when a specially treated oyster was opened and the first artificially induced pearl was discovered. Thus began one of the greatest, most successful international enterprises. Jewelry establishments everywhere vigorously opposed this process, but, despite all such harassment, the Mikimotos courageously continued to carry on their experiments which ultimately enabled them to perfect the process for the artificial mass production of pearls. They even succeeded in controlling the size and shape of these scientifically produced pearls. The Mikimotos realized, as the public was soon to do, that a cultured pearl was indeed the genuine article; but instead of its being a chance of nature, it was scientifically induced. Even when he had succeeded in establishing the soundness of the basic principles of his work, Mikimoto's troubles were not over. The difficulties incidental to the introduction of the irritant had been over-come, but the oysters so treated were originally placed in metal containers attached to rafts, let down into the water, and im-mediately beset with grave dangers. The water had to be ex-actly the correct temperature; if it was too cold, the oysters succumbed forthwith. Drifting seaweed and other sea hazards strangled them, and miscellaneous exterior attachments dam-aged them, making it necessary for the oysters to be pulled up repeatedly to be examined. These and other difficulties were happily transcended, however.

Today hundreds of girl operators work in sheds at *Ago Bay* inserting the mussel shell irritant into the oysters, while others are skillfully employed matching the near-perfect pearls or pre-paring them for final stringing.

The *Toba* pearl-diving girls, or *"ama,"* plunge into the water with their oyster buckets and remain under the surface long periods of time. They warily defy the sharks by wearing white swimsuits (frequently just the trunks) which frighten off the killers. One "girl" is a 57-year-old grandmother. Others are young and attractive. The day of the *"ama"* is fast dying as more oysters busily making pearls are suspended in wire cages from oil drums. The *"ama"* will go back to searching the floors of the bays for abalone and mussels as they have done for cen-turies.

There is a jaunty monumental statue of Grandfather Miki-moto on *Pearl Island,* wearing a derby hat, crested kimono, and carrying a cane. A cairn of stones marks the historic spot where he and his wife discovered the first cultured pearl.

Tourists are welcome to visit the *Pearl Museum* on *Toba's Pearl Island.*

Mikimoto now has its own jewelry stores in all the big Jap-anese cities, including main stores in the *Ginza* and the *Arcade* of the *Imperial Hotel,* **Tokyo;** the *Shin Osaka Building* in **Osaka;** the *Kobe International House* in **Kobe;** and others in **Nagoya, Fukuoka, Kyoto,** and **Sapporo.**

I must remind you that when buying pearls to be sure to

keep your specified stores tax exemption card on hand. It will save you the 16 per cent Japanese Commodity Tax which otherwise would be added to your purchases.

Kyoto

The Japanese have an innate fondness for styling their cities, streets, parks, and geographical settings after locations outside Japan—**Atami,** the "Riviera of Japan" ... **Osaka,** the "Chicago" and *Biwa,* the "Lake Lucerne of Japan" ... *Asakusa,* the "Coney Island" or "Broadway of Japan," the *Ginza* is the "Fifth Avenue, Piccadilly or Champs Elysees of Japan," and in the Land of the Rising Sun one calls the lovely, feudal capital, **Kyoto,** the "Paris of Japan," which latter liaison is official, since the European "City of Light" and the Asian "Celestial City" have recently, officially, been linked as "sister cities," although **Kyoto** was also later named "sister city" to another famed old place, Boston, thus giving it a highly incongruous set of sisters.

Foreigners, no less than Japanese, have been raving about **Kyoto** for ages. It's a truly great place, possessed of more character and charm than any other Japanese city.

Center of Japan's civilization for 1,000 years, the old capital teems with historic and religious sites, relics, works of culture, and art. Picturesquely nestling in a placid valley, with mountains looming on three of four sides, **Kyoto** is watered by the ancient *Kamo River,* in whose stream face-bathing women of the old court could hope to become **Kyoto** *bijin*—local beauties. This ancient city is the Mecca of the nation and the Eastern world, to which all lovers of the past and searchers for beauty repair.

Fortunately, this superb repository of human worth was spared the fire bomb attacks of wartime bombers, which humane indulgence was brought about through the insistence of American scholars, particularly *Harvard University*'s Orientalist Dr. Langdon Warner, who during his life was a great lover of Japan.

Despite its vast age **Kyoto** is an easy place in which to get about. The city is laid out in nine wards on a north-south, east-west basis, the northern end bumping up against *Lakes Mizoro* and *Takara*. A mountain wall fans out from *Arashiyama* to the west past *Mt. Atago*. The *Yodo River* flows through the flat countryside nearby.

In ancient times, Japan's capital was situated in a different city as each new regime took over. In 709 **Nara** was chosen as a seemingly permanent capital. In 784, however, a new capital was selected on a site approximating the modern *Mukomachi Station* in **Kyoto**. Ten years later another site was selected in what is now the center of the city. This new capital city was first described poetically as *Heian-kyo*—the "Capital of Peace"; it then became, successively, *Miyako*—"Capital" or "Imperial Capital," and then, simply **Kyoto**, "Capital of the West."

Kyoto, originally surrounded by a low earthen wall and ditch, pierced by 18 gates, was laid out in A.D. 805 following Chinese building rules. Its largest, most important, east to west streets were named consecutively from *Ichijo*, "First Street," to *Kyujo*, "Ninth Street."

Kyoto, unhappily, was disaster-prone. In 960 A.D. the first *Imperial Palace* was burned to the ground and, in 1177, the second *Palace* was engulfed with flames and burned to a crisp. In the 13th and 14th centuries civil war embroiled the area and after a short interval of peace from 1467 to 1474, the region again erupted in bloody fratricidal strife. For the next 100 years, up to about 1568, the Court lived on mere crumbs of its former glory.

In 1569 a great warrior-statesman of that forlorn feudal period entered with his forces, and undertook the physical and morale rebuilding of the *Imperial Palace*, city, and court, which tasks were completed by his successor, the great, if bloodthirsty, Hideyoshi. This man, Oda Nobunaga, restored the temples, laid out the streets anew, and renewed the sheen on the luster of the olden days. With the transfer of the nation's administration to **Edo (Tokyo)** under the Tokugawa Shogunate, **Kyoto's** bright star was eclipsed once again. But even today it

KYOTO

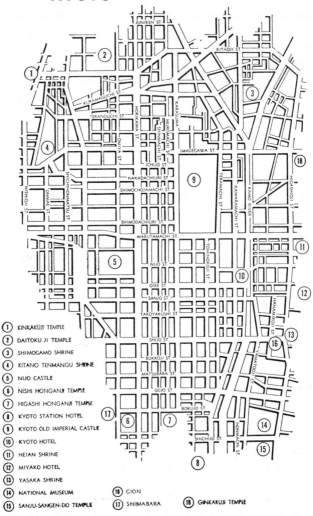

1. KINKAKŪJI TEMPLE
2. DAITOKU JI TEMPLE
3. SHIMOGAMO SHRINE
4. KITANO TENMANGU SHRINE
5. NIJO CASTLE
6. NISHI HONGANJI TEMPLE
7. HIGASHI HONGANJI TEMPLE
8. KYOTO STATION HOTEL
9. KYOTO OLD IMPERIAL CASTLE
10. KYOTO HOTEL
11. HEIAN SHRINE
12. MIYAKO HOTEL
13. YASAKA SHRINE
14. NATIONAL MUSEUM
15. SANJU-SANGEN-DO TEMPLE
16. GION
17. SHIMABARA
18. GINKAKUJI TEMPLE

is a great city, still the site for the ceremonial crowning of each Emperor.

Kyoto is many things: a lovely gold and silver pavilion; the jade-hued *Oji River;* an old weeping willow-lined back street where the damascene, ivory, cloisonné, silk, pearls, gems, and scrolls of the past are just as much in evidence now as in the

past; a garden style restaurant where the tea ceremony precedes a tasty dinner served by kimono'd girls with centuries old habits of taste; hillsides sparkling with masses of cherry blossoms in spring and maple tints in fall; a five-tiered pagoda rearing against the skyline side by side with roofs of modern hotels, offices, and department stores; a temple with a squeaky "Nightingale walk" where fierce old feudal samurai slashed with two-handed swords; a quiet moss-filled garden where shaven-headed priests chant and meditate; a gay July festival where great-wheeled, pinnacled carts are tugged through vast crowds by sweating men; and a collection of old, crumbling houses in an area where each family devotes its life and handed-down skills to silk weaving, pottery making, embroidery, and making lacquerware.

Kyoto is the city of an *Imperial Palace,* of a garden with 16 rocks, only 15 of which can be seen no matter where one stands, of a school where *Geisha* learn their intricate skills, of castles, temples, shrines, and Buddhist sanctuaries for nuns and monks. It is a city of restaurants, shops, flower arranging schools, red stands for viewing the moon, factories, ivory figurines, bambooware, obi cloth, human hair wigs, Buddhist rosary beads, and fantastic objects in wood, bronze, clay, metal, precious stone, gold, cloth, and rock.

Kyoto is a shrine to the Fox God, a temple to the love of a courtesan for an uncaring Emperor, an alley where young painted women clop along in the evening mists, a great bell that booms out 108 strokes at midnight each New Year's Eve, a whiff of powdered tea ceremoniously prepared in a dim, straw-matted room, the sun rising above the Eastern Hills, and the *Sanjo Bridge* known to warriors, priest, *Geisha,* and plain folk for almost 800 years.

It is all of these and more, a state of mind, a breeze from a glorious past, and an atmosphere rivaled by few places on earth.

Kyoto, in my humble estimation, is one of the truly fascinating cities of the world. It has great charm and a fascinating personality. Its character is veritably unique. This superb old city, justifiably one of Japan's greatest attractions for foreign visitors, is a modern center of industrial art and, next to **Tokyo,** attracts more visitors than any other Japanese city. No city is regarded with more veneration and affection by the Japanese themselves.

Kyoto, a city of seemingly eternal festivals which take place at all seasons of the year, is less affected by western influences than any other Japanese city outside of *Hokkaido.* **Kyoto** is a shopper's paradise. Its western style hotels, gourmet's restaurants, and exciting night clubs are pleasing equally to the Japanese and to foreign visitors. **Kyoto,** Japan's leading city of industrial arts, is only 317 miles from **Tokyo,** 25 miles from **Osaka,** and 47 miles from **Kobe.**

KYOTO TODAY. The population, like the city itself, has had its vicissitudes. In the late 17th century, the city boasted of just over half a million inhabitants, a number which, by the late 19th century, had diminished to its lowest point with 275,000. Since then, the population has spurted until today it is approximately 1.3 million and still increasing. It is indeed a boom town with great buildings, including magnificent new hotels, springing up all over the city.

Kyoto is justly renowned for its silk weaving industry, an economic activity traced back to the 8th century. The Chinese influence flourished in Japan's silk industry during the 17th century when, and for centuries thereafter, all the silk garments used by the great Japanese families were ordered woven by the Nishijin method which involves painstaking fingernail weaving in brocade patterns. Present procedures for imprinting the dyed silk fabrics were invented in the 17th century.

Kyoto porcelain and lacquerware are famous for their delicacy and superb workmanship. Lacquerware is another specialty outstanding for its beauty and quality. The silver and

gold lacquerware have been evolved from secret processes involving a mixture of dust and lacquer. Leading local dealers in the fine arts are listed in the chapter on "Shopping."

Embroidery was introduced into Japan from **China** and was unknown to the western world until the mid-19th century. The dyeing industry, originally a hand operation but now mechanical, is just as artistic and attractive as in the "good old days."

The *Asakusa* of **Kyoto,** though less obvious and blatant than its namesake in **Tokyo,** is found in and around *Shinkyogoku Street.* Here we find the cinemas, the hordes of small bars, shops, coffee houses, and *pachinko* gambling dens. This brilliantly lit street, animated with seething movement, is popular with visitors and natives alike.

Kyoto invites you to stroll through its intriguing streets and fascinating lanes. Nowhere else in Japan is the opportunity to absorb local color so prolific as here. **Kyoto** is like a huge small town. Though blessed with all the big city amenities of huge hotels, fine shops and big business, it is basically a community of small "homey" wooden or stucco houses lining the sheath-like lanes. Small shops indent the neighborhood house. Here we find the greengrocer, butcher, and the antique shops spilling over into the narrow thoroughfares. If time permits, take a walk about. You won't get lost and you will enjoy it.

Ponto-cho Street, one of **Kyoto's** best known and most picturesque, extends from the *Shijo Bridge* to the *Sanjo Bridge,* running through the finest amusement center, the area of the *Geisha* teahouses and the *Kaburenjo Geisha School.* As I have noted in the piece on *Geisha,* this is the "home training grounds" for all Japanese *Geisha,* which leads one to expect and find special *Geisha* attractions. There are two *Geisha* schools, on opposite sides of the river. The oldest and best known is the *Gion-machi;* its rival is the *Ponto-cho.* Should you be here between April fifteenth and May fifteenth, you may enjoy the *Geisha* performances of the *Kamogawa Odori,* "Dance of the Kamo River." At the time of the *Spring Festival,* the *Geisha* participate in the *Miyako Odori,* the famous "Cherry Dance," at the *Kaburenjo Theater.* The cast is a large one and the costumes are brilliant.

Theaters and Noh Stages: The best known theaters are the *Minamiza* and the *Shochiku Gekijo.* While I believe you will find the *Noh* performances quite ponderous, I would point out that there are three well-known *Noh* stages: the *Oe,* the *Kongo,* and the *Kawamura Stages.*

Festivals: There are more than 50 gay festivals celebrated here each year, most of them with religious overtones. With more than four a month, you are almost bound to stumble on one or another festival when you visit this ancient capital.

The KYOTO TOWER, Japan's second highest building, is opposite the station. It has two observation towers complete with souvenir shops and snack bars.

Kyoto is blessed with more beautiful buildings, temples, shrines, and gardens than any other city in Japan. There are more than 900 such edifices that could command your attention. It would be impossible to attempt to visit or even see more than a fraction of this number, even though your visit might be an extended one. I heartily recommend, however, that you not be discouraged by the words "temples and shrines" because here particularly one finds structures of outstanding beauty. Many of these entrancing buildings contain historic religious relics of breathtaking beauty and fascinating interest.

The OLD IMPERIAL PALACE is set in a sylvan park of heroic proportions. While the original *Palace* dated from the late 8th century, the present building was constructed, some two miles north of *Kyoto Station,* in 1855. The original *Palace* was destroyed by a great fire. Its replacement was a replica of the original, but this, too, met a similar sad fate by flames. The present *Palace* follows the artistic architectural simplicity of its predecessors. I must hasten to caution you that the *Palace* may, without special permission, be visited during only two periods of the year, between April sixth and tenth and from November twenty-sixth through December second. It is possible, without

too much difficulty, to obtain the necessary permission by applying directly to the *Office of the Imperial Household*. Your
local guide will know about this procedure. So will the information desk of your hotel. If interested, you have but to inquire.

The *Palace* is of great interest. The "Serene and Cool
Chamber" *(Seiryoden)* is a tricky piece of architectural genius.
A cold riverlet was changed in its course to flow under the
chamber to give it an ancient **Kyoto** version of air conditioning.
The room is constructed entirely of Japanese cypress, with
elaborate paintings on the sliding doors. In the *Ceremonial Hall*,
we find a richly ornate throne used by numerous emperors for
official functions. The stairs are flanked by two trees, one a
citrus tree called *Ukon*, the other a cherry tree known as *Sakon*
—the names of the Imperial guards who were, in ancient times,
on duty where the trees now grow.

The KATSURA IMPERIAL VILLA AND GARDEN,
submerged in an atmosphere of peace and repose, consist of
seven pavilions, each a marvel of design and delicate décor,
which blend themselves into the background of pines, palms,
maples, and shrubs. A placid lake is a harmonious extension of

the setting. A tea room overlooks the waters. Situated on the edge of town, just three miles from the *Kyoto Station,* the *Katsura Imperial Villa and Garden* were built in the late 16th century. The *Villa*'s connected buildings are superb architecturally, but it is the artistic gardens, however, that I think will capture your fancy. They are the work of the great landscape gardener, Enshu Kobori. Hideyoshi Toyotomi, who had the villa built and gardens laid out, gave Enshu great latitude and unlimited funds for his work. So perfect are the gardens that from whatever position they are viewed, one has the feeling of being in the most perfect place. To see the *Katsura Imperial Villa* one must apply for a permit at least two days in advance. Your hotel can arrange the details.

The NATIONAL MUSEUM contains several excellent small bronzes, a good exhibit of well-lighted figures of Kannon, magnificent screens, and the *Gion Festival Scroll,* one of the finest in the world.

The NIJO DETACHED PALACE (NIJO CASTLE). The two foregoing names are used interchangeably for this incredibly ornate royal residence set in 70 acres of fascinating gardens and arbors, surrounded by massive stone walls and a moat. Many students of architecture and design compare the splendor of *Nijo Castle* with its 15th-century counterparts, the decorative baroque castles of Europe.

The great Iyeyasu Tokugawa had *Nijo Castle* constructed to be his town house, and through the later centuries it has played an important role historically. It was here, for example, that the Emperor Meiji pronounced his abolishment of the Shogunate. During the late 19th century many of the fine artistic objects and works within the palace were either badly damaged or destroyed. Much of the original art work has been restored.

Within the grounds is a typical Japanese water garden, a beautiful cascade, and attractive designs of rocks and trees. The castle is composed of five separate buildings connected by galleries. Even such powerful figures as the shoguns feared assassins and took elaborate precautions to guard their lives from these villains. The galleries were fitted with an intricate alarm system which transformed normal footsteps to simulate the warbling notes of a nightingale. Yes, imagine—a "bird-like" warning for a warrior!

The first four buildings, devoted to public and reception rooms, are particularly noteworthy because of their elegant and highly ornate decorative schemes. The doors, screens, ceilings, and friezes depict settings of nature including trees, bamboo, animals, and birds. The fifth, and last, building was the shogun's private living quarters. The décor of this building is somewhat less elaborate than that of the other four, but even here the ornamentation is picturesque and colorful.

The KINKAKUJI TEMPLE (GOLDEN PAVILION), an extraordinarily lovely edifice, was originally constructed as a villa by 14th-century noblemen and later elaborated upon by the third Shogun of the Ashikaga house, Yoshimitsu. On the

Shogun's death, and under his posthumous orders, the villa was transformed into this Buddhist temple. The gardens, lake, stream, and arboreal settings remain little changed since the 14th century. The various buildings frequently have been attacked by flames, and though restorations have been frequent and accurate, the physiognomy is somewhat altered. The beautiful *Golden Pavilion,* adorned on its summit by a bronze phoenix, stood intact for more than 500 years until, in 1950, it was willfully burned to the ground by a demented arsonist, an acolyte priest. It was accurately restored in 1955. The story of the *Pavilion*'s destruction was the theme of a novel, "The Temple of the Golden Pavilion," by Japan's famed young novelist, Yukio Mishima. This novel is available in a superb English translation. Within the temple proper, the setting is awesomely rich and impressive. There are images of three Buddhist deities, numerous statues, and great paintings. The *Main Hall* may be reached from two entrance gates, the *Somon* and the *Chumon.* The camellia tree in the front garden is more than 300 years old; the pine tree in the shape of a boat in the rear garden is believed to be more than 550 years old.

The NISHI HONGANJI TEMPLE is worthy of your visit, as it is thought by many to be, architecturally, the best Buddhist temple in Japan. Shinran, who lived in the late 12th and early 13th centuries, was the founder of the Buddhist Jodo-Shinshu sect, of which the *Nishi Honganji Temple* is today the secular senior headquarters. Shinran, of noble birth, claimed early in life that he had received direct inspiration from the priest Honen, founder of the Buddhist sect of *Jodo,* who had died some years earlier in 1212. Apart from his visionary asceticism, Shinran was also a man of the world. After he had fallen in love with a high-born girl, he decided that the priests of his new sect need not bother with celibacy, dietary laws, or other restrictive habits. It is understandable that this sect was not always looked upon with great favor by the devout. However, late in the 16th century, it acquired the protection of Hideyoshi, the Napoleon of Japan, who chose **Kyoto** as the permanent headquarters of Jodo-Shinshu Buddhism.

The *Main Hall (Hondo),* rebuilt in 1760, is a veritable art museum. Among Shinran's many talents was the ability to do artistic work himself. At the age of 71, he carved a sitting statue of himself which is to be seen today in the *Founder's Hall*. Gruesomely enough, he willed that his statue should be covered with lacquer in which his own ashes should be mixed. This was done. Despite the many vicissitudes faced by the sect, the devoted followers of Shinran zealously and successfully guarded his self-carved effigy. The *Seimon Gate*, reconstructed in 1643, is considered one of the finest gates in Japan. In the temple belfry hangs an ancient, renowned bell. Within the temple are the *Sparrow Chamber*, the *Wild Geese Chamber*, the *Stork Chamber*, and other picturesquely named rooms, the artistic motif of each furnished by its name. Wild geese, for example, are reproduced with gold leaf, and sparrows have been worked into the scheme in paintings and carvings. The *Stork Chamber*, now used as an audience hall by the abbots, was first used by Hideyoshi as his office. Much of its art work was created by the fine Japanese masters of the 17th and 18th centuries. In a section of the grounds, 16th-century buildings constructed by Hideyoshi include his lovely tearoom.

The GINKAKUJI TEMPLE (SILVER PAVILION) was built in 1479. Its intended silver plating was never applied; hence, the alternative name cannot be considered as accurate. Shogun Yoshimasa had the temple erected as a villa. The garden, which is composed of huge mounds of sand, is a classical example of a very unusual type of small Japanese landscaping in perfectly elegant taste. The little tearoom in the *Hall of Buddha* has served as a prototype for Japanese tearooms built since that time.

The HEIAN SHRINE of the late 19th century is multiply notable: (1) the large building is a replica, on a reduced scale, of the first 8th-century *Imperial Palace;* (2) it is the scene of two important festivals, including the *Jidai Matsuri* April 15th and October 22nd; (3) its garden is invitingly beautiful; and (4) the crimson *Otemmon Gate*, of two stories, is delightfully decorative, its crimson paint in vivid contrast with the blue tiles of the roof.

The CHION-IN TEMPLE. It is difficult to write of the

temples of **Kyoto** without a generous sprinkling of superlatives lacing the descriptions. The *Chion-In Temple* evokes almost all the colorful adjectives that one has at his command. Both in size and splendor, this headquarters of the Jodo sect of Buddhism is remarkable. It is renowned not only throughout the Buddhist world but through the Christian world as well. The gardens are lovely. They were designed by the landscape master, Enshu Kobori. Like so many of the other vast wooden structures, the temple was burned down on numerous occasions. The supernatural effects of the umbrella, under the eaves, supposed to have been left there by a deified young man, have apparently worked, however. This charm is believed to ward off conflagrations. It has lived up to advance notices, as the present buildings have gone undamaged since 1633. The corridor floors of the temple, like so many others, give off a curious bird-like sound when walked upon. The melodic bell in the belfry booms out its deep toned call each year during the week of April nineteenth to twenty-fifth in tribute to Honen, whose tomb is near by.

The SANJU-SANGEN-DO TEMPLE is an oblong shaped 13th-century Buddhist temple some 130 yards long. The present structure, which dates from 1251, has been declared a National Treasure. It is one of the oldest temples in the city. In many ways I have found the *Sanju-sangen-do Temple* to be the most intriguing that I have visited. The principal image is a *Thousand-handed Kannon* in a sitting posture, but it is not only this statue and those of the traditional 28 followers which are remarkable. The most amazing spectacle is that of the one thousand and one "holy women," each with 40 arms raised in blessing. Japanese often state that if one peruses the faces of these statues he is certain to find one bearing a resemblance to one of his relatives. These gilded images, all of an identical eight-foot seven-inch height, are arranged in spectacular tiers for the entire length of the building. They form an amazing picture. *Sanju-sangen-do* means "thirty-three spaces" and is significant as the number of intervals between the pillars of the temple. The ancient archery field to the rear of the temple has a curious background. Here archers tested their endurance and skill in a competition designed to see who could shoot the greatest number of arrows, between sunrise and sunset, across the entire length of the range, a distance of some 400 feet. The samurai Daihachiro, in 1696, shot more than 13,000 arrows during the daylight hours, with more than 8,000 of them reaching their mark.

The RYOANJI TEMPLE's 15th-century *Zen* type of garden is a classical one. Americans are not always immediately impressed with the simplicity of the *Zen* gardens, but they do grow on us and their charm soon captures our affection. In these gardens, barren rocks are arranged on sand in such a manner as to give the impression of vast space. From any spot one stands, one of these rocks is always invisible. The *Ryoanji Temple* occupies an important niche in Japanese history.

The ninth-century KIYOMIZU TEMPLE enjoys an exciting situation near the five-storied pagoda, *Yasaka.* The Tokugawan Shogun Iemitsu was an extraordinarily busy man. Among other things, he commanded that the *Kiyomizu Temple* be built in 1633. The main building emerges in spectacular Oriental-style flying buttresses from the edge of the sheer cliff of *Mount Otowayama.* An arduous 145 steps must be climbed to reach the wooden platform before the temple. The platform once achieved, however, affords a panoramic vista, overlooking the sheer drop, giving a magnificent view of the city.

The SAIHOJI TEMPLE possesses the oldest and rarest *Zen* gardens in Japan, completely covered with a deep carpet of rare varicolored mosses. Rigid in their over-all severity, rocks rising from the landscape have an uncannily beautiful effect. Other rocks, in the garden pond, symbolically represent islands where sailors rest during their long voyages. The quiet acres are called the "Moss Garden" and "The Philosopher's Garden" alternatively.

The HIGASHI HONGANJI TEMPLE, built early in the 17th century on a site near the present *Kyoto Railroad Station,* was conceived as the principal temple of the Jodo-Shinshu Buddhist sect. The present tall, graceful edifices were built late in the 19th century.

GION CORNER (Kyoto Visitors Club). For the small fee of $2.00, you may participate in the cultural activities of this newly formed group, organized by the hotels, travel agents, department stores, and public carriers. *Gion Corner,* located on the first floor of the *Yasaka Hall, Gion,* presents authentic insights into the Old and New Japan, presenting theater and art forms, court music and dancing, tea ceremonies, flower arrangements, puppet shows, and the *Geisha* and *Maiko-san.* For information call 6-1115 or the *Kyoto City Tourist Association,* 23-1936.

The Suburbs of Kyoto

ARASHIYAMA is one of the most scenic delights in Kyoto Prefecture. Whatever the season, it is worth a visit easily made in half an hour by car from the center of town, a bit less by electric rail. The entire hillside is covered with cherry, maple, and pine trees. In the spring, when the cherry trees are in bloom, the sight is most rewarding. In the fall, the area is aflame with tinted foliage, while all during the year it is covered with the green of the pines. Should your tastes be such that shooting the rapids appeals to you, this is the place for it. This exciting experience takes places from **Kameoka** to **Arashiyama,** a distance of nine exotic miles, winding up at the base of this beautiful hill.

The HOZU RAPIDS. The far end of the rapids at **Kameoka** can be reached by car from **Kyoto** in three quarters of an hour. The thrill of shooting the rapids is not marred by danger. The boats for this sport are completely safe, and the crews who man the flat-bottomed craft are skilled and capable. The river meanders picturesquely through rock-studded gorges and valleys.

Nara

NARA is a venerable city, 25 miles from **Kyoto,** with a jewel-studded history glittering with mementoes of a glorious past. Its historical relics and fame as an art center are second only to that of its illustrious neighbor. Though **Nara** now has a population of but 80,000, it shares with **Kyoto** the honor of having been an ancient capital of Japan, when, for 74 years during its eighth-century zenith, it reigned as the capital of all Japan. Today it is of the greatest interest to the visitor because of its idyllic natural setting, its showplace of the largest Buddha in Japan, its temples and shrines, its *Deer Park,* and its artistic products. **Nara's** foremost specialty is gorgeous lacquerware. Other superb products are ink sticks, writing brushes, fans, lanterns, beautiful, lifelike wooden dolls, and skillfully worked deer horns. Should time permit, you can spend a comfortable night at the excellent *Nara Hotel,* or you may visit this area quite conveniently from **Kyoto** by private car or motor coach.

Nara's setting is serene. Its lovely *Deer Park* and ponds afford a foreground of loveliness while *Mounts Kasuga* and *Wakakusa* in the background add to the charm of the locale. *Mount Kasuga* is the collective name for the several mountains in its group which form a sacred area believed to be the home of the gods. *Mount Wakakusa* is covered only with grass, the burning of which on the fifteenth of January each year provides a most awesome spectacle. The views from both *Mount Kasuga* and *Mount Wakakusa* are excellent. *Mount Wakakusa* is particularly recommended for a romantic moonlit night.

NARA (DEER) PARK. One of the most famed of the local attractions is the picturesque *Sarusawa Pond.* This prelude to *Nara Park* is a most romantic sheet of shallow water stocked with carp and turtles, lumbering fellows loafing around the pond's willow tree-fringed edge. The view of *Kofukuji Temple* mirrored in *Sarusawa Pond* is the most memorable of the photographic gems of the *Nara Park* area. The five-storied *pagoda,* in the *Kofukuji Temple* grounds just north of the pond, is the second highest in Japan, 165 feet. This structure was built in 1424 as an exact replica of an earlier pagoda which stood on this site and was burned to the ground. The park, second to none in all Japan, consists of beautiful meadows, gentle hills, and verdant woodland. The 150 tame deer provide a fascinating attraction to visitors, who take keen delight in feeding the gentle, sloe-eyed animals. These lovable creatures roam the park freely all during the day, willing photographic subjects for avid shutterbugs. Each deer has its own sleeping quarters, and when the sweet doleful sound of Japanese taps is heard, the little darlings form an orderly procession to return to their "homes" to retire together for the night. Each fall the horns of the deer are cut, an annual event which has become such a popular occasion with the natives as to resemble a full-fledged festival. *Nara Park* is a focal point for much of the local sight-seeing; everything is convenient to it.

In the NATIONAL MUSEUM adjacent to the park we find treasured paintings, expert sculptures, and richly engraved gems.

The TODAIJI TEMPLE, known as the GREAT EASTERN TEMPLE, contains the fabulous *Daibutsu,* or *"Great Buddha."* This awesome bronze image, the largest in Japan, is allegedly the biggest bronze statue in the world. The *Todaiji Temple,* belonging to the Kegon sect of Buddhism, has been chosen by them as their number-one temple and general headquarters.

Everything in the *Todaiji Temple* suggests awesome size. The hall of the *Great Buddha* is said to be the largest wooden building in the world. The original hall, burned in the late 12th century, was first reconstructed 15 years later. After it had been destroyed again and again by warring generals, fires, and storms, the present building was constructed in 1708. The 13-foot-high octagonal *Bronze Lantern,* standing before the hall, is considered to be an outstanding object of Japanese art of the 8th-century *Tempyo Period.*

The DAIBUTSU, or *"Great Buddha,"* the holiest object of

the temple, is held in reverential awe by the Buddhist populace. Great difficulties were encountered in attempting to cast such a mammoth image, and several failures were endured. Never daunted, the devout Buddhists continued their efforts and the statue was successfully cast in A.D. 749. The *Great Buddha* sits serenely with legs crossed and hands held in typical palms up Buddha posture. The significance of the hands as Buddhist symbols is of interest. In this case, the right hand posture is believed to impart ease of mind to the devout, while the left hand is believed to grant the wishes of the pious. When viewed at close range, the perspective is such as to make the heroic proportions seem even larger. The pedestal stands ten feet high, and the statue itself is 53.5 feet high. The face is sixteen feet in length and 9.5 feet in width, while the eyes are approximately four feet wide. The mouth is just less than four feet in width, the ears are 8.5 feet long, and the hands just under seven feet in length.

Back of the *Great Buddha,* a great gilt halo shines, while to

the right and left in front of the image are two unusual statues of wood. The one to the right deals out good fortune, and the one to the left imparts wisdom as well as good luck. These two statues are believed to be of the late 17th century. By all means don't miss the wooden Buddha in the rear of the hall. This image, known as *Komokuten,* one of the "Four Heavenly Guardians," is busy stamping fiercely on a despicable demon. *Komokuten* is popularly believed to eliminate anything which stands in the way of Buddhism and its followers. In the other rear corner, another of the guardians is busy torturing yet another ill-fated demon. Immediately to the right of the *Buddha* is a pillar in which a small square hole is to be found. It is believed that anyone who can pass through this opening is certain of entering paradise. Rykrisp, anyone?

The background of the *Buddha* is both illustrious and stormy. The dedication, which took place in April of A.D. 752, was one of the most celebrated in the history of the world. The Empress Regnant Koken attended ostentatiously with her mother and father, the ex-Emperor and Empress Shomu, plus the entire court and thousands of Holy Men and Women. One hundred years later, the *Great Buddha* lost its head to an earthquake. It was replaced six years later. In 1180, the *Great Hall* was burned and a hand and the head of *Daibutsu* were melted in the conflagration. A mid-16th century earthquake again beheaded *Daibutsu.* Since 1692, however, things have been relatively quiet in the *Daibutsu Great Hall.*

The SANGATSUDO (THIRD MONTH) TEMPLE, the oldest building of the *Todaiji Temple,* founded in 733, contains many priceless articles including the statue of the Fukukenjaku Kannon, made from dry lacquer. The statue is surrounded by more than a dozen other celebrated figures. Fukukenjaku Kannon has the imposing chore of sparing the populace from suffering. Apart from its rich lacquer, the statue contains a vast number of perfect pearls, astonishing agates, and sparkling crystals. *Sangatsudo*'s alternate name, *Third Month Temple,* is derived from the annual services for the *Hokke Scripture* held in March.

The SHOSOIN TREASURE DEPOSITORY stands in solitary splendor less than a quarter of a mile from the *Great Buddha Hall.* It reminds me, and I'm sure will you, too, of nothing if not a huge log cabin. It is executed in the Azekusa style, cleverly designed to preserve and protect its contents. There are three rooms which contain more than three thousand 8th-century priceless items, including jewels, glassware, silverware, musical instruments, wearing apparel, masks, and mirrors. This vast treasure was the property of the Emperor Shomu, who bequeathed it to the *Todaiji Temple.* The treasure is now the property of the *Imperial Household Agency.* A new concrete building is being erected to house the contents even more effectively. Not long ago a United States Senator suggested that a periodic inventory be taken of the gold in Fort Knox. Bravo! The Japanese do not have to be reminded of such important chores, however. The *Shosoin Treasure Depository* has an annual fall inspection when the storehouse is thoroughly cleaned and punctiliously checked by a representative of the *Imperial Household.* He performs this chore with great gusto and ceremony, not only checking each item carefully against the inventory but, when he is finished, all of the openings are ceremoniously sealed. It is curious to note how the ancient Japanese intuitively knew how to care for their priceless possessions. Timbers are piled triangularly within the Treasury building. When the humidity is high, the timbers absorb the damp, preventing humidity from desecrating the storage area. When the air is dry, the timbers exude enough moisture to provide a perfect balance. The entire building is constructed without the use of nails. A favorite pastime of the good-luck conscious Japanese is to toss pebbles lightly towards the chinks. Little stones that remain and do not fall to the ground bring the tosser great good fortune.

The KASUGA SHRINE, the 8th-century headquarters of the Fujiwara family, consists of four unbelievably beautiful and very tiny vermilion shrines. The galleries which surround and connect the shrines are also of great attraction. I don't know of another shrine or public building that has such a spectacular approach as that which leads to the handsomely colored and ornate *Kasuga Shrine*. The path is lined with thousands of impressive stone and metal lanterns which always present a picture of startling splendor, but when, at the bi-annual festivals of the *Setsubun* on February third and the *O-Bon* on August fifteenth, these lanterns are lit, they form a twinkling vista of fairyland proportions. The *Setsubun Festival* is the occasion of the *Kagura* sacred dance performed by young girls in the sacred dancing hall of the *Shrine*.

KASUGA-WAKAMIYA SHRINE, just south of the *Kasuga Shrine*, is also distinguished by its great collection of stone lanterns beautifying its approach. The famous *"On-Matsuri"* *Festival*, December seventeenth each year, is the foremost of the **Nara** festivals. On this day, simulated warriors clad in old armor and others wearing costumes of the 8th century perform impressively.

The THREE-STORIED PAGODA located above *Sarusawa Pond* dates from the 12th century. It is considered one of the most graceful pagodas in existence.

Other of the Important Cultural Properties, objects, temples, and shrines in the area are:

TO-KONDO, next to the *Five-Storied Pagoda,* containing the *Buddha Yakushi,* was originally of the 8th century, re-constructed early in the 15th century. *Hokuendo,* near the *Three-Storied Pagoda,* is an octagonal 8th-century hall, most recently redone in the 13th century. NAN-ENDO, near the *Three-Storied Pagoda,* contains a wooden statue of Fukuken-jaku Kannon. The NATIONAL MUSEUM OF NARA was built in the late 19th century to house ancient objects of art not otherwise protected. YADORIGI is famous as a tree which has been so treated horticulturally as to include a variety of trees and bushes such as wisteria, camellia, nandin, cherry, maple, and elder. Lovers come here and tie bits of paper to this agglomerated arbor since it is believed particularly favorable to those in love. TAMUKEYAMA SHRINE, of the 8th century, was rebuilt in the 17th century after having been destroyed by fire. The NANDAIMON *(Great South Gate)* is a magnificent structure 22 yards high guarding the *Todaiji Temple.* The original gate was 10th century; the present one, 12th century. The 8th-century KAIDAN-IN, near the *Great Buddha,* is guarded in its corners by the Four Heavenly Guardians. The BELFRY, near the *Great Buddha,* is renowned for its ponderous bell. NIGATSUDO *(Second Month)* TEMPLE, an 8th-century temple near the *Belfry,* is named in commemoration of the religious rite which was originally held in February. The ELEVEN-FACED KANNON, two of them, one known as the "Large Kannon" and the other as the "Small Kannon," are housed in the *Nigatsudo Temple.* SHIN-YAKUSHIJI TEMPLE, of the middle 8th century, houses a seated image and an Eleven-Faced Kannon. The KAIRYUOJI TEMPLE, near the station, was largely built early in the 8th century, but that which we may see today is thought to be of the 12th century. The HOKKEJI TEMPLE, near the *Kairyuoji Temple,* is best known for its Eleven-Faced Kannon and because it was built for the nuns of the country. The AKISHINODERA TEMPLE was begun in the 8th century, but the present buildings are of the 12th and 13th centuries. The head of the *Gigeiten* image housed in the temple is of the *Tempyo Period* while the body is of the *Kamakura Period.* The SAIDAIJI TEMPLE, of the 8th century, contains statues of the Four Heavenly Guardians. The *Saidaiji Temple* houses a wealth of 8th century treasures, including the statue of *Shaka-muni* and the *Twelve Silk Scrolls.* The YAKUSHIJI TEMPLE contains statues which go back to the 7th century. The temple, originally built in A.D. 680, was moved to its present site early in the 8th century; it was burned on several occasions, however, and most of the present buildings are from the 13th century.

DREAMLAND, the Japanese answer to Disneyland opened in 1961, has been designed for the young at heart of all ages. It was built in an incredible six months at the staggering cost, by Japanese standards, of 11 million U. S. dollars. The site of *Dreamland,* a vast 123,000 square feet will be remembered by many a G.I.; it was a housing area for dependents of U.S. military personnel during the 1945–52 postwar period of occupation. The Japanese are elated to point out that their wonder park is a combination of history, fun, adventure, legend, and fantasy. Conveniently situated a mile from the *JNR's Nara Station, Dreamland* is composed of five separate villages known as *Adventure Land, Fantasy Land, Frontier Land, Main Street,* and *Tomorrow Land.* Not to be outdone by Mickey Mouse's creator, the Japanese have encircled *Dreamland* with a real honest-to-goodness old-fashioned railway and have also supplemented this transportation with a monorail train. There is a genuine Mississippi paddle wheel steamer. In *Dreamland,* the visitor will see a faithfully reconstructed *samurai* (warrior) home, ancient Japanese shops, and a reproduction of an Old World tea house complete with *Geisha* service.

Promoter Kunizo Matsuo, entertainment man supreme, was a long and faithful student and admirer of the creator of Mickey Mouse, Pluto, Minnie Mouse, Donald Duck and the other animated masterpieces. Watching Disney's work in **Tokyo** over television he conceived *"Dreamland,"* an admirable mixture of the East and the West. Disneyland, frankly, does not have to worry, however, about this Japanese copy.

Man-made canals, lifelike beasts in natural "jungle" settings, a feudal castle, and "Sleeping Beauty Castle," an olden-times shrine, Japanese dwellings, "Miracle House," an 18th-century U.S. whaling boat, fountains, and a big big amusement park all lie flamboyantly in the confines of this truly interesting *"Dreamland."* Open from ten A.M. to ten P.M., the admission is sixty American cents (two hundred yen) for adults and half price for children twelve or under.

Osaka

OSAKA is a busy, bustling, vibrant city second only to **Tokyo** in size. Close to three million ambitious people dwell in this thriving industrial center of Japan, important economically and noted as a seaport. **Osaka,** an amazingly modern city graced with two fine hotels, enjoys a unique setting at the mouth of the *Yodo River* with numerous canals winding through the city such as to lend it the nickname of the "Venice of Japan." The horizon is notable for its numerous skyscrapers; streets like the tree-lined *Midosuji* are milling with activity. Private cars, taxis, buses, and streetcars nervously move about in great agitation from early each morning until evening. Despite the farsighted postwar plans for the city's rebuilding which encompassed wide streets and pleasant boulevards, the tremendous morning and evening rush-hour traffic far over-taxes the existing facilities.

Situated 18 miles from **Kobe,** 15 miles from **Nara,** and about 25 miles from **Kyoto, Osaka** commands an imposing setting slightly inland from *Osaka Bay.*

Osaka's renaissance as a world trade center is particularly impressive when one takes into consideration that the original strength of the commerce of this area was its economic intercourse with China. That gigantic land formerly was the principal purchaser of the Osakan products, including heavy machinery, various appliances, fabrics, yarn, and clothing.

This "Chicago of Japan," is well known to many American businessmen who make their way to **Osaka** and come away with bulging order books as well as arrangements for exchange of ideas, machinery, and produce. Despite its great industrialization and emphasis on economic matters, this city has for several centuries been the drama center of Japan. Even today **Osaka** and nearby **Takarazuka** are leaders in drama and musical entertainment for Japan. The greatest castle in the country is *Osaka Castle,* built by Hideyoshi Toyotomi in 1584.

Much of the area's commercial growth can be attributed to

Hideyoshi, whose life span carried him from 1537 to 1598. It was he who encouraged the surrounding districts to make **Osaka** the headquarters for their businesses. The city prospered for 267 years under the Tokugawan Shogunate, but the greatest population growth has taken place since 1889.

While it is quite true that only **Hiroshima** and **Nagasaki** were hit by atomic bombs, this does not mean that other Japanese cities did not suffer severe bombing damage. They did. **Yokohama, Tokyo, Kobe,** and **Osaka,** to name four, suffered incredible damage and costly casualties. Two-thirds of the population of **Osaka** either were casualties or left the city to seek a more healthy wartime climate. It is now known that the city was ticketed for "A-bomb No. 3." Since the war, however, the population has increased materially, many of the former inhabitants having moved back, and vast numbers of others have migrated to this prosperous city. Because of its tremendous industrial upsurge, the modern metropolis little resembles the **Osaka** of a few decades ago. Today it is a completely international industrial city, smothered with a great blanket of factories and commercial buildings. The night life is sophisticated and hilariously gay, and, in certain quarters, nefariously naughty. It is quite curious that the section of the city that today is particularly noted for gay night clubs, intimate bars, girly-girly shows, movie houses, theaters, and good restaurants was used as a burial ground for executed criminals until less than 80 years ago.

The main shopping center is in the *Shinsaibashi* and *Sakai-suji* areas, the former being a long broad thoroughfare stretching on both sides of the *Shinsaibashi Bridge,* lined with countless retail shops, including two noted department stores.

OSAKA CASTLE, the 16th-century product of the dreams and desires of Hideyoshi Toyotomi, is the principal tourist attraction of the city. As early as 1868, trouble descended on the great castle. When Emperor Meiji was busy abolishing the shogunate, troops of the Tokugawa Shogunate razed the magnificent *donjon* while retreating. The castle was not rebuilt in its present form until 1931. The concrete fortress, seven stories high, re-creates a splendid medieval spectacle, exuding an aura of antiquity even though served by a modern elevator. The exhibits in the *Historical Museum* are worth seeing if time allows.

Hideyoshi though merciless was a crafty and skilled leader of men. He encouraged the *daimyos* (feudal barons) to contribute to the cost of transporting great rocks from far off places to enhance the strength and beauty of the castle. Tens of thousands of men worked for more than three years arduously transporting and placing these great boulders in the castle's walls. The feudal barons competed among themselves as to who could supply the largest pieces of masonry. Some of these stones may still be seen in the original walls. The rocks of the most heroic proportions are named *Higo-ishi,* contributed by Lord Higo and measuring some 47 by 19 feet, and the *Octopus Stone (Tako-ishi),* which is 37 feet long and 19 feet high. It remains a mystery today how the giant monoliths of Stonehenge, England were transported under ancient conditions to their present resting place near Salisbury. The question also arises as to how these equally enormous rocks were manhandled from so many distant places. And once here, how were they raised into position? Today, the castle with its moat, soaring serrated roofs, cornices, and great stone base remains silent on this subject.

TENNOJI PARK, close to *Tennoji Station,* is the site of the city *Zoo,* a fine *Botanical Garden,* the *Art Museum,* sports and amusement areas. The 14-acre *zoo* is most realistic; the ferocious beasts parade about in full view of the visitors. The *Art Museum* is cram-packed with ancient *objets d'art.*

TAKARAZUKA. The story of the evolution of this city from a mediocre carbonic cold spring spa into a world-famed, internationally-renowned amusement center is one which is studded with romance to defy the imagination of even an Horatio Alger, Jr. The present pre-eminence of **Takarazuka** can be attributed to the brilliant clairvoyance, in 1919, of a young Japanese businessman, Mr. Ichizo Kobayashi, who dreamed big entertainment dreams. The town is unprepossessingly located on the *Muko River,* near *Mount Rikko,* between **Kobe** and **Osaka.** Kobayashi decided that he should first convert **Takarazuka** into a multi-attraction amusement center, and he well knew that to realize such a dream he must have multitudes of patrons, who could be in attendance only if their transportation to **Takarazuka** were to be provided rapidly and inexpensively. He constructed a small railway network linking this district with the nearby populated areas. The tiny but ultra-efficient railway, known as the *Keihanshin Kyuko Electric Line,* spans the distance from **Osaka** to **Takarazuka** in a brief 37 minutes, while the run to **Kobe** is completed in 35 minutes. Watch out, however; it is extremely crowded during rush hours!

AMUSEMENT CENTER AND ALL-GIRL OPERA. The foremost fame of **Takarazuka** is its *All-Girl Opera.* This company is owned, strangely enough, by the *Keihanshin Kyuko Railway Company.* A performance of the *Takarazuka Girls' Opera Company* is worth traveling halfway around the world to see. The settings are unbelievably stupendous, the costuming is rich and colorful, the choreography, musical arrangements, and orchestral effects unbelievably fascinating. The musical shows, comedy, operetta, and opera performed by the *Takarazuka Company* are in both western and Japanese styles. Normally half the show is a modern western stage revue and the other half is Japanese in atmosphere. The girls take both male and female parts. There are four **Takarazuka** companies, one of which is in performance at all times locally, while one performs in **Tokyo** at the *Takarazuka Theater,* one is on tour, and one is always in the process of rehearsing a new show. The girls are carefully selected young beauties averaging 20 years of age who undergo a stern two years of training in the *Music School* attached to the *Opera House.* The curriculum covers singing, acting, dancing techniques, deportment, and languages. The end results justify the fastidious means since the presentations are acknowledged to be the most exciting in the Far East. The precision troupes, known as *Zukettes,* have demonstrated their disciplined dancing all over the western world. The *Recreation Auditorium,* largest of the structures within the amusement center, encompasses three theaters, the largest of which is the *Opera House* used for the girls' company, seating 4,000 spectators and said to be the largest of its kind in the Orient. The next of the *Auditorium's* theaters is devoted to the cinema, and the third is used for a Japanese version of vaudeville. A very small fee will permit you to be amused in all three of these theaters.

The amusement park is large and exciting and includes: public and secluded baths, a *zoo* with built-in baby sitters, gardens, exciting carnival rides, refreshment booths, and shooting galleries. The *Takara Baien* plum orchard is ablaze with blooms in February and early March. Should you wish to linger longer amid the amusement attractions, there is an excellent western style hotel containing 70 rooms, where you may rest comfortably as long as you wish. A golf course is nearby.

Kobe

To many visitors traveling by sea, **Kobe** is their first point of contact with Japan. This is true of those voyagers who have arrived from Europe by way of the *Suez Canal.* This port city on *Osaka Bay* is rimmed with a natural back drop of picturesque mountains. It is the second busiest port in Japan and the most important gateway to southwest Japan. Japan's 6th largest city with a population of nearly a million and a quarter, **Kobe** is noted for its equable climate. By virtue of the rapidly expanding domestic airline network, this area is now a virtual suburb of **Tokyo,** the flying time being an hour and a half, or less. Practically without exception, all of the world steamship lines are represented here, and more than 200 foreign firms and agencies are located in the city to handle the enormous export and import trade which is now greater than that of **Yokohama.**

This port city was a favorite center of our bombers' attention during the Pacific War. Though one will not see any appreciable number of scars in the city, more than 60 per cent of the metropolis was flattened by Allied bombs.

Two favorite local trips are: (1) to *Mount Maya,* its summit 2,298 feet above sea level, and (2) to *Mount Rokko* of 3,057 feet altitude. The former is reached by cable car and ropeway to the summit, near which the 7th-century Buddhist temple *Toritenjoji* is nestled in a thicket of Japanese cedars. *Mount Rokko,* offering a small but thoroughly enjoyable pleasure center, may be ascended on foot, by motor, or by cable car. The golf course and clubhouse are inviting. *Mount Rokko* is a busy wintertime center for skaters and skiers.

The KOBE PORT TOWER, on the port's central pier, rises 358 feet above the water. The third-floor rotating restaurant provides an excellent observation platform.

ARIMA SPA, 1,200 feet up the north side of *Mount Rokko,* known for its salt and iron hot springs, acid gas springs, and cold carbonic acid gas springs, is particularly popular with the Japanese.

HIMEJI, 35 miles from **Kobe,** may well be visited to enjoy

the splendors of the remains of one of Japan's greatest citadels, the 15th-century castle constructed by the great Sandanori Akamatsu. *Shirasagijo,* better known as the "Egret Castle," is surrounded by delightful grounds, a segment of which is a public park. **Himeji,** which is both a manufacturing and shopping center of the district, is a busy communications focal point.

The Inland Sea National Park

I know of no place other than Japan where a body of water, with its islands and islets, has been declared a national park. The *Inland Sea National Park* is unique.

The *Inland Sea* is bordered on the east and the north by Japan's principal island of *Honshu.* Its southerly boundary is the island of *Shikoku,* its western boundary the great island of *Kyushu,* with its famed seaside resort area of **Beppu.** Within the *Inland Sea,* there are innumerable, and smaller, bodies of land. To the east and to the west of the large island of *Shikoku* are great channels connecting the *Inland Sea* with the *Pacific Ocean.* The islands and the shore line are indented and decorated with a natural charm and beauty that varies not only with each season but also with the period of the day. From the **Osaka-Kobe** gateway, the waterway extends some 300 miles to the coast of *Kyushu.* Some of Japan's most magnificent scenic beauty and richest associations of the past are to be found in this area.

Among the islands of the *Inland Sea* are some so small as to be merely delightfully tree-clad rocks; others are of sufficient size to include communities of considerable size. Because of the dependency of the natives on the sea, the coasts here have been the main source of supply for the sailors of Japan for centuries past. The waters are shallow and the fishing excellent. From the bordering towns and villages, hardy fishing fleets ply for a wide variety of fruits of the sea including crayfish, oysters, mullets, and others not so well known to us. Many Nisei-Americans of Japanese ancestry came originally from this "Aegean Sea of Japan."

While there are at least seven shipping lines which service all the important points of the *Inland Sea,* I believe that the best by far is the *Kansai Kisen Line.* Theirs is a large fleet. If I may extend a word of fatherly caution to you, I might point out that all of their ships are seaworthy and all are excellent by Japanese standards. Their newest ones, however, were completed in 1960 and 1964—the *M.S. Kurenai Maru, M.S. Murasaki Maru* and *M.S. Kohaku Maru*—and are among the finest vessels on which I have ever sailed. These sleek, streamlined beauties are equipped with excellent restaurants, a recreation hall complete with Cinemascope screen, a sky room, and an excellent bar. The speed of these vessels enables the *Kansai Kisen Line* to provide that one of the news ships is available daily for the run from **Osaka** and **Kobe** to **Beppu,** and reverse.

The various interesting routings of the line allow one to include such extraordinary views as the very lovely *Miyajima* and *Yashima,* the angry whirlpools at *Naruto, Shodoshima* with its magnificent masses of flowers and autumnal-tinted *Kankakei* crags, and the incomparable spa of **Beppu** with its hot springs and boiling geysers. It can be said with little fear of contradiction that the towns, villages, coast lines, and islands of the *Inland Sea* afford some of the most spectacular scenery in all of Japan.

While there are night and other day *Inland Sea* services with connections at various points, I recommend the daylight run from **Osaka-Kobe** to **Beppu** or vice versa. One may leave **Osaka** at 7:20 in the morning, **Kobe** at 8:40, and, after a stop at **Matsuyama** in the late afternoon, arrive at **Beppu** at 9:10 P.M. This is the most attractive way to see the *Inland Sea* in its various moods and with its natural splendors at their best. Overnight runs are not scenically rewarding. Despite the grimly early hour of the departure, you need not worry about your comfort. The breakfast, lunch, and dinners served aboard the ships are outstanding. The staterooms provided for first class passengers will enable you to rest comfortably at your pleasure during the day. Radios and ship-to-shore telephones are standard stateroom equipment. The public rooms are most comfortable.

PLACES OF INTEREST IN THE INLAND SEA

AWAJI ISLAND, 32 miles long and 17 miles across at its widest point, is the first major island seen after departure from **Osaka-Kobe.** Unless yours is a long, leisurely vagabond trip, you will probably not wish to take time to stop at *Awaji.* If you do, however, it is well known for its traditional *Bunraku* (life-size puppet shows) put on by local farmers and fishermen. **Sumoto,** the largest town on the island, situated on the east coast, owes its existence to the manufacture of roof tiles and buttons, the growing of onions, and the catching of sardines.

Shikoku

SHIKOKU is the smallest of the four principal islands of Japan, though it is by far the largest of the islands within the *Inland Sea.* Its population is approximately five million, and it covers an area of more than 7,000 square miles. *Shikoku* is adorned with a 6,500-foot mountain and decorated with fine forests, lovely gardens, tranquil rivers, splendid views, and the oldest hot spring resort in Japan. The air and sea transportation between *Shikoku* and both *Kyushu* and *Honshu* is efficient and frequent. The internal traffic is handled by four main railway lines which operate to all points of the island.

TAKAMATSU, *Shikoku's* principal port, is a pleasant city of some 150,000 inhabitants. The main street and the side lanes are extraordinarily colorful. *Ritsurin Park,* with its landscape gardens, zoo, art gallery, and commercial and industrial museum, is worth a visit. The cable car ride to the summit overlooking the city and the harbor is picturesque. There are two attractive Japanese inns, each of which has a few western style rooms. Should you stop over between ships, I can recommend that you dine at either the *Kawaroku* or the *Tokiwa Honkan.* You may choose either sukiyaki or a western style meal.

MEGISHIMA is a tiny, attractive island two miles from

Takamatsu, from which port there is a regular frequent ferry service to this gem-like island which is the setting for one of the old Japanese fairy tales.

MATSUYAMA is noted particularly for its 16th-century castle and the ancient **Dogo Spa** on a hillside within the city limits. The castle, heroically rising from a hill in the center of the town, has a fine three-storied tower. The climate is excellent throughout the year. There is an excellent rail service from **Takamatsu.**

KOCHI. Unless your visit to Japan is a prolonged one and your urge to wander far from the beaten path is compelling, it is not at all probable that your schedule will permit a thorough exploration of *Shikoku,* the smallest of Japan's four islands. There are, however, attractions here about which you should be informed.

In **Kochi** there is to be found a fierce breed of magnificent dogs known as *Tosa-Inu,* of heroic size comparable to the Great Dane. These ferocious dogs have the physique of a boxer and the biting grip of a bulldog. Originally developed by the *samurai* of antiquity as bodyguards, these highly prized animals are bred today as fighting dogs. No other dogfights are currently permitted in Japan but the fierce combats between the *Tosas* are not only legal, but the fights, usually held Saturday afternoons, are well attended and accompanied by brisk betting. The bouts are conducted along similar lines to those of *sumo* wrestling, even to the point where the beasts sport a topknot, much like the obese human competitors. The dogs have been trained to assault each other's throats while assiduously guarding their own. A referee who enforces the strict rules governing the contest is the sole arbiter in declaring the winner. *Tosa* matches are determined both by superiority of strength as well as by the weakness of one or the other of the combatants. Dogs may not whine or whimper but they may growl gutturally. The bout is of 30 minutes' duration and if, in that period, one dog has not overpowered the other, the referee will determine the victor on the basis of displayed weakness or fear.

OSHINO is not far from **Kochi** and here, too, we find the unusual, this time a fowl. The spectacular *naga-o-dori* roosters are native to **Oshino** where they have been bred for centuries. You have seen these incredible creatures portrayed on picture post cards. They are quite normal in every other respect, but their flowing white tails stream out behind them for 20 feet or more.

TOKUSHIMA is the home town for the production of some of Japan's most ingenious puppets, and for the *Awa "Crazy" Dance* each summer.

BULL FIGHTING is native to other of the *Shikoku* cities and villages, but it is not the type of toreador sport we know about. The Japanese version sees bulls competing against bulls. Makes more sense, doesn't it?

SHODO-SHIMA, located some twenty miles from **Takamatsu,** is one of the largest of the *Inland Sea* islands whose principal port, **Tonosho,** is conveniently available by steamship from **Osaka, Kobe,** and **Takamatsu.** Because of its "off the beaten path" setting, the island has, so far, escaped much of the modern trend in Japan and retains considerable of its ancient Old World charm, customs, costumes, manners, and morals. Flowers, beautiful shrubs, and ancient trees abound. In the spring, the cherry blossoms are a riot of color, while the azaleas bloom in early summer. The olive trees and the brilliantly colored maples decorate the autumn months. It is said that some of the giant rocks for *Osaka Castle* came from this area.

YASHIMA, known as the "Roof Garden of the *Inland Sea,*" was an island a few miles from **Takamatsu.** It is *now* a peninsula, having been joined to *Shikoku* by a strip of land. The view from the plateau which juts three miles into the sea is excellent. It is reached by a combination of electric train and cable car from *Takamatsu Pier*. The great sea battle between the feudal clans of Genji and Heike was waged here and the drowned Heike, so the legend says, became sea crabs. Maybe not, but take a look at the "faces" on the *Inland Sea* denizens and you'll see how the legend got started.

Kyushu

KYUSHU is the most southern and westerly of Japan's four principal islands. The climate of *Kyushu* is mild, and its scenic landscapes, particularly on the northwest and south coasts, are notable even in a country famed for such natural attractions.

BEPPU, the "Riviera of *Kyushu*," is its most important resort area and the terminal for the *Inland Sea* cruise ships. It is happily located on the main rail line to *Honshu*. **Beppu** may be reached from **Tokyo** and **Osaka** by plane to nearby **Oita** with which it is connected by helicopter. More than 300 outstanding hotels and Japanese inns are to be found in **Beppu** and vicinity. The setting over the azure blue waters of the *Inland Sea* is strikingly impressive. The city rises gracefully from the sea with its warm soft sand beaches extending to the mountains beyond.

Mount Takasaki, rising from the sea three miles from the piers, is the home of some 700 monkeys, who flock from the heights down to the park area to be fed twice a day. The feeding of the monkeys is a memorable experience and a photographer's paradise. These little mimics have, as their principal items of diet, tangerines and peanuts. Visitors may purchase these staples at roadside stands and from vendors in the park. I must warn you in advance that these clever little fellows are extraordinarily sly. If, for example, you should purchase a package of peanuts and start to feed a monkey one peanut at a time, you must be careful not to place the bag in an outer coat pocket. As surely as you do, either the one that you are feeding or one of his accomplices will dash up and steal the entire sack. The trick is to empty the contents into various inner pockets so that you can prolong the feeding fun. These little rascals are more persistent and persuasive beggars than the bears in the pits at Berne, Switzerland. The monkeys' dining habits, incidentally, are impeccable. They even remove the rinds from the tangerines! After the morning and afternoon feeding times, the little fellows return to the heights of the mountain. Local caretakers string up a pennant to indicate when the monkeys have descended.

There are innumerable local hot spring bathhouses, but none is more attractive than that in the *Suginoi Hotel*. The sands on the beaches are also considered to have curative powers. It is not unusual for Japanese visitors to bury themselves up to their necks in the warm, soothing sand to read or sleep in lazy comfort. There are also "sand baths" where one may be immersed in piping hot sand.

The hot springs swimming pool adjacent to the anchor point of the cable car running to the pleasure ground above is enormous, 165 by 82 feet. It is used for training international and professional swimming champions, and is not always open to the public, but during the late spring, summer, and early fall, visitors may swim daily in the water which has a temperature varying from 78 to 83 degrees.

On the outskirts of **Beppu** are a series of "hells" which are combinations of geysers and boiling, churning miniature lakes of mud and water. *Umi-jigoku (Sea Hell)* is the largest and one of the least active of this type of phenomenon. Its temperature approximates the boiling point. *Chinoike-jigoku (Boiling "Blood Pond" Hell),* an agitated churning small body of water with its colors varying in a chameleonlike manner from dirty yellow to a brilliant vermilion red, is constantly adorned with a steam halo. *Chi-no-ike (Pond of Blood),* 540 feet deep, offers water at a sizzling 170 degrees. *Tatsumaki (Tornado Hell)* is undoubtedly the most incredible of the geysers. Were it not controlled by artificial means, the boiling waters would be ejected to enormous heights, but a stone roof prevents this spectacular performance. The *Tatsumaki* is an "Old Faithful" in that its intervals between eruptions never vary. *Wani (Crocodile Hell)* presents a series of tepid pools.

Mount Tsurumi, 4,536 feet in height, towers behind **Beppu.**

Midway up the slope is **Kankaiji,** where one may enjoy a magnificent panorama of **Beppu,** *Beppu Bay,* and the entire countryside.

The immediately surrounding area includes the spas **Hamawaki, Kamegawa, Shibaseki, Kannawa, Myoban,** and **Hotta,** variously noted for their saline, iron carbonate, nitric acid, alum, and sulphur springs.

From whatever vantage point one views **Beppu,** vaporous columns are seen rising from open fields, wooded areas, and residential and hotel sections. The city and countryside are virtually alive with molten mud, boiling waters, and natural steam. It is quite possible to cook by the natural steam which emerges from the ground below.

The ASO NATIONAL PARK is a unique mountainous area which includes *Mount Aso* (5,253 feet) and *Mount Kuju* (5,900 feet). While *Mount Aso* is not handsome as mountains go, it does possess a tremendously active volcanic crater even though four of its five craters are now peacefully somnolent. *Naka-dake* is a churning, gurgling mass of molten lava which last erupted in 1933. Motor excursions may be made from **Bochu** to the summit of *Mount Aso* where one finds *Aso Kanko,* a marvelous Alpine chalet with an outdoor hot springs swimming pool.

NAGASAKI, on the west coast of *Kyushu,* is not only the best known of the cities of *Kyushu* but also one of the most favorably situated. Located on *Nagasaki Bay,* a short distance from the *China Sea,* its approach by sea is sheltered by a series of picturesque islands.

Nagasaki is the nation's most ancient port with a fascinating historical background. Through this portal the customs, religious background, and philosophy of the west first entered isolated Japan as early as the 16th century. Her port played a vital role in the early development of trade with the western world and also heralded the advent of Christianity into Japan.

Nagasaki was sorely wounded by the second atomic bomb attack. Because of its sheltered location and surrounding hills, the damage here, though horrible and heart-rending, was por-portionately much less than that suffered at **Hiroshima.** Since the holocaust of August 9, 1945, the city has been completely rebuilt, but, unlike **Hiroshima** which has been greatly mod-ernized and reconstructed without attention to charm, **Naga-saki** has retained its exotic Eastern character.

One of the city's splendors, and visitors' paradises, is *Kaza-gashira Hill* which overlooks the port. The summit, reached by cable car, rewards the visitor with an opportunity to dine or spend the night at an excellent restaurant-hotel, the *Yataro,* where at night diners and sojourners may watch the brilliantly lit city below, the blinking lights of the liners anchored in the bay, and the silhouettes and shimmering lights of the islands beyond.

The same surrounding hills which served as an effective buf-fer for the atomic bomb also do much to temper the excellent climate. The summer's heat is moderated by the zephyrus sea breeze, while the winter is not severe. The city's resi-dential section, impressively situated, is reminiscent of **Naples'** *Vomero* area. The dwellings and apartments rise tier on beau-tiful tier from the waterfront *Bund.*

The Mitsubishi enterprises are famous throughout the world. This one-time family institution is heavily involved in retail business and in various manufacturing enterprises. This opu-lent name appears every place in Japan. Their local shipbuild-ing activities are particularly ambitious, being the greatest economic enterprise of the area. While, as a nation, Japan ranks first ahead of Great Britain and America in the shipbuilding world, it is also said that more merchant oceangoing tonnage is produced here by this one firm than any place else in the world. Because of the prime importance of **Nagasaki's** ship-building activities and also as a result of its aircraft production, collaterally generated by Mitsubishi, this doomed town was singled out for the second devastating atom bomb although it was an alternate target. The weather around the prime target—**Yawata,** a steel works community dubbed "Japan's Pittsburgh"

—was "socked in" that fatal morning, thereby dooming the Madame Butterfly city.

Don't fail to sample **Nagasaki's** famous and delectable *kasutera* cake, introduced to Japan by the Spaniards in the 1600's. This special spongecake, also known as *kastera,* also is claimed to have been introduced by Portuguese sailors.

The "modern" history of **Nagasaki** began with the landing of Portuguese sailors in 1543. These seafarers brought with them guns and pistols most welcome to the Japanese during this tempestuous *Muromachi Period* of fierce fighting among the warlords. The Portuguese and Japanese struck up an instantaneous mutual affection. Six years later, the renowned Jesuit priest, Francis Xavier, arrived accompanied by a group of adventuresome Spanish merchants. He wrote originally, "These people are the best we have so far discovered; no better could be found among the infidels." As a result of his zealous efforts and the good influence of the other Portuguese and Spaniards, *Kyushu* was the first of the islands to embrace Christianity which then spread to the other principal islands to such an extent that even the powerful general Oda Nobunaga officially recognized the Christians. Other warlords went so far as to dispatch emissaries halfway around the world to **Rome** to be received in audience by the Holy Father. The fanatical Spaniards, however, first had difficulties with the more broad-minded Portuguese and subsequently, by virtue of their arrogance and high-handed methods, ran afoul of important Japanese including Hideyoshi. Soon the Christian religion was banned. The devout followers were forced underground, and observance of their religion had to be carried on surreptitiously. Notwithstanding, trade between Japan, **Portugal,** and **Spain** continued to flourish. Shortly after 1600, the Dutch East India Company came, followed a few years later by British traders. Until the early part of the 17th century, the persecution of the Christians had been relatively mild, but under the third shogun, Iemitsu, the situation took a turn for the worse. He clamped down on the Christians like a vise. Because of their revolt against their persecutors, the Jesuits in *Kyushu* were subsequently massacred.

In 1639 the Japanese ports were closed to the popular Portuguese, the Spaniards having been banned by edict in 1624. For 200 years, Japan was again virtually isolated from the world. By the middle of the 17th century, the only trade carried on by Japan with the western world was with **Holland.** The Dutch were permitted to send one ship a year to *Kyushu.* Normal trade continued, however, with neighboring **Korea** and **China.** This isolation continued until Commodore Perry came along to break the bars of the Bamboo Curtain.

SUWA PARK and SHRINE, northeast of the city, are of particular interest to us Americans because it was in this park in 1879 that General and Mrs. Ulysses S. Grant planted a banyan tree which stands today as an arboreal monument to their visit. The intrepid western scholars who brought the word to the Japanese on medical and botanical sciences are also commemorated here in stone. The shrine is particularly noteworthy because of its 30-foot bronze *torii* and its association with the *Autumn Festival.*

The ROMAN CATHOLIC CHURCH OF OURA was erected in the 16th century as a memorial to 26 fearless and devout Christians who were martyred. The church was badly damaged by the atomic bomb.

The ROMAN CATHOLIC CATHEDRAL OF URAKAMI was another atom-bomb victim, but its ruins are of historic interest. This great cathedral, dedicated in 1941, and the largest in Japan, stood in tribute to the great number of Christians who were persecuted but whose faith never wavered. The cost of the cathedral was defrayed by the local Christians. A new cathedral will soon duplicate the original.

PEACE PARK AND CULTURAL CENTER. The recently completed gleaming white *Cultural Center* is near the green marble *Memorial Monument* marking the center of the atomic explosion. A large area is being properly prepared to serve as a *Peace Park* to commemorate the minute, day, and year (August 9, 1945 at 11:30 A.M.) when death rained from the sky. The *Peace Statue* is impressive.

MADAME BUTTERFLY'S HOUSE is almost unique. The hillside home of the operatic beauty is paralleled only by the London residence, near Baker Street Station, of A. Conan Doyle's fictional Sherlock Holmes. *"Madame Butterfly"* is an Italian musical drama based on an American play set in Japan. "Madame Butterfly's house" is nestled amid a magnificent but tiny Japanese garden with a splendiferous view of the bay. One can hear, in reverie, the haunting strains of Puccini's music as Pinkerton visits the octagonal summer house. It is possible vividly to envision the little *Geisha* who pined her heart out here for her handsome but faithless naval officer. The fact that the vast commercial Mitsubishi organization bought the house and donated it to the city of **Nagasaki** and that it once was the property of an English resident, a Mr. Glover, in no way lessens the sentimentality of a visit to Madame Butterfly's home. Puccini was never here.

Nagasaki's principal festivals are the *Suwa Shrine Festival (O-Suwa Matsuri)*, held early in October; the *Bon Matsuri*, known alternatively as the *Feast of the Lanterns* and the *Festival of Departed Souls*, which takes place July 13, 14, and 15; *Peiron*, which takes place in early June; and *Hata-age*, the *Kite-Flying Festival*, in April. (See Chapter Seven.)

FUKUOKA-HAKATA (KITAKYUSHU) is the largest commercial and industrial center in *Kyushu's* province of Fukuoka. These are twin cities à la Minneapolis and St. Paul, with the *Naka River* playing the Japanese version of the mighty Mississippi. These cities, with several suburbs, have now amalgamated into one metropolis known, as of 1964, as **Kitakyushu.** **Kitakyushu** is a typical large Japanese industrial city and trading port with busy commercial, shopping, and amusement centers located around the *Higashi-Nakasi* area. Of the five universities which are found in this enlightened city, one is devoted exclusively to women.

Historically, **Hakata** figured in the battles of the 13th-century Mongol invasions, when the fierce forces of Kublai Khan were twice repelled. The first time that Kublai Khan's forces were routed was by virtue of superior Japanese numbers and strength. The second time a combination of an anti-invasion wall and a fortuitous typhoon—the *"Kamikaze"*—took care of the invaders.

The two city parks are known as the *Higashi-koen (East Park)* and the *Nishi-koen (West Park)*, the former being particularly noteworthy for its pine forests and the impressive monument constructed in honor of the victories over the Mongols. The *West Park* is chiefly noted for its enchanting view over *Kyushu's Hakata Bay* and the azure blue waters of the sea beyond.

The HAKOZAKI HACHIMAN SHRINE of the Hachiman sect is of unique construction, especially its 16th-century gate in which no nails are used. The shrine houses a fine exhibition of mementoes of the Mongol invasions.

The **Fukuoka-Hakata** professional baseball team, the *Nishitetsu Lions,* is the only professional baseball nine in *Kyushu.*

MOJI, at the northeastern extremity of *Kyushu,* is washed by the waters of the *Shimonoseki Strait,* the northwestern extremity of the *Inland Sea.* **Shimonoseki** is the first town one reaches in *Honshu* when traveling from *Kyushu.* **Moji** and **Shimonoseki** are connected by underwater tunnels which carry the coastal trains of the *National Railways,* as well as vast numbers of vehicles and pedestrians. For centuries **Moji** was an insignificant village, but since 1887 when it became a terminus of the *Kyushu* railroad, it has been one of the busiest trading ports in *Kyushu.* Today the port is a significant one in international commerce. It was also because of the area's proximity to **China** and **Russia** that **Moji** became increasingly important during the wars at the end of the 19th century and the beginning of the 20th century. **Moji** is now an industrial city of extreme importance, boasting of steel and iron works and a flourishing export-import business.

UNZEN-AMAKUSA NATIONAL PARK lies directly

south of **Nagasaki** as the sea gull flies but is some three or more hours by the roundabout land route. This national park, the center of the *Shimabara Peninsula,* includes the islands of the *Amakusa* group and the waters of *Ariake* and *Chijiwa Bays.* *Mount Unzen,* a now extinct volcano, is a mélange of peaks, the loftiest of which, *Mount Fugen-dake,* rising to some 4,500 feet, may be reached by cable car. In the park are innumerable springs, geysers, and recreational facilities. In certain areas, the park's coloration is multi-hued, not unlike the *Grand Canyon* of the *Colorado River.* Arthritis and skin disease sufferers claim great relief from the *Unzen* springs.

UNZEN SPA is an internationally famous resort delightfully situated 2,400 feet above the sea. Its elevation moderates both the summer and winter temperatures. The combined resort includes *Furu-yu (Old Springs), Shin-yu (New Springs),* and *Kojigoku (Little Hell).* The beaches of *Chijiwa, Obama, Katsura,* and *Shimabara* are invitingly situated at the base of the *Unzen-Amakusa Park* mountains. They may be reached by car from **Unzen Spa** in less than an hour.

SHIMABARA. Were it not the site of the sad trials of the early persecuted Christians, **Shimabara** perhaps would be of little interest to the outside world. But the Christians were persecuted, and it was here, in 1638, that they fought their last-ditch battle against the troops of the Tokugawa Shogunate. The ruins of the castle associated with the Christian rebellion are just west of the modern *Shimabara Station.* The entire area immediately to the south, as far as **Kuchinotsu,** is associated with the travail of the Christians.

Shimabara is a peninsula port lying across the bay to the west of **Kumamoto.** Ships ply from here to **Omuta** on *Ariake Bay* and to ports to the south on *Yatsushiro Bay.* The bays are alive with delightful islands well known for white sandy beaches and a profusion of pine trees. Probably the most beautiful of the islands are those of the *Tsukumo* group which owe their origin to the eruption of *Mount Bizan* in 1792. Vast quantities of lava formed the submarine base for these beauties.

Hokkaido

The fourth, least known, most northerly, and one of the most attractive of Japan's four main islands is *Hokkaido*. The southern tip of *Hokkaido* lies a "fur piece" (as we adopted Hoosiers say) directly north of **Tokyo,** 878 miles as the crow flies from the capital to the southern tip of this lush island and another 269 miles to its most northerly prefecture. My favorite golf pro, Bob Harris of Sunset Ridge, is neither verbose nor one given to making exaggerated statements. After having returned from occupation duty there, he told me that he thought this island was one of the most beautiful spots he had ever seen, and even now he emphasizes again and again how utterly natural and unspoiled *Hokkaido* is. I, too, think it is a perfectly delightful island.

Cape Oma, Honshu's most northerly point, and *Matsumae, Hokkaido's* most southerly point lie more or less directly opposite one another across *Tsugaru Straits,* though in a direct north-south line the narrowest gap between *Hokkaido* and *Honshu* is eleven miles due north of *Cape Oma.*

The ship service between *Honshu* and *Hokkaido* is quite good, with a variety of routes being available. *Hokkaido* is interlaced with excellent rail communications. You will have no problem getting about. There are five principal ferry services between *Honshu* and *Hokkaido,* the crossings varying from a trip of a few hours up to as much as two and a half days from the south. I rather suspect, however, that you will not be wandering around footloose and fancy free in northern *Honshu* ready to hop a boat for *Hokkaido.* Should you wish to follow my advice and visit *Hokkaido,* you will no doubt want to fly from **Tokyo** to **Sapporo,** the capital. The air service is excellent.

As one would correctly suspect, *Hokkaido's* climate is definitely different from any and all of the other three main islands. *Hokkaido's* winters are long, cold, and crisply dry. One may expect the first of the lacy snow petals to tumble wistfully down in October, and the fluffy white stuff may be seen daily for at least six months thereafter. The western prefectures enjoy the most mountainous collections of snow, with depths of ten or more feet on the ground for long periods of time. To the east, under the soothing influence of the *Pacific Ocean,* the winter's snow is generally in evidence but to a much lesser degree.

Hardy serious skiers flock to *Hokkaido* where the runs and the resorts are among Japan's best, with the snow being ideal for skiing. Excellent ice skating is thrown in for good measure. Unlike *Honshu,* which has the questionable blessing of voluminous summer rains, August is *Hokkaido's* driest month, with the average daytime temperature being only 70 degrees Fahrenheit. Just ideal. On the other islands, the loveliest months of the year are September and October, while in *Hokkaido* they are the dampest months. The transition from winter to full-blown spring comes about with abrupt suddenness with the melting away of the last snow. Should you be planning a summer trip to Japan, I can recommend that the months from June through September are ideal for visiting this northern paradise.

THE AINUS. The unusual feature of *Hokkaido's* populace most generally discussed by the returning visitor is the famous, intensely interesting, now scanty aboriginal population known as the *Ainu.*

It is curious that these tiny, lovable people have their history completely intertwined with Japan but actually are not in any manner, way, shape, or form, Japanese. There is just no physical connection between these people and their hosts, for they must be considered guests of the Japanese à la "The Man Who Came to Dinner." The *Ainus* have broad features and blue eyes. By nature generously endowed with hair, they let it grow long, sporting fantastic beards and moustaches. There are numerous theories relative to the origin of the *Ainus,* but none has been fully substantiated. The generally held theory is that they originated in the north, quite probably in **Siberia** and entered Japan via *Sakhalin Island.* This is partially borne out by the fact that names of *Ainu* origin are found in the Siberian coastal districts. Others theorize that the *Ainus* conceivably are of Manchurian or Mongolian extraction, but my own anthropologic advisors tell me I can state, with no fear of contradiction, that they are Caucasians. Q.E.D. Whatever their ethnological background, they populated *Hokkaido* centuries before the forebears of the modern Japanese. In the early records, the *Ainus* are referred to as *"Emishi,"* which was, not by coincidence, the name by which *Hokkaido* was then known.

Modern *Ainus* are charming, quiet, well-mannered, and most anxious to please the visiting tourist. For a very small fee they will be delighted to show you their homes and indoctrinate you in their way of life. Their fishing boats are a source of great pride to them, and they gladly display them. The homes of the chiefs, even more noteworthy than those of the followers, may be visited. The present manners and habits differ widely from those of long ago since the *Ainus* have, in a simple way, become quite modernized. Their villages are widely scattered throughout *Hokkaido,* but the two most accessible and most interesting are **Shiraoi,** near *Noboribetsu Spa,* and **Chikabumi,** near **Asahigawa.** The women tattoo blue moustaches on their upper lips. The bear is the *Ainu* god. The *Ainus* today have all but disappeared, and those remaining, if they can be considered pure stock, ply the tourist trade by showing their old artifacts and carving souvenir bears holding fish in their mouths.

Hokkaido, like Japan in general, owes the United States much for its development from a semi-primitive state of existence into a modern entity graced with pleasant amenities and a comfortable way of life. The island was barren and undeveloped until the 1868 *Meiji Restoration,* when even the capital, **Sapporo,** was but a mere village. The Meiji government, however, in its progressive way, was alert to the island's tremendous potential. Soon American engineers and agricultural experts, many from the New England states, were invited to Japan to survey and help develop *Hokkaido.* The tremendous local advances in agriculture may be attributed largely to Horace Caprin, an expert agrarian who was sent to Japan in 1872 by President Grant. In four years this brilliant man taught the is-

landers modern American agricultural methods. He transformed many of them from the tiniest of tiny farmers to learned
agriculturalists able to emerge from virtual one-man operations
to mass methods and to convert much of the wasteland to richly
producing acreage. It was he who inspired the city planning for
Sapporo and who introduced the innovation of streets and boulevards which crossed each other at right angles. Professor W. G.
Clark, another American, played a prominent part in the development of *Hokkaido*. It was he who was responsible for the
University of Hokkaido and its farseeing scientific development.
He has been commemorated by a 15-foot granite column near
Sapporo's capitol building, which bears a bronze plaque in-
scribed, tersely: "Boys, Be Ambitious." The Hokkaidans have
become just what he besought them to be during his stay there.

Hokkaido's land area, approximately 21 per cent of Japan's
total, is administered by a governor.

On *Hokkaido* we find the *Daisetsuzan National Park,* the
most extensive in Japan, and the *Ishikari River,* 227 miles in
length. The cultivation of rice and other agricultural products
is the principal activity of the island, though there are some
coal mines, and commercial fishing is also important. In a minor
league sort of a way, some timber is cut, and cattle raising and
dairy farming play a small part in the economic life of the
island.

The earliest records in which credence may be placed are
from the mid-7th century. At that time, a chief from *Hokkaido* led an assault against *Shukushin,* which is now a possession of the U.S.S.R. For a considerable period of time until the
mid-15th century, *Hokkaido* was a favorite hideout for the
legions of defeated enemies of Yoritomo. Ultimately, the losers
got together and formed a group who became powerful followers of the Tokugawa Shogunate. As a result, they were given
land to be under their exclusive control in the southwest of
Hokkaido. When other supporters of the Shogunate were defeated in 1868, they, too, took refuge in **Hakodate.**

HAKODATE, together with its environs, declared an open

port in 1859, is the home of the fishing fleet of the island. *Hokkaido University* features a *Fisheries School* with a specially trained faculty who give courses in the theory and practice of commercial fishing and marketing. Hakodate's surroundings are charming and exquisitely attractive.

The *City Hall* is near the railway station, while the fine residential area is located to the east of *Mount Hakodate*. The manufacturing center is to the north. The *Archaeological Museum* of *Hakodate Park* is of some interest, while *Hakodate Fort (Goryokaku)* is perhaps best known for the resistance against government troops put forth here by a naval force in 1868. The cherry trees of **Hakodate,** clustered about the fort, make a showy display in April. The moat freezes in the wintertime.

Yunokawa Spa, approximately four miles away, may be reached by electric train, motorbus, or taxi.

The TRAPPIST MONASTERY FOR MEN is a short distance from **Oshima-Tobetsu,** some sixteen miles from **Hakodate.** Men visitors are welcome each day. The Trappists are famed for their butter and their dairies.

The TRAPPIST CONVENT FOR WOMEN, about 60 miles from **Hakodate,** may be visited daily but by women only.

All members of the *Trappist Monastery* and *Convent* have taken vows of silence.

ONUMA PARK AND LAKES lie 17 miles north of **Hakodate.** The three lovely lakes *Onuma, Konuma,* and the tiny *Junsai-numa* lie within *Onuma Park,* popular as an all-season playground. The lakes are studded with tiny islands whose enchanting scenery may best be enjoyed by boat. You will have no difficulty in renting a craft should you care to make such an excursion. The volcanic rock structure of the shores of *Onuma* and *Konuma* conspires to create a weird but fascinating effect. The lakes freeze to a smooth solid surface early in the winter, and skaters delight in wending their frosty way among the islands.

SHIKOTSU-TOYA NATIONAL PARK, which lies north of **Hakodate** and *Uchiura Bay*, is known for *Mount Yotei (Ezo-Fuji), Lake Toya,* and *Lake Shikotsu. Yotei* is among the highest of *Hokkaido's* peaks and a favorite target of Japanese Alpinists, who strike out from **Kutchan** when attempting to attain its summit. Its slopes provide excellent runs for skiers. The base is generously dressed with trees, though the format changes about halfway up the slope to rock and lava formations. The crest is usually powdered with snow throughout the year.

LAKE TOYA, graced with an inviting island in its center and **Toyako Spa** on its shore, is equidistant between **Hakodate** and **Sapporo.** The accommodations at the spa are limited to Japanese inns.

LAKE SHIKOTSU, best reached from **Sapporo,** offers the most exquisitely beautiful setting of the picturesque natural scenic attractions of *Hokkaido.* It is located on the 820-foot summit of a hill, surrounded by higher peaks whose cliffs plunge steeply to *Shikotsu's* shimmering waters. Its very seclusion adds to its total charm. Should you plan to arrive at *Lake Shikotsu* by train from **Sapporo,** the station to look for is *Chitose,* where taxis and motor coaches are available. *Shikotsu's* trout literally fight with each other to get on your hook, and the delicious crawfish called *zari-gani* are found almost exclusively here. *Marukoma Spa* on the shore of *Lake Shikotsu* has *Mount Tarumae* as its smouldering backdrop.

NOBORIBETSU SPA, both celebrated and ecstatically situated, is readily available from **Sapporo** and **Hakodate,** some 70 miles from the former and 129 miles from the latter. The spa and its surroundings abound in hot springs and other awesome natural phenomena. The *Valley of Hell (Jigoku-dani)* is a vast crater housing a heaving mass of boiling water from which a constant halo of steam emanates. This sinister scene is in violent contrast to the placid verdant greenery of the nearby hovering mountain slopes. Above the crater is a seething mud and water lake from which emerges the *Oyu-numo* sulphur springs. The extraordinary lake, encircled by steep cliffs, has a fatal fascination for suicide-bent individuals, many of whom have hurled themselves to their death in this boiling ebony mess. The volcanic peak across the lake is in a constant state of activity. Clouds of smoke continuously belch forth.

Noboribetsu Spa, frequently thought of as the "**Beppu** of *Hokkaido*," is maintained principally for tourists and for those whose various ailments are thought to be benefited by the hot springs. Here every imaginable medical facility is available. The *Takimoto Hotel*'s private hot spring baths are not only large and impressive, but the modern way of doing things has not reached here as in the moving outside world. These steaming baths are used by related and unrelated men, women, boys, and girls all together and all completely in the nude. Fun! Should you participate—and why not?—be sure to remember that you bathe before you enter the bath. It might be paradoxical, but nonetheless it is certainly a rude lapse of etiquette to start soaping up in the communal bath.

SAPPORO, capital city of *Hokkaido*, is the island's center of government, education, trade, and commerce. A modern city, it reflects the strong American influence exerted in its planning and construction. **Sapporo's** suburbs are extensive, with numerous suburban trains running as far as 45 miles into the country. There are three railway stations in town, all owned by the *National Railway Line (JNR)*.

Among the points of interest in **Sapporo** are:

The NAKAJIMA PARK, near the center of the city, is graced by ponds decorative in the summer and excellent for ice skating in the winter.

MARUYAMA PARK, whose baseball park has been used by visiting American teams.

The AINU MUSEUM, known as the Bachelor Museum and dedicated to the English Minister John Bachelor, in the *Hokkaido University Botanical Gardens,* where some 20,000 items pertaining to the strange but gradually dying out *Ainu* race of people are on exhibit. The BEAR PITS are intriguing.

The N.H.K. TELEVISION AND OBSERVATION TOWER soars 480 feet above the city. Its observation tower is 295 feet above the ground.

It is fitting that the capital city of *Hokkaido* should best be thought of in connection with the island's most famous sport, skiing. Here we find some of the best ski slopes in Japan and the highest ski jump in the Orient. The latter has been used for both domestic and international competitions.

JOZANKEI SPA is located 980 feet above sea level on the upper reaches of the *Toyohira River*. The splendid rock scenery is particularly noteworthy as is the popular skiing. The waters of the hot springs not far from the city are, as is the local custom, piped to the various hotels and homes.

DAISETSUZAN NATIONAL PARK is the largest in Japan. Much of its park area is completely virgin territory to overseas visitors and almost entirely unknown even to its Japanese visitors. Almost exactly in the geographical center of *Hokkaido,* the *Daisetsuzan National Park* includes lofty volcanic ranges, four of whose peaks exceed 7,000 feet. Snow capped *Mount Asahi* soars to 7,513 feet, making it *Hokkaido*'s most altitudinous. Magnificent primeval forests and vast areas bedecked with Alpine flowers cover the lower slopes of the mountains. To compensate for its lack of lake scenery, the park possesses several large rivers which wind their way through the valleys amid enchanting scenery. The *Ishikari River,* rising in the *Daisetsuzan Mountains,* is the longest in *Hokkaido,* with its course meandering 227 scenic miles before it flows into the *Sea of Japan* at the port town of **Ishikari.** *Lake Shikaribetsu,* on the southeastern borders of the park, is its lone body of water. Surrounded by precipitous cliffs, on a clear calm day, the lake reflects, under azure blue skies, their images in its shimmering waters. **Kohan Spa** and **Yamada Spa** are on the shores of *Lake Shikaribetsu.*

The motor routes to the park are varied and breathtaking. They all show us impressive mountains and forest scenery, waterfalls, and gorges. The popular **Sounkyo Spa** route, starting from **Kamikawa**, is dominated by great cliff formations and thundering waterfalls. *Mount Asahi* may be seen in the background. The route via **Fukiage Spa** is particularly favored by winter sports enthusiasts. Excellent skiing is available on the *Tokachi* mountain slopes.

AKAN NATIONAL PARK, third in size of *Hokkaido*'s national parks, is also most attractive and secluded. The mountain and forest landscape is enhanced by beautiful crater lakes. Their steeply wooded shores and tree covered islands create an impression of remote mystery. The park embraces two districts: *Kutcharo* which includes *Lakes Mashu* and *Kutcharo,* and *Akan* including *Lake Akan. Kutcharo*'s two lakes are separated by a group of volcanic hills with **Kawayu Spa** cuddled at their base. While summer is really the ideal time to visit *Akan National Park,* winter sports enthusiasts will find skating and skiing. *Lake Akan* is in a captivatingly lovely setting surrounded by steeply forested hills with a score of picturesque tree-covered islets on its placid surface. Apart from its scenic beauty, the lake is noted for a rare and curious weed, spherical in shape and green in color, which acts as a barometer to indicate the state of the weather. When the weather is fair, it emerges clearly above the lake's surface, but when the weather is bad, the weed submerges. This water plant is officially protected. Nobody may cut, harvest, or collect it. Two peaks, *Me-Akan* and *O-Akan,* rise from the lake's southern shore. *Mount Me-Akan* is volcanic, while *O-Akan* is now extinct. Both **Kawayu** and **Teshikaga Spas** have small but excellent Japanese inns.

LAKE MASHU, a lovely crater lake facing the 2,180 foot *Mount Mashu,* is completely encircled by sheer volcanic cliffs. The reflections of the green-hued mountains and the wooded island in its center combine to give the lake a romantic atmosphere.

LAKE KUTCHARO, the second largest in *Hokkaido,* with a tree covered island several miles in circumference, is encircled by steep forest-clad hills. There are boating and fishing facilities.

KUSHIRO is the canning, paper manufacturing, and lumber export city of *Hokkaido,* near *Akan National Park.*

CHAPTER 13

The Philippines

THE PHILIPPINES archipelago consists of over 7,107 enchanting islands spread over a vast area covering 1,155 miles north to south and 695 miles from east to west. 2773 of the Philippines' islands have been named, but only 466 are more than a mile square. The archipelago is divided into three basic regions: LUZON—site of the capital, **Quezon City; Manila;** the *Tagaytay Ridge* resort; *Bataan; Corregidor,* the last bastion to hold out valiantly against the Japanese in the bleak early months of World War II; cool **Baguio** high in the hills; **Banaue,** site of the man-made mountain rice terraces, one of the wonders of the world; and far to the south, at **Albay,** *Mount Mayon* with its perfect cone; THE VISAYAN ISLANDS—known for *Leyte Gulf;* **Cebu,** where the navigator-discoverer, Ferdinand Magellan, once planted the Spanish flag and claimed the archipelago for his king; **Iloilo,** *Negros, Bohol,* **Dumaguete, Bacolod,** and **Tacloban,** centers of the rich sugar and timber industries of the nation; and MINDANAO—which includes Zamboanga, where, according to legend and song, "the monkeys have no tails"; Davao; Cotabato; and Lanao.

To the north of the Philippines lies **Taiwan (Formosa),** and **Borneo** is to the south. The *China Sea* washes the islands' west coast, and the *Pacific Ocean* laps the east coast of the archipelago.

The tourist literature of the *Board of Travel and Tourist Industry* picturesquely pinpoints the varied charm and romance of the Philippines in the following paragraph: "*Intramuros,* Manila's walled city . . . a volcano sitting quietly in a lake . . . moss-grown churches . . . flower-laden city in the mountains . . . 4,000-year-old rice terraces . . . pearl diving in the southern seas . . . sparkling waterfalls . . . shimmering lagoons . . . shining green plantations . . . villages on stilts . . . a volcano rising like a green pyramid . . . ancient rites and festivals . . . names echoing the age of island empires, of dancing princesses, of Spanish conquistadores, of treasure-laden galleons, and of private lords" . . . but the foregoing is only part of the story which deserves more detail in the telling. The Philippines have been "discovered" so many times in their long eventful history—by aboriginal peoples, Indonesians, Malays, Chinese, Spanish, Americans, and, unhappily, last of all by the Japanese—that the word "rediscovery" seems more appropriate in discussing travel in this alluring area.

The warmhearted Filipinos are avidly anxious for you to come to their lovely island to "discover" or "rediscover" as you please. The Philippines fully intend to double their tourist business in the immediate future, so say the officials of the *Tourist Commission* who seek a minimum of 100,000 tourists annually, sure to spend, they believe, the U.S. dollar equivalent of thirty-six million. No stone is being left unturned to bring about the fulfillment of this ambitious goal. One merit point already earned and in effect is the new favorable tourist rate of 3.2 pesos to the dollar. The tourist drive kicked off, interestingly enough, during 1961, the year that marked the first centennial of the birth of the Philippine national hero, the Malay poet-patriot, José Rizal.

Americans constitute the bulk of the nation's visitors, a whopping seventy per cent or more. We are especially welcome because of our natural friendship and the intertwined histories of our two friendly nations.

PHILIPPINE
ISLANDS

SOUTH
CHINA
SEA

LUZON

- LAOAG
- VIGAN
- BONTOC
SAGADA - BANAUE
- BAGUIO

- CABANATUAN

- QUEZON CITY
BATAAN PENINSULA - MANILA
- TAGAYTAY
CORREGIDOR - ANTIPOLO
CAVITE
LIPA - PAGSANJAN FALLS

PHILIPPINE SEA

- NAGA

LUZON

MINDORO

PANAY LEYTE

PALAWAN

NEGROS

MINDANAO

Early in his tenure of office, the Commissioner of Tourism realized that Manila still did not have nearly enough first class hotel accommodations (less than 1,000 first class bedrooms in the capital and only 500 outside) and that there was an urgent need to beautify the airport, develop historic and scenic sights, and better the existing transportation facilities. He energetically set out to rectify all of these situations with spectacular initial results, and the aggressive program is continuing.

Another splendid scheme instituted by the hardworking Mr. Modesto Farolan, Commissioner of Tourism, is the regional training center on tourism in Manila which began in 1961. Here selected trainees from the Philippines, Viet Nam, Thailand, Singapore, Malaysia, Indonesia, Taiwan, and Korea study techniques of the tourist industry. Japan and Hong Kong, which are more advanced in the hotel and restaurant business, participate, as does Switzerland, which provides a top hotel man for one seminar, while Spain contributes a leading chef. There is also a high degree of cooperation from the *American Hotel Association*. As a result of all of this, tourism in the beautiful islands obviously will soon pick up and fly into high gear.

HOTELS in the Philippines are equipped to meet international standards, with all first class hotels both in the capital and the provinces being air conditioned and operating either on the American or European plan.

RESTAURANTS AND NIGHT CLUBS are numerous and good, there being proportionately more dining and entertainment facilities of an upper grade than there are good hotel rooms available. Even so, there is still considerable latitude for improvement in the public catering and lodging departments. Hotels are not yet on a collective par with the standards set by the other countries in the Far East.

Incoming steamers and planes bringing tourist groups are accorded special festive attention, visitors being greeted by local ladies in colorful Filipino *mestiza* dresses with high puffed shoulders and embroidered bodices. Lady tourists are frequently given an orchid corsage *(waling-waling)* or a garland of sampaguitas, the Philippine national flower, while gentlemen are sometimes handed a packet of famous Manila cigars.

The *Travel Center of the Philippine Tourist and Travel Association,* located in **Manila** on the ground floor, corner *General Luna* and *Muralla, Intramuros* (Walled City), is designed for the sole purpose of affording visitors every assistance and convenience while in The Philippines, especially while in the capital. Its competent staff will help you obtain any conceivable information which might be desired. This wonderful institution will do more than undertake the ordinary services in your behalf. It will, for example, handle the mailing or shipment of your souvenirs and purchases before or after your departure free of charge and will also receive or send telegrams or mail. What a boon this is to the time conscious traveler.

CLIMATE. A typically tropical climate prevails in the islands, and **Manila** is generally quite hot with an average year round temperature of eighty degrees and a humidity which averages from 65% in the dry season to 98% in the rainy months. There is an almost constant sea breeze in **Manila,** particularly in the bayside hotel area and all along beautiful *Dewey Boulevard.*

The hottest months are May and June when the maximum daytime temperatures push 90° and the thermometer reads over 80° at night. In December and January, maximum temperatures are 83.5°, with pleasant, wind-blown evenings. During the other months, the daytime maximums are from 84° to 88°, with nights being in the mid-seventies. The hill and mountain resorts are pleasantly cool throughout the year. The average rainfall in May is 5.03 inches, with June, July, August, and September having 10.04, 16.38, 17.07, and 13.76 inches respectively. October experiences a rainfall of about 7.66 inches.

CLOTHING. One should, of course, dress as for hot weather at home. During the day, a high degree of informality is achieved. Men will be quite comfortable in sports shirts and trousers, while the ladies may make themselves at home in summer cottons. It is also considered proper for visitors to wear the beautiful native *mestiza* dress, almost a national costume . . .

light, shimmery, and chic, with fascinating "butterfly wings" attached at the shoulders. Evenings men can comfortably wear the wonderful *barong tagalog,* known more simply as the "Manila shirt," woven, usually, from pineapple or banana fibers, worn outside the trousers, and quite frilly with hand-stitched embroidery. The Manila shirt is eminently suitable for evening wear, even for formal occasions. Regardless of whether or not you "go native," at least go light. Take along featherweight, wrinkle-resistant, easily washable garments.

LOCAL TRANSPORTATION in the Philippine cities, particularly **Manila,** is generously endowed with taxis, buses, and *jeepneys,* but if I were you, I'd stay with the taxis. Even though the *jeepneys* are swift and colorful, the cabs are better, and there won't be a fellow passenger alongside, perhaps carrying a live or dead animal, a basketful of cackling hens, or a quarter of a pig freshly butchered.

Taxis, though more expensive than the bus or *jeepney,* are cheap by our standards and, in general, operated on the meter principle.

The gayly painted *calesas* and *caritellas,* drawn by trotting ponies with lots of jangling silver ornamentation, provide a colorful ride in the olden style. These vintage vehicles rent for about 75¢ an hour or 10¢ for eight to ten blocks, though the cochero will ask to get, and expect to receive, slightly more than that.

Private cars may be rented relatively inexpensively and are useful for sightseeing. The best may be found in front of the *Manila Hotel* but, better yet, should be hired through your travel agent's local representative.

Manila, like so many other cities in the Far East, appears to have no closed season on pedestrians, so watch your step and look lively! Cars are driven on the right side of the street.

Getting out of the big city and into the provinces is a fairly simple undertaking by car, bus, rail, or air to places with names both pronounceable and unpronounceable. The *Philippine Air Lines* (PAL) operates a year-round daily morning round-trip

flight to the summer capital of **Baguio,** which in the India of another era the British would have termed a "hill station." During
the hot season, **Baguio** is serviced by many additional scheduled
flights. PAL also operates daily flights to the major southern
cities, with more than ninety domestic flights serving 49 points
throughout the archipelago.

The *Manila Railroad* has an air conditioned car on its daily
northern run to San Fernando in La Union Province, by which
train, with a change-over to a car at **Damortis,** one can drive up
the spectacular *Benguet Trail* to **Baguio.** There is also an air
conditioned railroad car in the *"Bicol Express"* that threads its
way southward down the narrowing peninsula to the **Legaspi**
tip toward *Mount Mayon.*

The *Baguio Bus Company* dispatches buses from **Manila** to
Baguio leaving the capital at hourly intervals from 5:30 A.M.

Two bus companies using late model coaches with wide
windows, individual foam rubber seats, and carrying 24 to 36
passengers provide first class services from **Manila** to the important tourist resorts in northern **Luzon.** The coaches of the
Luzon Bus Line and *Benguet Auto Line* (sister companies)
depart for **Baguio** at eight A.M., twelve noon, and one P.M.
on a five hour trip that costs $2.50 one way or $4.50 round trip.
The *Pangasinan Transportation Company* maintains a schedule
of four daily departures for the famed *"Blue Beach"* at
Lingayen, a four hour trip costing $1.77 each way. **Dagupan
City** is the nearest connecting point to the *Hundred Islands
National Park,* another scenic seaside resort area.

A hydrofoil sightseeing trip is operated around *Manila Bay*
Saturday, Sunday, and holiday afternoons. Departures every half
hour from the new *Luneta* landing beyond the *Army-Navy
Club.*

Choosing to visit some of the other islands by ship, one may
be accommodated by several different steamship lines including
the *Compania Maritima* and the *Philippine Steam Navigation
Company* which are among the twelve firms that operate inter-
island steamers, several times a week, with calls at **Cebu,**

Zamboanga, Cotabato, Davao, Jolo, Basilan, Dumaguete, and other ports. The entire inter-island trip takes about twelve days. The *"Don Julio"* is an air conditioned vessel which runs between Manila, Iloilo, and Bacolod. As a general rule, the inter-island vessels are terribly overcrowded. Travelers going on them would be well advised to do so with a merry spirit of adventure and a hearty resistance to crowds.

POPULATION. The nearly twenty-seven and a half million Filipinos include an admixture of Chinese, Spanish, and Indonesian, but the predominant strain is Malay.

The word *Igorot* merely means "savage," and the native tribes of the Philippines are split among the *Benguets, Bentoes, Ifugaos, Ibalois, Kankanai, Kalingas,* and *Apayaos.*

LANGUAGE. The country is rich in mellifluous tongues with romantic sibilant tones heard on all sides. There are three official languages—English, Spanish, and Tagalog—with English being the language of the school systems. Almost everyone speaks or understands our mother tongue. There are close to one hundred dialects spoken in The Philippines of which nine are sufficiently distinct to be thought of as individual languages. Most newspapers, books, and periodicals are printed in English.

RELIGION. 83% of the Filipinos embrace Catholicism as their religion, 10% are Protestants, and 4% Muslims. The remaining 3% include Buddhists, Taoists, and a handful of other more obscure faiths.

HYGIENIC CONDITIONS are generally good. Tap water is safe, and pasteurized milk is available. Except in the best places, care should be exercised with raw vegetables.

SPORTS EVENTS are regularly scheduled at the *Araneta Coliseum,* the *Rizal Memorial Stadium,* and the bigger college gymnasiums. Spectator sports like basketball, baseball, volleyball, tennis, swimming, and boxing are highly popular. The Filipinos have turned out world ranking boxing champions including Pancho Villa, Ceferino Garcia, Tiger Flores, Young Montana, and the lightweight champ, Gabriel "Flash" Elorde. Basketball is considered the national sport, and the Filipinos,

Olympic contenders each time out, are the best in Asia. Polo and golf are played at the more exclusive clubs, while horse racing, contested at the *Manila Jockey Club,* and at the *Santa Ana Race Track,* is **Manila's** favorite Sunday sport.

Jai alai, one of the world's swiftest sports imported from the Basque region of Old Spain, is a thriller to watch. At the *Fronton* one can dine pleasantly and dance in the air conditioned *Sky Room,* watching *jai alai* from the balcony and betting, from a few centavos up, by messenger. *Jai alai* is not played on Sunday.

"Sipa," a unique ball game involving the deft use of the instep and expert footwork in general, may be viewed Sunday afternoons at the *Rizal Public Playground.* Another weekend sport is cock fighting which takes place in the city's suburbs as well as in almost every provincial *barrio* or country town. Arrangements for hunting and fishing can be readily made through the *Philippine Gun and Tackle Club.*

For those who wish to play, not watch, golf is available for members and their guests, with guest cards easily arranged. Try the famed *Wack-Wack Golf and Country Club,* the *Manila Golf Club,* or the *Muni* (Municipal) *Golf Links,* which virtually surrounds the walled city, a stone's throw from the *Bay View, Luneta,* and *Manila Hotels,* and is open to the public.

The fabulous *Araneta Coliseum* in **Quezon City,** seating thirty thousand people, is the world's largest single domed auditorium. Here one can enjoy spectacular sports events, ice shows, jazz jamborees, and the Philippine appearances of top western world entertainers.

THEATERS. There are a large number of modern first and second class air conditioned cinemas in the city showing the latest American, European, and Filipino films, open seven days a week, including holidays, with seven or eight shows daily. The best theaters are the *Capital, Lyrion, Escolta, Ideal State, Ever, Universal, Odeon,* and *Galaxy* on *Rizal Avenue* and the *Gaiety* on *M. H. del Pilar.*

CLUBS. **Manila** is a city rich in club life, with its *Army and Navy Club, Elks Club, Manila Boat Club, Manila Overseas*

Press Club, National Press Club, Manila Club, Manila Golf Club, Philippine Columbian Club, Manila Polo Club, Manila Yacht Club, Nomad Sports Club, Rotary Club, Swiss Club, University Club, and *Casino Espanol de Manila,* not to mention the various civic and fraternal organizations familiar to us all everywhere.

SHOPPING is dealt with at length in Chapter Six, but I must mention here that **Manila** is a delight for the lover of fancy handicrafts as well as the curio and souvenir hunter. An occidental city in an Oriental setting such as **Manila,** the "Pearl of the Orient," naturally abounds with a cornucopia of attractive wares to please the casual and the discriminating shopper alike.

TIPPING. In The Philippines, tips are included in the bill for waiters, are optional for bartenders, unnecessary for door-men, headwaiters, shoe shine boys, and taxi drivers . . . leaving only hotel porters, barbers, bell boys, and chambermaids.

MISCELLANEOUS TRIVIA. The *American Embassy,* one of the largest the U. S. has, employs one thousand people, most of them loyal Filipinos . . . Squatters' shacks are called *barong-barong* . . . Cigars have been locally manufactured for two hundred years . . . A local grocery is called a cold store because it always incorporates refrigeration . . . The plaintive love song you'll hear is styled among the Filipinos as a *kundiman* . . . The Philippines have their own thriving motion picture in-dustry, their own Hollywood, local Oscars, and beauties . . . The touch-me-not plants found everywhere are called *makahiya* . . . **Manila** has seven English language newspapers . . . Some of the best, if unappetizingly served, food in the islands is served in what are called *panciterias* . . . What we term Philippine mahogany is broken down into *narra, molave, ipil, lauan, tanguile, kamagong,* and *baktikan* . . . The Philippines' flag has the Sun of Freedom and stars for *Luzon, Mindanao,* and the *Visayans* . . . The combination butterfly-sleeve blouse and wrap-around skirt goes under the local terminology of *patadiong* . . . The farmers' wide-brim sun-protecting straw hat is called *salakot* . . . A *sari-sari* is a general store, frequently owned by a Chinese . . . The *University of Santo Tomas* is 25 years older than *Harvard University* . . . The common man, once called *tao,* is now politically referred to as the Philippines' "Juan de la Cruz" . . . The siesta is almost mandatory for all Filipinos . . . And the festivals, dear to the heart of the native folk, will delight you as well.

LOCAL CUSTOMS. Filipino hospitality is proverbial, best summed up in the Spanish words *"Mi casa es su casa"* (My house is your house), and friendships, the harbinger of such hospitality, are easily struck up and can be lasting. During fiestas, every house is stocked with food, and every passerby is welcomed. The biggest occasions next to the fiestas, weddings, and anniversaries are life's more somber occasions, wakes and funerals.

DANCING in the Philippines is virtually a national sport, and what dancing it is. Try to see any of the following: the *Bakya,* the wooden shoe dance; the *Bulaklakan,* for married women only to perform; the *Carinosa,* Visayan courtship dance; the *Dugso,* Mindanao ritual dance; the *Itik-Itik,* Duck-Duck imitations; the *Kuratsa,* Visayan dance; the *Maglalatik,* from the coconut region of *Laguna de Bay;* the *Pandanggo Sa Ilaw,* with coconut oil lamps balanced on both the head and hands; the *Pandanggo Sa Sambalilo,* the sun hat dance; the *Sakuting,* mock fight with sticks; the *Subli, Tagalog* fiesta dance; and

the *Tinikling,* a nimble bird imitation dance step around carefully laid bamboo poles.

Among the Mindanao Moslems, there are those who dance the *Asik,* the slave dance originally from Mecca; the *Kaprangkamanis,* a dance to entertain royalty; the *Sagayan,* an inspirational dance for warriors to prepare them for battle; the *Singkil,* the exquisitely intricate princess dance performed with fans between crisscrossed bamboo bars; and the *Tahing Baila,* a dance that imitates fish movement under water. And, since the Philippines were so long a part of Spain, there are the *Habenera Botolena* for weddings and *barrio* (rural town) festivals; the *Jota Moncadena,* a Luzon-Spanish folk dance; the *Mazurka Boholana,* a popular dance of the Visayan Island province of Bohol; and the *Polkabal,* a Filipino version of polka and waltz mixed. A great native dance series called the *"Bayanihan"* (native homeland dances) has been performed with tremendous success abroad.

HISTORY. On June 24, 1572, the City of **Manila** was formally founded, named, so one story says, from the pale green cabbage-like plant found floating in the bisecting *Pasig River* known as "nila" and "May" meaning "There are." Hence, *May* (there are) *nila* (green plants in the river) or, more simply, **Manila.** Some Filipinos still refer to their capital as *Maynila.*

The big man in the Philippines' early days was Spain's Governor-General, Miguel López de Legaspi. Before he died in 1572, this early conquistador had succeeded in bringing under the Spanish hegemony almost all of what today consists of the 115,000 square miles of **The Philippines.**

With an extraordinary show of power, tact, and friendliness, de Legaspi won a heterogeneous group indeed to his side including the dwarf-size descendants of three distinct aboriginal tribes, who came from the Asian mainland; the Indonesians, who paddled up from the warm waters of the South Seas; the Malays, a race believed to have been a Hindu-Mongolian mixture originating in southeast Asia; and the Chinese, who came in great numbers to settle in northwest and central *Luzon.*

During most of the 350 years after the mid-16th century, the Spaniards ruled the Philippines as supreme masters, with all attempts to dislodge them failing dismally. The Filipinos, a coalition of Japanese and Filipinos, the Dutch, and Chinese pirates failed to make a dent in frequent forays against the Spaniards. The great Chinese, Lim-Ah-Hong, tried desperately to capture **Manila** but failed pathetically. The Mohammedan Moros from the south attacked the Christian Filipinos during the entire period of the Spanish reign, and twice during the blood-filled 18th century seized and held the capital for two years.

The Philippines were called "New Spain" from which countless Spanish galleons, rich with treasure, lifted anchor as they headed homeward to Europe.

During the twilight of the Spanish rule, powerful patriots came to the fore, chief of whom was Dr. José Rizal, poet-savant-writer-philosopher, who paid for his "treason" before Spanish rifles on December 30, 1896. There were others who continued the struggle for island liberty, including Apolinario Mabini, "The Sublime Paralytic," Andres Bonifacio, M. H. del Pilar, and the old "Fox of the Isles," General Emilio Aguinaldo, who used U. S. weapons in an insurrection against the Spanish and later turned these same weapons against the Americans.

The Americans arrived in 1898 when Admiral Dewey uttered the famous order, "Fire when ready, Gridley." The swift naval action was over at a terrible cost in Spanish lives, causing Dewey to add, more sympathetically, to his officers and men, "Don't cheer long; the poor fellows are dying."

The first U. S. administrators of **The Philippines** following our successful conquest were Army officers, the last military governor being Lt. General Arthur MacArthur, father of General Douglas MacArthur. On July 4, 1901, the Honorable William Howard Taft was inaugurated as the first Civil Governor. Self-rule for the islands, under U. S. supervision, was gradually introduced, English replacing Spanish as the scholastic language. A Philippine Commission was set up as the Upper

House, composed of both American and Filipinos appointed by the President of the United States, which was later replaced by a bicameral legislative system with both House and Senate being elective. In 1935, the Commonwealth of The Philippines was established, giving the country an elected president and placing control of almost all of the internal affairs in the hands of the people. In this latter form of government, the United States was represented by a presidential appointee from Washington, the U. S. High Commissioner.

Between 1941 and 1945, the Japanese cruelly occupied the Philippines, giving the long predestined status of sovereignty for the island people a nasty setback. A puppet government, established by the Japanese under Jose P. Laurel, was harassed throughout the increasingly turbulent war years and made no headway with a people determined to be free.

The Japanese left the "Pearl of the Orient" blackened, embarking in their final days in a savagery that has come to be known unforgettably to the Filipinos as the "Rape of Manila." The city was horribly and maliciously destroyed, especially the best parts south of the *Pasig River*.

The "Pearl" is now fast regaining its original luster, and, best of all, on July 4, 1946, the United States kept its wartime promise, permitting the islands to become the Republic of the Philippines, sovereign and free at last.

LUZON

MANILA sprawls on the wide curving crescent of *Manila Bay,* where the sunsets behind *Corregidor* are world famous, soul stirring, and breathtaking. The city is an interesting blend of old and new, where tradition speaks louder than the passage of time.

There is much to see, much to do in this gleaming white cosmopolitan city of now more than two million people, noted for its large number of educational institutions, fine markets, beautiful churches and cathedrals, wide sweeping flower-

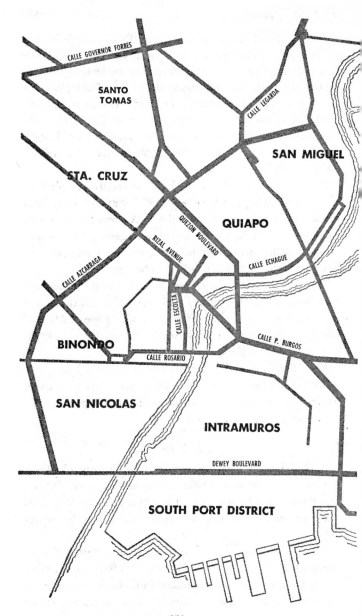

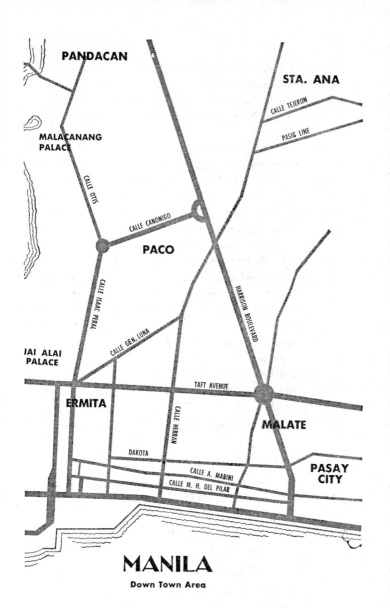

MANILA

Down Town Area

bordered boulevards, and attractive residential areas. The beauty of *Manila Bay* at sunset will live long in your memory.

One of the first sights to greet the visitor, whether landing at *South Pier* or arriving by air, as he comes directly down *Dewey Boulevard* is:

INTRAMUROS, the walled city, which was all there was to **Manila** when the first Spanish arrived. They subsequently built a thick wall around the walled city, a chore that took forty laborious years. Outside their formidable walls, the Spaniards dug a deep moat running to the *Bay*, which was filled in in 1903 and later converted into a huge garden which endured until the senseless *Battle of Manila.*

Intramuros, the city within a city, is bounded to the north by the *Pasig River* and on the other three sides by the *Municipal "Muni" Golf Links* and is famed for its fine old churches and historical sights. It suffered a dreadful fate in February of 1945 when Japanese marines and U. S. cavalrymen engaged in a death struggle. American artillery banged away at the huge walls until avenues of entry were punctured and U. S. infantrymen poured into the blackened gaps. On entering, our boys found Phase One of the ghastliness of the *"Rape of Manila."*

ST. AUGUSTINE CHURCH was the only church in the *Intramuros* area to escape Japanese wartime ravages. It is a

monument to Filipino craftsmanship, the oldest church in the nation, dating back to 1571. Inside repose the bones and ashes of Legaspi, the Chinese patriot Lim-Ah-Hong, and of many Spanish civil and ecclesiastical dignitaries. *St. Augustine* is a favorite church of tourists of all faiths.

The MANILA CATHEDRAL, a modern replica of the original structure of 1879, started as an humble Spanish wooden parish church far back in the late 16th century. Victim of fire and earthquake on several occasions, it has in its over four hundred years of fascinating history been rebuilt six times in all. Visitors will marvel at the only organ of its kind in the Orient, with 5,600 pipes and a set of seven bells, equipped with an automatic chimer, the gift of one of Europe's top bell makers. The *Manila Cathedral,* damaged in the war by the Japanese who fought tooth and nail around it, is located in the *Intramuros.*

MALACANANG PALACE, richly colorful home of the Chief Executive of the Republic, was previously occupied by numerous Spanish Governors and the American Governors General who succeeded them. The Palace derives its name from **Malaya,** its architecture from **Spain,** and the concepts of democratic government practiced by its present inhabitants from the United States and the western world. *Malacanang Palace* thus bears the imprints of two nations and is the contemporary home of the Filipino President. It is well worth a visit which one can make without difficulty. The gardens and grounds are bursting with brilliant hued blooms. Don't forget your camera.

FORT SANTIAGO was largely destroyed during the war which is perhaps just as well. In one of its narrow cells, Dr. José Rizal spent the last few days prior to his execution at the Luneta in 1898. Less than fifty years later, its grim dungeons echoed to the death screams of brave Filipino resistance fighters and guerrillas, tortured to death by the Japanese. The ruins may be seen.

DR. RIZAL'S MONUMENT, a model of simplicity, was

erected long ago on the spot where the bullets felled him that late-19th century December morning. The monument was built in elliptical *Luneta Park,* where many of the rank and file of the city congregate daily to watch the sun dip into *Manila Bay.*

The NEW LUNETA PARK, across *Dewey Boulevard* from the *Rizal Monument,* is the location of the huge *Quirino Grandstand* where the impressive parades and processions of significance wind up. *Luneta* stretches from the lawn of the *Manila Hotel* to the *Army and Navy Club House.* Here, by day, one may watch whole families relaxing and playing, and, at night, after the last glow of the tropical sunset has blurred into the soft night, the lovers arrive, hand in hand, arm in arm, and stroll or sit under the trees in an idyllic setting. Behind the grandstand in the lovely bay beyond the sea wall, rental motorboats are available for those who prefer to absorb their sunsets afloat.

DEWEY BOULEVARD, sweeping along the bay past beautiful parks, residences, and apartment buildings, is one of the finest and longest drives in the Orient, named, of course, after our American naval hero of 1898. On this boulevard one finds some of the best hotels, night clubs, and restaurants in the city. The boulevard, always impressive, is more beautiful toward nightfall when the first lights of evening begin to wink.

TAFT AVENUE, a handful of blocks inland, is another thoroughfare on which is located, among many other handsome buildings, both government and private, the *University of the Philippines.*

The AMERICAN MILITARY CEMETERY AND MEMORIAL, *Fort William McKinley,* in **Rizal,** makes one proud to be an American. Here 17,182 Filipinos and Americans rest in quiet dignity in a setting of unsurpassed beauty.

The CHINESE CEMETERY, in the extreme northwest section of the city beyond the *San Lazaro Race Course* and adjacent to the city's *North Cemetery,* is noted for its fabulous, highly ornate mausoleums.

The UNIVERSITY OF SANTO TOMAS, used by the Japs as an Allied internment camp during World War II, is centuries old, having been founded before *Harvard College*. The grounds of the university are spacious and well groomed, giving one the impression of a huge palace with lovely gardens.

The FORBES PARK RESIDENTIAL QUARTER, called "Millionaires' Row," is as magnificent and beautiful a dwelling area as is to be found anywhere. Do take half an hour to drive slowly through this well manicured area.

The MANILA POST OFFICE commands a most beautiful setting. Facing lovely plaza-like squares and backing up to the river, the *Manila Post Office* lends architectural dignity to the capital.

QUIAPO CHURCH is worth a visit to see the superb shrine of the *Black Nazarene*.

The NORTH AND SOUTH PORT DISTRICTS, separated by the *Pasig River* on *Manila Bay*, are fascinating and virtually "downtown." Tied up to the piers and at anchor in the sheltered *Bay*, one can see ships from all the world ports.

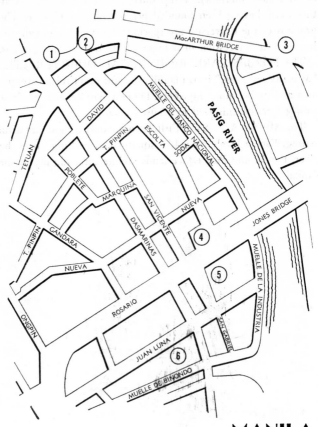

MANILA

ESCOLTA SHOPPING AREA

① PLAZA STA. CRUZ
② PLAZA GOITI
③ PLAZA LAWTON
④ PLAZA MORAGA
⑤ PLAZA CERVANTES
⑥ BANK OF AMERICA

MANILA
ERMITA SHOPPING AREA

MANILA BAY

⑦ ELLINWOOD CHURCH	⑮ U. S. EMBASSY
⑧ ST. PAUL COLLEGE	⑯ BETHEL TEMPLE
⑨ UNIVERSITY OF PHILIPPINES	⑰ BURNHAM GREEN
⑩ MEDICAL SCHOOL	⑱ HOLY TRINITY
⑪ ASSUMPTION CONVENT	⑲ DOCTOR'S HOSPITAL
⑫ PHILIPPINES GENERAL HOSP.	⑳ UNITED NATIONS PARK
⑬ UNITED NATIONS ORGANIZATION	㉑ LUNETA PARK
⑭ ATENEO LAW COLLEGE	㉒ MANILA HOTEL

QUEZON CITY, adjoining and contiguous with **Manila,** is a more modern version of the capital.

The BALARA FILTERS PARK, **Quezon City,** is a picnic and entertainment ground very popular with the Filipinos. A delightful spot to absorb local color.

GENERAL EMILIO AGUINALDO's HISTORIC HOME, just outside the city limits, is dedicated to the life and times of Filipino revolutionary history.

The PLAZA SANTA CRUZ, in the heart of the northside shopping area, is teeming with, and rich in, local sights.

The MEMORIAL TO THE UNKNOWN SOLDIER is in *Fort Santiago* near the *Manila Cathedral.* The *Memorial* is eternally adorned with flowers.

The UNIVERSITY OF THE PHILIPPINES, **Quezon City,** is neither as old nor as large as *Santo Tomas,* but it is beautifully situated and is worthy of your attention.

ESCOLTA, **Manila's** main shopping thoroughfare is a buzzing beehive of activity. Avid shoppers crowd the sidewalks and mill about under the arches. The street reverberates with the frenzied scooting in and out of thousands of impatient *jeepneys,* the pounding of hoofs, and the jangling of the shrill bells on the colorful, tassel-fringed horse drawn traditional *calesas.*

CHINATOWN in **Manila** is not as large as many Chinatowns located throughout Southeast Asia, but it is equally fascinating. About a mile long, it is typified by the sights, smells, and ceaseless activity of other Chinatowns.

The AMERICAN EMBASSY. As one drives along the *Bay* on *Dewey Boulevard* toward **Pasay City,** one passes on the seaward side the attractive *American Embassy* and the amazingly modern Embassy Office Building which is the Philippine headquarters of the U. S. Veterans Administration.

The BOTANICAL AND ZOOLOGICAL GARDEN, fascinating and postwar, is where one sees Amara, a black bear; Tenth World, a big Nippon monkey; Dingoy, a fine young tiger; and Melvin Jones, a strapping lion.

TAGAYTAY RIDGE is 36 colorful miles from downtown Manila. The drive to *Tagaytay* is one of the most interesting in the Orient. After having passed **Pasay City,** one plunges into the countryside passing through numerous attractive villages, characterized by stilt houses. All around one sees the water buffalo ploddingly at work. One may wish to stop at *Las Pinas Church* which houses the centuries old bamboo organ. In the area, one passes little coves and harbors in which are the fishing boats with their extended curved masts by which the fishing nets are manipulated. Numerous flower, fruit, and produce markets line the road to *Tagaytay Ridge*. The altitude of 2,000 feet above sea level blesses *Tagaytay* with a climate whose temperature is always ten to fifteen degrees cooler than that of **Manila.** The *Ridge* commands a grandiose view of *Lake Taal* and *Taal Volcano*. From the *Ridge* looking into the lake, one peers down into the crater's mouth, the lowest volcanic crater in the world and certainly one in a setting that is incomparable. The volcanic eruption of 1911 was the last of the eighteen eruptions known to *Taal Volcano*. Because of its geological formations, it is believed that the entire lake was once a crater which virtually makes *Taal Volcano* a crater within a crater. The area is extraordinarily colorful, the waters of the lake being a glistening azure blue.

Steam and smoke rise gently from the lowlands adjoining the lake.

The *Taal Vista Lodge* on *Tagaytay*'s highest point has a first class restaurant and is an excellent place to obtain lodging for the night.

THE PROVINCES OF LUZON

LOS BANOS, in the province of Laguna, is a peaceful sleepy town at the foot of a cloud-kissed slope. Numerous hot springs seep out of the base of *Mt. Makiling*.

The BOTANICAL GARDENS, found on the slopes of *Mt. Makiling,* are a beautiful *National Park* and site of the *College of Agriculture* and *School of Forestry* of the *University of the*

Philippines. Enchanting countryside is encountered on the trip out from the capital.

The PAGSANJAN FALLS. The eastern side of Laguna Province is distinguished by steep gorges, branching rivers, and splendid cascades, the most famous of which is the *Pagsanjan Waterfall* near the small picturesque town of **Pagsanjan,** only two hours' drive from **Manila.** One can reach the falls only by water, which boat trip is a thrilling adventure, for here one may shoot fourteen frothy white-water rapids and nineteen smaller falls before one touches, safely, at the end near the largest falls in which a rainbow is apt to be trapped if the angle of the sun is right. The *Pagsanjan Falls* are considered one of the outstanding beauty spots of the Philippines.

LAGUNA DE BAY, largest inland body of water in the Philippines, is a potential flood hazard to the capital during the rainy season. Fine duck hunting is available in the *Laguna de Bay's* reedy marshes. One may stay overnight at a good lodge on *Cielito Lindo,* an island in the lake.

ANTIPOLO, 800 to 1,000 feet above **Manila,** is, in May, the focal point for thousands and thousands of the devout. In **Antipolo's** massive old church, the town's patron saint, Our Lady of Peace and Good Voyage, is the object of these yearly pilgrimages. The image was brought to the Philippines in 1620 by a Governor of Spain. Legend has it that the local people are kept safe from marauders—Chinese, Dutch, and Japanese—by their faith in this saint. **Antipolo,** with its shrine and waterfalls, is only an hour's ride from **Manila** via a first class highway.

BATAAN and CORREGIDOR evoke memories of the valiant stand of the Filipino-American forces against superior Japanese forces in 1942. *Bataan* is a peninsula, *Corregidor* a rock, an island, a fortress like **Gibraltar,** standing like a sentinel, a cork in the bottle of *Manila Bay.* In olden days, ships stopped there to have their papers checked and, if need be, corrected. Hence, the name *Corregidor* from the Spanish *corregir . . .* to correct. From **Manila** one can be flown or go by boat to *Corregidor,* a National Shrine. and see the famed tunnels and gun emplacements; and in another few minutes by air, one may journey on to *Bataan,* start of the infamous "Death March" of U. S. prisoners of war after the peninsula yielded to the then victorious Japanese military leaders.

CALAMBA, the quaint birthplace of the Filipino hero of Malay descent, Dr. José Rizal, may be visited.

Other diverting spots half a day's to a day's round-trip distance from **Manila** include the YANGCO TEXTILE MARKET, FORT McKINLEY just beyond the *Manila Polo Club,* the picturesque PARANAQUE SALT BEDS, the scenic NOVALICHES WATERSHED, the BAT CAVES at **Montalban,** the HOT SPRINGS at **Pandi,** and the beaches along the *Cavite* shore.

BAGUIO is an hour from **Manila** by air or five hours by car. Its 5,000 foot altitude, sighing pine forests, distant glimpses of the *Benguet* copper mines at night, excellent eighteen hole golf course, military reservation at *Camp John Hay,* and picturesque *Igorot* tribesmen make it an ideal spot for a weekend outing or a sustained and crisply cool vacation. The *Philippine Military Academy,* the nation's West Point, is located here.

In **Baguio,** *Burnham Park,* decorated with a shimmery blue lagoon, is popular with promenaders. The *Mansion House* is the summer residence of the Philippines' President; the grounds can be visited by securing permission from the guards on duty.

The *Baguio Country Club,* for members and their guests, is a haven for sports lovers, with an eighteen hole golf course, tennis courts, bowling alleys, swimming pool, guest cottages, flower gardens, and a well appointed club house.

TRINIDAD VALLEY is nestled in the sheltering embrace of great mountains three hundred feet below **Baguio,** from which fertile area one gets the Philippines' largest cabbages, berries, and beans.

BANAUE in Ifugao is the site of the great rice terraces of the Ifugao *Igorots* which are often called the "eighth wonder of the world." Whole mountain ranges are terraced for the cultivation of rice carved eons ago by bare Malay hands from the harsh

mountainsides. Towering like gigantic stairways to the cloud-filled sky, these Banaue rice terraces extend almost ten times as long as the Great Wall of China, by actual measurement an incredible 14,000 miles long, a distance more than halfway around the earth. The work on the Banaue rice terrace complex began circa 2000 B.C. and is, even now, continuing every day. Imagine! These are among the steepest mountains of the world, some rising sheerly almost straight up, to defy man and agriculture, but they, too, are terraced.

The AMBUKLAO HYDRO-ELECTRIC DAM, an hour's drive from **Baguio,** is one of the largest in the whole Far East and the second highest rock filled dam in existence.

Near **Lingayen** one can see the scene of the first successful U. S. landings in late January of 1945, the start of the campaign to liberate Manila and all Luzon from the Japs. The whole area is dotted with monuments to hard-fought battles and lost soldier lives, hallowed ground for Filipinos and Americans alike. Here peacetime bonds were forged afresh in the blood, fire, and pain of war.

Toward **Bontoc** is the route down which the chewed up remnants of the Japanese armies of General Tomoyuki Yamashita fled. Yamashita, who was called the "Tiger of Malaya," was hanged by order of General Douglas MacArthur for criminal responsibility for the February 1945 "Rape of Manila."

MOUNT MAYON, rising eight thousand feet in perfect cone formation in Albay Province, is reputed to be the world's most perfect cone, a volcano that can easily be reached from **Manila** by overnight, or day, train trip and by motor car through areas of coconut plantations and thick virgin forests carpeting a rugged and mountainous countryside. Planes take but ninety minutes or less from **Manila** to Albay. In the immediate neighborhood of *Mount Mayon* are the famous *Tiwi Hot Springs* resort, the ruins of volcanically destroyed **Cagsawa,** *Calayucay Beach Resort,* the bay fishing area of *Legaspi Gulf,* and the beautiful *Lake Bulusan* resort and *Rizal Beach* in Sorsogon. *Mayon* last went wild in 1814 when its eruption was horribly destructive, completely inundating **Cagsawa** with lava.

BULUSAN LAKE RESORT nestles on the eastern slopes of *Bulusan Volcano* in Sorsogon Province about 1800 feet above sea level and is called, rightly, one of the most splendid tourist spots in the Philippines. It is a forest-enclosed mountain lake, surrounded by huge lauan and molave trees, orchid plants, and other brilliant flowers.

VISAYAN ISLANDS

CEBU, the Philippines' oldest city, is a trade center of the *Visayans,* its lasting fame symbolized by the cross planted there by a Portuguese explorer-navigator in the service of Spain during a voyage of discovery more than four hundred years ago, a relic still plainly visible in the public plaza. For his discovery, Ferdinand Magellan paid with his life, slain on little *Mactan* across the strait from **Cebu** by native warriors with poisoned spears while fighting a minor skirmish against the great Filipino chieftain, Lapu-Lapu.

PALAWAN, a beautiful island, most westerly of the large

islands, is bedecked with magnificent forests of over 150 different species of woods, many of them rare. *Palawan* has certain birds and animals not found in any other Philippine island including wild peacock, squirrel, porcupine, armadillo, mouse deer, and skunk. *Palawan* has an underground river which flows for miles through a deep cave before it finally reaches the sea. Birds who build edible nests, which are exported in large quantities to **Formosa** and **Hong Kong** where they are worth five times their weight in silver, are found in the cliffs by the seashore and in caves inland. This area is the genesis of that Oriental delicacy, the Chinese "bird's nest soup."

Near its capital city of PUERTO PRINCESA, Palawan Province maintains a model penal colony at IWAHIG, where the prisoners are "colonists." Accompanied by their families, they work out their sentences, with reductions of "imprisonment" for good behavior. Incidentally, treatment is so noteworthy that even with the chaos of the island battle between the Japs and the Filipinos, none of the colonists sought to escape.

MINDORO, whose name comes from *"mina de oro"* meaning "Mine of Gold," is noted for its tamarau, found only in the mountains, which are so thickly jungled that even today Japanese soldier-stragglers are still being flushed out, ignorant of their nation's surrender in 1945. This tamarau, an animal which looks like a cross between a carabao and a deer, is found nowhere else in the world.

The MARINE GARDENS OF PUERTO GALERA are another of *Mindoro's* scenic spots.

ILOILO, the port city of *Panay Island* and the western *Visayans,* is modern and cosmopolitan, with some of the residential homes ranking among the most beautiful in the entire Philippines. **Iloilo** is particularly noted for its lovely fabrics, the *jusi* and *piña* cloth.

BACOLOD CITY and DUMAGUETE are in Occidental and Oriental Negros respectively. The former is the sugar capital of the Philippines and a prosperous, charming metropolis whose sugar centrals are among the largest and most modern in the world. The two cities are known for their beautiful women . . . flashing eyed, light brown *señoritas* and *señoras* with masses of long black, hair-pinned tresses and luscious well-formed bodies, the better shown at fiesta time in the butterfly wing *mestiza* dresses. **Dumaguete** is famed for *Silliman University,* the oldest private American institution in the Philippines, set amidst coconut groves lining the seashore.

TAGBILARAN, capital of *Bohol Island,* offers a large variety of Philippine handicrafts, the vendors presenting a picturesque sight as their frail *bancas,* filled to the gunwales with their wares, crowd around the incoming inter-island ships.

MINDANAO

Come south! The warm glittering waters await you, as do the sun stained beaches, the fronds of the wind-waved coconut palms, the nipa thatch huts, the many coral islands, and the eternal blue skies which are perfectly reflected in the deep blue seas.

CAGAYAN DE ORO, **Mindanao's** northern gate in Misamis Oriental, is known for its copra and is but a few hours' drive from **Del Monte** in Bukidnon, the Philippines' major pineapple production region.

BUKIDNON, in the pineapple country, consists of seven plateaus of varying heights, separated from one another by seven deep canyons and three valleys. From the plateaus rise seven mountains, three of them extinct volcanoes, one almost a perfect cone looking for all the world like a miniature *Mt. Mayon.*

TACLOBAN. Here one can see where General MacArthur's American invasion forces first splashed ashore to redeem the General's famous pledge "I shall return."

ZAMBOANGA, where the monkeys are supposed to have no tails—but do, is noted for its soft weather, beautiful parks, drowsy rolling surf, fine beaches, lovely orchids, palm fringed sand strips, and natural swimming pools. **Zamboanga** is also known for its Moslem temples, *moro vintas* (a distinctive type of broad-sailed sailing craft), expert fishermen, stilted grass houses built over the sea, exquisite pearls, black coral and silver jewelry, and brass items. Here one sees hanging gardens, lily pool rock gardens, ancient *Fort Pilar*, the Spanish outpost of the 17th century not far from the beautiful shrine of *Our Lady of Pilar*, and the Moslem village and mosque of *Taluksangay* where Moros perform ceremonial dances.

The Mariposa or butterfly orchid, common to Zambo, is cheap and grows wild. Here also one can see Moro water gypsies; *Pasonanco Park* with its natural beauties; *San Ramon Penal Farm* (like *Iwahig Penal Colony* on *Palawan*); the famed *Black Coral and Kunzle & Streiff* shops, where one can feast one's eyes or buy beautiful salad dishes and dinner plates of thick, iridescent mother-of-pearl selling for less than $1.75 each! Imagine?

JOLO is unforgettable, with its colorful costumes, fragile houses on the water's edge, palm trees, the *Public Market*, the *Little Intramuros*, and the rising blue mountain backdrop.

COTOBATO is best approached at dusk up the river of the same name, passing the mysterious Moslem villages where one may buy exquisite woven baskets, Malayan *krisses* (ripple-edged daggers), inlaid gold and silver work, lovely brassware, and, by pre-arrangement, one may witness the authentic Moorish dances, the *kolintangs*, to the tune of graduated brass instruments.

DAVAO offers the *Blue Lagoon*, a legendary pond of incredibly blue water surrounded by white birch-like trees, about 2.5 miles from town, the fine basket and textile weaving of neighboring *Upi Village, Talomo Beach, Mt. Apo*, the highest pinnacle in the Philippines, the *Bago* hemp *(abaca) Experimental Station* out of whose fabulous fibers come that tough famous Manila hempen rope, the native fruit tree station at **Manambulan,** the *Davao Penal Colony,* and the famed *San Miguel* local brewery.

Davao is a sprawling frontier town, the city that hemp built, more Christian than Moslem, a modern city in every respect, proudly conscious of its great past. The luxurious new *Davao Insular Hotel* promises to make the city and the surrounding area an important tourist and holiday resort.

SASA is a clean, busy, pretty little port with *Mount Samal* in the background, a place of bougainvillaea and star-apple groves, presenting a spectacular view of *Mount Apo.*

Elsewhere in the **Mindanao** area are the *Del Monte Golf Course,* said to be the best in the islands; the breathtaking scenery of **Malaybalay;** the *Matepilca Ranch,* the vast holding of the Fortich family where many different types of cattle are bred; *Lake Pinamaloy,* sacred to the natives (perhaps because of crocodiles) and called "Widow's Tears" by local folk; the shopping center of **Marawai City** (once called **Dansalan**), a place rich in native lore, rituals, native dances, and handicrafts; and, near **Iligan City,** that major area attraction, *Maria Cristina Falls,* a magnificent cascade of over 300 feet located near the city.

SANGA-SANGA in the *Tawi-Tawi* group is the site of the country's southernmost airport in a tropical paradise; a Badjao village of water gypsy people is nearby.

Other places of interest in the area include *Turtle Island,* inhabited only by a turtle colony; *Bird Island,* with its exclusively winged population in the *Balabac* group; the *Biacnabato Caves,* with their majestic, near regal, stalactite chandeliers; the unique salt springs of **Nueva Vizcaya;** and the *Encantado* (Enchanted) *River* of **Port Lamon** in Surigao Province.

CHAPTER 14

Singapore and Malaya

FEDERATION OF MALAYSIA

SINGAPORE

SEDUCTIVE SINGAPORE'S POPULATION OF 1,600,000 is as colorful an agglomeration of humanity as has ever been dipped into an international melting pot. None of the cities of the world is more cosmopolitan or more entitled to be called the "crossroads of the world" than **Singapore**. Almost seventy-five per cent of the island's inhabitants are Chinese. One also finds a large group of Malays (15%), Indians, Ceylonese, Pakistanis, Eurasians, and Europeans (particularly British).

The costumes seen in Singapore are as divergent as the people. My favorite dress, the Chinese *cheongsam* split up the sides approaching cute slender hips, is everywhere. One also views females in vivid-hued Indian saris, Chinese *samfu,* Punjabi trousers and smocks, pencil skirts and blouses, toreador pants and shirts, a Malaya sarong *kebaya,* and Chinese trousers and coats. The predominant men's garb is the coolie costume with yard-wide Chinese laborer straw hats, but there are also Malay *Songkok* velvet caps, Sikh turbans, *Kadazan Siungs* (female hats) and flaring pantaloons, the Indian *Chooridar* working garb, a *Baju* horseman's costume, western business suits, or, for more formal occasions, white sharkskin or Palm Beach coats over light woolen black dress trousers.

Other countries or cities may claim to be more Chinese, Malayan, Indian, or European, but none is more of all of them than Singapore. Here one finds a complete blending of the cultures, customs, costumes, cuisines, festivals, religions, and traditions of the peoples of the world. Seldom has a city so completely captured my fancy as has Singapore. It is beautiful, sparkling clean, delightfully picturesque, grubby, modern and ancient . . . a thriving metropolis side by side with dense jungle, rubber plantations, agricultural communities, and fishing villages.

The natives of Singapore like to feel that their visitors sightsee by eye, by ear, and by sensory perception. The sounds of Singapore are as interesting as the sights. The cries of the street vendors and the singsong bargaining in *Chinatown,* where the tapping of sticks on hollow bamboo according to rhythm indicates what is being offered for sale, are mixed with the exotic smells of produce by day or the tempting fragrance of the frangipani and gardenia blossoms by night.

Standing in the palm shaded esplanade overlooking the harbor and the open roadstead, one has but to turn one's head slightly to see the skyscraper outline of the bustling downtown area, while five minutes away is a Malay village built on stilts in the water and five minutes or less in the other direction one finds an authentic *Chinatown.*

GEOGRAPHY. Diamond-shaped Singapore is, in effect, a trilogy, being a formerly independent state with Great Britain's maternal blessing, an island, and an ancient and modern city which is now an integral part of the Federation of Malaysia.

Lying at the southern tip of the *Malay Peninsula,* Singapore is separated from the mainland by the *Straits of Johore* which water is spanned both by a road and a rail causeway, each three-quarters of a mile in length. Twenty-six miles long from east to west and fourteen miles wide, *Singapore Island,* together with its adjacent islets, occupies an area of some 225 square miles situated eighty-five miles north of the Equator. Though it is basically flat, there are, on *Singapore Island,* several ranges of low-lying, gently undulating hills, the highest peak of which is 581 feet above sea level. The island's eastern shores are sandy and excellent for salt water bathing. The city's busy business area, lying at the southern end of the island, is complemented by numerous native quarters as well as by one of the most splendiferous European style residential areas I have ever seen. Its parks and playgrounds are well manicured and attractive.

Sumatra lies immediately west of Singapore, **Java** to the south, and **Borneo** to the south and east.

More than fifty-four per cent of the total population was, in 1961, under nineteen years of age, with more than twenty-five per cent of government revenue being devoted to the education of this youthful segment of the population. Schools are rapidly being built but cannot keep apace with the exploding population. Schools and teachers must function in two shifts daily, but despite this doubling up, facilities and the supply of instructors are inadequate.

CLIMATE. Singapore, a land of eternal summer, is ever green and punctuated with gay blooms and dotted with gently waving palm trees. There are no seasons as such. Singapore's average maximum temperature throughout the year is 84 degrees Fahrenheit. At the peak of the noon day heat, the temperature usually attains a maximum of 87° F., or sometimes a little bit higher. The average daytime minimum is 75 degrees, though the mercury seldom drops below 74° F. A delightful facet of the local climate is the gentle breeze which wafts across the island every evening after sunset, bringing with it an invigorating freshness. Singapore nights are invariably pleasantly cool.

HISTORY. Singapore, whose early Malay name, *Tumasik,* meant "Sea Town," derives its modern name not as one would suspect from the Malay or Chinese language but from the Sanskrit, being a combination of two ancient words—*singa* meaning "lion" and *pura* meaning "city." The ancient Java-

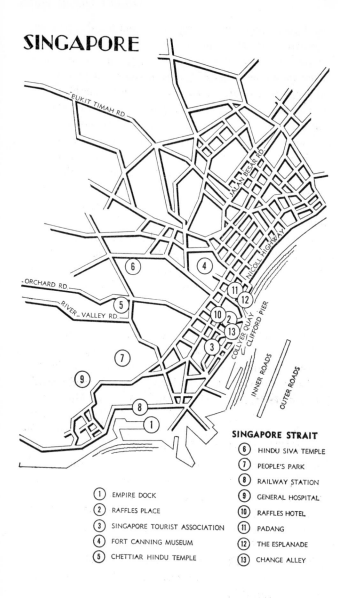

SINGAPORE

BUKIT TIMAH RD.

JALAN BESAR RD.

NICOLL HIGHWAY

ORCHARD RD.

RIVER VALLEY RD.

COLLYER QUAY

CLIFFORD PIER

INNER ROADS

OUTER ROADS

SINGAPORE STRAIT

① EMPIRE DOCK
② RAFFLES PLACE
③ SINGAPORE TOURIST ASSOCIATION
④ FORT CANNING MUSEUM
⑤ CHETTIAR HINDU TEMPLE

⑥ HINDU SIVA TEMPLE
⑦ PEOPLE'S PARK
⑧ RAILWAY STATION
⑨ GENERAL HOSPITAL
⑩ RAFFLES HOTEL
⑪ PADANG
⑫ THE ESPLANADE
⑬ CHANGE ALLEY

nese legend, probably apocryphal, chronicles the naming of *Singapura* as follows: The nobleman Sang Nila Uttama, a direct descendant of Alexander the Great, enroute by sea from **Palembang** to the *Island of Bentan,* encountered a terrific storm and was driven ashore on *Tumasik.* When he and his followers landed, they saw a great beast which Sang Nila Uttama described as being "very swift and beautiful, its body bright red, its head jet black, its breast white, and rather larger than a he-goat in size." When told that the beast which he admired so much was a lion, Uttama is said to have replied, "If the animals here look so smart and fierce, it would indeed be a good country in which to found a kingdom." He did, and named it *Singapura.*

During the 13th and 14th centuries, the island flourished under a succession of five kings who lived, successively, in a palace located on what is now known as *Fort Canning Hill.* The tomb one may see today near the site of the old *Royal Palace* is believed to be that of one of the sovereigns, Iskander Shah.

The tranquility of Singapore's early history was shattered in 1377 when the city was destroyed in a devastating war between the ferocious armies of the Palembang and Javanese kingdoms. The battle turned out to be such an orgy of fire and bloodshed that as a result a still living legend was born: Much of Singapore's soil is deep red in color, which vermilion hue is attributed to its having been saturated by the 14th-century blood which flowed so freely in the battle. The Javanese, having completely conquered the island, inexplicably lost all interest in it and left its inhabitants to their own devices. For centuries thereafter, Singapore remained in obscurity.

During the 16th and 17th centuries, the Malay chieftains, known as *Temenggongs,* who governed the island, fell under the rule of the Sultans of **Johore.** According to another ancient myth, one of the Sultans offered Singapore as a gift to a Scotchman, Alexander Hamilton, who, with uncharacteristic lack of foresight, declined it.

By the 19th century, Asiatic maritime activities had progressed, and Singapore had gained a new and unsavory reputation as a pirate haunt. The buccaneers' nefarious activities were something less than a blessing to Singapore. It was decades after the British had taken over before the pirates were completely swept from the surrounding seas.

The whole history of southeast Asia, and to a lesser degree of the entire world, was changed on the 28th of January in 1819. It was on that momentous day that Thomas Stamford Bingley Raffles, an official of the British East India Company, disembarked from his trading vessel to set foot for the first time on Singapore's blood red soil. Raffles, who was later knighted to become a "Sir," found a desolate island on which a mere 150 fishermen eked out their meager existence. Outside of the tiny village, the island of sinister reputation and shady past was overrun with mangrove swamps. The 19th century, however, was the imperial era of Britain's greatest glory. In her program of colonial expansion, she could neither make a mistake nor be denied. Englishmen everywhere were with uncanny perception ferreting out rich and strategic areas in which to found Crown Colonies. Sir Stamford, as he was best known, was a forthright man of dynamic action endowed with great vision and indomitable courage. He was morally certain that under British stewardship Singapore would become a successful seaport, where the East and West would meet to trade and where vessels from all over the world would come and go free of all inhibiting restrictions. He was right. Even today Singapore is a free port.

So skilled was Raffles in his negotiations with the *Temenggong* representing Johore's incumbent Sultan that by the sixth of February, nine days after landing, he had entered into an agreement which leased the island to the British East India Company.

Sir Stamford's actions did not meet with either immediate or universal approval at home, however. There were a number of British who doubted the wisdom of his action, which disapproval, momentarily at least, sent a cloud scudding across the complacent sky of Sir Stamford's dream of building Singapore into a strategic and commercially valuable port. He need not have worried. Under his wise and energetic administration, Singapore prospered.

In 1824, Sir Stamford Raffles renegotiated a favorable treaty with the Sultan which ceded, in perpetuity, Singapore and the small islands within ten miles of its coast (except those in the *Straits of Johore*) to the East India Company. British sovereignty on the island was thus established.

Between 1823 and 1830, the new British settlement was incorporated with **Malacca** and **Penang** as Straits Settlements under the British rule of **Bengal,** India, and in 1851 control of Singapore was turned over to the Governor General of India. In 1867, the British government assumed direct control of Singapore under a governor who served also as high commissioner of the then nine mainland Malay states. By the middle of the 19th century, Singapore had attained worldwide fame as a trading outpost, shipping center, and renowned naval base.

Curiously enough, such absolute faith was placed in Singapore as a naval stronghold that all of its formidable fortifications and defenses were constructed to defend it exclusively against attack from the sea. Such singleness of thought and action was quite unlike the British who were normally quite perspicacious in their planning.

No armada would have ever been so audacious as to attack Singapore from the sea. But the usually sagacious British savants never gave a moment's thought to the grave possibility of attack from the jungles of the *Malay Peninsula* from which Singapore is separated only by the narrow *Straits of Johore*. Thus it was, unhappily, from Malaya that the Japanese jungle fighters accomplished the cruelest defeat ever inflicted on the British. On February 15, 1942, the Crown Colony was surrendered to the Japanese.

In his memoirs, General Lord Ismay vividly describes Sir Winston Churchill's choleric rage when, after hearing of the impending Japanese attack on Singapore, he learned for the first time that there were no defenses to protect the island from the north.

On September 5, 1945, Singapore was liberated by forces of the Southeast Asia Command under Lord Louis Mountbatten (now Earl Mountbatten). A British military garrison administered Singapore for a period of seven months after which, on April 1, 1946, Singapore became a separate colony.

Powerful forces then began working for Singapore's complete independence. By 1955, a new constitution was adopted and free elections held, and in March of 1957 talks were begun in London which ultimately resulted in complete self-government for Singapore. The Constitution, adopted in 1958, came into full force with the general elections of May, 1959. In August of 1963, culminating several years of intensive negotiations and frequent frustrations, Singapore, together with North Borneo and Sarawak, became an integral part of the Federation of Malaysia.

LANGUAGE. Singapore is the only country in the world whose official language, Malay, is the tongue of a minority group. Despite the fact that almost seventy-five per cent of Singapore's population is Chinese, Malay is the language of the government, the schools, and the inscription on all legal documents. Chinese, Tamil, and English are the other most frequently spoken languages. There is no linguistic barrier for tourists, as English is understood almost everywhere.

FETES, FAIRS, AND FESTIVALS. Singapore literally oozes with local color. Is it any wonder? Under Holidays, Festivals, and Special Events, Chapter Seven, I have listed some of the almost limitless colorful events which take place throughout the year. One may readily realize the number of holidays that must be on Singapore's calendar when, to name but a few, there are religious and national holidays of Muslims, Christians, Buddhists, Confucianists, Jews, Hindus, Parsees, Sikhs, Taoists, and Zoroastrians. Photographic fans will never fail to find superb settings and magnificent coloration for their lenses.

HEALTH AND WEALTH. Singapore is a healthy, happy place to live, to work, and to visit. Disease is virtually unknown; there are no epidemics and no illness indigent to the island. The industrious inhabitants have a national per capita income of $1,200 (Singapore, or Straits, dollars), making it by far the richest state in the Asian area. Water may be safely drunk from the tap, as it is soft, clear, and of the purest content.

SHOPPING. By virtue of its status as a tax free port, Singapore shops offer prices that are startlingly low. Not only may one seek local souvenirs with confidence that rock bottom prices will be secured, but one's everyday necessities and travel needs may be purchased at prices that are lower than at point of origin. Color film of all types and sizes may be purchased less expensively, for example, in Singapore than in Chicago. Swiss watches, German cameras, electric shavers, and almost all other standard merchandise manufactured the world over may be purchased in Singapore at astoundingly low prices.

In Chapter Six, I have listed specific shops and stores, but in Singapore, perhaps more than elsewhere, much of the excitement and fun of shopping is the search for shops and bargains.

Exquisite souvenirs may be sought and found in shops along *Raffles Place, Battery Road, High Street,* and *North* and *South Bridge Roads.* To find intriguing Indian, Malayan, and Javanese art and curio shops, you have but to seek out *Orchard Road, Tanglin Road,* and *Arab Street.* The finest in handmade bags and shoes of alligator and reptile skins may be found in *Stamford Road,* while China crafts will be found in *North* and *South Bridge Roads, Battery Road, Stamford Road,* and *Orchard Road.* In *Chinatown,* one finds genuine Chinese art, antiques, furniture, Chinese silk clothing, and embroidery.

On the banks of the *Singapore River,* which flows through the heart of the town, one finds the *Malay Arts and Crafts Center.* In front of the marine police station is another center for purchasing Malayan products including *Kelantan* silverware, jewelry, sarongs, and beautifully handwrought Malay swords (*kris*).

CHANGE ALLEY is a name and an area with which to conjure. It is the "Petticoat Lane"–"Thieves Market" type of

bargain hunter's paradise. Even if one comes just to look-see, don't miss *Change Alley*. It is a visit to a chaotic, almost frantic, shopping center . . . and bargain like mad.

The ARCADE opposite *Clifford Pier* is another shopper's happy hunting ground where one may buy the latest type transistor radios, cuff links, yard goods, or what-have-you.

LOCAL TRANSPORTATION. Singapore's taxi system is excellent. The cars, though compact, are sufficiently roomy to be comfortable and are immaculately clean. The more than three thousand taxis are readily identified by circular disks bearing the letters "H.C.S." and by their ubiquitous meters. Meter fares are meticulously controlled, with the first mile or part thereof costing forty Singapore cents (U.S. 13¢). Additional half miles, or part thereof, are charged on the basis of twenty Singapore cents each. Should you hire a taxi by the hour, the fare is four Singapore dollars (U.S. $1.33) for the first hour and prorated fractionally each quarter hour thereafter.

Private cars are for hire at reasonable rates. Your local travel agent can make these arrangements for you.

Remember, please, the rule of the road in Singapore is *keep to the left.* Be sure when stepping into a street to *"look right."*

Buses are everywhere, but with taxis being so inexpensive and readily available, you probably won't have occasion to ride one. The *Malaysian Railway* which joins Singapore with **Johore Bahru** is modern and efficient, but the drive is so attractive that I think you would prefer to make this trip by private car.

TRISHAWS are available. This ancient Oriental mode of transportation is unique. It consists of a native propelled bicycle with a "side car" arrangement for two people. Try one just for the fun of it . . . or at least have your picture taken in one.

SAMPANS are used for water transport between the ships in the harbor or roadstead and the shore. Do be sure to hire a sampan for a turn about the harbor. You will find it a refreshing experience, with the view from the harbor toward Singapore being magnificent. Sampans cost $2.50 (Singapore) per hour per person (U.S. 83¢) and may be hired at *Clifford Pier.*

FLYING. An aerial view of Singapore is fascinating and will give one a better "bird's eye view" and topographical understanding of the area than ten thousand written words. Should you wish to take a flight, phone 84-447, the *Royal Singapore Flying Club,* and arrangements can be made easily and inexpensively.

WHAT TO WEAR. The best advice on this subject is "be comfortable." Singapore by day is quite informal. Men may wear light, plain white sports shirts and tropical-weight slacks or shorts, while ladies will be happy in light wash dresses. British women occasionally wear hats and gloves in the daytime, but I don't think American women will want to. When planning an evening out to dine, be sure to inquire before going out as to whether or not tie and jacket are required in the restaurant of your choice. If so, there is no exception to the rule.

TIPPING prevails in Singapore as it does the world over. A gratuity of ten per cent of your restaurant bill will be appreciated. Porters, bell boys, room boys, and others will be happy with less than their opposite numbers at home. Twenty Singapore cents is the minimum that I would suggest. Two Singapore dollars (U.S. 66¢) is a very big tip.

NEWS. One finds several English language newspapers in Singapore. Take your choice. It is quite probable that one's hotel room boy will have handed over the morning newspaper at breakfast. If not, the hotel desk will have newspapers for sale as well as late copies of the Asian editions of *Time, Newsweek, Life,* the *Saturday Evening Post,* and other English language publications.

INTERNATIONAL ORGANIZATIONS. Travel men and women will be interested to know that *SKAL* has an active chapter in Singapore. The phone number is 21-131, extension 2. *Rotarians* may learn the latest word on weekly luncheons by calling 30-286, while *Lions* may call 25-083 or 28-608 for information on their club. The *Junior Chamber of Commerce* may be reached by dialing 22-104. The *YMCA* may be reached by calling 33-793 and the *YWCA* by calling 35-850. The *American Club*'s phone number is 23-507.

SPORTS AND RECREATION. As an island state, it is only natural that Singaporeans and their visitors should spend much of their recreational time in or on the sea. Water sports include swimming, fishing, yachting, sculling, water skiing, skin diving, spear fishing, and coral and shell collecting. In Singapore, water activity takes place under the stars by moonlight as well as by day. The beaches at *Changi, Bedok, Loyang,* and *Pasir Ris* are readily available for swimming (at high tide) and picnicking. The *Singapore Swimming Club* has a huge, Olympic pool which I heartily recommend. A private club, notwithstanding, visitors may secure guest cards with little difficulty. There are also four huge public swimming pools. One may hire a launch at *Clifford Pier* to enjoy excellent swimming off the neighboring islands. Be sure to hire a guide for such an expedition. If you are interested in fishing parties, skin diving, spear fishing, or collecting corals and shells, you may make the necessary arrangements to do so through *"Sudong Coral,"* a store in *Cold Storage Arcade,* which will plan parties and organize guided visits to the small neighboring islands.

There are numerous other sports facilities including bad-minton at *P.W.D. Kalang Sports Club* (phone 28-311, ext. 52), golf at the *Royal Island Club* (phone 56-955) or the *Royal Singapore Golf Club* (phone 67-140), both of which have inviting swimming pools and attractive tennis facilities. Since both are private clubs, one should anticipate the desire to use their facilities and write ahead requesting a guest card. (Mention of one's home club affiliations is helpful.) One may watch go-cart racing at the *Karting Club of Singapore* (phone 67-879) and horse racing at the *Singapore Turf Club* (phone 92-331), motor racing at the *Singapore Motor Club,* polo at the *Singapore Polo Club* (phone 54-530), sculling and yachting at the *Royal Singapore Yacht Club* (phone 70-453), shooting at the *Singapore Gun Club,* squash at the *Cathay Hotel,* and public tennis at the *Farrer Park Athletics Center* (phone 31-664) or the *YMCA* (phone 33-793). There are rugby, soccer, hockey, and cricket matches on the colorful *Padang.*

The SINGAPORE TURF CLUB, a most pretentious race course in a superb setting, offers exciting racing. Founded in 1842, the present race track was built in 1932. The *Singapore Turf Club*'s history is not only one of equines but includes bloody battles during World War II. During their long occu-pation, the Japanese used the grandstand as a prisoner of war camp, cavalry depot, and veterinary research station.

The *Turf Club* is not just a race course, grandstand, and club house as we know them but also a village for the 1,500 people who work there in one capacity or another. The village contains both a mosque and a temple for the spiritual require-ments and shops to fill the physical needs of the workers and their families.

The track is one and an eighth miles around, and races are

contested at distances from three-quarters of a mile to a mile and three-quarters. The horses are imported from Europe and Australia, with the jockeys being Australian, British, and local lads. Races take place on Wednesdays and Saturdays. Should you wish to enjoy the so-called "sport of kings" from the club house, which is limited to members and guests, be sure to apply to the *Turf Club Town Office* at 146 Robinson Road where one may usually secure a member's guest badge. Should time not permit taking care of this formality in advance, you may visit the secretary's office at the race course on the afternoon of the sport.

The "WORLDS"—the *"Great World,"* the *"Happy World,"* and the *"New World"*—are the most unusual entertainment centers in the world. Each of these amusement centers contains movie houses, theaters, Chinese opera *(wayang),* dance halls, *joget* platforms (for the Malay dance where the partners never touch one another), restaurants, amusement stalls, bazaar type shopping booths, and every conceivable form of entertainment. Spend at least one evening in one or more of the *Worlds.*

The ANEKA RAGAM RAKYAT *(People's Variety Concert)* sponsored by the *Ministry of Culture* for the benefit of Singaporeans and their visitors is held fortnightly, usually on Sunday evening. Great open air stages in different parts of the island are the scenes of productions created by local talent. Literally thousands of people in all manner of costumes come to witness these entertainments which are free of charge. Be sure to bring your camera.

The CINEMAS are large, almost garish, air conditioned, and present the latest films from both East and West.

PORT. Singapore is the second busiest harbor in the world, handling annually some 40,000 vessels totaling more than 66,000,000 net tons. The port is used by 76 major shipping lines covering freight and passenger services to and from all parts of the world.

For the nautically inclined or statistically minded, a few marine facts might be of interest. The *Singapore Harbor Board* premises cover 950 acres with over three miles of wharves and jetties, forty acres of covered storage space, sixteen miles of special gauge railway, and an internal road system of twelve miles. Efficient oil and coal bunkering, fresh water, stevedore, ship chandler, laundry, and pest exterminating services are available locally.

Pilots are not obligatory in entering *Singapore Harbor,* but they are generally used by deep-sea vessels when berthing.

Six lighthouses, 21 light beacons, 27 unlit beacons, eleven light buoys, and 13 unlit buoys mark the entrances, deep water channels, and shoals in the port.

The *Harbor Board* maintains its own police force, a well equipped fire brigade, a fire boat, and a salvage tug with a range of 3,000 miles. It has extensive ship repair facilities, and its dockyard can accommodate ships up to 850 feet in length and up to 45,000 gross registered tons . . . very big vessels, indeed.

The SINGAPORE RIVER, a mile and three quarters long, passes through the heart of the city. The lighters, known locally as *Tonkangs,* crowd the river like vast collections of lumbering water buffalo. There are hundreds and hundreds of them. It is these *Tonkangs* and the *Bugis* boats with flaring sails and burdensome cargo, manned by almost naked Chinese, which unload the bulk of the thousands of freighters from all over the world in the roadstead. The *Singapore River* scene is a sight unrivaled in local color.

Among Singapore's many sights are:

BOTANICAL GARDENS. Not even *Kew Gardens* in London can outrival Singapore's *Botanical Gardens* where the most beautiful selections of the world's flowers are to be found. The orchid collection, blooming the year round, is unforgettable. These gardens form an idyllic, quiet, restful, and beautiful spot in which to stroll amidst exotic beauty. One may purchase a sack or so of peanuts for a pittance on entering the *Botanical Gardens* and amuse oneself feeding the monkeys who roam at random through the gardens. Singapore and Malaya abound with rubber trees. It is of interest to note that the first rubber sapling planted in this part of the world was brought from *Kew Gardens* in London and planted in the *Botanical Gardens* in 1877. As a result of this original rubber planting and ultimate cultivation, both the Malayan states and Singapore have built and maintained their economic importance.

TIGER BALM GARDENS (HAW PAR VILLA). Even after one sees this spectacular monstrosity, it will seem unreal. The late Aw Boon Haw who rose from rags to riches as one of the world's most legendary millionaires started life as a poor boy without a farthing, but through the manufacture and sale of patent medicines and cure-alls, and subsequently as a newspaper tycoon and insurance magnate, built one of the great fortunes of the world. The Aw jade collection, representing the joint effort of the late brothers Aw Boon Par and Aw Boon Haw, may be seen in the Aw mansion in *Tanglin Road*. This jade collection is the greatest in the world, with all stones being beautifully arranged in cabinets according to the dynasties of China. All of the worthwhile dynasties are represented. The mansion also houses some of the finest known Chinese paintings and etchings. Singapore's *Tiger Balm Gardens* are comparable to the collections of the same name in **Hong Kong.** If your time is limited and you visit both Singapore and **Hong Kong,** don't bother to see both *Tiger Balm Gardens.* They are the same, though one or the other is a required sight. The effect of the *Tiger Balm Gardens* is so weird, ugly, grotesque, and impossible as to be fascinating. On a hillside facing the seashore, the *Tiger Balm Gardens* include a collection of unique sculptures of concrete, plaster of paris, and papier mâché painted in the most riotous colors. These alleged "works of art" depict legends, stories, themes from ancient Chinese mythology and modern interpretations of old proverbs. One sees statues of real and imaginary animals, gods and goddesses, centaurs, and women with heads of fowl. There are also sculptured re-enactments of torture chambers, murders, and mayhem.

NICOLL HIGHWAY, running from *Queen Elizabeth Walk*

to *Mountbatten Road,* includes the two-mile-long *Merdeka Bridge.* A drive along *Nicoll Highway* from east to west will leave an image of lasting loveliness in the garden of your memories. The esplanade separating the highway from the harbor is ever ablaze with brightly hued flowers punctuated with gently waving palm trees and affords an unusually fine vantage point from which to view the ship-jammed harbor and the handsome silhouette of the downtown section.

The PADANG AREA. As one approaches the *Padang,* the old majestic *Britannia Club* comes into view. The *Padang's* wide expanse of Kelly green lawn is flanked on one side by the *Singapore Cricket Club* and on the other by the *Singapore Recreation Club.* Back of the *Padang* at *Empress Place,* one views the venerable collection of brooding British administrative and government buildings including *Victoria Memorial Hall* and *Theater,* the imposing *Supreme Court,* the legislative *Assembly House,* the newer *Government Tourist Office,* and the *Immigration Building.*

The ASSEMBLY HOUSE, built in 1827, now the home of the State Assembly, is behind *Victoria Memorial Hall*. *St. Andrew's Cathedral*, across the street, was built by convict labor in 1856. Within the grounds of *St. Andrew's Cathedral*, snake charmers frequently set up shop. These sly crafty fellows not only charm the snakes but intersperse their acts with feats of juggling and displays of magic. The *Municipal Building* is nearby.

Between the *Padang* and the sea, one finds the *Cenotaph* and the *Queen Elizabeth Walk* adjacent to the harbor. Nearby is the tiny memorial pagoda to the memory of Major-General Lim Bo Seng, a Malayan patriot who was tortured and subsequently killed by the Japanese during their occupation of Singapore in World War II.

The ESPLANADE, mentioned previously, is not only cool and pleasant but boasts of an outdoor restaurant which is an excellent place to dine, enjoy the passing parade, and view the busy harbor and the city's waterfront.

FORT CANNING HILL, behind the *National Museum* in *Stamford Road*, is the current headquarters of the Singapore garrison and was the site of the first government house and early palace of the local kings.

As one continues past the *Padang*, crossing *Cavanagh Bridge* over the *Singapore River*, one turns left and right to enter *Collyer Quay* in the heart of downtown Singapore where one sees the *Hong Kong and Shanghai Bank*, the *Union Building*, the *Ocean Building*, *Asia Building*, *Singapore Tourist Association*, and *The First National City Bank of New York*.

Famed *Raffles Place* is back of *Collyer Quay*, and between the two is the colorful bazaar shopping street, *Change Alley*.

Clifford Pier is in front of *Collyer Quay*.

RAFFLES PLACE, in the heart of town, is a distinguished square surrounded by banks, insurance companies, exchange marts, and busy offices. There are a number of shops in the area.

EATING STALLS. In the restaurant chapter I have mentioned these unique Singapore institutions, which are not little flimsy "beaneries" with a few pounds of vittles to disseminate . . . not at all. On the contrary, they are solid local institutions. The Chinese and Malays patronize the stalls as do fine feathered foreigners including the European and Australian inhabitants. The principal areas for the Chinese eating stalls are *Albert Street, People's Park,* the *Bedok* corner on the sea front, and *Koek Road.* The Malayan eating stalls are located in *Beach Road.*

VAN KLEEF AQUARIUM is one of the most modern and well stocked aquariums in the world. Fully air conditioned, this fish museum presents a twilight atmosphere in which one sees a myriad of tropical fish, sea animals, and the flora and fauna of the deep in a natural sea bed surrounding. This huge collection of exotic fish includes species from various parts of the world, but the majority of the *aquarium's* specimens may be seen in the waters around Singapore's shores and those of her neighboring islands.

The SINGAPORE MUSEUM is a small but well documented museum illustrating the background and history of modern Singapore as well as exhibiting collections of local flora and fauna. This museum is most general in its coverage and includes archeological specimens and illustrations of the modern and ancient ways of life in Singapore.

MODERN HOUSING DEVELOPMENTS. You will be intrigued with the housing development schemes at **Kallang** and **Queenstown** which consist of multi-storied apartment buildings designed to relieve the choking congestion in *Chinatown* by providing low cost comfortable housing.

BUKIT TIMAH NATURE RESERVE is one of several reserves set aside in Singapore for the propagation, protection, and preservation of the flora and fauna indigenous to Singapore, as well as for the preservation of objects and places of aesthetic, historical, and scientific interest. These reserves have well maintained paths where one may stroll leisurely in the shelter of two-hundred-foot trees. *Bukit Timah Nature Reserve,* on Singapore's highest hill 581 feet above sea level, is ornamented with the best primary evergreen rain forest in the area.

TEMPLES, CHURCHES, AND MOSQUES. There are sixteen mosques, thirteen temples, and thirty churches in Singapore including Armenian, Christian Science, Catholic, Methodist (English and Chinese), Presbyterian, Queen of Peace, and Seventh Day Adventist churches. Catholic and Methodist churches predominate among the Christian religious edifices.

SIANG LIM SIAN SI TEMPLE, in *Kim Keat Road,* is a most elaborate Buddhist place of worship built 55 years ago at a cost of more than half a million dollars. It has recently been greatly restored. Save for the *Ayer Hitam Temple* in Penang, this is the largest Buddhist temple either in Singapore or Malaya and contains exquisite marble artistry and wood carvings comparable to those one would see if one could currently visit Peking.

SAKYA MUNI GAYA TEMPLE, a Buddhist temple in *Race Course Road,* is better known as the "Temple of a Thousand Lights," which lights surround the temple's fifty-foot-high three-hundred-ton image of Lord Buddha. In the temple one finds the replica of a footprint, carved in teakwood and ornamented in mother-of-pearl, which is believed to have been left on a mountain in Ceylon by Lord Buddha.

SRI MARIAMMAN TEMPLE, Singapore's oldest Hindu place of worship, dates back to circa 1843. In 1936, the original plan which included a simple chaste façade was altered in appearance to the highly decorative front that visitors find so intriguing today.

The HOLY SULTAN MOSQUE, in one of the Malay quarters, is the center of worship for Singapore's 100,000 followers of Mohammed. Should you visit the *Holy Sultan Mosque,* which I urge, it is considered an act of courtesy to observe the custom of washing your face, ears, hands, and feet in holy water before following the High Priest (Imam), barefooted, into the *Mosque.*

CHETTIAR TEMPLE in *Tank Road* comes into prominence every year at the time of the Hindu festivals.

MOUNT FABER, rising steeply to its 350 foot eminence above the shore, is topped by a signal station for local shipping but is more interesting as a vantage platform from which one may enjoy a spectacular panorama of the shipping in the harbor, the adjacent city, all of the Island of Singapore, the hills of **Johore** to the north, and the islands of the *Rhio Archipelago* to the south. The spectacular tropical sunsets can be absorbed to good advantage on *Mount Faber*.

THE GAP, comparable in description to *Mount Faber,* is another favorable spot from which to enjoy the roseate hued sunsets.

FISHING KELONGS, in the sea near the shore, consist of a series of upright bamboo stakes set in straight lines leading to huts perched several hundreds yards out in the water. Known collectively as *kelongs,* these contraptions specifically are local fish traps into which large nets are lowered at night while bright lights are shown in such a way as to attract the fish which are quickly hauled in and the entire catch immediately sent on its way to nearby markets.

BEAUTIFUL RESIDENTIAL AREAS. New expensive estates, as large and delightful as one will ever see, are found in the *Holland* and *Dunearn Road* areas. Older but equally attractive estates are located in the *Tanglin* area. In both areas, the back estate acreages are under agricultural cultivation, and all have well manicured gardens and lawns.

THE RURAL AREA outside of the Singapore city limits numbers well over 500,000 inhabitants who are engaged in fishing, farming, and working on rubber plantations. Because of its unchanging climate, as many as twelve vegetable crops a year are possible including lettuce, cabbage, onions, sweet potatoes, spinach, cucumbers, fruit, and tobacco. Fish, poultry, pork, eggs, and vegetables are available in quantities sufficient to make Singapore self-sufficient in these products.

Much of the beef and almost all of the oranges must be imported, with the former coming from Australia and the latter, believe it or not, from California. Rice, spices, and dried foods are imported from Malaya.

The SINGAPORE WAR MEMORIAL on a gentle hill in the *Memorial Cemetery* overlooks the *Straits of Johore* north of Singapore City and commemorates the twenty-four thousand members of the armed forces who died during World War II but who were not interred in known graves. The inscription on the memorial reads as follows:

"1939–1945"

"On the walls of this memorial are recorded the names of 24,000 men and women of many races united in the service of the British Crown, who gave their lives in Malaya and neighboring lands and seas and in the air over southern and eastern Asia and the Pacific but to whom the fortune of war denied the customary rites accorded to their comrades in death. They died for all free men."

The UNIVERSITY OF SINGAPORE numbers more than two thousand students of all races, one third of whom are women, who study the arts, education, law, science, medicine, dentistry, and pharmacy. Classes are taught in English.

NANYANG UNIVERSITY, founded by Chinese merchants in 1953, is Chinese, with classes being conducted in that language. A wide range of courses is taught including commerce, chemistry, physics, mathematics, political science, economics, history, geography, literature, languages, and education. Twenty per cent of the almost two thousand students are women. The university buildings and gardens are as beautiful as those of any university in the world, the grounds including five hundred acres, almost 150 acres of which have been horticulturally developed.

MARKETS. All Singapore seems, with the exception of the busy European type downtown sector, as though it is one great, huge, colorful, strident indoor and outdoor market. The stalls, bazaars, and shops are presided over by men and women in every conceivable type and color of costume. They sell "just everything" from refreshing crushed ice to preserved shark fins, pharmaceutical beetles, and dried mushrooms. In open stalls, one finds shashlick, shish kabob, freshly squeezed fruit and vegetable juices, spices, rice in a variety of forms, fish, prawns, cucumbers, beans, celery, Chinese cabbage, raw mustard, and other exotic concoctions. Accidentally, one will stumble over markets in *Chinatown,* the Malayan villages, and other native quarters. The principal ones are: *Beach Road Market, Changi Market, Joo Chiat Market, Grange Road Market, Kandang Kerbau Market, Maxwell Market, Orchard Road Market, Siglap Market,* and *Telok Ayer Market.*

You will be pleasantly surprised, even amazed, at the attractiveness of the outdoor, and near outdoor, markets where the food is so well displayed and usually handled hygienically.

The Malay village of GEYLANG is the most picturesque of the rural villages.

Singapore's CHINATOWN is typically crowded, with the family washing hanging from the windows on long bamboo poles. Throngs of people live, work, and play in a cacophony of constant pattering to the tune of the harsh cries of street vendors. Late afternoon and evening is a good time to see *Chinatown,* where one's presence will cause no lifted eyebrows, visitors being taken in stride. *Chinatown's* food stalls sell sweet sour pork, fried prawns, beancurd, scarlet sausage, chicken, duck, and delectable vegetables. Drink purveying stalls, wheelbarrows of fruit, and armies of hawkers are all active. The odor of joss sticks permeates the atmosphere, and the clackety-clack of wooden sandals is interspersed with the *wayangs* (open air opera) and the singsong of ancient Chinese music.

The RESERVOIRS. *McRitchie, Pierce, Mandai,* and *Murnane* are calm jungle-side, concrete-lined lakes. The latter reservoir holds 56,000,000 gallons of water, said to be the largest covered reservoir in the world.

MALAYA

MALAYA, an independent country since August 31, 1957, is a gentle, lush, richly verdant, sun-splashed land of 51,000 square miles, populated like **Thailand,** its neighbor to the north, by some of the world's most friendly people. Malaya's seven million mainland inhabitants, who enjoy Asia's highest standard of living, dwell in eleven of the fourteen states of the Federation of Malaysia whose capital is the brash, beautiful, booming **Kuala Lumpur.**

The Federation of Malaysia is comprised of the eleven states of Malaya plus the island state of Singapore and the British protectorates of Sarawak and North Borneo, the latter now called Sabah. The 1964 population of the Federation was close to eleven million.

Malaya's inhabitants are a potpourri crosscut of the Far East with some 3,500,000 Malays, 3,300,000 Chinese, 750,000 Indians, representative population segments of Pakistanis, Europeans, Eurasians, and a smattering from nations throughout the world. The aborigines, though not numerous, are still to be found leading a nomadic life in Malaya's central jungles.

RACIAL TERMINOLOGY. Citizens of Malaya are known as Malayans or Malaysians whether they are ethnically Chinese, Malays, Pakistanis, Indians, or members of other races. A Malay is a member of an ancient race who could be a citizen of Indonesia or Borneo as well as of Malaya.

The RELIGIONS OF MALAYA are the religions of the world. Christian churches will be found representing the Catholics, Episcopals, Baptists, Unitarians, and, in Asia, the ubiquitous Methodists, as well as gathering places for the ancient religions of the Siamese, Sikhs, and Jews. There are Buddhist temples, Hindu, and Chinese places of worship and every type of mosque.

CLIMATE. Temperatures in the lowlands are pleasantly warm. Daytime temperatures seldom rise higher than ninety degrees, with the nights averaging a comfortable seventy degrees. In the hill stations of the *Cameron Highlands,* tempera-

MALAY PENINSULA

tures seldom exceed eighty degrees Fahrenheit or drop below forty degrees. Malaya knows no rainy season as such, though as a general rule one may count on its being dry from January through March, clear from April through August, with frequent rains from September through December. On the east coast, the greatest precipitation may be expected from November through January. The quantity and periods of rainfall vary greatly throughout the area, but of one thing you can be morally certain: when it rains in Malaya, it does so with tropical ferocity, frequently accompanied by thunder and lightning, but only for a while. The sun breaks through again within a matter of a couple of hours.

CLOTHING. A lightweight wardrobe is all that is ever required in Malaya. During the day women will be quite comfortable in light cotton dresses, while men will be happy in light, plain colored sports shirts and slacks. Should your tropical wardrobe need replenishing, Malayan materials are inexpensive and of good quality. Local tailors can run up almost anything you need in a day or two. In the better hotels and restaurants men are expected to wear a tie and jacket in the evening, while a normal street or cocktail dress will be just fine for milady. Smaller places are less formal.

GEOGRAPHICALLY, the *Malay Peninsula* stretches 700 miles southward from **Thailand** to **Singapore,** with scores of exotic islands lying off its variegated coast line. There is credible evidence that the *Malay Peninsula* was once joined by land to its now neighboring islands of **Sumatra, Java, Bali,** and **Borneo.** Numerous Malay rivers, of which *Pahang* on the east coast is the largest, flow into the surrounding waters of the *China Sea* and the *Strait of Malacca.* The *Peninsula*'s main ridge of mountains, serving as its spinal column, punctuates the *Peninsula* midway from east to west.

FLORA, FAUNA, AND ANIMAL LIFE. While many tropical lands include barren wastes or dismal, infertile rock-covered reaches, this is not so with Malaya. Quite on the contrary, 75% of the country is a verdant wonderland with evergreen jungle forests generously endowed with a vast variety of plant and animal life. The Malayans point out with great pride that the splendor of their plant and animal life is un-equalled elsewhere in an area of comparable size. Sleek black panthers and ferocious spotted leopards inhabit the jungle areas as do mighty elephants and rugged rhinoceroses. Exotically colored orchids bloom throughout the land in wild profusion.

HYGIENE. Malaya, like **Singapore,** is one of the healthiest places in the world. There are no diseases indigenous to this area. You may drink the tap water without fear, and the food at roadside stalls is safe, though some dishes may possibly be too spicy "hot" for western tastes.

INTERNAL TRANSPORTATION. The *Malaysian Airways* links all major Malaysian cities one with the other and with **Singapore.** *Thai International Airways* flies from **Singapore** to **Kuala Lumpur** and **Bangkok** several times a week. **Kuala Lumpur** is also served by *British Overseas Airways Corporation* (BOAC), *Cathay Pacific Airways* (CPA), *Garuda Indonesian Airways,* K.L.M. *Royal Dutch Airlines,* and *Qantas Empire Airways.*

On the MALAYSIAN RAILWAY one meets such interesting people, including as wide a variety of colorful racial groups as has ever been assembled. The countryside viewed from the folksy air conditioned trains is magical. The principal railway route is from **Singapore** to **Johore Bahru** and the west coast cities of **Kuala Lumpur, Ipoh,** and **Penang,** with connections onward to **Thailand.** Trains are pulled by the latest 1,500-horse-power diesel-electric locomotives. The *International North-South Express* is known picturesquely as the "Golden Blowpipe," a nod to the favorite weapon of the aborigines. Nightly service is provided with modern air conditioned sleeping compartments for two. Branch lines serve **Klang, Port Swettenham,** and **Teluk Anson.** Station masters along the line can arrange to have a car with chauffeur waiting to drive you to one of the hill stations (mountain resorts). Should one wish to visit *Fraser's Hill* or the

Cameron Highlands, the drives are from the *Kuala Kabu Road* and *Tapah Road* stations. The rail journey from **Gemas** through the heart of the primeval jungle of Central Malaya to **Kuala Lipis** and **Kota Bharu** is bewitchingly fascinating.

A first class sleeping-car service is operated twice weekly in each direction between **Penang** and **Bangkok, Thailand,** with connections from **Kuala Lumpur** and **Singapore.**

TAXIS are plentiful and cheap. Fares, depending on the size of the car, range from ten to thirteen and one-half U.S. cents per mile for city driving.

TRISHAWS are in evidence in **Penang,** where passengers are transported on a sedan-like seat in front of the pedaller, and in **Kuala Lumpur** and other Malayan cities, where the passengers sit abreast of the driver. I suggest that for a special sort of a thrill you try a ride in a *trishaw.*

ROADS in Malaya are good. One may be driven comfortably from **Singapore** through **Kuala Lumpur** to **Penang** in a chauffeur-driven car through some of the world's most exotic scenery in less than two days.

NATURAL RESOURCES. Malaya produces more than one-third of the world's rubber and tin.

ENTERTAINMENT. Western style night clubs are non-existent, although the better hotel dining rooms and restaurants provide music, dancing, and occasionally some type of cabaret. There is much more intriguing entertainment awaiting you in Malaya than the trite night club variety, however. Amusement parks, known as *"Worlds,"* are to be found in Malaya which are similar to the three *"Worlds"* I have described in **Singapore.** On the east coast of Malaya, one may see performances of skilled men who spin giant tops and fly huge brilliantly hued kites and perform the *bersilat,* a virile art of self-defense. The Malay dramas, *Makyong* and *Manora,* and the *Wayang Kulit* (shadow play) may be seen. Inquire locally of your travel agent or at the hotel for details of the time and place of performances. In country villages, the traditional saucer dance is presented, while on special occasions groups of Malayan Indians perform

their fire-walking ceremonies. The intricate Chinese lion dance
is performed in the streets on festival days.

Cinemas, to be found everywhere in Malaya, are air conditioned and present the latest American, British, French, Chinese,
Indian, and Malayan films.

SPORTS. Malayans are avid sports addicts and participate in
and watch enthusiastically almost every known game. Horse
race meetings are held throughout the year at courses in **Kuala
Lumpur, Penang,** and **Ipoh.** One may watch soccer, rugby,
cricket, and play tennis or golf. Salt water swimming and skin
diving in the ocean and fresh or salt water swimming in
splendid sanitary pools are at your disposal.

WEEKLY HOLIDAYS are observed on Friday in the states
of Perlis, Kedah, Kelantan, Trengganu, and Johore, while Sunday is the day of rest in the other states. Christmas Day, December 25th, is a national holiday. New Year's Day is not, though
the Chinese New Year is celebrated for two days. Good Friday
is celebrated as a holiday, but Easter is not. Mohammed's
birthday, August 23rd, is a national holiday as is Independence
Day, August 31st.

BACKGROUND AND HISTORY. Malayans, unfortunately,
have not proved to be brilliant historians. Accurate archives
were not chronicled in this smiling land. What is known of the
Peninsula's historical background indicates that from its earliest
beginnings external influences were brought to bear on this
polyglot land. Evidences are everywhere that the Thais (nee
Siamese), Chinese, and Indians took turns dominating Malaya.
Bali, Java, and Borneo all played a part in the early history of
Malaya. Centuries ago there were numerous Malays in **Sumatra,**
many of whom subsequently returned to the Peninsula. Busy
Arabian missionaries succeeded in converting almost 100% of
the early population to the Moslem faith. The Portuguese took
over Malacca, Malaya's oldest state, in the 16th century, the
Dutch in the 17th century, and the British in the 19th century.

Malaccan historians, Malaya's most prolific, indicate that the
state seems quite definitely to have been founded in the 14th

century by a Malayan nobleman fleeing the catastrophe in Singapura.

The exciting modern history of Malaya, however, stems from 1857, when, precisely one hundred years before the independence of Malaya was proclaimed, **Kuala Lumpur** was founded.

The country, now so tranquil, was not always so. With the founding of the lusty city destined to become the capital of the country, events began to transpire rapidly, but in the formative years the Malays and the Chinese did not live in the close harmony they enjoy today. Piracy was rampant, and the Chinese and the Malays fought each other just to be doing something if no better excuse was available. As almost any student of colonialism could foretell, the British, then in the zenith of their empire building, stepped in as a peacemaker among the warring factions and to add this rich area to its burgeoning Asian outposts. **Singapore** was by then a going proposition. What could have been more logical than to take over the whole *Peninsula?*

There are evidences that tin has been produced in Malaya for more than five hundred years, but it was not until the latter part of the last century that rubber trees were first introduced to Singapore and Malaya.

From south to north, the west coast Malayan states are:

JOHORE, lying immediately across the narrow *Straits of Johore* from **Singapore.** The capital of this verdant lowland state of just less than 950,000 population who live on 7,335 square miles is **Johore Bahru.**

MALACCA is the most historical and one of the three smallest states, both in population and area, encompassing less than 650 square miles populated by less than 300,000.

NEGRI SEMBILAN has a population of 370,000.

SELANGOR, of which **Kuala Lumpur** is state as well as national capital, is the second most populous with over a million inhabitants.

PERAK is the most populous of the Malay states with over a

million and a quarter inhabitants and is the second largest state in area. Its capital is **Ipoh.**

PENANG, the island state, tiniest of all with but 110 square miles of enchanting land surrounded by the sea, has a population of well over half a million. **George Town,** commonly called **Penang,** is the island's glamorous capital.

KEDAH's capital is **Alor Star,** its population three quarters of a million.

PERLIS, the most northerly of the states, is the least populous with less than 100,000 citizens and the second smallest with just over three hundred square miles. **Kangar** is its capital.

PAHANG, the most southerly of the eastern states and the largest in area, has almost 14,000 square miles with a population of 315,000.

TRENGGANU has **Kuala Trengganu** as its capital, a population of almost 300,000, and an area of over 5,000 square miles.

KELANTAN boasts of a population of more than half a million and close to 6,000 square miles of area.

FORM OF GOVERNMENT. Each of the original eleven peninsular states has its own ruler (sultan) and elected assembly. The supreme head of the Government, with headquarters in **Kuala Lumpur,** is His Majesty the Yang di-Pertuan Agong, a constitutional monarch elected by the Malay rulers (sultans) from among their own number for a terms of five years. The parliament is made up of an elected House of Representatives, and a Senate comprised of elected and appointed members. The Yang di-Pertuan Agong appoints the Prime Minister from among the membership of the House, a post which normally goes to the leader of the house majority. Malaya is a part of the Federation of Malaysia.

SINGAPORE, long-time British Crown Colony was not, contrary to popular western misconception, a part of Malaysia until August 1963. Each of the Federation members—Singapore, Malaya, Sarawak, and North Borneo—has its own democratic form of government which differs somewhat from the format of the original eleven states.

The Federation of Malaysia's present "labor" pains will soon become growing pains, and, it is hoped, in due course this political group will sprout into healthy adolescence. Meanwhile Indonesia's Sukarno is giving the Federation a hard time.

JOHORE, rich in major crops and natural minerals, is the most southerly of the Malay states and, because of its proximity to **Singapore,** best known to foreign visitors. **Johore Bahru,** its capital, lapped by the waters of the *Straits of Johore,* is reached across the causeway by car or *Malaysian Railway* in less than an hour from *Raffles Square.*

A day's visit from **Singapore** to **Johore Bahru** and surrounding southern **Johore** will prove rewarding. His Highness the Sultan's two splendid palaces are like pages from the Arabian Nights. *Istana Besar,* the sumptuous ceremonial palace, is situated on a gently undulating hillside amid the brilliantly colored *Istana Gardens.* Its vividly green, meticulously manicured lawns offer a verdant setting for a riot of flowers. Not now used as a royal residence, *Istana Besar* is open to the public (permission to visit, however, must be secured in advance) and is a virtual museum crammed with fascinating mementos of the colorful history of **Johore** and the personal souvenirs and costumes of its sultans and sultanas. It is in *Istana Besar* that His Highness the Sultan receives foreign dignitaries, presides at ceremonial functions, and state receptions. The decorative motif of the palace is in exquisitely good taste, rich and regal in its bearing. One may spend a fascinating hour or two browsing through this palace and its grounds. The Sultan resides in stately *Istana Bukit Serene,* majestically located on a gentle hill surrounded by a vast estate of lush green countryside. His Highness, the present Sultan, is a man of great personal charm and magnetism. Educated in England and on the Continent, his English is impeccable and his interest in people and things deep and genuine. It is one of the heartwarming pleasures of my more than three decades of world travel to have been entertained by His Highness in *Istana Bukit Serene.* The Sultan's private stables of thoroughbred and palamino horses are on the *Palace* grounds as is his collection of fabulous automobiles including Cadillacs, Rolls-Royces, Mercedes Benz, Buicks, and others. His Highness breeds birds, and his aviary contains a large exotic tropical array. The Sultan's private zoo, containing splendid species of the numerous animals indigenous to **Johore,** is open to the public. One will find the *Botanical Gardens* of great interest.

Johore Bahru's government building on an impressive hill overlooking the causeway is the seat of the local government. From its observation tower, one commands an impressive panoramic vista of **Singapore,** the *Straits of Johore,* rubber estates, pineapple groves, the *Istana Besar,* and, in the distance, the *China Sea.*

One should also visit the handsome, stately *Abu Bakar Mosque.*

If time permits, a drive along the waterfront will reveal the colorful gathering places for the **Johore** residents, and a short distance inland, reached by a good road, is *Kota Tinggi,* well known for its nearby cascading waterfall, a popular haunt for local picnickers. Bring a basket lunch.

SELANGOR is not only one of the Federation's richest states, but its capital, **Kuala Lumpur,** is the nation's capital as well.

KUALA LUMPUR, founded more than one hundred years ago by Chinese tin miners on a finger of land at the confluence of the *Klang* and *Gombak Rivers,* takes its name from the appearance of these merging waters . . . "muddy mouths." Twenty-eight miles from the sea at **Port Swettenham,** K.L., as the capital is generally known, snuggles between purple hills rising three to six thousand feet above it and is best viewed from the *Tengku Abdul Rahman Park.* A score or more skyscrapers stud K.L.'s horizon, most of which have been built since the 1957 proclamation of independence. K.L. is still a city of vivid contrasts with the boisterous effect of the new buildings being tempered by Moorish style mid-Victorian structures such as the massive government secretariat with its renowned clock tower. Much of the city retains it easy Old World atmosphere. *Victory Avenue* is broad and lined with palm trees; the heart of the city is decorated with vivid flowers and green trees. *Lake Garden,* in the heart of town, is set amid gentle hills, lacy trees, and blooming flowers, all surrounded by magnificent homes. Ultramodern buildings front on mining pools, and from the heart of town to vegetation choked jungle is but a matter of minutes.

The impact of the Japanese occupation which began in January of 1942 was felt more shockingly in K.L. than elsewhere. Kuala Lumpurians still talk about it with bated breath as something that couldn't have happened . . . but did.

K.L.'s present population of nearly 500,000 is rapidly growing. Vast blocks of flats encroach on the old Chinese and Malay villages. Brightly colored chauffeur-driven cars, busy taxis, and *trishaws* roam the downtown streets. On one river bank, at the site of the original founding, a typical Chinese city is still to be found where the streets are one continuous marketplace ajar with the inevitable shrieking noise that seems to be the hallmark of the Chinese. In *Petaling Street,* Chinese merchandise and food are on sale as are cameras and field glasses from Germany, radios and electronic devices, novelties and goods of all sizes and shapes. The Malay village is less boisterous, smaller, built on stilts, and dwarfed by great mosques.

Mountbatten Road is a busy shopping thoroughfare in which one finds the breathtaking *Arts and Crafts Center* featuring the work of village artisans: rich sarong brocades with traditional design and handwrought silverware.

In K.L., as in the other Malayan cities, the Chinese predominate. They are the merchants, business, and professional people. The Malays are content to work in the paddy fields, as fishermen, and in the tin mines or on the rubber plantations.

The NEW AIRPORT is fabulous. Large enough to accommodate the largest jets, its air conditioned main building is the last word in airport design.

The RAILWAY STATION is unique. One's first thought on seeing this highly ornate edifice is of another mosque which, in appearance, it could readily be were it not a busy metropolitan terminus. This overly decorative structure is Moorish in design, with arches, towers, onion-like domes, and columns. On festival nights, it is lighted. Inside, it's a teeming "working" railroad station.

ISTANA NEGARA is the official residence of the Yang di-Pertuan Agong, the constitutional monarch of the Federation, where the ceremonial changing of the guard at eight A.M. on Tuesdays is worth getting up to see.

The RELIGIOUS STRUCTURES of K.L. undoubtedly are the most varied in the world. Headed by the *Sultan's Mosque* and the *Cathedral of St. John,* there are houses of worship of almost every known civilized religion.

The NATIONAL MUSEUM *(Lake Gardens)* and NATIONAL ART GALLERY *(Ampang Road)* feature interesting relics of Malaya's history and the work of modern artists.

The SUNDAY MARKET, held Saturday nights at **Kampong Bahru,** is a concentrated colorful market attended by natives galore.

Costumes of all types are seen in K.L., but those which predominate are *cheongsams,* trousered *samfu,* and the saffron robes of the monks.

Stall-like restaurants are found throughout the city in which native delicacies are dispensed. Try the *satay,* served on bamboo skewers.

Driving out of town, scores of thousands of rubber trees, tapped to collect the latex from which sheet rubber is made, may be seen along the roadside. Modern tin dredges are side by side with old Chinese women panning for tin by the most ancient, though simplest, method.

The BUKIT BINTANG is the K.L. version of a *"World"* amusement park.

The CHIN WOO STADIUM's Olympic size swimming pool is adjacent to an excellent Chinese restaurant.

One can arrange to secure a guest card to the SELANGOR CLUB (popularly known as the "Spotted Dog" because of its typical English warty club architecture) without too much difficulty. Originally exclusively British, this is one of the largest private clubs in the world, with more than one thousand active members, now open to all Malayans regardless of their native race.

The SELANGOR TURF CLUB is the setting for K.L.'s horse race meets, held frequently throughout the year.

The SELANGOR CLUB PADANG (separate and distinct from the *Turf Club*) is the site of cricket and tennis matches.

The BATU CAVES about seven miles from town are unusual. The limestone rocks from which the caves are formed rise to a sheer height of more than four hundred feet. The entrance is reached by a flight of almost perpendicular stairs. The cavernous interior is eerie and worth the climb if you are fit and under forty!

Near K.L. are two interesting housing projects, the satellite town of PETALING JAYA with a population of more than 50,000 and JIN-JANG, a huge Chinese "new village."

PENANG, Malaya's island state, also known as *Prince of Wales Island,* is generally conceded to be one of the loveliest islands in the tropics, referred to with good reason as "the paradise of the East," the "pearl of the Orient," and the "holiday island of the Far East."

Penang has been a free port since 1876. All comments which I have made relative to the purchase of tax free merchandise in **Singapore** and **Hong Kong** apply to **Penang,** where watches, cameras, and other heavy dutiable items may be purchased at extremely low rates.

Penang's harbor is a miniature **Hong Kong,** agog with an agglomeration of sea craft from the tiny *perahus* of the local traders and *Bugis,* the Malay fishing boats, to ocean-going Chinese junks, busy ferryboats, tankers, cargo liners, freighters, and modern cruise liners, all of which add to the sophistication of the setting.

GEORGE TOWN, capital and principal city of **Penang** and referred to frequently as **Penang,** numbers among its almost 250,000 population members of almost all of the races of the world. It is a "busy as a beaver" city of indubitably Oriental character punctuated with the largest number of churches, mosques, and temples per capita of any city in the world. There are more than one hundred temples alone.

The KEK LOK SI *Monastery* and *Temple* at **Ayer Itam** near **George Town** is one of the handsomest of the Buddhist buildings of the Far East, built with money donated by Buddhists in Malaysia, Burma, Thailand, and Indonesia. *Kek Lok Si* is unique outside of Tibet.

The Thais have four temples of their own in **Penang,** and one may see a Ceylon type Burmese temple containing a huge reclining *Buddha.* The most noteworthy of the others are the *Capitan Kling Moslem Mosque* in *Pitt Street,* and the *Snake Temple* at *Sungei Kwang* nine miles from **George Town** in which a number of snakes reside. During the day, these reptiles appear to be doped by the incense, sleeping on the altars, incense burners, and rafters. The snakes, thought by the worshipers to have a touch of godliness, are known as the "divine ones." During the day, worshipers leave eggs on the temple floor, and at night when the atmosphere is cleared, the snakes squirm down to gorge to their slithering hearts' content.

The *Nattukottai Chettiar Temple* in *Waterfall Road* is the largest of the Hindu houses of worship. Other temples include the *Sri Marianman* in *Queen Street,* the *Siva* in *Dato Kramat,* and the *Subramanian Temple.*

PENANG HILL, 2,722 feet above sea level, is reached in twenty-four minutes by a funicular railway journey of one mile four hundred and thirty-five yards. The view over the ocean, the nearby islets, and the mainland's purple mass of *Kedah Peak* is a pleasant one. The atmosphere is rarified, and the view is particularly enchanting of an evening. North and west of **George Town** are to be found a series of the most beautiful beaches and coves. The azure blue waters lap gleamingly white and golden sand beaches surrounded by gently waving palm trees and tropical vegetation.

The distance around the island, 46 miles of resplendent scenery, can be readily traversed by car in three hours, passing rubber and coconut plantations, fishing villages, exquisite gardens, and waterfalls.

The BOTANICAL GARDENS, five miles from **George Town,** grow in lovely surroundings bisected by a gurgling stream emanating from the waterfall which cascades several hundred feet above. The lily pond is one hundred yards from the motor road.

The GREAT WORLD AMUSEMENT PARK is conveniently located on *Maxwell Road* near the intersection of *Penang Road* and has all of the attractions of the other *"World"* amusement parks of **Singapore** and Malaya.

The cinemas are air conditioned and numerous.

Penang is connected to the mainland by railway ferry to **Prai** and by all purpose ferry to **Butterworth.**

In addition to the bazaar type of shopping center, there are department stores, excellent shops, and attractive restaurants.

MALAYA'S NATIONAL PARK, lying between the *Cameron Highlands* and the east coast, is readily reached by the

"Golden Blowpipe" express train to *Tembeling Station,* thence by local bus and park service boat to the headquarters at **Kuala Tahan.**

If yours is the venturesome type of soul that has ever driven you to want to stalk elephants and tigers, angle for great game fish, shoot churning rapids, and live a life of jungle adventure, this is your cup of tea . . . but only with a camera. All game is fully protected from hunters, though one may fish.

Unlike hunting safaris or other jungle visits, advance arrangements for a visit to Malaya's *National Park* are not extensive. Your travel agent can arrange the trip easily by applying to the Chief Game Warden, Federation of Malaysia, Kuala Lumpur, Malaya.

PORT SWETTENHAM, **Kuala Lumpur's** seaport, is 28 miles west of **Kuala Lumpur.** Should yours be a cruise ship or a cargo liner docking at **Port Swettenham,** take a taxi or train to K.L.; you'll be there in no time at all after passing through superb scenery.

The HILL STATIONS are mountain resorts with comfortable lodging, sports, and hunting facilities.

CAMERON HIGHLANDS, one of three hill resorts, was established in the 1890's by Mr. W. Cameron and today is one of the famous health resorts of Asia. Because of its altitude, almost a mile high, the *Highlands* area is never hot. Its scenery encompasses waterfalls and brilliant flowers including roses, carnations, dahlias, geraniums, fuchsias, gladioli, violets, orchids, and jungle flora. There are a golf course, tennis, and badminton courts at **Brinchang.** Swimming may be enjoyed in a natural jungle pool. One may stop in one of several hotels, two inns, or private bungalows which frequently are rented out.

FRASER'S HILL, 65 miles north of **Kuala Lumpur,** enjoys the same cool climatic conditions of the *Cameron Highlands.* Though smaller than the *Cameron Highlands, Fraser's Hill* nevertheless provides equally exotic scenic effects, golf and tennis facilities, and government owned bungalows which are clean and comfortable.

Taiwan

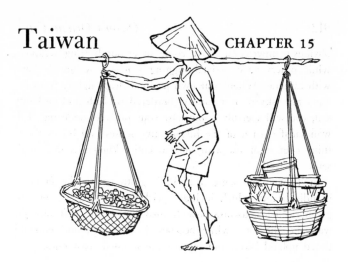

FREE CHINA'S PROVINCE OF **Taiwan** is better known to the west as **Formosa.** It is said that a gardenia would emanate the same ecstatic aroma by any other name. So, too, is the case with this paramecium-shaped island of the smiling semi-tropics.

The name *Taiwan* translates into "Terraced Bay," an aptly descriptive name as evinced by the island's generous patchwork quilt of rice terraces that yield two and sometimes even three heaping crops of nutritious rice each year. The Japanese who occupied the island from 1895 to 1945 called it *Takasadan,* meaning "The Land of High Mountains," in deference to the pinnacled thicket of peaks, many of which reach up well over 8,000 feet, with others attaining an altitude in excess of 10,000 feet. The entire island is only 240 miles in length and 85 miles in width at its widest point.

Portuguese explorers gasped with astonishment and joy when, after long dreary months at sea, they spied the shimmering beauty of the land rising up over their prows which they quickly named *Ilha Formosa,* meaning simply "Island Beautiful."

International travelers have been dropping by Taiwan, Ilha Formosa, Takasadan, or Formosa for centuries. Some visitors, obviously unwelcome, have come in armor bearing weapons, while others have arrived lugging suitcases weighted down with cameras. When your own jet liner drops lightly from the aqua blue sky onto a runway bordered by lush and cushiony soil, you will speedily know why your predecessors came. Taiwan satisfies each of the historic five senses and leaves something over to arouse a mysterious entity known as the "sixth sense" as well.

In Taiwan the sense of sight is glutted with the fantastic islandic beauty which includes prickly mountain battlements, green ricefields, tossing tassel-headed sugar cane, soft sunlight warming the long white beaches, jade colored and emerald tinted upland lakes, and picturesque serrated coast lines.

Taiwan's fabulous old Chinese towns and cities have successfully survived the Dutch, Portuguese, and Japanese influences, and the ordinary everyday life of the contemporary natives, as well as the celebration of the symbolical joyous festivals, constantly reminds one that the authentic Old China lives and breathes just as vigorously and deeply today as does its spiritual descendant, the New China. Many world travelers of wide experience believe the Formosa of today is as thoroughly Chinese as the mainland ever was.

One's smell and taste senses will be satisfied here by delectable

Chinese cooking nonpareil. There are gourmets who find the Taiwan cuisine a veritable rival to the French *cordon bleu*.

The sense of touch will be gratified by a visit to any shop, store, or bazaar, where the mere superficial handling of fine Chinese silk, teak, mahogany, shell, jade, or bambooware item, delicate ivory figurine, or article of lacquerware will of itself be a rich experience.

And one's sense of hearing will come alive with an endless and curious Tower of Babel jangle, the dialects of the happy people shrieking in excitement, the soft swish of the whirring pedicabs' tires, and the padded footfalls of the coolies on the warm asphalt, the cries of the hawkers, the sizzle of rich foods, the gurgle of feet pushing through a flooded paddy, or the sloshing of a patient, plodding water buffalo in the cloud reflecting, watery rice field, the weird music of Chinese opera, the baffling cacophony of the temple gongs, the rat-a-tat-tat of the festival firecrackers, an essentially joyous, wonderfully Chinese sound, as dear as anything on earth to the native hearts, young and old alike.

The island's activities are genuinely representative of the uniquely interesting and widely respected Chinese way of life. Taiwan's cultural and artistic background is dominated by oriental features, though located in a comfortably modern, westernized, thoroughly beautiful setting.

Taiwan is the real, authentic China which one may visit today, untainted by the so-called "People's Republic" of the mainland.

China is the Croesus-rich repository of fine, illustrious, and beautiful creations of the centuries old culture of the Far East . . . the innovator, the teacher, and pioneer nation, oozing with countless eras of heroic history and overflowing with centuries of superb artistic achievement.

Taiwan's scenic beauties are unsurpassed, her hospitality and Old World charm untarnished, and her food is palate-pleasing, literally out of this and several other worlds. The island's existing accommodations are impressive, though extremely limited, and the entire experience of a visit to Taiwan is exhilarating.

The foregoing, grouped together, adds up to the swift realization of an almost mystic sixth sense which can be spelled out in the simple, though marvelously expressive, word "atmosphere," a local color indigenous to Formosa.

Taiwan, gifted with a Chinese treasure chest of atmosphere, is on the Orient's "Main Line" running from **Japan** in the north to **Hong Kong** and **Manila** in the south.

Taipei's *Sungshan International Airport* is one of Central Asia's largest, its 9,000-foot runway capable of receiving safely any aircraft flown today. The layout and construction of the runways, taxiways, and lighting systems conform to the most exacting of United States civil and military standards. Modern instrument landing systems are available, if needed, which have been installed to the rigid technical specifications carefully prescribed by the ICAC *(International Civil Aviation Committee)*. To accommodate the rapidly swelling number of air passengers, an ultramodern air terminal on the site of the original *Sungshan International Airport* is being rapidly completed. The new two-story terminal is big enough to accommodate 3,000 busy people simultaneously. In it one finds air-line offices, a bank, a post office, two restaurants each capable of serving 500 persons at once, and a 1,000-person waiting room, all designed to please in beautiful modern Chinese décor and entered through a gate fitted with traditional Chinese style windows grilled with glazed tile.

Taiwan is easily accessible, served by five international carriers: the *Civil Air Transport* (CAT) which operates frequently scheduled flights to **Taipei** from **Seoul, Tokyo, Hong Kong, Manila,** and **Bangkok;** *Northwest Orient Airlines; Cathay Pacific Airways* (CPA) which range between **Hong Kong** and **Tokyo,** stopping at **Taipei;** and *Thai Airways International* which plies the skies between **Bangkok** and **Hong Kong** to **Tokyo** and **Taipei.** CAT also operates daily domestic flights from **Taipei** to **Taichung** in central Formosa, **Hualien**

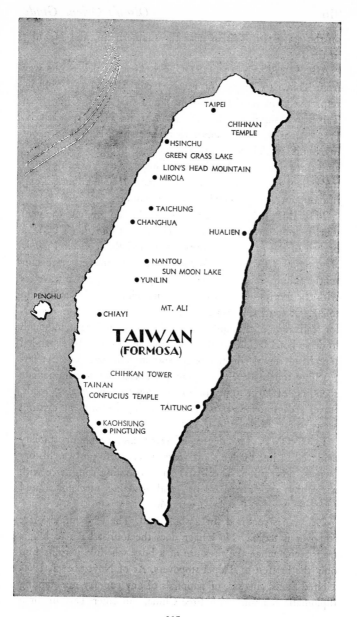

on the east coast, **Tainan** near the southern tip, and **Makung** in the *Pescadores.*

AIR FARES AND SCHEDULES. Airplane tickets one way from **Tokyo** to **Taipei** (or reverse) cost $106.40 and $149.30, respectively, in tourist (economy) and first class, while from **Taipei** to **Hong Kong** the fares are $70 and $89.60 respectively. Prop planes fly from **Taipei** to the Japanese capital in about five hours, while two hours are consumed flying to **Hong Kong** and three hours to **Manila.** The impatiently swooshing jets make the trips to **Tokyo** in two and one-half hours, **Hong Kong** in one hour and to **Manila** in ninety minutes.

THE IMPORTANCE OF TOURISM. To promote the vital tourist industry, the *Taiwan Tourism Council* (TTC), a branch of the provincial government, and the *Taiwan Visitors Association* (TVA), a collection of private interests, are currently pulling out all the stops to acquaint prospective travelers with the glories of Taiwan. These agencies expect to attract up to 200,000 tourists annually by 1968, and the outlook, moreover, for realization of this ambitious goal is sunshine bright, although to do so hotel facilities will, in the interim, have to be expanded tenfold or more, which is a colossal undertaking, but the far-reaching tourist development program calls for the immediate spending of large sums of money constructing hotels, roads, travel accommodations, and for bettering facilities at existing scenic spots, historical and cultural areas.

ECONOMY. The degree of social and economic stability achieved in just twelve short years of Taiwan's postwar history beggars description. The island has a booming commerce with a healthy agricultural return, and amazing mechanical and scientific progress has been wrought.

No visa is required for a short visit. The 72 hour visa-free stopover is terrific. No longer does the tourist have to hug a transit visa when the pressure of a busy schedule permits him only the briefest of Taipei stopovers. As of November 1, 1960, United States citizens, or nationals of any country maintaining diplomatic relations with Free China, can enter Taiwan for a three-day visa-free stopover, providing confirmed onward ticket is held. One can see a lot (all one wishes) of the "Island Beautiful" in 72 hours. Only a smallpox vaccination is needed for entry.

The New Taiwan Dollar (NT$) is the coin of the realm, available in notes of 100, 10, 5, and one, and in coins of 50, 20, and 10 cent denominations. One United States "greenback" equals forty Taiwanese dollars. Exchange is unrestricted, and you can reconvert upon departure up to fifty U.S. dollars.

INTERNAL TRANSPORTATION. Taiwan, which looks like a tobacco leaf someone carefully dropped on the map, is bursting with local transportation. The train and bus services are fantastically good and unbelievably cheap. The interior airlines offer tops in domestic service.

Diesel express trains, their coaches equipped with reclining seats, served by pert stewardesses in fetching, eye-arresting *cheongsam* dresses, go everywhere on the island. They speed from **Keelung** in the north to **Kaohsiung** in the south in just six hours. The shockproof, virtually vibrationless, through trains carry air conditioned coaches, Pullmans, and diners. Train attendants courteously offer hot towels, newspapers, magazines, and hot tea at no extra charge. Western style meals and drinks are at your command in the dining cars.

Buses on the *"Kin Ma"* and similar express highways are treats on wheels, with reclining seats, pretty stewardesses, free towels, tea, newspapers, magazines, and music-filled interiors. The coaches glide along over smooth slick asphalt highways in full view of the fabulous scenery outside. Well-kept highways penetrate every part of the island and all are served by these superduper motor coaches.

Taxi service is speedy, safe, courteous, reasonable, and highly efficient, operating 24 hours a day on call from the hotels in two to three minutes' time. Some 2,000 vehicles are in the cab service on an island-wide basis; fifty per cent of them are on the streets of Taipei. Some of the cars were manufactured in Japan, others imported from the United States and western

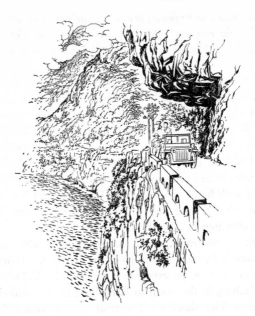

Europe, while an increasing number are being turned out by Formosa's only car manufacturer, the *Yue Loong Engineering Company.*

The first taxi mile costs U.S. 15¢, and there's a nickel added, roughly, for every additional quarter of a mile. Patronize the metered taxis, naturally, for most of their drivers not only are scrupulously honest but understand some English.

The local pedicab industry is gradually dying out, but the breed is a hardy one and lingers on. A number of these old vehicles are still available, and for a song. You can bargain for the fare.

Taiwan's first expressway linking **Taipei** and **Keelung** opened in 1963. It is the country's first highway available to motorized vehicles only.

The two main harbors, KEELUNG in the north and KAOHSIUNG in the south, handle the passenger and freight traffic of many of the world's great steamship lines such as the

American President Lines, the *States Marine,* the *Pacific Far East,* the *Messageries Maritimes,* and Japan's *O.S.K.* among others. Many noted ocean liners on world cruises call at **Keelung,** bringing hundreds of visitors in for visits to the handsome port, only an hour's easy drive from **Taipei.**

LANGUAGES. All Chinese use the same written language, but the differences lie in the myriad spoken dialects. Mandarin, the singsong national language, all tones and a mile wide, is in common island use, although many of the locals naturally prefer their own tongue. One hears Amoy or Hakka dialects, and the trained ear can easily discern the accents of the man from **Shanghai, Canton, Fukien, Peiping, Hunan,** and even as far out west on the China mainland as **Szechuan.** The local English that is spoken in the first class hotels, restaurants, stores, or travel agencies varies from fair to fair *Harvard.*

CLIMATE. Bisected by the Tropic of Cancer, **Formosa** is a country with a decidedly subtropical climate. In the balmy south, the sun hangs in the shimmering blue sky 330 days a year. There is, in general, a month or two of somewhat chilly weather during January and February which comprises the Formosan "winter," which, incidentally, is much like that of Washington, D.C. The average temperature, year round, in the north is 70.9 degrees F. and in the south 75.5 degrees F. The northern portion has the most rainfall with quite a concentration of Jupiter's "blessings," especially around the port city of **Keelung,** a most rained-on city. Taiwan, which is in the Pacific earthquake belt, is touched by numerous tremors, but few are more than mild and anemic in nature. None are dangerous. Typhoons sometimes swoop down from the rain-filled skies during the summer months, July through September. These disturbances, when they do hit, which is seldom, are mild.

I would personally recommend visiting Taiwan from October through December in the sparkling fall, or from March to late May in the mid to late spring. During the real winter months, keep a raincoat handy. Bring a sweater or light wrap for cool early spring and late fall evenings. Dress in Formosa is never formal at all except during special occasions.

HYGIENIC CONDITIONS. **Taipei** is a clean and healthy city, a statement true of Taiwan generally. Water, however, should not be drunk from the tap. Your hotel and/or restaurant will provide you with bottles of iced water or piping hot tea which Chinese hotels always provide free of charge.

TIPPING is an accepted practice in Taiwan. A ten to fifteen per cent gratuity in hotels and restaurants will be gratefully received. In barber shops, bathhouses, and other service institutions, where the charges are very low, the tip can be somewhat above the ten to fifteen per cent level.

LAUNDRY is done expertly and with garuda-like rapidity. Eight hour service is commonplace, but if your needs so dictate, laundry will be returned in as little as four hours.

GEOGRAPHICAL LOCATION. Taiwan, in the western *Pacific,* is included in the *Pescadores,* of which there are 77 islands in all; save for Taiwan and *Penghu,* however, the others are minuscule and of little, if any, significance. Taiwan is situated 100 miles east of the China mainland, 730 miles north of **Manila,** 1,302 miles southwest of **Tokyo,** and 500 miles northeast of **Hong Kong.**

A steep mountain range dominates Taiwan's central section . . . "like a huge fish fin thrusting far out of the water." The island's high point is *Yu Shan* (also known as *Jade Mountain* or *Mount Morrison*), towering a breathless 13,180 feet above sea level. Some sixteen rivers refresh the island which gleams with ponds, pools, and reservoirs, natural and man-made, mountain locked and exquisite. An unbroken line of snow-capped mountain spires running from north to south rise 10,000 to 12,000 feet into the air, smiling frostily down on the lush, green, terraced fields far below. The more beautiful eastern side of the great range is precipitously steep, while the western skirt floats down gradually to the vast granary of the island's energetic millions.

HISTORICAL BACKGROUND. Once teeming with aborigines, head-hunters, cannibals, and wild tribes, probably of Malayan stock, the "Island Beautiful" today has descendants of these early settlers among its population who are a colorful, exotic, and utterly friendly folk, loosely gathered in what is known as the Seven Tribes: *Ami, Taiyal, Paiwan, Bunnun* (or *Bunun*), *Saiset* (or *Saishet*), *Tsue* (alternatively *Tsou*), and the *Yami.*

The first Chinese to step on the island's shores was an officer who arrived in A.D. 607. He was followed by a wealth of Chinese who literally drifted across the *Taiwan Straits* from the coastal Fukien Province. The "foreigners," western European folk that is, did not dock until 1544 when the first sea weary Portuguese mariners blinked in utter disbelief on seeing "Ilha Formosa." The Dutch arrived in 1624 followed by the Spanish, but the hardy thick-skulled Dutch threw the Spaniards into the sea the very same year they arrived.

1661 was Formosa's big year when the legendary General Cheng-kung, commonly known in textbooks as "Koxinga," landed and blasted out the Dutch to bring the island under Chinese hegemony.

The political situation continued in a state of status quo until, in the wake of the Sino-Japanese conflict, the *Pescadores* including Formosa were ceded to Japanese rule which continued until 1945 when, in accordance with the Cairo Declaration and the Potsdam Conference, Formosa and the Pescadores reverted to China.

Formosa broke into the world's bold black headlines in 1949 following news of the disasters to the Republican Chinese armies on the mainland when Chiang Kai-shek's forces broke and yielded before the enormous Communist Chinese onslaught. Shattered remnants of the once regally proud and battlewise divisions streamed to Formosa as a sanctuary to join forces with the 180,000 aborigines who had outlasted the Japanese rule. These Chinese soldiers immediately built up a stout anti-Communist defense that enjoys the support of almost all of the free world.

Formosa supports some ten million people today including the original Chinese, the aborigine settlers, and the new arrivals of 1949–50.

The Chinese live a free life on this beautiful island where Chinese history and culture are truly mirrored in a peaceful, prosperous, and progressive place. Formosan art, architecture, culture, and history are all distinctly and indisputably Chinese.

Taiwan is historically, ethnically, politically, and legally a part of China. It has been so with only minor exceptions since the Sui dynasty A.D. 561–618.

THE LEGENDARY HEROES. GOHO was a gigantic figure of a man to whom must go credit for putting an end to the gory aboriginal head-hunting practice, although in so doing his own head was lopped off. It's a long story. Ask your guide to tell it to you locally.

KOXINGA was no less famous than Goho, and his memory, too, is revered today. He was the surviving son of Iquan, famed China trader, and, it is alleged, a Japanese mother. At twenty-two, loyal to the Ming dynasty, he became, in rapid succession, an earl, a marquis at twenty-four, and an admiral. At thirty-one, he became a full prince and a commander of the fleets. On his thirty-fifth birthday, he fought and won the greatest battle in Oriental naval history against the hated Manchus.

The Dutch were to feel the full fury of his long pent-up hate and thirst for revenge. The result of Koxinga's retaliation could mean only disaster for Dutch arms, though elements of their forces held out in a brave and memorable nine months' siege of *Fort Zelandia* before capitulating to a magnanimous conqueror. Then, at the age of only thirty-eight, lord of all he surveyed, this mysterious young Eastern "Alexander the Great" disappeared and, dying a strange death, left after him the legend and fame of being one of China's greatest leaders.

SPORTS. One of the world's great athletes at Rome's 1960 Olympic Games in the decathlon's grueling events was a young Taiwanese, C. K. Yang, supposedly of aboriginal ancestry. This silver medalist came but a slender handful of crucial points behind the great Californian, Rafer Johnson.

For athletic-aware tourists, both spectator and participant sports are plentiful in Taiwan. Visitors can indulge to their heart's content in golf, tennis, boating, yachting, swimming, fishing, mountain climbing, water skiing, hiking, biking, and hunting . . . but please, no heads!

Those who prefer to sit down and applaud strong, swift young men will have plenty to cheer for in Taiwan watching first class soccer, basketball, baseball, volleyball, American style football, boxing, swimming, tennis, golf, badminton, and track and field events.

Swimming, the ever refreshing sport, is particularly attractive at *Tamsui,* a beautiful beach near **Taipei;** *Fulung,* a well-protected surf beach an hour and a half from **Taipei;** *Keelung,*

forty-five minutes from **Taipei** on the sea; *Green Lake (Pitan),* seven miles from **Taipei;** and, farther south, the famous, inviting *Sun Moon Lake.*

The *Taiwan Golf and Country Club* in *Tamsui,* a scenic single hour's drive from **Taipei,** is justly regarded as one of the Far East's finest and most picturesque links. The annual CAT International Golf Tournament is held here, within sight of both a gurgling river and the azure blue *Pacific Ocean*. The celebrated "Double Tenth" (October 10th, the national holiday that commemorates the founding of the Chinese Republic by the world-famous Dr. Sun Yat-sen) is also marked by a big golf tourney.

Taipei has a tricky nine-hole municipal golf course on whose fairway guests are always welcome.

There are two marvelous, beautifully conditioned, red clay tennis courts at the *Grand Hotel* which are open for play the year round, while others are found at the fashionable *Cosmo Club*.

Soccer is enthusiastically played, particularly on October 31st, when the locally revered President Chiang Kai-shek's birthday is celebrated in the Cup Matches which honor him. This affair draws the finest teams in Asia.

Basketball also honors the Generalissimo, with one of Asia's best basketball tournaments being held on October 31st.

From October 25th through the 31st, the annual provincial track and field meet is staged in which event the world first heard of the great decathlon specialist, C. K. Yang. Taiwan athletic rivalry is keen not just in track and field events but also in basketball, volleyball, swimming, American style football, tennis, and basketball.

TAIPEI

TAIPEI, a city of close to a million souls, is the capital of the Republic of China, situated virtually at sea level, surrounded by serene mountains and bounded by three impressive rivers, the *Hsintien, Tamsui,* and *Keelung.* Taipei must be thought of as an ancient Oriental city with modern conveniences rather than as a modern city with a venerable Oriental background.

Although Taipei has been an established city for more than two centuries, it was only in 1920 that it became a corporate entity and not until 1949, when the Nationalist Chinese Government established its seat here, did Taipei become a world household word.

Taipei is the sister city of Houston, Texas, each having adopted the other. There is a sizable *Chinatown* in our Texas city, while a number of Houstonites live and work in the Chinese Nationalist capital.

Taipei, meaning "City of the North," was once a walled fortress like so many cities on the China mainland. Taipei's great walls were unseemingly thick and were pierced by five gates, one of which the Japanese pulled down during their fifty year occupation, the other four of which, however, remain standing today.

At the extreme northerly end of the island of Taiwan, Taipei, midway between its east and west coasts, is best known for its:

FIVE CITY GATES constructed during the Manchu dynasty, four of which remain in their original settings although the wall has long since disappeared.

The MARTYR'S SHRINE, commemorating the nation's war dead, stands in front of the magnificent *Grand Hotel* and is the scene of ceremonial occasions when visiting guests of the state lay wreaths at the shrine.

The LUNG SHAN TEMPLE, *Dragon Hill,* was constructed originally in the early 18th century, but was damaged extensively in the Second World War after which it was redone into a prepossessing edifice characterized by gilded columns and ornately carved ceilings. *Lung Shan,* dedicated to the Goddess of the Sea and the Goddess of Mercy, is of great architectural, historical, and religious significance.

CONFUCIUS' TEMPLE, in the *Ta Lung Tung* district, is typically Chinese in architectural design. The commemorative services held annually on September 28th are dedicated to the birthday of the immortal educator-teacher, Confucius. Always worthy of a visit, the September 28th anniversary is of particular interest.

The BOTANICAL GARDENS, exhibiting tropical plants, flowers, and trees, are an inviting setting for an afternoon stroll.

In the confines of the gardens, one finds the *National Art Hall,* the *National Central Library,* and the *National History Museum.* The *National Science Hall* is a completely new spectacular edifice, the dome of which has been built to emulate the breathtaking *Temple of Heaven* in **Peiping.**

PRESIDENTIAL SQUARE, in the heart of Taipei, is surrounded by the *Bank of Taiwan,* the *Courthouse, Friends of China Club,* and other national and international quarters.

CHENG HUANG TEMPLE, Tihua Street, is the repository of the "Protector God" of the island's people. On the founder's birthday, the devout gather from all over Taiwan to worship at this temple.

The ZOO, with an impressive collection of animals and birds, is situated near the *Grand Hotel.* In the center of the *Zoo,* atop its principal hill, one finds an ancient building which was used by the government during the Manchu dynasty.

The CHUNGSHAN KIDDY PLAYGROUND, hard by the *Zoo,* includes a popular stream on which the youngsters enjoy thrilling boat rides. Ice skating is unknown in Taiwan; hence the kiddy playground includes a roller skating rink and features a well patronized swimming pool.

The TAIWAN HANDICRAFT PROMOTION CENTER exhibits many products resulting from the fertility of the creative genius and skill of the Chinese. Any of the variety of exhibited objects may be purchased.

The Suburbs of Taipei

KEELUNG, a fine bathing area graced with soft sand beaches, is readily reached by car in forty-five minutes.

PEITOU, nine miles north of **Taipei,** is a renowned resort community famous for the therapeutic qualities of its sulphur, natural, and acidified hot springs. It is a favorite weekend rendezvous for local inhabitants and a focal point for gay blades seeking the ultimate in carnal pleasures.

MOUNT TA TUN, readily reached from *Peitou* or *Yangming Shan,* is 3,700 feet above sea level. Its crest, snow covered in winter, affords seascape views to the north and an excellent panorama of **Taipei** to the south.

YANGMING SHAN *(Grass Mountain)*, ten miles from **Taipei**, is blanketed with verdant scenery and a cool yet soft and velvety climate. Its hot springs and scenic attractions make the *Grass Mountain* one of Taiwan's most loved resorts. Springtime sees the *Yangming Shan* area wreathed in gorgeous cherry blossoms and flaming azaleas.

SHIHLIN INSTITUTE OF HORTICULTURE, in the immediate suburbs of **Taipei** not more than ten minutes drive from the *Grand Hotel*, contains butterfly and Madame Chiang Kai-shek orchids as well as thousands of other species of flowers including magnificent chrysanthemums.

TAMSUI, three quarters of an hour from the *Grand Hotel* by car, is blessed with beautiful beaches and the finest golf course on the island.

PITAN *(Green Lake)*, seven miles from **Taipei**, is known for the excellence of its boating facilities. Fishing and swimming in the emerald green waters are equally excellent. The lake is overhung with brooding cliffs.

WULAI, fifteen and one-half miles south of **Taipei**, is best known for its collection of aborigines. Here under the sprays of a cataract the original aboriginal dances are zestfully performed by barefoot girls decked out in colorful finery complete with shell bead headbands. One may ascend *Wulai Mountain* laboriously in a unique push car which operates on a narrow set of tracks. Enjoy the views on the way up, however; the descent is one big swoosh, somewhat like being hurtled downward on a toboggan.

CHIHNAN TEMPLE, of the Taoist faith, less than an hour from **Taipei**, is midway up the slope of *Monkey Hill* and is reached by climbing the so-called "Thousand Steps," which actually, according to my best count, include something over 1,400 risers. To avoid the arduous climb, you can be carried up in a sedan chair or be driven up the road which leads to the back of the temple.

YUANTUNG TEMPLE, *Chungho Hsiang,* is remarkable for the colossal letter of Buddha which has been engraved on the rocky ledge dominating the setting above a nunnery. There is a three story pagoda near the marble encrusted main building. The front gate of the temple is adorned with replicas of two great animals.

KUANYIN SHAN *(Mount Goddess of Mercy)* is most famous for the flaming forests of red maples which decorate the hillside in the autumn. The temple, standing almost a thousand feet above sea level, is midway up *Kuanyin Shan.*

FULUNG, the beach resort area not far from **Taipei,** has been particularly blessed by nature, having towering cliffs protecting the beach on three sides which barricades favorably control both the wind and the waves.

All of fabulous Formosa is scenically beautiful and interesting. For the busy American traveler, however, I believe that forty-eight hours spent in the **Taipei** area will give one a sufficiently gratifying finger-on-the-pulse feel of Old China.

For those whose time and zest permit, or demand, more of Taiwan, the next logical point to visit would be:

Central Taiwan

TAICHUNG, in central Taiwan, is the seat of the provincial government. This rapidly growing city is best known for its *National Palace Museum* possessed of invaluable national treasures.

PAKUASHAN, CHANGHUA, in central Taiwan, is particularly noteworthy for being the site of the world's largest statue of Buddha. Made of brick and concrete, **Pakuashan's** *Buddha* rises to a majestic 72 feet above its 14-foot base, making the apex of the *Buddha's* snug but ornate headpiece 86 feet above the surrounding concrete walk. The sitting *Buddha,* hands in serene repose, has a nose almost 6 feet long, a mouth 6 feet wide, eyes which are nearly 4 feet across, and ears which are more than 10 feet in length.

SUN MOON LAKE, fifteen miles southeast of **Taichung,**

2,400 feet above sea level, is one of Taiwan's most exotic points of interest, a honeymooners' paradise which takes its name from the natural shape which looks for all the world like two heavenly bodies strung together. Forest canopied mountains cluster around the gemlike lake in which an islet is embedded. This idyllic little island seems, fantastically, to change its shape by the hour; this seemingly unnatural phenomenon has a logical explanation, however. It is brought about by the waters of the calm lake rising and falling with the lunar tides. All sorts of boats are for hire on the *Sun Moon Lake* which, even today, is still the locale for a large number of aborigines. The aboriginal lodges, huts, *Wenwu Temple,* and the *Yuan Kuang Temple* are all worth visiting. The strange little people will be delighted to perform quaint and colorful folk dances for you.

South Taiwan

Proceeding southward from **Taichung** and the *Sun Moon Lake,* the avid visitor's next objective is **Tainan,** while between **Taichung** and **Tainan** one finds *Mount Ali,* the 9,184-foot soaring mountain which is reached by an old-fashioned chug-chug train. In March and April, the exotic orchids here are as plentiful as May flowers and buttercups in America. In April one sees vast forests of flowering cherry trees on the slopes of *Mount Ali.*

TAINAN, the ancient "City of the South," was once the capital where the mighty Koxinga trained his armies. The *Koxinga Shrine* and *Chihkan Tower* are points of interest worth visiting. From the top of the tower, the city and the surrounding countryside spread out invitingly.

KAOHSIUNG is split by the *"River of Love"* on the banks of which romantic couples may, of a pleasant evening, be seen strolling hand in hand.

The unusually scenic EAST COAST is celebrated for the *Suao-Hualien Highway* which has been carved out of the solid rock of the mountainside and is operated as a one-way highway banked by incredible precipices. The highway commands spectacular views of the ocean.

TAROKO GORGE, the Amalfi Drive of the Far East, pierces numerous tunnels and caves.

The EAST-WEST CROSS-ISLAND HIGHWAY takes off from the *Taroko Gorge* and crosses the central mountain range transcending passes in excess of 10,000 feet above sea level.

CHAPTER 16

Thailand

Thailand's people, eye-catchingly handsome, bask in their delightful closely knit ties with happiness. They exude such an unbounded *joie de vivre* that it imparts a feeling of mellow contentment to all who are around them. The sun is never masked by Thai clouds; it is always shining on Thai lips, in Thai eyes, and on Thai faces. In exotic, colorful, sun-drenched, wonderful Thailand, the smile is both proverbial and ubiquitous.

The well-proportioned raven haired Thai men and women carry themselves easily erect and are possessed of the priceless asset of dazzling white teeth that gleam forth from deeply bronzed attractive faces. The women wear either attractive Thai sarongs known as *pa-zin* that wrap tightly about the waist, cling to the hips, and drape softly to the feet and the *sabai chieng* (draped breast cloths), or smart, chic western costumes which their fine figures flatter. Men dress simply, wearing work clothes, shirts and pants, or well-tailored suits. Only on special occasions do the men don the colorful puffy-legged *panung* of Thai tradition. In the fields, both sexes wear the palm-leaf lampshade hats.

931

While the happy Thai smile is something that will gladden your heart the moment you set foot in this brilliant sunny land, a heartwarming custom that will soon come to your attention is the *wei,* that gracious traditional Thai form of greeting which consists of folding the hands before one's chest, face, or forehead and bowing politely from the waist. The polite *wei* is accompanied by the words *"Swaddi"* ("hello," "hi," or "so long") and *"Koh Khoon"* ("thank you").

The one word which must inevitably be predominant when thinking of or attempting to describe Thailand is "color"— vivid, brilliant, and multi-hued. No other section of the world is endowed with as gorgeous a riot of pleasing, captivating, rainbowlike tints. The sky is azure blue, the lawns are Kelly green, and many buildings are sparkling white with vividly contrasting roofs, eaves, doors, and frescoes of brilliant reds, oranges, yellows, greens, blues, indigos, or violets. Blood red and deep purple bougainvillaea, yellow champa blooms, many-tinted orchids, and saffron-robed Buddhist monks add brilliance to the tinctorial, picturesque panoramic vista of Thailand.

Thailand has two erstwhile names: the well-remembered *Siam* and an ancient less known one, *Sukhothai,* meaning "The Dawn of Happiness." The present name stems from the old *Prathet Thai* (free nation). The present name, Thailand, means "Free Land," a suitable soubriquet. **Bangkok,** the breathtakingly wondrous capital, is known to the Thais as *Krung Thep,* "City of Angels."

The CLIMATE is hot, that's all there is to it. Considering the normal lofty elevation of the mercury in local thermometers, however, it is refreshing to know that in the non-rainy season humidity is unknown, and during the wet season it rains only part of the time. I have spent entire days in March, the hottest month, photographing in the direct rays of the Thai sun without experiencing the slightest discomfort.

In **Bangkok** and the central Thai area there are three seasons. The hottest period is from February to June. During the rainy season from July through October, the southwest monsoon blows and the almost daily (seventeen to twenty days a month) tropical showers lower the temperature comfortably. The cooler season lasts from November to February during which months the local climate may be compared to Southern California. Sixty-two degrees Fahrenheit in December is the lowest temperature which one may normally expect to experience, and the highest temperature usually recorded, 96°, is in March. Average minimum temperatures range from 67° in December and January to 76° from April through October, with February, March, and November being a bit cooler. The lowest average daily temperature is 78° in December; the highest is 87° in March. Maximum temperatures in November and December will not reach 90°, though at least one or two days a month will be in the nineties during the other months.

CLOTHING needs are minimal, with tropical garments being worn throughout the year. For men, seersucker, Palm Beach, dacron, and other lightweights are excellent for informal wear, with sharkskin recommended for dress up. Cottons or other washables are always comfortable for women. With the exception of the more elegant establishments, completely informal dress is quite in order even during the evenings. Check with your own hotel or travel agent before going out to dinner as to whether or not a coat and tie will be expected. It usually is not. From July to October a very light raincoat will be useful, with a sweater, stole, or other light wrap being recommended for evenings from November to February. Please note that when visiting the *Grand Palace* men *must* wear coats and neckties and ladies *must* wear dresses . . . no slacks.

GEOGRAPHICALLY, Thailand resembles an elephant's head with the trunk swinging south into the *Isthmus of Kra* which leads into **Malaysia,** with which Federation this land enjoys a common border. Lying north and northwest of **Cambodia,** Thailand shares a long frontier with **Laos** to the north and east and with **Burma** to the west and northwest. The *Isthmus of Kra* is washed on one side by the *Bay of Bengal* and on the other by the *Gulf of Thailand.* Though **Bangkok** is some

thirty miles from the sea, it is a busy seaport. The fertile Thai plains abound with rich vegetation, and its mountains touch the clouds. Thailand's concentrated, dense forests break the monsoon flow and prevent great river-overflowing disasters such as have been the ancient and traditional curse of neighboring **China**. In Thailand's sunless jungles, one can find slinking cats, snarling tigers, spotted leopards, nimble deer, lumbering elephants, careening crocodiles, species of wild boar and bear, and those lethal vipers, the cobra and black krait. Thailand's great *Chao Phya River,* the "Lord River," bisects the capital and flows into the *Gulf.*

POPULATION AND NATURAL RESOURCES. The more than twenty-three million Thais enjoy an abundant life. Despite the fact that they consume vast quantities of rice, fish, tropical fruits, and other nutritious foods, they maintain their sylph-like physical silhouettes. Thai agrarians produce close to six million tons of traditional rice per annum of which 20% is exported, with corn and soy beans just beginning to enter the agricultural picture as economic factors. The export of teakwood, rubber, rice, and tin is the mainstay of the country's economy.

The Chinese exert a strong influence in Thailand. There are divergent statistics relative to the ethnic antecedents of the population, but it may be assumed, reasonably accurately I am sure, that while less than 4% of the population is Chinese many Thais trace some branch of their ancestral tree to **China**. In modern Thailand, as throughout Asia, the Chinese have dipped their skilled hands into the commerce of the country. Not only are the Chinese big businessmen, owning or directing export and import houses, being moneylenders of acknowledged acumen, and money-changers par excellence, but they are also proprietors of restaurants, portable eating and drinking stands, and the inevitable open-front Chinese shops. The native Thais have not, historically, been outstandingly successful, or even interested, in commerce, preferring the agrarian life almost exclusively, but the old order is now changing rapidly. While a large segment of the Thai population is lackadaisical and devoid of ambition beyond today's needs, this does not apply to the hard core of excellent Thai business men and women who are converting their country into an economic, educational, and cultural maelstrom.

The happy-go-lucky Thais are frantically friendly. They want desperately to be liked. Many, fond of all visitors, know only two English words: "hi" and "bye." I am sure that some Thais, the youngsters particularly, don't even know what these words mean. Frequently, as one comes along, they will shout "bye," waving and smiling like mad, and, as one passes, they shout "hi." The basic Thai philosophy of living leisurely for today only is held by a majority of the people and could quite conceivably be a normal product of the soft breezes, lulling atmosphere of the tropical climate, and the year round heat. Paradoxically, however, the Thais are not the "Step 'n' Fetchit" type of dawdlers who are just downright lazy nor are they like sleepwalkers mincing somnolently along. On the contrary, the Thais in their daily activities dart about like parakeets loose in a living room. Little boys and girls swimming, playing with kites, boxing, or enjoying other sporting activities do so with great gusto. Notwithstanding, a predominant Thai racial characteristic encompasses a mass lack of ambition. Almost 80% of the natives are engaged in farming their own plots of land on which they harvest one or two highly productive rice crops a year in addition to more frequent crops of day-to-day fruit or vegetable necessities, which leave the Thais with full bellies and absolutely no desire to do more. Everyone in Thailand eats abundantly and well. When called upon to create a surplus, improve the efficiency of their operations, expand, or turn to city life, they smile and, in essence, reply, "Why? We have everything we need." It is quite true that few, if any, Thais have the remotest ambition beyond being happy, healthy, and well fed today. The appeal for the Thais to protect themselves against the proverbial rainy day in the future evinces an abysmal lack of interest. The healthy, happy Thais provide for their own ill and aged with loving, tender care.

The TOURIST INDUSTRY is booming and has become a considerable source of foreign exchange revenue.

HYGIENIC CONDITIONS. This corner of Southwest Asia would gladden the heart of the most persnickety public health official anywhere. As in neighboring **Malaysia,** epidemic is unknown, and there is no illness which is native to Thailand. I must hasten to point out, however, that the Thais, through centuries of self-immunization, have built up a massive resistance to certain bacterial assaults which we do not share. Though the Thais in all walks of life are immaculately clean in their personal habits, donning spotlessly clean, freshly pressed or laundered clothing at least once, and frequently twice, daily, there are scores of thousands of the populace who live on the *klongs* and in rural areas where the canals are used for the disposal of sewage, bathing, brushing their teeth, doing their laundry, and as a source for cooking and drinking water. They not only thrive on this unusual procedure, but the *klong* dwellers present a radiant picture of perfect health. We could not drink one drop of *klong* water without dire results. In Thailand, drink boiled or bottled water everywhere. I would suggest that you eschew fresh, uncooked vegetables and fruit that you cannot peel yourself, except in the very best hotels and restaurants.

Thailand's hotels and restaurants, though inadequate in number, are superb. Bangkok's air conditioned *Rama* is one of the greatest hotels in the world. The *Intercontinental, Erawan* and the *Oriental* are excellent. Fine restaurants are to be found both in and out of the hotels.

RELIGION is a vitally important element in the well-being and happiness of these delightful people. With few exceptions, the Thais are all Buddhists . . . the most steadfast and devout Buddhists in the world. Buddhism is a religion which takes various forms in different countries. In Thailand, it has become an integral and essential part of the everyday life of the people, while in Japan it is not. As practiced by the Thais, Buddhism is a soft, gentle religion with no dire injunctions in respect to earthly behavior, no stern pronouncements of the hereafter, and no admonitions about toeing the spiritual mark. In Thailand, there are no religious strictures apropos of passing the faith along evangelically. These people realize that missionary zeal, unhappily, often hurts rather than helps, and bewilders more frequently than it beckons.

The Thais have a respectful reverence for the Buddhist faith. Their temples, which they prefer to call *wats,* are the most beautiful houses of worship in the world, being models of airi-ness and using space and color in effective though seemingly mad mixtures.

A Thai friend once told me, "Nothing scares or threatens us except the demons and the devils, but we have those fellows under control. We use them to guard our temples and palaces, keeping out the real evil spirits who could do us harm. We are thus insured of happiness."

There are more saffron-robed, shaven-headed Buddhist priests, monks, and acolytes per capita in Thailand than any other place. All young Thai boys vow to devote a minimum of three months of their lives to the temples where they serve their religion as acolytes dressed in the same type of soft orange colored robes as their elders. In this troubled world, it is gratifying as well as inspirational to see young men devote a period of their youth to their religion rather than going into the army or into big city gangs. The present King served Buddhism, abiding by the same rules, restrictions, and rituals of the temple as do his subjects. Many men remain with the priesthood, which, in Thailand, is an ancient and honorable calling, for life.

BUDDHIST BOWLS. The swarms of tangerine-clad monks impart confidence to the spiritual well-being of the populace of Thailand. One sees more colorful monks in **Bangkok** than sober-sided priests in **Rome.** The monks are in evidence everywhere—on the streets, in the parks, on public conveyances, bridges, barges, and in the temple grounds.

It is an adventure richly rewarding in human interest to arise early in the morning in Thailand to visit a residential area or take a boat on the *klongs*. Between the hours of six and eight A.M., one may watch the monks pass from house to house, or boat to boat, carrying a large bowl into which the Buddhist faithful pour all types of food . . . rice, fish, chicken, curries, beef, pork, cakes, or other choices. The broad streets, narrow byways, and fascinating canals teem in the morning's early hours with bowl-toting monks. Some are followed by "bowl boys" caring for an overflow of extra generous donations. In each of the larger Buddhist temples, one finds an orphanage-school where the youngsters "live in" and receive both a general and religious education. The students who apprentice them-selves to the priests and monks have, among their other daily duties, the carrying of an extra bowl or two for their mentors. Even the King, when he served his term as a monk, went bare-footed from house to house collecting food in his bowl.

The edibles collected must be in the temple by eight o'clock and are consumed not only for breakfast but also carefully stored for lunch and dinner.

If one should doubt the power of religion, or the strength of Buddhism, in this joyful land, one has but to look at the Thai calendar to see how it abounds in religious festivals, just as the cities and countryside abound in temples, or *wats*.

LOCAL PUBLIC TRANSPORTATION is abundant and adds generously to the variegations of the Thai coloration motif. Buses are painted different colors depending on their points of origin and destinations, but they are quite crowded, hot and dusty, and bewildering. I doubt that you will choose to ride the buses. The trams, also brightly tinted, present less of a problem even though they are of ancient vintage. It is fun, however, to take a streetcar to *Chinatown,* remaining on the same car for the round trip, absorbing a wealth of local atmos-phere in the process.

Taxis, of which the majority are now up-to-date four-wheeled vehicles with yellow license plates, are plentiful, though three-wheeled, motor-propelled cabs are to be seen. Until recently, payment for taxi rides in Thailand was a matter of barter and exchange, but not so any more. All **Bangkok** taxis had meters installed in mid-April of 1961. The fares are so cheap that it is almost impossible to take a taxi ride (not a sightseeing trip) within the city limits that could cost as much as a dollar. There is sure to be a language barrier between you and your driver. Before entering a cab, have your hotel doorman or desk clerk write the name and address of your destination or destinations for your driver.

Private cars with chauffeur may be hired by the hour, day, or night. A guide is optional. Ask your travel agent to make the arrangements for a sightseeing car for you, unless you are on a preplanned trip or tour.

The *samlor,* or pedicab, still exists, although traffic is now so dense as to make riding in these human-propelled vehicles less attractive than previously. A *samlor* ride costs little, a short ride running from 6 to 9 bahts, a much longer one from 10 to 15 bahts (from thirty to seventy-five U.S. cents).

TRAFFIC moves on the left. Beware! *"Look right"* when crossing streets.

AIRLINES. **Bangkok's** *Don Muang Airport* is served by twenty international airlines, with *Thai Airways* offering regular flights to all Thailand's major cities, some of them on a daily basis, others operating less frequently.

RAILWAYS. Thailand is crisscrossed with railways employing reasonably comfortable passenger trains, with overnight sleeper accommodations from **Bangkok** to **Chiengmai** and **Nongkhai** in the north and to **Ubol** in the northeast. Internationally, there are services from **Bangkok** to the Malay border with connecting air conditioned trains to **Penang, Kuala Lumpur,** and **Singapore.** It is a two day trip by train from **Bangkok** to **Singapore.**

CURRENCY is covered in Chapter Eight, but I would like to re-emphasize that the words "baht" and "tical" are both basic units of Thai foreign exchange, used interchangeably to describe the same monetary denominations, which is frequently confusing. There are one hundred satangs in one tical or baht, and an old accurate saying goes, "A Thai tical is an American nickel."

SPORTS in Thailand abound for both spectators and participants alike, with the Thais being particularly skilled at soccer which one may watch in the *National Stadium*.

KITE FLYING, which takes place on an open heath back of the *Grand Palace,* is contested in the springtime and should more properly be called "kite-fighting" since in Thailand this is a highly competitive sport, with all sizes being flown from little bitsy postage stamps to great lumbering B-52-like behemoths. The wind is brisk toward nightfall, and the kites have been designed to take full advantage of every tiny zephyr of breeze to rise missile-like from a standing start. Kite strings have been treated to give them cutting edges consisting of bits of glued-on broken glass. Many are streamed simultaneously from both ends of the "combat area," and when they have attained altitude the "male" and "female" kites from opposite ends of the field are permitted to sail toward one another. When the kites mingle over midfield, the deftness with which the kites are maneuvered and the artistry that is exhibited in cutting the rival kites from their strings is an extraordinary exhibition which I think you will enjoy.

FIGHTING. The Thais regale in all types of fighting—including kites as noted above, fish, cocks, crickets, and most of all human beings, i.e. Thai boxing, offered in **Bangkok's** two principal stadiums, the *Lumpini* and *Rajadamnoen.* The former offers the local version of the sport on Tuesdays and Saturdays, while the latter presents its program of the manly art of legalized mayhem on Thursdays and Sundays. Thai boxing matches are unique and exciting, the antics of both the fans and the boxers being intriguing. The participants fight with their fists, knees, elbows, insteps, and feet. The spectacle is an absolutely incredible one.

I believe that one may get a better idea of this sport in reading the following summation of the Thai boxing rules as set forth in the official program:

RULES. Fists, elbows, knees, and feet may be used to attack and defend. Biting, hair pulling, and spitting are not allowed.

PAY HOMAGE. According to tradition, boxers may pay homage to their teachers before commencing a contest. This is done by the boxers prostrating themselves on the floor, followed by various boxing poses. Keen followers of boxing may tell from the homage and poses in which camp the boxer has trained.

AMULETS AND FETISHES. Collections of supernatural superstitious magical substances used to guard or protect the wearers from harm and cuts are worn and tied to the upper arm of the boxer.

MONGKOLS are circlets made of rattan covered cloth which are worn on the head of the boxer during the time of paying homage.

GLOVES. A glove weighs four ounces only.

CLOTHES. Trunks shall be in blue or red material. Grease and ointment are forbidden.

THE RING shall not be less than sixteen feet or more than twenty-four feet square.

A CONTEST consists of five rounds, each round of three minutes duration, with a two minute rest period between.

KNOCKOUT. A boxer is deemed to have lost the contest when he is knocked down and unable to continue the contest for a period of ten seconds.

TECHNICAL KNOCKOUT. The referee may award the fight to a boxer whose opponent in the referee's opinion is so injured it may lead to serious complications should the fight continue.

DRAW. If both boxers earn equal scores during the contest, the fight may be declared a draw.

JUDGES' VOTES. A boxer who obtains the majority of the judges' votes shall be declared the winner.

RETIREMENT. A boxer may win a contest when his opponent is unable to continue to box, or he "retires."

FOUL. Biting, hair pulling, wrestling, falling down over opponent, embracing, swinging opponent down, catching, locking opponent's arm or head, holding the rope, or intentional falling without receiving a blow or kick.

The boxers' names are terrifyingly descriptive. Here is an excerpt from a program of March, 1962: "Smashing, Two Fisted, Lion Hearted, Deangg Mudung of **Bangkok,** the morning star of the *Sidsingh Camp,* the interesting ferocious product of the cauliflower industry of **Cholbury** in rural Thailand, a dare devil hot shot who worships the 'do or die' motto. Once in the ring it is either his opponent who is carried out or he is carried out to the hospital." Ugh! Another fighter of note was called "Whole-Souled, Magnificently Battling Sturdy Tiger of Nongkai Pridi Phusavat," who, according to the program, comes out "with knee caps flashing, insteps hardened, and his elbow points crying out for action."

HORSE RACING. The *Royal Bangkok Sports Club* is a combination race course, where the thoroughbreds perform on Saturdays, and a smart country club. Here one has for his pleasure excellent tennis courts, an interesting though short golf course which winds in and out of the race track infield, an Olympic size swimming pool, and all the amenities of a fine private country club. Should you be interested in the facilities of the club, address yourself to the secretary, a thoroughly gracious gentleman. In the past the club has been generous in welcoming foreign visitors. A section of the stand serves as a private club house from which members and their guests may watch the races. This area includes lovely terraces, bars, restaurants, library, reading, and card rooms. If you are a racing devotee and are to be in **Bangkok** on a Saturday, it would be well to communicate by mail with the Club Secretary in advance. Racing takes place at the *Turf Club* on Sundays.

SWIMMING for western visitors is limited to fine pools, though the natives swim daily in the *klongs* and river. Forty-five to one hundred miles from **Bangkok,** there are excellent soft surf beaches, the best of which are at **Bangsaen** and **Pathaya. Hua Hin,** 140 miles from **Bangkok,** is Thailand's most popular beach resort and one of the finest in the world. The foregoing all enjoy excellent climate, fine golf courses, tennis courts, the whitest imaginable sand beaches, and the crystal clear invigorating salt water of the *Gulf of Thailand.* These resorts are reached either by rail or road, with special weekend rail excursions leaving **Bangkok** late Friday night and returning Sunday afternoon. Excellent hotels and cottages are available at the beaches. The food is good.

CAMERAS. Nowhere else in such a limited area may one put his color film to such abundant use as in Thailand, especially in **Bangkok.** When you return from the Orient and have your color films developed, you will never be able to persuade your relatives, neighbors, and friends that the films haven't been doctored . . . so magically emblazoned is Thailand. In the *Grand Palace* and *Palace Grounds,* one may use only still cameras; no movies are allowed. In one chapel, that of the *Emerald Buddha,* no cameras of any kind are permitted. With the foregoing two very minor exceptions, you may "shoot" to your heart's content.

HISTORICALLY, the Thais, their forebears the Siamese, and the venerable Sukhothais were only a little more skilled in the chronicling of historical events than their neighbors to the east and south, the Malays and the Cambodians. From available records, it appears, however, that Thailand's earliest occupants probably trudged over the mountain barriers from south-central China as early as the 6th century, with other larger evacuations taking place after the released fury of the well known Kublai Khan had whiplashed great segments of China and Korea. Unfortunately for Kublai Khan, the terror of the Chinese and Koreans and would-be terror of the Japanese, he fell victim to the original *kamikaze* (which I have explained in Japan's chapter), or "divine wind," which shattered his bellicose dreams of world domination.

The Negrito tribes which migrated from the north en route to **Indonesia, Malaysia,** and the **Philippines** could have been among the first to settle in the Thai area, and many are believed to have lingered and settled down.

The Mons, followed by the Khmers, were the first permanent inhabitants, living in the valleys of the *Chao Phya* and *Mekong Rivers.*

The inhabitants who today are called Thais were long-time vassals of the Khmer rulers but gradually emerged from the yoke of serfdom and in the 13th century built the first Thai settlement of their own, calling it *Sukhothai.*

During this crucial stage in the nation's development, the great King Ram Khamheng ascended the throne, dominated the scene, and gave the Thais their first formal written language, an adaptation of the Khmer alphabet, and, more important, introduced Buddhism to the country.

In 1350, the Thais' forward progress was interrupted by the secession of Prince Ramatibodi, the "Alexander the Great" of ancient Thailand, who marched his armies through the *Isthmus of Kra* all the way to the *Indian Ocean,* which spelled the death knell of *Sukhothai.* It was Ramatibodi who later gave his countrymen their first set of codified laws and founded the capital of **Ayudhya** which persevered for 417 years, three hundred of them bloody ones. In due course, the Thais, oppressed by both the Burmese and the Khmers, succumbed to the stronger of the two, the Burmese.

The Thais came into contact with Europeans at the start of the 16th century, meeting first the Portuguese, then, early in the 17th century, the Dutch and English, and ultimately the French, who had literally tiptoed on egg shells into Thailand from Indochina.

At this time, a great adventurer loomed on Thai's historical horizon, a strange and powerful Greek Catholic spy for the French King Louis XIV by the name of Constantin Falcon, who rose to power by virtue of his financial wizardry in court circles and became advisor to the Thai King and then his First Minister. Falcon's role in Thailand was to convert the Thai monarch and his country to Catholicism and to deepen the French influence at the expense of the Dutch.

Temporarily at least, the French forged to the front, but their victory was short lived. The loyal Thais deposed the King, ousted Constantin, and grew disgusted with and suspicious of foreigners. For the next 150 years, the Thais duplicated the Japanese feat of isolation, even bettering that of the Tokugawa Shogunate.

The Burmese threat returned with a vengeance, and **Ayudhya** fell, the old capital being Biblically sacked and its inhabitants either slaughtered or forced to flee for their lives in dismal defeat. From this disaster only one young general and a handful of his faithful followers escaped. Phra Chao Tak Sin, a man like Robert Bruce of Scotland, bided his time, gained strength, struck back, and won. He established his capital at **Thonburi,** directly across the river from modern **Bangkok,** on the site of what is known as the *Temple of the Dawn (Wat Arun).* He became King only to lose his mind and shortly thereafter his life to assassins. In his place, another young Thai general, Chao Phya Chakri, sprang. He established his capital in **Bangkok** in 1782 and, in turning King, chose the name of Rama I, founding the Thai dynasty that rules to this very day. He does indeed deserve to be called the "Ataturk" or "Kemal" of Thailand, no less than the poor unfortunate Phra Chao Tak Sin merited being called Thailand's Robert Bruce.

Founder of modern Thailand, King Mongkut, in the early 1800's, opened wide arms to the waiting west. Though his knowledge of the west was much greater than any other Oriental, he was to learn more, for this was the monarch played so illustriously by Yul Brynner in "The King and I." Mongkut learned much about the west from the erudite Anna H. Leonowens, whose own life made such interesting reading in "Anna and the King of Siam" by Margaret Landon.

Mongkut opened Thailand more to western ways but in so doing cleverly parried off and out-jockeyed all colonial attempts to dominate him and subjugate his ancient land. As remarkable a man as he was, he was luckily followed by two only slightly less remarkable monarchs, his son, King Chulalongkorn, and King Vajiravudh, and the work of modernization continued in government, administration, education, commerce, and social reform. These reigns were followed by a depressing era of lean days for Thailand, however, when the philosophy "I am the State, the State is I" was doomed; the absolute monarchy was finished. In 1932, an army officers' junta seized the reins of power and set up a constitutional monarchy which provided for a parliament, half of whose members were elected, the other half being appointed. Thus, for the first time, Thailand enjoyed at least a limited measure of democracy, but the immediately ensuing years can best be described as an era of serene chaos, with plots, counterplots, coup d'etats, successful revolutions, and abortive uprisings following thickly, one after the other.

King Prajadhipok abdicated in 1935, being succeeded by his nephew, King Ananda Mahidol, who reigned until his death on June 9, 1946.

The present King, His Majesty Phumipon Adulyadet, was born in Cambridge, Massachusetts on December 5, 1927, and in 1949 married his Queen, Sirikit, from which union four children have sprung, three daughters and the Crown Prince, H.R.H. Prince Vachiralongkorn, who was born on July 28, 1952.

In World War II, the pliable Thais made an ill-fated alliance with Japan after a ludicrously brief period of token battling with the invaders. The world quite properly judged this affair a marriage of convenience since the Thai sympathies had always been with the west and Thai guerrillas were famous for their bravery and ruthless terrorization of the occupying Japanese. There is many an American alive today who, lost or strayed in Thailand during the war, owes his life to the resourceful help of these kind, gentle people. The United States recognized the Thai position for what it necessarily had to be under Axis domination and, liberating the country, immediately extended a most cordial hand in all postwar relations.

The present Thai government was set up by the Revolutionary Party under the present Prime Minister, Field Marshal Sarit Thanarat, on October 20, 1958, with the aim of introducing far-reaching administrative reforms to insure honesty and integrity in public affairs, stabilize the economy, improve the standard of living of the people, and better utilize the general natural resources of the country. So far, great success has been achieved in meeting each of these commendable goals.

The Thai government, comprised of the Prime Minister, two Deputy Prime Ministers, and fourteen Cabinet Members (also referred to as "Ministers"), is a constitutional monarchy with sovereign power originating in the people and exercised through the chief executives, the national legislature, and the judiciary.

CULTURE in Thailand is remarkable in its expression, enduring in its quality, and interesting both to the appreciative Thais and their welcome visitors. Thai culture is a mixture of Chinese and Indian, but it would take an amazingly introspective scholar to be able to venture a bold guess as to where one ends and the other begins, or even which is which.

The important thing is that the end result has become a blend which is eminently successful . . . and unmistakably Thai.

Thai dancing, Thai music, Thai drama, and Thai painting are all refreshing, exotic, unique, and worthwhile for even the most casual observer and a source of unending richness for the deeply concerned student.

MUSIC in Thailand is whatever and wherever you find it and like it. Temple music, classical drama music, and classical dancing music is singsong in quality, while popular music, imported from the west, transcends the scale from western opera and light opera to cool, torrid jazz, Dixieland, bop, and rock 'n' roll. The Thai King, a mean tootler on the "licorice stick" (clarinet), "digs" them all, having once played a duet with Benny Goodman.

Thai DANCING, blended with Thai drama, is world renowned and indubitably has its roots buried in the Indian past, possibly as far back as the 6th century. The ornate, unique, and rich costumes of the Thai dancers, themselves worth the spectacle, consist of golden baggy pantaloons, bejeweled and heavily embroidered tight-fitting jackets, "space men's helmets," ferocious goggle-eyed masks, and gay colored sashes and scarves, all highly ornamented, rich in gold and jewels.

Thai dancing comes under four classifications. The *Khon,* or masked play, with an all-male cast, is the acknowledged ancestor of the age-old Indian epic, the *Ramayana,* after which the *Khon* is patterned, and is characterized by off-stage dialogue, expressive and silent gestures, fevered dances, and abruptly struck poses which are dearly beloved by the enthusiastic audiences.

The *Lakon,* best described as being operatic ballet, the most graceful and least stylized form of Thai dancing requiring an all-female cast, is the best known of the Thai dancing. The *Lakon* chorus sings a dialogue-telling story, with the entire presentation reminding one somewhat of a western ballet. Although the *Lakon* is less vigorous than the all-male *Khon,* it is far more graceful and no less emotional in content, nor less attractive or interesting.

The *Rabam* is a character dance, while the *Likay* is the modern form of *Lakon.*

Thai classical dancing may be seen in the *Erawan* or *Rama Hotels,* the *Silpakorn Theatre (Fine Arts Department),* the *Phakavali Institute,* the *Buddhai Sawan School of Fencing,* and, as announced from time to time, in night clubs.

Thai PAINTING may best be seen in the beautiful Thai temples.

CLASSICAL THAI DRAMA is an evolution of ancient Sanskrit myth composed of dialogue, choral singing, graceful gestures, and dignified movements. In the Thai drama, as in *Khon,* the actors and actresses wear extraordinarily elaborate costumes and have their faces hidden by grotesque masks.

WAT is usually translated as "temple," but since the Thais prefer to think of their temples as monasteries, *wat* may mean either temple or monastery.

The BOT is the holiest section of a *wat* and is the only place where monks may be ordained. This consecrated area is surrounded by eight sacred boundary stones. A *wat* may be authentic and not have a *bot*.

A CHO FA and a NAGA are decorative birdlike animals and serpents of divine mythological origin found on *wat* roofs.

The GARUDA (KRUT), according to ancient mythology, was half bird and half man whose transportation was instantaneous. The *garuda* closed his eyes, wished to be at some place, and, on opening his eyes, was there. The *garuda,* known locally as the *krut,* is found on Thailand's royal standard.

A CHEDI (PHRA CHEDI) is an edifice surmounted by a dome which tapers into a spire containing the ashes of members of the Royal Family and of outstanding non-regal people.

A STUPA locally describes a *chedi* of Indian origin and usage.

A PRANG (PHRA PRANG) is an Indian *stupa* but of Cambodian type architecture.

A VIHARA (VIHAN) is a meeting hall.

YEAKS (YAKS) are huge, fantastic, multi-colored demigods found guarding Thailand's temples.

NORASINGH are the half-human, half-lion figures seen in the decorative scheme of the palace grounds, temples, and adorning street light poles.

WAT ETIQUETTE is not strict, and the Thais are both friendly and understanding. The *wat* floors are immaculately clean, however, and they should be kept that way. The native Buddhists always remove their shoes when entering a temple, and, while it is not an irrevocable rule that visitors must do likewise, it is the courteous thing to do and we, as Americans, are courteous.

During my rather considerable experience in the fascinating world of travel, I have time and again heard people say, "If you've seen one cathedral, you've seen them all; if you've seen one temple, you've seen them all; and if you've seen one shrine, you've seen them all."

In Thailand nothing could be further from the truth. Nothing. Each of the splendiferous *wats* of Bangkok is rich in decorative ornateness and has its own sublime character, personality, and beauty. Thailand is a vast show place, and **Bangkok** is its sparkling jewel. There is no other city within the realm of my experience that is so rewarding for the camera fan. A part of the radiant sparkling quality of the coloration of the *wats* and palaces is achieved by making brightly colored pottery, dishes, and plates, breaking them, and setting the broken pieces into the roofs and walls.

BANGKOK

BANGKOK, one of the most beautiful, interesting, and attractive cities of the world, exudes magnetic charm and titillating personality. This "City of Angels" *(Krung Thep),* as it is also known, sprawls delightfully on both banks of the *Chao Phya River* and, though some thirty miles from the sea, is one of Asia's busiest seaports. It is a city of shimmering and scintillating sights and sounds richly ornamented with gleaming public buildings, elaborately adorned colorful temples, handsome houses, and broad six-lane flower bedecked boulevards lighted at night by decorative lamps in half-human and half-lion form. **Bangkok** is a city of modern splendor, of blazing neon business signs; it is also a city of multi-hued demigod *yeaks* and blue demons.

There is a vast introspective western misconception of the Thai capital. Almost without exception, visitors expect to see a brooding, foreboding city hacked out of the impenetrable jungle with the city's inhabitants living in semi-squalor on the banks of filthy canals in an atmosphere permeated with incredibly bad odors. Nothing could be further from the truth.

Wherever one casts his eyes in modern **Bangkok,** there is a most attractive public or private building, a palace, a temple, or a handsome home. The City of Angels is a metropolis of eye-pleasing contrasts.

The Thais point with great pride to the fact that their crime rate is one of the lowest in the Orient, and the visitor, male

BANGKOK

1. TURF CLUB
2. PRAMANE GROUND
3. SPORTS CLUB
4. POLO CLUB
5. LUMPINI PARK
6. TACHIN STATION
7. GRAND PALACE
8. WAT PO
9. WAT PHRA KEO
10. BANGKOK STATION

952

or female, is safer out alone after dark in their country than in one's own home town.

Bangkok is a city where, on the river's west bank in the **Thonburi** area near the site of the original capital, one finds Thais living an amazing life in stilted houses on the *klongs*. For scores of miles, one sees boats of all sizes and shapes ranging from tiny four-foot sampans to great junk-like vessels which serve as general stores, fruit and vegetable markets, hardware stores, butcher shops, fish stores, floating restaurants, and souvenir shops. On the colorful *klongs,* one sees hundreds of naked boys and girls who swim like fish from early morning until late at night.

Bangkok is a city of fetes, fairs, and festivals, the locale of the procession of golden barges down the river to the *Temple of the Dawn* in October; **Bangkok** is a city of almost two million happy, live-and-let-live people. It is a city where Oriental splendor lies side by side with European-style houses of business, magnificent homes and stilted native houses, of five institutions of higher learning, a sports center, a city of eastern magic and religious belief, an Arabian Nights Damascus, and a spiritual Oriental Rome. **Bangkok** is a city of fun, romance, adventure, and gaiety in a fantastic setting . . . of a cacophonic *Chinatown* and a *Snake Farm* with white igloos . . . of saffron-robed monks and modern air conditioned hotels and restaurants.

Among the points of great interest in Thailand's number one city are:

The GRAND PALACE, built by Rama I, is one of the most spectacularly beautiful and colorful man-made structures in the world. In common with the other great structures of **Bangkok,** the *Grand Palace* is so brilliantly colorful as to defy description, or even belief. The glistening white walls are in vivid contrast to scintillating royal purples, saffron, orange, yellow, and other bright blues.

The *Grand Palace* is reminiscent of the pomp and splendor of Old Siam, its ornate buildings characterized by their many-

tiered golden roofs and glass encrusted spires thrusting into the ethereal, eternally blue skies. The most impressive of the *Grand Palace* buildings open for inspection is *Chakri Hall,* erected in 1868 for receptions and used today for Royal Audiences. *Dusit Hall* was the work of Rama I and is said to be the most splendid structure within the *Grand Palace* grounds. The *Throne Hall,* site of the coronation of His Majesty King Phumipon, is to the left as one enters the main gate.

The *Grand Palace* and the *Wat Phra Keo (Royal Chapel of the Emerald Buddha* within the *Palace Compound)* are the only local buildings which pose even a slight visitation problem. Be sure to ascertain through your local agent, or tour conductor, the hours next available to visit the *Grand Palace.* Whatever the weather, gentlemen must wear a coat and tie when visiting the *Grand Palace,* and ladies must wear a conservative dress; no slacks, shorts, or open sandals will be permitted. Within the *Grand Palace* grounds, one may take still pictures but not moving pictures.

A section of the *Grand Palace* was once a forbidden city one mile square and wonderfully spectacular, dominated by its towering shrine surrounded by high-fretted walls, garlanded with serpentine eaves and steeply gabled roofs.

I particularly recommend that you be sure to see the fresco adorning the long wall parallel to the *Temple of the Emerald Buddha* seen as one passes from the *Palace* to the *Temple*. This long ornate painting created in 1783 depicts an epic struggle between two legendary groups, the demons and the monkeys.

As Jimmy, my favorite Thai guide, puts it, "After you've seen that fresco, you can write your own fairy tales and go back to America and make a fortune on creative imagery." He's right. This fresco must have been the product of a Jules Verne type of mind.

One sequence depicts a regiment of the demons' allies called from another planet to hurl spears on the pestiferous monkeys who had the demons under murderous siege. The military intelligence of the monkeys was extraordinarily good, however, as they had received advance word of this heinous attempt to annihilate them. The monkeys retaliated, years before the Wright Brothers, by getting a number of their own troops airborne, and as the spears cascaded down from the fiendish arms of the outer space demons, the monkeys caught the weapons and cleverly deflected them into the bodies of the earthly demons below.

The fresco's most amusing, and sensuous, pictorial sequence involves some high skulduggery. A local deity had assured the head demon that if he could reflect peacefully for seven days without losing his temper, he would be granted immortality. The demon forthwith retired to a quiet glen below his palace and for six days withstood every possible temptation which could possibly cause him to lose his temper. The deity had enjoined the monkeys from causing the demon bodily harm during his peaceful meditations, but the monkeys were permitted to harass him, which they did with heinous vengeance. The monkeys called the demon king names, spat in his face, tweaked his ears, and were as ornery as only legendary monkeys could be. For six days and six nights, the chief demon withstood the urge to vent his normal righteous wrath. The monkeys were frantic. They couldn't permit the king of their deadly enemies to achieve immortality. But the anthropoids' chief, the red monkey, was not a leader to be treated lightly. He conceived a magnificent idea and proceeded to execute it by crossing the moat and climbing the steps to the palace parapet where a group of the demon's wives were gathered with their retinues. These bare-bosomed beauties form an inviting panel in the fresco. The red monkey hypnotized the group and swept the head demon's favorite curvacious wife into his arms. He carried her stealthily down the steps, across the moat, and into the glen below. When the pair reached the great demon's meditating area, the red monkey awoke the wife from her hypnotic sleep, who, when awakened, was being held in rapturous embrace. The red monkey was making violent love to her. Realizing her horrible predicament, the queen shouted, "Husband, husband, the red monkey is making love to me; what are you going to do about it?"

With that, the great demon roared in wrathful indignation and drove the red monkey away . . . but in so doing, he lost his place in mythical immortality.

Another test of the ingenuity of these two armies was posed when the great demon turned himself into a grotesque figure the size of a mighty mountain and opened his cavernous jaws to make them resemble the mouth of a yawning cave. He then caused great winds to blow, and the monkeys, caught in the turbulent storm, stampeded to the false security of the "cave" only to march pell-mell into the mammoth stomach of the great demon. The red monkey was not to be outdone. He caused himself to become the size of a mountain and grasped the great demon by the nape of the neck and pulled him erect, slashing his distended belly with a tremendous sword. In the fresco, one sees legions of monkeys spewing forth from the slit gut of the great demon, which, no doubt, served him right.

Bangkok's magnificent temples, more than three hundred in number, are architecturally unique. These colorful *wats,* cradles of religion and religious interpretation for the Buddhist faithful, glittering like the sunlight, have multi-tiered roofs and curved gables, with oddly attractive snake-like up-pointing spires and squat bell-bottomed steeples.

The PANTHEON, within the *Compound,* is the *Shrine of Kings* in which repose statues of the Thai monarchs who have guided the destinies of this happy land since 1782.

WAT PHRA KEO *(Royal Chapel of the Emerald Buddha),* in the grounds of the *Grand Palace,* is the repository of the *Emerald Buddha,* thirty-one inches of beautiful emerald-colored jasper, seated high on a solid gold throne. The solid jasper *Buddha,* reputedly of Ceylonese origin, is attired in ornamental clothing made of precious metal which varies with the season. *Wat Phra Keo,* the loveliest and most famous of the temples of Thailand, is a commanding three-tiered structure surmounted by a golden roof and decorated with murals depicting the life story of the Lord Buddha with scenes from the *Ramayana,* Hindu writings similar to the Homeric epics of Greece. *Wat Phra Keo* is of typical Thai architecture, guarded by kingsize demon sentinels, weapons in hand, lips curled in ferociously dentured grins, and adorned with crested helmets. The nine ornate columns represent the major planets, the huge lacquered doors are inset with mother-of-pearl, and the inner gates are masterpieces of art. The courtyard is brilliantly bedecked with painted stone serpents and animals, bronze beasts, and decorative pillars. Within the *Wat* are other magnificent works of art including golden fawns which are part bird, part wild beast, and part human.

The numerous wind bells, each pitched to a different soothing note, add a pleasant harmony to one's visit.

Wat Phra Keo is open to the public on Sunday mornings for worship and for visitors during the week. The *Emerald Buddha* may not be photographed from inside the *Wat,* but distant views may be made from the steps through the doorway.

WAT ARUN *(Temple of the Dawn),* the most spectacularly situated of the *wats* of **Bangkok,** is considered to be, next to the

Wat Phra Keo, the most beautiful *wat* in the world. A striking example of Thai decorative art, *Wat Arun* is situated on the site of the historical ancient capital of Thailand established by Phra Chao Tak Sin after he escaped from the ruined city of **Ayudhya** in 1767. On the west bank of the river, a visit to *Wat Arun* may best be included after a morning's tour of the *klongs.*

Wat Arun's four porcelain pavilions rising majestically from the river's edge depict phases in the life of Buddha from his birth, education, and conversion to his death. The broken-dish frescoes, the statue of the Moon God on a milk white horse, and the steeply terraced steps add to the sublime picture of *Wat Arun,* crowned by five tall *prangs* and a Khmer-styled pagoda.

WAT PO *(Temple of the Reclining Buddha)* is the internationally famous home of the 150-foot-long *Reclining Buddha,* which symbolizes the passing from present-day existence into nirvana. *Wat Po* supports a collection of multi-tiered steeples which house Buddha images and the ashes of Thai V.I.P.s. *Wat Po* is ornamented with numerous Chinese stone statues, a gallery containing tens of scores of Buddhist images, and a bas-relief on which is inscribed the epic of *Ramayana.* Near the *Reclining Buddha* is the Bhodi Tree, an object of reverential devotion by the Thais, thought to be a tree having sprung from the one under which Lord Buddha once sat.

WAT RAJABOPIT is best known for its antique mother-of-pearl inlaid door panels dating back to the early days of **Ayudhya** from which they were salvaged.

WAT SRAKET, just outside the old city wall, was built by King Chulalongkorn and houses one of the largest Buddhas in Thailand, as well as a treasure trove of Buddhist icons, statues, and paintings, some originals and others copies of authentic works. *Wat Sraket's* roof tiles are brilliantly colored, its symmetry of almost pure Grecian line. For a week toward the end of October and the start of November, *Wat Sraket* plays host to a famed fair to which thousands flock for worship and more temporal enjoyment. In the *Wat,* one can see what is supposed to be a bone of the Buddha himself, brought from India in 1899.

WAT SUTAT, close to the *Grand Palace,* is the repository of eighty life-size figures of Lord Buddha which can be seen in a gentle half-light. The massive main halls and the elaborate multi-tiered roofs and other outstanding works of art are said to be the creations of King Rama II. In the square in front of *Wat Sutat* is the scarlet-red teakwood *Giant Swing.*

WAT RAJAPRADIST, overlooking the *Saranrom Garden,* is a small but richly exquisite temple of Carrara marble, gold, rubies, and sapphires. The exterior is superb, while the interior is of regal simplicity.

Other magnificent *wats* you will wish to see if your time in **Bangkok** permits are: *Wat Indra Vihan, Wat Bovornives, Wat Trimit, Wat Yanawa,* and *Wat Kalayanamit.*

The LAK MUANG is a small brick structure opposite the *Pramane Ground* that houses the *Guardian Spirit* of **Bangkok.** This yellow stucco shrine is surmounted by an impressive, *wat*-like spire. The *Lak Muang* is considered by gamblers to be their special oracle. They come in droves to ask for divine intervention in behalf of their speculations. Here one may buy and release captive birds.

RAJADAMNOEN AVENUE is the most impressive in the city . . . and in all Asia. This six-lane thoroughfare begins at the *Shrine of the Emerald Buddha,* passes the *Pramane Grounds,* and sweeps majestically through **Bangkok,** passing fine new office buildings, theaters, government bureaus, and the Thai boxing emporium. The half-lion, half-man statues atop the light poles add a distinct decorative overtone to the boulevard.

The NATIONAL LIBRARY, opened to the public in 1905, was the gift of the children of King Mongkut, one of Thailand's most able leaders and erudite scholars, to the nation in memory of their father. In front of the *Mahathad Temple* facing the *Pramane Grounds,* the *Library* houses one of the greatest collections of old books and manuscripts in the world, including prayer books, religious works, books on law, old maps, and records.

The NATIONAL MUSEUM, once the *Royal Palace* of the Prince-Successor, known as the Prince of Wang Na or the Second King, was built in 1782, but it was not until 1884 that the then reigning sovereign, King Chulalongkorn, set aside three buildings for the *Museum.* In 1926, the entire compound was given to the *Museum* by King Prajadhipok.

The *Museum* houses a colorful collection of antiquity including 10th-century tablets, lacquered and gilt bookcases, 14th-century illustrated manuscripts and stone inscriptions, Buddha and Hindu images, royal palanquins, theatrical costumes and masks, musical instruments, and ancient weapons. The mother-of-pearl inlaid objects for which Thailand is noted are in great evidence in the *National Museum.*

THAI HOUSES. One will find authentic, traditional Thai houses of more than passing interest. One of the most interesting Thai teak houses is owned by the American, Jim Thompson, a Thai silk fancier. His house, in Soi Kasemsan, is opposite the *National Stadium.* Jim Thompson's establishment, a combination of five genuine Thai homes, includes outstanding collections of old Siamese paintings and antiques.

Another genuine old teak house, named *Suan Pakkard Palace*, can be found on *Sri Ayudhya Road*. Built by a Prime Minister of King Mongkut, *Suan Pakkard Palace* is now in the possession of a Thai princess. The *Lacquer Pavilion* in the garden was the library of a monastery and is the only one of its kind known to be in existence. The black and gold murals seen inside are traditional. The antiques in the main house are of interest.

Your local travel agent or the information desk of your hotel can tell you about the days that these two houses will be open. Generally speaking, Mr. Thompson's home is open twice a week on Mondays and Thursdays from nine A.M. until noon. Financial benefits from the guided tours go to a school for the blind.

WAT BENCHAMABOPIT *(Marble Temple)* is another of **Bangkok's** handsome and outstanding buildings. *Benchamabopit's* Italian Carrara marble walls are surmounted by many-tiered golden roofs. The inner courtyard houses a collection of Buddha images from various Eastern countries. Scores of naked youngsters dive and swim from the golden domed *Wat's* boat landing.

The SARANROM GARDEN was built as an adjunct to a royal palace. Today this well kept garden is surrounded by pavilions for conventions, meetings, and festivals. Ulysses S. Grant stayed here on his post presidency world tour, and today the *American University Alumni Association* has weekly luncheons, Saturdays, at 12:15 P.M., to which visitors are invited.

SAOWAPHA INSTITUTE *(Snake Farm)* on the road between **Bangkok** and its busy airport resembles from a distance the architectural design and coloration of many of the *wats* and public buildings. It is surrounded by a sea of snow-like snake igloos. Wonderful work has been done here with anti-snake-bite serum. Visitors may watch the attendants feed the scaly horrors on Mondays at two P.M., and venom being extracted on Thursdays at ten A.M. I shudder just thinking about it.

KHAO DIN PARK (DUSIT ZOO) contains a growling, roaring, whining collection of exotic Thai animals, including a large number of pixy-like gibbons, and that pinkish-white old fellow who goes through life billed as the "Royal White Elephant of Thailand." (He was knighted in 1959, becoming a peer of the realm.)

FEHUKAO THONG (GOLDEN MOUNT) is one of the principal landmarks of **Bangkok.** Wherever one drives in the capital, the big *Phra Chedi,* crowning splendor of the *Golden Mount,* is visible.

LUMPINI PARK is a favorite gathering place for large numbers of local Thais. During the afternoons and evenings, a half hour's stroll through the park will prove interesting.

The DEMOCRACY MONUMENT is situated on *Rajadamnoen* between rows of ultramodern buildings.

The THRONE HALL, a gleaming white two story edifice entirely of marble, is currently used as the *National Assembly Hall.*

The FINE ARTS DEPARTMENT is the state school for youthful aspirants in classical drama, music, and Thai ballet.

Visitors may secure special permission to watch these classical courses of instruction.

THE KLONGS AND FLOATING MARKETS. Though there are a number of *klongs* within the city proper, with the continuation of the road widening projects these canals are doomed to extinction, the waterways being rapidly filled in to make room for more and wider streets. When one speaks of **Bangkok's** *klongs,* therefore, it is of the canals and their floating markets stemming from the west bank of the river across from **Bangkok** proper in **Thonburi** that reference is made.

To take advantage of the scenic splendor and heartwarming human interest of the floating markets, one must rise early and be on the way either by public sightseeing boat or chartered private launch not later than seven A.M.; 6:30 A.M. is preferable. The markets are held each morning from about seven A.M. until ten A.M. except on Buddhist holidays. Leaving **Bangkok,** one starts downstream toward the sea entering the labyrinth of *klongs* from the river. The canals penetrate jungle-like areas and open sections as they flow past the native stilted houses.

One passes scenes of primitive home life with entire families descending their front steps into the canals for communal bathing, washing of pots and pans, and gathering water for cooking. The produce boats are flatbottom scows, little sampans, long dugout canoes, and junks. Absolutely everything is sold from these boats. One may purchase ice either by the cake or shredded, bakery goods, fresh fruit, fish, vegetables, meat, ceramic products, hardware items, flowers, yard goods, dresses, and the famous straw lantern shade hats. There are coffee vendors, postmen delivering mail, kids off to school, floating restaurants exuding savory odors, and one sees the monks making their early morning "bowl rounds" by boat.

The *klong* vendors are almost exclusively Thai women, except the butchers who are Chinese men. Thais are not permitted to slaughter any living thing. Amidst the colorful floating stores, naked youngsters swim about gaily and frequently catch onto moving boats to be tugged far along the canals and even into the open river to await a ride back or a long tiring swim home.

Returning from the visit to the *klongs,* one will see the *Wat Benchamabopit* and *Wat Arun, Temple of the Dawn.* This is also the best time to see the—

ROYAL BARGES which are huge, gaily decorated wooden boats with magnificently carved bows, seldom used but most effective when displayed in the marine parade at festival time. The largest of the Royal Barges, 150 feet in length, may be fitted with the *Royal Throne* for the king on ceremonal occasions.

TRIPS FROM BANGKOK

Thailand's most popular seaside resorts, readily accessible by car or rail, are the previously mentioned BANGSAEN, PATHAYA, and HUA HIN. All are pleasantly cool pleasure paradises.

AYUDHYA, Thailand's ancient capital, sixty miles from **Bangkok,** placidly reposes in a fertile plain that is the national rice bowl. Reached from **Bangkok** by car, train, or boat on the

Chao Phya River, **Ayudhya** offers the prospect of a most interesting day sightseeing trip from the capital. Your hotel chef will be delighted to prepare a picnic lunch which may be enjoyed amid the ancient ruins of the city that became Thailand's capital in 1350. Thirty-three sovereigns reigned here until 1767 when the city was literally leveled. Today the city is little more than a dreamy provincial town with an aura of ancient grandeur, where one may close one's eyes and, in reverie, reconstruct the frantic days when the Burmese came storming in murderous attack, destroying everything before their military avalanche. Ancient books point out, "The canals of that old city, **Ayudhya,** literally ran red with blood, the blood of butchered people." Now the sacked buildings are smoke-blackened ruins over which the jungle is making creeping stealthy inroads. The reddish walls of the regal royal palace are crumbling as are the government buildings and temples. In a hazy sort of a way, **Ayudhya** resembles *Angkor Wat,* with monasteries, *chedis,* a colossal bronze Buddha image, and a reclining image. Restorations are currently in process, and it is hoped that the area will not only be preserved but completely rebuilt.

NAKORN PATHOM. As one heads southwest toward the *Isthmus of Kra* from **Bangkok's** contrasting city of *klongs,*

Emerald Buddha, fighting crickets, houses on stilts, and air conditioned movie palaces, **Nakorn Pathom** is the first big city which becomes visible some 36 miles away. One's eyes will be caught by the vast *Phra Pathom Chedi,* its spire of 380 golden glazed tiles surmounting a huge bell-like shrine, the largest pagoda in southeast Asia. *Phra Pathom Chedi* was built in the middle of the 19th century by King Mongkut over the ruins of an ancient sanctuary. The first Buddhist mission sent to Thailand by the Indian King Asoka, patron of the ancient Indian arts, was founded in **Nakorn Pathom** circa 200 B.C. It is believed that the Buddhist drive to embrace all of the elephant-headed country struck out from this southwestern coastal town.

KANCHANABURI, about 70 miles from the Thai capital, is the terminus of a rail line, the last fair sized outpost of the central plains before the land ridges into the mountains. It was from **Kanchanaburi** that Allied prisoners were sent forth by their Japanese captors to build a railway over the high hills separating Thailand from Burma. A well tended *Allied Cemetery* is a grim reminder of those days. Here one can see the original bridge over the *River Kwai,* the inspiration for the famous book and film, though the bridge is of steel, not wood.

RAJBURI, 50 miles from **Bangkok,** is the pottery center of Thailand. Local clay is ideally adapted for the potter's wheels which turn out endless ceramic products, including large quantities of water jars, a number of which are used in almost every Thai home for preserving the drinking supply. The populated areas of **Songkhla, Pekhet,** and **Haadjai** are also in the vicinity, beyond which tall leafy mountains heave their majestic bulk, dropping beyond to the powder-fine white sand beaches on both the *Gulf of Thailand* and the *Indian Ocean* on either side of the narrow neck of the *Isthmus of Kra.* This is one Thai locale that is not predominantly Buddhist but Muslim. **Rajburi** may be reached in about two hours by car from **Bangkok.**

BANG PA-IN, near **Ayudhya** on the banks of "Lord River," is a royal summer residence located where King Chulalongkorn constructed Old Thai buildings reminiscent of Europe, being an odd agglomeration of a small Gothic church, Renaissance hall, medieval water tower, and Greek temples. Here one may shed a tear over a pathetic little monument erected by a distraught king to his beloved queen who was drowned long ago in a corner of the palace moat.

LOPBURI, 90 miles from **Bangkok** over the same rail and road route as **Ayudhya** and **Bang Pa-in,** is another ancient Thai city, once a Khmer outpost in a golden day when that once mighty empire was paid tribute by Siam. **Lopburi's** triple pagoda, *Prang Sam Yod,* a sight worth seeing, was constructed of laterite in the architectural style of *Angkor Wat.* King Narai, then residing at **Ayudhya,** had **Lopburi** constructed, in the 17th century, as the site of his summer palace, which is still in evidence. One can also see the queer Renaissance style house of the master plotter, prime minister, and Greek adventurer, Constantin Falcon. Nearby, on the road to **Lopburi** at **Saraburi,** one finds the footprint of Buddha to which hordes of the devout flock in February.

CHIENGMAI, 510 miles north of **Bangkok** by road, is Thailand's second city and is reached by plane in less than three hours, by train in seventeen hours, and by road in two days. **Chiengmai's** 75,000 inhabitants live happily in a mountain valley, one thousand cool feet above the *Gulf of Thailand,* astride the *River Ping,* surrounded by towering mountains. Founded more than 900 years ago and known as the "Northern Capital," **Chiengmai** is famous for its Thai cotton and splendid handicraft, especially handwrought silver and lacquerware. Sections of **Chiengmai** are inhabited by clusters of artisans who have made a common cause of the concentrated pursuit of their crafts which include *Silver Village, Weaving Village,* and *Umbrella Village.* It is said that Thailand's most beautiful maidens are to be found in this city.

The *wats* of **Chiengmai** are almost as renowned and eye-pleasing as those of **Bangkok.** *Wat Chedi Luang* is considered by connoisseurs of things beautiful to be one of the most beautiful in Thailand. *Wat Suan Dawk* is the repository of the ashes of the ancient kings of the north. The 600-year-old *Wat Phra Sing* is a thing of beauty. *Wat Chedi Jet Yod* is at least eight centuries old, while *Wat Koo Tou* houses the most venerable Buddha image in the country. *Wat Koo Tao* is characterized by its unusual shape, reminiscent of a pumpkin pyramid.

Except for midsummer, this northern climate is ideal, with October to February being enhanced by a profusion of red roses, the pride and joy of **Chiengmai's** populace.

NAKORN SRITHAMARAJ, considered to be the oldest continuously inhabited city in Thailand, is the home of Thailand's most distinctive craft, *"Niello,"* an art that that has been nurtured in Thailand for more than eight centuries. There is a large collection of outstanding temples in **Nakorn Srithamaraj,** the best known and oldest of which is *Wat Mahathat.*

TOURIST ORGANIZATION OF THAILAND (TOT), Mansion 2, Rajdamnern Avenue, phone 24641, cable address "TOT" BANGKOK, is one of the world's friendliest and most efficient government tourist organizations. TOT's information desk is open seven days a week, holidays included, from 8:30 A.M. to 4:30 P.M. Its personnel will be delighted to provide you with information and particulars apropos of all phases of traveling, life, and customs in Thailand.

TOT also maintains a shopping center at Sri Ayudhya Road, phone 48379, featuring a tempting selection of Thai souvenirs and handicrafts, including Thai silk, cottons, jewelry, bronze ware, dolls, and attractive articles made of straw and carved wood.

To visit Thailand is to endow our earthly existence with a generous bit of heaven. To know the Thais, even though through brief impersonal encounter, is to love them.

Thailand no longer enjoys diplomatic relations with her neighbor **Cambodia.**

CHAPTER 17

Viet Nam

Saigon, **Viet Nam's** capital and principal port of entry either by sea or air, is one of the most brilliantly beautiful cities that I have ever visited. Its broad, flower-bedecked, tree-lined boule vards are invitingly decorated with street cafes, its residential section is handsome, well groomed, and colorful, and its shops are smart. The men of **Saigon** are handsome, and the beautiful girls are adorably costumed in the *ao dai,* the long form-fitting, slit-sided multicolored tunics over long white satin pantaloons which are the most attractive native costumes in the world.

Saigon is the glamorous lustrous "Paris of the Orient." As one of my Vietnamese friends explains it, "Our country is French in appearance but Oriental at heart."

CLIMATE. Viet Nam is a year-round vacationland, but October through April are its finest months. During this period, the days are not excessively hot, and the evenings are cooled by maritime breezes. From May through September, heavy rains occasionally fall, with the climate from March through August approximating that of Washington, D.C.'s midsummer. It must be noted, however, that during the so-called rainy season it does not rain all of the time, the downpours being limited to late afternoon. Should it be convenient for you to visit **Saigon** only during the hot or rainy season, don't let this deter you. A light raincoat will do the trick. The good hotels and restaurants are all air conditioned.

CLOTHING. One needs only light informal clothing in Viet Nam. Sports shirts and slacks will be just fine for the men and summer cottons for the girls. Evenings are pleasantly cool. Men will usually want a coat and tie for dinner.

HYGIENE. The Vietnamese are clean, intelligent, and attractive people. Public places and private homes are immaculately clean. While water is quite safe to drink in the good hotels and restaurants, the water supply is not universally up to our standard. Bottled water should be used as a wise precautionary measure.

LOCAL TRANSPORTATION is excellent, with French Renaults and Peugeots constituting the majority of the taxi fleet, which cabs are easily recognizable by their two-tone cream and blue paint jobs and black and white license plates. The drivers are courteous and the fares cheap. The ubiquitous Orient *trishaw* is here but is called locally "cyclo-pousse." There are lots of them. Try one.

One can arrange easily for sightseeing in a private car with chauffeur and an *ao dai*-clad beauty for a guide who speaks impeccable English, perfect French, and Vietnamese.

HOTELS in Saigon are the finest imaginable. The ultra-modern *Caravelle* and the attractive *Majestic* are among the world's best.

RESTAURANTS everywhere in Viet Nam are excellent. One may sample of the finest in French, Vietnamese, and Chinese foods.

The GEOGRAPHICAL LOCATION of Viet Nam is south of Red China and west of Laos and Cambodia. The entire eastern and southern coast lines of Viet Nam are washed by the waters of the *South China Sea*.

The 1954 Geneva cease fire agreement split ancient Viet Nam at the seventeenth parallel, an unjust political situation that has left the citizens understandably unhappy.

The country is now divided into two almost exactly equal parts. Northern Communist Viet Nam occupies 62,000 square miles with a population of sixteen million, while the Republic of Viet Nam, south of the seventeenth parallel, encompasses 65,000 square miles and includes fourteen million citizens. Viet Nam as a whole is twice as large as New England, while South Viet Nam by itself is the size of the state of Washington.

The POPULATION includes two million aborigines who live in the mountain areas and are descendants of the original populace who inhabited Viet Nam several thousand years ago. The Chams, aborigines who now inhabit the southern portion of central Viet Nam, have a brilliant history to which temples and palaces attest.

HISTORICAL BACKGROUND. Unlike their Cambodian neighbors who pay little attention to written history, the Vietnamese have a recorded history that stretches back centuries and a legendary history that goes back to 2,879 B.C.

The Viets emigrated from central China. *Nam* means south; hence, *Viet Nam* means the "Viets of the South." The first name of the country was *Nam Viet,* and the country was known as such until 111 B.C.

From 111 B.C. and until A.D. 938, Viet Nam was dominated, except for two short periods, by the Chinese.

The years from A.D. 939 to A.D. 1883 are known by the Vietnamese as their era of great national dynasties. During that period the country was unified; its economic, administrative, and military organizations were perfected; and the famous *Temple of Literature* was erected in **Hanoi.** Universal literary examinations began in the 11th century after the founding of the *National University.* The *National Legal Code* was promulgated in the 15th century when the agrarian reforms were put into effect.

Unfortunately, the Vietnamese ignored the Industrial Revolution and retained an aloof self-styled "splendid isolation." Their progress thwarted, Viet Nam was unable to fend off the advances of France, and in 1863 and 1867 Viet Nam's southern provinces became French colonies and in 1884 all of Viet Nam became a French protectorate. Life under the French was not happy, nor was the Japanese occupation a savory period in Viet Nam's history.

The post World War II era has been a troubled, confusing, and unhappy one for these gentle people. The *Viet-Minh* perpetrated a cruel hoax on the Vietnamese when, under the guise of fighting for freedom and independence for all of Viet Nam, they were, in reality, doing their utmost to lead the country into the open arms of communism. Through a ruse, the old time Communist, Nguyen Ai Quoc, took the name of Ho Chi Minh and usurped leadership of the *Viet-Minh* which had been founded as a league for the independence of Viet Nam. Instead, it took effective steps to enslave the entire population. During the Indo-Chinese War of 1946–54, the Vietnamese were faced with horrible decisions. They had either to fight side by side with the *Viet-Minh* whom they knew were Communist in sympathy or refuse to fight for freedom against their own best interests. It may readily be seen that the Vietnamese were never given a clearcut choice between communism and genuine independence and freedom. In their fight for liberation from France, the Vietnamese were inadvertently also striking a blow for communism which the vast majority of them detested worse than the plague.

Ultimately, on May 8, 1954, the French surrendered **Dien Bien Phu,** and an armistice agreement was signed whereby the French High Command abandoned approximately half of the territory and almost sixty per cent of the population of Viet Nam to the *Viet-Minh*.

This was a sad development for the free world and a dreadful situation for the Vietnamese people.

Except for the hard core of Communist leaders, almost all of the *Viet-Minh* officers and men who fought the war for freedom against the French fought as their ancestors had against the Mongol armies of Kublai Khan in the 13th century— heroically and against overwhelming superior material strength.

What a pyrrhic victory! Their sacrifices and their victory ultimately benefited the Communist leaders.

By virtue of the Geneva Agreement, the country was divided at the 17th parallel, as previously noted, and for a period of three hundred days, ending in May of 1955, free choice of residence was to be left to the Vietnamese who wished to go either to the north or the south. Few if any Vietnamese from the south went north. 880,500 refugees succeeded in fleeing to the south abandoning all of their belongings and frequently risking their lives to do so. The *Viet-Minh* did everything possible, including physical violence, to prevent any of the non-Communists escaping to the south.

Ngo Dinh Diem was called upon by ex-Emperor Bao Dai, then Chief of State, to head the government of Viet Nam. He took over. On October 23, 1955, the Free Republic of Viet Nam was born in all its glory. The same Ngo Dinh Diem was elected President by an overwhelming majority, and on October 26, 1955, the Republic was officially proclaimed by the President. One year later, the Vietnamese Constitution was adopted by the Assembly.

The political situation in Viet Nam, as this edition goes to press, is disturbed. It is hoped that normal travel conditions will soon again prevail. In the meantime be sure to check with your travel agent before planning to visit Viet Nam.

SAIGON

SAIGON, a city of more than two million inhabitants, including **Cholon,** does not possess the wealth of sightseeing attractions, either natural or man made, as do **Bangkok, Tokyo, London, Paris,** and **Rome,** but it is a fascinatingly beautiful city, a bit of **Paris** transplanted, that I heartily recommend that you visit and see. Much of the pleasure of your sightseeing in **Saigon** will be derived from the local color, the variety of the costumes to be seen, and the joy of being in an intriguingly modern, yet Old World, city.

Under the domination of the French from 1867 through 1954,

Saigon was a gaudy, bright-light metropolis characterized by uninhibited revelry, bawdy houses, and gay gambling casinos. Today the city is circumspect, stately, and completely respectable. It is thoroughly European in aspect, but encompasses as a part of its metropolitan area the completely Chinese city of **Cholon** which adds an authentic Oriental ingredient to the capital's attractive atmosphere.

Among the local sights and sounds are the itinerant barbers and dentists busily plying their trades in the streets, the *trishaws* and bicycles creating confusing chaotic traffic patterns, the streetside service stations for bicycles with spare parts and equipment hanging on a convenient tree, stall vendors hawking soup, dried meat, and sugar cane juice, and the typically French picture of long unwrapped loaves of bread tucked under an arm or attached to a bicycle tandem.

Though **Saigon** is not on the sea, it is one of the great ports of the Orient, being connected to the sea by the *Saigon River*. If you arrive in Viet Nam by ship, your sightseeing begins forty miles up the river as your ocean liner leaves the *South China Sea* and traverses a passage lined with verdant mangroves. Sampans and river junks filled with rice, fish, sand, or wood glide by in Oriental file. Should you arrive by air, your local agent can later arrange a river sightseeing trip by motorboat covering some twenty miles of the busy local waterways.

Tu Do, the main street, emerges at one end at the *Hotel Majestic* overlooking the busy riverfront, passes blocks of smart shops and sidewalk cafes, and comes to an end at the spacious French square dominated by a Catholic cathedral and the *Caravelle Hotel.* A late afternoon stroll on *Tu Do* is particularly packed with local color.

The CENTRAL MARKET consists of innumerable bazaar type stalls under one huge city-block-square building as well as numerous stalls lining the streets in the vicinity. Here visitors may purchase all of the specialties of Viet Nam, and the local citizens can buy all of the home necessities for the maintenance of everyday life.

CHOLON is **Saigon's** *Chinatown,* a separate city but contiguous with the capital. Absolutely authentically Chinese, the character of **Cholon** is different from the Chinese sections of many other Oriental cities. The streets are wider, the din of the cacophony less frantic, and the crowded street stalls less conspicuous.

The FLOWER MARKET, in the heart of town, stretches for several blocks. Stall after stall bursts with blooms of all descriptions.

The BOTANICAL GARDENS are a photographer's paradise. Take plenty of film. It is said that **Saigon's** collection of orchids and equatorial plants is the most lavish in the Orient. The *Zoo* is located in the *Botanical Gardens*.

The NATIONAL MUSEUM traces the history of the art and culture of the Vietnamese from the 5th century onward. Not only does **Saigon's** *Museum* contain examples and exhibits of its own country but there are presentations of the art of Japan, China, Tibet, Cambodia, Thailand, Laos, Indonesia, and Malaya. In the foreign section of the *Museum,* one may see an absolutely priceless Japanese carving of an elephant and rider, while in the Cambodian section there are stone carvings typical of a golden era in Asian art.

Bas-reliefs, precious stones, inscribed metals, coins, ceramics, wood carvings, paintings, musical instruments, vehicles, and historical documents are also to be seen in the *Museum*.

TOMB AND TEMPLE OF MARSHAL LE VAN DUYET. Of the Chinese and Vietnamese temples, shrines, and pagodas, none is more fascinating than that of Marshal Le Van Duyet where, in addition to the place of worship, one may see the arms, war costumes, and palanquins of the 18th century, as well as the observance of an interesting ritual. When the devout come to pray, they carry cans containing forty or fifty incense sticks with them. Several are lighted at the entrance and placed in ceramic urns beautifully carved in bas-relief, themselves artistic articles of great value. After having left their lighted joss sticks, as they are known, in the urns to ward off evil spirits, the devout prostrate themselves on woven mats before the Buddha, and from their kneeling position methodically shake the can of sticks, each of which is numbered. As a result of this manipulation, one stick will eventually fall from the can. The number of the fallen stick is noted, and the worshipper proceeds to a receptacle containing written fortunes each of which is also numbered. The fortune number corresponding to the fallen joss stick is taken and read. If the fortune is a favorable one, the fortunate worshipper leaves happy. If the fortune is an unfavorable one, all is not lost, as there is a special prayer box in which it may be deposited . . . and there's always tomorrow.

It was in this temple that I first saw a number of aristocratic older Vietnamese ladies who had mouthfuls of absolutely black teeth. It seems that in ancient times when well-born Vietnamese girls were being introduced to society, they were required to paint their teeth black with an indelible stain. If for any reason the girls refused to do so and kept their teeth a natural gleaming white, they were doomed to spinsterhood; young men simply wouldn't seek them out for nuptial vows. Fortunately for all concerned, this ugly custom no longer perseveres. The Vietnamese girls now have the brightest, shiniest teeth that I have ever seen gleaming from their lovely mouths.

INDEPENDENCE PALACE is a great white stone struc-

ture set amid plush lawns and verdant gardens. Its entrance is best viewed from the broad busy boulevard which sweeps across **Saigon** to the *Palace* gates. It is not open to the public.

Short Trips From Saigon

BIEN-HOA and THU-DAU-MOT. **Bien-Hoa** and **Thu-Dau-Mot** are art centers where skilled Vietnamese craftsmen make the pottery and lacquer pieces for which **Saigon** is noted. **Bien-Hoa,** twenty miles from **Saigon,** is the pottery center where visitors are graciously received at the *Applied Arts School* any day of the week, Sunday included. **Thu-Dau-Mot** is the lacquer work center where visitors can watch the processes through their many painstaking stages. The lacquer-craft art is one that has been passed down through lacquerwork families for centuries. Now Vietnamese craftsmen combine modern methods with the techniques of antiquity. In **Thu-Dau-Mot,** one will find studios where craftsmen will undertake special orders for special, individually chosen designs.

The excursion to **Bien-Hoa** and **Thu-Dau-Mot** may very easily be accomplished in a day's time. I would suggest driving first to **Bien-Hoa** in the morning, taking luncheon on the bank of the *Dong-Nai River,* proceeding after lunch to **Thu-Dau-Mot,** and returning to **Saigon** in the late afternoon. This trip encompasses only sixty miles of travel.

DALAT, a popular mountain resort 180 miles from **Saigon,** is readily accessible from **Saigon** either by road or air. Named after the river which flows through it, the *Da,* and the local tribal name, *Lat,* the city's beauty is enhanced by the lacy waterfall which is both a lovely tourist attraction and an attractive picnic spot. The river is now named the *"Camly."*

While the visitor may reach **Dalat** from the capital in less than an hour by air, the drive is well worth the travel time. The road passes through vast rice growing areas, banana groves, rubber, tea, and coffee plantations, and the vast dense jungles of the *Blao Pass,* where sights and sounds of the jungle may be seen and heard, plus, occasionally, a glimpse of a startled deer.

Dalat, with an altitude of five thousand feet above sea level, boasts an almost perfect climate of eternal springtime completely free of excessive heat. From May through October, the bright sunshine is interwoven with heavy rains, while the dry season is from November to May. **Dalat's** area of approximately one hundred square miles includes some sixty thousand persons, not counting about twenty thousand local picturesque primitive tribesmen. One may enjoy visiting these tribespeople and sharing with them the tribal wine drunk through a bamboo pipe from an earthenware pot. **Dalat** is decorated with palatial homes, flowers of all types including gladioli, chrysanthemums, roses, pansies, marigolds, geraniums, orchids of all types and descriptions, and Viet Nam's pride and joy, the bougainvillaea. Cherry blossoms bloom at Christmastime.

The **Dalat** area produces fruits and vegetables of all kinds in profusion, but the winter *pièce de résistance* is locally grown strawberries just oozing with flavor, served à la Française with "crème Chantilly."

The *Dalat Palace* and the *Dalat Hotels* are both good western type hostelries which are heavily booked at all times, but particularly at Christmas and Easter.

SPORTS. The *Sports Club* for tennis and boating and the *Dalat Golf Club* for golfing are two fine clubs for which guest cards may be readily obtained. There are innumerable hiking paths, while swimming, sailing, and fishing may be enjoyed in the lakes and rivers. Excellent mountain stream fishing abounds, and big-game hunting parties radiate from **Dalat.**

The new TWO STORY MARKET is a most unusual shopping center for the Orient. One may view and purchase all the local arts and crafts here.

The vivid beauty of the **Dalat** area cannot be overemphasized. It is generously endowed with purple mountains, the sparkling waters of five lakes, waterfalls, and innumerable private and public gardens.

HUE, the imperial city of yesteryear, lazily located on the

River of Perfumes and silhouetted by the *Mountain of the King,* is the former capital of Viet Nam.

One of the romantic experiences of a lifetime is to ride on this radiant *River of Perfumes* at night when the moon is up, the stars are bright, and the wind is fresh and free. Your sampan will be propelled by a graceful, lovely boat girl with a crystal clear voice who will hum or sing melodically as she slowly propels the boat. As the night progresses, tiny boats follow their river routes selling chicken soup, fresh fruit, and lotus grains cooked in sugar water.

Among the ancient attractions of **Hue** are:

The ROYAL TOMBS, six in number, which were built by successive Vietnamese emperors. In most instances emperors had their tomb construction begun during their lifetimes leaving instructions for the completion after their demise. Thus, the character and décor of the tombs vary according to the personality of the emperors. Common to all, however, are the great bronze urns and the rampant dragons who slither down long flights of stairs on each side of the entrance. Pink lotus pools and square lakes whose smooth waters reflect the shadows of the gently swaying trees surround the *Tombs.*

The TOMB OF THE EMPEROR GIA-LONG is characterized by two *cenotaphs,* one for the emperor himself and one for his queen, an honor then not usually bestowed upon a spouse.

The EMPEROR MINH-MANG lived in his tomb some years before his death.

TU-DUC, an emperor-poet, spent much of his leisure time writing poetry at his sarcophagus in a lovely little structure bedecked with lotus blossoms constructed over a lake near his tomb-to-be.

The IMPERIAL CITY is divided into two sections, one for private living quarters and the other resplendent with palaces separated from the private living quarters by large moats. Visitors today may walk into the former royal residences through a large porch on which the emperors stood to review their troops and to preside at public meetings. The palaces, guarded by nine cannons, are treasured for their riches, tradition, and art.

Index

Index